Disabled children

a legal handbook

Available as an ebook at www.lag.org.uk/ebooks

The purpose of the Legal Action Group is to promote equal access to justice for all members of society who are socially, economically or otherwise disadvantaged. To this end, it seeks to improve law and practice, the administration of justice and legal services.

Disabled children

a legal handbook

SECOND EDITION

Steve Broach, Luke Clements and
Janet Read

with Rebekah Carrier, Camilla Parker,
Louise Price, Martha Spurrier and Polly Sweeney

Legal Action Group
2016
the access to
justice charity

This edition published in Great Britain 2016
by LAG Education and Service Trust Limited
3rd floor, Universal House, 88–94 Wentworth Street, London E1 7SA
www.lag.org.uk

First edition published 2010

British Library Cataloguing in Publication Data
a CIP catalogue record for this book is available from the British Library.

This book has been produced using Forest Stewardship Council (FSC) certified paper. The wood used to produce FSC certified products with a 'Mixed Sources' label comes from FSC certified well-managed forests, controlled sources and/or recycled material.

Print ISBN   978 1 908407 00 9
ebook ISBN   978 1 908407 12 2

Typeset by Regent Typesetting, London
Printed in Great Britain by Hobbs the Printers, Totton, Hampshire

Introduction

This handbook is about the legal rights of disabled children, young people and their families in England. For the purpose of this handbook and unless otherwise stated, a 'child' is a person aged under 18 and a 'young person' is a person between the ages of 16 or 18 and 25. The law in relation to this important group is complex and frequently misunderstood by those who have duties and responsibilities towards them. The level of complexity has been increased by new legislation, in particular the Children and Families Act 2014, which sits on top of much of the previous statutory scheme rather than creating a new coherent scheme for all disabled children and young people. Many families also lack essential information about legal matters which substantially affect their lives and about the ways the law might be used to assist them.

Our aim in writing this book is to provide an up-to-date legal guide which can make a contribution towards safeguarding the rights and furthering the interests of disabled children and those close to them. To this end, we have focused on issues which research, as well as our direct contact with children and their families, indicates are particularly important to them. Throughout the book, we try to suggest how the law may be used as a tool to solve problems that disabled children and their families frequently encounter and to help them achieve a quality of life enjoyed by those who do not live with disability.

The handbook seeks to be an authoritative guide to the law and of value to all those working in this field – be they in the charitable, independent or statutory sectors: advisers, advocates, lawyers, social and health care professionals as well as for those in academia – students and educationalists.

Above all, however, we want this text to be available to families with disabled children and disabled children and young people themselves so that they may use it directly themselves or jointly with an advocate, lawyer or chosen representative. It has been our experience that many disabled young people and their parents access and make very effective use of books and articles about relevant law. This being so, we are delighted that the contents of this book should shortly be available to them free of charge on the internet enabled by the Council for Disabled Children, as they were with the first edition.

The book begins with a chapter which lays down the principles that underpin the approach we take and outlines some basic information about the characteristics and circumstances of disabled children and their families in the UK. It identifies problems that they commonly encounter, the barriers that get in the way of living an ordinary life and some of the interventions and arrangements that are seen to bring about change for the better. Chapter 2 provides an introduction to what we have termed the 'legal fundamentals': the sources of law and the legal framework that apply to this group of children and their families. The subsequent chapters give detailed consideration of the law in specific areas that have been shown to be crucial: children's services, education, health, housing, decision-making, carers services, equality and non-discrimination, the transition to adulthood and remedies. None of these are, however, discrete topics capable of being considered in isolation from one another. In the lives of children and families as well as in legal and organisational terms, there are substantial overlaps and connections between them. In an effort to make at least some of those connections clear, we have relied heavily on cross-referencing throughout the book.

It is, of course, impossible in one text to do justice to the complexity of the lives, needs and aspirations of disabled children and their families. Similarly, a book of this length cannot cover all aspects of the law relating to every dimension of their lives or everything that might happen to them. Inevitably, choices have had to be made about what to limit and what to leave out altogether. For example, while this book is concerned throughout with the well-being and safety of disabled children, we do not deal specifically with procedures in relation to child protection. Also, this edition does not cover disabled young people in the criminal justice system or social security entitlements. Finally, we have taken the difficult decision for this edition to limit the focus of the book to England only, recognising the increasing divergence in law and policy in this area between England and Wales.

In the writing and editing of this handbook we have benefited greatly from those who have given advice and who have read and provided constructive feedback on the drafts of this edition and the first edition. We are particularly grateful to the following colleagues:

Clare Blackburn, Jamie Burton, Mary Busk, Jeanne Carlin, Keith

Clements, Louise Franklin, Jo Honigmann, Christine Lenehan, Liz Martin, Imogen Proud, Frank Redmond, John Selby, Jacqui Shurlock, Ben Silverstone, Vida Simpeh, Nick Spencer, Philippa Stobbs, Janet Sunman, Zoe Thompson, Peter Woods, Helen Wheatley, Lucia Winters, Ian Wise QC and Victoria Wright. Our thanks go to Anne Pinney who generously shared unpublished research on disabled children who live away from their families.

Steve Broach would like to thank the following law students at BPP Law School in London who provided valuable research assistance: Edward Martin, May Poon, Adam Porte, Natasha Silverman and Colin Miles-Witcher.

This second edition has been greatly improved by the input from a group of expert contributors who have led on updating or drafting several of the chapters, and whose names appear alongside ours on the cover. We are confident our readers will appreciate the difference their expertise has made.

We are grateful to the Council for Disabled Children for funding and creating a website to make the contents of this book freely available online. We also thank our Legal Action Group publishers and in particular Esther Pilger for her extraordinary patience in the face of successive deadline extensions.

We would welcome all comments, corrections and feedback on this book – particularly suggestions of additional materials – which can be emailed to Steve Broach at sbroach@monckton.com. Despite the extensive assistance we have had in compiling this book, all the mistakes remain our own.

We have endeavoured to state the law as at 1 November 2015

Steve Broach
Luke Clements
Janet Read

December 2015

Legal entitlements

As set out in chapter 2, the law in relation to disabled children is found in many sources – international conventions, Acts of Parliament, regulations, statutory guidance and so on. Many of these sources of law overlap and there remains significant confusion about what public bodies *must* do to support disabled children (duties) and what they *may* do (powers), an issue again explored in chapter 2 at see paras 2.45–2.49.

To help clarify this confusing picture, we provide below a list of *some* of the key 'entitlements' to which disabled children, young people and their families have the benefit. An entitlement arises where one or more public body has a relevant duty – whether this duty is owed to all disabled children or only to some, for example those with a certain level of need or those in a certain age group.

This summary is only a very general guide, and readers should consult the relevant chapter for necessary background information in relation to each entitlement. It should also be borne in mind that even if a public body only has a power, not a duty, to confer a particular benefit on a disabled child or their family so that no entitlement to the benefit arises, that power still has to be exercised rationally, reasonably and fairly: see para 2.49. There are also an extensive range of 'general' duties (see para 2.48), for example duties on local authorities and partners, such as Clinical Commissioning Groups, to co-operate to ensure that disabled children's needs are met (see paras 2.52–2.55).

In general terms, disabled children are entitled to have their needs assessed and a person-centred plan put in place to ensure these needs are met, if found to be sufficiently substantial by the assessment. Local areas may seek to address needs using less formal arrangements than those prescribed by the law. To the extent that disabled children and families are satisfied with the outcomes of these arrangements, this may be acceptable. However, if (as is too frequently the case) disputes emerge between families and public bodies as to the level of services and support to be provided, it is essential to be able to identify with precision exactly what the law requires – in other words, for families to know their rights and to be able to enforce them. This will be even more important when, as now (late 2015), services and support are likely to be reduced as a result of overall reductions in public expenditure.

Disabled children are entitled to ...

Children's services

- An *assessment*, at least under the Common Assessment Framework but probably an assessment by a social worker if they have significant needs: see paras 3.30–3.46.
- A *child in need plan* following an assessment, which should be a 'realistic plan of action (including services to be provided)': see paras 3.108–3.127.
- *Services or direct payments to meet their assessed needs*, where these are 'necessary': see paras 3.62–3.65.
- *Suitable accommodation*, if their parent or parents are prevented (for whatever reason) from providing them with suitable accommodation or care: see paras 3.136–3.143.
- A *personal adviser and pathway plan* after the age of 16 if they are 'leaving care': see paras 10.49–10.60.
- *Transition assessments* as they move towards adult social care: see paras 10.14–10.37.

Education

- *Reasonable adjustments* from their school or education setting to help address any barriers they might face to learning: see paras 4.96–4.98 and 9.39–9.42.
- *Support at school for any medical conditions* they may have: see paras 4.93–4.94.
- *'SEN support'* at their early years setting, school or college to meet their special educational needs, if they do not have an Education, Health and Care plan (EHC plan): see paras 4.103–4.109.
- An *education, health and care needs assessment* if it *may be* necessary for their special educational provision to be made in accordance with an EHC plan: see paras 4.110–4.133.
- An *EHC plan*, where their statutory assessment shows that it *is* necessary for their special educational provision to be made in accordance with such a plan: see paras 4.134–4.163.

- All the *special educational provision* quantified and specified in their EHC plan: see para 4.158.
- A *transition plan* following the annual review of their statement or EHC plan at age 14: see para 10.9.
- *Not be excluded from school*, other than as a 'last resort': see paras 4.220–4.229.
- *Suitable education otherwise than in school* if they are out of school for whatever reason, regardless of any resource constraints: see paras 4.210–4.217.
- *Free, suitable home-to-school travel arrangements*, if they are an 'eligible' child: see paras 4.230–4.241.

Health

- An *assessment of their healthcare needs*: see paras 5.39–5.42.
- In particular, *all the health provision specified in their EHC plan*, if they have one: see paras 5.43–5.46.
- *NHS continuing care*, if their health needs are complex: see paras 5.89–5.99 (children) and 10.66–10.70 (adults).
- A *Personal Health Budget*, in particular if they are eligible for continuing care: see paras 5.105–5.106.
- *Age-appropriate child and adolescent mental health services*, if they have mental health needs: see para 5.127.
- *Palliative care*, if they have a life-limiting condition: see paras 5.140–5.145.

Housing

- *Suitable accommodation if they are 'homeless'*: see paras 6.12–6.15.
- *Social housing allocated in accordance with the local authority's allocations policy*, see paras 6.18–6.34.
- A *Disabled Facilities Grant* to adapt their home, if such a grant is necessary to facilitate access or make the home safe: see paras 6.41–6.72.

Decision-making

- *Respect for their increasing capacity to make their own decisions as children*; see paras 7.7–7.15.
- The right to be *involved in all decisions made about them*: see para 7.16.
- The right to *respect for their confidential information*: see paras 7.23–7.26.

- *A presumption that they can make all decisions for themselves when they turn 16*: see para 7.34.
- The right to *support to help them make decisions themselves*: see para 7.41.
- If they lack capacity to take a decision, *all decisions to be taken in their best interests*: see paras 7.47–7.54.
- An *Independent Mental Capacity Advocate* in certain situations: see paras 7.55–7.57.

Equality and non-discrimination

- *Access to almost every aspect of public life without discrimination*, whether direct, indirect or for a reason relating to their disability: see chapter 9.
- *Reasonable adjustments* to help support their access on an equal footing to their non-disabled peers: paras 9.39–9.42.

Parents, family and friends caring for disabled children are entitled to ...

- Be *free from discrimination arising 'by association'* with the disabled child: see paras 9.29–9.35.
- A *carer's assessment* to help them sustain their caring role and to remain in (or return to) work and to participate in education, training and leisure activities: see paras 8.8–8.14.
- *Services to meet their needs as carers* if the assessment shows there to be an eligible need in a relevant area of their life: see paras 8.15–8.25.
- *Have their caring role taken away*, if they are a young carer (see paras 8.38–8.39) or if they are an adult carer who no longer feels able to continue caring (see para 8.9).
- *Transition assessments* as the disabled child they are caring for moves towards accessing adult social care: see paras 8.59–8.61 and 10.38–10.41.
- *Childcare* that is suitable for disabled children up to the age of 18: see paras 8.24–8.25.

Authors and contributors

Steve Broach is a barrister at Monckton Chambers in London. He has a wide-ranging public law practice with a particular focus on the law and policy affecting children and disabled people. Steve has appeared in many of the cases in front of the Supreme Court regarding disabled people. He was awarded young barrister of the year at the Legal Aid Lawyer of the Year Awards in 2011. Steve is co-author of *Children in Need: local authority support for children and families* (2014, LAG, 2nd edition). Prior to becoming a barrister, Steve worked extensively in the voluntary sector on behalf of disabled children and adults. Steve blogs regularly on the issues covered in this book at www.rightsinreality.wordpress.com

Luke Clements is Cerebra Professor of Law and Professor of Law and Social Justice at Leeds University and a consultant solicitor specialising in public and human rights proceedings on behalf of socially excluded groups. Luke is a leading expert on UK social care law, the rights of disabled people and carers. He regularly writes for academic journals and he is author of *Community Care and the Law* (2016 pending, LAG, 6th edition) and *Carers and their rights* (2015, Carers UK, 6th edition).

Janet Read is an Associate Professor (Reader) Emeritus at the University of Warwick Medical School and an Honorary Professor at Cardiff Law School. Her work focuses on the human rights of disabled children and adults and their families and the development of a provision to enable them to exercise those rights. She is the co-author (with Luke Clements) of *Disabled People and the Right to Life* (Routledge, 2008), *Disabled Children and the Law* (2006, JKP) and *Disabled People and European Human Rights* (2003, Policy Press). For around ten years her research has also focused on the relationship between socio-economic factors and childhood disability in the UK and other countries. Janet has held a number of practice and management posts in the public and voluntary sectors.

Rebekah Carrier is a solicitor and director of Hopkin Murray Beskine. Her specialist work in housing and public law has included successful challenges to local housing policies as well as to decision making and central and local government policy impacting on housing, for example ensuring that families including disabled children needing their own bedroom are not affected by the bedroom tax. She acted in the case of *R (SG) v Secretary of State for Work and Pensions* in which the Supreme Court found that the benefit cap breached the obligations in the United Nations Convention on the Rights of the Child. Her work involves using the law creatively to prevent homelessness and ensure that her clients obtain not just a roof over their heads but appropriate housing that meets their needs. Rebekah receives referrals from and has provided training for voluntary organisations including women's refuges, organisations supporting disabled children and their families, and projects working with refugees and victims of trafficking. Rebekah contributed to chapter 6: Housing.

Camilla Parker is a legal and policy consultant, specialising in the areas of mental health, mental capacity, disability and human rights. She has a particular interest in the human rights of young people in need of mental health care, which is the subject of her doctoral research at Cardiff Law School. Camilla was the main author of *The legal aspects of the care and treatment of children and young people with mental disorder: a guide for professionals* (DH/National Institute for Mental Health in England, January 2009) and worked as a consultant for the Department of Health on the revision of the children and young people's chapter in the Mental Health Act 1983 Code of Practice (2015). She is a qualified (non-practising) solicitor and member of the Law Society's Mental Health and Disability Committee. Camilla wrote chapter 7: Decision-making.

Louise Price is a barrister at Doughty Street Chambers, London. Louise's practice includes a range of complex civil and public law work. She is a specialist in the areas of discrimination and equality and has particular experience of claims in the spheres of employment, education and service provision. Her public law practice focuses on regulatory law and issues arising out of the provision or retention of information. Louise is a contributor to *Professional Discipline and Healthcare Regulators* (2012, LAG) and *Munkman on Employer's Liability* (2013, Lexis Nexis). Louise updated chapter 9: Equality and non-discrimination.

Martha Spurrier is a barrister at Doughty Street Chambers, London specialising in public law and civil claims against public authorities. She has particular expertise in human rights and her practice is focussed on cases involving public authorities, inquests, prisons, community care, children's and women's rights, mental health and mental capacity. Martha has acted at all levels, including the Supreme Court and the European Court of Human Rights. Prior to joining Doughty Street, Martha was in-house counsel at Mind and the Public Law Project. She is author of *Freedom to Write: a user's guide* (2012 English PEN: 2012) and a contributing editor of *Rights and Freedoms* (2013, Halsbury's Laws). Martha regularly contributes to *Legal Action*, the *Solicitors' Journal*, *INQUEST* and *European Human Rights Law Review*. Martha updated chapter 5: Health.

Polly Sweeney is an associate solicitor at Irwin Mitchell, Bristol specialising in community care, health care and medical treatment and education law (including representing parents at special educational needs and disability tribunals) and cases in the Court of Protection regarding mental capacity, best interests and deprivation of liberty. Polly is a member of the Law Society's Mental Health and Disability Committee. She updated chapter 4: Education with Steve Broach and wrote chapter 11: Remedies.

Contents

Table of cases

Table of statutes

Table of statutory instruments

Table of international and European legislation

European legislation

CHAPTER 1

Understanding disabled children's lives

continued

Key points

- Disabled children and their families have the same human rights as others, including the right to the same quality of life as those who do not live with disability.
- The social model of disability assumes that some of the most oppressive and limiting aspects of disabled people's lives are caused by social, environmental and political factors which can be changed.
- The state has core responsibilities to promote the human rights of disabled children and their families and to counter the discrimination they experience.
- Around 7 per cent of children in the UK are disabled, using the Equality Act 2010 definition. The majority live at home with their families.
- Disabled children and their families are worse off financially and have markedly poorer standards of living than those families who do not live with disability. Expenditure is higher but opportunities for earning through paid employment are reduced, particularly for mothers. Many families are in debt and live in unsuitable housing.
- Families provide high levels of care for their disabled children.
- Disabled children and their families face substantial barriers in everyday living and experience high levels of social exclusion.
- Many children and their families have difficulty in accessing services to meet their needs. Provision is complex and information about entitlements frequently unavailable.
- The combination of high levels of need, poor circumstances and lack of support services can have an impact on the health, wellbeing and opportunities of all family members.
- The early times when disability is identified are stressful for many families.
- While many parents report that they are satisfied with their disabled children's schools, many also experience problems in accessing suitable education provision.
- Many disabled young people face considerable difficulties in transition from childhood to adulthood and from children's to adult service provision.
- A minority of disabled children live away from their families for some or all of the year: in residential schools, healthcare settings or 'looked after' by local authorities.

continued

> • Children and their families need person-centred services which
> promote full social participation and enable them to maximise
> their health, well-being and life chances.

Introduction

1.1   This handbook provides a comprehensive review of the law, particularly social care, education and healthcare law, as it applies to disabled children and their families. We have aimed to write something
that is useful for everyone interested in the lives of disabled children whether they are lawyers or non-lawyers. We hope that families
themselves, as well as individuals and organisations representing
their interests will continue to make use of it.

1.2   The nature of the difficulties faced by disabled children and their
families means that a handbook devoted solely to the law would be
a rather inadequate tool. In order to understand how the law can be
used to help them, we need first to appreciate the common problems
they encounter and the services and other arrangements that would
make a positive difference to their lives. The purpose of this chapter
is to set out some of the most important principles and 'facts of life'
as they affect disabled children and those close to them. In order to
do this, we draw on the ideas and expertise of disabled children and
their families, on official reports and on research about their circumstances and experiences. The aim is that anyone unfamiliar with the
issues disabled children and their families face, can get up to speed
fairly quickly, that individuals and organisations working on their
behalf can have access to reliable source material and that disabled
young people and their families can check out their individual experience against the broader picture.

1.3   Throughout the guide, 'children' is used to mean those from birth
to 18 years unless it is otherwise specified. In certain specific contexts
a child becomes a 'young person' at around 16. We make this clear
throughout the text. The words 'young adults' refer to adults up to
the age of 25 years.

1.4   Some parents known to the authors of this handbook have discussed the difficult balancing act involved in trying to raise awareness of the problems families face without unwittingly feeding the
prejudices of those who view their lives as overwhelmingly negative.

Recognising the adversity that disabled children and their families face need not involve undermining the integrity of their personal and family life. Equally, challenging inadequate support for one child or family can lead to improvements for all families.

Underpinning principles

An ordinary life

1.5   An underpinning principle of this handbook and of the rights-based approach it adopts is that disabled children and those close to them are entitled to enjoy the same human rights as others. This can be summarised as the right to live an ordinary life.

1.6   Disabled children's and their families' needs and priorities may be different in some ways from those who do not live with disability. This does not mean that they should be precluded from participating in ordinary social, economic and cultural experiences enjoyed by others. Disabled children and their families, however, may need additional supports and different arrangements to enable them to participate in things that are part and parcel of an ordinary life. Living an ordinary life carries with it the presumption that like any children, those who are disabled should usually be brought up in a family setting – one of the principles embedded in the Children Act 1989 (see chapter 3 at para 3.12).

The social model of disability

1.7   In the past 30 years, disabled writers and activists have developed an approach known as the 'social model of disability'.[1] While there are of course differences in emphasis and understanding between some of those developing these ideas, there are a number of common areas of agreement. The social model of disability has contributed to re-shaping the way that disability is understood and has been influential

---

1   For example T Shakespeare, *Disability rights and wrongs revisited*, Routledge, 2013; N Watson 'Theorising the lives of disabled children: how can disability theory help?' (2012) 26(3) *Children and Society* pp192–202; M Oliver and C Barnes, *The new politics of disablement*, Palgrave Macmillan, 2012; J Morris, *Pride against prejudice*, Women's Press, 1991.

in relation to government policy,[2] international treaties[3] and international classification systems of health, illness and disability.[4]

1.8   The social model makes a distinction between impairment and disability. 'Impairment' is used to refer to a person's physical, sensory and intellectual characteristics or limitations. 'Disability' on the other hand, is seen as the restriction, disadvantage or oppression experienced by those living with impairment. In the words of the United Nations Convention on the Rights of Persons with Disabilities (UNCRPD):

> ... disability results from the interaction between persons with impairments and attitudinal and environmental barriers that hinder their full and effective participation in society on an equal basis with others[5]

Crucially, this approach challenges the notion that a child's impairment or medical condition is solely or even primarily responsible for any restrictions they face. It argues that many of the common problems they encounter are not a necessary consequence of living with impairment. By contrast, a much greater emphasis is placed on the disabling impact of the physical, social, cultural, political, and legal environment. It reminds us of the importance of context in shaping people's lives and opportunities: individual characteristics including impairments, are important, but the context in all its complexity, has the power to increase or reduce the disability that children and their families experience. This context includes the services that are available to them. This handbook adopts this approach and, therefore, pays particular attention to the circumstances in which disabled children and their families live and to features of the social context that act as barriers to their living ordinary lives. It emphasises the importance of arrangements and services that enable disabled children and their families to flourish: circumstances which aim to create equality of opportunity between those who live with disability and those who do not.

---

2   Prime Minister's Strategy Unit, *Improving the life chances of disabled people*, The Stationery Office, 2005.

3   UN Convention on the Rights of Persons with Disabilities (2006).

4   World Health Organisation, *The international classification of functioning, disability and health: children and youth version*, 2007.

5   UN Convention on the Rights of Persons with Disabilities (2006), Preamble, para (e).

The relevance of human rights

1.9 In addition to the influence of the social model of disability, there has also been growing recognition of the importance of a human rights approach to enhance understanding of the experience of disabled children and to bring about improvements in their lives.[6] This approach has been summarised as follows:

> At its most basic, it affirms without qualification that disabled people are not 'other': they are unquestionably included within the category and meaning of what it is to be human, and may, therefore, expect all the rights derived from that status. By employing such a normative and unifying approach, the things that happen to disabled children and adults, the lives they lead and the goals they aspire to, may be evaluated against norms or benchmarks established by consensus and sometimes by law, as universal *human* rights.[7]

In keeping with the fundamental purpose of the UNCRPD, our goal should be to try to reduce barriers that hinder the full participation of disabled children and their families in society and to ensure their enjoyment of the human rights and freedoms that everyone should be able to expect.

1.10 In chapter 2 we consider, in outline, the international human rights treaties of greatest relevance to the issues considered in this handbook – the European Convention on Human Rights (ECHR), the UN Convention on the Rights of the Child (UNCRC) and the UNCRPD (see paras 2.10–2.37 below). Reference is also made to the rights safeguarded by these conventions at key points in this text, where they are of particular relevance. It is important, however, to be aware of specific key human rights principles that underpin many of these specific rights – and these include:

- the core responsibilities of the state;
- the principle of non-discrimination;
- the principle of dignity;
- the principle of independent living;
- the principle of choice;
- the principle of cost effectiveness.

---

6 J Bickenbach, 'Disability rights, law and policy', in G Albrecht, K Seelman and M Bury (eds), *The Handbook of Disability Studies*, Sage, 2001.

7 L Clements and J Read, 'Life, disability and the pursuit of human rights', in L Clements and J Read, *Disabled people and the right to life*, Routledge, 2008, p6.

The core responsibilities of the state

1.11   Given that many of the factors that restrict disabled people are social-ly created, it follows that addressing these and the consequent exclu-sion and disadvantage they experience is a core responsibility of the state. As the UN has observed, in a binding (2003) statement:[8]

> The obligation of States parties to the Covenant to promote progres-sive realization of the relevant rights to the maximum of their avail-able resources clearly requires governments to do much more than merely abstain from taking measures which might have a negative impact on persons with disabilities. The obligation in the case of such a vulnerable and disadvantaged group is to take positive action to reduce structural disadvantages and to give appropriate preferential treatment to people with disabilities in order to achieve the objectives of full participation and equality within society for all persons with disabilities. This almost invariably means that additional resources will need to be made available for this purpose and that a wide range of specially tailored measures will be required.

1.12   This core obligation, which is given further emphasis in General Comments to the UN Convention on the Rights of the Child,[9] is on the state, not on families or charities. Families are already 'disabled by association'[10] and many carers experience similar levels of social exclusion to those for whom they provide care. This has been recog-nised by guidance concerning the rights of carers,[11] which states that social workers should not 'assume a willingness by the carer to continue caring, or continue to provide the same level of support'. The law reflects this approach, placing duties on the state to provide a level of support to all disabled people (children and adults) that respects their human rights.

The principle of non-discrimination

1.13   The principle of non-discrimination runs wider than the obligations under the Equality Act 2010 (see chapter 9) and is essentially the core obligation in the UN Convention on the Rights of Persons with Dis-abilities (see, for example, articles 3, 4, 5 and 6) to provide for true

---

8   General Comment 5 concerning persons with disabilities and the International Covenant on Economic, Social and Cultural Rights, para 9.

9   General Comment 9, para 20.

10   *Coleman v Attridge Law* C-303/06 [2008] All ER (EC) 1105, ECJ, considered at paras 9.4–9.5.

11   Department of Health, *Practice guidance to the Carers (Recognition and Services) Act 1995*, LAC (96)7, para 9.8.

equality of disabled people before the law, to effective legal protection and the right to 'reasonable accommodation'. It brings with it the requirement, for example, that the arrangements for disabled children should not be inferior to those for non-disabled children; that disabled children should not be inappropriately excluded from mainstream schooling;[12] and that all disabled children be treated equally whatever their impairments or conditions.

The principle of dignity

1.14   The concept of 'dignity' is central to many human rights treaties and bodies[13] and is often expressed in terms of respect for 'personal autonomy'/'physical integrity' and of a right to a level of support that does not lead to 'indignity', and that compensates for the disabilities faced by disabled people.[14] In England, the binding legal basis for the duty on the state to ensure that disabled children are treated 'with dignity' derives from articles 3 and 8 of the ECHR: the basic obligation is to ensure that no one is subjected to degrading treatment (article 3) and that 'respect' is shown for a person's private life (article 8). In this context, 'private life' has a broad ranging meaning encompassing a 'person's physical and psychological integrity' and their 'relations with other human beings' and their immediate environment.[15]

1.15   The European Court of Human Rights (ECtHR) has expressed the obligation this imposes in the following terms:

> In a civilised country like the United Kingdom, society considers it not only appropriate but a basic humane concern to try to improve and compensate for the disabilities faced by a person in the applicant's situation. In my opinion, these compensatory measures come to form part of the disabled person's physical integrity.[16]

1.16   Much has also been said of the obligation to protect dignity in domestic court judgments, including:

---

12 See paras 4.220–4.229 in relation to school exclusions.
13 See, for example, the comments of the European Court of Human Rights in *Pretty v United Kingdom* (2002) 35 EHRR 1 at [65].
14 Judge Greve in her concurring opinion in *Price v UK* (2002) 34 EHRR 1285 at 1296 and see *R (A, B, X and Y) v East Sussex CC and the Disability Rights Commission (No 2)* [2003] EWHC 167 (Admin); (2003) 6 CCLR 194 at [86].
15 *Botta v Italy* (1998) 26 EHRR 241.
16 The concurring opinion of Judge Greve in *Price v United Kingdom* (2002) 34 EHRR 1285 at 1296.

The recognition and protection of human dignity is one of the core values – in truth the core value – of our society and, indeed, of all the societies which are part of the European family of nations and which have embraced the principles of the Convention. It is a core value of the common law, long pre-dating the Convention.[17]

1.17   The principle of dignity, therefore, requires action to promote the inclusion of disabled children and their families in all aspects of social, economic and political life. It requires that the state treats disabled children as individuals in their own right – and not as objects. It means that (where necessary) urgent action be taken to ensure that they do not experience indignity due, for example, to inadequate bathing[18] or toileting[19] facilities or an inability to access their home or communities (see para 3.77 and paras 6.41–6.77 below in relation to the duty to adapt disabled children's homes to meet their needs). However, the principle of dignity has its limits, including resource considerations where article 8 of the ECHR is involved.[20] Resources play no part in the duty to avoid degrading treatment contrary to article 3 of the ECHR.

The principle of independent living

1.18   The right to independent living – at its most basic – means that disabled people should not be excluded from mainstream society, for example by being placed unnecessarily in a care home or hospital. The concept of independent living is, however, much more expansive and is expressed in article 19 of the UN Convention on the Rights of Persons with Disabilities (a convention the UK has ratified – see para 2.28 below) in the following terms:

17 Munby J (as he then was) in *R (A, B, X and Y) v East Sussex CC and the Disability Rights Commission (No 2)* [2003] EWHC 167 (Admin); (2003) 6 CCLR 194 at [86].

18 See Complaint nos 02/C/8679, 8681 and 10389 against Bolsover DC, 30 September 2003, where the local government ombudsman held that the ability to manage 'bathing with dignity' was the entitlement of everybody. See also Complaint no 07C03887 against Bury MBC, 14 October 2009, where the local government ombudsman referred to the 'breathtaking insensitivity' of the council in failing to secure immediate arrangements to enable a mother to bathe her disabled sons.

19 See, for example, *R (Bernard) v Enfield LBC* [2002] EWHC 2282 (Admin); (2002) 5 CCLR 577, where Sullivan J found a violation of article 8 due to delayed provision of proper toileting for the applicant – holding (at [33]) that such facilities 'would have restored her dignity as a human being'.

20 *McDonald v United Kingdom*, Application no 4241/12, (2015) 60 EHRR 1, (2014) 17 CCLR 167.

    a. Persons with disabilities have the opportunity to choose their place of residence and where and with whom they live on an equal basis with others and are not obliged to live in a particular living arrangement;

    b. Persons with disabilities have access to a range of in-home, residential and other community support services, including personal assistance necessary to support living and inclusion in the community, and to prevent isolation or segregation from the community;

    c. Community services and facilities for the general population are available on an equal basis to persons with disabilities and are responsive to their needs.

1.19   The courts have held that preserving independence should be a fundamental aim of all social care interventions,[21] that inappropriate institutionalisation is a form of discrimination against disabled people[22] and that while cost may be a factor in deciding whether a care home placement is to be preferred to a community living alternative, it is unlikely ever to be permissible for it to be the determinative factor.[23] These rights apply equally to disabled children as to disabled adults. Indeed disabled children have the protection that their best interests must be treated as a primary consideration in all actions and decisions affecting them.[24]

The principle of choice

1.20   Respect for a person's identity and physical integrity (as protected by article 8 of the ECHR[25]) brings with it a requirement to respect their choices and preferences. Where the state provides support or

21 *R v Southwark LBC ex p Khana and Karim* [2001] EWCA Civ 999; (2001) 4 CCLR 267 and see also *R (B) v Cornwall CC* [2009] EWHC 491 (Admin) at [10]. The Department of Health's *Care and Support Statutory Guidance* (2014) lists, at para 1.15, 'supporting people to live as independently as possible, for as long as possible' as expressed in the UN Convention on the Rights of Persons with Disabilities, article 19, as a 'guiding principle'.

22 *Olmstead v LC* 527 US 581 (1999), in which the US Supreme Court held that the Americans with Disabilities Act 1990 gave disabled people a qualified right to live in the community rather than in institutions.

23 See, for example, *Gunter v South West Staffordshire PCT* [2005] EWHC 1894 (Admin); (2006) 9 CCLR 121 at [20].

24 UN Convention on the Rights of the Child, article 3, which informs the rights protected by article 8 of the ECHR and the other ECHR rights; see the extensive discussion by the Supreme Court in *R (SG) v Secretary of State for Work and Pensions* [2015] UKSC 16; [2015] 1 WLR 1449.

25 See, for example, *Botta v Italy* (1998) 26 EHRR 241, considered at paras 1.14, 2.15, 5.77 and 9.143.

otherwise intervenes in a disabled person's life, it should, so far as is consistent with its other obligations, ensure that its action promotes the disabled person's and their family's aspirations. A key aspect of this obligation is the duty to take full account of the wishes of the disabled child and the family – in every aspect of the support provided – be it from health, social care, education and so on. This means that the family's and disabled child's preferences should not be sacrificed merely because they are in conflict with what a council considers to be 'best'[26] and that planning should be 'person centred' and where possible should yield to the personal preferences of the family and disabled child.

The principle of cost-effectiveness

1.21   While respect for individual and family preferences is an important principle in relation to meeting the needs of disabled children, it is subject to the principle of 'cost-effectiveness'; as a general rule, choice does not trump 'cost'. Where the state has an obligation to meet a disabled child's needs (eg special educational or social care needs), if it is able to meet these fully in one way, it is permitted to refuse to meet them in an alternative, more expensive, way. The principle of cost effectiveness is in reality an essential component of the state's core obligation to 'promote progressive realisation' of the rights of disabled people 'to the maximum of [the state's] available resources': such an obligation requires it to devise cost effective procedures that ensure as many people as possible benefit from its limited resources. However, 'cost-effectiveness' should not lead to a minimalist approach to meeting disabled children's needs. Critically, although cost may trump choice, it must not trump dignity or other fundamental human rights. The courts may hold, however, that a disabled person's sense of dignity can be overridden if the service or provision which they consider will uphold their dignity is significantly more expensive than an alternative service which can properly meet their needs.[27]

---

26 For a graphic example of this, see *R (CD) v Anglesey CC* [2004] EWHC 1635 (Admin) considered at paras 3.141 and 10.11.

27 *McDonald v United Kingdom* (2015) 60 EHRR 1.

Consulting disabled children and young people and their families

1.22   A fundamental requirement under the obligation to show respect for a person's private and family life (in ECHR article 8) is to involve them in decisions which concern them, regardless of the nature of their impairments and the extent of their support needs. This duty is reflected in the guidance concerning the assessment of children's social care and special educational needs (see respectively chapter 3 at paras 3.26 and 3.33 and chapter 4 at paras 4.123–4.129 below). The courts have emphasised the absolute importance of communicating with disabled people to ascertain their wishes, feelings and preferences[28] and made it clear that this obligation includes proper consultation with family members noting that in many situations:

> the devoted parent who ... has spent years caring for a disabled child is likely to be much better able than any social worker, however skilled, or any judge, however compassionate, to 'read' his child, to understand his personality and to interpret the wishes and feelings which he lacks the ability to express.[29]

1.23   Disabled children and members of their families should, therefore, be listened to about both the barriers that get in the way of living an ordinary life and the things that would remove these barriers and help them. They should also have the right to participate so that their ideas are central to any decision-making. This applies to the planning and operation of services as well as to assessment and service-delivery at an individual level.[30] Whatever the nature of the issues that they are facing and whatever the type of service they are dealing with, children and their parents have the right to expect that professionals and service-providers treat them with respect and recognise the knowledge and expertise that they have gained through experience.

1.24   Individuals within families may have different priorities and different wishes, but all have a right to be heard. While parents may understandably have to prioritise such things as care, finance, housing, health and education, it should come as no surprise that children

---

28 See for example, *R (A and B) v East Sussex CC (No 2)* [2003] EWHC 167 (Admin); (2003) 6 CCLR 194.

29 *Re S* [2002] EWHC 2278; [2003] 1 FLR 292 at [49].

30 For example, A Franklin and P Sloper, *Participation of disabled children and young people in decision-making relating to social care*, Social Policy Research Unit, University of York, 2007; Triangle *A bit good but a bit not good too. Children and young people's views about specialist health services*, Triangle Services, Brighton, 2012.

may put a premium on play, leisure, friendships and school.[31] In recent years, there has been greater recognition of the importance of seeking the views of disabled children and young people themselves and understanding their perspectives. In the past, these were often neglected, particularly if children did not use standard forms of communication. There are now many tried and tested ways of finding out what disabled children and young people want, using forms of consultation and communication appropriate to their needs.[32] Seeking the advice of those who know them best about how to find out the detail of what is important to them is crucial.[33]

1.25   An obligation to consult with children and young people inevitably invites a discussion about their capacity to understand, the weight that should be given to their views and their right to make decisions about certain matters – not only in their dealings with public bodies but also in the context of their families. In all families, children and adults develop their own ways of negotiating decisions large and small and dealing with conflicts of view and differing individual priorities. The approaches they adopt will vary considerably depending for example, on their personal, social and cultural backgrounds, the ages of those involved, their circumstances, the decisions to be made and so on. Like other families, those with disabled children and young people also develop their own ways of dealing with these matters but, as we shall see later in this chapter, they are often having to sort out complex issues in particularly challenging circumstances. It is reasonable to assume that the application of the law to day-by-day decision-making in the family is probably not an all-consuming preoccupation for most of the time. The rights that children, young people and young adults have to make decisions about

---

31 B Beresford, R Parveneh and P Sloper, *Priorities and perceptions of disabled children and young people and their parents regarding outcomes from support services*, Social Policy Research Unit, University of York, 2007.

32 For example, A Knight, A Clark, P Petrie and J Statham, *The views of children and young people with learning disabilities about the support they receive from social services: a review of consultations and methods*, Thomas Coram Research Unit, University of London, 2006; The Communication Trust and Early Support, *Misunderstood. Supporting children and young people with speech, language and communication needs*, 2012; J Bradshaw 'The use of augmentative and alternative communication apps for the iPad, iPod and iPhone: an overview of recent developments', (2013) 18(1) *Tizard Learning Disability Review*, p31; Council for Disabled Children and Participation Works, *How to involve children and young people with communication impairments in decision-making*, 2015.

33 G Hanrahan, *Moving into adulthood and getting a life. Becoming an adult: A guide to the Mental Capacity Act for families of young people with learning disabilities*, Oxfordshire Family Support Network, 2014.

matters that affect them and to be free from unwarranted restriction or from having their views disregarded in the private as well as the public sphere are, however, of utmost importance.[34] The way that the law approaches questions of mental capacity and decision-making in relation to disabled children, young people and young adults both within their families and in relation to external organisations is covered in chapter 7.

Disabled children and their families: numbers, characteristics and circumstances

1.26   Data about the population of disabled children and their families are collected for different purposes and this affects not only the type of information gathered but also the ways in which the children and their characteristics are described.[35] For example, while there is considerable overlap between children defined as 'disabled' according to the Equality Act 2010 and those identified as having special educational needs (SEN), the two groups are not the same.[36] At an individual level, how children are defined can also affect what others see as their primary needs and whether they can access all services that they and their families may need.

The population of disabled children

1.27   Using a disability definition equivalent to that in the Equality Act 2010, there are about 0.9 million disabled children aged 0–18 in the UK or approximately seven per cent of the child population.[37] A study

---

34 For a discussion of these issues written by parents of disabled young people, see for example: G Hanrahan, *Moving into adulthood and getting a life: a guide to the Mental Capacity Act for families of young people with learning disabilities*, Oxfordshire Family Support Network, 2014.

35 Department for Work and Pensions, *Making disability data work for you*, 2014.

36 Some estimates indicate that three quarters of disabled children are also assessed as having special educational needs. See for example, J Porter, H. Daniels, J Georgeson, J Hacker and V Gallop, *Disability data collection for children's services*, Department for Children, Schools and Families Research Report, 2008; S Parsons and L Platt, *Disability among young children. Prevalence, heterogeneity and socio-economic disadvantage*, Centre for Longitudinal Studies, Institute of Education, University of London, 2013.

37 Department for Work and Pensions, *Family Resources Survey*, 2012/2013.

using data from the *Family Resources Survey (FRS)*[38] found that the children's most commonly-reported difficulties are with memory, concentration, learning and communication. It also showed that many children have difficulties in more than one area of daily living: around a third of disabled children experience between two and four difficulties and more than 10 per cent experience five or more difficulties.

1.28   Since the 1980s there have been changes in the population of disabled children. Increasing numbers of those with multiple and complex impairments are living longer and being cared for at home. This is due, in part, to improved survival rates for low birth weight and extremely premature babies.[39] This trend has significant implications for the children and their families as well as for services attempting to meet their needs. When children have higher support needs or complex impairments, some parents may have to take responsibility, for example, for administering medication, tube feeding, assisted ventilation and resuscitation procedures, as well as other treatments and interventions.[40] It is estimated that around 18,000 children and young people in England have multiple and complex impairments which result in their needing some form of palliative care.[41] In addition, recent years have seen a marked reported increase in numbers of children identified as having autistic spectrum disorders[42] and attention-deficit hyperactivity disorder (ADHD).[43] It is important to acknowledge that when disabled children have multiple impairments, it is not uncommon for some of their needs and difficulties to go unrecognised by service providers and practitioners because the diagnosis of one condition may overshadow another. For example, attention has been drawn to the neglect of the mental health needs

---

38   C Blackburn, N Spencer and J Read, 'Prevalence of childhood disability and the characteristics and circumstances of disabled children in the UK: secondary analysis of the Family Resources Survey', (2010) *BMC Pediatrics* 10, p21.

39   A T Gibson, 'Outcome following preterm birth', (2007) 21(5) *Best practice and research clinical obstetrics and gynaecology*, pp869–882; EPICure, *Population based studies of survival and later health status in extremely premature infants*, 2008.

40   C Glendinning, C Kirk, S Guiffrida and D Lawton, 'Technology-dependent children in the community: definitions, numbers and costs', (2001) 27 *Child: Care, Health and Development*, pp321–334.

41   H Cochrane, S Liyanage, R Nantambi, *Palliative care statistics for children and young adults*, Department of Health, 2007.

42   S Levy, D Mandell and R Schultz, 'Autism', (2009) 374 *The Lancet*, pp1627–1638.

43   E Taylor, 'Developing ADHD', (2009) 50 *Journal of Child Psychiatry and Psychology*, pp126–132.

of those with learning disabilities[44] despite the fact that around 36 per cent of learning disabled children and young people have been diagnosed as having a psychiatric disorder.[45]

Family composition

1.29   The majority of disabled children are brought up at home by their families of origin and almost two-thirds of them live in two-parent households. The proportion being brought up in lone-parent households (32 per cent) is significantly greater, however, than that for non-disabled children (22 per cent).[46] A number of studies have highlighted disabled children's increased chances of being brought up by lone parents, the majority of whom are mothers,[47] but the reasons for this are not clear. Some research suggests that any increased risk of separation or divorce is most likely to be seen when a disabled child is very young, particularly between the ages of 12 months and two years[48] but it needs to be recognised that this is also a time when there is a risk of relationship breakdown for those who have young non-disabled children. In addition, one study found that while families with children with cognitive delay were more likely to experience changes in family composition and marital status than those with more typically developing children, the increased levels of family change could be put down to differences in socio-economic circumstances rather than being specifically related to the child's

44   C Burke, *Feeling down. Improving the mental health of people with learning disabilities,* Foundation for People with Learning Disabilities, 2014; C Blackburn, J Read and N Spencer, 'Children with neurodevelopmental disabilities', *Annual Report of the Chief Medical Officer 2012, Our Children Deserve Better: Prevention Pays,* Department of Health, October 2013, chapter 9.

45   E Emerson and C Hatton 'Mental health of children and adolescents with intellectual disabilities in Britain', *British Journal of Psychiatry,* November 2007, 191 (6) pp493–499.

46   Department for Work and Pensions, *Family Resources Survey,* 2012/2013.

47   H Clarke and S McKay, *Exploring disability, family formation and break-up: reviewing the evidence,* Research Report No 514, Department for Work and Pensions, 2008; C Blackburn, N Spencer and J Read, 'Prevalence of childhood disability and the characteristics and circumstances of disabled children in the UK: secondary analysis of the Family Resources Survey', (2010) *BMC Pediatrics* 10, p21.

48   H Clarke and S McKay, *Exploring disability, family formation and break-up: reviewing the evidence,* Research Report No 514, Department for Work and Pensions, 2008; D Risdal and G Singer, 'Marital adjustment in parents of children with disabilities: a historical review and meta-analysis', (2004) 29 *Research and Practice for Persons with Severe Disabilities,* pp95–103.

disability.[49] However lone parenthood comes about, it is crucial to be aware that it has considerable implications for the children and families concerned. As we discuss later, it is associated with increased levels of poverty together with restricted access to essential goods and services. When combined with the high parental workloads associated with caring for some disabled children, this means that some lone parents and their children are very hard-pressed indeed.

1.30   Recent research has also pointed to the clustering of childhood and adult disability within households.[50] A 2010 study reported that almost half of disabled children, compared with about a fifth of non-disabled children, live with a parent who also is disabled. In addition, around a quarter of disabled children live with one or more siblings who are also disabled.[51] While further research is needed to help understand how this comes about, it is crucial to recognise the level of need and additional difficulties that may arise when parents and children in the same household are disabled.

Socio-economic disadvantage, low income and debt

1.31   A 2013 UK government report drew attention to the fact that the association between poverty and child disability means that disabled children in the UK are significantly more likely to live under conditions that have been shown to impede development, educational attainment and adjustment and increase the risk of poor health, additional impairment and social exclusion.[52] In other words, in addition to the impact of living and growing with disability, the well-being, choices and life chances of many disabled children and their families are also insidiously eroded by living for substantial periods without the basic resources that would allow them a reasonable standard of living.

49 C Hatton, E Emerson, H Graham, J Blacher and G Llewellyn, 'Changes in family composition and marital status in families with a young child with cognitive delay', (2010) 23(1) *Journal of Applied Research in Intellectual Disabilities*, pp14–26.

50 H Clarke and S McKay, *Exploring disability, family formation and break-up: reviewing the evidence*, Research Report No 514, Department for Work and Pensions, 2008; C Blackburn, N Spencer and J Read, 'Prevalence of childhood disability and the characteristics and circumstances of disabled children in the UK: secondary analysis of the Family Resources Survey', (2010) *BMC Pediatrics* 10, p21.

51 C Blackburn, N Spencer and J Read, 'Prevalence of childhood disability and the characteristics and circumstances of disabled children in the UK: secondary analysis of the Family Resources Survey', (2010) *BMC Pediatrics* 10, p21.

52 Department for Work and Pensions, *Fulfilling potential. Building a deeper understanding of disability in the UK Today*, 2013.

Many families who are not living on the lowest incomes nevertheless deal with the increased demands of living with disability without sufficient human and material resources to offset them.

1.32   Prevalence of childhood disability is socially patterned: its distribution follows a social gradient with the highest prevalence found among children whose parents are the least well off.[53] As a group, disabled children in this country and elsewhere are in substantially more disadvantaged financial and material circumstances than non-disabled children.[54] The reasons for this are not fully understood.[55] There has been a long-standing debate on whether disability should be seen as a cause or a consequence of socio-economic disadvantage, though characterising the explanation in this way is an over-simplification. Recent research using longitudinal data, has indicated, however, that young non-disabled children living in socio-economically deprived households have a greater risk of developing disabling chronic conditions later in childhood than those in better off circumstances. The odds of their developing a disabling condition increases significantly as the level of socio-economic disadvantage rises.[56]

1.33   In addition, a considerable body of research draws attention to the impact that the presence of a disabled child in a household has on both income and expenditure. Growing up with disability and caring for a disabled child involves the need for substantial additional expenditure.[57] Simultaneously, however, the demands of caring

53 N Spencer, C Blackburn and J Read, 'Prevalence and social patterning of limiting long-term illness/disability in children and young people under the age of 20 years in 2001: UK census-based cross-sectional study', (2010) 36(4) *Child, Care, Health and Development*, July 2010, pp566–573.

54 C Blackburn, N Spencer and J Read, 'Prevalence of childhood disability and the characteristics and circumstances of disabled children in the UK: secondary analysis of the Family Resources Survey', (2010) *BMC Pediatrics* 10, p21; N Spencer, C Blackburn and J Read, 'Disabling chronic conditions in childhood and socioeconomic disadvantage: a systematic review and meta-analyses of observational studies', *BMJ Open*, 2015.

55 S Parsons and L Platt, 'Disability among young children. Prevalence, heterogeneity and socio-economic disadvantage', CLS Working Paper 2013/11, November 2013.

56 C Blackburn, N Spencer and J Read, 'Is the onset of disabling chronic conditions in later childhood associated with exposure to social disadvantage in earlier childhood? A prospective cohort study using ONS Longitudinal Study for England and Wales', *BMC Pediatrics*, 26 June 2013.

57 The Children's Society, *4 in every 10. Disabled children living in poverty*, 2011; M Woolley *How do they manage? Income and expenditure of families with a severely disabled child*, Family Fund, 2004.

reduce the options available to the adults in the family, particularly mothers, to bring in income by having paid employment.[58]

1.34   Calculations using FRS data indicate that when all groups in the population are taken together, the income for a household with a disabled child is around 13 per cent lower than for households with non-disabled children. There are variations between some groups, however, and the lowest incomes are to be found among lone parents, black and minority ethnic families and those with disabled parents and disabled children in the same household.[59]

1.35   The combination of all of these factors means that in many households there is a shortfall between income and necessary expenditure. As a consequence, living standards in families with disabled children are lower across the board than those of their non-disabled peers. On almost every measure of material deprivation, disabled children are more likely than other children to live in households which are unable to afford things that are generally regarded as important and ordinary for children in the twenty-first century, such as having more than one pair of shoes, access to outside play space, participating in a leisure activity once a month or buying some basic toys.[60] In some surveys, substantial numbers of families report being unable to afford adequate food and heating.[61] Standard consumer durables such as cars, central heating, washing machines and dryers are essential items for families with disabled children if they are to meet their children's needs and offset the additional demands of living with disability. For those on low incomes, they are expensive to buy and maintain. Heavy usage of some items means that running costs and wear and tear are high too.[62] Given their circumstances, it is unsurprising that households with disabled children (26.5 per cent) are also more likely than those with non-disabled children (16.2 per cent) to report one or more debts. The highest proportion of families

---

58 E Emerson and C Hatton, 'The socio-economic circumstances of children at risk of disability in Britain', (2007) 22 *Disability and Society*, pp563–580; S McKay and A Atkinson, *Disability and caring among families with children*, Research Report No 460, Department for Work and Pensions, 2007.

59 C Blackburn, N Spencer and J Read, 'Prevalence of childhood disability and the characteristics and circumstances of disabled children in the UK: secondary analysis of the Family Resources Survey', (2010) *BMC Pediatrics* 10, p21.

60 C Blackburn, N Spencer and J Read, 'Prevalence of childhood disability and the characteristics and circumstances of disabled children in the UK: secondary analysis of the Family Resources Survey', (2010) *BMC Pediatrics* 10, p21.

61 Contact a Family, *Counting the Cost*, 2014.

62 Contact a Family, *Counting the Cost*, 2014.

reporting being behind with payments are those where there are both disabled children and disabled adults.[63]

1.36   Organisations representing the interests of disabled children and their families have drawn attention to the fact that the material hardship many face has worsened in recent years.[64] Research commissioned by the Equality and Human Rights Commission has assessed the cumulative impact of government changes to public expenditure, taxation and benefits on specific groups within the whole population between 2010 and 2015. The study found that the impacts of tax and welfare reforms both in cash terms and as a percentage of net income are more negative for families with a disabled child than for those with non-disabled children. These negative impacts are particularly marked for those already on low incomes, with the hardest-hit being households where there is both a disabled child and a disabled adult.[65]

Housing problems

1.37   Restricted financial resources are also partly responsible for many disabled children and their families living in poor or unsuitable housing.[66] Disabled children are more likely to live in rented accommodation and with fewer rooms than non-disabled children. Lack of space and poor access both outside and within the home are commonly reported problems. Even when families are living in accommodation that might be judged reasonable according to general criteria, it is often unsuitable for disabled children and their carers. Physical barriers inside and outside the home can make it difficult for children to take part in ordinary childhood and family activities. Inaccessible toilets, bathrooms and kitchens as well as a lack of space for storing

---

63 C Blackburn, N Spencer and J Read, 'Prevalence of childhood disability and the characteristics and circumstances of disabled children in the UK: secondary analysis of the Family Resources Survey', (2010) *BMC Pediatrics* 10, p21.

64 Contact a Family, *Counting the Cost*, 2014.

65 H Reed and J Portes, *Cumulative Impact Assessment: A Research Report by Landman Economics and the National Institute of Economic and Social Research (NIESR) for the Equality and Human Rights Commission*, Equality and Human Rights Commission, Research report 94, 2014.

66 C Blackburn, N Spencer and J Read, 'Prevalence of childhood disability and the characteristics and circumstances of disabled children in the UK: secondary analysis of the Family Resources Survey', (2010) *BMC Pediatrics* 10, p21; E Emerson and C Hatton, *The socio-economic circumstances of families supporting a child at risk of disability in Britain in 2002*, Institute of Health Research, University of Lancaster, 2005; B Beresford and D Rhodes, *Housing and disabled children: round-up: reviewing the evidence*, Joseph Rowntree Foundation, 2008.

essential equipment are problems faced by many.[67] Some of the most severe housing difficulties are experienced by families with the lowest incomes and those from black and minority ethnic groups. Families who find themselves in unsuitable housing but who are unable to access financial assistance for adaptations frequently overstretch themselves by moving house or by undertaking building work at their own expense. See further chapter 6 in relation to disabled children's housing needs.

Living with disability: parents' and children's experience

At home

1.38   In addition to managing the higher costs of living with often very limited resources, families also have to meet their disabled children's needs for care. The care of a disabled child frequently makes demands that exceed what is required of parents of non-disabled children. Studies have recorded the on-going and long-term nature of the caring commitments and have described the often high levels of personal and practical care being provided by parents to their disabled sons and daughters of all ages.[68] While needs vary depending on the individual child, their circumstances, age and impairments, caring for them may involve help with bathing, washing, eating, toileting, mobility and communication. Parents may also be responsible for managing dietary requirements, administering medication, using technological equipment and procedures as well as undertaking physiotherapy and other activities designed to keep children well or assist learning and development. Some children need careful supervision if they are to be safe while others need a great deal of fine-tuned attention, guidance and stimulation if frustration or distress is to be kept at bay.

---

67   B Beresford and D Rhodes, *Housing and disabled children: round-up: reviewing the evidence*, Joseph Rowntree Foundation, 2008.

68   For example B Dobson, S Middleton and A Beardsworth, *The impact of childhood disability on family life*, Joseph Rowntree Foundation/York Publishing Services, 2001; S McKay and A Atkinson, *Disability and caring among families with children*, Research Report No 460, Department for Work and Pensions, 2007; G M Griffiths and R P Hastings, '"He's hard work but he's worth it". The experience of caregivers of individuals with intellectual disabilities and challenging behaviour: a meta-synthesis of qualitative research', (2014) 27(5) *Journal of Applied Research in Learning Disabilities*, pp401–419.

1.39   Getting out and about and doing things that other adults and children regard as ordinary often needs a great deal of planning and organisation. Going shopping, getting a haircut or having a day out can be made difficult by a combination of such things as transport problems, an inaccessible physical environment, a restricted budget and the need to transport bulky equipment – as well as parental fatigue.

1.40   Caring for a disabled child is a workload undertaken in private, day after day, and for some children, during the night too.[69] Often it has to be accomplished by parents who also have to attend to the needs of other family members, particularly other children. Parents of disabled children may find that informal arrangements with family and friends such as 'child-swaps' or babysitting are less easy to come by. Formal childcare, as we shall see later, is also not as easily available as for non-disabled children. In households where money is very tight, parents do not have the option of paying for some extra help or buying in something that makes life a little easier or more enjoyable for the children and adults. Consequently, unless they are provided with support from statutory services, less well off families often have only their own muscle-power, energy and ingenuity to fall back on.

1.41   The patterns of care in households with a disabled child tend to reflect childcare arrangements in families more generally. In both lone-parents and two-parent households, the caring workload overall tends to be weighted towards mothers and this has an impact on their employment and career opportunities.[70] Women with disabled children are less likely than other mothers to be in paid work. When working, they are less likely to be employed full-time. Overall, couples with disabled children are less likely both to be in paid work compared with couples who have non-disabled children.[71] While fathers' employment rates are less affected than mothers', twice as many couples with a disabled child are jobless, compared with those who do not have a disabled child.[72] In addition, studies point

69 J Heaton, J Noyes, P Sloper and R Shah, 'The experience of sleep disruption in families of technology-dependent children', (2006) *Children and Society*, pp196–208; Family Fund, *Tired all the time. The impact of sleeping difficulties on families with disabled children*, 2013.

70 N Coleman and L Lancely, *Lone parent obligations: supporting the journey into work*, Department for Work and Pensions Research Report 736, 2011.

71 S McKay and A Atkinson, *Disability and caring among families with children*, Research Report No 460, Department for Work and Pensions, 2007.

72 S McKay and A Atkinson, *Disability and caring among families with children*, Research Report No 460, Department for Work and Pensions, 2007.

to the difficulties reported by men who are the single wage-earners in couple households. They describe tensions around the conflicting demands of employment and the need to provide care or to attend to other matters related to their disabled child.[73] (see chapter 8, paras 8.10–8.11 and 8.17 for carers' rights in relation to support for paid employment).

1.42   Some parents, particularly those raising children alone, feel that the level and range of care and the commitments involved with bringing up a disabled child mean that employment outside the home is simply not practical.[74] For others, the lack of affordable and suitable childcare for disabled children of all ages, and a lack of suitably trained staff to deliver it, are significant barriers to taking up work or, indeed, simply having time out from their caring responsibilities to attend to other important issues. Childcare costs for disabled children also tend to be considerably higher than for those who are non-disabled.[75]

1.43   While there is a great deal of evidence about the taxing workloads managed by parents, it is important to stress that studies have indicated time and time again that parents are not prone to characterising their disabled children as burdensome. Research has repeatedly highlighted the strength of parents' understanding, love and appreciation of their children. They are acutely aware of the limitations placed upon them and their restricted opportunities. Parents tend to focus on the personal and practical arrangements which would enable their families to achieve a decent quality of life.[76] Studies also indicate that parents know only too well that many others do not see their children in the same way. Managing other people's misunderstanding of their children and hurtful attitudes towards them can

73 J Harrison, M Henderson and R Leonard (eds) *Different Dads: fathers' stories of parenting disabled children*, Jessica Kingsley Publishers, 2007; Contact a Family, *Fathers*, 2008.

74 Department for Work and Pensions, *Fulfilling potential. Building a deeper understanding of disability in the UK Today*, 2013.

75 For example, Daycare Trust, *Listening to parents of disabled children about childcare*, 2007; H Cheshire, V Brown, I Wollny, E Ireland, S Scott, P Jessiman, C Blackburn, J Read, S Purdon, and D Abbott, *Impact evaluation of the Disabled Children's Access to Childcare Pilot (DCATCH)*, Research Report DFE-RR168, Department for Education, 2011.

76 For example, Contact a Family, *Our Family, Our Future*, 2009; G M Griffiths and R P Hastings, '"He's hard work but he's worth it". The experience of caregivers of individuals with intellectual disabilities and challenging behaviour: a meta-synthesis of qualitative research', (2014) 27(5) *Journal of Applied Research in Learning Disabilities*, pp401–419.

be yet another problem to be dealt with.[77] Around a third of parents report that one of the main barriers their children face is still the attitudes of others.[78] Disabled children and their families report that they often experience insensitive reactions by other people and that public spaces and arrangements that may suit the majority are not designed to include them.[79]

1.44   Rates of reported bullying are higher for young disabled people than for other young people[80] and there has been a growing body of evidence that disabled children have an increased risk of exposure to violence[81] and abuse.[82] Disabled children in a large-scale US study were found to be 3.4 times more likely overall to be abused or neglected than non-disabled children, with similar levels of mistreatment identified in smaller-scale UK studies.[83]

1.45   There is frequently a substantial gap between the aspirations and activities regarded as ordinary for non-disabled children and their disabled peers. Across their childhoods, many disabled children are excluded from age-appropriate experiences that may be regarded as important for all children, and they have a far greater chance of having a more restricted and confining social and personal life. Leisure, play and time with friends are often more limited for disabled children and young people.[84] The *Life Opportunities Survey* allows us to

---

77   J Read, *Disability, the family and society: listening to mothers*, Open University Press, 2000; S Ryan, '"I used to worry about what other people thought but now I just think ... well I don't care": shifting accounts of learning difficulties in public places', (2008) 23 *Health and Place*, pp199–210.

78   Department for Work and Pensions, *Fulfilling potential. Building a deeper understanding of disability in the UK Today*, 2013.

79   S Ryan, '"People don't do odd, do they?" Mothers making sense of the reactions of others towards their learning disabled children in public places', (2005) *Children's Geographies*, pp291–306.

80   Department for Work and Pensions, *Fulfilling potential. Building a deeper understanding of disability in the UK Today*, 2013.

81   L Jones, M Bellis, S Wood, K Hughs, E Mc Coy, L Eckley, G Bates, C Mikton, T Shakespeare and A Officer, 'Prevalence and risk of violence against children with disabilities: a systematic review and meta-analysis of observational studies', (2012) *The Lancet*, pp899–907.

82   K Stalker, and K McArthur, 'Child abuse, child protection and disabled children: a review of recent research', (2012) *Child Abuse Review*, pp24–40.

83   National Working Group on Child Protection and Disability, *'It doesn't happen to disabled children': child protection and disabled children*, NSPCC, 2003.

84   For example P Murray, *Hello! Are You Listening? Disabled teenagers' experience of access to inclusive leisure*, Joseph Rowntree Foundation, 2002; H Clarke, *Preventing social exclusion of disabled children and their families*, Research Report RR782, DfES, 2006; G Bielby, T Chamberlain, M Morris, L O'Donnell and C Sharp, *Improving the wellbeing of disabled children and young people through*

compare the participation and restrictions experienced by disabled children and their non-disabled peers aged 11–15 years. There were substantial differences between the two groups in relation to personal relationships, education, transport and leisure or play, with disabled children and young people being disadvantaged in all areas.[85] Children and young people with complex impairments and high support needs and those who have learning disabilities and behaviour that may challenge, frequently experience a high degree of social exclusion.[86] Earlier, we referred to the impact on parental employment of lack of available childcare for disabled children of all ages. Another consequence of limited access to childcare is that the children have fewer opportunities to mix with others and benefit from the activities they enjoy.[87]

1.46 Parents may also express concern about the impact on their non-disabled sons and daughters of the circumstances that go along with living with disability.[88] In addition to research on the experience of parent carers, there has been growing recognition of the amount of care and support that some siblings offer to their disabled brothers and sisters. Sometimes, they may provide help or assistance directly to their disabled brother or sister; at other times, they may do things to support a parent who is undertaking most of the care. (See chapter 8 at paras 8.26–8.59 below for the law in relation to young carers). Whether or not brothers and sisters are involved in care, there has been a recognition of the need to understand their experiences and to learn from their perspectives.[89] Studies which have consulted

improving access to positive activities, Centre for Excellence and Outcomes in Children and Young People's Services, 2009.

85 Office for National Statistics, *Life Opportunities Survey. Interim Results 2009/2010*, ONS, 2010.

86 J Morris, *That kind of life? Social exclusion and young disabled people with high levels of support needs*, Scope, 2001; E Emerson and S Einfeld, *Challenging behaviour*, 3rd edition, Cambridge University Press, 2011.

87 For example, Council for Disabled Children, *Extending inclusion. Access for disabled children and young people to extended schools and children's centres: a development manual*, DCSF Publications, 2008; Daycare Trust, *Listening to parents of disabled children about childcare*, 2007.

88 Contact a Family, *Siblings*, 2011.

89 Contact a Family, *Siblings*, 2011; C Connors and K Stalker, The *views and experiences of disabled children and their siblings – A positive outlook*, Jessica Kingsley Publishers, 2002; R Hastings, *Children and adolescents who are siblings of children with intellectual disabilities or autism: research evidence*, Sibs, 2014.

siblings directly report mixed reactions to their situations.[90] Many speak positively about their relationship with their disabled brother or sister and have straightforward attitudes towards their impairments and support needs. Others, as might be anticipated, do not get on so well. Some report being upset by the attitudes of other people towards their brother or sister and it is also not uncommon for them to describe being teased or bullied themselves. A review of research on siblings of children with learning disabilities or autism, concludes that overall, the evidence indicates that neither the well-being of the majority nor their relationships with a disabled brother or sister are negatively affected. It has been suggested, however, because some research indicates that there is a risk to the well-being of some siblings of children with high levels of behaviour problems, we might do well to pay particular attention to this group. Research on siblings is limited in a number of respects, however, and this leaves gaps in our knowledge about this group of children and young people.[91]

1.47　　　In many families, the health of parents may suffer. As a group, parents of disabled children are reported to experience higher levels of stress and lower levels of well-being than those of non-disabled children.[92] Some studies have highlighted the negative impact on the emotional well-being of parents of any behavioural difficulties their children may have.[93] Mothers of some groups of disabled children have been found to be particularly vulnerable to poorer health and well-being and some studies have suggested that this increased risk may be attributed in part at least, to the socio-economic disadvantage that frequently goes hand-in-hand with disability.[94]

90 N Atkinson and N Crawforth, *All in the family: siblings and disability*, NCH Action for Children, 1995; K Stalker and C Connors, 'Children's perceptions of their disabled siblings: "She's different but it's normal for us"', (2004) *Children & Society*, pp218–230.

91 R Hastings, *Children and adolescents who are the siblings of children with intellectual disabilities or autism: Research evidence*, Sibs, 2014.

92 P Sloper and B Beresford, 'Families with disabled children', (2006) 333 *BMJ*, pp928–929. M Hirst, 'Carer distress: a prospective, population-based study', (2005) 61 *Social Science and Medicine*, pp697–708.

93 R Hastings, 'Parental stress and behavior problems of children with developmental disability', (2002) 27(3) *Journal of Intellectual and Developmental Disability*, pp149–160.

94 E Emerson, C Hatton, G Llewellyn, J Blacker and H Graham, 'Socio-economic position, household composition, health status and indicators of well-being of mothers with and without intellectual disabilities', (2006) 50 *Journal of Intellectual Disability Research*, pp862–873.

Dealing with services

1.48   In addition to the caring work and the practical and financial problems to be tackled at home, parents of disabled children have to have dealings with a wide range of health, education and social care professionals and their organisations. Good services can make an essential contribution to the health, development and well-being of disabled children. They can also be a powerful mediator of stress for parents and other family members. Parents have consistently reported, however, that dealing on a regular basis with poor services and those that are difficult to access can be one of the most stressful aspects of bringing up a disabled child. Contact with such services and battling for what they feel their child needs, often constitutes additional, tiring and frustrating work for already over-stretched families. Over a considerable period of time, a number of themes have consistently emerged from studies which have explored parents' and children's experience as service users.

1.49   There are high levels of unmet need for provision, with many finding that they are not eligible for services that would help them, or that the things that are provided are not suitable. It is not uncommon for families to have lengthy waiting times for an assessment and, subsequently, for the provision of essential equipment, adaptations and other services. Waiting times for services and equipment also vary considerably from area to area. Parents say that they have to be very persistent and active if they are to access provision that they feel would really help their child and other family members. Often children and young people with a range of complex needs – for example those with learning disabilities who also experience mental distress or challenging behaviour are not well served. Many families report that they need to travel some distance to access services for their child.[95]

95 For example, M Hirst, 'Carer distress: a prospective, population-based study', (2005) 61 *Social Science and Medicine*, pp697–708; G M Griffiths and R P Hastings, '"He's hard work but he's worth it". The experience of caregivers of individuals with intellectual disabilities and challenging behaviour: a meta-synthesis of qualitative research', (2014) 27(5) *Journal of Applied Research in Learning Disabilities*, pp401–419. Ofsted, *The special educational needs and disability review 090221*, September 2010; Care Quality Commission, *Health Care for Disabled Children and Young People*, 2012; E Brawn and C Rogers, *Keep us close. Ensuring good, inclusive and accessible local services for disabled children and their families*, Scope, 2012; J Sunman, *A Local Experience of National Concern*, Oxfordshire Family Support Network, 2014; Care Quality Commission, *From the pond into the sea: Children's transition into adult health services*, 2014.

1.50   Services are commissioned and delivered by specialists working in systems of baffling complexity which undergo regular reorganisation. There are problems associated with co-ordination and joint planning between key agencies and disciplines at all levels, resulting in serious problems for children and their parents in relation to essential provision. Studies and official reports have repeatedly called for better service co-ordination and have pointed to the importance of families having a key worker or lead practitioner who acts as a reliable point of contact to help them through the maze and ensure that essential services are delivered.[96] Some of the provisions of the Children and Families Act 2014 which are explained later in this guide, represent the most recent attempt on the part of government to address the problems of fragmented health, education and care services for disabled children and their families.[97]

1.51   In addition to the difficulty of accessing specialist services for their children, families also report that they often meet barriers or problems when they use universal facilities and services which should be accessible to all. Exclusionary practices and limited appreciation of theirs and their children's needs and rights can create considerable difficulties.[98]

1.52   Attention has also been drawn to the particular barriers which disabled parents face and the difficulty of accessing services to assist them in their parenting roles.[99] Their difficulties may often be exacerbated by the lack of effective collaboration between children's and adult social services. Given that recent research has highlighted a clustering of childhood and adult disability in a significant proportion

96 For example, V Greco and P Sloper, 'Care co-ordination and key worker schemes for disabled children: results from a UK-wide survey', (2004) 30 *Child: care, health and development*, pp13–20; 2004; P Sloper, J Beecham, S Clarke, A Franklin, N Moran and L Cusworth, *Models of multi-agency services for transition to adult services for disabled young people and those with complex health needs*, Social Policy Research Unit, University of York, 2010; Children's Workforce Development Council, *Lead professional: practitioners' and managers' guides*, 2007, refreshed March 2010; HM Government, *Working together to safeguard children: A guide to inter-agency working to safeguard and promote the welfare of children*, March 2015.

97 Department for Education/Department of Health (2015) *Special Educational Needs and Disability Code of Practice: 0 to 25 Years*, January 2015.

98 For example, *The Parliamentary hearings on services for disabled children*, October 2006; Contact a Family, *Putting families with disabled children at the heart of the NHS reforms in England*. 2011.

99 CSCI, *Supporting disabled parents: a family or fragmented approach?* Commission for Social Care Inspection, 2009.

of households,[100] it is reasonable to assume that many disabled parents and their disabled children are vulnerable to having serious levels of unmet need.

Problems with information

1.53   Across the whole of childhood and through transition to adulthood, disabled children and their families say that they have difficulty in finding useable information at a time when they need it.[101] It is difficult for families to find essential information about such things as access and entitlements to services and benefits; approaches to managing aspects of a child's condition, development or behaviour; different services to meet different needs; the responsibilities of various organisations; and where to find key contacts. For whatever reasons, it has proved difficult for service-providers to develop systems that are sufficiently sophisticated and user-friendly to cope with both the complexity of the information to be delivered and the diversity of circumstances of those needing it. The important requirement for a new 'local offer' in every local area in England under the Children and Families Act 2014 is a legislative response to this problem.[102]

1.54   A number of studies have described what families regard as the key elements of effective information systems.[103] Parents say that they want short, clear, written guides to local services with more in-depth materials geared to key periods in their children's lives. They also need information on other important matters such as benefit entitlements, disabling conditions and interventions of proven value to their children. Parents want information to be jargon-free and in different formats.

1.55   Government, service-providers and organisations for disabled children and their families have increasingly been using the internet

---

100   C Blackburn, N Spencer and J Read, 'Prevalence of childhood disability and the characteristics and circumstances of disabled children in the UK: secondary analysis of the Family Resources Survey', (2010) *BMC Pediatrics* 10, p21.

101   W Mitchell and P Sloper, *User-friendly information for families with disabled children: a guide to good practice*, York Publishing Services, 2000; Contact a Family, *We're listening*, 2003.

102   Children and Families Act 2014 s30.

103   W Mitchell and P Sloper, *User-friendly information for families with disabled children: a guide to good practice*, York Publishing Services/Joseph Rowntree Foundation, 2000; Contact a Family, *We're listening*, 2003.

to disseminate information.[104] While this is undoubtedly making a positive difference to many, there was initially some concern about the position of families on low incomes on account of their having more limited internet access than others.[105] It was argued that the 'digital divide' might actually exacerbate existing inequalities.[106] This situation may be changing, however, as smart phones, already many people's preferred means of accessing routine information, become more affordable. However good the provision of information becomes, many parents say that it is not enough on its own. They stress the importance of having a person who can act as a key contact for information and other purposes, to make sure that they get what they and their children need.

1.56   A time when information (among other things) is particularly crucial is when children and families find themselves at a critical transition stage – ie a point when something important changes and a significant adjustment of circumstances and arrangements is required. This is sometimes related to a child's age or development, to external arrangements and services, to family circumstances or to a combination of some or all of these. These transitional periods merit attention because of their potential to be hazardous and stressful for the children and adults concerned. Typically at one of these points, the territory is unfamiliar and new knowledge and information have to be found, absorbed and applied to get a satisfactory outcome for the child and family. While these challenging periods may vary with individuals and their circumstances, there are some transitional stages which are predictable and which affect most children and families: (1) the early years when disability may be identified; (2) accessing education; and (3) the transition to adulthood.

104 See for example, Special Educational Needs and Disability Regulations 2014 ('SEND Regs 2014') SI No 1530 reg 57, which requires that a local authority must publish its 'local offer' by placing it on its website, in line with Children and Families Act 2014 s30.

105 C Blackburn and J Read, 'Using the internet? The experiences of parents of disabled children', (2005) *Child: care health and development*, pp507–515.

106 C Blackburn and J Read, 'Using the internet? The experiences of parents of disabled children', (2005) *Child: care health and development*, pp507–515; K Baxter, C Glendinning and S Clarke, 'Making informed choices in social care: the importance of accessible information', (2008) 16 *Health and Social Care in the Community*, pp197–207.

The early years

1.57   For almost all parents, the time when their child was identified as being disabled is highly significant. This remains the case whether disability is identified in the early years of a child's life or later. Parents' accounts suggest that the process of finding out that they have a disabled child is experienced as exceptionally stressful by many.[107] In this section, we focus mainly on the experience of pre-school children and their families, given that improvements in diagnostic techniques mean that more disabled children are being diagnosed at a younger age. We recognise, however, that some parents and their children may be dealing with these issues at a later time.

1.58   As negative perceptions of disability are so widespread, it is not surprising that some parents initially approach the experience of finding that they have a disabled child with at least some of the negative attitudes that they may later come to modify or reject. It is not uncommon for people to describe feeling shocked and overwhelmed.[108] Some may be unsure whether they can cope with what they think will be demanded of them and others may not wish their lives to change in ways that they assume will happen. Many of these concerns are of course entirely understandable, given the attitudes that many encounter and the scarcity of good quality service provision for disabled children in many areas. Personal reactions are diverse and complex but many parents report that getting to know their child through a loving, care-giving relationship means that their initial attitudes change.

1.59   In addition to any personal reactions they may have, studies have identified issues related to the nature and organisation of services that present problems for some parents during the early years. There tends to be agreement among key organisations for disabled children and their families, however, that early years services have improved for at least some groups of children.[109] Some of the progress has been attributed to the highly praised Early Support Programme that operated across the whole of England from 2002–2015 and which introduced a key worker system to help families access the services they needed.

---

107   B Dobson, S Middleton and A Beardsworth, *The impact of childhood disability on family life*, Joseph Rowntree Foundation/York Publishing Services, 2001; *Right from the start*, Scope, 2003.

108   B Dobson, S Middleton and A Beardsworth, *The impact of childhood disability on family life*, Joseph Rowntree Foundation/York Publishing Services, 2001.

109   *The Parliamentary hearings on services for disabled children*, October 2006.

1.60   Notwithstanding the positive support received by some, there are still concerns about the pitfalls for children and families at this crucial time. Common problems include: the stress involved in the process of getting a confirmed diagnosis of their child's impairment or condition;[110] insensitive or inappropriate practice on the part of some professionals and service providers; a lack of information at the right time about key services and benefits; a lack of consistency and co-ordination between multiple service providers; exclusion from key mainstream and community service providers and facilities.[111] As we have seen, some of these barriers are experienced by parents and their children throughout childhood but in the early years they are likely to be dealing with them for the first time and in a situation where both the idea and experience of living with disability are new. Parents can spend a great deal of time and energy trying to find their way around the complex maze of unfamiliar services. Some studies point to the particular difficulties experienced at this time by families from minority ethnic groups and those whose first language is not English.[112]

1.61   Depending on the child's condition, parents may also be extremely concerned about the child's health or even survival. As health and other professionals assess their child and plan and provide interventions, they may find themselves attending frequent appointments with a range of unfamiliar specialists in different settings. Arrangements may be particularly demanding if the child has quite complex impairments. One report illustrated this with reference to the experience of the family of a 13-month-old child who had, over a nine-month period, attended a total of 315 service-based appointments in 12 different locations.[113]

110 Care Quality Commission, *Special review. Healthcare for disabled children and young people*, 2012.

111 Department for Education and Skills, *Together from the start: practical guidance for professionals working with disabled children (birth to third birthday) and their families*, 2003; *The Parliamentary Hearings on Services for Disabled Children*, 2006.

112 C Hatton, Y Akram, R Shah, J Robertson and E Emerson, *Supporting South Asian families with a child with severe disabilities*, Jessica Kingsley Publishers, 2004.

113 Department for Education and Skills, *Together from the start: practical guidance for professionals working with disabled children (birth to third birthday) and their families*, 2003.

1.62   Parents may also have to learn new, sometimes highly technical skills for the first time as they begin to care for their child at home.[114] It is not difficult to see how in this situation, some other aspects of family life may be put on hold.

1.63   As they undertake this taxing level of activity and try to test out the living arrangements that work for them, they may also find that money worries can be a further cause of stress. The impact of the higher costs of disabled living and reduced income can bite quite early. There may be an immediate impact on parents', particularly mothers', choices about working outside the home. As we have seen, suitable and affordable day care is often hard to come by, making the demands of caring and working very difficult to manage (see chapter 8 on carers' rights). As we noted earlier, considerable numbers of lone parents manage all of this unaided by a partner. We have also seen that the first two years of a disabled child's life, may be a time when some adult relationships come under pressure.[115]

1.64   Successive governments have recognised the importance of early intervention to support children and families and to improve long-term outcomes for them. Recent work has drawn attention to the fact that while children with learning disabilities are at greatly increased risk of developing behaviour difficulties, often resulting in a poorer quality of life for children and their families, far too few are provided with effective, evidence-based early interventions.[116]

Getting an education

1.65   Like all children, disabled children have a right to suitable education. In 2014, the English government introduced a number of measures to reform the system of education for children who have special educational needs (SEN) and disabilities. These recent changes are explained later in this handbook (see chapter 4). In this section, we consider the majority of disabled children and young people who go to day schools within travelling distance of home. The experience of

---

114 S Kirk and C Glendinning, 'Developing services to support parents caring for a technology-dependent child at home', (2004) 30 *Child: care, health and development*, pp209–218.

115 H Clarke and S McKay, *Exploring disability, family formation and break-up: reviewing the evidence*, Research Report No 514, Department for Work and Pensions, 2008.

116 Challenging Behaviour Foundation, *Early intervention for children with learning disabilities whose behaviours challenge*, Briefing Paper, 2014.

those who attend residential schools is considered in a later section about children who live away from home.

1.66   The term 'special educational needs' (SEN) was introduced into policy and law in the early 1980s following the Warnock report.[117] Children were deemed to have special educational needs if they had a significantly greater difficulty in learning than most children of the same age. Those with higher levels of need that required the local authority to arrange additional or different educational provision were given a statement of SEN produced in accordance with prescribed statutory procedures. In 2015, 15.4 per cent of children in England were identified as having SEN and just under three per cent had a statement or an EHC plan.[118] Pupils with SEN are drawn disproportionately from more disadvantaged backgrounds and there is substantial variation between geographical areas in the proportion of children deemed to have SEN.[119] Almost all children with SEN who do not have statements (these are now being converted to 'education, health and care (EHC) plans' – see paras 4.134–4.163 below) are educated in mainstream schools while 4 in 10 of those with a statement are placed in special schools. Autistic spectrum disorder is the most common primary need for children with statements. Among pupils placed in special schools, the most frequent primary needs are identified as severe learning difficulty (24.7 per cent), autistic spectrum disorder (21.5 per cent) and moderate learning difficulty (17.8 per cent).[120]

1.67   Some children with SEN and disabilities and their parents undoubtedly have good experiences of well-managed, high quality education services[121] and the majority of parents report that they are satisfied with their children's educational provision as a whole.[122] A recent review of evidence by the Department for Work and Pensions, indicates that in the past few years, levels of educational attainment for children with SEN at key stages 2 and 4 have improved overall though the gap between those without SEN and those who have SEN with a statement has widened. The proportion of disabled 19-year-

117 Department of Education and Science, *The report of the committee of enquiry into the education of handicapped children and young people* (the Warnock Report), Cmnd 7212, HMSO, 1978.

118 Department for Education, *Statistical release. Children with special educational needs 2015. An analysis,* 2015.

119 Ofsted, *The Special Educational Needs and Disability Review 091221,* 2010.

120 Department for Education, *Statistical release. Children with special educational needs 2015. An analysis,* 2015.

121 Ofsted, *The Special Educational Needs and Disability Review 091221,* 2010; Lamb Inquiry, *Special educational needs and parental confidence,* DCSF, 2009.

122 Lamb Inquiry, *Special educational needs and parental confidence,* DCSF, 2009.

olds without a Level 3 qualification has also fallen in recent years from 74 per cent to 53 per cent and is converging towards the average for non-disabled young people.[123]

1.68   Despite these improvements, a range of research studies[124] and official reports[125] suggest that substantial numbers of children and their parents are not well-served in the education system, and encounter serious problems as they try to navigate what is a very complex system. Common themes emerge from these sources. Parents report experiences that are stressful and difficult and they often describe protracted battles to gain access to what they regard as essential services for their children. While many parents may value the confidence and security derived from having a statement/plan, they can feel disadvantaged in a system that is unfamiliar and difficult to understand. Some parents and children have difficulty in finding the information they need, preparing the necessary written submissions as well as reading and commenting on professional reports. Being in disagreement with the school, individual professionals or the local authority and going through procedures to resolve disputes is also experienced as highly stressful. Even when parents are satisfied with how processes work and with the outcomes, they often report that they have had to be engaged very actively with the system and to have worked very hard to make progress for their children. A 2014 report by the local government ombudsman[126] identified six key main areas of concern:

1) delays in the process which can often lead to other problems, such as the loss of education;
2) inadequate assessment and review of statements of SEN;
3) poor planning of an individual's SEN support, particularly in the key transition phases;
4) failure to provide specific SEN support, such as qualified specialists;

123 Department for Work and Pensions, *Fulfilling potential. Building a deeper understanding of disability in the UK Today*, 2013.
124 R Tennant, M Callanan, D Snape, I Palmer and J Read, *Special educational needs disagreement resolution services: national evaluation*, Research Report DCSF-RR054, DCSF, 2008. See also C Penfold, N Cleghorn, R Tennant, I Palmer and J Read, *Parental confidence in the special educational needs assessment, statementing and tribunal system: a qualitative study*, Research Report RR117, DCSF, 2009.
125 Lamb Inquiry, *Special educational needs and parental confidence*, DCSF, 2009; Ofsted, *Special education needs and disability review*, 2010.
126 Office of the Local Government Ombudsman, *Special Educational Needs: preparing for the futures*, 2014.

5) unlawful exclusions, children wrongfully excluded from the educational system due to their SEN; and

6) failure to ensure suitable SEN provision in a council's area.

There is also increasing recognition that between local authorities there is not only substantial variation in the proportion of children identified as having SEN but also in the nature and quantity of services provided for them.[127]

1.69   Within education for children with SEN and disabilities, a key issue remains the setting where they should be educated. From the late 1970s onwards, there has been a growing challenge to the then established wisdom that it was both necessary and desirable for disabled children to be educated in separate schools from their non-disabled peers. By the mid–1990s, the inclusion of disabled children in mainstream schools had gained official support.[128] Increasingly, law, policy and practice assumes that mainstream schooling is the appropriate option for disabled children unless there is a particular reason why their needs cannot be met in this way. In recent times, inclusion in education has come to be seen as one crucial aspect of disabled children's right to social inclusion more generally. As might be expected, there is variation in the reactions of disabled children and adults and their families to these shifts in thinking and to the experiences of both inclusive and separate education.[129] Some of these variations may be explained by the different educational needs of some groups of disabled children: for instance, children with autistic spectrum disorders compared with those who have physical or sensory impairments.

1.70   Parents of disabled children have to make difficult choices about what they regard as being in their children's interests at any particular time. They have to consider the information that is available to

127 J Lewis, A Mooney, L Brady, C Gill, A Henshall, N Willmott and J Statham, *Special educational needs and disability: understanding local variation in prevalence, service provision and support*, DCSF Research Report DCSF-RR211, 2010.

128 Department for Education and Employment, *Excellence for all children, meeting special educational needs*, The Stationery Office, 1998.

129 M Priestly and P Rabiee, 'Hope and fears: stakeholders' views on transfer of special school resources towards inclusion', (2002) 6 *Inclusive Education* pp371–390; C Rogers, 'Experiencing an "inclusive" education: parents and their children with "special educational needs"', (2007) 28 *British Journal of the Sociology of Education*, pp55–68; Ofsted, *Inclusion: Does it matter where pupils are taught? Provision and outcomes in different settings for pupils with learning difficulties and disabilities*, 2006.

them, take all circumstances they can into account and decide on what seems to them to be the best option for their children.

1.71   The government in England has argued that it has introduced its most recent reforms in response to the evidence that the existing system was complex and that it was often difficult for children and young people to get the help they needed at the right time.[130] Statements are being phased out and replaced by a single assessment process and a combined EHC plan in an effort to integrate the planning and delivery of education, health and social care from birth to 25 years of age. In addition, the stated aims of the reforms are to involve parents more in assessments, to give them greater control over the funding allocated to their children and to offer greater choice of school placement.[131] See chapter 4 at paras 4.21–4.31 for an overview of the reforms. It is too early to tell what the impact of the reforms will be but experience dictates that there is no credible 'quick fix' in a system which has to attempt to meet the differentiated needs of a complex population of disabled children within the resources that local and central government deem to be available.

Transition to adulthood

1.72   The limited opportunities afforded to young disabled people during the transition to adulthood and beyond, have long been a cause for serious concern. Research and official reports have consistently documented the things that make it an exceptionally hazardous time for many disabled young adults and their families. It is little wonder that it has become common for many disabled young people and their parents known to the authors, to refer to this period in their lives as 'the transition cliff'. Bringing about improvements in the experience of transition and their lives as young adults, is held to be a key focus of the current reform of the law, including the extension of the scope of EHC plans to the age of 25. Consistent themes emerge from

130 Department for Education, *Increasing options and improving provision for children with special educational needs (SEN)*, 2014.
131 Department for Education, *Support and aspiration: A new approach to special educational needs and disability*, 2011.

the large number of official reports[132] and research studies[133] on the experience of transition.

1.73   While there have been some improvements in the experience of disabled young people (see below), it is all too easy for many to leave school and find themselves living a different life from that they would wish and one that is significantly more restricted than their non-disabled peers. For many, there are low expectations about what they have a right to look forward to as adults and a lack of meaningful consultation with them and their families about their aspirations and the decisions to be made. If they are to maximise their health, well-being and life chances as adults, disabled young people together with their families, will need to have the opportunity to identify the outcomes they want and to plan the arrangements and services that will enable them to happen. Identifying young disabled people's needs and wishes in relation to post-school education, health, social care, independent living and employment is fundamental.

1.74   Despite the raft of existing legal duties intended to ensure that this type of assessment and planning take place in a timely fashion (see chapter 10), there is widespread under-recognition of need, inadequate planning and poor co-ordination between services. There is variation in practice in different areas of the country, and young people and their parents may find that they have to be extremely

132 For example, HM Treasury and Department for Education and Skills, *Aiming high for disabled children: better support for families*, 2007; Commission for Social Care Inspection, *Growing up matters: better transition planning for young people with complex needs*, 2007; Department for Education, *Support and aspiration. A new approach to special educational needs and disability*, 2011; Department for Work and Pensions, *Fulfilling potential. Building a deeper understanding of disability in the UK Today*, 2013.

133 For example, M Knapp, M Perkins, J Beecham, S Dhanasiri and C Rustin, 'Transition pathways for young people with complex disabilities: exploring the economic consequences', (2008) 34 *Child: care, health and development*, pp512–520; J Beecham, T Snell, M Perkins and M Knapp, *After transition: health and social care needs of young adults with long-term neurological conditions*, PSSRU Research Summary 48, London School of Economics, 2008; S Beyer, A Kaehne, J Grey, K Sheppard, and, A Meek, 'The transition of young people with learning disabilities to employment: what works?' (2008) 14:1 *Journal of Developmental Disabilities*, pp85–94; P Sloper, J Beecham, S Clarke, A Franklin, N Moran and L Cusworth, 'Transition to adult services for disabled young people and those with complex health needs', *Research Works*, 2011–02, Social Policy Research Unit, University of York; B Beresford, N Moran, P Sloper, L Cusworth, W Mitchell, G Spiers, K Weston and J Beecham, *Transition to Adult Services and Adulthood for Young People with Autistic Spectrum Conditions*, Working Paper no DH 2525, Social Policy Research Unit, University of York, 2013; J Sunman, *A Local Experience of National Concern*, Oxfordshire Family Support Network, 2014.

well informed and persistent to gain access to the supports that they need. Important systems, organisations and funding streams are often complex, and many young people and their parents do not feel clear about the options available to them. The young people who do best, tend to be those who have family, friends, and significant other people in their lives who are able to help shape and sustain their aspirations through school and give them active practical help and advice as they negotiate their way through post-school provision.

1.75   Disabled 16-year-olds' aspirations about post-school education and employment have risen and are now not significantly different from those of their non-disabled peers but sadly for many, these aspirations are not translated into comparable attainments in post-school education or employment. However positive their aspirations may have been at 16, by the time they reach the age of 26, there is a widening gap between them and their non-disabled peers in terms of their subjective sense of well-being as well as their confidence about their abilities in relation to employment.[134] Data from the 2011 Youth Cohort Study shows that by the time they reach 18, 30 per cent of those who had a statement of SEN when they were in Year 11, and 22 per cent of those who had declared that they were disabled, were not in any form of education, employment or training, compared with 13 per cent of their non-disabled peers.[135] In the UK, there are around 200,000 disabled young people age 16–24 in this category.[136]

1.76   The difference in the rate of unemployment between disabled and non-disabled young people is reduced as the level of qualifications increases. Earlier in this chapter, we saw that while there have been improvements overall in the school-age educational achievements of disabled children and young people, the poor educational outcomes of many continue to be a cause for concern. This may account in part, for the restricted options that are available to some young people in transition and early adulthood, particularly in employment. There is also variation in employment by the type of impairment a young person has. Young people with learning disabilities and those who face mental health issues consistently have fewer opportunities.[137]

134 T Burchardt, *The education and employment of disabled young people,* Joseph Rowntree Foundation, 2005.

135 Ofsted, *Progression post-16 for learners with learning difficulties and/or disabilities,* 2011.

136 Department for Work and Pensions, *Fulfilling potential. Building a deeper understanding of disability in the UK today,* 2013.

137 Department for Work and Pensions, *Fulfilling potential. Building a deeper understanding of disability in the UK today,* 2013.

1.77 Improving access to appropriate courses in further and higher education may be crucial to some disabled young people's future well-being and success.[138] Funding arrangements for further education (FE) have often been regarded as complex and difficult to manage.[139] Ofsted found that the multi-agency assessments carried out by local authorities to determine a young person's support needs and programme requirements prior to transfer to post-16 education, were frequently of an inadequate standard and that many young people entitled to them had not been assessed at all.[140] Provision varied considerably from area to area and for those with the highest levels of need, there was very little choice locally. While the inspectorate found good provision in a range of specialist and mainstream settings, they found too little attention paid to learning opportunities linked to future employment. Funding restrictions meant that some students were only able to have around three days per week foundation learning which was not adequate to prepare them for other destinations, including employment. In addition, Ofsted drew attention to the absence of systematic ways of collecting information about what happened to young people once they had left their FE college or of monitoring the effectiveness of this provision in supporting progression.

1.78 An increasing number of disabled young people are entering higher education (HE) and once there, their attainments are comparable to those of non-disabled students. Having a degree level qualification also significantly improves a young person's employment prospects, bringing them almost in line with their non-disabled peers in this respect. In 2010/11, 40,000 disabled people qualified from full-time HE courses. Those who receive a disabled student allowance (DSA) are less likely to leave a course early than those who do not.[141] The DSA is used to purchase equipment and other forms of study support to enable disabled students to participate fully as learners (see chapter 10, paras 10.91–10.93). In 2014, the government proposed changes to the DSA which would entail institutions of HE taking greater responsibility for meeting disabled students' learning

---

138 National Audit Office, *Oversight of Special Education for Young People age 16–25*, 2011.

139 Department for Education, *Support and aspiration: A new approach to special educational needs and disability*, 2011.

140 Ofsted, *Progression post-16 for learners with learning difficulties and/or disabilities.* 2011.

141 Department for Work and Pensions, *Fulfilling potential. Building a deeper understanding of disability in the UK today*, 2013.

and support needs as part of the way that they discharge their duties under the Equality Act 2010.[142] Following a challenge to this proposal by a range of groups and organisations, the government postponed the introduction of these changes until the academic year 2016/17 and made them subject to the outcome of a public consultation.[143]

1.79   In terms of social care support, young people and their families will almost certainly come across problems as responsibilities for their support and assistance are transferred from children's to adult services. Some services which young people have had access to as children are discontinued and are not replaced by age-appropriate provision for young adults. Local authority financial restrictions have had a substantial negative impact on adult social care[144] and as a consequence many disabled young adults have inevitably been deemed ineligible for social care services or only offered a limited range of supports. Health services too, have frequently seemed unequal to the task of co-ordinating and delivering healthcare to young people and young adults with complex needs. [145]

1.80   As with any young adult, options for greater independence in adulthood can encompass a wide range of arrangements depending on the circumstances, needs and wishes of those concerned and the resources made available to them. For example, a young person's choices about living separately from their family of origin will be affected among other things, by the accommodation and supported living opportunities available to them, money, their educational opportunities, their culture and social background, their relationships inside and outside the family and so on. Some young people and their families may wish to continue to live together but want the chance to pursue separate interests, activities and lifestyles; some young people may favour group living with others of a similar age, some may want to work towards getting a place of their own and so on. Available evidence suggests, however, that choices are severely restricted for many young disabled adults who find that they continue to be very dependent on their parents for every day living

142 Department for Business, Innovation and Skills, *Written Ministerial Statement by David Willetts, Minister for Universities and Science*, 7 April 2014.

143 Department for Business, Innovation and Skills, *Written Ministerial Statement by Rt Hon Greg Clark, Minister of State for Universities, Science and Cities*, 12 September 2014.

144 ADASS, *Annual Budget Survey*, June 2015.

145 Care Quality Commission, *Special review. Healthcare for disabled children and young people*, 2012; Care Quality Commission, *From the pond into the sea: children's transition into adult health services*, 2014.

arrangements whatever anyone might otherwise wish. Long-term unemployment and reliance on benefits has a range of negative personal and financial consequences for many disabled young adults and their families.[146]

1.81   While many disabled young people experience an unsatisfactory transition to adulthood and adult services, the experiences of three groups merit particular attention on account of their circumstances or unmet needs. Firstly, because other people may have a limited view of what is appropriate and possible, those with complex impairments and high support needs may be allowed a very restricted range of opportunities and aspirations and are likely to be offered only segregated services as young adults. Recent work following the revelations of abuse at Winterbourne View hospital in 2011, has drawn attention to the limited community-based provision available to young people with learning disabilities whose behaviours challenge. Some may have autism or mental health issues in addition.[147] Families of these young people have pointed to the risk of their being placed inappropriately in hospital settings when other options are not available in the post-school period.[148] In 2013, more than 20 per cent of people occupying in-patient beds for mental and behavioural healthcare were between the ages 18–24 years, a sharp rise from the proportion who were under 18 (5.7 per cent).[149]

1.82   By contrast, the second group comprises young people who have lower support needs, including those with mild learning disabilities and those with a diagnosis of autism but with no learning disability. Their needs may not be met because they are regarded as ineligible for support services. They may find themselves in jeopardy as a result.[150]

146 M Knapp, M Perkins, J Beecham, S Dhanasiri and C Rustin, 'Transition pathways for young people with complex disabilities: exploring the economic consequences', (2008) 34 *Child: care, health and development*, pp512–520.

147 National Audit Office, *Care services for people with learning disabilities and challenging behaviour*, 2015.

148 J Sunman, *A Local Experience of National Concern*, Oxfordshire Family Support Network, 2014.

149 Health and Social Care Information Centre, *Learning Disabilities Census Report*, 2013.

150 Prime Minister's Strategy Unit, *Improving the life chances of disabled people*, TSO, 2005; Commission for Social Care Inspection, *Growing up matters: better transition for young people with complex needs*, 2007; B Beresford, N Moran, P Sloper, L Cusworth, W Mitchell, G Spiers, K Weston and J Beecham, 'Transition to adult services and adulthood for young people with autistic spectrum conditions', Working Paper no DH 2525, Social Policy Research Unit, University of York, 2013.

1.83   The final group of young people are those who have spent time in residential placements away from their families and neighbourhoods. The majority on leaving school return to their areas of origin. Most appear either to return to live with their families or to have some form of residential care and it is reported that choices offered to them are limited and frequently not well-planned.[151]

Children who live away from home

1.84   While the majority of disabled children live with their families of origin and go to day schools, a minority live away from home for all or some of the year. Some are in boarding schools in term-time and go home to their families for holidays and some weekends; some are weekly or two-weekly boarders; some stay at school 52 weeks a year (see chapter 4 at paras 4.202–4.205); some are in healthcare settings and others are 'looked after' (see chapter 3 at paras 3.144 and 3.147) by local authorities. These categories of placements and settings are not entirely separate as there may be some overlap. For example, a looked-after child may go to residential school.

1.85   There is no doubt that for a long time, disabled children who lived away from home were a very neglected group who did not feature in the main policy agendas.[152] The past ten years have seen some attention being given to this population of children and young people in research and official reports,[153] but the information that we have about them remains inadequate, for example, about the numbers and characteristics of children and young people, the triggers and pathways that take them to particular settings away from home, their

---

151 P Heslop and D Abbott 'Help to move on – but to what? Young people with learning difficulties moving on from out-of-area residential schools or colleges', (2008) 37 *British Journal of Learning Disability*, pp12–20.

152 J Morris, *Gone missing? A research and policy review of disabled children living away from home*, Who Cares Trust, 1995.

153 For example, D Abbott, J Morris and L Ward, *Disabled children and residential schools: a survey of local authority policy and practice*, Norah Fry Research Centre, University of Bristol, 2000; A Pinney, *Disabled children in residential placements*, DfES, 2005; Regional Partnerships, *Analysis of Out of Authority Placements*, July 2008; P McGill, 'Residential schools for children with learning disabilities in England: recent research and issues for future provision', (2008) 13(4) *Tizard Learning Disability Review*; P Heslop and D Abbott, 'Help to move on – but to what? Young people with learning difficulties moving on from out-of-area residential schools or colleges', (2009) 37 *British Journal of Learning Disability*, pp12–20; Health and Social Care Information Centre, *Learning Disabilities Census Report*, 2013.

educational and other personal outcomes, and what happens to them as they reach adulthood.[154]

1.86   A report by the Office of the Children's Commissioner for England provides an extremely useful summary of the information that is available on disabled children in residential education.[155] It indicates that there has been a year on year decline in numbers of children boarding in recent times. In 2014, there were 6,070 children and young people placed in residential special schools of all types. Across all sectors, there are 379 schools catering for children and young people from the ages 2 to 25 years. There is a concentration of schools in the south of England and over half of the children who are boarders are placed in the southern regions of the country. A total of 192 residential special schools have dual registration as children's homes. Dual registration is required if any child stays for more than 295 days per year. Children in these settings are generally assumed to have more complex and higher support needs than those in other boarding schools and it is also thought that a higher proportion are likely to be looked-after children. Independent providers account for 88 per cent of dual registered schools, and they provide for 79 per cent of children needing such settings.

1.87   The information provided by the annual school census on individual pupils at residential school, is severely limited as it excludes details on the characteristics of those attending independent boarding schools. These schools make up nearly half of all residential schools. The information collected about children and young people at other boarding schools indicates that 75 per cent were boys and that 60 per cent of pupils were aged 12 to 16 years. In terms of the children's primary special educational needs, 29 per cent were identified to have emotional, behavioural and social difficulties, 18 per cent autistic spectrum disorder and 14 per cent hearing impairment. More than a quarter of boarders were placed over twenty miles from home and nearly a third in schools outside their own authorities. 10 per cent of boarders in the non-independent schools were looked-

---

154 Audit Commission, *Out of authority placements for special educational needs*, Audit Commission Publications, 2007; Department of Health, *Valuing people: a new strategy for learning disability for the 21st century*, TSO, 2001; Commission for Social Care Inspection, *Growing up matters: better transition for young people with complex needs*, 2007; A Pinney, *Children with learning disabilities whose behaviours challenge. What do we know from national data?*, Challenging Behaviour Foundation and the Council for Disabled Children, 2014.

155 The Office of the Children's Commissioner, *The views and experiences of children in residential special schools: overview report*, 2014.

after children, the majority of whom (61 per cent) were there through a voluntary agreement under section 20 of the Children Act 1989.

1.88   Not all looked-after disabled children go to residential special schools. Again, it is widely recognised that the information that we have about the whole group of looked-after disabled children is incomplete.[156] While the special educational needs profile of children who are looked after by local authorities, is in many respects similar to all children with SEN, there are some differences. Those who are looked after are most likely to have been assessed as having behavioural, emotional and social disorders. In 2014, this applied to 40 per cent of looked after children who had statements of SEN. They were also more likely to have moderate learning difficulties (17.7 per cent) compared with their peers who were not looked after (15.5 per cent). A major difference was also that only 8.7 per cent of looked-after children with SEN were identified as having autistic spectrum disorders compared with 21.9 per cent of all children with statements of SEN.[157] Even though the information on the whole population is fragmented, some research has indicated that looked-after disabled children are likely to remain in care for longer than their non-disabled peers, less likely to return home and have a higher risk of being placed inappropriately. For many, there appear to be barriers to achieving permanent and stable living arrangements.[158]

1.89   We do not know enough about disabled children placed in health-care settings. However, the learning disability census introduced in the wake of revelations in 2011 of abuse of people with learning disabilities at Winterbourne View hospital, has begun to fill major information gaps about a particular group of children and young people. It provides an annual snapshot of all children and adults with a learning disability, autistic spectrum disorders and/or behaviour that challenges, who are in in-patient settings. Of the 3,250 counted in the 2013 census,[159] 185 were under 18 years of age. While these facilities are supposed to be mainly for short-term assessment and treatment, the census shows that many do not operate in that way.

156 A Pinney, *Disabled children in residential placements*, DfES, 2005; C Baker, *Permanence and Stability for Disabled Looked After Children*, Institute for Research and Innovation in Social Services, 2011.

157 A Pinney, *Children with Learning Disabilities Whose Behaviours Challenge. What do we know from national data?*, Challenging Behaviour Foundation and the Council for Disabled Children, 2014.

158 C Baker, *Permanence and stability for disabled looked after children*, Institute for Research and Innovation in Social Services, 2011.

159 Health and Social Care Information Centre, *Learning Disabilities Census Report*, 2013.

A 2014 report which analysed additional unpublished data from the learning disability census on the 236 children and young people aged under 19 years, found that 41 per cent stayed in hospital for up to three months and 74 per cent for up to a year. 14 children and young people had been in these units for five years or more.[160] 29 per cent of the children were placed more than 100 km from home. Frequency of the use of restrictive practices such as restraint and seclusion were issues of concern. At the time of writing, all available evidence indicates that efforts to meet the formal government target of moving people from the assessment and treatment units to appropriate community-based provision have failed.[161] This failure has led to the publication of a government consultation on a series of proposals, including for law reform, to drive change for this particularly vulnerable group.[162] While the focus of this programme is clearly on adults, it is important to many families with children who look towards their sons' and daughters' future lives with considerable concern.

1.90   Too little is known about what determines whether children leave home and live apart from their families for some or all of the time. Some parents and children feel that a placement in residential school, for example, is a positive choice and one which works to the child's benefit.[163] Unfortunately for others, a placement away from home (whether in a school or some other setting) appears to happen more because other preferred services (including appropriate child and family support) are not available.

1.91   There are indications that the age of the young person may be a factor in placement decisions. Information on looked-after children and those in residential schooling shows that the majority are beyond primary school age[164] and that there are also substantial numbers of teenage boys assessed as having emotional, behavioural and social

---

160 A Pinney, *Children with learning disabilities whose behaviours challenge. What do we know from national data?*, Challenging Behaviour Foundation and the Council for Disabled Children, 2014.

161 National Audit Office, *Care services for people with learning disabilities and challenging behaviour*, 2015; J Sunman, *A local experience of national concern*, Oxfordshire Family Support Network and Healthwatch Oxford, 2014.

162 Department of Health, *No voice unheard, no right ignored – a consultation for people with learning disabilities, autism and mental health conditions*, March 2015; Department of Health, *Government response to No voice unheard, no right ignored – a consultation for people with learning disabilities, autism and mental health conditions*, November 2015.

163 The Office of the Children's Commissioner, *The views and experiences of children in residential special schools: overview report*, 2014.

164 Lamb Inquiry, *Special educational needs and parental confidence*, DCSF, 2009.

disorders, challenging behaviour and autism in residential schools. Many parents look after their children with little outside support for years before taking a decision to find some form of residential provision. A limited amount of research on residential schooling as well as anecdotal accounts suggest that as some children get older, particularly if they have high support needs or challenging behaviour, their families may not feel that they can continue to provide the levels of support and care that they require.[165] It is sometimes suggested that even when a child goes away from home for primarily social or family reasons, some parents may find residential schooling a preferable and less stigmatising option to other provision.[166]

1.92   In some cases, residential schooling is required only because there is no suitable educational provision to meet the child's needs in his or her own locality. As rates of placement in residential school vary substantially from one local authority to another,[167] it is reasonable to conclude that decisions have as much to do with local policy and resources as with children's educational needs. The same point may be made in relation to out-of-area services for looked-after disabled children and young people.

1.93   Studies of children with complex needs who spend substantial periods in healthcare settings have suggested that a lack of appropriate community-based services for them and their families contributes to their being admitted and remaining in hospital for long stays.[168] Even if a hospital admission may be appropriate for some children, and young adults who face a health crisis, this should not become a long-term option simply because there is nothing else available or because the fact that funding does not follow the patient, means there is no financial incentive for local areas to bring them home.[169]

165 D Abbott, J Morris and L Ward, *Disabled children and residential schools: a survey of local authority policy and practice*, Norah Fry Research Centre, University of Bristol, 2000.
166 D Abbott, J Morris and L Ward, *Disabled children and residential schools: a survey of local authority policy and practice*, Norah Fry Research Centre, University of Bristol, 2000.
167 D Abbott, J Morris and L Ward, *Disabled children and residential schools: a survey of local authority policy and practice*, Norah Fry Research Centre, University of Bristol, 2000.
168 K Stalker, J Carpenter, R Phillips, C Connors, C MacDonald, J Eyre and J Noyes, *Care and treatment? Supporting children with complex needs in healthcare settings*, Pavilion Publishing, 2003; J Sunman, *A Local Experience of National Concern*, Oxfordshire Family Support Network and Healthwatch Oxford, 2014.
169 National Audit Office, *Care services for people with learning disabilities and challenging behavior*, 2015.

1.94　　　Lengthy out-of-area placements are likely to result in some children and young people becoming cut off from their families.[170] It appears, however, that the majority of children in residential special schools go home regularly and that many schools see facilitating contact between children and their families as an important element of their work.[171] Despite this, maintaining contact can be particularly challenging for some, due, for example, to distance, transport arrangements and expense.

1.95　　　While some children and young people may benefit overall from placements away from home, some may not. Some placements may deny a child the chance to participate in ordinary features of life. Many families and children have concerns about safeguarding and protection from abuse in residential settings[172] and this is small wonder given the recent evidence that has come to light about some health settings. In any event, being separated from family is clearly a significant matter for any child. This makes it crucial that it is not a placement that happens because of deficits in other community-based services or that arrangements do not isolate a child from significant family and community relationships. Some studies indicate that young disabled people are very likely to return to their family or area of origin after they have finished in residential school, making the maintenance of those personal links even more crucial.[173]

Services for disabled children and their families

1.96　　At the beginning of this chapter we said that disabled children and those close to them are entitled to enjoy the same human rights as others. Even though some of their needs and priorities may be different from those who do not live with disability, this does not mean that they should be prevented from participating in ordinary experiences that others may take for granted. Disabled children and their

170　D Abbott, J Morris and L Ward, *Disabled children and residential schools: a survey of local authority policy and practice*, Norah Fry Research Centre, University of Bristol, 2000.

171　A Pinney, *Disabled children in residential placements*, DfES, 2005.

172　The Office of the Children's Commissioner, *The views and experiences of children in residential special schools: overview report*, 2014; J Sunman, *A local experience of national concern*, Oxfordshire Family Support Network and Healthwatch Oxford, 2014.

173　P Heslop and D Abbott, 'Help to move on – but to what? Young people with learning difficulties moving on from out-of-area residential schools or colleges', (2009) 37 *British Journal of Learning Disability*, pp12–20.

families may need additional supports and different arrangements to enable them to participate in things that are part and parcel of an ordinary life. The aim of policies and services should be to enable them to maximise their health, well-being and life chances and to promote opportunities for full social participation. This includes universal services and organisations as well as those that are more specialist or targeted. Universal services are required by the reasonable adjustments duty in the Equality Act 2010 to make adjustments to improve their accessibility to disabled children.[174]

1.97   As far as services and other arrangements are concerned, it has long been accepted as good practice that one size does not fit all and that a much more flexible approach to meeting children's and families' needs is required. The principle is well established that children and their families, jointly with relevant professionals, should be able to identify outcomes that are important for living an ordinary life and then, together, plan arrangements and services which enable those outcomes to be achieved. The test as to whether the plan works, is whether the outcomes are realised. The child and the family, rather than service providers, commissioners and other professionals, should be at the centre of this process which should be driven by their needs, choices and aspirations. The professionals and their organisations should collaborate effectively with each other in order to plan and deliver.[175] It is also well-established that what is provided does not need to take the form of familiar services, though sometimes it may – some children and families, for example, may wish to access existing short break facilities because they find them beneficial.[176] While some parents and their children may be clear about what would work best for them, others may find it helpful to gain from the ideas and experiences of other families and organisations representing their interests, as well as service providers. For example, a range of information materials and case studies are now available to assist young people and their families as they decide what might be the most preferable options for them in the transition to

---

174 Equality Act 2010 ss20–22. See chapter 9 at paras 9.39–9.42.

175 See for example, Department for Education and Skills, *Together from the start: practical guidance for professionals working with disabled children (birth to third birthday) and their families*, 2003. HM Government, *Working Together to Safeguard Children: A guide to inter-agency working to safeguard and promote the welfare of children*, March 2015; G Hanrahan, *Moving into adulthood and getting a life: getting started*, Oxfordshire Family Support Network, 2014.

176 C Hatton, M Collins, V Welch, J Robertson, E Emerson, S Langer and E Well, *The impact of short breaks on families with a disabled child over time*, DFE-RR173, 2011.

adulthood.[177] As we have seen earlier in this chapter, however, it is not always easy for young people and their families to access the appropriate and up-to-date information they need.

1.98 These basic ideas were first taken forward in the field of adult social care with the development of what became known as the 'personalisation agenda'. Personal budgets and 'self-directed support', key features of personalisation, are now being introduced and promoted for disabled children and their families.[178] A personal budget is a sum of money that is allocated to an individual or family to spend on help and support to meet their assessed eligible needs and to achieve agreed outcomes. According to the personalisation principles, this aims to give the child and family more control. Families can access their personal budgets through a direct payment or, if they do not wish to do this, can manage them with the assistance of a third party, including the local authority. Direct payments for disabled children and their families are not new. Instead of having local authority social care services provided in kind, families have been able to choose to have a direct payment equivalent to the cost so that they may purchase them themselves.[179] To begin with, personal or individual budgets only applied to social care support funded by social services but at the time of writing, they are in the process of being extended to some forms of health and educational provision. Families are also able to have a personal budget as part of an EHC plan, covering all three types of provision.[180]

1.99 Some children, young people and their families have undoubtedly found that direct payments and personal budgets suit them very well and are satisfied with the type of support offered and the degree of control they have.[181] It is important, however, to recognise that they are unlikely to suit everyone. While many may subscribe to the principles of personalisation, of having a greater degree of flexibility and control and of shifting the existing balance of power more in their

177 See for example, K Sibthorpe and T Nicoll, *Making it personal. A family guide to personalisation, personal budgets and education, health and care plans*, Kids/In Control, 2014; G Hanrahan, *Moving into adulthood and getting a life*, Oxfordshire Family Support Network, 2014; Challenging Behaviour Foundation, *Positive Behaviour Support Planning*, 2015.

178 K Sibthorpe and T Nicoll, *Making it personal. A family guide to personalisation, personal budgets and education, health and care plans*, Kids/In Control, 2014.

179 These were first made available by the Carers and Disabled Children Act 2000.

180 K Sibthorpe and T Nicoll, *Making it personal. A family guide to personalisation, personal budgets and education, health and care plans*, Kids/In Control, 2014.

181 J Waters and C Hatton, *Measuring the outcomes of EHC plans and personal budgets*, Lancaster University and In Control, Summer 2014.

favour, not everyone believes that personal budgets are the necessary vehicle to achieving this and to bringing about the promised
improvements in people's lives. Some raise questions about whether
personal budgets may place additional stress on some families who
are already overstretched, and also draw attention the fact that the
new system will not solve the problem of the shortfall of skilled support to meet some children's needs. [182] There is no doubt, too, that
like any other system, the new arrangements may fall foul of auster-
ity measures, leaving children and families without adequate support. A personal budget is after all, only available to pay for assessed,
eligible needs (see chapter 3 at paras 3.103–3.107).

1.100   Some families' concerns about new policies come from their
experience of the harsh day-to-day reality of trying to obtain what
they believe their children need and should have a right to, rather
than because they lack vision. In a recent workshop organised by the
Challenging Behaviour Foundation, parents and children were asked
to say what they would like and they produced the messages shown
opposite.

Conclusion

1.101   This chapter has emphasised that disabled children and those close
to them are entitled to enjoy the same human rights as others and
to expect a quality of life comparable to that of their peers who do
not live with disability. However, as can be seen from the level of
social exclusion that they experience and the barriers they face, the
aspiration of a more ordinary way of life is still beyond the reach
of many disabled children and their families. Challenging the social
exclusion and discrimination faced by these children and families
and bringing about positive change for their benefit is a considerable
task requiring on-going political, social and legal action. This book
focuses on the contribution that the law can make towards the col-
lective effort of bringing about improvements in the lives of disabled
children both individually and as a group, and in particular how the
law can be used as a tool to help children and their families achieve
the goals that they value.

182 For example, J Sunman, *A local experience of national concern*, Oxfordshire
Family Support Network, 2014.

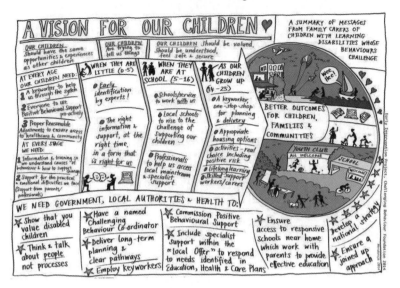

Graphic produced by family carers and illustrated by Pat Mendonca, courtesy of The Early Intervention Project (The Challenging Behaviour Foundation and the Council for Disabled Children), 2014.

CHAPTER 2

Legal fundamentals

Key points

- There is a wide range of domestic (UK) and international sources of law creating powers and duties in relation to disabled children.
- These powers and duties are influenced by an expanding range of international human rights conventions affecting disabled children.
- The extent to which services *must* be provided to disabled children will depend on whether there is a 'specific' or 'general' duty to do so.
- Where a public body has a power to provide services (rather than a duty to do so), that power must be exercised fairly, rationally and reasonably.
- Since the Children Act (CA) 2004, services for children (health, education, social care) are becoming more integrated.
- In particular, all the relevant agencies now have additional duties to co-operate to improve the well-being of all children (including disabled children).
- However, important separate legal duties remain in relation to children's services, education and health (see chapters 3, 4 and 5 respectively).
- Where agencies are or may be in breach of their duties, routes to redress include complaints processes, specialist tribunals and (where the problem is sufficiently serious and urgent) judicial review in the High Court (see chapter 11).
- Funding through legal aid may be available for children and families when a legal challenge becomes necessary (see chapter 11).

Introduction

2.1   There is a wide and expanding range of domestic and international sources of law affecting disabled children and their families, much of which has come into force in the last fifteen years. This chapter describes in outline terms the different sources of law and considers some of the most important powers and duties on public bodies (these are set out in more detail in the succeeding chapters). It explores the distinction between duties (things public bodies have to do) and powers (things public bodies may do) and considers how the legal structures of the agencies providing services to disabled children and their families are changing, in many cases bringing agencies closer together. Finally, it considers the different routes to redress for children and families who have been denied the services and support they need, including the potential for legal aid funding for some of these challenges – issues explored more fully in chapter 11.

2.2 In recent years, and most notably through the Human Rights Act (HRA) 1998, international human rights law has become as important a source of law for disabled children and their families as domestic legislation, regulations and statutory guidance. Each of these sources of law is explored in turn below.

The common law and judicial review

2.3 A distinctive feature of our legal system is the 'common law', being the law developed by judges through the decisions in court. It is a particular feature of the English legal system that any gaps left by legislation can be filled by the courts. The role of the common law is to ensure that the law reflects the standards of our society – and so it can evolve over time as social standards shift.

2.4 With the current debate on the potential repeal of the HRA 1998 (see para 2.10 below), it is particularly important that common law rights are widely understood. Indeed the Supreme Court has emphasised that the first place to look to identify rights should be domestic law, including the common law, rather than the European Convention on Human Rights.[1]

2.5 The most important common law rights for disabled children, young people and families will be the rights that can be enforced through judicial review (see chapter 11 below at paras 11.88–11.103). In short, judicial review is the process by which the courts assess the lawfulness of the actions and decisions of public bodies. In *Council of Civil Service Unions v Minister for the Civil Service*,[2] Lord Diplock clearly outlined the classification of the grounds of judicial review:

- **Illegality:** acting outside statutory powers or in breach of a statutory duty.

---

1 *R (Osborn) v Parole Board* [2013] UKSC 61; [2014] AC 1115 at [54]–[57].
2 [1985] AC 374.

- **Irrationality:** failing to take relevant matters into account, considering irrelevant matters, acting 'unreasonably'.[3]
- **Procedural impropriety:** acting unfairly, breaching a legitimate expectation, actual or apparent bias.

2.6   As a shorthand, it can be said that public bodies are required by the common law to act rationally, reasonably and fairly in everything they do. However, these categories are not fixed in stone, and indeed the grounds of judicial review often merge into one another.[4]

2.7   A further important ground of challenge has arisen with the arrival in English law of EU and human rights principles. This is proportionality, which requires that decisions pursue legitimate aims to which they are rationally connected and that a 'fair balance' is struck between the interests of the individual and those of the wider community.[5] Where there is a human rights issue in the case, proportionality is often the most powerful ground of review of any judicial review ground because it requires the most intense focus on the decision and its consequences. Whether proportionality is also a legitimate ground of review in relation to common law or statutory rights not protected by the European Convention on Human Rights is the subject of ongoing debate.[6]

2.8   Some of the most important grounds of challenge to public law decision-making in the social welfare field (other than proportionality) are:

- **Failure to follow the policy and objects of a statutory power:** This is the *Padfield* principle.[7] So for example, the purpose of Part III of the Children Act (CA) 1989 is that 'local authorities should provide support for children and families'.[8] Everything done under this Part of the CA 1989 should further this purpose (see chapter 3).

---

3 The bar for 'unreasonable' decision-making is set high – to be unlawful on this basis a decision would generally have to be so unreasonable that no reasonable decision-maker would take it. This is known as '*Wednesbury* unreasonableness' from the leading case of *Associated Provincial Picture Houses Ltd v Wednesbury Corporation* [1948] 1 KB 223.

4 See *Boddington v British Transport Police* [1999] 2 AC 143 at 152E–F for some examples of grounds which can fit into different categories.

5 See *Huang v Secretary of State for the Home Department* [2007] UKHL 11; [2007] 2 AC 167 and *Bank Mellat v HM Treasury* [2013] UKSC 39; [2014] AC 700 for the principles of proportionality.

6 See *Pham v Secretary of State for the Home Department* [2015] UKSC 19; [2015] 1 WLR 1591 and *R (Keyu) v Foreign Secretary* [2015] UKSC 69.

7 From the leading case of *Padfield v Ministry of Agriculture, Fisheries and Food* [1968] AC 997.

8 See *R (M) v Gateshead MBC* [2006] EWCA Civ 221; [2006] QB 650 at [42].

- **Failure to take all relevant matters into account:** often referred to as *Tameside* irrationality.[9] A good example of this principle in action comes from the judgment of the Court of Appeal in *R v Ealing LBC ex p C*.[10] In that case, the local authority had failed to carry out a sufficiently detailed assessment of the needs of a disabled boy, in particular his need for suitable accommodation. The Court of Appeal held that 'Important practical problems were simply not addressed' in the decision-making. Lord Justice Judge concluded as follows:

  > In my judgment, both the decision and the decision making process were flawed. Unless the repetition of an assertion is to be regarded as a proper manifestation of a reasoning process, there was none here. Certainly there was no analysis of the accommodation problems faced by this disabled boy and his mother and his brother. The decision is therefore susceptible to judicial review on the basis that it is unreasonable in the *Wednesbury* sense. To adapt Lord Diplock's observation in *Tameside*:
  >
  > > 'Did the council ask themselves the right question and take reasonable steps to acquaint themselves with the relevant information to enable them to answer it correctly?'
  >
  > The answer to the first is no: the right question or questions were not asked. The answer to the second question equally is no: reasonable steps were not taken by the council to enable the question to be answered correctly.[11]

- **Fettering of discretion:** a term which continues to strike fear into the hearts of many council officers and other public officials. The basic principle is that public bodies must not operate an inflexible policy but must always give consideration to exercising their powers; see *R (Lumba) v Secretary of State for the Home Department*.[12] It is essential that policies governing statutory powers do not automatically determine the outcome; see *R v Hampshire CC ex p W*.[13]

2.9   Another key common law right for disabled children, young people and families is the right to a fair consultation; see chapter 1 at paras 1.22–1.25 generally on the importance of proper consultation in this

---

9 From the leading case of *Secretary of State for Education and Science v Tameside MBC* [1977] AC 1014.

10 (2000) 3 CCLR 122.

11 Judgment at 130F–I.

12 [2011] UKSC 12; [2012] 1 AC 245 per Lord Dyson at [21]: 'It is a well established principle of public law that a policy should not be so rigid as to amount to a fetter on the discretion of decision-makers'.

13 [1994] ELR 460 per Sedley J.

area. The requirement on public bodies to consult fairly is an aspect of the common law duty of procedural fairness. It is now well understood[14] that a fair consultation requires the following:

- Consultation must take place at a 'formative stage', ie sufficiently early in the decision-making to influence the outcome.
- The public body must provide 'sufficient reasons for any proposal to permit of intelligent consideration and response'.
- 'Adequate time' has to be allowed for consideration and response by consultees – with what is 'adequate' depending on all the circumstances. For example, while a six-week consultation period may generally be 'adequate', this may not apply if the six weeks ran over the school summer holidays and the issue affected disabled children and their families.
- The public body must ensure that the outcome of the consultation is 'conscientiously taken into account' in the final decision. However, consultation is not negotiation and providing the public body gives rational reasons it may proceed with a decision even if the majority of consultees disagree.

International human rights conventions

European Convention on Human Rights

2.10   For the purposes of this book, the most important human rights convention is the European Convention on Human Rights (ECHR), because it has been incorporated into UK domestic law through the HRA 1998. Before the HRA 1998 came into force in 2000, individuals who felt that their ECHR rights had not been respected had to go to the European Court of Human Rights (ECtHR) in Strasbourg, a lengthy and time-consuming process. Now, cases alleging breaches of ECHR rights are routinely dealt with by the domestic courts. Although the current government has expressed its intention to repeal the HRA 1998, at the time of writing (November 2015) no proposed legislation has been published and it is far from certain that any such legislation will be approved by parliament – particularly if it breaks the link with the ECHR. Until parliament repeals or amends the HRA 1998, it retains its full effect.

---

14   See *R v North and East Devon Health Authority ex p Coughlan* [2001] QB 213, approved by the Supreme Court in *R (Moseley) v Haringey LBC* [2014] UKSC 115; [2014] 1 WLR 3947.

2.11 Several articles of the ECHR are of relevance to disabled children and their families, of which the most important is undoubtedly article 8, the right to respect for family, home and private life. The following section considers this article – as well as articles 3 and 5, which are also of importance in certain situations. Article 2, the duty to protect life, is not considered separately, but much of the analysis concerning article 3 (below) applies with even greater force to situations where there are arguable grounds that the state might have been culpable (by neglect or otherwise) in a death.[15]

Article 3

2.12 Article 3 places a duty on public bodies to take action to ensure that no one is subjected to torture, inhuman or degrading treatment. If a state official (for example a police or prison officer) subjects someone to seriously unpleasant treatment, this could amount to a violation of the duty under article 3. However, the same may occur if the state fails to take action to prevent such treatment occurring (even if the perpetrator is not a state official) since there is a 'positive obligation on states to ensure (so far as they are able) that no-one suffers from torture, inhuman or degrading treatment'. Accordingly, if the criminal justice system fails to punish the perpetrators of unlawful violence, this may amount to a violation.[16] For example in *R (B) v DPP*,[17] a decision by the Crown Prosecution Service not to prosecute (simply because the victim had mental health problems) was held to constitute 'degrading treatment of the victim' contrary to article 3.

2.13 *Đorđević v Croatia*[18] concerned the harassment by school children of someone with learning disabilities and his mother, with whom he lived. The harassment included shouting obscenities, spitting, pushing him against an iron fence, hitting him with a ball and on one occasion burning him with a cigarette. The police and authorities were aware of this harassment but took no effective action and this

---

15 See for example, *Edwards v UK* Application no 46477/99, 14 March 2002.

16 See for example *Atalay v Turkey* (2008) Application no 1249/03, 18 December 2008.

17 [2009] EWHC 106 (Admin).

18 Application no 41526/10, 24 July 2012: see also *Commissioner of Police of the Metropolis v DSD and others* [2015] EWCA Civ 646, where the Court of Appeal considered the extent of the 'positive obligation' to investigate such – suggesting that there is 'a sliding scale: from deliberate torture by State officials to the consequences of negligence by non-State agents' – with the state having a greater 'margin of appreciation' as to the action it takes at the 'bottom of the scale' than at the top: judgment at [45].

failure was held to amount to a violation of the positive obligation under article 3.

Article 8

2.14   Article 8 protects a person's family life, private life, home and correspondence. Article 8 is what is termed a 'qualified' right. By this it is meant that although the state (for example a local authority, the police, etc) should not generally interfere with a person's privacy, their family life or their home, there may be situations where this is permitted (for example if a child is being abused or a home is being used for illegal purposes). The ECHR, however, stipulates that any such interference with this right must be (among other things) 'proportionate' – or perhaps rather must not be 'disproportionate'. For example, in *Kutzner v Germany*,[19] two sisters were taken into care because the parents had learning disabilities. The court held that this was a 'disproportionate' interference with the article 8 right to family life because, before taking this action, the government had failed to consider providing extra support to the family to enable them to remain living together.

2.15   The courts have given a very broad meaning to the idea of 'private life'. They have held it to encompass not only the idea of having one's privacy respected – but also the notion of one's identity; one's 'ability to function socially';[20] one's 'physical and psychological integrity';[21] and of the right to develop one's personality and one's relations with other human beings 'without outside interference'.[22] Action (or inaction) by the state that may make a person unwell (for example through pollution[23]) will, therefore, engage the article 8 right as may a refusal to allow access to a person's social services file – if that contains information about his or her childhood (ie their 'identity').[24] The court has also held that creating barriers which restrict a disabled person's freedom of movement may also interfere with a person's article 8 rights (the right to develop relations with one's environment/other people).[25] In this latter context, it has been

19   (2002) 35 EHRR 25.
20   *R (Razgar) v Secretary of State for the Home Department* [2004] 2 AC 368 per Lord Bingham at [9].
21   *Pretty v UK* (2002) 35 EHRR 1.
22   *Botta v Italy* (1998) 26 EHRR 241.
23   *Hatton v UK* (2003) Application no 36022/97.
24   *Gaskin v UK* (1989) 12 EHRR 36.
25   *Botta v Italy* (1998) 26 EHRR 241.

argued that an understanding of the nature of this right has, for disabled people, become aligned with many of the concepts associated with the 'social model' of disability (see paras 1.7–1.8).[26]

2.16   Article 8 places both a 'negative' and a 'positive' obligation on the state. The negative obligation is that the state must not interfere with the rights protected by article 8 unless it is pursuing one of the specified legitimate aims and even then it must not act in a disproportionate way – so the interference must be no more than strictly necessary. An example of a 'negative' interference would be taking away someone's home, or removing someone's children into care. But the state also has 'positive' obligations to take action in some cases – most obviously to protect those who are in some way at risk of abuse. In *Đorđević v Croatia*[27] (considered above at para 2.13), it was not only the person with learning disabilities who was harassed by the school children: his mother (his carer) also suffered because she witnessed what was being done to her son and the ECtHR held that this amounted to a violation of her right to family life (to 'dignity and the quality of life') under article 8.

2.17   The positive obligations under the ECHR extend not merely to protecting vulnerable people from harm and prosecuting their abusers. There is also in certain circumstances a positive obligation on the state to take action to ensure the fulfilment of article 8 rights. For example, where a child's welfare is at stake, 'article 8 may require the provision of welfare support in a manner which enables family life to continue'.[28] Article 8 may also require states to take action to 'ameliorate and compensate' for the restrictions that disabled people experience – as Judge Greve of the ECtHR held in *Price v United Kingdom*:

> In a civilised country like the United Kingdom, society considers it not only appropriate but a basic humane concern to try to improve and compensate for the disabilities faced by a person in the applicant's situation. In my opinion, these compensatory measures come to form part of the disabled person's physical integrity.[29]

2.18   It has been held that the 'very essence of the Convention is respect for human dignity'[30] and with this understanding comes an obligation on public bodies to ensure that the supports made available to

---

26 L Clements and J Read, 'The dog that didn't bark', in L Lawson and C Gooding (eds), *Disability rights in Europe: from theory to practice*, Hart Publishing, 2005.

27 Application no 41526/10, 24 July 2012.

28 *Anufrijeva v Southwark LBC* [2004] QB 1124 per Lord Woolf at [43].

29 (2002) 34 EHRR 1285: a case that concerned article 3 – ie, the right not to be subjected to 'degrading treatment'.

30 *Pretty v UK* (2002) 35 EHRR 1 at [65].

disabled people ensure they are not left in squalid or undignified circumstances. In *R (Bernard) v Enfield LBC*[31] for example, the court found a violation of article 8 through the delay in provision of proper toileting – holding that providing accessible toileting facilities to a disabled woman 'would have restored her dignity as a human being'. Similarly, in *R (A, B, X and Y) v East Sussex CC and the Disability Rights Commission (No 2)*, Munby J (as he then was) held that the:

> Recognition and protection of human dignity is one of the core values – in truth the core value – of our society and, indeed, of all the societies which are part of the European family of nations and which have embraced the principles of the Convention.[32]

2.19   While the courts will scrutinise carefully any failure of a public body to treat an individual with appropriate 'dignity' – they are very aware (some might say – 'too aware') of the fact that public bodies have limited financial resources. Accordingly, where the body has considered all the relevant factors and acted within the law – the courts are reluctant to interfere with their decisions as to what is an appropriate level of support for a particular individual.[33]

Article 5

2.20   A further ECHR right which has taken on increasing prominence in the disability sphere is article 5. Article 5 severely limits the situations in which people can be deprived of their liberty and imposes strict procedural rules on public bodies whenever they seek to deprive someone of their liberty. The court has held that a person is 'deprived of their liberty' if they are subject to continuous supervision and control and are not free to leave, there is no valid consent and the state has responsibility for the deprivation.[34] The strictness of the requirements of article 5 mean that even if it is thought to be in a disabled person's best interests to be 'subject to continuous supervision and not free to leave' – this must be justified by independent evidence and scrutiny.

---

31 [2002] EWHC 2282 (Admin); (2002) 5 CCLR 577 at [33].

32 [2003] EWHC 167 (Admin); (2003) 6 CCLR 194 at [86].

33 See for example *McDonald v UK* (2015) 60 EHRR 1; (2014) 17 CCLR 187 where the ECtHR reiterated that its policy was to give 'a wide margin of appreciation' to individual states in relation to the reasonableness of such polices – but see also L Clements (ed), 'Disability, Dignity and the Cri de Coeur', [2011] *EHRLR Special Disability Rights Issue*, pp675–685.

34 *P v Cheshire West and Chester Council* [2014] UKSC 19; (2014) 17 CCLR 5.

2.21   The process for authorising the detention of disabled children/ young people can be complex. If the child is 'accommodated' and has a history of absconding, then in certain situations the local authority can place them in secure accommodation with the approval of a court (CA 1989 s25). In some situations, a child or young person can be detained ('sectioned') under the Mental Health Act 1983 and, in some further situations, where the child lacks the necessary mental capacity to choose where they want to live, their detention can be approved by virtue of the provisions in the Mental Capacity Act 2005 if aged 16 or over.[35] If under 16, then their deprivation may have to be approved by the High Court – although in certain situations it appears that it is possible for the child's parents to give consent to the placement.[36] This is a complex area of law, full consideration of which lies outside the scope of this book – but it is explored further in chapter 7 at paras 7.49–7.52.

Other key conventions: children and disability

2.22   Alongside the ECHR, two other international human rights conventions are of direct relevance to disabled children. These are the UN Convention on the Rights of the Child (UNCRC) and the UN Convention on the Rights of Persons with Disabilities (Disability Convention). There is now a widely recognised requirement that the ECHR rights should be read in 'harmony' with the other international conventions, meaning that a breach of one of the rights contained in the international conventions may well result in a breach of the ECHR, which would be unlawful under the HRA 1998.[37] The international conventions should also inform how the courts interpret any domestic laws that are ambiguous.

---

35   Reforms to this complex and unsatisfactory scheme are being considered by the Law Commission, see Law Commission Consultation Paper No 222, *Mental Capacity and Deprivation of Liberty*, 2015.

36   *Trust A v X and others* [2015] EWHC 922 (Fam); [2015] Fam Law 636: a controversial decision coinciding with the writing of this book – and one that may be refined/reconsidered in due course. See discussion in chapter 7 at paras 7.51–7.52 and Box 3.

37   See *Neulinger v Switzerland* (2010) 28 BHRC 706 and see discussion by Lord Wilson in *Mathieson v Secretary of State for Work and Pensions* [2015] UKSC 47 at [41]–[45].

The UN Convention on the Rights of the Child (UNCRC)

2.23   The UNCRC is the most widely ratified of the UN conventions and is, therefore, as close as possible to a universally agreed international human rights treaty. Although the UNCRC is not part of English law (it has not been 'incorporated' in the way that the HRA 1998 'incorporated the ECHR), its provisions are subject to what is known as an 'interpretative obligation'. This means that English law must be interpreted as far as possible so as to give it a meaning that does not conflict with the requirements of the UNCRC (or indeed any other international treaty the UK has ratified – for example the Disability Convention considered below.[38] In a 2006 judgment, Baroness Hale explained this idea (in the UK context) in the following terms:

> Even if an international treaty has not been incorporated into domestic law, our domestic legislation has to be construed so far as possible so as to comply with the international obligations which we have undertaken. When two interpretations of these regulations are possible, the interpretation chosen should be that which better complies with the commitment to the welfare of children which this country has made by ratifying the United Nations Convention on the Rights of the Child.[39]

2.24   In 2015, the Supreme Court reiterated this principle.[40] Lord Reed for example asserted that 'It is not in dispute that the Convention rights protected in our domestic law by the Human Rights Act can also be interpreted in the light of international treaties, such as the UNCRC, that are applicable in the particular sphere'.[41]

2.25   Articles in the UNCRC of particular relevance to disabled children include:

- Article 2: non-discrimination.
- Article 3: the best interests of the child to be a primary consideration.[42] This article has been the subject of significant litigation. In 2011, the Supreme Court referred to the central importance of 'best interests' and whilst it accepted that this was not without limits, it considered that it 'must rank higher than any other. It

---

38 See, for example, *Mabon v Mabon* [2005] EWCA Civ 634; [2005] Fam 366.

39 *Smith v Smith and another* [2006] UKHL 35; [2006] 1 WLR 2024 at [78].

40 *R (SG) v Secretary of State for Work and Pensions* [2015] UKSC 16; [2015] 1 WLR 1449 and see for example S Broach, *'Enforcing human rights – what the Benefit Cap judgment means for future cases'* on the 'RightsinReality' blog.

41 *R (SG) v Secretary of State for Work and Pensions* [2015] UKSC 16; [2015] 1 WLR 1449 at para 83.

42 See UN Committee on the Rights of the Child, *General comment No 14 on the right of the child to have his or her best interests taken as a primary consideration,* May 2013 for more on UNCRC article 3.

is not merely one consideration that weighs in the balance along-side other competing factors. Where the best interests of the child clearly favour a certain course, that course should be followed unless countervailing reasons of considerable force displace them'.[43]

- Article 4: states to use the 'maximum extent' of available resources to realise children's economic, social and cultural rights.
- Article 12: the right to participation.
- Article 24: the right to the 'highest attainable standard of health'.

2.26 Article 23 of the UNCRC relates specifically to disabled children. It requires states to recognise that disabled children should enjoy 'full and decent' lives. It further recognises the right of disabled children to 'special care'. Such support is to be provided to disabled children free of charge where possible, subject to resources. The aim of such support should be to allow every child to achieve 'the fullest possible social integration and individual development'.

2.27 The UN Committee that oversees the UNCRC (like all other such UN treaty committees) from time to time issues advice (known as 'General Comments') on the way the convention should be inter-preted. In its General Comment No 9, for example, it stressed the particular importance of the requirement in article 23 that a child with disability and her or his parents and/or others caring for the child receive 'special care and assistance' and noted that this support should be 'free of charge whenever possible'.

The UN Convention on the Rights of Persons with Disabilities (Disability Convention)

2.28 The UK ratified the Disability Convention in 2009. In accordance with the general principles discussed above, the rights enshrined in the Disability Convention should be taken into account when interpreting domestic law or European law and the ECtHR has itself recognised that the Disability Convention is an important reference point for the interpretation of article 8 of the ECHR.[44] The Court of Appeal has said that the Disability Convention has the potential to

---

43 Lord Kerr's judgment in *ZH (Tanzania) v Secretary of State for the Home Department* [2011] UKSC 4; [2011] 2 AC 166 – and see also *R (SG) v Secretary of State for Work and Pensions* [2015] UKSC 16; [2015] 1 WLR 1449.

44 See *Glor v Switzerland*, Application no 13444/04, 30 April 2009 and *Alajos Kiss v Hungary*, Application no 38832/06, 20 May 2010.

'illuminate' the approach to discrimination and justification under article 14 of the ECHR.[45]

2.29   Important articles in the Disability Convention for disabled children include:

- Article 3: general principles, including 'respect for inherent dignity' and 'full and effective participation and inclusion in society'.
- Article 9: accessibility.
- Article 19: independent living and inclusion in the community.

2.30   As with the UNCRC, there is a specific article in the Disability Convention (article 7) relating to disabled children. Article 7(1) requires states to:

> Take all necessary measures to ensure the full enjoyment by children with disabilities of all human rights and fundamental freedoms on an equal basis with other children.

2.31   Article 7(2) reinforces the UNCRC article 3 requirement that in all actions concerning a disabled child, the child's best interests shall be a primary consideration.[46] Similarly, article 7(3) reinforces the right to participation under UNCRC article 12, requiring states to provide 'disability and age-appropriate assistance' to help disabled children realise this right.

2.32   Furthermore, article 23(3) specifically requires that disabled children have equal rights in respect of family life, and requires states to provide 'early and comprehensive information, services and support' to prevent 'concealment, abandonment, neglect and segregation' of disabled children. Under article 23(5), where the immediate family is unable to care for a disabled child, the state must make 'every effort' to find alternative care within the wider family or in a family setting in the community.

2.33   Article 24 of the Disability Convention concerns education. In particular, it requires states to establish an 'inclusive education system'. Disabled people have a right to be educated 'on an equal basis with others in the communities in which they live': article 24(2)(b).

2.34   The UK government has entered a reservation to article 24 in relation to residential education[47] in the following terms:

---

45 *Burnip v Birmingham CC* [2012] EWCA Civ 629; [2013] PTSR 117 at [22].

46 A breach of both article 7(2) of the Disability Convention and article 3 of the UNCRC was found by the Supreme Court in *Mathieson v Secretary of State for Work and Pensions* [2015] UKSC 47.

47 The issue of residential special school provision is discussed further at paras 1.86–1.87 and 4.202–4.205.

The United Kingdom reserves the right for disabled children to be educated outside their local community where more appropriate education provision is available elsewhere. Nevertheless, parents of disabled children have the same opportunity as other parents to state a preference for the school at which they wish their child to be educated.[48]

2.35 The UK government has also made a declaration in relation to article 24 to provide a definition of the meaning of 'inclusion':

The United Kingdom Government is committed to continuing to develop an inclusive system where parents of disabled children have increasing access to mainstream schools and staff, which have the capacity to meet the needs of disabled children.

The General Education System in the United Kingdom includes mainstream and special schools, which the UK Government understands is allowed under the Convention.[49]

2.36 This declaration reflects the government's position that the law relating to special educational needs, now in Part 3 of the Children and Families Act 2014, establishes an 'inclusive education system' while preserving a role for special schools to meet the needs of children with more complex needs. This question is further considered at paras 1.68–1.71 and more fully in chapter 4.

2.37 The UK has also ratified the Optional Protocol to the Disability Convention, which permits individuals and groups to petition the UN Disability Committee in Geneva where there are alleged violations of rights protected by the Disability Convention. As is normal with international conventions, there is a prior requirement to exhaust domestic remedies before sending a 'communication' to the Disability Committee.[50] However, this still raises the prospect that where the rights enshrined in the Disability Convention are not incorporated into domestic law and cannot properly be read into the ECHR, then a remedy may be obtained through the Disability Committee.

The hierarchy of domestic law

2.38 The legal regime relating to the rights of disabled children is made up of three categories aside from the common law (see paras 2.3–2.9 above). The most important are the relatively few statutes (known

---

48 Accessible at www.un.org/disabilities/default.asp?id=475.
49 Accessible at www.un.org/disabilities/default.asp?id=475.
50 Optional Protocol, article 2(d).

also as 'Acts' and as 'primary legislation') and these spell out the basic rights and duties: the Children Act 1989 being a prominent example. Beneath the layer of primary legislation lie an extensive range of 'subordinate' or 'secondary legislation' often labelled regulations, orders and rules. Primary and secondary legislation are 'law' because they have both been approved by parliament.

2.39   Statutes or 'primary' legislation are the most important of our 'laws' – and the role of the courts is to interpret the intention of parliament when enacting these laws and to give effect to their ordinary meaning: but also, in doing so, to endeavour to interpret them in a way that does not conflict with international human rights standards. Subordinate or secondary legislation (for example the SEND Regs 2014) has the same legal force as primary statutes. These rules and regulations are made under a specific statute by the relevant government minister and are subject to approval by parliament. Rules and regulations will normally go into more detail than the statute under which they are made, prescribing such matters as processes to be followed, timescales and so on.

2.40   The final category is guidance, which is, essentially, advice issued by government to explain what the law requires and to suggest how it may be complied with. Unlike the law (which we must all obey), guidance does not have to be followed slavishly if there are good reasons to depart from it. Problematically, however, some guidance is more binding than other guidance.

2.41   Guidance that carries the label 'statutory guidance' or 'Code of Practice' have for various legal reasons much more force – indeed they are often referred to as 'binding' on the public bodies to which they are addressed. *Working Together to Safeguard Children* (March 2015) is an example of statutory guidance and is referred to extensively in chapter 3. At page 6 of the guidance, it states that it is 'issued under section 7 of the Local Authority Social Services Act 1970, which requires local authorities in their social services functions to act under the general guidance of the Secretary of State'. In *R v Islington LBC ex p Rixon*,[51] the court set out precisely what local authorities have to do with guidance issued under section 7 of the 1970 Act:

> Parliament in enacting s7(1) did not intend local authorities to whom ministerial guidance was given to be free, having considered it, to take it or leave it ... Parliament by s7(1) has required local authorities to follow the path charted by the Secretary of State's guidance, with liberty to deviate from it where the local authority judges on admissible

51 (1997–98) 1 CCLR 119 at [123].

grounds that there *is* good reason to do so, but without freedom to take a substantially different course.

2.42   More recently, in *R (TG) v Lambeth LBC*,[52] the Court of Appeal said that '[i]t is inaccurate to describe guidance given under section 7 of the 1970 Act ... as apt to be followed "probably" or only "as a matter of good practice". In the absence of a considered decision that there is good reason to deviate from it, it *must* be followed'[53] (emphasis as original).

2.43   It is often in statutory guidance that we find the most important duties in relation to disabled children – for instance, the duty to assess social care needs and produce a plan to show how those needs will be met under Children Act (CA) 1989 s17.[54] Very similar considerations apply to codes of practice issued by the government – of which the most obvious example is the *Special Educational Needs and Disability Code of Practice* which is referred to extensively in chapter 4. On page 1 of the code, it states 'the guidance in this code must be considered and that those who have regard to it will be expected to explain any departure from it'. This is a less binding form of guidance than guidance such as *Working Together* which public bodies are required to 'act under' – but nonetheless guidance to which public bodies must 'have regard' has always to be considered.

2.44   Where government issues 'practice guidance', for instance the short breaks practice guidance (see paras 3.95–3.97), it is less coercive and public bodies have more freedom to deviate from it – where they have sound reasons for so doing. Nevertheless, the advice it contains is something that must be taken into account when that body makes a decision and if the decision is at significant variance from the approach required in the guidance, the courts may (in the absence of compelling reasons to the contrary) be prepared to find the decision to be made unlawfully.[55] In *R (Ali) v Newham LBC*,[56] the court held that in the circumstances of that case non-statutory guidance on tactile paving for people with visual impairments had to be followed and it was unlawful for the local authority to depart from it.[57]

---

52   [2011] EWCA Civ 526; (2011) 14 CCLR 366.
53   Judgment at [17].
54   HM Government, *Working Together*, 2015.
55   *R v Islington LBC ex p Rixon* (1997–98) 1 CCLR 119 at 131E.
56   [2012] EWHC 2970 (Admin); (2012) 15 CCLR 715.
57   At [39], the court referred to the following factors as influencing whether non-statutory guidance must be followed: 'the authorship of the guidance, the quality and intensity of the work done in the production of the guidance, the

Powers and duties

2.45   Public bodies such as local authorities are 'creatures of statute'. This means that they can only do things that they are permitted or required to do by Acts of Parliament and secondary legislation. There is, however, an important broad power in Localism Act 2011 s1, which gives local authorities 'power to do anything that individuals generally may do' (described as a 'general power of competence').

2.46   This section looks at the different types of duties and powers, because understanding how these duties and powers operate is critical to determining whether disabled children and families have an entitlement to a particular service or benefit. In general terms, 'a power need not be exercised, but a duty must be discharged',[58] but as is set out below the nature of an individual power or duty is often much more subtle and nuanced.

2.47   First, legislation frequently places mandatory duties on public bodies, signified by the use of language such a 'shall' and 'must'. Some of the things parliament requires public bodies to do are expressed as 'specific' duties; a key example of this is CA 1989 s20(1), which requires local authorities to provide accommodation to *every* child who meets the qualifying criteria. Where a specific duty arises, it is appropriate to speak of the child as having a 'right' to a service.

2.48   Other duties are expressed in more general terms; for instance, CA 1989 s17(1), which creates a general duty to assess and provide services for children 'in need' (see chapter 3). This duty has been held by the courts not to be owed to each individual child in need but generally to all children in need in the local authority's area.[59] Therefore, a child in need cannot rely on section 17 alone to claim a right to a service, although this right may be found in other legislation (see paras 3.51–3.78). General duties are also often described as 'target' duties,[60] meaning that parliament has set local authorities a 'target' but has not intended a failure to meet that target to give rise to a legal challenge for an individual aggrieved person. Target duties cannot be

extent to which the (possibly competing) interests of those who are likely to be affected by the guidance have been recognised and weighed, the importance of any more general public policy that the guidance has sought to promote, and the express terms of the guidance itself'.

58   *R (G) v Barnet LBC* [2003] UKHL 57; [2004] 2 AC 208 per Lord Nicholls at [12].

59   *R (G) v Barnet LBC* [2003] UKHL 57; [2004] 2 AC 208.

60   C Callaghan, 'What is a "target duty"?', (2000) 5 *Judicial Review*, pp184–187.

ignored and a public authority must 'do its best'[61] to achieve compliance with the duty in every individual case.

2.49   When an Act or regulation uses the word 'may' or 'can' (rather than 'must' or shall'), it gives the public body a 'power' to act but not a 'duty'. An example is the power to make direct payments in relation to special educational provision considered in chapter 4 at paras 4.196–4.198. No individual can claim a right to a service which a public body only has a power to provide. However, public bodies must exercise their powers rationally, reasonably and fairly and it may be that certain powers have to be exercised in certain situations, including to avoid a breach of a person's human rights (for example, the power for local authorities to accommodate families together under CA 1989 s17(6) if the family are homeless and cannot access other accommodation by reason of their immigration status[62]). What public bodies cannot do is to decide never to use a power, or decide only to use it in a specific way: this is known, in legal jargon, as 'fettering a discretion'; see para 2.8 above. So if parliament has given a public body a power to do something, then each time the opportunity arises when it could use this power, it must consider whether or not to exercise it. The public body cannot decide never to use the power, or never to use it for the benefit of certain groups of people, for to do so would be to act against the will of parliament. See further the discussion of these requirements, which stem from the 'common law', at para 2.3–2.9 above.

Key local structures/processes

2.50   The basic structure of the agencies responsible for delivering services to children and families was set in place by the Children Act (CA) 2004. In particular, the CA 2004 created:

- A Children's Commissioner for England, whose primary function is 'promoting and protecting the rights of children in England'.[63]

---

61 *R v Radio Authority ex p Bull* [1998] QB 294 at 309. See *R (West) v Rhondda Cynan Taff CBC* [2014] EWHC 2134 (Admin); [2014] ELR 396 for breaches of general duties in relation to nursery education for young children.

62 See *R (Clue) v Birmingham CC* [2010] EWCA Civ 460; (2010) 13 CCLR 276.

63 CA 2004 s2(1) as amended by Children and Families Act 2014 s107.

- Lead Members for Children's Services: elected councillors in every children's services authority with direct responsibility for children's services, reporting to the council leader.[64]
- Directors of Children's Services: senior officers with management responsibility for all children's services, including education and children's social services.[65]

2.51   Since the 2010 general election, there has been a rolling back of some of the requirements initially imposed by the CA 2004. For instance, the regulations requiring the production of a children and young people's plan have been revoked.[66] Although the statutory duty on local authorities to establish a Children's Trust Board remains in force,[67] there is no longer any statutory guidance on how this duty should be exercised.

2.52   Chapter 1 has described the difficulties that families have in finding their way around complex services that do not co-operate effectively with one another: see paras 1.48–1.52. While the importance of effective collaboration between different services has long been recognised, research and official reports testify to the fact that it has proved difficult to achieve.[68] In an attempt to deal with this problem, the CA 2004 imposed important interlocking duties on relevant agencies to safeguard and promote the well-being of children. Under CA 2004 s10, each children's services authority is required to make arrangements to co-operate with its relevant partners. The list of relevant partners is extensive and includes all the relevant health agencies, the youth offending team and education institutions. Relevant partners are required to co-operate with the authority in the making of these arrangements and the aim of these arrangements must be to improve the well-being of children in terms of the five 'Every Child Matters' outcomes.[69]

2.53   The authority and its relevant partners are each required by CA 2004 s11 to make arrangements to ensure that 'their functions are discharged having regard to the need to safeguard and promote the

64 CA 2004 s19.

65 CA 2004 s18.

66 See the Children's Trust Board (Children and Young People's Plan) (England) (Revocation) Regulations 2010 SI No 2129. However, a number of local authorities have chosen to retain their plans on a voluntary basis.

67 CA 2004 s12A.

68 Audit Commission, *Services for disabled children: a review of services for disabled children and their families*, Audit Commission Publications, 2003.

69 CA 2004 s10(2).

welfare of children'.[70] This convoluted wording has some similarities to the general equality duty under the Equality Act 2010: see paras 9.97–9.115. What it means in practice is that in carrying out any functions, whether at a strategic or an individual case level,[71] public bodies such as local authorities and clinical commissioning groups must do so having regard to the need to promote children's welfare. Any agency taking a decision not to provide services to an individual disabled child or to tighten eligibility to services generally must be able to show how such a decision fits with this duty.

2.54   The Supreme Court has held[72] that the CA 2004 s11 duty translates the spirit of article 3 of the UNCRC into domestic law – the requirement to treat children's best interests as a primary consideration in all decisions affecting them (see para 2.25 above). In *R (B) v Barnet LBC*,[73] the local authority was held to have breached the CA 2004 s11 duty in relation to its treatment of a severely disabled child with inappropriately sexualised behaviour. The requirements of CA 2004 s11 were summarised by Lady Hale in *Nzolameso v Westminster City Council*[74] as follows:

> The decision-maker should identify the principal needs of the children, both individually and collectively, and have regard to the need to safeguard and promote them when making the decision.[75]

2.55   The CA 2004 builds on the existing co-operation duty in CA 1989 s27, which is specific to individual cases. It enables local authorities who need co-operation from a partner agency (for example an NHS or housing authority) to request help and it places a duty on the partner agency to comply with the request provided it is 'compatible with [the bodies'] ... statutory or other duties and obligations and does not unduly prejudice the discharge of any of their functions'.

2.56   The Health and Social Care Act 2012 introduced important reforms to the operation of the NHS nationally and locally. These are considered in more detail in chapter 5. An obvious change was the

---

70   CA 2004 s11(2), see paras 3.49 and 3.60. The education functions of a children's services authority are excluded from the CA 2004 s11 duty, because this duty is mirrored in relation to those functions by Education Act 2002 s175.

71   See *Nzolameso v Westminster City Council* [2015] UKSC 22; [2015] 2 All ER 942 at [24] for the application of the CA 2004 s11 duty both at the policy or strategic level and in individual cases.

72   *ZH (Tanzania) v Secretary of State for the Home Department* [2011] UKSC 4; [2011] 2 AC 166 per Lady Hale at [23].

73   [2009] EWHC 2842 (Admin); (2009) 12 CCLR 679.

74   [2015] UKSC 22; [2015] 2 All ER 942.

75   Judgment at [27].

transformation of primary care trusts into clinical commissioning groups.[76] The 2012 Act also created the NHS Commissioning Board,[77] known as 'NHS England', which has responsibility for commissioning certain specialist services for disabled children. Health and Wellbeing Boards[78] operate jointly across local authorities and clinical commissioning groups and are responsible for the production of joint health and wellbeing strategies[79] to inform commissioning decisions.

2.57   The 2012 Act also established Healthwatch England[80] and a network of local Healthwatch[81] organisations.[82] The remit of Healthwatch covers the breadth of health and social care services children and young people might use. Healthwatch has the power to give advice to the secretary of state, local authorities and NHS England. It can also undertake special inquiries or projects to look at potential systemic failures in more detail. Local Healthwatch has the power to conduct 'Enter and Views' in health settings to speak to children and young people using the service and observe policies and practices.[83] This power is not available in relation to children's social care settings.[84]

'Parental responsibility'

2.58   A number of the rights and duties covered in this handbook are affected by the concept of 'parental responsibility' – see for example the duty to accommodate children under CA 1989 s20(1)[85] or the rights in relation to certain mental health treatment.[86]

2.59   'Parental responsibility' is defined in CA 1989 s3(1), referring to 'all the rights, duties, powers, responsibilities and authority which by

---

76 Health and Social Care Act 2012 s10.
77 Health and Social Care Act 2012 s9.
78 Health and Social Care Act 2012 s194.
79 Health and Social Care Act 2012 s193.
80 Health and Social Care Act 2012 s181.
81 Health and Social Care Act 2012 ss182–189.
82 See Healthwatch, *Healthwatch, children and young people: An overview of the network and the role of Healthwatch England* and Healthwatch, *Healthwatch, children and young people: The role of local Healthwatch* (both November 2014).
83 Health and Social Care Act 2012 s186.
84 Local Authorities (Public Health Functions and Entry to Premises by Local Healthwatch Representatives) Regulations 2013 SI No 351 reg 11.
85 See chapter 3 at paras 3.136–3.143.
86 See chapter 5 at para 5.126.

law the parent of a child has in relation to the child and his property'. The basic principles governing who has parental responsibility are:

- Where a child's father and mother were married to each other at the time of the birth, each have parental responsibility automatically.[87]
- Where a child's father and mother were not married to each other at the time of his birth:
  - the mother has parental responsibility automatically; and
  - the father has parental responsibility if he acquires and does not lose it under the CA 1989 (see below).[88]

2.60 Specific provisions apply to govern other situations, for example women in civil partnerships or married to another woman at the time of treatment for assisted reproduction.[89]

2.61 Fathers who were not married to a child's mother at the time of the child's birth can gain parental responsibility in the various ways specified in CA 1989 s4.[90] Unmarried fathers can now most simply acquire parental responsibility for their children born after 1 December 2003 by registering themselves as the father on their child's birth certificate.

2.62 Local authorities can obtain parental responsibility for a child through a court order in family proceedings. Special guardians[91] will also have parental responsibility; while this will be shared with the parents the special guardian is entitled to exercise parental responsibility to their exclusion other than in certain specified circumstances.[92]

Routes to redress

2.63 This chapter of the first edition of this Handbook provided guidance on routes to redress, including judicial review, complaints procedures and the tribunal. These issues, along with the availability of legal aid, are now covered in more detail in chapter 11 on remedies.

---

87 CA 1989 s2(1).
88 CA 1989 s2(2).
89 CA 1989 s2(1A) and Human Fertilisation and Embryology Act 2008 s42.
90 See also CA 1989 s4ZA for acquisition of parental responsibility by a second female parent and s4A for acquisition of parental responsibility by a step-parent.
91 See CA 1989 s14A–G.
92 See CA 1989 s14C(1).

Children's services

continued

Key points

• All 'disabled' children are children 'in need'. This status is not affected by the reforms introduced by Part 3 of the Children and Families Act 2014.

• The primary duty on children's services authorities is to assess the needs of children in need, including disabled children.

• Once needs have been assessed, a children's services authority has a duty to provide services to meet the assessed needs if certain conditions are met, in general terms where it is deemed 'necessary' to do so. In deciding whether it is 'necessary' to meet a child's needs, a local authority is entitled to take account of the resources available to it – but once it is accepted that it is 'necessary' to meet a particular child's needs then they must be met. At this stage, cost is only relevant to the extent that needs may be met in the most cost-effective way.

• If the outcome of the assessment is continued social care involvement, there must be a support plan setting out what services are to be delivered, and what actions undertaken, by whom and for what purpose.

• Where the criteria in Children Act 1989 s20(1) are met, disabled children must be accommodated.

• Children accommodated under CA 1989 s20 have additional rights while 'looked after' and on 'leaving care'.

• Decisions not to assess, provide support or accommodate disabled children can be challenged through the complaints procedure, and (where sufficiently urgent and/or important) through an application for judicial review.

Introduction

3.1   Disabled children are children first, and as such should be able to access all the services available to all children – for example nurseries, playgroups, playgrounds, leisure services, children's centres and mainstream schools. The requirements that there should be a sufficient supply of such services and that they should be accessible to all children regardless of impairment are considered at para 3.28 below and chapter 9 respectively.

3.2   This chapter is concerned with the provision of additional services to disabled children by local authority children's services departments. These are different from those provided by the NHS and are sometimes known as 'social care services'. They cover a variety of arrangements and provision aimed at helping disabled children and their families to live an ordinary life. This chapter sets out the local authority duties to assess the needs of disabled children and discusses the complex issue of when the authority has a duty to provide services to meet the child's assessed needs. It also deals with duties on authorities to accommodate disabled children and the additional rights which should be enjoyed by disabled children who are 'looked after' as a result of being accommodated or who are 'leaving care'. There is a specific focus on short breaks as a particularly important service for disabled children and families.[1] Disabled children's rights to health services, including NHS continuing care, are considered in chapter 5. Right to childcare are considered in chapter 8, see paras 8.24–8.25.

3.3   This chapter, like all those that follow, should be read with the realities described in chapter 1 in mind. As we have noted (see paras 1.48–1.52 above), for many families the social care system is one of baffling complexity and dealing with it amounts to additional, tiring and frustrating work. Not infrequently, the system requires parents to attend multiple meetings where they repeat the same information to a range of unfamiliar specialists in different settings. In one case, a family of a one-year-old child attended (over a nine-month period) 315 service-based appointments in 12 different locations (see para 1.61).

3.4   In 2014/15, two Acts of major significance to disabled people and carers came into force. The first is the Children and Families Act (CFA) 2014 which creates a new system to address the educational needs and related health and care needs of disabled children and young people aged 0–25. The second is the Care Act 2014, which although primarily an Act concerning disabled adults and their carers also contains important provisions on transition to adulthood.

3.5   Both Acts have the potential to improve services and support for disabled children, young people and their families. However, neither

---

1 Short breaks are 'part of a continuum of services which support children in need and their families. They include the provision of day, evening, overnight and weekend activities for the child or young person, and can take place in the child's own home, the home of an approved carer, or in a residential or community setting'. See DCSF, *Short Breaks: Statutory guidance on how to safeguard and promote the welfare of disabled children using short breaks*, April 2010, para 2.1.

provides the kind of coherent statutory scheme which could ensure that the needs of disabled children and their families are met in every case.

Key changes under the Children and Families Act 2014

3.6 The key provisions of the CFA 2014 and its Code of Practice[2] for disabled children's social care are addressed throughout this chapter.[3] In summary, they include:

- The replacement of 'statements of special educational needs' by Education, Health and Care (EHC) plans (paras 3.121–3.127 below).[4]
- The duty on local authorities to have in place a 'local offer', setting out the provision (including care provision) which is expected to be available both within and outside the local authority's area at the time of its publication (para 3.28 below).
- The duty on local authorities to keep social care provision made inside and outside their area under review (para 3.28 below).[5]
- The duties in relation to integration and joint commissioning with the NHS (para 3.24 below).[6]
- The duty to provide children, young people and parents with 'advice and information about matters relating to the disabilities of the children or young people concerned'.[7]

3.7 Although these are important developments, they do not affect the fundamental aspects of the statutory scheme for disabled children's social care. For example, unlike in relation to education and health

---

2 Department for Education/Department of Health, *Special Educational Needs and Disability Code of Practice: 0 to 25 years*, January 2015 ('the SEND Code').

3 For further information see Council for Disabled Children, *The role of social care in implementing the Children and Families Act 2014*, 26 March 2015.

4 EHC plans differ from statements by containing details of a child/young person's health and social care needs as well as their special educational needs: they also have the potential to continue until the age of 25.

5 CFA 2014 s27(1). The SEND Code states at para 4.20 that '[l]ocal authorities should link reviews of education, health and social care provision to the development and review of their local offer and the action they intend to take in response to comments'.

6 See the SEND Code at chapter 3. These build on the co-operation duties imposed by Children Act 2004 ss10–11, see chapter 2 at paras 2.52–2.54.

7 CFA 2014 s32(2).

services, there is no new duty to provide social care services in the CFA 2014. Neither the CFA 2014 nor the Care Act 2014 remove any social care rights that existed before their implementation (indeed both make material improvements). In relation to the social care rights of disabled children, however, the main contribution made by both Acts is to improve the co-ordination of social care support with education and health services rather than creating any new entitlements.

3.8   A further development under the CFA 2014 with potentially far-reaching implications (including for social care) is the duty imposed by section 19. This requires local authorities to 'have regard' to (ie consider) a series of matters, most notably 'the need to support the child and his or her parent, or the young person, in order to facilitate the development of the child or young person and to help him or her achieve the *best possible educational and other outcomes*'[8] (emphasis added). This strongly suggests that it will no longer be acceptable for a local authority to simply aim for 'sufficient' or 'adequate' provision (including social care provision) for a child or young person.[9]

Statutory scheme: disabled children as 'children in need'

3.9   The law and procedures related to the provision of social care services for disabled children and their families is complex and is covered in detail below. An overview of the assessment and care provision duties of local authorities is provided overleaf to help explain the process.

3.10   Both for disabled children who have an EHC plan (see paras 3.121–3.127 below) and those who do not, the key legislation governing the provision of additional services to disabled children is the Children Act (CA) 1989 and the Chronically Sick and Disabled Persons Act (CSDPA) 1970. The CA 1989 establishes the assessment duty (see paras 3.30–3.46 below) which is generally crucial as the gateway to services and support. The CA 1989 also requires the pro-

---

8   CFA 2014 s19(d).
9   However, the section 19 duty is only engaged when a local authority is exercising a function under CFA 2014 Pt 3. This may, therefore, lead to disputes in individual cases – for example it may be said that a stand-alone assessment under CA 1989 s17 does not engage the section 19 duty, whereas a social care assessment undertaken as part of an EHC assessment process plainly must.

vision of certain specific services, particularly residential and foster care short breaks.

3.11   Assessments made under CA 1989 should also determine whether a child is eligible for support under CSDPA 1970 (see paras 3.62–3.78 below).[10] As the 2015 statutory guidance[11] explains:

> When undertaking an assessment of a disabled child, the local authority must also consider whether it is necessary to provide support under section 2 of the Chronically Sick and Disabled Persons Act (CSDPA) 1970. Where a local authority is satisfied that the identified services and assistance can be provided under section 2 of the CSDPA, and it is necessary in order to meet a disabled child's needs, it must arrange to provide that support.

3.12   Section 17(1) of the CA 1989 places a duty on local authorities to safeguard and promote the welfare of children within their area who are 'in need'. So far as is consistent with this duty, local authorities must promote the upbringing of such children by their families.[12] Local authorities are empowered to provide 'a range and level of services' to meet the needs of 'children in need'. The work of authorities under CA 1989 Part III should be directed at (among other things) providing effective family support.[13]

3.13   The definition of 'children in need' is to be found at CA 1989 s17(10), which provides that a child is to be taken as 'in need' if:

(a) he is unlikely to achieve or maintain, or to have the opportunity of achieving or maintaining, a reasonable standard of health or development without the provision for him of services by a local authority ...; or

(b) his health or development is likely to be significantly impaired, or further impaired, without the provision for him of such services; or

(c) *he is disabled.* (emphasis added).

3.14   It is important to note that unlike other categories of children 'in need', there is no additional requirement for 'disabled' children to require support from the local authority to meet this definition. If a child is 'disabled', he or she is automatically a child 'in need'. At section 17(11), the definition of 'disabled' for the purposes of CA 1989 Part III is given as follows:

---

10 As specifically provided for by CA 1989 Sch 2 para 3(a).

11 HM Government, *Working Together to Safeguard Children: A guide to interagency working to safeguard and promote the welfare of children*, March 2015, p18.

12 CA 1989 s17(1)(b).

13 CA 1989 Sch 2 para 7(a)(i).

For the purposes of this Part, a child is disabled if he is blind, deaf or dumb or suffers from mental disorder of any kind or is substantially and permanently handicapped by illness, injury or congenital deformity or such other disability as may be prescribed.

3.15   The definition is outdated and excessively medical in its approach. It does, however, have the practical advantage of being extremely broad. In particular, the phrase 'mental disorder of any kind' encompasses a wide range of conditions, including Asperger syndrome/high-functioning autism, attention deficit hyperactivity disorder (ADHD) and attention deficit disorder (ADD) as well as impairments such as learning disability, mental illness and personality disorder. All such conditions fall within Mental Health Act 1983 s1(2), which defines 'mental disorder' as including 'any disorder or disability of the mind'. Additionally, a mental disorder will generally amount to a disability within the definition in the Equality Act 2010 s6 and, accordingly, any difference in treatment of such persons will be liable to challenge, as unlawful, disability discrimination.[14]

3.16   If it is not accepted that a child is 'disabled', a child may still be a 'child in need' by virtue of requiring services for the reasons specified in section 17(10)(a) or (b). This alternative route to entitlement will also be relevant to siblings of disabled children, who may be 'in need' as a result of the impact on them of living in a family coping with disability. If so, services can be provided for the sibling directly (subsequent to their own assessment) as well as following the assessment of the disabled child under CA 1989 s17(3), which allows services to be provided to any family member of a child 'in need'. For the rights of siblings of disabled children who are 'young carers', see chapter 8 on carers at paras 8.26–8.59.

3.17   It should be born in mind that there is a low threshold for social care assessments,[15] which should be carried out if a child *may be* 'in need' (one of the potential outcomes of the assessment being a decision that he or she is not in fact 'in need'). Although it will not be unlawful for a local authority to prioritise the speed with which it undertook certain assessments (for example on the basis of urgency), it would be unlawful for a local authority to have 'eligibility criteria' for assessments, see para 3.54.

14 See for example *Governing Body of X School v SP and others* [2008] EWHC 389 (Admin) and see also chapter 9 below regarding the definitions of 'disability' and 'discrimination' under the Equality Act 2010.

15 By analogy see *R v Bristol CC ex p Penfold* (1997–98) 1 CCLR 315 which concerned a very similar obligation in the NHS and Community Care Act 1990, s47.

3.18   While many children will have had a medical diagnosis of an impairment or condition prior to a local authority assessment taking place, legally, this is not a requirement.

3.19   The latest statistics (for 2013–14) suggest that about 10 per cent of all children recognised by local authorities to be 'in need' have disability or illness as their primary need.[16]

'Within their area'

3.20   The duty in CA 1989 s17(1) is owed to children who are 'within the area' of a particular local authority. This does not mean that a child has to be 'ordinarily resident' in that local authority – the ordinary residence provisions of the Care Act 2014 do not apply to the CA 1989. In particular, it is possible (and indeed in London likely) that a child can be within the area of more than one authority. An example of this is found in *R v Wandsworth LBC ex p Stewart*[17] where the children were held to be 'within the area' of both Lambeth (where they were living) and Wandsworth (where they went to school). What is plainly needed is for the authorities to co-operate in cases like this to make sure that one authority takes the lead, typically the authority where the child lives; this is supported by the co-operation duty in CA 1989 s27.[18]

3.21   If a child in need is placed in accommodation outside his home area, he remains the responsibility of the placing authority for the duration of that placement: CA 1989 s105(6). The implications of this for the responsibility to provide adult care services have been addressed by the Supreme Court.[19] However, if a child in need leaves a local authority's area voluntarily (for example because they are part of a travelling family) then the authority continues to have the power to provide them with services outside their area.[20]

---

16 Department for Education, *Statistical First Release: Characteristics of children in need in England, 2013–14*, 29 October 2014, p7. This found that there was a total of 397,600 children assessed as 'in need' in England in 2014 – which would indicate that about 40,000 of these were disabled children. Given that there are about 700,000 disabled children in England, this would suggest that the vast majority of disabled children go unrecognised as children 'in need'.

17 [2001] EWHC 709 (Admin); [2002] 1 FLR 469.

18 The High Court in *Sandra Stewart* stated (at [28]) that in these cases where children are within the area of more than one authority 'there is a manifest case for co-operation under section 27 of the Children Act and a sharing of the burden by the authorities'.

19 In *R (Cornwall Council) v Secretary of State for Health and another* [2015] UKSC 46; [2015] 3 WLR 213.

20 *R (J) v Worcestershire CC* [2014] EWCA Civ 1518; [2015] 1 WLR 2825.

Social work service/key workers

3.22   Local authorities in England must appoint a director of children's services[21] whose functions include children's social services functions. As a matter of public law, it is a requirement that directors are provided with sufficient staff in order to discharge their functions.[22] Where harm results from delay caused by staff shortages, it will constitute maladministration.[23]

3.23   A duty exists on the Lead Member for Children[24] and the director of children's services to 'co-operate with those leading the integration arrangements for children and young people with SEN or disabilities to ensure the delivery of care and support is effectively integrated in the new SEN system'.[25]

3.24   The CFA 2014 requires that local authorities exercise their functions with a view to ensuring the integration of educational provision and training provision with health care provision and social care provision.[26] Authorities must also make joint commissioning arrangements[27] with 'partner commissioning bodies'[28] about the education, health and care provision to be secured for children and

---

21 Children Act 2004 s18.
22 Local Authority Social Services Act 1970 s6(6) makes this obligation explicit in relation to directors of adult services – requiring that they secure the provision of 'adequate staff' for assisting them in the exercise of their functions.
23 Report on complaint no 05/C/18474 against Birmingham City Council, 4 March 2008, where the ombudsman referred to Birmingham's 'corporate failure to ensure adequate resourcing and performance of its services to highly vulnerable people' (para 55).
24 The council's elected cabinet member with responsibility for children's services.
25 SEND Code, para 3.70.
26 CFA 2014 s25.
27 The SEND Code states at para 3.9 that: 'Joint commissioning arrangements must cover the services for 0–25 year old children and young people with SEN or disabilities, both with and without EHC plans. Services will include specialist support and therapies, such as clinical treatments and delivery of medications, speech and language therapy, assistive technology, personal care (or access to it), Child and Adolescent Mental Health Services (CAMHS) support, occupational therapy, habilitation training, physiotherapy, a range of nursing support, specialist equipment, wheelchairs and continence supplies and also emergency provision.' Joint commissioning arrangements must also include arrangements for securing the education, health and care provision specified in EHC plans: SEND Code, para 3.11,
28 Being the NHS Commissioning Board ('NHS England') and each clinical commissioning group for the area: CFA 2014 s26(8).

young people with special educational needs and disabled children and young people.[29]

Key workers

3.25   Given the difficulties that parents and children have in obtaining information and accessing fragmented and unco-ordinated services, it is little wonder that many families value the allocation of a particular worker to them and refer to the positive impact that a capable and conscientious key worker can have on their lives.[30] The SEND Code states that '[l]ocal authorities should adopt a key working approach, which provides children, young people and parents with a single point of contact to help ensure the holistic provision and co-ordination of services and support'.[31] Models of service and the recommended roles for key workers vary, but central key worker tasks include being the single point of contact for the family, the key source of information and guidance, the mediator and facilitator with other professionals across agency boundaries and the co-ordinator of provision, as well as acting as an advocate and source of personal support. An individual in this position is well placed not only to provide essential information but also to act as a guide through complex service structures, to take the strain of negotiation from the parents and to help them to access services. Key workers can be effective in relieving the stress often experienced by parents. While the first official recommendation that children and their families should have a single professional to act as their main point of contact was made in 1976,[32] research over subsequent decades has highlighted how patchy developments have been in this respect.[33] The government

29 CFA 2014 s26.
30 Audit Commission, *Services for disabled children: a review of services for disabled children and their families*, Audit Commission Publications, 2003; R Townsley, D Abbott and D Watson, *Making a difference? Exploring the impact of multi-agency working on disabled children with complex healthcare needs, their families and the professional who support them*, Policy Press, 2003; P Sloper, P Greco, V Beecham and R Webb, 'Key worker services for disabled children: what characteristics of services lead to better outcomes for children and families?', (2006) 32 *Child: care, health and development*, pp147–157.
31 SEND Code, para 2.21.
32 Court Report, *Fit for the future: report of the committee on child health services*, Cmnd 6684, HMSO, 1976.
33 V Greco and P Sloper, 'Care co-ordination and key worker schemes for disabled children: results of a UK-wide survey', (2004) 30 *Child: care, health and developments*, pp13–20.

in England has long professed a commitment to key workers and has issued a range of guidance documents on the role of the 'lead professional'.[34]

Basic principles of assessment

3.26   In the following paragraphs, we detail the legal duties of local authorities in relation to assessment by reference to the 2015 statutory guidance, *Working Together to Safeguard Children*[35] ('*Working Together*'). The guidance (as we note below) has significant limitations and must be seen in the context of the wider set of public law principles that underpin all assessments of disabled children and their families.[36] These include the requirement that:

- Assessments should be needs-led rather than dictated by available provision.
- In consultation with all the children and adults concerned, the assessment process should identify first, the barriers that inhibit the child and family living an ordinary life and second, what can be done by the support agencies to tackle them.[37]
- Assessment should take account of the needs of the whole family and individuals within it; while some services may be provided directly to a disabled child, others may be offered to parents or siblings (see chapter 8 for duties to adult and child carers).
- The agreed provision or arrangements following assessment may not necessarily take the form of what are usually seen as social care services.[38]
- There has also been a growing emphasis on assessment practice that adopts an outcome focus. This means that the practitioner

---

34 See, for example, Children's Workforce Development Council, *Lead professional: practitioners' and managers' guides*, 2007, refreshed March 2010, and HM Government, *Working Together to Safeguard Children: A guide to inter-agency working to safeguard and promote the welfare of children*, March 2015, para 9.

35 HM Government, *Working Together to Safeguard Children: A guide to inter-agency working to safeguard and promote the welfare of children*, March 2015.

36 For a more detailed discussion of good assessment practice, see J Read, L Clements and D Ruebain, *Disabled children and the law: research and good practice*, 2nd edn, Jessica Kingsley Publishers, 2006.

37 See, for example, Department for Education and Skills, *Together from the start: practical guidance for professionals working with disabled children (birth to third birthday) and their families*, 2003.

38 Department of Health, *Carers and Disabled Children Act: practice guidance*, TSO, 2001.

undertaking the assessment, together with the children and adults in the family, identifies a range of outcomes that are important to help the family live a more ordinary life. All involved then agree on the provision that could make those outcomes happen.[39] The effectiveness of any intervention is then judged on the extent to which the identified outcomes are achieved.

- Assessments should be undertaken and provision put in place promptly and children and their families should not have to wait for essential services.
- Early intervention is regarded as important in order to avoid families reaching crisis point.[40]
- Finally, because children grow and develop and family circumstances change, assessment of need should not be seen as a one-off event but should be repeated as required, while avoiding the burden that unnecessary repetitious assessments impose on families.

Registers of disabled children, the 'local offer' and sufficiency of social care provision

3.27   The CA 1989[41] requires that local authorities maintain a register of disabled children within their area (by means of a computer if needs be). There would appear to be considerable potential for such a database to be used dynamically to provide both targeted information for families and as a strategic resource (linked – for example into the assessments concerning the extent to which there are young carers/ parent carers within their area[42] as well as the sufficiency of childcare

---

39 See Department of Health, *Carers and Disabled Children Act: practice guidance*, TSO, 2001; J Cavet and P Sloper, 'Participation by disabled children in individual decisions about their lives and in public decisions about service development', (2004) 18 *Children and Society* pp278–290; P Rabiee, P Sloper and B Beresford, 'Desired outcomes for children and young people with complex health care needs and children who do not use speech for communication', (2005) 135 *Health and Social Care in the Community* pp478– 487.

40 HM Treasury and Department for Education and Skills, *Aiming high for disabled children: better support for families*, 2007.

41 Schedule 2 Part 1 para 2; regulatory powers under the Children Act 2004 s17 enabling the extension of this duty to encompass 'Children and Young People's Plans' appear to have been abandoned with the revocation of the regulations under that section.

42 ie CA 1989 s17ZA and s17ZD respectively and see also paras 8.7 and 8.32 below.

facilities suitable for disabled children[43]). Registration of a child's name on such a register is entirely voluntary.

3.28   CFA 2014 s27 additionally requires that local authorities assess and keep under review the sufficiency of social care provision (and educational/ training provision – see para 4.37) in their area for disabled children. Compliance with this and the other strategic duties will require local authorities to know their population of disabled children and young people, understand their social care needs and assess whether the level of social care services available is sufficient to meet those needs. Information as to social care services inside and outside the local authority's area is required to be published as part of the 'local offer'.[44] In *R (L and P) v Warwickshire CC*,[45] the court held that, in breach of its statutory duty, the authority had failed to maintain a disability register, noting that:

> ... unless this local authority has such a register and knows more or less precisely how many disabled children there are in the county it cannot make a fully informed decision about budgetary allocation or as to the terms of a proposed Local Offer.[46]

3.29   Even where registers are well-maintained, the fact that registration is voluntary means that they are not guaranteed to be a reliable source of information on the population of disabled children in a local area. Local authorities will need, therefore, to draw on other data.[47]

Duty to assess

3.30   The CA 1989 contains no explicit duty on children's services authorities to assess the needs of disabled children and their families.[48] However, in *R (G) v Barnet LBC and others*,[49] the House of Lords held

43   Childcare Act 2006 s6(2)(a)(ii); see also paras 8.23–8.25 below.
44   See CFA 2014 s30 and SEND Regs 2014 Sch 2 para 13. See further chapter 4 at paras 4.72–4.78.
45   [2015] EWHC 203 (Admin); [2015] ELR 271.
46   [2015] EWHC 203 (Admin); [2015] ELR 271 at [83].
47   See for example, Department for Work and Pensions, *Making disability data work for you*, 2014.
48   There has for some time been an express duty to assess in the primary legislation for adult social care: see NHS and Community Care Act 1990 s47 and now Care Act 2014 s9.
49   [2003] UKHL 57; (2003) 6 CCLR 500 – the view was expressed by Lords Hope, Nicholls and Scott and influenced in part by the requirement in CA 1989 Sch 2 para 1 that: 'Every local authority shall take reasonable steps to identify the extent to which there are children in need within their area'.

that such an obligation to assess under CA 1989[50] had to be inferred to exist.[51]

3.31 As noted at para 4.123 below, where a local authority is under a duty to undertake an 'EHC assessment', this will include a specific duty to assess their social care support needs.[52]

3.32 Where a local authority carries out an EHC assessment, it must seek advice, which must include 'advice and information in relation to social care'.[53] In the opinion of the authors of this book, it will not be sufficient for children's services to discharge the advice-giving duty in relation to an EHC assessment by simply stating that a child is 'not known' to social care. The request for advice must constitute a referral for the purposes of CA 1989 s17 and so, the proper response where a child is not previously known to social care will be to carry out an assessment in accordance with the *Working Together* guidance (see paras 3.33–3.36 below) so that there can be meaningful input to the EHC assessment process. Where a new or revised social care assessment is necessary this should be carried out alongside the overall EHC assessment process. The SEND Code calls for a 'tell us once' approach[54] and emphasises the need for co-ordinated assessment processes[55]. The SEND Code states further that 'EHC needs assessments should be combined with social care assessments under Section 17 of the Children Act 1989 where appropriate'.[56]

50 The issue in *R (G) v Barnet* was whether CA 1989 s17 created a specific duty to provide services, in particular accommodation. Lord Nicholls was in the minority who held that such a duty did arise; however, his view that there was also a duty to assess was shared by Lord Hope and Lord Scott, who were in the majority. Lord Hope referred (at [77]) to CA 1989 Sch 2 para 3, which allows a children's services authority to assess the needs of a child who appears to be in need at the same time as any assessment under CSDPA 1970 and (then) Education Act 1996 Part IV (a special educational needs assessment, now replaced by an education, health and care assessment).

51 The ombudsman has also identified a public law duty to assess under the CA 1989 – see for example Complaint no 12 015 730 against Cambridgeshire County Council, 12 November 2013, in particular para 44.

52 CFA 2014 s36 and SEND Regs 2014 regs 3–10. The duty only arises where the authority is of the opinion that: (a) the child or young person has or may have special educational needs; and (b) it may be necessary for special educational provision to be made for the child or young person in accordance with an EHC plan.

53 SEND Regs 2014 reg 6(1)(e).

54 SEND Code, para 9.33.

55 SEND Code, paras 9.30–9.31.

56 SEND Code, para 10.18.

Guidance on assessment – *Working Together* (2015)

3.33   The principal guidance on the duty to assess the needs of children who are or may be 'in need' is found in a 2015 policy document, *Working Together*.[57] The guidance is problematical in that it is primarily concerned with the duties to safeguard children from abuse and neglect and provides only limited practical advice concerning the provision of support to disabled children and their families. The perception that *Working Together* is directed at children subject to abuse or neglect (and not the needs of disabled children and their families for support) is reinforced by its requirement[58] that every local safeguarding children's board publishes a 'threshold document' setting out (amongst other things) the 'criteria, including the level of need, for when a case should be referred to local authority children's social care for assessment and for statutory services under section 17 of the Children Act 1989 (children in need)'. However, the statutory duty to disabled children as children 'in need' is clear and *Working Together* can be read in a way which supports the positive implementation of this duty (especially if applied sensitively by professionals who have the necessary expertise) in cases where there are no concerns about the child's parenting.

3.34   The purpose of assessment is said by *Working Together* 'always' to be to gather important information about a child and family, analyse their needs, decide whether the child is a child in need and provide support to address those needs to improve the child's outcomes.[59] Moreover, '[e]very assessment should be focused on outcomes, deciding which services and support to provide to deliver improved welfare for the child'.[60] Key features of the guidance on assessment include:

- The clear statement that '[w]here an assessment takes place, it will be carried out by a social worker'.[61]

57 HM Government, *Working Together to Safeguard Children: A guide to inter-agency working to safeguard and promote the welfare of children*, March 2015, issued under section 7 of the Local Authority Social Services Act 1970, which requires authorities 'to act under' such guidance.

58 *Working Together*, p15, para 18.

59 *Working Together*, p19, para 29. The final point is expressed in the guidance as 'to improve the child's outcomes *to make them safe*' (emphasis added). This illustrates the problem with conflating the guidance on children 'in need' and children 'at risk' as has been done through the reissued *Working Together* guidance.

60 *Working Together*, p25, para 52.

61 *Working Together*, p18.

- The requirement for a 'timely' assessment, and the specific obligation for a decision to be made about the type of response required within *one working day* of a referral being received.[62] It is also emphasised that '[f]or children who need additional help, every day matters'.[63]
- The imposition of a maximum timeframe for assessments to conclude[64] of *45 working days*: the presumption being that a single assessment will take place within this timeframe which is proportionate to the needs of the individual child. Importantly, the guidance states that '[w]hatever the timescale for assessment, where particular needs are identified at any stage of the assessment, social workers should not wait until the assessment reaches a conclusion before commissioning services to support the child and their family'.[65]
- Every assessment must be informed by the views of the child as well as the family and children should, wherever possible, be seen alone.[66] Assessments of disabled children may, therefore, require more preparation, more time and potentially specialist expertise in communication.[67] This obligation to engage with the child in the assessment process is reinforced by CA 1989 s17(4A),[68] which requires an authority to ascertain and give due consideration to a child's wishes and feelings before deciding what (if any) services to provide to that child.[69] The High Court has stressed that even if a disabled person was felt to be 'completely' prevented from communicating their wishes and feelings, the assessors had a duty to

---

62 *Working Together*, p26, para 58.
63 *Working Together*, para 10. A point endorsed by the SEND Code (para 9.35) that '[f]or social care, help and support should be given to the child and family as soon as a need is identified and not wait until the completion of an EHC needs assessment'.
64 Defined as the point where 'it is possible to reach a decision on next steps': *Working Together*, p26, para 60.
65 *Working Together*, p26, para 61.
66 *Working* Together, p26, para 62; see also para 22: 'Anyone working with children should see and speak to the child; listen to what they say; take their views seriously; and work with them collaboratively when deciding how to support their needs'.
67 Department of Health, *Framework for the assessment of children in need and their families practice guidance*, 2000, para 3.128
68 As inserted by CA 2004 s53.
69 In this respect the statutory scheme reflects the requirements of UNCRC article 12.

ascertain those wishes and feelings by any possible means.[70] See paras 1.22–1.25 for more on the fundamental duty to consult with disabled children on decisions about their lives.

3.35   *Working Together* stresses[71] that a 'good assessment' is one which investigates three 'domains':

- the child's developmental needs;
- parenting capacity; and
- family and environmental factors.

Important 'dimensions' within these domains for a disabled child are likely to include health, education, emotional and behavioural development and self-care skills (child's developmental needs), ensuring safety (parenting capacity) and housing, family's social integration and community resources (family and environmental factors). Assessments should be holistic; as *Working Together* states (p23, para 42), '[e]very assessment should reflect the unique characteristics of the child within their family and community context'.

3.36   The minimum standards detailed in *Working Together* must be followed (since it is statutory guidance) in the absence of cogent reasons – and even in such cases, the scope for departure is severely limited.[72] What is important is that the assessment carefully and accurately sets out and evaluates all the child's needs so a proper decision can be made as to what services (if any) are required to be provided to the child and/or family to meet those needs (see paras 3.62–3.65 below on the duty to provide services to meet assessed needs).

Early help

3.37   In recent years, a number of good practice guidance documents have encouraged local authorities to move away from detailed assessments of 'children in need' towards a more flexible approach, often using what has been termed the 'Common Assessment Framework' (CAF)[73] – sometimes referred to as a type of 'Early Help' assessment.[74] Such

---

70 *R (A and B) v East Sussex CC (No 2)* [2003] EWHC 167 (Admin); (2003) 6 CCLR 194.

71 *Working Together*, p21, para 36.

72 See for example *R (TG) v Lambeth LBC* [2011] EWCA Civ 526; (2011) 14 CCLR 366 at [17] and *R v Islington LBC ex p Rixon* (1997–98) 1 CCLR 119 at 123, 15 March 1996, QBD. These cases are considered at paras 2.41–2.42 above.

73 Department for Children, Schools and Families, *Common assessment framework (CAF)*, 2006

74 *Working Together* p13, para 8.

simplified/streamlined assessment programmes appear to have a number of benefits[75] including their potential to be used (and shared) by all professionals who have involvement with the relevant child. While such an approach has practical advantages, the fundamental legal duty towards children 'in need' (including disabled children) is to assess their needs in a manner consistent with *Working Together*. If families are happy with a less rigorous approach, this may be acceptable in practice. However, any authority that neglects its assessment duty where a family is less than happy with the approach is likely to find itself criticised by the High Court or the Ombudsman.

3.38   *Working Together* formalises the concept of an 'Early Help' assessment. This should be undertaken by a lead professional, for example a family support worker, health visitor or special educational needs co-ordinator, who should 'provide support to the child or family, act as an advocate on their behalf and coordinate the delivery of support services'.[76] Although *Working Together* refers to a child who is 'disabled and has specific additional needs' as an example of a child who may benefit from 'Early Help',[77] this section of the guidance is aimed at 'all professionals, including those in universal services'.[78] *Working Together* is clear that if a 'disabled' child (or any other child who may be 'in need') is identified, 'a referral should be made immediately to local authority children's social care'.[79] The guidance, therefore, suggests that 'Early Help' is a low level approach different from the duty to assess children 'in need' which falls on local authority children's services departments. Indeed, *Working Together* refers to 'Early Help' in the context of the general co-operation duty in CA 2004 s10, see para 2.52 above.

3.39   The scope of the duty to assess disabled children as children 'in need' was, however, considered by the High Court in *R (L and P)*

75 Department for Children, Schools and Families, *Early Support*, 2004 – but see P Gilligan and M Manby, 'The common assessment framework: does the reality match the rhetoric?' (2008) 32 *Child and Family Social Work*, pp177–187; S White C Hall and S Peckover, 'The descriptive tyranny of the common assessment framework: technologies of categorization and professional practice in child welfare', (2009) 39 *British Journal of Social Work*, pp1197–1217; H Bonnick, 'Framework for optimism', (2010) *Community Care* 8, p8.
76 *Working Together*, p14, para 9. It is plain from p12 of the guidance that the 'Early Help' approach is intended to reflect the general duty on local authorities and other relevant bodies to co-operate in order to improve the well-being of children found in Children Act 2004 s10.
77 *Working Together*, para 5.
78 *Working Together*, para 3.
79 *Working Together*, para 11.

v Warwickshire CC[80] where the court considered that 'the guidance should not be read as insisting that every disabled child should initially be the subject of a full-blown social worker assessment'. In the court's opinion, the legislative scheme did not require that every child with a 'mental disorder' should be entitled automatically to receive a section 17 assessment conducted by a social worker. In the judge's view, there was nothing wrong with the local authority's approach that disabled children with lower level needs could be assessed under the CAF. This leaves open the question of the threshold at which a local authority must offer a social work assessment rather than an 'Early Help' assessment.

Parent carers and young carers needs assessments

3.40   The CA 1989 (as amended by the CFA 2014) places specific and significant duties on local authorities to assess the needs of carers with parental responsibility for disabled children as well as young carers and these duties are considered in chapter 8. These assessments must inform the decision on the package of support to be provided to the family under CA 1989 s17.

Local protocols

3.41   *Working Together* also requires the publication by local authorities and their partners of 'local protocols for assessment'.[81] The protocol must be consistent with the statutory guidance and set out clear arrangements for the management of cases after referral to the children's services department. In particular, the protocol for each authority should (amongst other things):

- ensure that assessments are timely, transparent and proportionate to the needs of individual children and their families;
- set out how the needs of particular groups, including disabled children, will be addressed in the assessment process;
- clarify how social work assessments will be informed by other specialist assessments, for example education, health and care assessments under the CFA 2014;
- ensure any specialist assessments are co-ordinated so that the child and family experience is a joined up assessment process and a 'single planning process focused on outcomes; and

---

80 [2015] EWHC 203 (Admin); [2015] ELR 271, see [72].
81 *Working Together*, p27, paras 65–67.

- set out the process for challenge by children and families by publishing the complaints procedures.[82]

3.42 The local protocol is, therefore, an essential document for all those concerned with how assessment should operate in any particular local area. There is an express requirement in *Working Together* for local authorities to publish the local protocol[83] and, given the overarching theme of transparency,[84] it should be expected that the protocol is easily available, including on the authority's website and as part of the 'local offer' website (see para 3.28 above). *Working Together* states clearly that the 'local authority is publicly accountable for this protocol' (para 67).[85]

Assessment case-law

3.43 The duty to assess under CA 1989 s17 has been the subject of significant litigation, which has reinforced its nature as being 'substance' rather than 'form'. Although these cases were decided by reference to guidance that pre-dated the 2015 *Working Together* guidance, the principles they establish would appear to be of continued and direct relevance.

3.44 In *R (AB and SB) v Nottingham CC*,[86] it was held that a failure by an authority to have in place a 'systematic approach' for conducting a core assessment[87] was an 'impermissible departure from the guidance'. In the court's opinion it was essential that the result of such an assessment must be that individuals could see 'what help and support the child and family need and which agencies might be best placed to give that help'.

3.45 Assessments must also identify and address foreseeable future needs as well as present needs: *R (K) v Manchester CC*.[88]

---

82 All from *Working Together*, p27, para 67.
83 *Working Together*, p27, para 65.
84 See for example the SEND Code at para 11.1: 'Relations between education, health and social care services and young people should be marked by open communication so that parents and young people know where they are in the decision-making process, their knowledge and experience can be used to support good decision-making and they know the reasons why decisions have been made.'
85 *Working Together*, p27, para 67.
86 [2001] EWHC 235 (Admin); (2001) 4 CCLR 294 at 306G–I.
87 The previous guidance distinguished between 'initial' and 'core' assessments, a distinction abandoned under *Working Together*.
88 [2006] EWHC 3164; (2007) 10 CCLR 87.

3.46   A failure to carry out a lawful assessment according to the guidance may result in the court requiring that a new assessment be undertaken.[89] A failure to involve a disabled child in his or her assessment may also render the process unlawful, as was the case in *R (J) v Caerphilly CBC*[90] where it was held that severely challenging behaviour exhibited by a young man did not absolve the authority of its duties to engage him in the assessment.

Duty to provide services

3.47   There is an expectation in the law and guidance that where disabled children are assessed as having substantial needs, these needs will be met through the provision of services. However, given the longstanding gulf between need and available resources, it is important for families to know when there is a *duty* on a children's services authority to meet need following assessment. This section seeks to answer this question.

3.48   In relation to the general expectation that assessed needs will be met, the general duty (see para 2.48 for the meaning of this term) on local authorities is to provide services so as to minimise the effects of disabled children's disabilities and give them the opportunity to lead lives which are 'as normal as possible'.[91] Furthermore, the clear expectation of *Working Together* is that an assessment which identifies significant needs will generally lead to the provision of services. This is demonstrated by the definition of the purpose of assessment which includes 'to provide support to address those needs to improve the child's outcomes to make them safe'.[92] Further, the guidance states that '[e]very assessment should be focused on outcomes, deciding which services and support to provide to deliver improved welfare for the child'.[93]

3.49   The duties under CA 1989 s17 are reinforced by the general duty to safeguard and promote the welfare of all children in the authority's area under Children Act (CA) 2004 s11. This in turn reflects the obligation imposed by article 3 of the UN Convention on the Rights

---

89   *R (G) v Barnet LBC* [2003] UKHL 57; (2003) 6 CCLR 500 per Lord Nicholls at [32].
90   [2005] EWHC 586 (Admin); (2005) 8 CCLR 255. This case is discussed in detail at paras 10.58–10.59.
91   CA 1989 s17(1) and Sch 2 para 6.
92   *Working Together*, para 29.
93   *Working Together*, para 52.

of the Child (UNCRC) that the best interest of children should be treated as a primary consideration in all actions and decisions which affect them.[94] They are also reinforced by CSDPA 1970 s2, considered throughout the following section of this chapter.

3.50   It is not, however, necessarily the case that services must be provided to meet *every* assessed need. Whether a children's services authority has to provide services following assessment is dependent upon the nature and extent of the need assessed and the consequences of not providing the service. It is also important here not to confuse the decision that a need must be met with the decision on the *way* to meet the need. For example, a local authority may conclude that there is a need for a child and his or her carers to have a short break from each other. This need can be met in a variety of ways such as by way of a sitting service in the child's home, by the child attending a day service or activity away from the home and so on. The decision on the particular service or type of service to offer must be informed by consideration of the assessed needs of the particular child and family.

The service provision decision

3.51   As we have seen above, while local authorities are obliged to assess disabled children in accordance with the requirements of *Working Together*, they are not obliged to provide services as a consequence, unless a decision is reached that this should happen (ie because the duty under CSDPA 1970 s2 arises, or, under CA 1989 s17, services are required to safeguard or promote the welfare of the child).[95] The duty under CSDPA 1970 s2 is of particular importance because the courts have held that an individual child has no right to a service under CA 1989 s17.[96]

3.52   The process of 'so deciding' requires that authorities act rationally, follow agreed procedures which are explained to the child/family in question and produce a decision for which clear and logical reasons are provided. At law, therefore, there are two distinct issues:

94 See *ZH (Tanzania)* [2011] UKSC 4; [2011] 2 AC 166 at [23], where Baroness Hale held that CA 2004 s11 and similar statutory provisions translated 'the spirit, if not the precise language' of the obligation imposed by UNCRC article 3 into domestic law.

95 If a negative service provision decision is made, there is no obligation on the authority to specify what services would have met the assessed needs.

96 See *R (VC) v Newcastle CC* [2011] EWHC 2673 (Admin); (2012) 15 CCLR 194 at [21]–[27].

1) the process of deciding what services are required (referred to in this chapter as the 'service provision decision'); and

2) the legal consequences that flow once an authority decides that services are required (essentially the enforceability of that decision).

The use of eligibility criteria

3.53   Sadly these distinct processes (the service provision decision and the consequences of the decision) are sometimes confused. The confusion relates to the notion of 'eligibility criteria' – criteria which are used to determine eligibility: the confusion relates to the question: 'eligibility for what?'

3.54   As we have seen above, local authorities are under a statutory duty to assess the needs of each child 'in need'.[97] Accordingly, it would be unlawful for a local authority to impose its own 'eligibility criteria' to decide who shall have assessments. This would constitute an extra-statutory hurdle for a child to cross. However, once a child has been assessed, the law does not require that services be provided in every case.

3.55   Various statutory provisions require social services/children's services departments to provide support for disabled children. The most important of these comprise CA 1989 and CSDPA 1970 s2. However, other provisions do exist and one of these, Mental Health Act 1983 s117, is considered briefly at para 5.130.

3.56   The general duty[98] to provide support services under CA 1989 Part III (see para 3.48) is triggered by the authority 'determining' (s17(4A)) that the provision of services is 'appropriate' (s17(1)). The specifically enforceable duty[99] under CSDPA 1970 s2 (see para 3.49), is triggered by the authority being 'satisfied' the services are 'necessary'.[100] Arguably there is very little, if any, difference between these two tests. In practice, a local authority could (and perhaps 'should')[101] decide that

97 The High Court in *R (L and P) v Warwickshire CC* held that there was no duty to carry out a social work assessment of every disabled children, as some disabled children could be assessed simply via a CAF assessment or another form of 'Early Help' assessment; see para 3.39 above.

98 See para 2.48 for an explanation as to the nature of a 'general' or 'target' duty.

99 See para 2.47 for an explanation as to the nature of a 'specifically enforceable' duty.

100 *R v Gloucestershire CC ex p Barry* [1997] AC 584; (1997–98) 1 CCLR 40.

101 Not least, because CA 1989 Sch 2 permits an authority to assess a child's needs for the purposes of CSDPA 1970 s2 at the same time as assessing under CA 1989.

it will only 'determine' that the provision of services is 'appropriate' under CA 1989 Part III when it is satisfied these are necessary (ie the test for accessing support under the 1970 Act). If this is right then the same decision must effectively be made regardless of which Act the decision is being taken under.

3.57   It follows that it is reasonable for an authority to state that a disabled child will not as a general rule be 'eligible' for support services unless the authority is satisfied that these are necessary. This then requires that the authority explains the process by which it will decide whether or not a child is 'eligible' – ie the criteria it uses to make this judgment. The use of 'eligibility criteria' in this context has been held to be lawful by the courts.[102]

3.58   Such criteria must, however, promote the objects of the legislation, ie that so far as possible, disabled children be brought up by their families[103] and that the services provided should seek to minimise the effects of their disabilities and give them the opportunity to lead lives which are 'as normal as possible'.[104] Given that resources are limited, the criteria should also contain an element of 'prioritisation' – ie it is legitimate for authorities to target those in most need and to devote resources where they can have the most positive impact.[105] While the use of such criteria is well developed in relation to adult care law[106] this is not so for children's services. In *R (JL) v Islington LBC*,[107] Black J stressed the 'pressing need' for government guidance on eligibility criteria for children services, given that many local authorities have, at best, imperfect, and, at worst, unlawful criteria.[108]

102 *R v Gloucestershire CC ex p Barry* [1997] AC 584; (1997–98) 1 CCLR 40, and in the disabled children's context *R (JL) v Islington LBC* [2009] EWHC 458 (Admin); (2009) 12 CCLR 322.

103 CA 1989 s17(1)(b).

104 CA 1989 Sch 2 para 6.

105 In this context see also L Clements and P Thompson, *Community care and the law*, 5th edn, LAG, 2011, paras 23.38–23.41.

106 See for example the Care and Support (Eligibility Criteria) Regulations 2015 SI No 313.

107 [2009] EWHC 458 (Admin); (2009) 12 CCLR 322.

108 There has been no statutory guidance on eligibility criteria for disabled children's services since the Islington judgment. However, there has been non-statutory advice given to local authorities on the application of eligibility criteria in the context of short breaks, see para 3.95 below.

Flow diagram: Assessment and service provision decision: stages and questions

Assessment

If a child presents who may be 'in need' (for example, they may be disabled – see para 3.7 above) , the local authority *must* undertake an assessment and identify what needs for support or services the child and/or the family have (see paras 3.30–3.32 above). The assessment must be completed within a maximum of 45 working days (see para 3.34 above).

Following the assessment, the local authority must decide which of the various needs that have been identified it is 'necessary' to respond to (see para 3.56 below). This decision must then be set out in a care plan, described in the guidance as a 'child in need plan' (see paras 3.108–3.117 above).

Service provision

If the local authority decides that support must be provided, then the following questions should be asked in sequence:

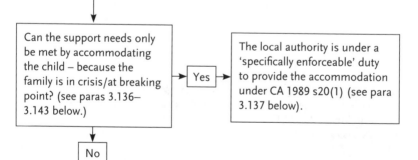

Can the support needs only be met by accommodating the child – because the family is in crisis/at breaking point? (see paras 3.136–3.143 below.) → Yes → The local authority is under a 'specifically enforceable' duty to provide the accommodation under CA 1989 s20(1) (see para 3.137 below).

No

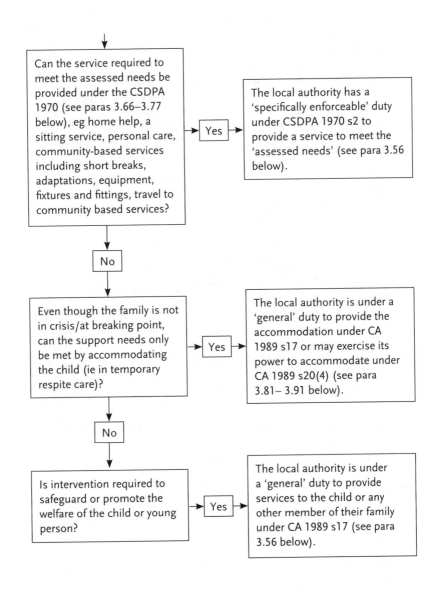

As Clements and Thompson observe, all too often these are:

> ... poorly publicised and formulated with little or no consultation. It appears that in many cases, access to support services is measured largely by assessing the imminence of family breakdown. Thus if it is imminent or has occurred, resources can be accessed, but not otherwise. Clearly such criteria cater for the needs of children suffering abuse or neglect but are likely to be inappropriate for many families with disabled children or young carers. In practice such policies deny support to families until such time as they fall into (or are at severe risk of falling into) the child protection regime: effectively therefore they cater, not for CA 1989 Part III (provision of services for children and their families) but for Part VI (child protection).[109]

3.59   It is permissible, therefore, for children's services authorities to operate eligibility criteria to limit access to services. However, the principles of public law and departmental guidance[110] demand that there must be a rational process for deciding which children are eligible for services and which are not. Eligibility criteria must therefore:

- be transparent because of the policy expectation – see, for example, the 'local offer' created by CFA 2014 s30 – and the need to comply with public law duties and an authorities' obligations under ECHR article 8; every 'local offer' must include information as to any eligibility criteria governing access to social care services for disabled children and young people;[111]
- explain in clear 'everyday language' how services are allocated on the basis of need;
- take account of the impact of disability on children and families; and
- have been the subject of consultation which has taken into account (among other things) the relevant equality duties, particularly the duty under Equality Act 2010 s149 (see paras 9.97–9.107).

3.60   The human rights obligations on public bodies (particularly ECHR article 8: see paras 2.14–2.19) additionally require that any criteria they operate must not be so strict as to deny support where there is

---

109 L Clements and P Thompson, *Community care and the law*, 5th edn, LAG, 2011 at para 23.39.

110 See in this context, Department for Children, Schools and Families, *Aiming high for disabled children: core offer*, 2008.

111 See SEND Regs 2014 Sch 2 para 18. If a local authority operated 'secret' criteria or otherwise refused to make their criteria transparent, this would not be 'in accordance with law', which is one of the requirements of ECHR article 8.

a real risk of significant harm[112] to the child or family if support is not provided (being harm that is more than minor or trivial).[113] In setting criteria, local authorities are obliged to treat the best interests of disabled children as a primary consideration, this obligation being imposed by UNCRC article 3 read with ECHR article 8, CA 1989 s17 and Children Act 2004 s11.[114]

3.61 The lawfulness of one example of eligibility criteria for disabled children's services was tested in *R (JL) v Islington LBC*[115] where the court held the criteria to be unlawful for a variety of reasons, including that:

- they sought to limit access to services regardless of the outcome of the assessment (through imposing an upper maximum limit on the support that could be provided – in this case respite care); and
- in formulating the criteria, the council had failed to have proper regard to its general disability equality duty under (what is now) the Equality Act 2010 s149.[116]

112 'Significant harm' is not defined in the CA 1989, but does not include 'minor shortcomings' or 'minor defects' in care being provided; Department of Health, *The Children Act 1989 Guidance and Regulations. Volume 1: Court Orders* (1991), para 3.12. See R White, A P Carr and N Lowe, *The Children Act in practice*, 4th edn, LexisNexis, 2008, paras 8.43–8.44 and HM Government, *Working together to safeguard children: a guide to inter-agency working to safeguard and promote the welfare of children*, 2010, paras 1.26–1.31 for more on the 'significant harm' threshold.

113 In *R v Gloucestershire CC ex p Mahfood* (1997–98) 1 CCLR 7, DC (a pre-Human Rights Act 1998 judgment), McCowan LJ expressed this proposition in the following way: 'I should stress, however, that there will, in my judgment, be situations where a reasonable authority could only conclude that some arrangements were necessary to meet the needs of a particular disabled person and in which they could not reasonably conclude that a lack of resources provided an answer. Certain persons would be at severe physical risk if they were unable to have some practical assistance in their homes. In those situations, I cannot conceive that an authority would be held to have acted reasonably if they used shortage of resources as a reason for not being satisfied that some arrangement should be made to meet those persons' needs.'

114 See *R (Sanneh) v Secretary of State for Work and Pensions* [2013] EWHC 793 (Admin) at [45]: 'There is no doubt that, in exercising its obligations under section 17, a local authority is bound to consider the article 8 rights to respect for family life of all relevant family members, but particularly the child in need; and it is bound to do so "through the prism of article 3(1)" of the UNCRC.' The obligation imposed by UNCRC article 3 has been considered by the Supreme Court in the 'Benefit Cap' case: *R (SG and others) v Secretary of State for Work and Pensions* [2015] UKSC 16; [2015] 1 WLR 1449. See further chapter 2 at para 2.25

115 [2009] EWHC 458 (Admin); (2009) 12 CCLR 322.

116 Formerly Disability Discrimination Act 1995 s49A; see paras 9.97–9.107.

Duty to meet 'assessed needs'

3.62   Once it has been decided that a child's or a family's needs meet the relevant 'eligibility criteria' (ie the local authority is satisfied that it is necessary to provide support services) then there is an obligation on the authority to provide services and support to meet the assessed need(s). Generally, but not always, this is a straightforward legal obligation. The complication arises from the nature and the 'enforceability' of the legal duties underlying the obligation. The services available under CSDPA 1970 and CA 1989 are considered separately below, but certain general points can be made:

- Services assessed as required under the 1970 Act must be provided, regardless of resources. In other words, once a child/family has been assessed as eligible for support under the 1970 Act, there is a specific duty (see para 2.27) to provide them with services to meet their assessed needs, a duty which cannot be avoided because of lack of resources.[117] As the court stated in *R v Kirklees MBC ex p Daykin* (1998):[118]

    Once needs have been established, then they must be met and · cost cannot be an excuse for failing to meet them. The manner in which they are met does not have to be the most expensive. The Council is perfectly entitled to look to see what cheapest way for them to meet the needs which are specified.[119]

    It follows that councils cannot, in such situations, seek to delay or attempt further rationing – for instance by placing a person on a waiting list[120] or suggesting that the case needs to go to a 'panel'.[121]

---

117   *R v Gloucestershire CC ex p Mahfood* (1997–98) 1 CCLR 40 at 15K and 16D–H per McCowan LJ.

118   (1997–98) 1 CCLR 512 at 525D.

119   See further *R (JL) v Islington LBC* at [106]: 'If the local authority is satisfied that it is necessary, in order to meet a child's needs, to make arrangements within a particular category on the section 2 list, it must make those arrangements. Once this point is reached, considerations such as a finite budget and sharing out resources to reach a greater number of people no longer play a part.'

120   See, for example, Local government ombudsman complaint no 00/B/00599 against Essex, 3 September 2001.

121   See paras 3.132–3.133 below concerning the requirement to identify support services where none are immediately available and paras 10.18–10.19 for further discussion about the questionable legality of 'allocation or funding' panels.

- If a service can be provided under either CA 1989 or CSDPA 1970, then it is provided under the 1970 Act.[122] In essence, the reason for this is that the more enforceable duty under the 1970 Act trumps the lesser duty under the 1989 Act – or put another way, a local authority cannot escape its obligations by choosing to provide a services under a less enforceable provision.
- As will be seen below, the broad range of services available under the 1970 Act means that most services for disabled children and their families are, therefore, provided under the 1970 Act.

3.63   Even if a service is assessed as needed under the 1989 Act (ie because it cannot be provided under the 1970 Act), this does not mean that a local authority need not provide it. Although in such cases there is a general duty[123] not a specific duty (see para 2.48), it is important to distinguish this from a mere 'power'. Local authorities should meet their duties (including their general duties) unless they have good reasons for failing so to do. The key considerations are likely to be:

- As above, local authorities must have clear, published criteria explaining how they will decide who should get support services; these criteria must have been the subject of consultation and have been subjected to a rigorous assessment of their potential impact on disabled people as required by Equality Act 2010 s149.
- Local authorities cannot adopt general exclusions or rigid limits or lists of services that will not be provided – for example, excluding all children with Asperger syndrome from disabled children's services, having caps or ceilings on the amount of service to be provided (eg a maximum of 100 hours per year of short breaks), or stating that 'out of county residential respite will not be provided'. To do any of these things would, in public law terms, be to 'fetter their discretion' to meet their general duties in such cases.[124] It may also involve a breach of the specific duty imposed by CSDPA 1970 s2.
- A local authority that is not providing a service to meet a need, must be able to demonstrate that it has complied in all material respects with the relevant guidance,[125] particularly the *Working Together* statutory guidance.

---

122 *R v Bexley LBC ex p B* (2000) 3 CCLR 15 and see also *R (Spink) v Wandsworth LBC* [2005] EWCA Civ 302; (2005) 8 CCLR 272.

123 *R (G) v Barnet LBC and others* [2003] UKHL 57; (2003) 6 CCLR 500.

124 See, for example, *R v Bexley LBC ex p Jones* [1995] ELR 42 at 55.

125 See, for example, *R v Birmingham CC ex p Killigrew* (2000) 3 CCLR 109 and *R v Lambeth LBC ex p K* (2000) 3 CCLR 141.

- The more severe the consequences of not meeting a need, the more 'anxiously' will the courts and the ombudsmen scrutinise the reasons given by the council for not responding to that need,[126] any actions taken in trying to meet the needs[127] and the process by which the council arrived at its decision.[128] As Munby LJ has noted, it may well be difficult for an authority to justify a decision to provide no services following an assessment of a child with moderate or complex disabilities.[129]

- Where a fundamental human right is likely to be violated by a failure to provide support – such as in particular the right to respect for personal dignity[130] or family life[131] under article 8 of the ECHR, the 'positive obligations' of the state may mean that an authority has no choice but to meet its general duty and provide the service: see paras 2.14–2.19.[132]

3.64   It should be emphasised that it will only be in rare cases that the service required cannot be provided under CSDPA 1970 (see below).

3.65   Legally, the relationship between the 1970 and the 1989 Acts is one that has attracted considerable judicial attention.[133] To put it succinctly (but perhaps for non-lawyers incomprehensibly!) – services provided under section 2 of the 1970 Act are in fact provided by a local authority in the 'exercise of their functions' under Part 3 of the 1989 Act.[134] This reinforces the fact that an assessment under the CA 1989 can and should lead to a decision on whether services have to be provided under the CSDPA 1970.

---

126 See, for example, *R v Lambeth LBC ex p K* (2000) 3 CCLR 141.

127 *R v Islington LBC ex p Rixon* (1998) 1 CCLR 119.

128 *R v Ealing LBC ex p C* (2000) 3 CCLR 122.

129 *R (VC) v Newcastle CC* [2011] EWHC 2673 (Admin); (2012) 15 CCLR 194 at [26].

130 *R (A and B, X and Y) v East Sussex CC* [2003] EWHC 167; (2003) 6 CCLR 194.

131 *R (Bernard) v Enfield LBC* [2002] EWHC 2282 (Admin); (2002) 5 CCLR 577.

132 See *Anufrijeva v Southwark LBC* [2004] QB 1124 at [43], where the Court of Appeal stated that: 'Article 8 may more readily be engaged where a family unit is involved. Where the welfare of children is at stake, article 8 may require the provision of welfare support in a manner which enables family life to continue.' The authors suggest that this will particularly be so where the family includes a disabled child.

133 For a review of the previous case-law, see L Clements and P Thompson, *Community care and the law*, 5th edn, LAG, 2011, paras 9.148–9.153.

134 The Care Act 2014 and Children and Families Act 2014 (Consequential Amendments) Order 2015 SI No 914. See also *R (Spink) v Wandsworth LBC* [2005] EWCA Civ 302; (2005) 8 CCLR 272.

Services under the Chronically Sick and Disabled Persons Act 1970

3.66 The CSDPA 1970 places a specific duty on a local authority to provide the support which a disabled child is assessed as needing – if that support comes within its scope (see below). As *Working Together* states:

> Where a local authority is satisfied that the identified services and assistance can be provided under section 2 of the CSDPA, and it is necessary in order to meet a disabled child's needs, it must arrange to provide that support.[135]

3.67 If the need for the support is (for example) five hours of home/short break care a week, then the local authority must provide five hours. It cannot delay[136] or 'trim'[137] the package for financial reasons. If the service that is required is not available for any reason, the authority must provide a suitable substitute support in the interim while taking urgent steps to ensure that the suitable service is made available.[138] If the family decide that it wants the need met by a direct payment (see paras 3.98–3.99 below) the amount of the payment must be sufficient to meet the need – but the local authority cannot insist that the family have a direct payment (ie the family can require the local authority to arrange or commission the support required).

3.68 CSDPA 1970 s2 provides a list of services that councils must provide to disabled children.[139] In practice, this includes services of great importance, such as short breaks (also known as 'respite care' and increasingly referred to as 'replacement' care), day activities, equipment, adaptations and so on. As noted above, if a service can be provided to meet an assessed need under CSDPA 1970 s2, there is a specific duty to provide it which cannot be avoided by an authority

---

135 *Working Together*, p18. See also to similar effect the SEND Code at para 3.49 in relation to EHC assessments and plans: 'Where a child or young person has been assessed as having social care needs in relation to their SEN or disabilities social care teams *must* secure social care provision under the Chronically Sick and Disabled Persons Act (CSDPA) 1970 which has been assessed as being necessary to support a child or young person's SEN and which is specified in their EHC plan' (emphasis as original).

136 Local government ombudsman complaint no 00/B/00599, 3 September 2001.

137 *R v Islington LBC ex p Rixon* (1997–98) 1 CCLR 119 at 129B.

138 *R v Islington LBC ex p Rixon* (1997–98) 1 CCLR 119 at 129B.

139 CSDPA 1970 s28A (although this has now been superseded in England by amendments to section 2 itself), inserted by the CA 1989, expressly extended the CSDPA 1970 s2 to children. From 1 April 2015, the CSDPA duty to disabled adults has been superseded by the Care Act 2014.

claiming to be acting under CA 1989 s17. The list of services which can be provided under CSDPA 1970 s2 is summarised below.

Practical assistance in the home

3.69   The provision covers a very wide range of home-based (sometimes called 'domiciliary') care services, although it does not cover health-care services even if these do not have to be provided by qualified health professionals.[140] In practice, the services provided under this provision include personal care in the home such as bathing, help using the toilet, moving and helping with feeding and routine house-hold chores. Importantly, this provision also includes respite/short break care if provided as a sitting-type service in the home or through home-based child support or play workers.

Home-based short breaks

3.70   Short break (or respite) care is a 'highly valued' service[141] – giving families and the disabled child the chance to have time apart – or at least time when the family is not providing care or supervision. It is identified in policy documents as well as by families themselves as one of the most important support services that can be provided.[142] The key element of good practice is that a service is arranged that is of benefit to all family members, including the disabled child. Home and community-based short breaks take a wide variety of forms such as sitting-in and befriending schemes for children and young people of all ages. Home-based short breaks are provided under section 2(6)(a) of the 1970 Act (ie as 'practical assistance in the home') and community-based support is provided under section 2(6)(c) (ie as recreational/educational facilities 'outside his home'. Some short breaks are linked to a disabled child's preferred leisure activities, for

---

140   *R (T, D and B) v Haringey LBC* [2005] EWHC 2235 (Admin); (2006) 9 CCLR 58.

141   For example: C Hatton, M Collins, V Welch, J Robertson, E Emerson, S Langer and E Wells, *The Impact of Short Term Breaks on Families with a Disabled Child Over Time*, Department for Education, DFE-RR173, 2011; Contact a Family, *What makes my family stronger*, 2009; Contact a Family, *No time for us: relationships between parents who have a disabled child – a survey of over 2,000 parents in the UK*, 2004; Mencap, *Breaking point: families still need a break*, 2006; Shared Care Network, *Still waiting*, 2006.

142   HM Treasury/Department for Education and Skills, *Aiming high for disabled children*, 2007 and see HM Government, *The Children Act 1989 Guidance and Regulations. Volume 2: Care Planning, Placement and Case Review*, DCSF Publications, 2015, chapter 6.

instance a play scheme at a local football club, horse riding, swimming etc. If a child has a need for short break/respite care which cannot be provided in their own home or a community-based setting and which has to be provided in a care home or foster placement (ie away from the child's home) then it will generally be provided under CA 1989 (see paras 3.81–3.91).

Wireless, television, library, 'or similar recreational facilities'

3.71 The use of the phrase in CSDPA 1970 s2(6)(b) of 'or similar recreational facilities' means that this provision could include such things as a computer, gaming consoles and other recreational equipment as well as 'talking books' (ie audio book service for people with visual impairments).[143]

Recreational/educational facilities

3.72 As with 'practical assistance in the home' above, this provision is particularly wide in its potential scope – covering community-based activities such as day centres and after-school or school holiday clubs as well as specific recreational/educational support activities that the assessment of need identifies as of importance to the child's development and sense of well-being. Clearly, services under this provision may also include an element of respite/short break, since if the child is being provided with care and support in the community, then he or she is having a short break from his or her family.

3.73 While local authorities fund the attendance of many disabled children at community-based day centres, play schemes, holiday clubs etc, not infrequently these facilities are used by other disabled children whose parents pay for the service themselves (ie without any local authority support). While this may be because their needs have been held to be insufficiently great to be eligible for support (see paras 3.53–3.61), it can be because there has been no proper assessment – and if this is the case, a request should be made for the authority to undertake one. A not uncommon indication that such an assessment is required is when the community-based service decides that it is unable to meet the child's needs because they are so demanding (for example, that there is a need for 1:1 care).

3.74 Services under this provision also include those which assist the disabled child 'in taking advantage of educational facilities' that are

143 Complaint 11 017 875 against Suffolk County Council, 11 October 2012, para 6.

available to him or her. Although this does not cover the actual provision of education, it is aimed at providing support that enables the disabled child to access education – for example, help with their personal care requirements while they pursue their studies,[144] as well as escorted travel to and from the education setting[145] and possibly the provision of additional facilities at the institution[146] (although these might also be required under the Equality Act 2010 – see paras 9.71–9.96 below).

Travel and other assistance

3.75   Local authorities must, when assessing a disabled child's need for community-based support, also consider that child's travel needs to enable him or her to access that service. It is not acceptable for a local authority to have a blanket policy that it will not provide such transport, for example by reference to an expectation that parents will always provide transport – or for it to state that a disabled child's mobility component of disability living allowance should be used to cover this. While local authorities are permitted to charge for services under the 1970 Act (see paras 3.155–3.156), the law requires that in assessing the charge, entitlement to the mobility component of disability living allowance must be ignored.[147]

3.76   If a disabled child needs travel assistance to a community-based activity – then that is clearly a 'need', regardless of whether the child is or is not receiving a social security benefit. Because of local authority misunderstandings about this question, Department of Health guidance[148] was issued in 2012 which states that the 'Department would like to make the position clear' that:

> ... local councils have a duty to assess the needs of any person for whom the authority may provide or arrange the provision of community care services and who may be in need of such services. They have a further

144 See Department of Health *LAC(93)12 – Further and Higher Education Act 1992.*

145 Note, however, the detailed statutory scheme in relation to school and college transport, see [Education chapter]. If transport to an education facility can be provided under the Education Act 1996 then this would normally take precedence over the CSDPA transport duty as such provision would not be 'necessary' for the purposes of the 1970 Act.

146 *R (M) v Birmingham CC* [2009] EWHC 688 (Admin).

147 Social Security Contributions and Benefits Act 1992 s73(14) and see also the local government ombudsman report Case no B2004/0180 against Newport City Council, 31 August 2006.

148 Department of Health, *Charging for Residential Accommodation and Non-Residential Care Services,* 2012, LAC(DH)(2012)03 (policy guidance) paras 9–11.

duty to decide, having regard to the results of the assessment, what, if any, services they should provide to meet the individual's needs. This duty does not change because a particular individual is receiving the mobility component of Disability Living Allowance.

Home adaptations, fixtures and fittings

3.77 This provision covers situations where an authority assesses a disabled child as needing adaptations to the home in which they live, or the provision of additional fixtures and fittings. These can include such things as ramps, grab handles, wheelchair accessible showers and can extend to major works such as through floor lifts and ground-floor extensions. The duty imposed by the CSDPA is to provide 'assistance' in 'arranging for' the carrying out of any adaptations or the provision of any additional facilities. Frequently, the authority may ask the family to apply for a disabled facilities grant to meet some or all of the cost of this work – and these grants are considered further below (see chapter 6 at paras 6.41–6.72). It is, however, important to note that the fact that a grant may be available does not detract from the core duty under the CSDPA 1970 – so (for example) if the cost of the works that are required exceeds the current maximum mandatory grant, or the work is required to a second home (eg because the parents have separated), then the council will have to consider making the additional sums available to comply with its duty under section 2 of the 1970 Act.[149]

Holidays, meals and telephones

3.78 Once satisfied that the child meets the authority's eligibility criteria for support, the authority must consider if this need for support can and should be met by the provision of (or assistance in obtaining) a holiday, meals and/or a telephone (including any special equipment necessary to enable it to be used including such things as minicoms and other electronic items). While it might be seen as anomalous to include such items, it is arguable that holidays – in particular – are of great importance to a child's development and a family's sense of well-being.[150] It is important for local authorities to keep in mind that

149 See, for example, local government ombudsman reports on Complaints 02/C/8679, 02/C/8681 and 02/C/10389 against Bolsover DC, 30 September 2003 and Complaint no 05/B/00246 against Croydon LBC, 24 July 2006, para 37.

150 One week's holiday a year away from the home is a core criterion within the Townsend Deprivation Index – see P Townsend, P Phillimore and A Beattie, *Health and deprivation: inequality and the North*, Croom Helm, 1988.

families with disabled children will have a right to support with the cost of holidays where this is accepted to be necessary to meet the child's needs – and that this can include the basic cost, not merely disability-related extra costs.[151]

Services under CA 1989 Part III

3.79   Although the range of services which can be provided under the 1970 Act is wide, there are some services that disabled children and their families need, that do not fall within the terms of that Act. One such service is the provision of accommodation for children and families together – for which a power is expressly provided in CA 1989 s17(6).[152] However, a more commonly encountered support service which cannot be provided through the 1970 Act is residential short breaks (still frequently referred to as 'respite').

3.80   Where a local authority considers that another authority (for example a local housing authority or a clinical commissioning group) could help it meet the needs of a child 'in need', then it may make a formal request for such assistance.[153] The partner authority must comply with the request unless it is incompatible with its legal duties or would 'unduly prejudice the discharge of any of [its] functions' to do so.[154]

Respite care/short breaks away from the home

3.81   As noted above, while much short break/respite care is provided under the 1970 Act in the home or community (or via Direct Payment (see paras 3.98–3.99 below), it may also be provided in residential units, in hospices or by foster carers. In *R (JL) v Islington LBC*,[155] the court confirmed that residential and other overnight short break care could not be provided under the 1970 Act and that, as a general rule, such support is provided by councils under CA 1989 s17(6) or

---

151 *R v North Yorkshire CC ex p Hargreaves (No 2)* (1997–98) 1 CCLR 331.

152 As inserted by Adoption and Children Act 2002 s116. Guidance on the operation of this power is given in England through LAC (2003)13. See chapter 6 for further information on housing and disabled children.

153 CA 1989 s27.

154 CA 1989 s27(2).

155 [2009] EWHC 458 (Admin); (2009) 12 CCLR 322.

s20(4).[156] It is also, however, possible that residential short breaks would need to be provided under the specific duty created by CA 1989 s20(1) to meet 'actual crises',[157] see paras 3.136–3.143 below.

3.82 This is of importance, since the duty under section 20(1) is not a 'target duty' but one that is specifically enforceable (see para 2.47). In the judge's opinion in the *Islington* case, however, the section 20(1) duty would only arise when a parent was 'immediately' prevented from providing a disabled child with suitable care and accommodation.[158]

3.83 Statutory guidance[159] has been published to assist with the decision as to the relevant statutory provision when residential short breaks are being provided. Chapter 2 of the guidance deals with short breaks involving the provision of accommodation. The guidance does not mention the CA 1989 s20(1) duty, considering instead whether a residential short break should be provided under CA 1989 s17(6) or s20(4). The importance of this distinction is that it is only where a residential short break is provided under CA 1989 s20 that the child may acquire 'looked after' status.

3.84 In simple terms, a child is 'looked after' if she or he is in the care of a local authority or if it is providing the child with accommodation (unless that accommodation is provided under s17 – for example as short break care).[160] See further, paras 3.144–3.147 below.

3.85 The guidance states that the decision as to which statutory provision applies to a residential short break:

> ... should be informed by their assessment of the child's needs and should take account of parenting capacity and wider family and environmental factors, the wishes and feelings of the child and his/ her parents and the nature of the service to be provided.[161]

---

156 Section 20(4) reads: 'A local authority may provide accommodation for any child within their area (even though a person who has parental responsibility for him is able to provide him with accommodation) if they consider that to do so would safeguard or promote the child's welfare.'

157 *R (JL) v Islington LBC* at [96].

158 *R (JL) v Islington LBC* at [95]–[96].

159 Department for Children, Schools and Families, *Short Breaks: Statutory guidance on how to safeguard and promote the welfare of disabled children using short breaks*, April 2010 ('Short Breaks Statutory Guidance'). This guidance was issued alongside the Care Planning, Placement and Case Review (England) Regulations 2010 (the 2010 Regulations) SI No 959, see para 1.6. See also chapter 6 of HM Government, *The Children Act 1989 Guidance and Regulations Volume 2: Care Planning, Placement and Case Review*, June 2015.

160 The formal definition of 'looked-after' status is found in CA 1989 s22(1).

161 Short Breaks Statutory Guidance, para 2.5.

The 'key question' is said to be 'how to promote and safeguard the welfare of the child most effectively'.[162] Depending on the circumstances of the child and family:

> ... the assessment, planning and review processes for children in need may be appropriate or the additional requirements for looked after children may be more appropriate.

3.86   The guidance provides a lengthy list of factors which local authorities should take into account in determining whether short breaks are to be provided under CA 1989 s17(6) or s20(4).[163] These include:

- any particular vulnerabilities of the child;
- the length of time away from home and the frequency of such stays;[164]
- whether short breaks are to be provided in more than one place;[165]
- the views of the child and views of parents;[166]
- the extent of contact between short break carers and the child's family and between the child and the family during the placement;[167]
- distance from home; and
- the need for an independent reviewing officer (IRO)[168] to monitor the child's case and to chair reviews.

3.87   Taking matters in the round, the guidance suggests at para 2.12 that children whose welfare will be best safeguarded by becoming 'looked after' during residential short breaks include:

---

162 Short Breaks Statutory Guidance, para 2.7.

163 Short Breaks Statutory Guidance, para 2.8.

164 The guidance states that 'the less time the child spends away from home the more likely it is to be appropriate to provide accommodation under section 17(6)'.

165 The guidance states that 'where the child spends short breaks in different settings, including residential schools, hospices and social care placements, it is more likely to be appropriate to provide accommodation under section 20(4)'.

166 The guidance states that 'some children and parents may be reassured by, and in favour of, the status of a looked-after child, while others may resent the implications and associations of looked-after status'. It is essential, however, that any such views must be properly informed, including as to the benefits which accrue from 'looked-after' status.

167 There is no further guidance on this point, although it can be assumed that where there is significant ongoing contact with family during short breaks then this points towards the service being provided under CA 1989 s17(6).

168 An IRO will not be appointed where accommodation is provided pursuant to CA 1989 s17(6) as appointment of an IRO is one of the requirements of 'looked-after' status.

- children who have substantial packages of short breaks sometimes in more than one setting; and
- children whose families have limited resources and may have difficulties supporting the child or monitoring the quality of care while they are away from home.

3.88 The guidance further highlights[169] that the relevant regulations for looked-after children[170] (see para 3.146 below) are modified in their application to some residential short breaks. The modified scheme applies where no single placement is intended to last for more than 17 days and the total of short breaks in one year does not exceed 75 days. However, this only applies where children receive short breaks in a single setting; where a child goes to multiple settings the full looked-after scheme applies.

3.89 There is a helpful table in the guidance[171] which summarises the different effect of residential short breaks being provided where regulation 48 does and does not apply:

- Where regulation 48 applies, the local authority must put in place a short break care plan 'addressing issues key to the safe care of the child' and must appoint an IRO. The visiting and review requirements are less onerous than when the child has full 'looked-after' status.
- Where regulation 48 does not apply, then the full requirements of the 2010 regulations take effect. The local authority must put in place a care plan, an IRO must be appointed and the child's case must be reviewed regularly.

3.90 Guidance is given on the requirements of a short break care plan in cases where regulation 48 applies. The plan should 'focus on setting out those matters which will ensure that the child's needs can be fully met while the child is away from his/her parents'. It should be linked to the child in need plan (see paras 3.108–3.135 above); the guidance makes clear that '[t]here should not be separate plans which duplicate information'. The guidance notes that '[p]arents must be fully involved in all aspects of agreeing the short break plan. As far as is practicable, children should also be involved in agreeing the plan'.[172]

---

169 Short Breaks Statutory Guidance, paras 2.16–2.23.
170 Care Planning, Placement and Case Review (England) Regulations 2010 SI No 959 reg 48.
171 Short Breaks Statutory Guidance, p16.
172 Short Breaks Statutory Guidance, paras 2.19–2.24.

3.91   Chapter 3 of the guidance deals with assessment, planning and review in the context of short break provision. While this chapter may still contain some valuable guidance, it is likely that much of it has been superseded by the *Working Together* statutory guidance discussed extensively in this chapter. There is guidance on the technical requirements relating to the provision of short breaks in different settings in chapter 4, although again this may now be somewhat out of date. Chapter 5 of the guidance highlights the right for families to obtain direct payments to meet a child's needs for short breaks instead of receiving a service direct from the local authority; see paras 3.98–3.99 below.

Short breaks generally

3.92   Children Act 1989 Schedule 2 para 6(1)(c) requires local authorities to provide services designed to assist family carers of disabled children 'to continue to [provide care], or to do so more effectively, by giving them breaks from caring'. Regulations[173] made under the Act in 2011 require that local authorities, when discharging this duty, have regard to the needs of family carers:

> ... who would be able to provide care for their disabled child more effectively if breaks from caring were given to them to allow them to:
> (i) undertake education, training or any regular leisure activity,
> (ii) meet the needs of other children in the family more effectively, or
> (iii) carry out day to day tasks which they must perform in order to run their household' (reg 3(b)).

These are, therefore, the statutory goals to which local authorities should be directing their provision of short breaks, both in terms of planning and commissioning services and in making decisions on individual cases. Despite this, evidence from the Every Disabled Child Matters campaign suggests that more than half of local authorities have cut spending on short breaks (respite services) for families with disabled children since 2011/12.[174]

3.93   Regulation 4 states that 'a local authority must provide, so far as is reasonably practicable, a range of services which is sufficient to assist carers to continue to provide care or to do so more effectively'. These services must include a range of daytime care, overnight care and leisure activities (regulation 4(2)). This range of services must be

---

173 Breaks for Carers of Disabled Children Regulations 2011 SI No 707.
174 Every Disabled Child Matters, *Short breaks in 2015: An uncertain future*, 2015.

set out in a 'short breaks services statement' (regulation 5).[175] This statement must include the range of services provided in accordance with regulation 4, any criteria by which eligibility for those services will be assessed, and how the range of services is designed to meet the needs of carers in the area.

3.94 Read as a whole, therefore, the 2011 regulations impose a duty on local authorities to secure a sufficient supply of a wide range of short break services and to publish clear and transparent information about these services and how they can be accessed.

3.95 Advice published by the Department of Education in 2011[176] provides a helpful summary for local authorities of the requirements imposed by the 2011 regulations – including a requirement that local authorities must consider 'the legal implications of the eligibility criteria they apply to short breaks services'. The advice suggests they should 'not apply any eligibility criteria mechanistically without consideration of a particular family's needs'.[177]

3.96 The advice also provides a helpful summary of the benefits of short breaks both for disabled children and parents: 'Children benefit from new interests, relationships and activities, while parents can catch up with "everyday activities" (sleep, cleaning, shopping), attend to their physical and psychological wellbeing, and maintain and develop social networks'. The advice reiterates a central theme of the 2011 regulations, being that 'short breaks should not just be there for those at crisis point'. The advice correctly notes that 'local authorities must give families the choice to access short breaks services using a direct payment'.

3.97 The advice describes the benefit of a 'local offer' of non-assessed short breaks to which families with disabled children can refer themselves. It notes the importance of having fair eligibility criteria for this kind of service but states that '[l]ocal authorities can provide families with access to short breaks services without any assessment'. However, it appears, from the authors' personal experience, that these low-level support services are being rolled back or cut completely at present as a result of reductions in central government funding for local authorities. This is supported by research carried out by the Every Disabled Child Matters campaign, see para 3.92 above.

175 The SEND Code requires at para 4.44 that the short breaks services statement should be published with the 'local offer' for each local authority.
176 DfE, *Short Breaks for Carers of Disabled Children: Departmental advice for local authorities*, March 2011.
177 DfE, *Short Breaks for Carers of Disabled Children: Departmental advice for local authorities*, March 2011, p4. See further chapter 4 of the advice.

Direct payments

3.98   Instead of the authority arranging for services to be provided to a disabled child and other family members, the parents (or the child if aged 16 or 17) can generally insist on having the support by way of a 'direct payment' and can then use that payment to buy the necessary services (including periods of residential short breaks/respite care away from the child's own home).[178] The right to insist on a direct payment applies regardless of whether the support is provided under the CSDPA 1970 or the CA 1989.[179] The statutory scheme governing direct payments derives from CA 1989 s17A and has been fleshed out by regulations[180] and detailed guidance.[181] Local authorities are under a duty to make a direct payment where:[182]

- the person appears to the responsible authority to be capable of managing a direct payment by themselves or with such assistance as may be available to them;
- the person consents to the making of a direct payment (local authorities cannot insist that a person has a direct payment);
- the responsible authority is satisfied that the person's need for the relevant service can be met by securing the provision of it by means of a direct payment; and
- the responsible authority is satisfied that the welfare of the child in respect of whom the service is needed will be safeguarded and promoted by securing the provision of it by means of a direct payment.

3.99   The regulations[183] place restrictions on the use of direct payments to pay a relative who lives in the same household as the disabled child (but no restriction if the relative lives elsewhere). Accordingly, paying such a relative, who may well know and have a good relationship with

---

178 Direct payments for those aged 18 or over are governed by Care Act 2014 ss31–33 and Care and Support (Direct Payments) Regulations 2014 SI No 2871.

179 This derives from the fact that services provided under section 2 of the 1970 Act are technically provided in discharge of a local authority's functions under CA 1989 Part III – see para 3.65 above.

180 Community Care, Services for Carers and Children's Services (Direct Payments) (England) Regulations 2009 SI No 1887.

181 Department of Health, *Guidance on direct payments for community care, services for carers and children's services England*, 2009 (amended 29 October 2010). In relation to adults, the guidance has been replaced by the Statutory Guidance to the Care Act 2014 (Department of Health), chapter 12 – but at the time of publication the 2009 guidance remains relevant to disabled children.

182 Regulation 7(1)(c).

183 Regulation 11.

the child, to provide care may be a very attractive option for families. If the relative lives in the same household, the presumption is that he or she may not be paid with the direct payment – unless the authority 'is satisfied that securing the service from a family member is necessary for promoting the welfare of the child'. In simple English, this means that the council can agree to such a payment, if it is satisfied that it is necessary – ie the threshold for reversing the presumption against such an arrangement is a relatively low one.

Direct payments and respite care/short breaks

3.100   Where a disabled person has been assessed as needing a service, then in general there is a duty to make the provision by way of a direct payment if so requested. In this context, the ombudsman has held it to be maladministration for a local authority:

- to require a parent carer to give reasons why he wanted a direct payment in lieu of a service, and for the authority to state 'that direct payments would not be paid for childcare and that childcare was the responsibility of the parents, whether or not children have a disability';[184] and
- to have a policy of refusing direct payments for certain services – such as short (overnight) breaks.[185]

3.101   Although direct payments cannot be used to purchase prolonged periods of residential respite care (being capped at a maximum of four consecutive weeks in any period of 12 months),[186] in practice as long as the residential care periods are less than four weeks long and are separated by at least four weeks of non-residential care, then successive such periods are permitted.[187]

---

184 Public Service Ombudsman (Wales), Complaint no B2004/0707/S/370 against Swansea City Council, 22 February 2007 – see in particular paras 78, 133 and 137.

185 Complaint no 08 005 202 against Kent CC, 18 May 2009 para 39 – in this case the council had refused on the grounds that it was able to provide these 'in house'.

186 Community Care, Services for Carers and Children's Services (Direct Payments) (England) Regulations 2009 SI No 1887 reg 13.

187 Department of Health, *Guidance on direct payments for community care, services for carers and children's services England 2009*, 2009, paras 101–103.

Independent user trusts

3.102   Although the Direct Payment Regulations[188] permit payments to be made to persons with parental responsibility for a disabled child, such arrangements must come to an end when the child becomes 18. At this stage, the payment must either be paid to the disabled person (if he or she wishes to continue with a direct payment) or if he or she lacks sufficient mental capacity to consent to the payment, then it can be paid to someone on his or her behalf – if (among other things) that third party agrees.[189] It follows that on a child becoming an adult, a change in the payment arrangements has to take place – although this need not be problematic. One way of seeking to avoid such disruption is for the carers of the disabled child to create a trust (or a company limited by guarantee) – variously called an 'independent user trust', 'user independent trust' and a 'third party scheme'. The trust then assumes responsibility for ensuring that services are provided to meet the assessed needs of the disabled person – for example, by employing care assistants and/or paying an independent agency etc. Not infrequently, the parents of a disabled child will be the initial trustees of such a trust. Such arrangements, which the courts have held to be lawful,[190] have some practical benefits over and above securing continuity of care arrangements during the transition into adulthood (see paras 10.49–10.60 below) – and these include the fact that the NHS is also permitted to make payments to such a trust.[191]

---

188 Community Care, Services for Carers and Children's Services (Direct Payments) (England) Regulations 2009 SI No 1887.

189 Direct payments to disabled adults and their carers are now governed by Care Act 2014 s31 (adults with capacity) and s32 (adults without capacity) and the Care and Support (Direct Payments) Regulations 2014 SI No 2871.

190 *R (A and B) v East Sussex CC (No 1)* [2002] EWHC 2771 (Admin); (2003) 6 CCLR 177.

191 For further consideration of such trusts, see L Clements and P Thompson, *Community care and the law*, 4th edn, LAG, 2007, paras 12.64–12.70.

Personal budgets and personalisation

3.103   Many children and families are advised that their entitlement to services takes the form of a 'personal budget'. The idea behind such an arrangement is that a personal budget can provide some of the benefits of a direct payment without the disabled person or the parent having to take on the full responsibilities of managing a direct payment. In theory, the individual is encouraged to decide in what other ways the money could be spent to maximise their child's sense of independence and well being. In this intermediate phase, instead of a direct payment being made, the monies are retained by the local authority and referred to as a 'personal budget': with the disabled person or their parents (if a child) encouraged to exercise as much control as they wish over directing how the budget is used.

3.104   All adults who are eligible for care services in England must be told the cost of their care arrangements (ie their 'personal budget') even if the services are arranged by or provided directly by the local authority.[192]

3.105   These principles are now embedded in statute in relation to disabled children who have an EHC plan[193] and this entitlement is considered at paras 4.184–4.195 below.

3.106   While many of the principles underpinning the personalisation agenda are admirable, it has had its critics[194] and the implementation has caused not insignificant difficulties – particularly in relation to what are termed 'resource allocation systems/schemes' (RAS). RAS (which it appears are being discarded by many local authorities[195]) endeavour to give the disabled person an indication of the resources that the council would be prepared to expend on his or her care – before the care planning process has been completed. They are sometimes referred to as 'upfront allocations' or 'indicative amounts'. The calculation is generally based on a questionnaire that the disabled

---

192 Care Act 2014 s25(1)(e).

193 CFA 2014 s49 – the SEND Code stating that (para 3.38): 'Young people and parents of children who have EHC plans have the right to request a Personal Budget, which may contain elements of education, social care and health funding.'

194 See, for example, I Ferguson, 'Increasing user choice or privatizing risk? The antinomies of personalization', (2007) 37 *British Journal of Social Work*, pp387–403, 2007, and L Clements, 'Individual budgets and irrational exuberance', (2008) 11 CCLR 413–430.

195 See L Series and L Clements, 'Putting the Cart before the Horse: Resource Allocation Systems and Community Care', (2013) 2 *Journal of Social Welfare Law*, pp207–226.

person has completed. This awards 'points' which are then converted into an indicative financial amount. The idea is that disabled people may opt for this sum – and then make their own arrangements – without having to go through the whole care planning process, which would involve the detailed assessment of the actual cost of a real care package.

3.107   Admirable as this may sound, in practice the process is often disempowering – so that families with disabled children do not appreciate that they do not have to accept the 'indicative amount' (which may be less than they are presently receiving or insufficient to enable them to have their care needs addressed satisfactorily).[196] In law, individuals are entitled to decline having a personal budget and to insist that their care package be provided by the local authority or that any sum they have (eg as a direct payment) be sufficient to purchase a satisfactory package of care to meet their needs. The fact that the local authority advises them that their care costs are above the 'indicative amount' generated by a RAS is simply irrelevant: the legal duty remains (as indicated at paras 3.62–3.65) to meet eligible assessed needs.[197]

Care plans: the 'how, who, what and when'

3.108   The assessment and care planning process requires that the local authority construct a care plan that (amongst other things) describes the services that will be provided in order to meet the disabled child's identified 'needs'. For example, an assessment may identify that the child needs adaptations to the house in order that they can access the bathroom, that they need regular home help support at meal times and that their parents need to have regular short breaks – in order to be able to sustain their caring roles. The care plan should specify

196 This was found by Black J to be the case in *R (JL) v Islington LBC* [2009] EWHC 458 (Admin), where (at [39]) she observed that she found it 'hard to see how a system such as this one, where points are attributed to a standard list of factors, leading to banded relief with a fixed upper limit, can be sufficiently sophisticated to amount to a genuine assessment of an individual child's needs'.

197 *R (KM) v Cambridgeshire CC* [2012] UKSC 23; (2012) 15 CCLR 374 – see for example the judgment of Lord Wilson at [28]: 'What is crucial is that, once the starting point (or indicative sum) has finally been identified, the requisite services in the particular case should be costed in a reasonable degree of detail so that a judgment can be made whether the indicative sum is too high, too low or about right.'

how these identified needs are going to be met. In relation to some needs, it may not be possible to state immediately how they will be met (for instance the adaptations) – and in this case the care plan should specify the steps that the local authority will take to ensure that the needs are met within a reasonable time.

3.109　　Although there is no general requirement in the Children Act 1989 to prepare a 'care plan' for a disabled child, the courts have held that such a document is required to be prepared since it is a 'the means by which the local authority assembles the relevant information and applies it to the statutory ends, and hence affords good evidence to any inquirer of the due discharge of its statutory duties'.[198] A 'plan of action' is also required by the *Working Together* statutory guidance, see para 3.111 below.

3.110　　An example of what a care plan should contain is given in the 2010 short breaks statutory guidance,[199] namely:

- have clear and realistic objectives;
- include ascertainable wishes and feelings of the child and views of the family;
- follow consideration of options, including but not limited to direct payments;
- state the nature and frequency of services, as far as is practicable, including health and social care in the same plan, especially if short breaks are provided from different agencies;
- state the child's health, emotional and behavioural development including full details about any disabilities and clinical needs the child may have and medications they may require;
- state the child's specific communication needs, especially for children who communicate non-verbally, and include the child's likes and dislikes with particular regard to leisure activities;
- include the results of all necessary risk assessments which could include, depending on the child's impairment, moving and handling, invasive procedures, and behaviour;
- state contact arrangements for emergencies;
- state commitments of professionals involved;
- refer to or summarise any other important documents about the child's development;
- confirm those caring for the child have been selected following the advice set out in government guidance on direct payments;
- outline arrangements to review the plan.

198　*R v Islington LBC ex p Rixon* (1997–98) 1 CCLR 119, 128D.

199　DCSF, *Short Breaks: Statutory guidance on how to safeguard and promote the welfare of disabled children using short breaks*, March 2010, para 3.16.

3.111   *Working Together* states that:

> ... [w]here the outcome of the assessment is continued local author-ity children's social care involvement, the social worker and their manager should agree a plan of action with other professionals and discuss this with the child and their family. The plan should set out what services are to be delivered, and what actions are to be under-taken, by whom and for what purpose.[200]

A care plan produced following an assessment under *Working Together* is frequently referred to as a 'child in need plan'. Previous (2000) policy guidance, the *Framework for the Assessment of Children in Need and their Families*[201] made the following comment concerning care plans:

> It is essential that the plan is constructed on the basis of the find-ings from the assessment and that this plan is reviewed and refined over time to ensure the agreed case objectives are achieved. Specific outcomes for the child, expressed in terms of their health and devel-opment can be measured. These provide objective evidence against which to evaluate whether the child and family have been provided with appropriate services and ultimately whether the child's wellbe-ing is optimal.

3.112   In *R (J) v Caerphilly CBC*,[202] it was held that care plans must 'set out the operational objectives with sufficient detail – including detail of the "how, who, what and when" – to enable the care plan itself to be used as a means of checking whether or not those objectives are being met'. In *R (AB and SB) v Nottingham CC*,[203] the council's care plan was struck down by the court because 'there was no clear iden-tification of needs, or what was to be done about them, by whom and when.'[204] The same approach was followed in *R (S) v Plymouth CC*,[205] where the assessments were quashed because they failed to result in a 'realistic plan of action' to meet the child's needs in relation to housing and respite care.

3.113   A 2014 ombudsman's report held (in similar terms) that an assessment of a disabled child must be more than merely a descrip-tive document: it must spell out with precision what the child's needs

200 *Working Together*, para 53.
201 Department of Health, *Framework for the Assessment of Children in Need and their Families*, 2000, para 4.37.
202 [2005] EWHC 586 (Admin); (2005) 8 CCLR 255. This case is discussed in detail at paras 10.58–10.59.
203 [2001] EWHC 235 (Admin); (2001) 4 CCLR 294.
204 [2001] EWHC 235 (Admin); (2001) 4 CCLR 294 at [43].
205 [2009] EWHC 1499 (Admin).

are, what the impact of the disability is on the child's carer(s) and whether the child and the carers needs can be met and can continue to be met into the future. The assessment must result in a care plan that identifies the child's needs, what is to be done about these needs, by whom and when. If a direct payment is made, it must specify precisely what need these payments are intended to meet, why this level of payment is considered appropriate, or what outcome this will result in.[206]

3.114   The fact that a care need requires non-routine arrangements, does not obviate the need for a local authority to provide services to meet it. This elementary point is illustrated by a 2011 ombudsman's complaint.[207] A disabled deaf child was found on assessment to have complex needs – including a need for respite care. This was a problem, since the council was unable to locate a carer who was able to provide support and who also had the necessary British Sign Language (BSL) skills. To this, the ombudsman commented, 'There is no evidence that it considered the obvious and sensible expedient of paying two people to work together, one to communicate with H and the other to provide for her care. Nor did it explore whether it could fund a carer to be trained in BSL'.

3.115   The importance of lawful assessments and care planning was highlighted in a 2013 local government ombudsman report[208] which concerned a profoundly disabled 14-year-old girl (her condition was degenerative; she was blind, profoundly deaf with severe physical and learning disabilities: she required constant supervision and was dependent on her parents to meet all her needs). Direct payments were being paid, and due to the need to keep the number of people involved in the daughter's care to a minimum – to reduce her stress – the direct payments were being used to pay her father to provide the care.

3.116   As a result of the daughter's needs increasing, the family requested a reassessment to increase the direct payments. The local authority began a core assessment, rejected the request for increased support (stating that the current funding was adequate) and stated that it would no longer be prepared to allow the father to be paid with the direct payments.

---

206 Local government ombudsman complaint number 13 002 982 against Birmingham City Council, 12 March 2014.
207 Complaint no 09 004 278 against Leeds City Council, 1 July 2011, paras 153–154.
208 Complaint no 12 015 328 against Calderdale Council, 20 November 2013.

3.117   In finding maladministration, the ombudsman noted that although the assessment described the daughter's complex 'exceptional' needs and that these were increasing – it said nothing about how these needs were to be met (other than by her parents). It described the impact on her parents but said nothing about their needs as carers. It acknowledged that her parents were best placed to provide the care (particularly given her communication difficulties) but gave no rational reason for requiring the direct payments to be used for an alternative carer. The ombudsman further noted that the council was unable to explain how it decided that the current package of care would meet the daughter's needs – and that the assessment contained no precise identification of her needs, nor what needed 'to be done about them, by whom and when'. The ombudsman considered that there had not been an 'adequate assessment' of the daughter's needs, nor her parents needs (as 'carers') at anytime in the previous ten years.

Reassessments and reviews

3.118   Local authorities must keep under review the care needs of disabled children and their families. A care plan should normally specify a 'review date' which will ordinarily be within 12 months – although where there is a material change in a disabled child's needs, a reassessment should be undertaken without delay. The local government ombudsman has held that once support needs have been put in place the level of service should continue until there has been a reassessment.[209] A reassessment/review should be undertaken to ascertain if the person's care needs have changed and if so – if there is a need to make changes to their care plan: a 'review must not be used as a mechanism to arbitrarily reduce' the level of a person's' care support.[210]

3.119   Despite the detailed requirements of the statutory scheme and the established principles of public law, reports by the local government ombudsman continue to demonstrate local authorities making serial errors constituting maladministration. A 2014 report concerning Birmingham City Council[211] is illustrative for this purpose:

---

209 Complaint no 11/010/725 against London Borough of Lambeth, 16 August 2012.

210 Department of Health, *Care and Support Statutory Guidance*, 2014, para 13.4.

211 Complaint no 13 002 982, 12 March 2014.

- A direct payment to provide 10 hours per month support was being made to the parent of a disabled child.
- Despite the mother's request that this be increased, the local authority did not reassess and indeed 'lost sight of this child' for almost five years, simply continuing to pay direct payments for the 10 hours per month.
- When finally a reassessment was completed – although it was flawed and not shown to the parent – it was used by the authority's 'panel' (see paras 10.18–10.19) to determine that the 10 hours of support per month remained adequate.

3.120 A complaint eventually resulted in a new assessment – but sadly this still contained errors and did not fully consider the child's needs and his mother's needs as a carer and (again) had not been discussed with her. There was no care plan to explain what need the 10 hours of direct payments is to address, and what outcome was expected from providing the support.'[212] In addition to recommending substantial financial compensation, the ombudsman advised that an independent social worker undertake (within a fixed timescale) an assessment of the child's needs and her mother's needs (as a carer).

Social care needs and EHC plans

3.121 Where a child has an EHC plan (see paras 4.134–4.163), the SEND Code provides specific detail as to the way the provision must be set out in the plan (sections H1 and/or H2). Section H1 must contain the provision which must be made under CSDPA 1970 s2 (see above paras 3.66–3.78). The SEND Code requires that provision in Section H1:

> ... should be detailed and specific and should normally be quantified, for example, in terms of the type of support and who will provide it (including where this is to be secured through a social care direct payment).[213]

It also reiterates that provision should be clearly linked to the achievement of the outcomes specified in the plan.

3.122 Section H2 of the EHC plan is reserved (in the case of children) for other provision not required by the CSDPA 1970 but which is

---

212 In the main report at para 63, the ombudsman noted that 'The assessments do not consider X's needs in accordance with Birmingham City Council's eligibility criteria for services provided under its Short Breaks Services Statement.'

213 SEND Code, p167.

'reasonably required by the learning difficulties or disabilities which result in the child or young person having SEN'.[214] The code suggests (p168) that this 'may include provision identified through early help and children in need assessments and safeguarding assessments for children'. Having reiterated that provision required under the CSDPA 1970 must be set out in Section H1, the code suggests two categories of social services which may need to be included in Section H2:

- Residential short breaks. This is plainly correct as this is not a service which can be provided under the CSDPA 1970; see para 3.81 above.
- 'Services provided to children arising from their SEN but unrelated to a disability'. It is far from clear what if any services would fall within this category in practice. Given the breadth of the CSDPA duty, it may well be that the only category of service which should routinely be included in Section H2 of EHC plans for children is residential short breaks.

3.123   The CFA 2014 imposes no new duty to make provision in relation to the social care element of an EHC plan. As the SEND Code notes:

> For social care provision specified in the plan, existing duties on social care services to assess and provide for the needs of disabled children and young people under the Children Act 1989 continue to apply.[215]

3.124   EHC plans must be reviewed at least every 12 months.[216] Each review should consider the social care provision made and 'its effectiveness in ensuring good progress towards outcomes'.[217] Although a representative of social care must be invited to the review and given two weeks' notice of the meeting, there is no absolute requirement in the SEND Code that they should attend. However, it is difficult to see how the requirements of the review can be achieved without direct input from children's social care in cases where there is any social care provision being made under the plan. The SEND Code states that 'EHC plan reviews should be synchronised with social care plan reviews, and must always meet the needs of the individual child'.[218]

---

214 The local authority may also choose to specify in section H2 other social care provision reasonably required by the child or young person, which is not linked to their learning difficulties or disabilities; SEND Code, p169. All social care provision for adults with EHC plans must be in section H2.

215 SEND Code, para 9.137.

216 CFA 2014 s44.

217 SEND Code, para 9.167.

218 SEND Code, para 10.20.

In relation to social services involvement in transitional plans see also paras 10.15–10.60 below).

3.125   The provisions of the CFA 2014 Part 3 have been extended in modified form to young people in youth custody (see paras 4.119–4.201 below). The SEND Code states that:

> Local authorities should also consider whether any social care needs identified in the EHC plan will remain while the detained person is in custody and provide appropriate provision if necessary. For example, if a detained child is looked after, the existing relationship with their social worker should continue and the detained child should continue to access specific services and support where needed.[219]

3.126   Local authorities may also need to carry out an assessment of detained children and young people to consider their post-detention education, health and care needs and whether an EHC plan will be required.

3.127   As noted at paras 11.60–11.61, CFA 2014 s51 provides no right of appeal to a tribunal in relation to the social care (or health) elements of the EHC plan. At the time of writing (November 2015), a pilot scheme had been established[220] to allow the tribunal to make non-binding recommendations in relation to social care (and health) provision. Disagreement resolution and mediation services should, however, cover social care disputes in relation to EHC plans in every local authority.[221] Complaints can also be made under the Children Act complaints procedure.[222]

Timescales for assessments and providing services

3.128   As noted above (para 3.34), *Working Together* requires social care assessments to be completed in a timely manner with an outside timeframe of 45 working days. Where delay occurs either in the assessment or the provision of services then the complaints process may be invoked (see paras 11.8–11.16) since this will at least put the process on a fixed timescale (ie that for investigating the complaint).

3.129   In relation to the provision of services, the common law requires that these be provided within a 'reasonable time'. What is a 'reasonable

---

219   SEND Code, para 10.67.
220   Under the Special Educational Needs and Disability (First-tier Tribunal Recommendation Power) (Pilot) Regulations 2015 SI No 358. The 13 pilot authorities are listed in the schedule to these regulations. See further, paras 11.75–11.80.
221   SEND Code, para 11.5.
222   SEND Code, paras 11.105–11.111.

time' is a question of fact, depending on the nature of the obligation and the purpose for which the decision is to be made.[223] Generally, the disabled child and/or the family will have a good idea of what is reasonable and what is not unreasonable (for example, how urgent the need is and what steps the council has actually taken to meet its obligations). Where the period seems excessive then the reasons why this is thought to be the case should be explained, in ordinary language, in any complaint. As *Working Together* notes, '[f]or children who need additional help, every day matters'.[224]

3.130   The local government ombudsman has investigated a considerable number of complaints concerning delayed assessments relating to home adaptations (see chapter 6). In a 1996 report,[225] for example, a delay of six months in assessing a disabled person's needs was held to be maladministration, and another 1996 report found seven months for an assessment and a further four months' delay by the authority in processing the disabled facilities grant approval to be maladministration.[226] In this complaint, the local ombudsman reiterated her view that if the authority has a shortage of occupational therapists, it should not use them for assessment purposes if this will result in unreasonable delay, stating, '[i]f such expertise is not available, councils need to find an alternative way of meeting their statutory responsibilities'. Where a delay arises because there is a physical shortage of services (for example, no place available at a day centre), the court will require that short-term alternative arrangements be made to meet the identified need as well as steps taken by the council to address the structural 'supply side' problem, if there is one (eg the shortage is not a 'one-off' but a chronic problem).[227]

3.131   In general, if the shortage is due to a budgetary problem, it will not be an acceptable excuse – as the court has noted:[228]

> Once a local authority has decided that it is necessary to make the arrangements, they are under an absolute duty to make them. It is a duty owed to a specific individual and not a target duty. No term is to

---

223 See, for example, *Re North ex p Hasluck* [1895] 2 QB 264; *Charnock v Liverpool Corporation* [1968] 3 All ER 473.
224 *Working Together*, p7, para 10.
225 Complaints nos 93/B/3111 and 94/B/3146 against South Bedfordshire DC and Bedfordshire CC.
226 Complaints nos 94/C/0964 and 94/C/0965 against Middlesbrough DC and Cleveland CC.
227 *R v Islington LBC ex p Rixon* (1997–98) 1 CCLR 119 at 128.
228 *R v Gloucestershire CC ex p Mahfood* (1997–98) 1 CCLR 7, DC, per McCowan LJ; and see also *R v Kirklees MBC ex p Daykin* (1997–98) 1 CCLR 512 at 525D.

be implied that the local authority are obliged to comply with the duty only if they have the revenue to do so. In fact, once under that duty resources do not come into it.

Delay and interim provision

3.132 The duty on local authorities is to meet the eligible needs of disabled children and their families – and this will frequently necessitate the support being provided prior to the completion of an assessment. A 2000 guidance document[229] made this point forcefully by criticising those councils that regarded assessments as an 'event rather than as a process and services were withheld awaiting the completion of an assessment'. The same guidance highlighted the need for 'action' in such cases – that 'services should be provided according to the needs of the child and family, in parallel with assessment where necessary, and not await completion of the assessment'.[230] This requirement is re-emphasised in the 2015 *Working Together* guidance. Having referred to the maximum timeframe of 45 working days, it states that:

> Whatever the timescale for assessment, where particular needs are identified at any stage of the assessment, social workers should not wait until the assessment reaches a conclusion before commissioning services to support the child and their family. In some cases the needs of the child will mean that a quick assessment will be required.[231]

3.133 The need for interim support pending completion of the care planning process is also stressed in *Working Together* – that children's needs are paramount and that every child should receive 'the support they need before a problem escalates'.[232]

The need for services to promote dignity

3.134 All support services provided by local authorities for disabled children and their families (including for 'accommodated children' – see following section) must comply with the obligations under the

229 Department of Health, Department for Education and Employment and Home Office, *Framework for the assessment of children in need and their families (policy guidance)*, 2000.
230 Department of Health, Department for Education and Employment and Home Office, *Framework for the assessment of children in need and their families (policy guidance)*, 2000, para 1.56.
231 *Working Together*, p26, para 61.
232 *Working Together*, p8, para 12.

European Convention on Human Rights (ECHR): the essence of which is the promotion and protection of the inherent dignity of all those in need. In *R (A, B, X and Y) v East Sussex CC*,[233] the High Court stated (at [86]) that:

> The recognition and protection of human dignity is one of the core values – in truth the core value – of our society and indeed all societies which are part of the European family of nations and which have embraced the principles of the [European Convention on Human Rights].

3.135   The obligations on children's services authorities to provide services to meet disabled children's assessed needs must, therefore, be seen in the context of the state's convention obligations and, in particular, the positive obligations under ECHR article 8, to ensure decent and dignified standards of living for disabled children, where possible with their families. The service provision decision, therefore, needs to be taken with due regard to all the general principles and human rights standards set out in chapters 1 and 2.

Duty to accommodate disabled children

3.136   As noted above (see paras 3.81–3.91), in general where a local authority facilitates short break/respite care in a way which involves the child spending a period in a residential care (or substitute family) placement, then this care is considered to be provided as a support service under CA 1989 s17. However, if the placement arises because 'the person who has been caring' for the disabled child is 'prevented ... from providing him with suitable accommodation or care' for whatever reason, then the care is provided under a different section of CA 1989, namely section 20(1). This distinction is important, because the duty to provide accommodation under CA 1989 s20(1) is a 'specifically enforceable' duty[234] and a child accommodated under this duty may well become 'looked-after' by a local authority (see paras 3.144–3.147).[235] Residential short breaks may also be provided under the authority's power to accommodate pursuant to CA 1989 s20(4)

---

233 [2003] EWHC 167 (Admin); (2003) 6 CCLR 194.
234 See para 2.29.
235 This arises if the child is in local authority care by reason of a court order or is being accommodated under CA 1989 s20, regardless of whether under subsection (1) or (4) for more than 24 hours by agreement with the parents (or with the child if aged over 16).

– but only if the qualifying criteria for the section 20(1) duty are not met on the facts of the individual case.

3.137 In *R (G) v Southwark LBC*,[236] the House of Lords confirmed that where the qualifying criteria in CA 1989 s20(1) are met (considered below), an authority is under a specific duty to accommodate a child under that section. This duty trumps the power to accommodate a child under CA 1989 s17(6) and children's services authorities cannot avoid their section 20(1) obligations by referring children in need of accommodation to housing authorities or providing 'help with accommodation' under CA 1989 s17. It will constitute maladministration if a local authority fails to undertake an assessment in relation to its CA 1989 s20(1) duty in an appropriate case – for example in relation to a disabled child whose mother is unable to cope with his challenging behaviour and wants the local authority to accommodate him.[237]

3.138 As noted above (see para 3.81), the High Court held in *R (JL) v Islington LBC*[238] that the 'prevention' referred to in CA 1989 s20(1)(c) had to be current, and that the duty only arose (in effect) at the point of crisis. Where a disabled child is placed away from home, including at a residential special school (see paras 4.202–4.205), it will therefore be a question of fact as to whether the placement is made pursuant to CA 1989 s20(1)(c).

3.139 It follows that the section 20(1) duty to accommodate may not be triggered until a family is close to 'breaking point' and the parents at risk of no longer being able to provide the necessary care to the disabled child (and potentially any non-disabled siblings). The precise wording of the relevant limb of the section 20(1) duty states that the duty to accommodate arises where the child requires accommodation as a result of:

(c) the person who has been caring for him being prevented (whether or not permanently, and for whatever reason) from providing him with suitable accommodation or care.

3.140 It is important to bear in mind that accommodation under CA 1989 s20(1) is *voluntary*, in other words that a child cannot be accommodated under this duty if a person with parental responsibility who is willing and able to provide accommodation objects (CA 1989

---

236 [2009] UKHL 26; (2009) 12 CCLR 437.
237 Report on complaint no 13/010/519 against Birmingham City Council, 31 March 2014.
238 [2009] EWHC 458 (Admin); (2009) 12 CCLR 322.

s20(7)).[239] The 'section 20 regime depends on parental consent and is non-coercive':[240] the parent retains full 'parental responsibility' (see paras 2.58–2.62) and may remove their child at any time from a local authority's accommodation (s20(8)). Consent obtained from parents for section 20 placements must be properly informed.[241]

3.141   Before providing accommodation, an authority must give due consideration to the wishes and feelings of the child, although these may not be determinative.[242] Authorities must additionally consider the child's wishes and feelings throughout any placement. Accordingly, in *R (CD) v Anglesey CC*,[243] the High Court criticised the respondent council for attempting to end a successful fostering arrangement for a 15-year-old severely disabled girl and requiring her to reside at an establishment 'to an extent substantially contrary to her wishes and feelings'.

3.142   In relation to children accessing overnight or residential short breaks, it should be remembered that these arrangements only engage the CA 1989 s20(1) duty if all the qualifying criteria are met. In particular, if the parents are not 'prevented' from providing suitable accommodation and care but the short breaks are being provided to promote the child's well-being and support positive family life, then the service is being provided under CA 1989 s17 or s20(4).

3.143   Where a local authority accommodates a disabled child outside their area, the placing authority retains responsibility for that child for the duration of the placement: CA 1989 s105(6).

Duties towards 'looked-after' disabled children

3.144   A disabled child who is accommodated under CA 1989 s20(1) duty (or indeed the section 20(4) power)[244] may become a 'looked-after' child for the purposes of CA 1989.[245] For this to apply, all that is required is

---

239 Unless the child is 16 or over and agrees to be provided with accommodation under this section: CA 1989 s20(11).
240 *Bedford v Bedfordshire CC* [2013] EWHC 1717 (Admin), and see also Cerebra Legal Entitlements Research Project, *Digest of Cases 2014*, Ben's Story at p47.
241 *Williams v Hackney LBC* [2015] EWHC 2629 (QB).
242 *R (Liverpool CC) v Hillingdon LBC* [2009] EWCA Civ 43 per Dyson LJ at [32], approved by Baroness Hale in *R (G) v Southwark LBC* [2009] UKHL 26; (2009) 12 CCLR 437 at [28].
243 [2004] EWHC 1635 (Admin); (2002) 7 CCLR 589.
244 But not under CA 1989 s17.
245 CA 1989 s22(1)(b).

that the accommodation is provided for a continuous period of more than 24 hours (CA 1989 s22(2)). As noted above (paras 3.80–3.90), a modified form of 'looked-after' status applies to disabled children receiving residential short breaks in a single setting for a limited period of time. A local authority does not acquire parental responsibility for children it is voluntarily accommodating; responsibility remains with the child's mother or parents (CA 1989 s2).

3.145 Local authorities do, however, have additional duties towards disabled children who are 'looked after' (as they do to all 'looked-after' children), including duties in relation to accommodation and maintenance.[246] In particular, there is a 'specific' duty (see para 2.47) on local authorities to safeguard and promote the welfare of the children they look after.[247] Local authorities must ascertain and give due consideration to their wishes and feelings when making decisions for looked-after children.[248] Furthermore, under CA 1989 s22C[249] authorities accommodating a looked-after child have to:

- place the child in what is, in their opinion, the most appropriate placement available;[250]
- place the child within the local authority's area, unless that is not reasonably practicable;[251] and
- ensure so far as is reasonably practicable that the placement is close to the child's home, does not disrupt the child's education or training and is suitable to the child's particular needs as a disabled child.[252]

3.146 Placements of children away from home are governed by the Care Planning, Placement and Case Review (England) Regulations 2010 (the 2010 Regulations).[253] Generally, under the 2010 Regulations, where a child becomes 'looked-after', the local authority must:

---

246 CA 1989 s23.

247 CA 1989 s22(3)(a).

248 CA 1989 s22(4)–(5).

249 Substituted, together with ss22A, 22B, 22D–22F, for s23 as originally enacted, by Children and Young Persons Act 2008 s8(1).

250 CA 1989 s22C(5). This duty applies if it is not reasonably practicable and/or consistent with the child's welfare to place the child with a parent, a person with parental responsibility or a person named in a child arrangements order: s22C(3)–(4).

251 CA 1989 s22C(9).

252 CA 1989 s22C(8).

253 SI No 959.

- assess their needs for services to achieve or maintain a reasonable standard of health or development and prepare a care plan;[254]
- ensure that a registered medical practitioner assesses the child's state of health and provides a written report of that assessment as soon as reasonably practicable;[255]
- prepare a placement plan setting out how the placement under section 22C will contribute to meeting the child's needs;[256]
- ensure that visits are made to the child at their placement by the local authority's representative within one week of the start of the placement, at intervals of not more than six weeks for the first year of any placement, and thereafter:
  - where the placement is intended to last until C is aged 18, at intervals of not more than three months, and
  - in any other case, at intervals of not more than six weeks;[257]
- carry out a review of the child's case within 20 working days of the date on which they become looked-after, with a second review to take place not more than three months after the first and subsequent reviews at intervals of not more than six months.[258]

3.147   The detailed requirements of the 2010 Regulations are themselves expanded upon by the 'Volume 2' Children Act statutory guidance.[259] Detailed reference to this guidance will be essential in any case involving a looked-after child. Guidance with particular relevance to disabled children becoming looked-after includes:

254 2010 Regulations, reg 4. See reg 5 and Sch 1 for the detailed requirements of the content of the care plan for 'looked-after' children and reg 6 for the process requirements.

255 2010 Regulations, reg 7.

256 2010 Regulations, reg 9. The plan must cover all the matters specified in Sch 2 to the 2010 regulations. If it is not reasonably practicable to prepare the placement plan before making the placement, the placement plan must be prepared within five working days of the start of the placement: reg 9(2). Under reg 14, a placement may generally only be terminated following a formal review of the child's case in accordance with 2010 Regulations, Part 6.

257 2010 Regulations, reg 28.

258 2010 Regulations, reg 33. Pursuant to reg 32, no significant change should be made to the child's care plan unless this change has been considered at a review, unless this is not reasonably practicable.

259 HM Government, *The Children Act 1989 Guidance and Regulations Volume 2: Care Planning, Placement and Case Review*, June 2015. There is also statutory guidance issued in March 2015 entitled *Promoting the health and well-being of looked-after children*.

- In drawing up a health plan[260] for a disabled child, consideration must be given to continuity of specialist care.[261]
- A thorough assessment of the child's disability-related needs must be undertaken to ensure that any requirements necessary for his/her accommodation are identified and arrangements made to ensure the suitability of that accommodation.[262]
- Foster carers can provide a disabled child with 'an important opportunity to live in his/her local community rather than be placed in more traditional forms of residential care which may be some distance from home'.[263]
- In all types of placement 'disabled children must have access to the same facilities such as recreation, living or garden areas, as other non-disabled children in the home and this will form an important criterion as to whether the accommodation is suitable'.[264]

Support for 'accommodated children'

3.148 CA 1989 ss85–86 require that where children are provided with accommodation otherwise than under the social care powers and duties (for example by an NHS body or the local authority's education department) for a significant period, the relevant children's services department must be notified.

3.149 CA 1989 Sch 2 para 8A[265] provides that '[e]very local authority shall make provision for such services as they consider appropriate to be available with respect to accommodated children'.[266] These services must be provided 'with a view to promoting contact between each accommodated child and that child's family'.[267] The particular services which can be provided include advice, guidance and

---

260 The health plan 'forms the health dimension of the care plan': para 2.16. The care plan will also include a personal education plan; see the SEND Code, para 10.6.

261 HM Government, *The Children Act 1989 Guidance and Regulations Volume 2: Care Planning, Placement and Case Review* ('Volume and Guidance'), June 2015, para 2.63.

262 Volume and Guidance, June 2015, para 3.26.

263 Volume and Guidance, June 2015, para 3.28.

264 Volume and Guidance, June 2015, para 3.29.

265 Inserted by Children and Young Persons Act 2008 s19.

266 CA 1989 Sch 2 para 8A(1). See also CA 1989 Sch 2 para 10 for the obligation on local authorities to support all children 'in need' living apart from their families to live with their families or achieve greater contact with them, where this is necessary in order safeguard and promote their welfare.

267 CA 1989 Sch 2 para 8A(3)

counselling, services necessary to enable the child to visit, or to be visited by, members of the family and assistance to enable the child and members of the family to have a holiday together.[268]

Duties towards disabled children 'leaving care'

3.150   In recognition of the unacceptably poor outcomes for formerly 'looked-after' children, the Children (Leaving Care) Act 2000 created a new scheme to oblige children's services authorities to continue to provide assistance to young people whom they had formerly been looking after, both disabled and non-disabled. The duties are in respect of 'eligible', 'relevant' and 'former relevant' children.

3.151   'Eligible' children are those who are 16 or 17 years old and have been 'looked-after' for 13 weeks from the age of 14, either continuously or in total.[269] In respect of 'eligible' children, children's services authorities are required to:

- assess the young person's needs and then prepare a 'pathway plan' to meet those needs;[270]
- appoint a personal adviser to co-ordinate services,[271] who must be independent of the authority and not the person with responsibility for the assessment or pathway plan: *R (J) v Caerphilly CBC*.[272]

The pathway plan 'must include any services being provided in respect of the young person's disability'.[273]

3.152   'Relevant' children are children aged 16 or 17 years old who have ceased to be 'looked-after' but otherwise would have been 'eligible'.[274] Children's services authorities have a duty to 'keep in touch' with relevant children and prepare pathway plans for them.

---

268 CA 1989 Sch 2 para 8A(4). See further CSDPA 1970 s2(6)(f) and para 3.78 above for the specific duty to support disabled children to have holidays

269 CA 1989 s19B and 2010 Regulations, reg 40.

270 CA 1989 s19B and 2010 Regulations, reg 41. The assessment should be completed within three months of the child reaching 16 or them becoming an eligible child after that age: 2010 Regulations, reg 42. See 2010 Regulations, Sch 8 for the detailed requirement of the pathway plan.

271 See 2010 Regulations, reg 44 for the functions of the personal adviser.

272 [2005] EWHC 586 (Admin); (2005) 8 CCLR 255.

273 HM Government, *The Children Act 1989 Guidance and Regulations Volume 2: Care Planning, Placement and Case Review*, March 2010, para 5.17.

274 CA 1989 s23A.

3.153 'Former relevant' children are young people who are over 18 but were previously 'eligible' or 'relevant' children.[275] Duties towards former relevant children are discussed in paras 10.49–10.60, where the 'leaving care' scheme is generally given more detailed consideration. The key guidance for young people 'leaving care' is the 'Volume 3' Children Act guidance.[276]

3.154 These duties sit alongside other duties in relation to disabled young people's social care needs, for example, the duty to maintain an EHC plan up to the age of 25 and the duties owed during and after the transition to adulthood under the Care Act 2014. These wider duties are covered in more detail in chapter 10 on transition to adulthood. In the opinion of the authors, the scheme lacks coherence, with too many overlapping obligations and a lack of clarity as to which takes precedence.

Charging for children's services

3.155 Children's services authorities have the power to charge for services provided under the CA 1989. Authorities may recover 'such charge as they consider appropriate' (CA 1989 s29(1)) and, in so doing, if the child is under 16, can take into account the financial circumstance of the parents, and if 16 or over, can take into account the child's means (s29(4)). However, no person can be charged while in receipt of income support or a range of other benefits (s29(3)). Furthermore, an authority cannot require a person to pay more than he or she can reasonably be expected to pay (s29(2)).

3.156 Children's services authorities can also charge for services provided under CSDPA 1970 s2. In practice (at the time of publication), few authorities do charge parents or children for services provided either under CA 1989 Part III or CSDPA 1970 s2.[277]

---

275 CA 1989 s23C.
276 DfE, *The Children Act 1989 guidance and regulations Volume 3: planning transition to adulthood for care leavers*, revised January 2015.
277 See L Clements and P Thompson, *Community Care and the Law*, 4th edn, LAG, 2007, paras 24.68–24.73 (not in current edition) and chapter 10 for further information on charging.

Safeguarding and child protection

3.157   Local authorities have extensive powers and duties under CA 1989 to protect children from harm. A key threshold for these powers and duties to arise is set out in CA 1989 s47, being that the local authority has reasonable cause to suspect that a child is suffering, or is likely to suffer, significant harm. It is vitally important that this safeguarding threshold is kept distinct from the far lower threshold described above at para 3.56 where it is 'necessary' to meet a disabled child's needs, or the even lower threshold for when a disabled child is 'in need' and entitled to a statutory assessment (see para 3.30).

3.158   The fact that these powers and duties are not considered in detail in this book should not be taken to indicate that effective and appropriate measures to safeguard disabled children are anything other than crucial (see para 1.44). In addition, as with any children, decisions about protecting disabled children from harm are often complex. A small number of recent cases indicate, however, that the existence of these powers may give rise to fear among parents that if they find themselves disagreeing with or complaining about the council, or taking action of which the council disapproves, then they may find themselves the subject of child protection proceedings. For a local authority to misuse their powers in this way, would of course, run contrary to the entire object and purpose of CA 1989 Part III, which is that 'local authorities should provide support for children and families'.[278]

3.159   In *A Local Authority v A (A Child)*,[279] Munby LJ made a number of observations about heavy-handed interventions by local authorities who believed that they were not merely 'involved' with such families but that they had 'complete and effective control ... through [their] assessments and care plans'. Of this attitude, Munby LJ observed that 'it needs to be said in the plainest possible terms that this suggestion, however formulated – and worryingly some local authorities seem almost to assume and take it for granted – is simply wrong in law.' He continued:

> 52 Moreover, the assertion or assumption, however formulated, betrays a fundamental misunderstanding of the nature of the relationship between a local authority and those, like A and C and their carers, who it is tasked to support – a fundamental misunderstanding of the relationship between the State and the citizen. People in the

278   *R (M) v Gateshead MBC* [2006] EWCA Civ 221 per Dyson LJ at [42].
279   [2010] EWHC 978 (Fam); (2010) 13 CCLR 404, at paras 50–51.

situation of A and C, together with their carers, look to the State – to a local authority – for the support, the assistance and the provision of the services to which the law, giving effect to the underlying principles of the Welfare State, entitles them. They do not seek to be 'controlled' by the State or by the local authority. And it is not for the State in the guise of a local authority to seek to exercise such control. The State, the local authority, is the servant of those in need of its support and assistance, not their master. ...

53 This attitude is perhaps best exemplified by the proposition that 'in the event that the parents were to disagree with the *decisions* of the local authority (which will always be based upon the opinion of relevant professionals) it would seek to *enforce its decisions* through appropriate proceedings if necessary' (emphasis added). This approach, ..., though reflecting what I have come across elsewhere, reflects an attitude of mind which is not merely unsound in law but hardly best calculated to encourage proper effect being given to a local authority's procedural obligations under Article 8 of the Convention ... . Moreover, it is likely to be nothing but counter-productive when it comes to a local authority 'working together', as it must, with family carers. 'Working together' involves something more – much more – than merely requiring carers to agree with a local authority's 'decision' even if, let alone just because, it may be backed by professional opinion.

3.160   Munby LJ referred to a number of other cases considered by the courts where a local authority had acted in such a high-handed way.[280] The local government ombudsman has also expressed concern about local authorities seeking to use their child and adult protection powers inappropriately. A 2008 ombudsman complaint[281] concerned a local authority in dispute with a disabled child's family over a care plan. The disagreement centered on the use of a hoist that the council considered necessary, but the family were not satisfied with the proposed arrangements and continued to carry the young man upstairs to be bathed. Although it was accepted that his family were devoted to him, nevertheless the local authority made an adult protection referral – asserting that this was putting him at risk. The ombudsman held that it 'beggars belief that the referral was made at all'.[282] In similar vein, a 2009 ombudsman complaint[283] concerned a mother

---

280 [2010] EWHC 978 (Fam); (2010) 13 CCLR 536 at [55].
281 Complaint no 07/B/07665 against Luton Borough Council, 10 September 2008.
282 Complaint no 07/B/07665 against Luton Borough Council, 10 September 2008, para 37.
283 Complaint no 07/C/03887 against Bury MBC, 14 October 2009.

who (because of a service failure by the council) had no option but to use a hose in the back garden to keep her sons clean. Instead of providing adequate bathing facilities, she was warned by the social services panel that cleaning them this way was 'abusive' – something that the ombudsman considered to be of 'breathtaking insensitivity' by a council that (in her opinion) exhibited an 'institutionalised indifference' not only to the disabled children's needs and the mother's plight but also to the council's duties and responsibilities.[284]

3.161   The proper procedures to be followed in relation to safeguarding children (including disabled children) can be found in the *Working Together* statutory guidance considered in detail earlier in this chapter in relation to the duty to assess disabled children as children 'in need'. The guidance sets out how organisations and individuals should work together to safeguard and promote the welfare of children and young people in accordance with the CA 1989 and the CA 2004. The general principles in the statutory guidance are also supplemented by specific practice guidance in relation to disabled children.[285]

3.162   *Working Together* mandates that the same approach to assessment should apply to all child cases, including those of children 'at risk'. The emphasis is on effective action to safeguard children: '[p]ractitioners should be rigorous in assessing and monitoring children at risk of neglect to ensure they are adequately safeguarded over time. They should act decisively to protect the child by initiating care proceedings where existing interventions are insufficient'.[286] This is undoubtedly correct, however in the context of disabled children it is vitally important that local authorities distinguish between cases of potential abuse or neglect and cases where families are simply struggling as a result of a failure to discharge the support duties outlined above.

3.163   The same requirement for a support plan focussed on outcomes is imposed by *Working Together* in child 'in need' and child 'at risk' cases.[287] However, in abuse or neglect cases the plan should be reviewed regularly both to see whether sufficient progress has been made to meet the child's needs and on the level of risk faced by the child.[288] The guidance highlights that prompt action may be required

---

284 Complaint no 07/C/03887 against Bury MBC, 14 October 2009, paras 40 and 43.

285 DCSF, *Safeguarding disabled children – Practice Guidance*, 2009.

286 *Working Together*, p20, para 32.

287 *Working Together*, p25, paras 52–56.

288 *Working Together*, p25, para 55.

in certain cases. In addition to the general requirement for an initial decision on the type of response required within one working day of a referral, there is a specific requirement imposed by CA 1989 ss 44 and 46 for action to be taken by the social worker, the police or the NSPCC in cases where removal of the child may be required.[289] These 'immediate protection' cases are addressed, including a process flow chart.[290] Guidance on the 'strategy discussion' required in cases where it is thought the CA 1989 s47 threshold[291] may be crossed is provided.[292] There is also guidance on how to carry out s47 enquiries and the potential outcome of s47 enquiries.[293] There then follows detailed guidance on child protection arrangements which are beyond the scope of this book.

Transition to adult social care

3.164   The scheme governing care and support for disabled adults and support for their carers established by the Care Act 2014 is addressed in chapter 10. This scheme creates three new types of transition assessment – a child's needs assessment,[294] a child's carer's assessment[295] and a young carer's needs assessment.[296]

3.165   The Care Act 2014 (by amendment of the CA 1989 and the CSDPA 1970) also creates an unusual set of duties on local authorities to continue to provide children's services to a disabled young person after the age of 18 if the Care Act transition assessment process has not been completed at the right time. These duties comprise:[297]

- CA 1989 s 17ZH, which requires that services provided under CA 1989 s17 must continue once a disabled child or young carer turns 18 until adult services have: (a) concluded that the individual does not have needs for care and support or for support, (b) begun to

289 *Working Together*, p26, para 59.
290 *Working Together*, pp31–32.
291 See above para 3.157
292 *Working Together*, pp36–38.
293 *Working Together*, pp39–42.
294 Care Act 2014 ss58–59; see chapter 10 at paras 10.28–10.37.
295 Care Act 2014 ss60–61; see chapter 10 at paras 10.38–10.41. Care Act 2014 s62 creates a power to meet the needs of carers of young people in transition to adulthood.
296 Care Act 2014 s64; see chapter 10 at paras 10.42–10.43.
297 Inserted by Care Act 2014 s66; and see also the *Care and Support Statutory Guidance*, 2014, chapter 16.

meet identified needs, or (c) concluded that they will not meet any identified needs, for example because they do not meet the eligibility criteria.

- CA 1989 s17ZI, which requires that where social care services are being provided as part of an EHC plan and that plan ceases to be maintained, children's services must continue until any of the situations identified at (a)–(c) above are reached (ie the adult care and support process is finalised).
- CSDPA 1970 s2A, which requires that CSDPA services must also continue until any of the situations identified at (a)–(c) above are reached.

3.166   The Care Act 2014 s66 is therefore an important mechanism to ensure that a disabled young person's transition from children's services to adult services is not a 'cliff edge'; that children's services can continue until it is appropriate for the baton to be passed to adult services. As the *Care and Support Statutory Guidance* explains:

> ... Under the Care Act 2014, if, having carried out a transition assessment, it is agreed that the best decision for the young person is to continue to receive children's services, the local authority may choose to do so. Children and adults' services must work together, and any decision to continue children's services after the child turns 18 will require agreement between children and adult services. ...[298]

3.167   The Care Act 2014 guidance states[299] that in cases where a young person is continuing to receive children's services over the age of 18, any safeguarding concerns should be addressed through adult safeguarding arrangements under the Care Act 2014 scheme.

---

298 *Care and Support Statutory Guidance*, 2014, para 16.71.
299 *Care and Support Statutory Guidance*, 2014, para 14.5.

CHAPTER 4

Education

continued

Key points

- Disabled children have a right to suitable, effective and appropriate education aimed at helping them achieve the 'best possible' outcomes.
- A large proportion of disabled children have 'special educational needs' (SEN). The new scheme to meet those needs is set out in Part 3 of the Children and Families Act (CFA) 2014.
- Local authorities have general duties to promote the welfare of disabled children and children with SEN and to promote the fulfilment by every child of his or her educational potential.
- There is a legal presumption in favour of mainstream education for disabled children and children with SEN.
- Most children with SEN in mainstream schools will have their needs met through a system of 'SEN support' under the SEND Code.
- The route to specialist provision is through a statutory assessment which may lead to an Education, Health and Care plan (EHC plan).
- Children, including children with complex needs, can also be educated at home.
- Children with SEN should not be excluded from school except as a 'last resort'; where they are excluded, their parents can generally appeal to a Governor's Committee and an Independent Review Panel or to the tribunal in some cases where disability discrimination is alleged.
- Local authorities owe a specific duty to children (including disabled children and children with SEN) who are out of school to offer suitable alternative provision.
- Disputes between parents and local authorities in relation to specific aspects of the SEN system can be resolved through an appeal to the First-tier Tribunal (Special Educational Needs and Disability).

Introduction

4.1   This chapter considers the rights of disabled children to education. The right education is fundamental to achieving good outcomes for disabled children, as it is for every child. Although the focus of this chapter is on children with special educational needs (SEN) it also considers the duties of schools towards children with disabilities that do not meet the definition of SEN.

4.2   This chapter focuses on the new SEN and disability scheme for children and young people aged 0–25 that was introduced through Part 3 of the Children and Families Act (CFA) 2014, in force from 1 September 2014. It is important to note however that many children and young people will continue to receive support under the old legal framework until they have transitioned to the new system, which should be completed by 2018.

4.3   At the time of writing (November 2015) there have been no Upper Tribunal decisions under the new scheme in Part 3 of CFA 2014, and there has only been one judicial review judgment considering the scheme.[1] As such this chapter focuses on Part 3 of CFA 2014, the relevant regulations (the SEND Regs 2014[2]) and the guidance in the Code of Practice which accompanies them.[3] Many of the tribunal decisions and case-law in relation to the old scheme under Education Act (EA) 1996 Part 4 covered in the first edition of this book will continue to be relevant to the interpretation of Part 3 of CFA 2014, although this will be tested by the courts and tribunals on a case-by-case basis.

4.4   The purpose of the reforms under Part 3 of the CFA 2014 is to create 'a system which is less confrontational and more efficient'.[4] However emerging evidence from the specialist charities in the field suggests that one year on, the reforms have not yet made a significant difference to levels of satisfaction with the SEN system.[5]

4.5   At the most fundamental level children with SEN are still hugely more likely to be excluded from school than other children:

- Pupils with SEN account for 7 in 10 of all permanent exclusions and 6 in 10 of all fixed period exclusions.

---

1   *R (L and P) v Warwickshire CC* [2015] EWHC 203 (Admin); (2015) 18 CCLR 458. See S Broach, *CDC Care Law Update 1*, Council for Disabled Children.

2   SI No 1530.

3   Department for Education/Department of Health, *Special educational needs and disability code of practice: 0 to 25 years; Statutory guidance for organisations which work with and support children and young people who have special educational needs or disabilities*, January 2015 ('SEND Code').

4   SEND Code, Ministerial Foreword, p11.

5   For example National Autistic Society, *School report 2015: A health check on how well the new Special Educational Needs and Disability (SEND) system is meeting the needs of children and young people on the autism spectrum*, October 2015; National Deaf Children's Society, *One year on: impact of changes to the special educational needs system on deaf children*, September 2015; Driver Youth Trust, *Joining the dots: Have recent reforms worked for those with SEND?* October 2015.

- Pupils with SEN without statements have the highest permanent exclusion rate and are around nine times more likely to receive a permanent exclusion than pupils with no SEN.
- Pupils with statements of SEN have the highest fixed period exclusion rate and are around nine times more likely to receive a fixed period exclusion than pupils with no SEN.[6]

4.6 It is also concerning that there has been a 2.5 per cent decrease in the numbers of children recognised to have SEN in the most recent year for which data has been reported by the Department for Education.[7] A potential implication of this is that children who would otherwise be identified with SEN are not being identified because of concerns about the resource implications.

Key definitions – CFA 2014 Part 3

• Special educational needs (SEN)

A child or young person has SEN if they have a learning difficulty or disability which calls for special educational provision to be made for him or her.[8]

A child of compulsory school age or a young person has a learning difficulty or disability if he or she:

- has a significantly greater difficulty in learning than the majority of others of the same age, or
- has a disability which prevents or hinders him or her from making use of facilities of a kind generally provided for others of the same age in mainstream schools or mainstream post-16 institutions.[9]

A child under compulsory school age has special educational needs if he or she is likely to fall within the definition above when they reach compulsory school age or would do so if special educational provision was not made for them.[10]

Difficulties related solely to learning English as an additional language are not SEN. When identifying and assessing SEN for children and young people whose first language is not English

6 Department for Education, *Statistical First Release: Permanent and Fixed Period Exclusions in England, 2013 to 2014*, July 2015.
7 Department for Education, *Statistical First Release: Special educational needs in England*, January 2015.
8 CFA 2014 s20(1).
9 CFA 2014 s20(2).
10 CFA 2014 s20(3).

requires particular care and schools should look carefully child or young person's performance in different areas of learning and development or subjects to establish whether lack of progress is due to limitations in their command of English or if it arises from SEN or a disability.[11]

• Special educational provision

CFA 2014 s21 defines special educational provision for children over two and young people as:

'educational or training provision that is additional to, or different from, that made generally for others of the same age in –
• mainstream schools in England,
• maintained nursery schools in England,
• mainstream post-16 institutions in England, or
• places in England at which relevant early years education is provided.'[12]

Special educational provision for a child aged under two means educational provision of any kind.[13]

• Disability

The definition of disability is set out in section 6(1) of Equality Act 2010, which states that a person (P) has a disability if:
a) P has a physical or mental impairment, and
b) the impairment has a substantial and long-term adverse effect on P's ability to carry out normal day-to-day activities.

Further detail in relation to this definition of disability is set out in chapter 9 at paras 9.11–9.22.

• Health care and social care provision

CFA 2014 s21(3) defines 'Health care provision' as the provision of health care services as part of the comprehensive health service in England continued under section 1(1) of the National Health Service Act 2006 (see chapter 5 for duties in relation to healthcare provision for disabled children).

Social care provision means the provision made by a local authority in the exercise of its social services functions.[14] This will include

---

11 SEND Code, para 6.24.
12 CFA 2014 s21(1).
13 CFA 2014 s21(2).
14 CFA 2014 s21(4).

provision such as short breaks and domiciliary care in the home. Further information in relation to social care duties can be found in chapter 3.

There can often be difficulties in identifying whether particular provision is special educational provision, health provision or social care provision. Some assistance is given by CFA 2014 s21(5), which makes clear that health care provision or social care provision which educates or trains a child or young person is to be treated as special educational provision (instead of health care provision or social care provision). As such it is likely that the majority of provision delivered to disabled children in schools will be special educational provision. However the relevant tests summarised above should be applied in relation to each and every type of provision a child receives, particularly if they have an EHC plan (see paras 4.134–4.163 below).

The SEND Code states that speech and language therapy and other therapy provision can be regarded as either education or health care provision, or both. It could therefore be included in an EHC plan as either educational or health provision. However, since communication is so fundamental in education, addressing speech and language impairment should normally be recorded as special educational provision unless there are exceptional reasons for not doing so.[15]

- **Young person**

A 'young person' is a person over compulsory school age but under the age of 25.[16] A child is of compulsory school age from the beginning of the term following their fifth birthday until the last Friday of June in the year in which they become 16, provided that their 16th birthday falls before the start of the next school year.[17] For example, if a child turns 16 in March 2016, they will be over compulsory school age (and therefore a 'young person') after Friday 24 June 2016.

15 SEND Code, para 9.74.
16 CFA 2014 s83(2).
17 SEND Code, glossary of terms, page 279.

The human right to education

4.7   Education is a fundamental human right. The right is contained in a number of international treaties, but most importantly within article 2 of Protocol 1 to the European Convention on Human Rights ('A2P1'), which states:

> No person shall be denied the right to education. In the exercise of any functions which it assumes in relation to education and teaching, the state shall respect the right of parents to ensure such education and teaching in conformity with their own religious and philosophical convictions.

4.8   The United Kingdom has entered a reservation in respect of A2P1 which provides that the second sentence of the right (relating to parent's wishes) is only accepted in so far as it is compatible with the provision of efficient instruction and training, and the avoidance of unreasonable expenditure. This qualification reflects the position in Education Act 1996 s9 which gives only a qualified right to parents to have their choices and views respected in relation to their child's education.

4.9   The scope of the right to education under A2P1 in relation to a disabled child has been considered by the Supreme Court in *A v Essex CC*.[18] This was a damages claim under A2P1 in relation to a period of 18 months when A was effectively without any education, apart from irregular speech and language therapy sessions and access to some educational toys. A has complex needs, including severe learning disabilities, autism and epilepsy. His needs were ultimately met successfully in a residential special school placement.

4.10   The Supreme Court held by a majority of 3–2 that it was not arguable that A2P1 gave A an absolute right to education to meet his special needs during the 18 months he was out of school. However, a different 3–2 majority of the Justices found that it was arguable that Essex had failed to provide educational facilities that were available that might have mitigated the consequences of the failure to meet A's special needs during this period. Despite this, the Supreme Court declined to extend time to allow this part of A's claim to proceed to trial. This judgment is complex, with all five Justices giving separate speeches, but it clearly demonstrates that at the very least in order to comply with A2P1 authorities must not neglect the educational needs of children with even the most complex SEN and must do what is possible to provide these children with some education, even

---

18   *A v Essex County Council* [2010] UKSC 33; [2011] 1 AC 280.

if less than suitable education, while a suitable placement for them is being found.

4.11 In relation to children with SEN like A who are out of school, the A2P1 right to education is supplemented by the powerful duties contained in EA 1996 s19 which require suitable alternative education to be provided regardless of resource difficulties – see below at paras 4.210–4.217.

4.12 As discussed in chapter 2 (see paras 2.22–2.37), recent cases[19] show that international human rights conventions are growing in significance in English law. The UN Convention of the Rights of Persons with Disabilities is one such international treaty and Article 24 sets out important rights for disabled children when accessing education. In particular:

> States parties recognise the right of persons with disabilities to education. With a view to realising this right without discrimination and on the basis of equal opportunity, state parties shall ensure an inclusive education system at all levels and life long learning directed to:
> a) the full development of human potential and sense of dignity and self-worth, and the strengthening of respect for human rights, fundamental freedoms and human diversity;
> b) the development by persons with disabilities of their personality, talents and creativity, as well as their mental and physical abilities, to their fullest potential;
> c) enabling persons with disabilities to participate effectively in a free society.

4.13 Article 24(2) states:

> In realising that right, states parties shall ensure that:
> a) persons with disabilities are not excluded from the general education system on the basis of disability, and that children with disabilities are not excluded from free and compulsory primary education, or from secondary education, on the basis of disability;
> b) persons with disabilities can access an inclusive, quality and free primary education and secondary education on an equal basis with others in the communities in which they live;
> c) reasonable accommodation of the individual's requirements is provided;
> d) persons with disabilities receive the support required, within the general education system, to facilitate their effective education; and

---

19 For example, see *R (SG and others) v Secretary of State for Work and Pensions* [2015] UKSC 16; [2015] 1 WLR 1449.

e) effective individualised support measures are provided in environments that maximise academic and social development, consistent with the goal of full inclusion.

4.14   In addition, there are also a number of important obligations relating to education in the UN Convention on the Rights of the Child including:

Article 28 (right to education)

Article 28 provides that states should recognise that all children shall have an equal right to education and in particular:

- primary education should be compulsory and available free to all
- States should encourage the development of different forms of secondary education including general and vocational education, make them available and accessible to every child, and take appropriate measures such as the introduction of free education and offering financial assistance in case of need;
- higher education should accessible to all on the basis of capacity by every appropriate means;
- States should make educational and vocational information and guidance available and accessible to all children;
- States should take measures to encourage regular attendance at schools and the reduction of drop-out rates.
- school discipline should be administered in a manner consistent with the children's human dignity.

Article 29 (educational development)

Article 29 provides that a child's education should be aimed at the development of:

- the child's personality, talents and mental and physical abilities to their fullest potential;
- respect for human rights and fundamental freedoms, and for the principles enshrined in the Charter of the United Nations;
- respect for the child's parents, his or her own cultural identity, language and values, for the national values of the country in which the child is living, the country from which he or she may originate, and for civilizations different from his or her own;
- the preparation of the child for responsible life in a free society, in the spirit of understanding, peace, tolerance, equality of sexes, and friendship among all peoples, ethnic, national and religious groups and persons of indigenous origin; and
- the development of respect for the natural environment.

4.15 Although these conventions are 'unincorporated' and so are not formally part of English law, where the obligation or right has a link to a direct right under the ECHR – for example, the right to education under A2P1 – then it is likely that they will be considered very carefully by the courts when deciding whether a public body has acted lawfully. They should also be taken into account in any case where domestic law is ambiguous. See further chapter 2 at paras 2.22–2.37.

Duty to participate to 18

4.16 The Education and Skills Act (ESA) 2008 raises the participation age so that all young people leaving year 11 are required to continue in education or training until at least their 18th birthday.[20] This does not necessarily mean that the young person has to remain in school and 'participation' can include:

• full-time study in a school, college or with a training provider;
• full-time work or volunteering (20 hours or more) combined with part-time education or training; or
• an apprenticeship or traineeship.

4.17 Every young person who reaches the age of 16 or 17 in any given academic year is entitled to an offer of a suitable place, by the end of September, to continue in education or training the following year.[21]

4.18 The aim of these duties is to ensure that every young person continues their studies or takes up training and goes on to successful employment or higher education. The Department of Education's statutory guidance for local authorities[22] states that:

> Most young people already continue in education or training after they finish year 11, because it gives them the best chance to get the skills and qualifications that employers and universities look for. However, the small group of young people not participating includes some of the most vulnerable. We want to give all young people the opportunity to develop the skills they need for adult life and to achieve their full potential.

---

20 ESA 2008 Pt 1.
21 Department for Education, *Participation of young people in education, employment or training*, September 2014, para 26.
22 Department for Education, *Participation of young people in education, employment or training*, September 2014. See Annex 1 to the statutory guidance for detailed information on duty to participate requirements.

4.19   There are a number of legal duties on local authorities to encourage and support young people to participate. These include:

- securing sufficient suitable education and training provision for all young people aged 16 to 19 and for those up to age 25 with a learning difficulty assessment (LDA) or Education, Health and Care (EHC) plan in their area;[23]
- making available to all young people aged 13–19 and to those up to age 25 with an LDA or EHC plan, support that will encourage, enable or assist them to participate in education or training;[24]
- promoting the effective participation in education and training of 16 and 17 year olds in their area with a view to ensuring that those persons fulfil the duty to participate in education or training;[25] and
- making arrangements to identify 16 and 17 year olds who are not participating in education or training.[26]

4.20   Local authorities are also under a duty to secure participation of young people through their wider functions[27] such as developing post-16 transport arrangements which ensure that young people are not prevented from participating because of the cost or availability of transport to their education or training.[28] Information in relation to post 16 education and training provision available to young people for children with SEN and disabilities up to the age of 25 must also be included in each local authority's 'local offer'[29] as described at paras 4.72–4.78 below. There are also duties on providers to promote good attendance,[30] to tell their local authority when a young person is no longer participating[31] and to secure independent careers guidance.[32]

---

23 Education Act 1996 ss15ZA and 18A (as inserted by the Apprenticeships, Skills, Children and Learning Act 2009) and see also CFA 2014 s27.
24 Education and Skills Act 2008 s68, as amended by CFA 2014 s20.
25 ESA 2008 s10.
26 ESA 2008 s12.
27 ESA 2008 s10.
28 Education Act 1996 s509AA.
29 CFA 2014 s30 and SEND Regs 2014 Sch 2.
30 ESA 2008 s11.
31 ESA 2008 s13.
32 Department for Education, *Participation of young people in education, employment or training*, September 2014, para 39.

The SEN and disability scheme 0–25

4.21   In March 2011, the government published a Green Paper titled 'Support and Aspiration: A new approach to SEN and disability'. This consultation recognised that the provision of services to families of children with SEND was often fragmented and challenging to navigate, and set out a series of wide ranging reforms to improve the existing scheme for accessing support. The consultation ultimately led to Part 3 of the Children and Families Bill, which received Royal Assent on 13 March 2014 and came into force on 1 September 2014 – arguably too short a timeframe to implement wholesale system reform, notwithstanding that many of the provisions had been the subject of earlier pilot schemes.

4.22   The new scheme is underpinned by a number of important general duties on local authorities, including duties to:

- promote the fulfilment by every child (and young adult for whom an EHC plan is maintained) of their educational potential;[33] and
- have regard to the need to safeguard and promote the welfare of children in carrying out their educational functions.[34]

4.23   On the day the new system came into force, Children and Families Minister Edward Timpson MP said:

Today is a landmark moment in improving the lives of children with SEND and their families. These reforms put children and parents at the heart of the system.

For too long, families have found themselves battling against a complex and fragmented system. These reforms ensure support fits in with their needs and not the other way round - they will result in a simpler and more joined up system that focuses on children achieving their best.

This is the beginning of a journey, and the vast majority of local authorities have told us they are ready and parents have been supportive over the changes.[35]

4.24   The feature of the new scheme which has received the greatest focus is that statements of Special Educational Needs (Statements) for children in schools and learning difficulty assessments (LDAs) for young people in further education and training are being replaced with a

---

33 Education Act 1996 s13A(1)(c).
34 Education Act 2002 s175. This mirrors the duty in section 11 of the Children Act 2004 in relation to other local authority functions, see chapter 2 at para 2.53.
35 Department of Education press release, 1 September 2014.

single combined education, health and care plan (EHC plan) which will be available from birth until age 25. Accordingly, the new scheme will extend the current age of eligibility for those with a statement of SEN and still in education from 16 to 25, although importantly it does not create any new legal right to education up to this age. Transitional arrangements are in place to support the implementation of the new system and are described below, see paras 4.42–4.71.

4.25   It is important to note however that only a small minority of children with SEN will have an EHC plan, as was the case with statements. For the reforms to benefit the majority of children with SEN it is therefore important to retain a focus on their other elements. Some of the other key changes include the introduction of a new system for 'SEN support' (replacing 'school action' and 'school action plus' in schools and extending the system to early years and further education) and the new 'local offer'. For children and young people with EHC plans, there are changes to appeal rights and mediation, the introduction of personal budgets and direct payments for education and a focus on outcomes and preparation for adulthood.

4.26   Prior to the implementation of the new system, the government set up pilots with 31 local authorities to test the proposals in the SEND green paper. This was known as the 'Pathfinders Programme'. It ran from October 2011 to September 2014 and its final report was published in July 2015.[36] The report found that overall, the data suggested that the process for accessing support has improved for families. However, there was no statistical change in the extent to which families thought the decisions reached were fair and there remained a significant percentage of families who are not satisfied. In addition, the surveys found little evidence of significant improvements in parental outcomes or in either children's health or quality of life. The extent to which the reforms will bring about the positive changes for children and young people with SEND that had been envisaged therefore remains to be seen. It will only be possible to obtain a complete picture of the difference the reforms have made once all children and young people have transitioned to the new system in 2018.

Section 19 – general principles

4.27   The SEND Code states that 'Section 19 of the Children and Families Act 2014 sets out the principles underpinning the legislation and the

---

36 Department for Education, *The Special Educational Needs and Disability Pathfinder Programme Evaluation Final Impact Research Report*, July 2015.

guidance in this Code of Practice'.[37] Section 19 establishes the following core principles which must underpin all decisions taken by local authorities when exercising their functions in relation to children and young people. It requires local authorities to have regard to the following matters:

(a) the views, wishes and feelings of the child and his or her parent, or the young person;

(b) the importance of the child and his or her parent, or the young person, participating as fully as possible in decisions relating to the exercise of the function concerned;

(c) the importance of the child and his or her parent, or the young person, being provided with the information and support necessary to enable participation in those decisions;

(d) the need to support the child and his or her parent, or the young person, in order to facilitate the development of the child or young person and to help him or her achieve the best possible educational and other outcomes.

4.28 Whenever a local authority is taking any decision in relation to children and young people with SEN or disabilities under CFA 2014 Part 3, it must have 'regard' to the above principles. In essence, this requires consideration of these principles when all decisions are taken.

4.29 The principles will apply to all decisions taken by local authorities under Part 3 of CFA 2014, from individual decisions as to what provision is required to meet a child or young person's needs in an EHC plan to macro decisions about commissioning of services and any criteria to be applied. While there may be boundary disputes as to whether health or social care decisions are taken in the exercise of the functions under Part 3 of CFA 2014, it is far less likely that there will be any such dispute in relation to educational decisions.

4.30 Although having 'regard' does not create a duty on a local authority to provide the 'best' provision or to agree to do something in accordance with a parent's wishes in every case, it does mean local authorities will need to evidence how they have had regard to these principles when making all decisions. Under section 19(d), the aim must be now the 'best possible...outcomes' for children and young people in every case.

4.31 A similar duty to the section 19 duty can be found in section 149 of the Equality Act 2010, the 'Public Sector Equality Duty' (PSED) which is discussed in chapter 9 at paras 9.97–9.115. It is likely that the courts will draw on the extensive PSED case-law in interpreting the section 19 duty.

37 SEND Code chapter 1, p19.

Working together and sufficiency duties

4.32   CFA 2014 Part 3 includes a number of important duties on local authorities and their partners to work together. These duties continue a theme in children's legislation dating back to the Children Act 1989 (section 27) and the Children Act 2004 (section 10); see further chapter 2 at paras 2.52–2.55.

4.33   In particular, whenever local authorities are exercising any of their functions under Part 3 of CFA 2014, they must do so with a view to ensuring the integration of educational provision with health and social care provision where this would promote the well-being of children or young people in its area who have SEN or a disability or it would improve the quality of special educational provision.[38] 'Well-being' of children and young people includes:

(a) physical and mental health and emotional well-being;
(b) protection from abuse and neglect;
(c) control by them over their day-to-day lives;
(d) participation in education, training or recreation;
(e) social and economic well-being;
(f) domestic, family and personal relationships;
(g) the contribution made by them to society.[39]

4.34   Similarly, local authorities and their health partners must make joint commissioning arrangements for education, health and care provision for children and young people with SEN and disability.[40] This must include arrangements for securing EHC needs assessments, securing the education, health and care provision specified in EHC plans and agreeing personal budgets.[41] The duty to have joint commissioning arrangements is an important development, as it requires local authorities and their health partners to be able to demonstrate firm arrangements that are clearly documented.

4.35   The SEND Code states that joint commissioning arrangements should enable partners to make best use of all the resources available in an area to improve outcomes for children and young people in the most efficient, effective, equitable and sustainable way.[42] This

---

38 CFA 2014 s25(1). See further the SEND Code, para 3.70 requiring councillors and senior officers to 'co-operate ... to ensure the delivery of care and support is effectively integrated in the new SEN system'.

39 CFA 2014 s25(2).

40 CFA 2014 s26(1).

41 CFA2014 s26(4).

42 SEND Code, para 3.4 and Commissioning Support Programme, *Good commissioning: principles and practice*, September 2010.

duty will be particularly important for disabled children who need to access provision holistically from education, health and social care.

4.36   In order to ensure that joint commissioning is informed by a clear assessment of local needs, each local authority must have a Health and Wellbeing Board who have a duty to promote greater integration and partnership working, including through joint commissioning, integrated provision and pooled budgets.[43] In order to understand the needs of its local population, Health and Wellbeing Boards must carry out Joint Strategic Needs Assessments (JSNA) which should include consideration of the needs of children and young people with SEN and disability in order to agree outcomes and joint commissioning decisions.[44]

4.37   Local authorities are also under a duty to keep education (and care) provision for children and young people with SEN and disabilities under review and consider the extent to which provision is sufficient to meet the needs of children and young people its area and for whom it is responsible.[45] They must consult with a range of people and bodies, including children, parents and young people in order to comply with these duties.[46] This duty will be important for parents and young people where there are concerns in a local area that provision may not be sufficient to meet needs. The assessment of sufficiency under CFA 2014 s27 must be informed by the comments made on the 'local offer' for the relevant area, see paras 4.72–4.78 below. As such it is vital that children, young people and parents use the 'local offer' comment facility to provide feedback on any gaps in the quality or quantity of local provision.

4.38   In addition, health bodies have a duty to bring certain children to the local authority's attention. This duty applies where a CCG, NHS trust or NHS Foundation trust forms the opinion that a child has, or probably has special educational needs or a disability. Where this arises, the health body must inform the child's parent that they have formed that opinion and give them the opportunity to discuss and then bring their opinion to the attention of the appropriate local authority.[47] By bringing the child to the attention of the local authority, this would then trigger the local authority's duty to consider when

---

43 SEND Code, para 3.21.
44 Local Government and Public Involvement in Health Act 2007 s116B.
45 CFA 2014 s27.
46 CFA 2014 s27(3).
47 CFA 2014 s23.

an assessment of the education, health and care needs is required (see below at paras 4.110–4.133).[48]

4.39   Parents, children and young people frequently face difficulties in ensuring that local authorities and their partners work together effectively and can face delays in accessing provision as result. The working together provisions under CFA 2014 include specific duties in relation to co-operation and assistance. In particular, a local authority must co-operate with its local partners and each of its local partners must co-operate with the local authority when carrying out any functions under CFA 2014 Part 3.[49] Partners include district councils, schools, youth offending teams and CCGs.[50]

4.40   These duties also extend to officers within the local authority to ensure that there is co-operation between education and social services departments.[51]

4.41   Finally, CFA 2014 s31 creates a duty to ensure co-operation in individual cases, similar to the duty imposed by Children Act 1989 s27 in relation to social care decisions for children 'in need' generally (see chapter 2 at para 2.55). Section 31 allows a local authority to request the co-operation of a wide range of partners including health bodies in any individual case. The partner body must comply with the request, unless they consider that doing so would (a) be incompatible with their duties, or (b) otherwise have an adverse effect on the exercise of their functions.[52] A person or body that decides not to comply with a request under section 31 must give the authority that made the request written reasons for the decision.[53]

Implementation and transfer to the new system

4.42   From 1 September 2014, all new entrants to the system (children and young people with SEN who do not yet have a statement or LDA) were able to access statutory assessments and plans in accordance with the new scheme under CFA 2014 Part 3. No new requests for assessments for statements under the Education Act ('EA') 1996 or LDAs under the Learning and Skills Act ('LSA') 2000 could be made

48   CFA 2014 s36.
49   CFA 2014 s28(1).
50   CFA 2014 s28(2).
51   CFA 2014 s28(3).
52   CFA 2014 s31(2).
53   CFA 2014 s31(3).

from this date. The process for requesting EHC needs assessments and plans for new entrants is set out at paras 4.110–4.163 below.

4.43   Children and young people that already have a statement or LDA should be transferred to the new scheme in accordance with the Department of Education's advice 'Transition to the new 0 to 25 special educational needs and disability system: Departmental advice for local authorities and their partners' September 2015 ('transition advice'), currently (November 2015) in its third edition.

4.44   All children and young people with statements of SEN must be transferred to new EHC plans by April 2018.[54] For young people with LDAs, the deadline for transfer is September 2016.[55] The legal test for an EHC plan remains the same as that for a statement under the EA 1996.[56] Accordingly, the government has stated that it expects that 'all those who have a statement of SEN and who would have continued to have one under the current system will be transferred to an EHC plan – no-one should lose their statement and not have it replaced with an EHC plan simply because the system is changing'.[57]

Statements of SEN during the transition period

4.45   Until 1 April 2018, for children and young people with existing statements and LDAs who are awaiting transfer, local authorities must continue to comply with the legal framework under the EA 1996 and the statement and old law continues to have affect until the transfer process has been completed.[58] During this transition period, local authorities must continue to maintain statements and review them at least annually.

4.46   Parents will also be able to request re-assessments of children and young people with statements under the EA 1996 pending transfer to an EHC plan. In these circumstances, local authorities can agree to conduct an EHC needs assessment instead of a re-assessment under the EA 1996 where it is appropriate to do to so and agreed by child's parent or young person.[59] The transition advice states that local authorities are encouraged to use this power where they can

---

54 Transition advice, para 2.1.
55 Transition advice, para 1.9.
56 CFA 2014 s37(1), and see further para 4.134 below.
57 Transition advice, para 1.8.
58 Children and Families Act 2014 (Transitional and Saving Provisions) (No 2) Order 2014 SI No 2270 Pt 5.
59 Children and Families Act 2014 (Transitional and Saving Provisions) (No 2) Order 2014 SI No 2270 art 23.

as it will allow children and young people to benefit from the new system earlier than planned and also help to reduce the burden of outstanding transfers.[60]

4.47   Where a request for a re-assessment of a statement is made, local authorities must inform the parents of their decision within six weeks. Re-assessments must be carried out where an assessment has not taken place within the last six months and it is necessary for the local authority to carry out an assessment.[61] This could include where there has been a change in the child's needs or the provision is no longer suitable.[62]

4.48   Up until the point where a local authority provides formal notice in writing that the 'Transfer Review' process to an EHC plan has started, parents and young people can continue to exercise rights of appeal to the First-tier Tribunal (Special Educational Needs and Disability) ('the tribunal')[63] in relation to:

- the description of needs in Part 2 of the statement;[64]
- the provision in Part 3 of the statement;[65]
- the school named in Part 4 of the statement;[66]
- if no school is named in Part 4 of the statement;[67]
- if the local authority refuses to change the name of the school following a parental request where the statement is at least one year old;[68]
- situations where the local authority refuses to carry out a re-assessment, provided an assessment has not taken place in the last six months;[69]
- situations where the local authority decides not to amend the statement following a re-assessment;[70]
- situations where the local authority decides not to amend the statement following an annual or other review;[71] and

60 Transition advice, para 3.9.
61 Education Act 1996 s329.
62 Department for Education and Skills, *SEN Code of Practice*, 2001, para 7.68.
63 Children and Families Act 2014 (Transitional and Saving Provisions) (No 2) Order 2014 SI No 2270 arts 8–10 and 19.
64 Education Act 1996 s326(1A)(a).
65 Education Act 1996 s326(1A)(b).
66 Education Act 1996 s326(1A)(b).
67 Education Act 1996 s326(1A)(c).
68 Education Act 1996 Sch 27 para 8(3)(b).
69 Education Act 1996 s328(3)(b).
70 Education Act 1996 s326(1)(c).
71 Education Act 1996 s328A(3).

- situations where the local authority ceases to maintain a statement.[72]

4.49 The procedure and time limits for appeals to the tribunal are described at paras 4.242–4.248 below.

4.50 Where an appeal to the tribunal has been issued, the local authority cannot commence the Transfer Review process until the conclusion of tribunal appeal.[73]

Local transition plans and timing of transfers

4.51 Provided all transfers take place before 1 April 2018, and subject to specific national requirements described at para 4.53 below, each local authority has discretion to determine when children and young people will be transferred to the new system during the transition period. The process for each local authority should be set out in a 'Local Transition Plan' which should include:

- information about who has been consulted in the development of the plan;
- the numbers of children and young people expected to transfer each year during transition;
- the order in which children and young people will be transferred;
- details of transfer review process;
- sources of independent information and advice.[74]

4.52 Local authorities should publish their Local Transition Plan on their website alongside the local offer (see paras 4.72–4.78 below).[75]

4.53 Between 1 September 2015 and 31 March 2018, local authorities must transfer the following groups of children and young people each year:

- children in year 9;
- children and young people leaving youth custody; and
- children and young people prior to moving from:
  - relevant early years settings to school (including where the child remains at the same institution),
  - infant to junior school,

---

72 Education Act 1996 Sch 27 para 11(2)(b).
73 Children and Families Act 2014 (Transitional and Savings Provisions) (No 2) Order 2014 art 16.
74 Transition advice, para 4.6.
75 Transition advice, para 4.7.

- primary to middle school,
- primary to secondary school,
- middle to secondary school,
- school (including school sixth forms) to a post-16 institution or an apprenticeship,
- mainstream school to special school, or
- special school to mainstream school.[76]

4.54   In addition to the above, between 1 September 2016 and 31 March 2018, the following groups of children and young people should be transferred:

- all children in Year 6;
- all children in Year 11;
- those moving from one local authority to another;
- children and young people who still have a non-statutory EHC plan (issued as part of the pilot of the new scheme prior to 1 September 2014).[77]

4.55   Where the transfer cannot be completed before 1 April 2018 (for example because of an ongoing tribunal appeal in relation to a statement), the provision set out in Part 3 of the plan will be treated as if it were specified in an EHC plan and the local authority must ensure that an EHC assessment is carried out and concluded as soon as reasonably practicable.[78]

Transfer process from statements to EHC plans

4.56   The process by which statements are transferred to an EHC plan is called the 'Transfer Review'.

4.57   A local authority must notify the child's parent or young person two weeks prior to the start of the transfer review process commencing. Once notice has been provided, the provisions under the EA 1996 in relation to appeals to the tribunal, reviews and re-assessments cease to apply, although a local authority must continue to maintain the statement (and ensure the special educational provision in Part 3 is delivered) until the final EHC plan is issued.[79]

---

76 Children and Families Act 2014 (Transitional and Saving Provisions) (No 2) Order 2014 SI No 2270 art 14.

77 Transition advice, para 4.13.

78 Children and Families Act 2014 (Transitional and Saving Provisions) (No 2) Order 2014 SI No 2270 art 17.

79 Transition advice, para 5.7.

4.58   The transfer review process must then be completed and an EHC plan issued within a further 18 weeks – so 20 weeks in total.[80] This is the maximum timescale that is allowed and steps must be completed as soon as practicable. Local authorities do not need to comply with these time limits in certain circumstances, including where advice has been requested during summer holidays, exceptional circumstances affecting the child, child's parents or young person, or they have been out of the local authority area for more than four weeks continuously during the transfer period.[81]

4.59   The timescales for transfer were originally set at 14 weeks but were extended on 1 September 2015 following an announcement made by the Minister, Edward Timpson MP at the beginning of the summer.[82] In a letter to Directors of Children's Services in July 2015 the Minister explained his reasons for extending the timescales:

> Transferring Statements and LDAs to EHC plans is a significant task that needs to be done well. Simply rebadging statements and LDAs as EHC plans isn't an option. We need to ensure that the needs of children and young people are properly identified and met. ... I have heard that the current timescales are putting a strain on the system that risks undermining the quality of person-centred assessment and EHC plans. We need to ensure that the needs of children and young people are properly identified and met through the provision you put in place; and that the processes enable you to undertake the task efficiently and to a high standard.

4.60   The government's transition advice states that in the academic year within which the local authority intends to transfer the child or young person from a statement to the new system, the transfer review should replace the annual review of the statement.[83] Where the transfer review does replace the annual review it must be completed within 12 months of the date the statement of SEN was issued or of the previous annual review of the child or young person's statement.[84]

4.61   As part of the transfer review process, the local authority must carry out an EHC needs assessment. The requirements for an EHC needs assessment are set out at paras 4.110–4.133 below. Parents and young people who are transferring from a statement may agree with the local authority to use existing advices and assessments where

---

80 Transition advice, para 5.2.
81 Transition advice, para 5.5. See further para 4.133 below.
82 Children and Families Act 2014 (Transitional and Saving Provisions) (Amendment) (No.2) Order 2015 SI No 1619.
83 See DfE Newsletter to Local Authorities at 14, October 2014.
84 Transition advice, para 4.15.

appropriate although it will be important to ensure that the advices are up to date and properly consider the requirements of an EHC plan and in particular the focus on outcomes. Parents are not obliged to agree to use existing assessments/advices and if they consider that fresh assessments/advices are required then the local authority must obtain these during the transfer review.

4.62   There has been significant confusion about this issue in many local areas but the position is clear – new advice must be obtained as part of the transfer review process unless all parties, including the parent(s), agree that previous advice is sufficient. Parents may well not agree to rely on previous advice, not least because it is unlikely to focus on outcomes, which are central to the new scheme. Previous advice may also be significantly out-of-date.

4.63   There must also be meeting between the local authority and the parents or young person as part of the transfer review process. In practice this meeting is often facilitated by the child or young person's school and will take the place of the annual review meeting. The meeting itself can take place at any stage during the transfer review process. Some local authorities will hold the meeting at the start in order to discuss the process and agree what advices/assessments should be obtained. Alternatively, local authorities might convene the meeting once all of the advices/assessments are received and a draft EHC plan has been issued to enable parents or the young person to provide their views.

4.64   Where a transfer review is conducted within 12 months of a transfer between phases of education, the local authority must complete the transfer review before:

- 31 March in the calendar year of the child or young person's transfer from secondary school to a post-16 institution; and
- 15 February in the calendar year of the child's transfer in any other case.[85]

4.65   During the transition period, a child or young person's statement must remain in place until:

- after the period within which a parent can register an appeal with the tribunal following a local authority's decision to cease the statement of SEN; or, if an appeal is registered, after the appeal has been determined;
- the statement of SEN is ceased because the young person leaves school;

85 SEND Regs 2014 reg 18.

- the transfer review has been completed for the child or young person and an EHC plan has been issued; or
- after the period within which a child's parent or young person can register an appeal following a local authority's decision not to secure an EHC plan and to cease to maintain the statement following a transfer review; or, if an appeal is registered, after a determination that an EHC plan is not required.[86]

4.66   The transfer review process will be formally concluded at the point that the finalised EHC plan is sent to the child's parent or young person, the school or other institution named in the plan and the responsible CCG or, where the local authority has notified the child's parent or young person of its decision that an EHC plan will not be issued and that it is proposing to cease to maintain the statement of SEN. From the point that the Transfer Review commences, parents and young people will have appeal rights under the new system. Appeal rights relating to statements of SEN under the 1996 Act will no longer be available to parents.[87]

Transfer process for young people with learning difficulty assessments

4.67   The process for transfer for young people with an LDA is different to that for children with a statement.

4.68   The transition advice states that until 31 August 2016 a young person up to the age of 25 in further education or training who receives support to meet his or her SEN as a result of an LDA and who does not intend to continue in further education or training beyond that period can choose either to:

- continue to receive support as a result of the LDA (where it is still required) until the end of his or her time in further education or training or until 1 September 2016, whichever comes first; or
- request an EHC needs assessment.[88]

4.69   If a young person intends to continue in education beyond 31 August 2016 they can choose either to:

- continue for the time being to receive their support as a result of their LDA (where it is still required); or
- request an EHC needs assessment.[89]

86 Transition advice, para 3.3.
87 Transition advice, paras 5.16–5.17.
88 Transition advice, para 4.21.
89 Transition advice, para 4.23.

4.70   During academic year 2015/16 local authorities must consider whether an EHC needs assessment is required for those young people who continue to receive their support as a result of their LDAs and that they believe will remain in further education or training beyond 31 August 2016.[90]

4.71   There are also separate arrangements for the transfer process for those in youth custody that are described in detail in the transitions advice at Part 6. See the discussion of the new scheme for detained young persons with SEN at paras 4.199–4.201 below.

The local offer

4.72   Under CFA 2014 s30, each local authority must publish a 'local offer' which sets out in one place information about provision they expect to be available across education, health and social care for children and young people in their area who have SEN or are disabled. One of the central purposes of this requirement is to make provision more responsive to local needs by directly involving children and young people and their parents in its development.[91] The 'local offer' is fundamental to the success of the reforms, given that a significant majority of disabled children and children with SEN will not have an EHC plan. A local authority must keep its 'local offer' under review and may from time to time revise it.[92]

4.73   The information that must be published in the 'local offer' is set out at regulation 53 of and Schedule 2 to the SEND Regs 2014. The regulations require detailed and comprehensive information including:

- the special educational provision and training provision which the local authority expects to be available in its area for children and young people in its area who have special educational needs or a disability;
- arrangements for identifying SEN;
- securing services, provision and equipment;
- approaches to teaching and adapting curriculum;
- provision to assist with preparation for adulthood and independent living;
- transport arrangements;

90 Transition advice, para 4.24.
91 SEND Code, para 4.2.
92 CFA 2014 s30(5).

- sources of information, advice and support;
- complaints procedures and mediation;
- information about availability of personal budgets;
- information about any criteria that must be satisfied before any provision or service set out in the local offer can be provided.

4.74 When preparing and reviewing its 'local offer', local authorities must consult a wide range of specified persons, including children, young people and parents, but also governing bodies of maintained schools, advisory boards of children's centres and CCGs.[93]

4.75 The consultation with children, young people and parents must include consultation about:

- the services children and young people with special educational needs or a disability require;
- how the information in the local offer is to be set out when published;
- how the information in the local offer will be available for those people without access to the Internet;
- how the information in the local offer will be accessible to those with special educational needs or a disability; and
- how they can provide comments on the local offer.[94]

4.76 The local authority must seek and publish at least annually comments on the 'local offer' from children, young people and parents. Comments can be made on 'the content of [the] local offer, including the quality of the provision that is included and any provision that is not included'.[95]

4.77 The 'local offer' must be published by placing it on the local authority's website.[96] Arrangements must also be made to enable (i) people without access to the Internet and (ii) different groups, including people with special educational needs or a disability to obtain a copy.[97]

4.78 The importance of ensuring 'local offers' meet these requirements was emphasised by the High Court in *R (L and P) v Warwickshire County Council*, where the local authority's proposed 'local offer' was the was found to fall 'a considerable distance short of the

---

93 SEND Regs 2014 reg 54.
94 SEND Regs 2014 reg 55.
95 SEND Regs 2014 reg 56.
96 SEND Regs 2014 reg 57.
97 SEND Regs 2014 reg 57(b).

statutory requirements'.[98] This was because there was no provision identified in the majority of the categories set out in Schedule 2 to the regulations.

Duties on schools

4.79   Schools and colleges and other educational institutions have wide ranging duties to identify and support children with SEN and disabilities, whether or not they have an EHC plan.

4.80   The key duties that are described in this chapter only apply to the following schools and other institutions in England unless otherwise stated:

- mainstream schools (which includes mainstream academies);
- maintained nursery schools;
- 16 to 19 academies;
- alternative provision academies;
- institutions within the further education sector;
- pupil referral units.

4.81   There are separate regulations governing non maintained (independent) schools.[99]

4.82   The duties owed by educational institutions are in general the responsibility of the 'appropriate authority'. For a maintained school, maintained nursery school, or institution within the further education sector, this will be the governing body. In the case of an Academy, this will be the proprietor/owner. For pupil referral units, the appropriate authority will be the management committee. It is important to identify who the 'appropriate authority' is in order to ensure that any concerns about compliance with these important duties are raised with the correct body.

Key duties

4.83   Under CFA 2014 s66(2), schools and other educational institutions must use their best endeavours to secure that the special educational provision called for by the pupil's or student's special educational needs is made. This duty applies to all children with SEN, including

---

98 [2015] EWHC 203 (Admin); (2015) 18 CCLR 458 at [78].

99 Non-Maintained Special Schools (England) Regulations 2015 SI No 728. See further, Department for Education, *The Non-Maintained (Special) Schools Regulations: Departmental advice for non-maintained special schools*, August 2015.

those without an EHC plan. This duty replaces section 317(1)(a) of the Education Act 1996 and expands its remit to further education institutions, academy schools and 16 to 19 academies. Where special educational provision is made for a child or young people at maintained school, a maintained nursery school, an Academy school, an alternative provision Academy or a pupil referral unit and no EHC plan is in place, the appropriate authority must ensure that the child's parent or the young person is informed.[100]

4.84   All schools and post 16 institutions are under a duty to co-operate with each responsible local authority, and each responsible local authority must co-operate with their partners, in the exercise of their functions.[101] This would include, for example, a request for advice for the purposes of an EHC needs assessments.

4.85   In addition, maintained nurseries and mainstream schools must ensure that children with SEN engage in the activities of the school together with children who do not have special educational needs.[102] However, this duty applies only in so in so far as is reasonably practicable and is compatible with:

- the child receiving the special educational provision called for by his or her special educational needs[103] – for example, the child may need 1:1 or small group work which takes them away the classroom for certain periods;
- the provision of efficient education for the children with whom he or she will be educated[104] – this exception should only be used rarely where there it is not possible for any adjustments to be made to avoid the incapability;[105] and
- the efficient use of resources.[106]

4.86   There are also a number of supplemental obligations on schools which are set out in the SEND Code. These include:

- Equality and inclusion: paragraph 6.8 of the SEND Code says that schools should regularly review and evaluate the breadth and impact of the support they offer or can access. Schools must co-operate with the local authority in reviewing the provision that is

---

100 CFA 2014 s68.
101 CFA 2014 s29(3).
102 CFA 2014 s35(2).
103 CFA 2014 s35(3)(a).
104 CFA 2014 s35(3)(b).
105 See paras 4.95–4.103 below and chapter 9 at paras 9.71–9.78 for the duty to make reasonable adjustments under the Equality Act 2010.
106 CFA 2014 s35(3)(c).

available locally and in developing the local offer. Schools should also collaborate with other local education providers to explore how different needs can be met most effectively. They must have due regard to general duties to promote disability equality, in other words the PSED (see chapter 9 at paras 9.97–9.115).

- Careers guidance for children and young people: paragraph 6.13 of the SEND Code states that maintained schools and pupil referral units must ensure that pupils from Year 8 until Year 13 are provided with independent careers guidance. Academies are also subject to this duty through their funding agreements.
- Identifying SEN in schools: paragraphs 6.14 to 6.35 of the SEND Code states all schools should have a clear approach to identifying and responding to SEN and should seek to identify pupils making less than expected progress given their age and individual circumstances, focusing on four broad areas of need:
  - communication and interaction;
  - cognition and learning;
  - social, emotional and mental health difficulties;
  - sensory and/or physical needs.
- The SEND Code states at para 6.63 that 'where, despite the school having taken relevant and purposeful action to identify, assess and meet the SEN of the child or young person, the child or young person has not made expected progress, the school or parents should consider requesting an Education, Health and Care needs assessment. To inform its decision the local authority will expect to see evidence of the action taken by the school as part of SEN support.'
- Involving parents and pupils in planning and reviewing progress: paragraphs 6.64 to 6.71 of the SEND Code states that schools must provide an annual report for parents on their child's progress. A record of the outcomes, action and support agreed through the discussion should be kept and shared with all the appropriate school staff. This record should be given to the pupil's parents. The school's management information system should be updated as appropriate.

The role of the SENCO

4.87   In mainstream schools and maintained nursery schools there is a duty on the appropriate authority to designate a member of staff at the school (to be known as the 'SEN co-ordinator' or 'SENCO') as having responsibility for co-ordinating the provision for pupils with special educational needs.[107] The SENCO will play a central role in ensuring that children and young people receive the special educational provision that they require.

4.88 It will be for the appropriate authority of the school to determine the particular role and functions of the SENCO but they may include a range of tasks including selecting, supervising and training learning support assistants, advising teachers at the school about differentiated teaching methods, and identifying the pupil's special educational needs and co-ordinating the making of special educational provision which meets those needs.[108]

4.89 SENCOs must also now meet minimum requirements for qualification and experience. This includes that they have been a qualified teacher working at the school and has been a SENCO for at least twelve months or has a postgraduate qualification in special educational needs co-ordination, for the time being known as 'The National Award for Special Educational Needs Co-ordination', awarded by a recognised body.[109]

SEN information reports

4.90 The governing bodies of maintained schools and maintained nursery schools and the proprietors of Academy schools are also now required to prepare a report containing SEN information (known as the SEN information report) about the implementation of its policy for pupils at the school with special educational needs.[110]

4.91 The information that must be contained in the SEN information report is set out in Schedule 1 to the SEND Regs 2014 and includes, for example:

- the kinds of special educational needs for which provision is made at the school;
- information in relation to mainstream schools and maintained nursery schools, about the school's policies for the identification and assessment of pupils with special educational needs;
- information about the school's policies for making provision for pupils with special educational needs whether or not pupils have EHC plans;
- information on where the local authority's local offer is published.

107 CFA 2014 s67(2).
108 SEND Regs 2014 reg 50.
109 SEND Regs 2014 reg 49.
110 SEND Regs 2014 regs 51–52.

4.92   The SEN information report must be published on the school's website.[111] It should act as an important reference point for parents and young people when deciding which school they wish to apply to attend or ask to be named in the EHC plan.

Duty to support pupils with medical conditions

4.93   CFA 2014 s100 introduced a new legal duty on maintained schools and academies to make arrangements to support pupils with medical conditions.

4.94   Statutory guidance[112] published in April 2014 on 'Supporting pupils at school with medical conditions' sets out arrangements for Individual Healthcare Plans and other key duties including:

- The school should have a named person with overall responsibility for policy implementation;
- All schools must develop a policy for supporting pupils with medical conditions that is reviewed regularly and is readily accessible to parents and school staff. The policy must include:
  - the procedures to be followed whenever a school is notified that a pupil has a medical condition
  - the role of individual healthcare plans, and who is responsible for their development, in supporting pupils at school with medical conditions
  - arrangements for children who are competent to manage their own health needs and medicines
  - the procedures to be followed for managing medicines
  - what should happen in an emergency situation
  - details of what is considered to be unacceptable practice (examples are provided in the guidance)
  - how complaints may be made and will be handled concerning the support provided to pupils with medical conditions.

Duties under the Equality Act 2010

4.95   Many children and young people with SEN will be disabled and will benefit from having the 'protected characteristic' of disability under the Equality Act 2010. This means that they have a right not to be discriminated against and can enforce a legal duty to make reasonable

---

111 SEND Regs 2014 reg 52.
112 See CFA 2014 s100(2) for the obligation on appropriate authorities to 'have regard' to this guidance.

adjustments on a wide range of bodies, including schools and other providers of education.

4.96 This duty is not limited to schools and extends to all educational bodies that a child or young person might attend who are required to make adjustments to their policies and their premises and to provide auxiliary aids and services to avoid young people with disabilities being placed at a substantial disadvantage.

4.97 The reasonable adjustments duty requires those subject to it to anticipate the likely needs of disabled learners and take steps that are reasonable to meet those needs – with the cost of those reasonable steps to be met by the body concerned.

4.98 A failure to make a reasonable adjustment amounts to unlawful discrimination and can be challenged in a court or tribunal.

4.99 The reasonable adjustments duty requires action in the following three areas; policies, physical features and auxiliary aids or services. This means that the education provider must undertake an assessment of the young person's needs and what detriment is being caused to them by the relevant policy or physical feature or the failure to provide the relevant aid.

4.100 In deciding whether an adjustment is reasonable, the educational body can take into account the cost of the adjustment sought, the organisation's resources and size and the availability of financial support.

4.101 Other duties under the Equality Act 2010 include a prohibition on direct discrimination (refusing to provide a service because the person is disabled) and on treating a person less favourably because of a reason connected with their disability without justification (described as 'discrimination arising from disability').

4.102 Further details in relation to duties under Equality Act 2010 are set out in chapter 9 at paras 9.71–9.87. There is a range of guidance about the implications of the Equality Act 2010 for schools and education providers from the Equality and Human Rights Commission.[113] There is also a guide to the Equality Act 2010 for schools that is specific to disabled children published by the Council for Disabled Children.[114]

---

113 For example EHRC, *Technical Guidance for Schools in England*, last updated July 2014.

114 P Stobbs, *Disabled Children and the Equality Act 2010: What teachers need to know and what schools need to do, including responsibilities to disabled children and young people under the Children and Families Act 2014*, Council for Disabled Children, March 2015.

SEN support – early years, schools, colleges

4.103 In January 2015, 15.4 per cent of pupils in schools in England have identified SEN (equating to 1,301,445 pupils) and 2.8 per cent of pupils in schools in England have statements or an EHC plan (equating to 236,165 pupils).[115] The majority of children with SEN will therefore not have a statement or EHC plan and their needs will be met through a scheme of 'SEN support',[116] a graduated approach to identifying and supporting pupils of SEN which will extend to young people in further education colleges/sixth forms.

4.104 Detailed information in relation to the SEN support system at each stage is set out in SEND Code:

- early years – paragraphs 5.36 to 5.60;
- schools – paragraphs 6.44 to 6.99; and
- further education – paragraphs 7.13 to 7.34.

4.105 All early years settings, schools and post 16 institutions should adopt an 'assess, plan, do, review' cycle. The SEND Code states at para 6.44 that:

> where a pupil is identified as having SEN, schools should take action to remove barriers to learning and put effective special educational provision in place. This SEN support should take the form of a four-part cycle through which earlier decisions and actions are revisited, refined and revised with a growing understanding of the pupil's needs and of what supports the pupil in making good progress and securing good outcomes. This is known as the graduated approach. It draws on more detailed approaches, more frequent review and more specialist expertise in successive cycles in order to match interventions to the SEN of children and young people.

4.106 The SEND Code makes clear at para 5.44 that:

> This cycle of action should be revisited in increasing detail and with increasing frequency, to identify the best way of securing good progress. At each stage parents should be engaged with the setting, contributing their insights to assessment and planning. Importantly, class and subject teachers are still responsible even when the pupil is away from the main class for parts of their provision.

4.107 All school and academy sixth forms, sixth form colleges, further education colleges and 16–19 academies are provided with resources to

---

115 Department for Education, *Statistical First Release: Special educational needs in England*, January 2015.

116 SEN support replaced School Action and School Action Plus following the implementation of the new scheme from 1 September 2014.

support students with additional needs, including young people with SEN and disabilities.[117]

4.108   SEN support requires support for transitions between schools and phases of education. Paragraph 5.47 of the SEND Code states that:

> SEN support should include planning and preparing for transition, before a child moves into another setting or school. This can also include a review of the SEN support being provided or the EHC plan. To support the transition, information should be shared by the current setting (in agreement with parents) with the receiving setting or school.

4.109   The guidance in the SEND Code on when schools or settings should seek an EHC plan is as follows:

> Where, despite the setting having taken relevant and purposeful action to identify, assess and meet the special educational needs of the child, the child has not made expected progress, the setting should consider requesting an EHC needs assessment.[118]

Education, health and care needs assessments

4.110   An EHC needs assessment for a child or young person aged between 0 and 25 can be requested by:

- the child's parent
- a young person over the age of 16 but under the age of 25,[119] and
- a person acting on behalf of a school or post-16 institution (the SEND Code states that this should be with the knowledge and agreement of the parent or young person where possible).[120]

4.111   The SEND Code states at para 9.9 that:

> In addition, anyone else can bring a child or young person who has (or may have) SEN to the attention of the local authority, particularly where they think an EHC needs assessment may be necessary. This could include, for example, foster carers, health and social care professionals, early years practitioners, youth offending teams or probation services, those responsible for education in custody, school or college

---

117 SEND Code, para 7.28.
118 SEND Code, para 5.49.
119 Where a young person lacks capacity, a request for an assessment must be made on their behalf by an 'alternative person', ie a parent or 'representative', see chapter 11 at paras 11.83–11.87.
120 CFA 2014 s36(1).

staff or a family friend. This should be done with the knowledge and, where possible, agreement of the child's parent or the young person. Where a child or young person has been brought to the local authority's attention, they must determine whether an EHC needs assessment is required.[121]

4.112   There is a right to request an assessment up to the young person's 25th birthday.[122]

Criteria for assessment

4.113   CFA 2014 s36 provides that when a request for an EHC needs assessment for a child or young person is made, the local authority must determine whether it may be necessary for special educational provision to be made for the child or young person in accordance with an EHC plan.

4.114   In making this determination, the local authority must consult the child's parent or the young person as soon as practical after receiving a request and notify the parent or young person that they have the right to express views to the authority (orally or in writing) and submit evidence.[123]

4.115   Where a local authority is considering whether to secure an EHC needs assessment, it must also notify:

- the responsible CCG;
- the officers of the local authority who exercise the local authority's social services functions for children or young people with special educational needs;
- in relation to a child, the head teacher of the school the child or if the child receives education from a provider of relevant early years education, the person identified as having responsibility for special educational needs (if any) in relation to that provider;
- in relation to a young person, the head teacher of the school or if the young person is a student at a post-16 institution, to the principal of that institution.[124]

4.116   The local authority must secure an EHC needs assessment for the child or young person if, after regard to the views of the parent or

---

121 CFA 2014 s36(3).
122 SEND Code, para 9.115.
123 SEND Regs 2014 reg 3.
124 SEND Regs 2014 reg 4(2).

young person and evidence submitted, the local authority is of the opinion that:

    (a) the child or young person has or may have special educational needs, and

    (b) it may be necessary for special educational provision to be made for the child or young person in accordance with an EHC plan.[125]

4.117   In relation to a young person over the age of 18, the local authority must consider whether he or she requires additional time, in comparison to the majority of others of the same age who do not have special educational needs, to complete his or her education or training.[126]

4.118   Paragraph 9.14 of the SEND Code sets out factors which local authorities must pay particular attention to when determining whether an EHC needs assessment is required. These include:

- academic attainment and rates of progress;
- nature, extent and context of the child or young person's SEN;
- evidence of action already being taken by placement;
- evidence that where progress has been made, it is only as a result of additional intervention and support above that usually provided;
- evidence of physical, emotional and social development and health needs.

4.119   Local authorities may develop criteria to help them decide whether to carry out an EHC assessment but must be prepared to depart from criteria where there are good reasons to do so.[127] They must not apply a blanket policy to particular groups/types of needs and must consider the child or young person's needs individually and on their merits, applying the tests in section 36.

4.120   Where the local authority determines that it is not necessary for special educational provision to be made in accordance with an EHC plan it must notify the child's parent or young person of:

- the reasons for the determination not to secure an EHC needs assessment;
- their right of appeal;
- the time limits for doing so;
- information concerning mediation;

---

125 CFA 2014 s36(8).
126 CFA 2014 s36(10).
127 SEND Code, para 9.16.

- the availability of disagreement resolution services and information and advice about matters relating to the special educational needs of children and young people.[128]

4.121   The local authority is not required to secure an EHC assessment if the child or young person has been assessed during the previous six months although can do so if it considers necessary.[129]

4.122   The local authority must make it determination regarding whether to secure an EHC needs assessment within six weeks of the request subject to exceptions outlined below.[130]

The assessment process

4.123   Where the local authority secures an EHC needs assessment for a child or young person, it must seek advice and information on the needs of the child or young person, what provision may be required to meet such needs and the outcomes that are intended to be achieved by the child or young person receiving that provision from the following persons on the following topics:

- the child's parent or the young person;
- manager, head teacher or principal of education institution;
- medical advice and information from a health care professional identified by the responsible commissioning body (usually the CCG);
- psychological advice and information from an educational psychologist;
- advice and information in relation to social care;
- any other person the local authority thinks is appropriate;
- any person the child's parents or young person reasonably request the local authority obtain advice from;
- from year 9 onwards – advice to assist with preparation for adulthood and independent living;
- where it appears that the child or young person is either visually or hearing impaired or both, the school or placement should consult with a person who is qualified to teach children or young people with visual or hearing impairment before they provide their advice.[131]

---

128 CFA 2014 s36(5) and SEND Regs 2014 reg 5(3).
129 SEND Regs 2014 reg 24.
130 SEND Regs 2014 reg 4(1).
131 SEND Regs 2014 reg 6.

4.124   When the local authority is requesting advice, they must provide the person or body with a copy of any representations made by the child's parent of the young person and any evidence submitted.[132]

4.125   Partners must respond within a maximum of 6 weeks of requests for advice,[133] although there are exceptions to the time limits as outlined at para 4.133 below.

4.126   SEND Regs 2014 reg 7 states that when securing an EHC needs assessment a local authority must:

- consult the child and the child's parent, or the young person and take into account their views, wishes and feelings;
- consider any information provided to the local authority by or at the request of the child, the child's parent or the young person;
- consider the information and advice obtained;
- engage the child and the child's parent, or the young person and ensure they are able to participate in decisions; and
- minimise disruption for the child, the child's parent, the young person and their family.

4.127   There is an emphasis in the SEND Code on ensuring all assessments have a person centred approach and there is effective co-ordination. Paragraph 9.22 states that the assessment and planning process should:

- focus on the child or young person as an individual;
- enable children and young people and their parents to express their views, wishes and feelings;
- enable children and young people and their parents to be part of the decision-making process;
- be easy for children, young people and their parents or carers to understand, and use clear ordinary language and images rather than professional jargon;
- highlight the child or young person's strengths and capabilities;
- enable the child or young person, and those that know them best to say what they have done, what they are interested in and what outcomes they are seeking in the future;
- tailor support to the needs of the individual;
- organise assessments to minimise demands on families;
- bring together relevant professionals to discuss and agree together the overall approach;

---

132 SEND Regs 2014 reg 6(3).
133 SEND Regs 2014 reg 8(1).

- deliver an outcomes-focused and co-ordinated plan for the child or young person and their parent;
- support and encourage the involvement of children, young people and parents or carers by:
  - providing them with access to the relevant information in accessible formats
  - giving them time to prepare for discussions and meetings, and
  - dedicating time in discussions and meetings to hear their views.

4.128   In addition, the local authority must not seek any of the advice referred to above if such advice has previously been provided for any purpose and the person providing that advice, the local authority and the child's parent or the young person are all satisfied that it is sufficient for the purposes of an EHC needs assessment.[134] See paras 4.61–4.62 above for the application of this provision to 'Transfer Reviews'.

4.129   When securing an EHC needs assessment the local authority must also consider whether the child's parent or the young person requires any information, advice and support in order to enable them to take part effectively in the EHC needs assessment, and if it considers that such information, advice or support is necessary, it must provide it.[135]

Timescales

4.130   If a local authority decides, following an EHC needs assessment, not to issue an EHC plan, it must inform the child's parent or young person within a maximum of 16 weeks from the request for an EHC needs assessment.[136]

4.131   Where the local authority decides to issue an EHC plan, the child's parent or young person must be provided with a draft plan and given 15 days to provide their views.[137]

4.132   The entire process of EHC needs assessment and EHC plan development, from the point when an assessment is requested (or a child

---

134 SEND Regs 2014 reg 6(4).
135 SEND Regs 2014 reg 4(9).
136 SEND Regs 2014 reg 10(1).
137 SEND Regs 2014 reg 13(1)(a).

or young person is brought to the local authority's attention) until the final EHC plan is issued, must take no more than 20 weeks.[138]

4.133 Where there are exceptional circumstances, it may not be reasonable to expect local authorities and others partners to comply with the time limits above. The SEND Regs 2014 set out specific exemptions. These include where:

- the local authority has requested advice from the head teacher or principal of a school or post-16 institution during a period beginning one week before any date on which that school or institution was closed for a continuous period of not less than four weeks from that date and ending one week before the date on which it re-opens;
- exceptional personal circumstances affect the child, the child's parent, or the young person during the time period; or
- the child, the child's parent, or the young person, are absent from the area of the authority for a continuous period of not less than four weeks during the time period referred to in paragraph.[139]

Education, health and care plans

4.134 CFA 2014 s37 states that a local authority must issue an EHC plan where, in the light of an EHC needs assessment, it is necessary for special educational provision to be made for a child or young person in accordance with an EHC plan.

4.135 Paragraph 9.54 and 9.55 of the SEND Code sets out the factors which local authorities should consider when deciding whether to issue a plan. These include:

- the child or young person's SEN and the special educational provision made for the child or young person;
- whether the information from the EHC needs assessment confirms the information available on the nature and extent of the child or young person's SEN prior to the EHC needs assessment; and
- whether the special educational provision made prior to the EHC needs assessment was well matched to the SEN of the child or young person.

138 SEND Regs 2014 reg 13(2).
139 SEND Regs 2014 regs 10(4) and 13(3).

4.136   Where, despite appropriate assessment and provision, the child or young person is not progressing, or not progressing sufficiently well, the local authority should consider what further provision may be needed. The local authority should take into account:

- whether the special educational provision required to meet the child or young person's needs can reasonably be provided from within the resources normally available to mainstream early years providers, schools and post-16 institutions; or
- whether it may be necessary for the local authority to make special educational provision in accordance with an EHC plan.[140]

4.137   Where a local authority decides it is necessary to issue an EHC plan, it must notify the child's parent or the young person and give the reasons for its decision.[141] The local authority should ensure it allows enough time to prepare the draft plan and complete the remaining steps in the process within the 20-week overall time limit within which it must issue the finalised EHC plan.[142]

Contents of the EHC plan

4.138   Paragraph 9.61 of the SEND Code sets out the key requirements and principles which apply to local authorities and those contributing to the preparation of an EHC plan. These include:

- EHC plans should be clear, concise, understandable and accessible and written so they can be understood by professionals in any local authority;
- EHC plans should be forward looking – for example, anticipating, planning and commissioning for important transition points in a child or young person's life, including planning and preparing for their transition to adult life.

4.139   The SEND Code states at para 9.62 that:

As a statutory minimum, EHC plans must include the following sections, which must be separately labelled from each other. The sections do not have to be in the order below and local authorities may use an action plan in tabular format to include different sections and demonstrate how provision will be integrated, as long as the sections are separately labelled.

---

140   SEND Code, para 9.56
141   CFA 2014 s36(9).
142   SEND Regs 2014 reg 13(2).

Format of EHC plan:

A the views, interests and aspirations of the child and his parents or the young person;

B the child or young person's special educational needs;

C the child or young person's health care needs which relate to their special educational needs;

D the child or young person's social care needs which relate to their special educational needs or to a disability;

E the outcomes sought for him or her;

F the special educational provision required by the child or young person;

G any health care provision reasonably required by the learning difficulties or disabilities which result in the child or young person having special educational needs;

H1 any social care provision which must be made for the child or young person as a result of section 2 of the Chronically Sick and Disabled Persons Act 1970 and

H2 any other social care provision reasonably required by the learning difficulties or disabilities which result in the child or young person having special educational needs (section H2);

I the name of the school, maintained nursery school, post-16 institution or other institution to be attended by the child or young person and the type of that institution or, where the name of a school or other institution is not specified in the EHC plan, the type of school or other institution to be attended by the child or young person; and

J where any special educational provision is to be secured by a direct payment, the special educational needs and outcomes to be met by the direct payment.

4.140 In addition, from year 9, the EHC plan must include (in sections F, G, H1 or H2 as appropriate) the provision required to assist in preparation for adulthood and independent living, for example, support for finding employment, housing or for participation in society.[143]

143 SEND Regs 2014 reg 12(3).

Outcomes

4.141   EHC plans must specify the outcomes sought for the child or young person in Section E.[144] This is a significant change from statements which lacked a focus on agreed outcomes. The outcomes section of an EHC plan is very important because the duty to maintain the plan after a young person's 18th birthday depends on whether the outcomes have been achieved. Despite their importance the outcomes section cannot however be appealed to the tribunal; the only legal remedy in relation to a flawed outcomes section of a plan is judicial review.

4.142   The SEND Code suggests at para 9.64 that:

> EHC plans should be focused on education and training, health and care outcomes that will enable children and young people to progress in their learning and, as they get older, to be well prepared for adulthood.

The SEND Code goes on to give the following general guidance on outcomes:

> EHC plans can also include wider outcomes such as positive social relationships and emotional resilience and stability. Outcomes should always enable children and young people to move towards the long-term aspirations of employment or higher education, independent living and community participation.

4.143   Paragraph 9.66 of the SEND Code provides a definition of outcomes as follows:

> An outcome can be defined as the benefit or difference made to an individual as a result of an intervention. It should be personal and not expressed from a service perspective; it should be something that those involved have control and influence over, and while it does not always have to be formal or accredited, it should be specific, measurable, achievable, realistic and time bound (SMART). When an outcome is focused on education or training, it will describe what the expected benefit will be to the individual as a result of the educational or training intervention provided.

4.144   Outcomes are not a description of the service being provided – for example the provision of speech and language therapy is not an outcome. The outcome is what it is intended that the speech and language therapy will help the individual to do that they cannot do now and by when this will be achieved.[145]

---

144 SEND Code, para 9.64.

145 SEND Code, para 9.66. For practical guidance, see Council for Disabled Children, *EHC Outcomes Pyramid*, September 2014.

4.145   In all cases, EHC plans must specify the special educational provision required to meet each of the child or young person's special educational needs. The provision should enable the outcomes to be achieved.[146]

4.146   The SEND Code addresses the relationship between shorter term targets and longer term outcomes at para 9.69:

> The EHC plan should also specify the arrangements for setting shorter term targets at the level of the school or other institution where the child or young person is placed. Professionals working with children and young people during the EHC needs assessment and EHC plan development process may agree shorter term targets that are not part of the EHC plan. These can be reviewed and, if necessary, amended regularly to ensure that the individual remains on track to achieve the outcomes specified in their EHC plan. Professionals should, wherever possible, append these shorter term plans and targets to the EHC plan so that regular progress monitoring is always considered in the light of the longer term outcomes and aspirations that the child or young person wants to achieve. In some exceptional cases, progress against these targets may well lead to an individual outcome within the EHC plan being amended at times other than following the annual review.

The draft EHC plan and requests for a particular school, college or other institution

4.147   Before issuing the final EHC plan, child's parents or the young person must be sent plans in draft and given 15 days to make representations including on particular school named.[147]

4.148   The SEND Code states at para 9.77 that when the local authority sends the draft EHC plan to the child's parent or the young person the following apply:

- The local authority must notify the child's parent or the young person that during this period they can request that a particular school or other institution, or type of school or other institution, be named in the plan. The draft plan must not contain the name of the school, maintained nursery school, post-16 institution or other institution or the type of school or other institution to be attended by the child or young person.[148]

---

146 SEND Code, para 9.68.
147 SEND Regs 2014 reg 13(1).
148 SEND Regs 2014 reg 13(1)(a)(i).

- The local authority must advise the child's parent or the young person where they can find information about the schools and colleges that are available for the child or young person to attend, for example through the local offer.[149]
- The local authority should also seek agreement of any Personal Budget specified in the draft plan.[150]

Placements under EHC plans

4.149   Where a particular school is requested, the local authority must consult with governing body and relevant local authority if out of area.[151]

4.150   The child's parent or the young person has the right to request a particular school, college or other institution of the following type to be named in their EHC plan:

- maintained nursery school;
- maintained school and any form of academy or free school (mainstream or special);
- further education or sixth form college;
- independent special school or independent specialist colleges (where they have been approved for this purpose by the Secretary of State and published in a list available to all parents and young people).[152]

4.151   CFA 2014 s39 provides that the local authority must name the requested school or other institution in the EHC plan names the school or other institution specified in the request, unless:

- the school is unsuitable for the age, ability, aptitude or SEN of the child or young person concerned; or
- the attendance of the child or young person at the requested school or other institution would be incompatible with:
  - the provision of efficient education for others, or
  - the efficient use of resources.

4.152   In determining whether attendance would be incompatible with the efficient use of resources, the local authority must consider the cost

---

149   SEND Regs 2014 reg 13(1)(b).
150   SEND Code, para 9.77.
151   CFA 2014 s39(2).
152   CFA 2014 ss38(3) and 41. Parents may also make representations for places in non-maintained early years provision and independent schools or colleges not on the approved list. These requests must be considered in accordance with EA 1996 s9. See SEND Code at para 9.84.

to the public purse generally when comparing the costs of the parents' requested school with the LA's own provision. The Upper Tribunal has clarified that:

- for maintained special schools and maintained specialist units, the place funding is ignored for the purposes of calculating relative placement cost;
- for maintained mainstream schools, the Age Weighted Pupil Unit (AWPU) is taken into account as an additional cost, as is any further funding provided to meet the child's needs.[153]

4.153   The SEND Code states at para 9.88 that where a parent or young person does not make a request for a particular nursery, school or college, or does so and their request is not met, the local authority must specify mainstream provision in the EHC plan unless it would be:

- against the wishes of the parent or young person; or
- incompatible with the efficient education of others.[154]

4.154   Mainstream education cannot be refused by a local authority on the grounds that it is not suitable: SEND Code, para 9.89.

4.155   If the local authority considers a particular mainstream place to be incompatible with the efficient education of others it must demonstrate that there are no reasonable steps that it, or the school or college, could take to prevent that incompatibility.[155]

Finalising and maintaining the EHC plan

4.156   Regulation 14 of the SEND Regs 2014 provides that the finalised EHC plan must be in the form of the draft plan, or in a form modified in the light of the representations made by the child's parent or young person.

4.157   When sending a copy of the finalised EHC plan to the child's parent or the young person, the local authority must notify them of:

- their right to appeal matters within the EHC plan;
- the time limits for doing so;
- the information concerning mediation;

---

153   *Hammersmith and Fulham LBC v L and F; O and H v Lancashire CC* [2015] UKUT 0523 (AAC), see summary at [6]-[9]. Although this was a decision in the context of Education Act 1996 s9 it would appear also to apply where the relevant statutory provision is CFA 2014 s39.

154   CFA 2014 s33(2).

155   CFA 2014 s33(3) and SEND Code, para 9.90.

- the availability of:
  - disagreement resolution services; and
  - advice and information about matters relating to the special educational needs of children and young people.[156]

4.158   CFA 2014 s42(2) provides that local authorities must secure the specified special educational provision in the EHC plan. Section 43 requires any of a wide range of schools, colleges and institutions to admit a child or young person if named in their EHC plan. If a local authority names an independent school or independent college in the plan as special educational provision it must also meet the costs of the fees, including any boarding and lodging where relevant.[157]

4.159   The specific duties in relation to maintaining the health and social care aspects of the plans are summarised in chapters 5 and 3 respectively.

Ceasing to maintain the EHC plan

4.160   Decisions to cease to maintain an EHC plan are governed by CFA 2014 s45. There are only two bases on which a local authority can decide to cease to maintain a plan:

- the authority is no longer responsible for the child or young person; or
- the authority determines that it is no longer necessary for the plan to be maintained.[158] The circumstances in which it is no longer necessary for an EHC plan to be maintained for a child or young person include where the child or young person no longer requires the special educational provision specified in the plan.[159]

4.161   Importantly, section 45(3) is clear that in deciding whether a young person over 18 no longer requires the special educational provision specified in the plan, 'a local authority must have regard to whether the educational or training outcomes specified in the plan have been achieved'. This is why the outcomes section of any plan is of critical importance, particularly a plan for a child who is approaching transition to adulthood.

4.162   If there is a decision to cease to maintain a plan, it must continue to be maintained until the end of the period allowed for bringing an

---

156 SEND Regs 2014 reg 14(2).
157 SEND Code, para 9.131.
158 CFA 2014 s45(1).
159 CFA 2014 s45(2).

appeal under section 51 against its decision to cease to maintain the plan or until the appeal is finally determined.[160]

4.163   Specific circumstances where a local authority must not cease to maintain a plan are set out in regulations 29–30 of the SEND Regs 2014. The procedure which must be followed in determining whether to cease to maintain a plan is mandated by regulation 31. In particular, the local authority must:

- inform the child's parent or the young person that it is considering ceasing to maintain the child or young person's EHC plan;
- consult the child's parent or the young person; and
- consult the head teacher, principal or equivalent person at the educational institution that is named in the EHC plan.

Reviews

4.164   CFA 2014 s44 requires local authorities to review EHC plans every 12 months starting on the date the plan was first made. Regulation 18 of the SEND Regs 2014 provides further specific circumstances where plans must be reviewed (see paras 4.165–4.167)

4.165   Where a child or young person is within 12 months of a transfer between phases of education, the local authority must review and amend the plan to include the placement the child or young person will attend following transfer no later than:

- 31 March in the calendar year of the child or young person's transfer from secondary school to a post-16 institution; and
- 15 February in the calendar year of the child's transfer in any other case.[161]

4.166   Where it is proposed that a young person transfers from one post-16 institution to another post-16 institution at any other time, the local authority must review and amend the EHC plan at least five months before that transfer takes place so that it names the post-16 institution that the young person will attend following the transfer.[162]

4.167   Where a child or young person is due to transfer from a secondary school to a post-16 institution on 1 September 2015 the local authority must amend and review the EHC plan before 31 May 2015.[163]

---

160 CFA 2014 s45(4),
161 SEND Regs 2014 reg 18(1).
162 SEND Regs 2014 reg 18(2).
163 SEND Regs 2014 reg 18(3).

4.168   Local authorities should consider reviewing an EHC plan for a child under five at least every three to six months to ensure that the provision continues to be appropriate. Such reviews would be in addition to the annual review and are not subject to the same requirements regarding invitations and obtaining advice. However, the child's parent must be fully consulted on any proposed changes to the EHC plan and made aware of their right to appeal to the tribunal – both if they do not agree with the proposed changes and if no changes are made.[164]

4.169   When undertaking a review of an EHC plan, a local authority must:

- consult the child and the child's parent or the young person, and take account of their views, wishes and feelings;
- consider the child or young person's progress towards achieving the outcomes specified in the EHC plan and whether these outcomes remain appropriate for the child or young person; and
- consult the school or other institution attended by the child or young person.[165]

4.170   Where the child or young person attends a school, the local authority can require the head teacher or principal of the school to arrange and hold the meeting. The local authority can ask a further education college to convene the review.[166]

4.171   The following persons must be invited to attend with at least two weeks' notice:

- the child's parent or the young person;
- the provider of the relevant early years education or the head teacher or principal of the school, post-16 or other institution attended by the child or young person;
- relevant local authority officers in relation to SEN and social care functions; and
- a health care professional identified by the responsible commissioning body to provide advice about health care provision in relation to the child or young person.[167]

4.172   The person arranging the review meeting must obtain advice and information about the child or young person from the persons invited

---

164 SEND Code, para 9.178.
165 SEND Regs 2014 reg 19.
166 SEND Regs 2014 reg 20.
167 SEND Regs 2014 reg 20(2) and (3).

to attend and must circulate it to those persons at least two weeks in advance of the review meeting.[168]

4.173　The child or young person's progress towards achieving the outcomes specified in the EHC plan must be considered at the meeting.[169] This requirement is particularly important for young people aged over 18 as the educational and training outcomes will determine whether the EHC plan ceases.

4.174　When the child or young person is in or beyond year 9, the review meeting must consider what provision is required to assist the child or young person in preparation for adulthood and independent living.[170]

4.175　Following the review, the head teacher or principal of the school or educational institution must prepare a written report which sets out any recommendations or amendments to be made to the EHC plan. The report must include the advice and information obtained prior to the annual review.[171] The report must be prepared within two weeks of the review meeting and sent to everyone who was invited to attend/prepared advice.[172]

4.176　When the local authority receives the report they must decide whether to:

- continue to maintain the EHC plan in its current form;
- amend it; or
- cease to maintain it.[173]

4.177　The local authority must notify the child's parent or the young person of their decision within four weeks of the review meeting and, if the decision is to continue the plan in its previous form or cease to maintain it, inform them of:

- their right to appeal;
- the time limits for doing so; and
- information concerning mediation and the availability of disagreement resolution services and information and advice.[174]

4.178　Where a local authority decides to make amendments following the annual review it must:

168　SEND Regs 2014 reg 20(4).
169　SEND Regs 2014 reg 20(5).
170　SEND Regs 2014 reg 20(6).
171　SEND Regs 2014 reg 20(7) and (9).
172　SEND Regs 2014 reg 20(9).
173　SEND Regs 2014 reg 20(10).
174　SEND Regs 2014 reg 20(11).

- send the child's parent or the young person a copy of the EHC plan together with a notice specifying the proposed amendments, together with copies of any evidence which supports those amendments;
- provide the child's parent or the young person with notice of their right to request that a particular school is or other institution is named in the plan;
- give them at least 15 days, beginning with the day on which the draft plan was served, in which to:
  - make representations about the content of the draft plan;
  - request that a particular school or other institution be named in the plan;
  - request a meeting with an officer of the local authority; and
  - advise them where they can find information about the schools and colleges.[175]

4.179   The local authority must then send the finalised EHC plan to the child's parent or young person, the governing body or principal of the school or educational institution and the CCG, as soon as possible and in any event within eight weeks of first sending the plan and proposed amendments to the parent and notify them of the matters specified at para 4.177 above.[176]

Re-assessments

4.180   Provided that an assessment has not been undertaken within the previous 6 months, and the local authority considers it is necessary, the local authority must carry out a re-assessment of the educational, health care and social care needs of a child or young person for whom it maintains an EHC plan if a request is made to it by:

- the child's parent or the young person;
- governing body, proprietor or principal of the school or institution which the child or young person attends; or
- the responsible CCG.[177]

4.181   The local authority may also secure a re-assessment of those needs at any other time if it thinks it necessary.[178]

---

175 SEND Regs 2014 reg 22.
176 SEND Regs 2014 reg 22.
177 CFA 2014 s44(2) and SEND Regs 2014 reg 24.
178 CFA 2014 s44(3).

4.182   The local authority must notify the child's parent or the young person whether or not it is necessary to reassess the child or young person within 15 days of receiving the request to re-assess.[179] Where the local authority does not consider it is necessary to re-assess they must notify them of:

- their right to appeal;
- the time limits for doing so;
- information concerning mediation and the availability of dis-agreement resolution services and information and advice.[180]

4.183   If, at any time, a local authority proposes to amend an EHC plan, it shall proceed as if the proposed amendment were an amendment proposed after a review, with parents or young people having the same appeal rights and entitlement to notification.[181]

Personal budgets

4.184   The SEND Code states at para 9.95 that: 'A personal budget is an amount of money identified by the local authority to deliver provision set out in an EHC plan where the parent or young person is involved in securing that provision.'[182] It can include funding for education, health and social care.

4.185   The new right to a personal budget and right to request a direct payment in respect of SEN provision offer new opportunities to parents and young people to be able to use funding available to access specialist interventions which may not ordinarily be commissioned or available within local authorities.

4.186   This is recognised in the SEND Code, which says at paragraph 9.61 that where a young person or parent is seeking an innovative or alternative way to receive their support services – particularly through a Personal Budget, but not exclusively so – then the planning process should include the consideration of those solutions with support and advice available to assist the parent or young person in deciding how best to receive their support.

4.187   It is therefore important that parents, young people and professionals working with them understand how personal budgets and direct payments work, and when they can be accessed.

179 SEND Regs 2014 reg 25(1).
180 SEND Regs 2014 reg 25(2).
181 SEND Regs 2014 reg 28.
182 CFA 2014 s49(2).

4.188   Parents and young people have a right to request a personal budget figure be included on the EHC plan.[183] Each local authority must have a policy on personal budgets as part of their local offer which should include:

- a description of the services across education, health and social care that currently lend themselves to the use of Personal Budgets;
- how that funding will be made available;
- clear and simple statements of eligibility criteria and the decision-making processes.[184]

4.189   The local authority is not required to prepare a personal budget for special educational provision which is secured by the local authority under an arrangement with a third party (such as the NHS) where the local authority pays an aggregate sum for the provision and a notional amount for that child's particular provision cannot be disaggregated without having an adverse impact on other services or if it would not be an efficient use of the local authority's resources.[185] This amendment appears to have been made to alleviate local authority concerns about the burden of having to prepare a personal budget in such cases.

4.190   A request for a personal budget can be made at any time during the EHC needs assessment process or when a draft EHC plan is prepared.[186]

4.191   There are four ways in which a personal budget can be delivered:

- direct payments – where individuals receive the cash to contract, purchase and manage services themselves;
- an arrangement – whereby the local authority, school or college holds the funds and commissions the support specified in the plan (these are sometimes called notional budgets);
- third party arrangements – where funds (direct payments) are paid to and managed by an individual or organisation on behalf of the child's parent or the young person;
- a combination of the above.[187]

4.192   The first step in setting a personal budget figure is for the local authority to provide an indication of the level of funding required. This is called an 'indicative budget' or 'indicative figure'. It can be

---

183 CFA 2014 s49(1).
184 SEND Code, para 9.96.
185 Special Educational Needs (Personal Budgets) Regulations 2014 SI No 1652 reg 4A.
186 Special Educational Needs (Personal Budgets) Regulations 2014 reg 4(1).
187 SEND Code, para 9.101.

calculated through a resource allocation scheme or banded funding system but this should only be a starting point and local authorities should be clear that any figure discussed at this stage an indicative amount only.[188]

4.193 The final allocation of funding budget must be sufficient to secure the agreed provision specified in the EHC plan and must be set out as part of that provision.[189]

4.194 Local authorities must consider each request for a personal budget on its own individual merits. If a local authority is unable to identify a sum of money for a particular provision they should inform the child's parent or young person of the reasons.[190]

4.195 The SEND Code states (para 9.106) that demand from parents and young people for funds that cannot, at present, be disaggregated should inform joint commissioning arrangements for greater choice and control.

Direct payments for SEN provision

4.196 As explained above, one of the ways in which funding from a personal budget can be accessed is through a 'direct payment'. A direct payment is a cash payment made by the local authority to the child's parent or young person to contract, purchase and manage services themselves.

4.197 A local authority may only make direct payments where they are satisfied that:

- the recipient will use them to secure the agreed provision in an appropriate way;
- where the recipient is the child's parent or a nominee, that person will act in the best interests of the child or the young person when securing the proposed agreed provision;
- the direct payments will not have an adverse impact on other services which the local authority provides or arranges for children and young people with an EHC plan which the authority maintains; and
- securing the proposed agreed provision by direct payments is an efficient use of the authority's resources. This means in practice a

---

188 See by close analogy *R (KM) v Cambridgeshire CC* [2012] UKSC 23; (2012) 15 CCLR 374, discussed at chapter 3 at para 3.107.
189 SEND Code, para 9.102.
190 SEND Code, para 9.106

local authority will only agree to make direct payment for special educational provision where it will not cost them anymore than if they provided the provision themselves or through their existing contracting arrangements.[191]

4.198   Where a direct payment is proposed for special educational provision, the early years setting, school or college must agree to a direct payment being used before it can go ahead.[192]

Children and young people in custody

4.199   Sections 70–75 of the CFA 2014 apply the scheme in a modified form to children and young people in custody up to the age of 18. This is an extremely important development given the widespread acknowledgment that outcomes for this group are even worse than those for other children and young people with SEN.

4.200   The SEND Code addresses these provisions at paras 10.60–10.150. Practice guidance is also available from the Council for Disabled Children.[193]

4.201   The central requirement of the scheme for detained children and young people are as follows:

- Local authorities must not cease an EHC plan when a child or young person enters custody. They must keep it while the detained person is detained and maintain and review it when the detained person is released.
- If a detained person has an EHC plan before being detained (or one is completed while the detained person is in the relevant youth accommodation) the local authority must arrange appropriate special educational provision for the detained person while he or she is detained.
- If it is not practicable to arrange the provision specified in the EHC plan, provision corresponding as closely as possible to that in the EHC plan must be arranged.

---

191 Special Educational Needs (Personal Budgets) Regulations 2014 reg 6(1).
192 Special Educational Needs (Personal Budgets) Regulations 2014 reg 9.
193 Council for Disabled Children, *Children and Families Act 2014: Children and young people with SEN in youth custody, Implementation Support Materials,* March 2015.

- Where a detained person does not have an EHC plan, the appropriate person[194] or the person in charge of the relevant youth accommodation can request an assessment of the detained person's post-detention EHC needs from the 'home' local authority. When considering a request the local authority must consult the appropriate person and the person in charge of the relevant youth accommodation. There is a right to appeal to the tribunal for the appropriate person.
- The local authority must secure an assessment of post-detention needs if the detained person has or may have SEN and it may be necessary for special educational provision to be made in accordance with an EHC plan on their release from detention.
- Advice and information must be sought from the usual range of sources as part of the assessment process, see para 4.123 above.
- The standard 20-week timescale for the completion of the EHC planning process applies, see para 4.132 above.
- Anyone else, including Youth Offending Teams and education providers in custody, has a right to bring the detained person to the notice of the local authority as someone who may have special educational needs and the local authority must consider whether an assessment of their post-detention EHC needs is necessary
- The local authority must promote the fulfilment of the detained person's learning potential while they are in custody and on their release, whether they have an EHC plan or not.
- The duties in the CFA 2014 no longer apply once a young person is transferred to the adult secure estate.

Residential and out-of-authority placements

4.202   Children with complex needs may at some stage require residential schooling – whether as a result of the complexity of their needs, family breakdown or indeed a combination of the two. When considering whether an educational need for a residential school placement arises the question asked is often whether the child needs a 'waking day' curriculum, and there are a number of court and tribunal decisions under the old scheme addressed to this question. However, the joined-up approach across education, health and social care which is supposed to be at the heart of the new scheme should reduce the

---

194 The detained person's parent, where the detained person is a child, or the young person, where the detained person is a young person.

tendency to focus on children's needs in silos. In practice an argument for residential schooling which has tended to gain more support in tribunal appeals is that there is no local provision that can meet the child's needs.

4.203   Where there is social care input into a residential school placement, it is likely that it will be made under CA 1989 s20 and the child will become 'looked after'.[195] In other cases where a child is placed in a residential special school with the intention that he or she should remain there for longer than three months, the Director of Children's Services must be notified.[196] The Director must then 'take such steps as are reasonably practicable to enable them to determine whether the child's welfare is adequately safeguarded and promoted' and consider whether to exercise any of their functions under CA 1989 in relation to that child.[197]

4.204   Many children in residential schools will be placed out of their 'home' authority. Other disabled children will be placed out of authority either as a result of family breakdown or to meet their social care needs. Responsibility for meeting these children's SEN remains with the authority where they are ordinarily resident. So if a child moves to a settled placement with foster parents then the responsibility for their SEN moves to the local authority in whose area the foster parents live.

4.205   Regulation 15 of the SEND Regs 2014 makes provision for the transfer of responsibility for EHC plans where a child or young person moves between local authorities.

Education otherwise than at school

4.206   Under section 7 of the Education Act 1996 parents have the right to educate children, including children with SEN, at home. However in practice a decision to home educate a child with SEN can often give rise to conflict between the local authority and the family. Moreover a family should never feel forced to home educate a child with SEN, given the duties on schools and local authorities covered in this chapter to ensure that those needs are met otherwise than at home.

---

195 *R (O) v East Riding of Yorkshire CC* [2011] EWCA Civ 196. See chapter 3 at paras 3.144–3.147 for the consequence of 'looked after' status.

196 CA 1989 s85. See further chapter 3 at paras 3.148–3.149.

197 CA 1989 s85(4).

4.207   Guidance on this sensitive area is given in the SEND Code at paras 10.30–10.38. The Code emphasises that:

- Home education must be suitable to the child's age, ability, aptitude and SEN.
- Local authorities should work in partnership with, and support, parents to ensure that the SEN of these children are met where the local authority already knows the children have SEN or the parents have drawn the children's special needs to the authority's attention.
- Local authorities should fund the SEN needs of home-educated children where it is appropriate to do so.[198]
- In cases where local authorities and parents agree that home education is the right provision for a child or young person with an EHC plan, the plan should make clear that the child or young person will be educated at home. If it does then under CFA 2014 s42(2) the local authority must arrange the special educational provision set out in the plan, working with the parents.
- In cases where the EHC plan gives the name of a school or type of school where the child will be educated and the parents decide to educate at home, the local authority is not under a duty to make the special educational provision set out in the plan provided it is satisfied that the arrangements made by the parents are suitable. The local authority must review the plan annually to assure itself that the provision set out in it continues to be appropriate and that the child's SEN continue to be met.
- Where a child or young person is a registered pupil and the parent decides to home educate, the parent must notify the school in writing that the child or young person is receiving education otherwise than at school and the school must then remove the pupil's name from the admission register.
- The local authority is required to intervene through the school attendance order framework 'if it appears ... that a child of compulsory school age is not receiving suitable education'.

4.208   Importantly, the SEND Code notes at para 10.34 that:

Local authorities do not have the right of entry to the family home to check that the provision being made by the parents is appropriate

---

198 The Code notes at para 10.30 that 'The high needs block of the Dedicated Schools Grant is intended to fund provision for all relevant children and young people in the authority's area, including home-educated children'. See further the Department for Education's undated document 'Revised Funding Guidance for Local Authorities on Home Educated Children'.

and may only enter the home at the invitation of the parents. Parents should be encouraged to see this process aspart of the authority's overall approach to home education of pupils with SEN, including the provision of appropriate support, rather than an attempt to undermine the parents' right to home educate.

4.209   The power for local authorities to arrange for special educational provision to be made otherwise than at school or college is contained in CFA 2014 s61. The local authority must be satisfied that 'it would be inappropriate for the provision to be made in a school or post-16 institution or at such a place'.[199] Before reaching its decision the local authority must consult the parent or young person.[200] It is important to note that the local authority may decide to arrange *part* of the provision otherwise than at school – for example it may be appropriate for certain therapies to be provided in another setting while the remainder of the special educational provision is made at school.

Duties to children who are without education (EA 1996 s19)

4.210   Any child (regardless of disability or SEN) who is out of the education system for any reason is owed the duty in EA 1996 s19 by their local authority. This duty is to 'make arrangements for the provision of suitable education at school or otherwise' for such a child. 'Suitable education' means 'efficient education suitable to his age, ability and aptitude and to any special educational needs he may have'.[201] As a consequence, a failure to provide adequate home tuition while a child is not in mainstream schooling will be maladministration.[202]

4.211   Given the number of children with SEN who are, for one reason or another 'out of the education system' it is of no surprise that there has been considerable attention as to the nature, extent and enforceability of the section 19 duty on LEAs. Any failure to comply with the section 19 duty will generally need to be remedied through judicial review, given the urgency of getting the child back into education. The nature of the section 19 duty has been clarified by a number of

---

199 CFA 2014 s61(2).

200 CFA 2014 s61(3).

201 Education Act 1996 s19(6).

202 See, for example, Local Government Ombudsman's Digest of Cases (Education) 2007/08, Report 05A15425 5192, where it was recommended that compensation of £7,000 be paid for the failure of support.

court and local government ombudsman decisions. These have established in particular that LEAs cannot plead a 'shortage of resources' as a reason for not making suitable arrangements for disabled children in such cases. More importantly still, in the landmark case of *Tandy*,[203] the House of Lords held that the duty under EA 1996 s19 is owed to each individual child who falls within the definition in the section and that 'suitable education' must be determined purely by educational considerations, disregarding any resource constraints an LEA may face.

4.212   The Department of Education has issued statutory guidance on 'Alternative Provision' for children who are out of school.[204] The first three key points made in this guidance are as follows:

- Local authorities are responsible for arranging suitable education for permanently excluded pupils[205], and for other pupils who – because of illness or other reasons – would not receive suitable education without such arrangements being made.
- Governing bodies of schools are responsible for arranging suitable full-time education from the sixth day of a fixed period exclusion.
- Schools may also direct pupils off-site for education, to help improve their behaviour.

4.213   The guidance goes on to state that 'While there is no statutory requirement as to when suitable full-time education should begin for pupils placed in alternative provision for reasons other than exclusion, local authorities should ensure that such pupils are placed as quickly as possible'.[206]

4.214   Further advice has been given by government on 'Ensuring a good education for children who cannot attend school because of health needs'.[207] The key points in this guidance are as follows:

203 *R v East Sussex CC ex p Tandy* [1998] AC 714.
204 Department for Education, *Alternative Provision: Statutory guidance for local authorities*, January 2013.
205 See paras 4.220–4.229 below in relation to school exclusions.
206 Department for Education, *Alternative Provision: Statutory guidance for local authorities*, January 2013, para 2.
207 Department for Education, *Ensuring a good education for children who cannot attend school because of health needs: Statutory guidance for local authorities*, January 2013.

Local authorities must:

• Arrange suitable full-time education (or as much education as the child's health condition allows) for children of compulsory school age who, because of illness, would otherwise not receive suitable education.

Local authorities should:

• Provide such education as soon as it is clear that the child will be away from school for 15 days or more, whether consecutive or cumulative. They should liaise with appropriate medical professionals to ensure minimal delay in arranging appropriate provision for the child.

• Ensure that the education children receive is of good quality ... allows them to take appropriate qualifications, prevents them from slipping behind their peers in school and allows them to reintegrate successfully back into school as soon as possible.

• Address the needs of individual children in arranging provision. 'Hard and fast' rules are inappropriate: they may limit the offer of education to children with a given condition and prevent their access to the right level of educational support which they are well enough to receive. Strict rules that limit the offer of education a child receives may also breach statutory requirements.

Local authorities should not:

• Have processes or policies in place which prevent a child from getting the right type of provision and a good education.

• Withhold or reduce the provision, or type of provision, for a child because of how much it will cost (meeting the child's needs and providing a good education must be the determining factors).

• Have policies based upon the percentage of time a child is able to attend school rather than whether the child is receiving a suitable education during that attendance.

• Have lists of health conditions which dictate whether or not they will arrange education for children or inflexible policies which result in children going without suitable full-time education (or as much education as their health condition allows them to participate in).

4.215   Many disabled children are failed by their schools either due to bullying or due to the inability of the school to provide suitable education. On occasions this results in their parents withdrawing them and subsequently making a complaint to the courts or local government ombudsmen. In *R (G) v Westminster CC*,[208] however, the Court of Appeal held that a father had not acted reasonably in withdrawing his son from school on the grounds he was being bullied when the school was taking reasonable steps to address his bullying. The court did hold that where a child was not receiving suitable education and there was no suitable education available that was reasonably practicable for the child, the authority would be in breach of EA 1996 s19.[209]

4.216   The ombudsman has, however, held in a different case that parents acted reasonably in removing their son from a school (and educating him at home) when the LEA and the school had comprehensively failed to comply with his statement of SEN, and indeed their associated SEN obligations under the EA 1996.[210] Likewise in a 2007 complaint the local government ombudsman considered that a mother's removal of her disabled son due to bullying was not unreasonable, given the LEA's maladministration in failing to use its mediation process to help to address the bullying and its failure to provide assistance to reintroduce child to his school or to find an alternative.[211]

4.217   The EA 1996 s19 duty has been considered by the High Court in cases involving children with SEN. In *R (B) v Barnet LBC*,[212] the court held that it was not reasonably practicable for a child to attend a school which the headteacher had said was unsuitable for her and as such there had been a breach of the section 19 duty. In a case such as this, there is then a duty on the LEA to make alternative provision which the court enforced in relation to B by way of a mandatory order. By contrast, in *R (HR) v Medway Council*,[213] the court approved the *Barnet* case but held that on the facts, the LEA had discharged its EA 1996 s19 duty by offering a placement in a hospital special school, even though an independent educational psychologist has said that this school was not suitable for HR. This was essentially because it was not sufficiently obvious that the school was unsuitable, given the LEA's evidence to the contrary. These two cases together suggest that even where a disabled child is out of school for a significant period

---

208 [2004] EWCA Civ 45; [2004] 1 WLR 1113.
209 Judgment at [46].
210 Local Government Ombudsman's Digest of Cases (Education) 2003/04, Report 02/A/13068.
211 Local Government Ombudsman's Digest of Cases (Education) 2006/07, Report 05/B/11513.
212 [2009] EWHC 2842 (Admin); (2009) 12 CCLR 679.
213 [2010] EWHC 731 (Admin).

the court will only intervene when it is obvious that the LEA has not offered 'suitable' education, particularly if there is an ongoing tribunal appeal pending (as there was in relation to both B and HR).

School admissions

4.218   Children with SEN but without a statement/EHC plan must aply for school admission in the usual way. This means that parents will need to address the relevant over-subscription criteria for schools where the demand for places exceeds the available supply. In most cases this means that preference is given to children living nearer the school, unless the child is adopted or looked after by the local authority or has a sibling at the school or there is an exceptional medical or social need for them to attend the particular school.

4.219   Parents can appeal to the independent appeal panel responsible for their particular admissions authority (usually the local authority) if they disagree with a school admissions decision. These appeals and the prior decision making by the local authority are regulated by two Codes of Practice, issued under School Standards and Framework Act 1998 s84.[214] Relevant bodies including admissions authorities and independent appeal panels must 'act in accordance' with the codes.[215]

Exclusions from school and colleges

4.220   As noted above, pupils with SEN account for 7 in 10 of all permanent exclusions and 6 in 10 of all fixed period exclusions from English schools. This statistic alone suggests, at the very least, indirect discrimination against disabled children contrary to the Equality Act 2010.[216] Exclusion, particularly for disabled children and children

---

214 Department for Education, *School Admissions Code: Statutory guidance for admission authorities, governing bodies, local authorities, schools adjudicators and admission appeals panels*, December 2014; Department for Education, *School Admission Appeals Code: Statutory guidance for school leaders, governing bodies and local authorities*, February 2012.

215 School Standards and Framework Act 1998 s84(3).

216 See in this context, the Local Government Ombudsman's Digest of Cases (Education) 2007/08, Report 06C06190, concerning an exclusion of a young person with SEN and the ombudsman's finding that the LEA had failed to have regard to the likelihood that the case facts engaged its general duties under the Disability Discrimination Act 1995.

with SEN, should be regarded as 'a draconian remedy of last resort'.[217] This is reinforced (although perhaps not as strongly as previously) in the regulations[218] and statutory exclusions guidance for schools in England.[219] In particular the guidance states that:

- head teachers[220] should, as far as possible, avoid excluding permanently any child with a statement of SEN or a looked after child (para 22);[221]
- where a school has concerns about the behaviour, or risk of exclusion, of a child with additional needs a pupil with a statement of SEN or a looked after child, it should, in partnership with others (including the local authority as necessary) consider what additional support or alternative placement may be required (para 24); and
- early intervention to address underlying causes of disruptive behaviour should include an assessment of whether appropriate provision is in place to support any SEN or disability that a pupil may have (para 18).

4.221 At para 15, the guidance states that a decision to exclude a pupil permanently should only be taken in response to serious or persistent breaches of the school's behaviour policy *and* where allowing the pupil to remain in school would seriously harm the education or welfare of the pupil or others in the school. By using the word 'only', the guidance creates a discrete and exclusive test for when a permanent exclusion is a justified and a lawful response. When asking whether the pupil acted as alleged, the standard of proof is the balance of probabilities and this means whether something is 'more likely than not' to have occurred.[222]

4.222 The guidance recognises (at para 22) that pupils with statements of SEN and looked after children are particularly vulnerable to the impacts of exclusion as well as having disproportionately high rates

---

217 J Ford et al, *Education law and practice*, 3rd edn, Jordans, 2010, para 8.38.
218 School Discipline (Pupil Exclusions and Reviews) (England) Regulations 2012, SI No 1033.
219 Department for Education *Exclusion from maintained schools, Academies and pupil referral units in England*, 2012. An updated version of this guidance was published in January 2015 and then withdrawn after threatened legal action, including in relation to failure to consult on important changes from the previous guidance. As such the 2012 guidance remains in force.
220 The term 'Headteacher' in the guidance and in this section applies also to a teacher in charge of a pupil referral unit and to a principal of an academy.
221 This must now be read as including a child with an EHC plan.
222 *Re B (Children) (Sexual Abuse: Standard of Proof)* [2009] 1 AC 11.

of exclusion. As such, it is essential that schools and local authorities comply with the guidance in relation to children with SEN and looked after children who are at risk of exclusion or who have been excluded.

4.223   For both fixed period and permanent exclusions, there is a duty to provide alternative education for the pupil from the sixth day of the exclusion. For a child with a statement of SEN or EHC plan, the local authority must identify an appropriate full-time placement in consultation with the child's parents who retain the right to express a preference for a school they wish their child to attend or make representations for a placement in any other school (para 45).

4.224   Notwithstanding these time-specific duties, it has been and is still all too often the case that provision of education for excluded children is inadequate. A 2004 local government ombudsman report,[223] for example, concerned a child who was excluded for violent and disruptive behaviour while the LEA was in the process of assessing his SEN. He was out of school for over a year. For the first half term no education was provided and after this he received tuition which varied between six and 12 hours a week. In the ombudsman's opinion this was grossly inadequate and could not be described as 'suitable education'.

4.225   A similar finding emerges from a 2010 report,[224] which concerned a six-month exclusion of a child who had mental health difficulties (and for whom an application for a statement of SEN was then made). The ombudsman found that during the exclusion period the education provided 'was well below the requirements of the statutory guidance', and observed (para 30):

> According to section 19 of the Education Act 1996, the Council was responsible for this once it became impossible for [the child] to attend School A .... Therefore, it is not sufficient for the Council to say that [she] remained on the school roll and so the local authority was not responsible for her education. That fails to reflect the reality of the

223 Local Government Ombudsman's Digest of Cases (Education) 2003/04, Report 01/B/6663, where it was recommended that compensation of over £2,000 be paid for the failure of support. See also the Digest of Cases (Education) 2007/08, Report 06C06190, which concerned the exclusion (for behavioural reasons) from a mainstream school of a young person with a statement of SEN. The ombudsman found there to be maladministration, not least because requests for a reassessment of his needs were ignored by the LEA because he was approaching year 11. The ombudsman also noted the failure of the LEA to have regard to the likelihood that these facts engaged its general duties under the Disability Discrimination Act 1995.

224 Complaint no 07A14912 against Barnet LBC, April 19 2010.

situation: that the school had become unsuitable for [her] and it was impossible for her to attend. Accordingly, the Council was responsible for arranging suitable educational provision.

4.226 The school's governing body must consider the reinstatement of an excluded pupil within 15 school days of receiving notice of an exclusion which brings the pupil's total number of excluded days to more than 15 in a term; or of a permanent exclusion; or of any exclusion which would result in a pupil missing a public examination or a national curriculum test. Parents of children who are permanently excluded (and excluded pupils aged 18 or over) can ask for the governing body's decision to be reviewed by an Independent Review Panel (IRP). The time limits are set out in paras 72 and 84 of the statutory guidance. There is also a right to make a claim under the Equality Act 2010 to the First-tier Tribunal (Special Educational Needs and Disability) if parents believe the permanent exclusion was the result of disability discrimination. This appeal right also exists for fixed term exclusions (see chapter 11, para 11.70 below). The tribunal has issued guidance on how to bring a disability discrimination claim in light of the changes.[225]

4.227 In their application for an IRP hearing, parents have a right to request that the local authority/academy trust appoints and pays for an SEN expert (para 117), regardless of whether or not the school recognises that their child has SEN (para 119). The statutory guidance sets out the nature of the SEN expert's role as 'analogous to an expert witness, providing impartial advice to the panel on how special educational needs might be relevant to the exclusion' (para 155). The focus of their advice should be on 'whether the school's policies which relate to SEN , or the application of these policies in relation to the excluded pupil, were legal, reasonable and procedurally fair' (para 156) and if a school does not recognise the pupils has SEN, also address this issue (para 157). The panel members should apply the tests of illegality, irrationality and procedural impropriety in relation to the decision to exclude (para 148).

4.228 Unlike an Independent Appeal Panel under the previous scheme, an IRP can only uphold the exclusion decision, recommend that the governing body reconsiders their decision or quash the decision if it considers it was flawed when considered in light of judicial review principles and direct that the governing body considers the exclusion again. However it cannot direct reinstatement, be this immediate

225 HM Courts and Tribunals Service, *How to claim against disability discrimination in schools - a guide for parents*, 2013.

or at some later date. If the IRP directs a governing body to reconsider its decision and the governing body does not offer to reinstate a pupil, the IRP can order a readjustment of the school's budget (or payment in the case of an academy) so that money follows the excluded pupil; a panel does not have this power where it has only made a recommendation. The main power in relation to exclusions therefore now vests in the school rather than in an independent body, which is a concerning development for excluded pupils. However, if a parent brings a claim of disability discrimination in relation to the permanent exclusion, the tribunal will expedite the timetable (unless the exclusion is being considered by an IRP) so that a decision can be reached in no more than six weeks; if successful, the tribunal can order reinstatement.

4.229   An example of an Independent Appeal Panel (the forerunner to the IRP) considering proportionality is found in *W v Bexley LBC Independent Appeal Panel*,[226] a case in which the IAP accepted the school's evidence that W had cut another student's folder with a knife and sliced this student's shirt with the knife while the student was wearing it. However, despite making this finding, the IAP concluded that permanent exclusion was a disproportionate response and that a fixed-term exclusion would have been more appropriate. As the IAP had no power to order a fixed-term exclusion, reinstatement was ordered.

School and college transport

4.230   The statutory provisions in relation to school transport in England are found in EA 1996 ss508A–509A. The school transport duties on local authorities in England are further explained in the relevant guidance.[227] There is separate guidance for post 16 transport which covers learners of sixth form age attending schools as well as sixth form colleges and other Further and Higher education institutions.[228]

4.231   Under section 508B, local authorities must arrange free suitable home-to-school travel arrangements for 'eligible' children of compulsory school age for whom no, or no suitable, free travel arrangements have been provided. Eligibility is generally determined by distance

226 [2008] EWHC 758 (Admin).
227 Department for Education, *Home to school travel and transport guidance: Statutory guidance for local authorities*, July 2014.
228 Department for Education, *Post-16 transport to education and training: Statutory guidance for local authorities*, February 2014.

from school. However, other groups of children can also be 'eligible', including here children with SEN, a disability or mobility problems who as a result of their difficulties cannot reasonably be expected to walk to school.[229]

4.232   Where a parent chooses to send his or her child to a school which is not the nearest appropriate school and is not named as the 'appropriate school' in the child's statement/EHC plan, the local authority may choose not to provide assistance with transport. This will arise where the local authority has made suitable arrangements for the child to become a registered pupil at a school nearer to his home.[230] Local authorities should not, therefore, adopt general transport policies that seek to limit the schools for which parents of children with statement/EHC plans may express a preference if free transport is to be provided. In most cases local authorities will have clear general policies relating to transport for children with statements/EHC plans; these should be made available to parents and more often than not are well publicised on local authority websites.

4.233   However, it is acceptable for the local authority to name the school preferred by the child's parents in the statement/EHC plan on condition that the parents agree to meet all of or part of the transport costs, so long as there is a nearer school which is held to be suitable. If there is no nearer suitable school the local authority is likely to owe the EA 1996 s508B duty to arrange free, suitable transport.

4.234   Home-to-school transport should not cause the child undue stress, strain or difficulty that would prevent the child benefiting from the education the school has to offer. The statutory guidance states that 'For arrangements to be suitable, they must also be safe and reasonably stress free, to enable the child to arrive at school ready for a day of study'.[231] Proper safeguarding procedures should be in place in relation to drivers and escorts.

4.235   If a child is not eligible for free home-to-school transport, the local authority may still make transport arrangements for them.[232] This includes children who are older or younger than compulsory school

229 Education Act 1996 Sch 35 para 2.
230 Education Act 1996 Sch 35B, para 2(c). Such children will therefore not be 'eligible' children for the purposes of section 508B.
231 Department for Education, *Home to school travel and transport guidance: Statutory guidance for local authorities*, July 2014 para 35.
232 See Education Act 1996 s508C. Guidance on the exercise of the section 508C power is given in Department for Education, *Home to school travel and transport guidance: Statutory guidance for local authorities*, July 2014 at paras 36 and 37.

age. Such arrangements do not have to be free of charge, but whether or not there will be a charge should be made clear in the authority's school travel policy. Local authorities may put in place school travel schemes in which case different rules in relation to eligibility for free home to school transport will apply .

4.236   Local authorities are under a duty to publish a post-16 Transport Policy Statement.[233] This must include specific provision for disabled learners.[234] In particular, it must 'specify arrangements for persons with learning difficulties or disabilities receiving education or training at establishments other than schools maintained by the authority which are no less favourable than arrangements specified for pupils of the same age with learning difficulties or disabilities attending such schools'.[235] The relevant statutory guidance expressly states that the overall intention of the 16 to 18 transport duty is to 'ensure that learners of sixth form age are able to access the education and training of their choice; and ensure that, if support for access is required, that this will be assessed and provided where necessary'.[236]

4.237   Education Act 1996 ss508F–H provide additional duties in relation to adult learners. Essentially, section 508F states that the local authorities should provide transport in order to facilitate the attendance of adults at further education or higher education institutions. They should also facilitate the attendance of an adult for whom an EHC plan is maintained. Any transport provided under section 508F should be provided free of charge.[237] This means that for many disabled young people the only ages at which they can be charged for school or college transport will be 16 and 17, ie when they are no longer 'eligible' children for the purposes of section 508B and before the adult transport duty under section 508F applies to them.

4.238   Disputes in relation to school transport will generally be resolved by local education transport panels, such panels being required to act fairly and to take into account any educational needs an individual learner may have.

4.239   The statutory guidance states as follows in relation to resolving school transport disputes:

> Local authorities should have in place both complaints and appeals procedures for parents to follow should they have cause for complaint

---

233 Education Act 1996 s509AA.
234 Education Act 1996 s509AB.
235 Education Act 1996 s509AB(2).
236 Department for Education, *Post-16 transport to education and training: Statutory guidance for local authorities*, February 2014 para 2.
237 Education Act 1996 s508F(1).

about the service, or wish to appeal about the eligibility of their child for travel support. The procedure should bepublished alongside the local authority travel policy statement. If an appellant considers that there has been a failure to comply with the procedural rules or if there are any other irregularities in the way an appeal was handled they may have a right to refer the matter to the Local Government Ombudsman. If an appellant considers the decision of the independent appeals panel to be flawed on public law grounds, they may apply for a judicial review.[238]

4.240 Whereas previously each local authority was free to adopt its own procedure for school transport appeals, the statutory guidance now includes at annex 2 a 'recommended review/appeals process'. This suggests that:

- At stage 1, a parent has 20 working days from receipt of the local authority's home to school transport decision to make a written request asking for a review of the decision.
- The written request should detail why the parent believes the decision should be reviewed and give details of any personal and/or family circumstances the parent believes should be considered when the decision is reviewed.
- Within 20 working days of receipt of the parent's written request a senior officer reviews the original decision and sends the parent a detailed written notification of the outcome of their review.
- A parent has 20 working days from receipt of the local authority's stage one written decision notification to make a written request to escalate the matter to stage two.
- Within 40 working days of receipt of the parents request an independent appeal panel considers written and verbal representations from both the parent and officers involved in the case and gives a detailed written notification of the outcome (within five working days).

4.241 There is a flow chart setting out the recommended process in the statutory guidance at page 36. However parents will need to check with their local authority whether the recommended process has been adopted or if a decision has been taken to depart from the guidance.

---

238 Department for Education, *Home to school travel and transport guidance: Statutory guidance for local authorities*, July 2014, para 35.

Appeals to the tribunal

4.242   As with the previous scheme under Part 4 of the Education Act 1996, the principal remedy in relation to disputes under CFA 2014 Part 3 is an appeal to the First-tier Tribunal (Special Educational Needs and Disability). The appeal right lies with parents in relation to children. For young people, those who have capacity in relation to the relevant decision can appeal in their own name while for young people who lack the relevant capacity the appeal can be brought by any 'representative' or their parent; see further paras 11.81–11.87.

4.243   The following decisions can be appealed to the tribunal:[239]

- a refusal to carry out an EHC needs assessment following a request;
- a refusal to make an EHC plan following an assessment;
- disputes in relation to sections B, F or I of the EHC plan (see para 4.139 above for these sections, which concern SEN issues only);
- a refusal to make requested amendments to an EHC plan following an annual review;
- a refusal to carry out a re-assessment following a request;
- a decision to cease to maintain an EHC plan.

4.244   In addition to the above, there is a pilot scheme from April 2015 in relation to certain local authorities[240] that provides the tribunal with the power to recommend the health care and social care needs and health and social care provision that should be specified in the EHC plan.[241]

4.245   It is important to note that a tribunal appeal must be lodged within two months of the decision letter from the local authority confirming one of the decisions above has been made.

4.246   Parents and young people who wish to make an appeal to the tribunal may do so only after they have contacted an independent mediation adviser and discussed whether mediation might be a suitable

---

239 CFA 2014 s51.

240 The local authorities included in the Pilot Scheme are: Barking and Dagenham London Borough Council, Bedford Borough Council, Blackpool Council, Cheshire West and Chester Council, Ealing London Borough Council., East Riding of Yorkshire Council, Hackney London Borough Council, Kent County Council, Lambeth London Borough Council, Liverpool City Council, Sandwell Metropolitan Borough Council, Stockport Metropolitan Borough Council, Wokingham Borough Council.

241 This scheme is governed by the Special Educational Needs and Disability (First-tier Tribunal Recommendation Power) (Pilot) Regulations 2015 SI No 358. See further, chapter 11 at paras 11.75–11.80.

way of resolving the disagreement.[242] This requirement does not apply where the appeal is solely about the name or type of the school, college or other institution named on the plan. It is important to note that there is no requirement to mediate before appealing to the tribunal, merely to consider mediation.

4.247   Where a parent or young person is required to obtain a mediation certificate, he or she must contact the mediation adviser within two months of written notice of the local authority's decision being sent, inform the mediation adviser that he or she wishes to appeal and inform the mediation adviser whether they wish to pursue mediation.[243]

4.248   Further information in relation to the tribunal process is set out in chapter 11, see paras 11.60–11.87.

Other enforcement methods

Judicial review

4.249   As explained in chapter 11 (see paras 11.88–11.103), where a child is suffering an ongoing disadvantage as a result of a school or local authority's breach of duty, for instance the duty on local authorities to provide suitable education for children out of school, it may be possible to achieve a remedy through an application for judicial review in the High Court. Care must be taken, however, to ensure that no other effective remedy can be obtained through another route, in particular through a tribunal appeal, otherwise the High Court is likely to either refuse permission for the judicial review to proceed or refuse to grant any relief at the end of the proceedings.

4.250   Judicial review proceedings should be brought as soon as possible and in any event, no later than three months after the decision complained about; the time limit can be extended in exceptional circumstances. As such families should take advice from a specialist solicitor as quickly as possible if an application for judicial review may be required. Legal aid may be available to meet the costs of an application for judicial review, depending on both the merits of the proposed application and an assessment of the financial means of the child, young person and/or parent(s). See further chapter 11 at paras 11.108–11.116 for a more extensive discussion of legal aid eligibility.

---

242 CFA 2014 s55(3). See further, chapter 11 at paras 11.48–11.59.
243 Special Education Needs and Disability Regulations 2014 reg 33.

Complaint to the secretary of state

4.251 Alternatively, a parent or child may make a complaint to the secretary of state if a local authority or governing body of a maintained school in England has acted unreasonably or is in breach of its duties. It is usually necessary to follow all internal complaints procedures before making a written complaint to the secretary of state and the complaint will not normally be able to be investigated if the child has left the school in question. An investigation by the secretary of state can take in excess of six months so this should not be used as a remedy in urgent cases. If the complaint is upheld, however, the secretary of state can issue directions to require the local authority or school to carrout its legal obligations properly. See chapter 11 at paras 11.22–11.35 for further information.

Complaint to the ombudsman

4.252 Complaints in relation to maladministration by local authorities can also be made to the local government ombudsman (www.lgo.org.uk) in England. Further information in relation to the role of the ombudsman in resolving disputes in relation to education issues can be found in chapter 11 at paras 11.36–11.43.

Decision-making for young people

4.253 CFA 2014 s80 and the related regulations[244] govern how decisions are made by and for young people aged over 16 under CFA 2014 Part 3. These provisions are discussed in chapter 11 at paras 11.81–11.87.

Further advice and support

4.254 Education law is notoriously complex and even in this lengthy chapter it has not been possible to cover all relevant issues. Parents, young people and others are strongly advised to seek independent advice on their own case.

4.255 Details of where further advice and support can be obtained can be found in chapter 11 at paras 11.118–11.128 along with information as to the availability of legal aid.

244 SEND Regs 2014 Part 6.

CHAPTER 5

Health

continued

Key points

- Disabled children have the same right as other children to access universal health services.
- Disabled children and young people with an education, health and care plan which includes health provision have a specific right to have this provision arranged by the NHS.
- NHS bodies have a duty to engage disabled children and their families in decisions about the planning and delivery of health services.
- NHS bodies and local authorities have duties to co-operate to ensure that disabled children's health needs are met.
- Disabled children may require a range of specialist health services, including therapy services and equipment.
- Where disabled children have particularly severe and/or complex health needs, the NHS will have the primary responsibility for providing them with 'continuing care'.
- Disabled children may also require Child and Adolescent Mental Health Services (CAMHS) input.
- It is always essential to determine whether a disabled child can and does consent to treatment, and to know if a child cannot or does not consent what the appropriate legal route is in each individual case.
- Children with life limiting conditions will require high quality palliative care.
- The transition from children's to adult health services is vital for the well-being of disabled young people and must be properly planned.

Introduction

5.1   Health services are critically important for many disabled children. It is often health services such as GPs, hospital-based services and health visitors that first identify that a child may have an impairment. Disabled children also need and have a right to access the same range of universal health services provided for other children. However, many disabled children also require additional specialist health services. These will range from therapeutic services such as physiotherapy to equipment and technology which may assist severely disabled children to lead more ordinary lives.

5.2   Historically, the health needs of children in general, and disabled children in particular, were not given national priority status.
However, in around 2009, this began to change with the introduction of NHS operating frameworks in England that explicitly stated
that children should be one of four national priorities for the NHS
in England, alongside cancer, stroke and maternity. The health and
well-being of children was also shown to be a priority with the publication in February 2009 of 'Healthy lives, brighter futures', the English government's first-ever strategy for children and young people's
health. Since then the Department of Health has published *Improving
Children and Young People's Health Outcomes: a system-wide response*
(February 2013), identifying the need for co-ordinated, tailored and
integrated care and promising greater efficiency and accountability,
with children, young people and their families being involved in
decisions about their care and the design of services.[1] At the same
time, the government published a pledge, supported by many signa-
tories including NHS England, the Care Quality Commission (CQC),
Healthwatch and Public Health England, to improve the health outcomes of children and young people, including by providing better
care for disabled children and young people.[2]

5.3   The prioritisation of children and young people's health needs
was reflected in the first mandate from the government to the NHS
Commissioning Board (NHS England), the body responsible for
supervising and developing health commissioning since the reorganisation of the NHS in April 2013.[3] That mandate, which ran from
April 2013 to March 2015, asked the NHS England to pursue as part
of its objectives the support of children with disabilities, including
ensuring access to services.[4] A further mandate published for the
period April 2015 to March 2016[5] set an objective that disabled children should have access to the services identified in their education,
health and care (EHC) plan (see below) and that 'parents of children

---

1 Department of Health with Department of Education and others, *Better health
   outcomes for children and young people: A system wide response*, February 2013.
2 Department of Health, *Better health outcomes for children and young people: Our
   pledge*, February 2013.
3 Issued under NHS Act 2006 s13A, as added by Health and Social Care Act
   2012 s23. Under s13A(7), NHS England must 'seek to achieve the objectives
   specified in the mandate'.
4 Department of Health, *A mandate from the government to the NHS
   commissioning board: April 2013 to March 2015*, November 2013.
5 Department of Health, *A mandate from the government to NHS England: April
   2015 to March 2016*, December 2014.

who could benefit have the option of a personal budget based on a coordinated assessment across health, social care and education'.[6]

5.4   Disabled children's health needs should also be addressed through the reforms introduced under Part 3 of the Children and Families Act (CFA) 2014,[7] despite the fact that the CFA 2014 is primarily focused on children's special educational needs.[8] Some of the key requirements of the CFA 2014 relating to health[9] include:

- The duty to assess some disabled children's health needs as part of an education, health and care needs assessment[10] (see para 5.41 below) and to specify provision to meet certain of those needs in an EHC plan (see 5.43–5.46 below).[11]
- The obligation to include '[h]ealth care provision for children and young people with special educational needs or a disability that is additional to or different from that which is available to all children and young people in the area' within the 'local offer' for every area (see 5.27–5.29 below).[12]
- New co-ordination duties, including a duty on local authorities and partner commissioning bodies to put in place joint commissioning arrangements (see 5.20–5.26 below).[13]
- A new duty on health bodies to bring children who have or probably have special educational needs or a disability to the attention of the appropriate local authority.[14]

---

6   Department of Health, *A mandate from the government to NHS England: April 2015 to March 2016*, December 2014, para 4.13.

7   See Department for Education/Department of Health, *0 to 25 SEND code of practice: a guide for health professionals, Advice for clinical commissioning groups, health professionals and local authorities*, September 2014.

8   See Council for Disabled Children, *Using the Children and Families Act 2014 to improve outcomes for children and young people with SEN and disability: a briefing for health services* for a summary of the health-related elements of the CFA reforms. See further Council for Disabled Children, *Making it happen: Improving outcomes for children and young people with SEN and disability, a resource for CCGs* to explain the CFA 2014 and its implications for health services.

9   See further the summary annexed to the letter from Jane Cummings for NHS England to CCG Accountable Officers dated 10 August 2015 (Publications Gateway reference: 02838).

10   CFA 2014 s36.

11   CFA 2014 s37.

12   CFA 2014 s30 and SEND Regs 2014 reg 53 and Sch 2 para 12.

13   CFA 2014 s26.

14   CFA 2014 s23. There is also a requirement on NHS bodies to inform parents if it is thought that a particular voluntary organisation is likely to be able to give the parent advice or assistance in connection with any special educational needs or disability the child may have, see s23(4).

- The appointment of a 'designated medical officer' (DMO) to support each clinical commissioning group (CCG) in meeting its statutory responsibilities for children and young people with SEN and disabilities (see para 5.17 below).[15] The DMO has a particular role to support schools with their duties under the *Supporting Pupils with Medical Conditions* guidance.[16]

5.5   This emphasis on the healthcare needs of disabled children is underpinned by international obligations – particularly those enshrined in article 25 of the UN Convention on the Rights of Persons with Disabilities (UNCRPD) and article 24 of the UN Convention on the Rights of the Child (UNCRC). However, despite this clear focus nationally and internationally, health outcomes for disabled children remain problematic. The UN Committee on the Rights of the Child has found that inequality in access to health services remains in the UK, with disabled children in particular facing barriers to the realisation of this basic right.[17] A 2011 Green Paper[18] recorded that families struggled to get the right support from health services and that the system could feel bureaucratic, impenetrable and inefficient[19] and, in March 2012, a Care Quality Commission review[20] found that it could take up to 15 years for children's disabilities to be diagnosed, that health service providers often failed to consult disabled children and their families and that there was a lack of 'joined up' thinking between different health providers.

5.6   In 2013, the Chief Medical Officer's report stated that, '[w]hile disabled children and young people can lead full and fulfilling lives, for many, disability is associated with limited development and social participation, and with poor educational, health and employment outcomes',[21] finding in particular that 'it is widely recognised that there is a serious lack of appropriate mental health provision' for

15 SEND Code, para 3.45.
16 Department for Education, *Supporting pupils at school with medical conditions. Statutory guidance for governing bodies of maintained schools and proprietors of academies in England*, September 2014; see further chapter 4 at para 4.93.
17 UN Committee on the Rights of the Child, *Concluding observations*, 2008.
18 Department for Education, *Support and aspiration: A new approach to special educational needs and disability*, CM 8027, TSO, 2011.
19 Department for Education, *Support and aspiration: A new approach to special educational needs and disability*, CM 8027, TSO, 2011.
20 CQC, *Healthcare for disabled children and young people*, 2012.
21 Chief Medical Officer, *Our Children Deserve Better: Prevention Pays*, 2013.

children,[22] of whom approximately 10 per cent have a clinically diag-
nosable mental disorder.[23] Similar findings were made by the House
of Commons Health Committee in 2014, which concluded that there
are 'serious and deeply ingrained' problems with the commissioning and provision of CAMHS.[24] The cuts in funding to CAMHS services are of particular concern: Young Minds has reported that, in the
period 2010–2013, two-thirds of local authorities in England reduced
their CAMHS budget.[25]

5.7   In addition to concerns about inadequate access to healthcare
generally, since the 1980s there has been considerable public, professional and legal debate about decisions to withhold or withdraw medical treatments which save or extend the lives of disabled children.
Prior to that time, it was common practice to bring about the deaths
of some infants with learning disabilities and physical impairments
and decisions about 'selective non-treatment' were largely confined
to the domain of medical practice and conduct. Without doubt,
some decisions and associated protocols were underpinned by the
assumption that disabled children's lives were of less value than their
non-disabled peers. In the early 1980s, a number of landmark legal
judgments confronted this practice and established that the courts
were the proper place to determine issues of principle in relation to
the right to life of disabled children.[26] Since that time, disabled people
and parents of disabled children have written extensively about the
value accorded to disabled children's lives and the implications of
this for medical and healthcare decisions.[27]

5.8   There continue to be cases brought before the courts by healthcare providers and parents seeking judgments on practice which may
result in the death of a child.[28] Where these challenges concern deci-

---

22 Chief Medical Officer, *Our Children Deserve Better: Prevention Pays*, 2013,
    chapter 9, p6.
23 Chief Medical Officer, *Our Children Deserve Better: Prevention Pays*, 2013,
    chapter 10, p2.
24 House of Commons Health Committee, *Children's and adolescents' mental
    health and CAMHS*, third report of session 2014–15, p10.
25 Young Minds, *Local authorities and CAMHS budgets 2012/2013*, 2014.
26 For a detailed discussion of these issues, see L Clements and J Read (eds),
    *Disabled people and the right to life: the protection and violation of disabled people's
    most basic human rights*, Routledge, 2008.
27 See for example, J Campbell 'It's my life–it's my decision?: assisted dying
    versus assisted living', in L Clements and J Read (eds), *Disabled people and the
    right to life: the protection and violation of disabled people's most basic human rights*,
    Routledge, 2008.
28 See by way of recent example *Re Jake (A Child)* [2015] EWHC 2442 (Fam).

sions as to the cost-effectiveness of embarking on expensive treatments, the courts have held that these are primarily for the NHS and not for courts to make.[29] However, when the NHS seeks to withdraw life-sustaining treatment (or to embark on a treatment regime that may accelerate death) then, if there is a dispute between the medical professionals and the parents or others,[30] the court should adjudicate.[31] In such cases, the test will be the child's 'best interests' – which must be given a wide interpretation, and although the guiding principle will be to prolong life, other factors are relevant including the pain and suffering caused by the treatment and the quality of the life which will be prolonged. Where this is considered to be intolerable, from the point of view of the person concerned, then life-prolonging treatment may not be in their best interests.[32] The views, wishes and feelings of the parent(s) should always be taken fully into account in the best interests assessment, including where the parent has significant learning disabilities.[33]

5.9   This chapter sets out the duties and powers governing the provision of health services to disabled children, both in terms of universal and specialist services. It also considers the duties to provide specific services, whether by way of continuing care to disabled children with severe and/or complex health needs, mental health services or palliative care for children with life-limiting conditions.

5.10   The principal statute that places obligations on health bodies to provide services, the NHS Act 2006, is not (unlike those that govern social care and education rights – see chapters 3 and 4 above) drafted in specific and individualistic terms. Nevertheless, it has been held by the courts to place fundamental and enforceable obligations on health bodies. Furthermore, disabled children with the benefit of an EHC plan, as introduced by the CFA 2014, have a specific right to have the health services specified in the plan arranged for them, as discussed further below.

---

29 *R v Cambridge Health Authority ex p B* [1995] 1 WLR 898, CA.
30 See, for example, *Re B (A Minor) (Wardship: Medical Treatment)* [1981] 1 WLR 1421; [1990] 3 All ER 927; *An NHS Trust v D* [2002] 2 FLR 677; [2000] 2 FCR 577.
31 *Glass v UK* (2004) Application no 61827/00, 9 March 2004.
32 See, for example, *Portsmouth NHS Trust and Derek Wyatt and Charlotte Wyatt* [2004] EWHC 2247 (Fam); *L (A Child) (Medical Treatment: Benefit)* [2004] EWHC 2713 (Fam). The Supreme Court considered the requirements of a best interests approach to decisions about end of treatment in *Aintree University Hospitals NHS Foundation Trust v James* [2013] UKSC 67; (2013) 16 CCLR 554.
33 *Re Jake (A Child)* [2015] EWHC 2442 (Fam) at [44].

Changes to the NHS

5.11   In 2011 the Department of Health published the NHS constitution.
The version currently in force was issued on 27 July 2015 after a
consultation process[34] on various amendments. The constitution sets
out what service users can expect from the NHS and what the NHS
expects from them in return – and as such is an important advocacy
tool. The Secretary of State for Health and all NHS bodies (such as
clinical commissioning groups, NHS trusts etc) must have regard
to the NHS constitution when they exercise functions in relation to
the health service.[35] Key aspects of the NHS constitution for disabled
children include:

- The first principle, that 'The NHS provides a comprehensive service, available to all irrespective of ... disability'.
- The statement, in relation to the value of 'respect and dignity',
  that 'We value every person – whether patient, their families or
  carers, or staff – as an individual, respect their aspirations and
  commitments in life, and seek to understand their priorities,
  needs, abilities and limits'.
- Four statements of rights:
  - 'You have the right to access NHS services. You will not be
    refused access on unreasonable grounds';
  - 'You have the right to receive care and treatment that is appropri-
    ate to you, meets your needs and reflects your preferences';
  - 'You have the right to expect your NHS to assess the health
    requirements of your community and to commission and put
    in place the services to meet those needs as considered neces-
    sary'; and
  - 'You have the right not to be unlawfully discriminated against
    in the provision of NHS services including on grounds of ...
    disability'.
- The commitment 'to make decisions in a clear and transparent
  way, so that patients and the public can understand how services
  are planned and delivered'.
- Statements about the right to decent quality of care and
  environment.
- Statements in relation to the provision of care with dignity and in
  a way that respects people's human rights.

34 Department of Health, *A consultation on updating the NHS Constitution*,
February 2015.
35 NHS Act 2006 s1B and Health Act 2009 s2 respectively.

- The statement that 'You have the right to be involved in planning and making decisions about your health and care with your care provider or providers, including your end of life care, and to be given information and support to enable you to do this. Where appropriate, this right includes your family and carers. This includes being given the chance to manage your own care and treatment, if appropriate'.

5.12 The reorganisation of the NHS resulting from the Health and Social Care Act 2012 means that the NHS in England is structured as follows:

- The Secretary of State for Health retains the overarching duty[36] to promote a comprehensive health service 'designed to secure improvement in the physical and mental health of the people of England ...'. The Secretary of State must particularly have regard to 'the need to reduce inequalities between the people of England with respect to the benefits that they can obtain from the health service'.[37]

- 211 clinical commissioning groups (CCGs)[38] are responsible for planning and purchasing local healthcare services, including secondary healthcare and mental healthcare services.[39] This includes children's healthcare services, children's mental healthcare services and maternity services. CCGs have a number of duties relevant to disabled children, including in relation to reducing inequalities[40] and promoting patient involvement[41]. While CCGs have significant GP representation, their members include other professionals and representatives of the public. CCGs commission services from hospitals, private and voluntary sector providers and community mental health services.

- NHS England acts as the commissioning body responsible for planning primary care and specialist services for which it would be inefficient to have local commissioning.[42] For example, there is

---

36 NHS Act 2006 s1, as substituted by Health and Social Care Act 2012 s1.

37 NHS Act 2006 s1C, as added by Health and Social Care Act 2012 s4.

38 As established by NHS Act 2006 s1I (as added by Health and Social Care Act 2012 s10), with the function of 'arranging for the provision of services for the purposes of the health service in England'.

39 See NHS Act 2006 s3, as amended by Health and Social Care Act 2012 s13 to transfer the primary responsibility for commissioning health services from the secretary of state to CCGs.

40 NHS Act 2006 s14T, as added by Health and Social Care Act 2012 s26.

41 NHS Act 2006 s14U, as added by Health and Social Care Act 2012 s26.

42 See NHS Act 2006 s1H, as added by Health and Social Care Act 2012 s9.

a clinical reference group within NHS England which deals with the commissioning of 'complex disability equipment', including specialist wheelchair services for disabled children.[43] NHS England holds the overarching duty to continue the promotion of a comprehensive health service in England concurrently with the Secretary of State.[44] NHS England also has a number of duties relevant to disabled children, including in relation to reducing inequalities[45] and promoting patient involvement.[46]

- Healthwatch England[47] and Local Healthwatch[48] are intended to act as 'consumer champion organisations' to increase patient involvement in health and social care provision. Local Healthwatch has the power to conduct 'Enter and Views' on children's health settings, which involve speaking to the children and young people using the services and observing policies and practices in action.[49]

- Public Health England (an executive agency of the Department of Health) has overall responsibility for addressing health inequalities and improving health outcomes in England.

- Monitor (the financial regulator for health services in England that sits alongside the CQC) acts as an independent regulator for quality in health and social care in England.[50] Monitor has a specific oversight role for NHS Foundation Trusts, which are independent legal entities with significant financial freedoms. A significant number of hospitals now have Foundation Trust status.

- As part of the shift of responsibility for public health, local authorities must establish Health and Wellbeing Boards.[51] The primary purpose of these boards is to encourage integrated working in the provision of health and social care services 'for the purpose of advancing the health and wellbeing of the people in [the] area'.[52]

43 See www.england.nhs.uk/commissioning/spec-services/npc-crg/ group-d/d01/.
44 NHS Act 2006 s1H(2).
45 NHS Act 2006 s13G, as added by Health and Social Care Act 2012 s23.
46 NHS Act 2006 s13H, as added by Health and Social Care Act 2012 s23.
47 Established under Health and Social Care Act 2012 s181, amending Health and Social Care Act 2008 Sch 1 and adding ss45A–45C.
48 See Health and Social Care Act 2012 ss182–189, amending the Local Government and Public Involvement in Health Act 2007 in various respects.
49 Healthwatch, *Healthwatch, children and young people: The role of local Healthwatch*, November 2014, p3.
50 See Health and Social Care Act 2012 ss61–71 and Sch 8.
51 See Health and Social Care Act 2012 ss194–199.
52 Health and Social Care Act 2012 s195.

5.13   In addition, from 1 October 2015, the responsibility for commissioning children's public health services has transferred from NHS England to local authorities.[53]

5.14   The reorganised NHS is governed by the following five principles set out in the NHS Outcomes Framework:

1) Preventing people from dying prematurely.
2) Enhancing the quality of life for people with long-term conditions.
3) Helping people to recover from episodes of ill health or following injury.
4) Ensuring people have a positive experience of care.
5) Treating and caring for people in a safe environment and protecting them from avoidable harm.

5.15   A key practical question for disabled children and their families will be whether their health needs are the responsibility of their local CCG or NHS England. In the vast majority of cases, the CCG will hold the responsibility, and where it does not it should refer the child and family to NHS England. There is a detailed 'Manual' which describes which elements of specialised services are directly commissioned by NHS England and which by CCGs, the most recent version of which was published in January 2014.[54]

5.16   One of the NHS England 'National Programmes of Care' is for 'Women and Children', which includes many specialist paediatric health services. There are published 'Commissioning Intentions' which set out NHS England's approach to its specialist commissioning remit.[55] The current version of this document indicates that specialist wheelchair services will now be commissioned by CCGs. An important service for many disabled children, which remains commissioned by NHS England, is Tier 4 Child and Adolescent Mental Health Services (CAMHS); see paras 5.107–5.124 below. These are highly specialised services with a primary purpose of the assessment and treatment of severe and complex mental health disorders in children. NHS England also commissions secure CAMHS services.

5.17   Under the reforms introduced by the CFA 2014, every CCG is required to appoint a 'Designated Medical Officer' (DMO), whose primary role is 'providing a point of contact for local partners, when

---

53   See the Local Authorities (Public Health Functions and Entry to Premises by Local Healthwatch Representatives) Regulations 2013 SI No 351 (as amended).

54   NHS England, *Manual for Prescribed Specialised Services 2013/14*, January 2014.

55   NHS England, *Commissioning Intentions 2015/16 for Prescribed Specialised Services*.

notifying parents and local authorities about children and young people they believe have, or may have, SEN or a disability, and when seeking advice on SEN or disabilities'.[56] The DMO should be a senior clinician, often a paediatrician, who will be responsible for ensuring that assessment, planning and health support is carried out.[57]

Children and families' views to inform health services

5.18   NHS bodies have a duty[58] to make arrangements to ensure that users of services are, either directly or through representatives, involved in:

- the planning of the provision of health services;
- the development and consideration of proposals for changes in the way those services are provided, if implementation of the proposal would have an impact on the manner in which services are provided or the range of services available; and
- decisions to be made by the NHS body affecting the operation of those services, if the decision would have an impact on the manner in which services are provided or the range of services available.

5.19   The views of disabled children, young people and their families are, therefore, expected to inform local design and delivery of health services. Frequently, however, disabled children have been found to be less actively involved in decisions about both their treatment and service development than children who are not disabled. Standard 8 of the National Service Framework (NSF) for Children (see below), required local and NHS bodies to ensure disabled children and their parents are routinely involved and supported in making informed decisions.[59] The importance of involving of children and families in decision-making was reinforced in England by the *Aiming high for disabled children* review[60] and by the Local Government and Public Involvement in Health Act 2007, as now amended to require the

56   SEND Code, para 3.45.
57   SEND Code, para 3.46.
58   Under NHS Act 2006 s242(1B)–(1F).
59   Department of Health, *National service framework for children, young people and maternity services: disabled children and young people and those with complex health needs*, 2004 ('Disabled Child Standard, Children's NSF'), pp5, 29, 30.
60   HM Treasury/DfES, 2007.

establishment of Health and Wellbeing Boards (see paras 5.12 above) which can provide important forums for the voices of disabled children and families to be heard. The requirement for the NHS to take account of the views of its users, including disabled children and their families, is also central to the NHS Constitution (see para 5.11 above).

Co-operation between health bodies and local authorities

5.20   An important issue for many disabled children and their families is, which body will take the lead responsibility for meeting their needs – the local authority or the relevant health body? The answer to this question is that health bodies and local authorities are expected to work together to meet the health needs of disabled children. This expectation comes from (among other sources):

- NHS Act 2006 s82, which states that in exercising their respective functions, NHS bodies and local authorities must co-operate with one another in order to secure and advance the health and welfare of the people of England and Wales.
- Children Act 2004 s10, which requires local authorities to co-operate with their 'relevant partners', including health bodies, to safeguard and promote the welfare of children in their area, as explained in the statutory guidance, *Working together to safeguard children: A guide to inter-agency working to safeguard and promote the welfare of children* (March 2015).

5.21   Further, CFA s26 requires local authorities and 'partner commissioning bodies' (including CCGs and NHS England) to make 'joint commissioning arrangements' about the education, health and care provision to be secured for children and young people with special educational needs and disabled young people. A lengthy list of requirements for these joint arrangements is imposed by CFA s26(3). There are further requirements in relation to co-operation between local authorities and NHS bodies imposed by CFA s25 (headed 'promoting integration'), ss28–29 ('co-operating generally') and s31 ('co-operating in specific cases').

5.22   For children 'in need' generally, including disabled children, local authorities have a clear obligation to take the lead in ensuring their needs are met, bringing in different agencies (including health) where necessary. However, for children with particularly severe and/or complex health needs, the NHS may be the lead agency – for example, when a child is eligible for 'continuing care' funding (see paras 5.87–5.100).

5.23   To deliver co-operation and joint working on the ground, 'key workers' or 'care co-ordinators' are essential (see chapter 3 at para 3.25). Standard 8 of the Children's National Service Framework (NSF) stated that the key workers should be 'the main point of contact with the family' and should take responsibility for co-ordinating review meetings and liaising with professionals to ensure all agreed support is delivered.

5.24   A multidisciplinary approach requires co-ordinated assessment, planning and commissioning. A 2013 publication from the Children and Young People's Health Outcomes Forum,[61] advises how agencies should work together so as to integrate health, social care, education and other services, and reinforces the requirements of Standard 8 of the Children's NSF. Additionally, the 2006 English *Joint planning and commissioning framework for children, young people and maternity services*[62] introduced a framework to help local commissioners (both health bodies and local authorities) to design a unified system in each local area to achieve a joined-up picture of children and young people's needs and for collaboration to achieve the best use of joint resources for 'better outcomes'.[63]

5.25   Since there is no explicit statutory obligation on the NHS or the local authority to act as the lead agency, there is obvious scope for a disabled child's needs to be allowed to 'drift' while each authority blames the other for a service failure. In such cases, a complaint (or if sufficiently urgent, an application for judicial review: see chapter 11) should be made against both authorities. The complaint or application for judicial review should be framed, not only in terms of the failure to meet the specific need but also in terms of the authorities' failure to 'work together' as required by NHS Act 2006 s82, Children Act 2004 s10 and multiple provisions of the CFA 2014, not least the requirement for joint commissioning arrangements in s26. The

61 *Improving Children and Young People's Health Outcomes: a system wide response*, English Guidance, February 2013.

62 HM Government, *Joint planning and commissioning framework for children, young people and maternity services*, 2006.

63 This is reinforced in Department of Health, *Improving Children and Young People's Health Outcomes: a system wide response*, February 2013, and Department of Health, *The commissioning framework for health and wellbeing*, 2007. See also *Commissioning a good child health service*, Royal College of General Practitioners, Royal College of Paediatrics and Royal College of Nursing, March 2013.

ombudsmen in general expect the authority that is in touch with the child to 'grasp the nettle' and secure the provision, before entering into protracted negotiations with the other authority on liability for the care costs.[64]

5.26   Such a complaint will also be appropriate when the dispute is between different NHS bodies (which are under a duty to co-operate with each other by virtue of NHS Act 2006 s72). The ombudsmen have found maladministration[65] where disputing health bodies have, in such a case, failed to agree which one of them would accept funding responsibility on an interim basis. In the current NHS structures, this would include a case where there is a dispute as to responsibility for meeting a disabled child's needs between a CCG and NHS England.

The 'local offer' and health

5.27   One of the key reforms introduced by the CFA 2014 is the requirement for every area to establish a 'local offer' covering education, health and care provision and other related services.[66] Although the duty to publish this information falls on the local authority, the local offer can only be an effective tool if health bodies, particularly CCGs, co-operate in its development. When preparing and reviewing a local offer, a local authority must consult a range of health bodies, including NHS England and any CCG within its area.[67] The central requirement to publish comments on the local offer[68] will include comments on health provision.

5.28   The health provision which must be included in the local offer is:

Health care provision for children and young people with special educational needs or a disability that is additional to or different from that which is available to all children and young people in the area, including –

---

64 Complaint no 96/C/3868 against Calderdale MBC.
65 Report by the Public Services Ombudsman for Wales and the Health Service Ombudsman for England of an investigation of a complaint about the Welsh Assembly Government (Health Commission Wales) Cardiff and Vale NHS Trust and Plymouth Teaching Primary Care Trust, Third Report, Session 2008–2009, HC 858, TSO, 2009.
66 CFA 2014 s30. See chapter 3 at para 3.28 for the local offer in relation to social care and chapter 4 at para 4.72 in relation to education.
67 SEND Regs 2014 reg 54(2).
68 SEND Regs 2014 reg 56.

(a) services for relevant early years providers, schools and post-16 institutions to assist them in supporting children and young people with medical conditions, and

(b) arrangements for making those services which are available to all children and young people in the area accessible to children and young people with special educational needs or a disability.[69]

5.29   The SEND Code also specifies that the local offer must include:[70]

- speech and language therapy and other therapies such as physiotherapy and occupational therapy and services relating to mental health;
- wheelchair services and community equipment, children's community nursing, continence services;
- palliative and respite care and other provision for children with complex health needs;
- other services such as emergency care provision and habilitation support;
- provision for children and young people's continuing care arrangements;
- support for young people when moving between healthcare services for children to healthcare services for adults.

Health services – fundamental duties

5.30   The NHS Act 2006 s1(1) requires the secretary of state to:

continue the promotion in England of a comprehensive health service, designed to secure improvement –

(a) in the physical and mental health of the people of England, and

(b) in the prevention, diagnosis and treatment of illness.

5.31   Section 3 of the 2006 Act, as amended, places a duty on each CCG to:

arrange for the provision of the following to such extent as it considers necessary to meet the reasonable requirements of the persons for whom it has responsibility:

(a) hospital accommodation,

(b) other accommodation for the purpose of any service provided under this Act,

(c) medical, dental, ophthalmic, nursing and ambulance services,

(d) such other services or facilities for the care of pregnant women, women who are breastfeeding and young children as the CCG considers are appropriate as part of the health service,

---

69 SEND Regs 2014 Sch 2, para 12.
70 SEND Code, para 4.40

(e) such other services or facilities for the prevention of illness, the care of persons suffering from illness and the after-care of persons who have suffered from illness as the CCG considers are appropriate as part of the health service,

(f) such other services or facilities as are required for the diagnosis and treatment of illness.

5.32   The 2006 Act requires, therefore, that there be a 'comprehensive' health service which all can access – including disabled children. This entitlement of universal access to the NHS is emphasised by the NHS constitution, see para 5.11 above.

5.33   Health services can be categorised into those delivered as 'primary care' and 'secondary care'. Primary care describes the health services that play a central role in local community including GPs, pharmacists, dentists and midwives. Primary care providers are usually the first point of contact for a patient and a continuing point of contact, even if the patient is receiving services from a hospital or from some other 'secondary' NHS facility.

5.34   Secondary care is acute or specialist healthcare provided in a hospital or other secondary care setting. Patients are usually referred from a primary care professional – for example, a GP. The 2013 *Who Pays?* guidance identifies who is responsible for the funding of a specific patient's needs.[71] In England, responsibility is primarily linked to registration with a GP, and for those who are not registered with a GP, it is based on where they are 'usually resident'.

The responsibilities of GPs and other primary health services

5.35   As with all children, GPs act as the main point of access or referral to all appropriate medical and health services that a disabled child may need. At the primary care level, these may include: medical services provided directly by the GP, physiotherapy, speech and language therapy, occupational therapy, early intervention rehabilitation programmes, general community nursing and health visiting. The GP also is responsible for referring a child for services in the secondary healthcare sector (and liaising with other healthcare professionals in this respect).[72] This can include obtaining a 'second opinion' on

71 NHS England, *Who Pays?* September 2013.
72 National Health Service (General Medical Services Contracts) Regulations 2004 SI No 291 reg 15(4)(b) (as amended).

a child's diagnosis and healthcare treatment – as well as referrals for in- and out-patient paediatric care in hospital settings and some interventions such as physiotherapy, speech and language therapy and occupational therapy which may also be provided in this sector as well as in primary care. Some children, particularly those with complex impairments, may require assessment, treatment and monitoring by a range of medical and healthcare specialists working in different in- and out-patient departments of hospitals.

5.36   The GP contract[73] requires, among other things, that they refer their patients for 'other services under the 2006 Acts'. Since the 2006 Act includes services provided by local authorities such as a home help service[74] (which could include a 'sitting service'), it follows that GPs are also obliged to make referrals to local authorities where a need for such social care support may exist.

5.37   As noted above, disabled children – especially if their impairment is diagnosed in hospital at birth – may be subjected to multiple health assessments to diagnose their condition to the satisfaction of the medical practitioners. However, they may then be – in effect – abandoned by the statutory services. This phenomenon has been expressed in the following terms:[75]

> As soon as a condition or impairment has been identified or diagnosed, service professionals may fade away without any support or significant information being provided for the family. All too often nothing further is done until a crisis develops.

5.38   The child may then be discharged with only limited liaison with the local GP surgery and the health visitor and without any proper co-ordination with the local authority concerning social care support services. In such cases, immediate contact should be made with the GP surgery to ensure that the child's and family's needs are addressed and that timely referrals can then be made to the relevant expert services as and when a need arises (for example, physiotherapy, speech and language therapy as well as social care support from the local authority).

---

73 National Health Service (General Medical Services Contracts) Regulations 2004 SI No 291 reg 15 (as amended).

74 NHS Act 2006 s254 and Sch 20 para 3 – which applies to both England and Wales and includes such a service for a disabled child.

75 J Read, L Clements and D Ruebain, *Disabled children and the law: research and good practice*, 2nd edn, Jessica Kingsley Publishers, 2006, p116.

Duty to assess healthcare needs

5.39   Notwithstanding the absence of an explicit provision in the NHS Act
2006 requiring a health body to assess the healthcare needs of a disabled child, there are a number of reasons why such a duty almost
certainly exists. The first concerns the analogous findings of the
House of Lords in *R (G) v Barnet LBC and others*[76] that a duty to
assess exists under the Children Act (CA) 1989, despite it lacking an
explicit obligation. The second and more cogent reason concerns the
general obligations imposed by the law on public bodies – essentially
that in order to exercise their duties towards disabled children, health
bodies must follow a process that is, by any other name, an assessment – ie the gathering of all relevant information about the child
and his or her care needs and the rational determination of whether
it is necessary to provide services to meet these needs.[77]

5.40   Assessment is, therefore, the means by which the health body
'assembles the relevant information and applies it to the statutory
ends, and hence affords good evidence to any inquirer of the due
discharge of its statutory duties'.[78] Further evidence of such a duty to
assess can be implied from the obligations created by CA 2004 s11
which requires health bodies and others to safeguard and promote
children's welfare and from the 2013 Department of Health guidance which includes a 'pledge' to improve the health outcomes of
children and young people, including by providing better care for disabled children and young people.[79] This builds on the previous child
health strategy in England, which made a commitment that 'by 2010,
all children with complex health needs will have an individual care
plan' – a commitment which rests on there being a duty to assess
a child's individual needs so that such a plan can be meaningfully
drawn up.[80]

---

76 [2003] UKHL 57; [2004] 2 AC 208.
77 In effect 'asking themselves the right question', one of the fundamental public
law requirements on all public bodies, see *Secretary of State for Education and
Science v Tameside MBC* [1977] AC 1014.
78 *R v Islington LBC ex p Rixon* (1997–98) 1 CCLR 119 at 128.
79 Department of Health, *Improving Children and Young People's Health Outcomes:
a system wide response*, 2013, and see also Department of Health, *Better health
outcomes for children and young people: Our pledge*, 2013.
80 Department for Children Schools and Families/Department of Health, *Healthy
lives, brighter futures*, 2009, p72 at 6.42.

Education, health and care needs assessments

5.41   Some disabled children with significant special educational needs will now have the benefit of the education, health and care needs assessment duty imposed by CFA 2014 s36 (EHC assessments). Although the local authority takes the lead in this assessment process and the key question to determine is whether it may be necessary for special educational provision to be made for the child or young person in accordance with an EHC plan,[81] the NHS still has an important role to play.

5.42   The process of carrying out EHC assessments is governed by the SEND Regs 2014 regs 3–10.[82] Under these regulations:

- Where the local authority is considering securing an EHC needs assessment it must also notify the responsible commissioning body.[83]
- Where the local authority decides to assess, it must seek 'medical advice and information from a health care professional identified by the responsible commissioning body'.[84] This information and advice must be considered by the local authority when securing the assessment.[85]
- NHS bodies must respond to requests for input into EHC assessments within six weeks, unless it is impractical for them to do so for one of a limited set of specified reasons.[86]
- If, following an assessment, the local authority determines not to secure an EHC plan for the child (see below and further at chapter 4, para 4.130) then the responsible commissioning body must be notified.[87]

---

81 CFA 2014 s36(8)(b).
82 SI No 1530. See further chapter 4 at paras 4.110–4.133.
83 SEND Regs 2014 reg 4(2)(a). The commissioning body must also be notified of the decision on whether or not to conduct an EHC needs assessment, see reg 5(2).
84 SEND Regs 2014 reg 6(1)(c) – unless such advice has previously been provided for any purpose and the person providing that advice, the local authority and the child's parent or the young person are satisfied that it is sufficient for the purposes of an EHC needs assessment, see reg 6(4).
85 SEND Regs 2014 reg 7(c).
86 SEND Regs 2014 reg 8.
87 SEND Regs 2014 reg 10(2).

Education, health and care plans

5.43   On completion of an EHC assessment (see above at 5.41–5.42 and further at chapter 4), the local authority must secure and maintain an education, health and care plan (EHC plan) for the child or young person where the assessment shows that it is necessary for special educational provision to be made in accordance with an EHC plan.[88]

5.44   Although the duty to put an EHC plan in place is dependent on the child or young person having significant special educational needs, the presence of an EHC plan can have important consequences for the child or young person's right to health services. Firstly, an EHC plan must include 'any health care provision reasonably required by the learning difficulties and disabilities which result in him or her having special educational needs'.[89]

5.45   Secondly and most importantly, the effect of the inclusion of health care provision within an EHC plan is to establish a specific right for the child or young person to obtain the specified provision. This is the consequence of CFA 2014 s42(3), which reads: 'If the plan specifies health care provision, the responsible commissioning body must arrange the specified health care provision for the child or young person'. The 'responsible commissioning body' will generally be the CCG, but as noted above (see paras 5.12–5.15) may also be NHS England for more specialised services. The SEND Code also states that young people and parents of children who have EHC plans have the right to request a personal budget, which may contain elements of education, social care and health funding.[90] See paras 5.105–5.106 below in relation to health personal budgets generally.

5.46   The preparation of EHC plans is governed by the SEND Regs 2014 regs 11 to 17. Relevant provisions of these regulations from the health perspective include:

•   When preparing an EHC plan, the local authority must take into account the evidence received when undertaking the EHC needs assessment, including information and advice from health professionals.[91]

88   CFA 2014 s37(1).
89   CFA 2014 s37(2)(d). An EHC plan may also specify other health care and social care provision reasonably required by the child or young person, see s37(3).
90   SEND Code, para 3.38.
91   SEND Regs 2014 reg 11.

- The plan must set out in section C 'the child or young person's health care needs which relate to their special educational needs'.[92]
- The plan must set out in section G 'any health care provision reasonably required by the learning difficulties or disabilities which result in the child or young person having special educational needs'.[93] This must be agreed by the responsible commissioning body.[94]
- Where the child is in or beyond year 9 at school, the plan must include health care provision 'to assist the child or young person in preparation for adulthood and independent living'.[95]
- Advice and information, including from health professionals, must be set out in the appendices to the plan (section K).[96]
- The final plan must be sent to the responsible commissioning body (and of course the parents or young person and the school) as soon as practicable and, in any event, within 20 weeks of the request for an EHC needs assessment,[97] unless any of the exemptions to this timeframe[98] apply.
- Commissioning bodies must liaise in the event that a child or young person moves to a new commissioning body's area but remains the responsibility of the same local authority.[99]

Health action plans

5.47   Health action plans (HAPs) for people with learning disabilities became official policy with the publication of *Valuing People* in 2001.[100] This required that people with learning disabilities be offered a HAP by the relevant health bodies – although primary responsibility rested with primary care nurses and GPs.

---

92 SEND Regs 2014 reg 12(1)(c).
93 SEND Regs 2014 reg 12(1)(g).
94 SEND Regs 2014 reg 12(2).
95 SEND Regs 2014 reg 12(3).
96 SEND Regs 2014 reg 12(4).
97 SEND Regs 2014 reg 13(2).
98 Being those specified in SEND Regs 2014 reg 10(4)(a)–(d) in relation to EHC assessments. See further chapter 4 at para 4.133.
99 SEND Regs 2014 reg 16.
100 Department of Health, *Valuing people: A new strategy for learning disability for the 21st century*, Cm 5086, 2001, at paras 6.15–6.18.

5.48   HAPs consider the person's needs for 'health interventions' such as oral health and dental care, fitness and mobility, continence, vision, hearing, nutrition and emotional needs as well as details of medication taken, side effects, and records of any screening tests. There needs to be, in each case, someone who supports the person with the development of their HAP – and this is referred to as a 'Health Facilitator' – ideally this person is chosen by the person with learning difficulties and may be a family member, friend, support worker or health professional. There is no standard format for a HAP but a number of examples exist. The 2001 guidance[101] states that HAPs are to be offered and reviewed at the following stages:

- transition from secondary education with a process for ongoing referral;
- leaving home to move into a residential service;
- moving home from one provider to another;
- moving to an out-of-area placement;
- changes in health status, for example as a result of a period of out-patient care or in-patient treatment;
- on retirement;
- when planning transition for those living with older family carers.

5.49   Good practice guidance on the preparation of HAPs has been issued by the Royal College of GPs.[102]

5.50   In 2008, the Joint Committee on Human Rights in its report *A Life Like Any Other*[103] called into question the commitment of (amongst others) health bodies to the implementation of the government's policy in *Valuing People* and this resulted in follow-up guidance in 2008[104] which acknowledged that 'achievement of the health-related targets in *Valuing People*' had been 'one of the areas where least progress' had been made.[105] This guidance made a commitment that in addition there would be annual health checks for people with learning disabilities (who are known to local authorities) through a

---

101 Department of Health, *Valuing people: A new strategy for learning disability for the 21st century*, Cm 5086, 2001, at para 6.16.

102 Matt Hoghton, *A step by step guide for GP practices: Annual health checks for people with a learning disability*, Royal College of GPs, 2010.

103 Joint Committee on Human rights, *A life like any other*, Seventh Report of Session 2007–08, HL Paper 40-I HC 73-I, The Stationery Office Limited, 2008.

104 Department of Health, *Health action planning and health facilitation for people with learning disabilities: good practice guidance*, 2008.

105 Department of Health, *Health action planning and health facilitation for people with learning disabilities: good practice guidance*, 2008, p1.

directed enhanced scheme. This scheme is available from GPs whose practices have agreed to undertake this additional function – in addition to their core obligations under the GP.[106]

Children's health services – the Children's NSF

5.51   In 2003, in an effort to drive up the standard of care provided to all children by the NHS and social services authorities in England, the government commenced publication of a *National service framework for children, young people and maternity services* (the Children's NSF),[107] which sets national standards and provides best practice guidance for children's health and social care. The Children's NSF, which comprises 11 separate documents focusing on distinct issues/ disabling conditions, is best considered as 'practice guidance' (see chapter 2 at para 2.44). As such it acts as a benchmark – setting a standard to which public bodies should aspire. A significant failure to reach the standards set out in the Children's NSF may be evidence of maladministration. Although the ten-year programme under the Children's NSF has now reached an end, the standards it set are still relevant guidance as to what disabled children and their families can expect from the NHS.

5.52   Part 1 of the Children's NSF set out five core standards concerning service provision for all children and young people and their parents and carers. Each core standard is summarised below.

Standard 1: Promoting health and well-being, identifying needs and intervening early

The health and well-being of all children and young people is promoted and delivered through a co-ordinated programme of action including prevention and early intervention wherever possible, to ensure long-term gain, led by the NHS in partnership with local authorities.

5.53   Under the Healthy Child Programme introduced to achieve Standard 1, the local NHS (now CCGs) must ensure that a systematic assessment of each child's physical, emotional and social develop-

---

106 Primary Medical Services (Directed Enhanced Services) (England) Directions 2006 as amended (eg, Primary Medical Services (Directed Enhanced Services) (England) (Amendment) Directions 2011); see further *Clinical directed enhanced services (DESs) for GMS contract. Guidance and audit requirements for 2012/13*, BMA/NHS Employers, 2012.

107 Department of Health, *National service framework for children, young people and maternity services: core standards*, 2004 (Core document, Children's NSF).

ment and family needs is completed by the child's first birthday and in the absence of regular contact a review takes place when the child is aged between two and three. Key issues must be identified and interventions required must be documented.[108] In addition all professionals working with children and young people need to be aware of health and developmental problems and proactive in identifying opportunities to promote a child's health and well-being. CCGs and local authorities also have a responsibility to tailor health promotion services to the needs of disadvantaged groups, including children in special circumstances, identified through a local population needs assessment.[109]

Standard 2: Supporting parenting

Parents or carers are enabled to receive the information, services and support which will help them to care for their children and equip them with the skills they need to ensure that their children have optimum life chances and are healthy and safe.

5.54   The markers of good practice for this standard include the provision of information and services to support parenting through local multi-agency partnerships, that parents whose children are experiencing difficulties receive early support and evidence-based interventions and that the local NHS and local authorities ensure that parents are involved in the planning and delivery of services, with representation from all local communities and groups.[110]

Standard 3: Child, young person and family-centred services

Children and young people and families receive high quality services which are co-ordinated around their individual and family needs and take account of their views.

5.55   This standard recognises that children have a right to be involved in decisions about their care. Particular effort should be made to ensure that children and young people who are often excluded from participation in activities are supported in giving their views and that parents' views are considered in planning and service development.[111] Formal working arrangements need to be in place for the provision of link workers, advocates to support children and young

---

108 Core Document, Children's NSF, p40.
109 Core Document, Children's NSF, p22.
110 Core Document, Children's NSF, p66.
111 Core Document, Children's NSF, p91.

people, interpreters and/or support workers for children in special circumstances or from minority groups, to represent their needs during individual consultations and on multi-disciplinary review and development groups.[112]

5.56 All children and young people have a right to care and support which meets their developmental needs and provides them with the opportunity to achieve, or maintain, their optimal standard of health, development and well-being, regardless of their individual circumstances or those of their families and communities.[113] To achieve this there needs to be a high degree of co-ordination between different children's service providers with the highest degree of integration and co-ordination required when a child or young person is suffering abuse or neglect and local safeguarding children procedures are being followed.[114]

Standard 4: Growing up into adulthood

All young people have access to age-appropriate services which are responsive to their specific needs as they grow into adulthood.

5.57 This standard is considered in chapter 10 at para 10.64.

Standard 5: Safeguarding and promoting the welfare of children and young people

All agencies work to prevent children suffering harm and to promote their welfare, provide them with the services they require to address their identified needs and safeguard children who are being or who are likely to be harmed.

5.58 Safeguarding and promoting children's welfare must be a priority. All agencies should ensure that the Local Safeguarding Children Board (LSCB), is effective in safeguarding and promoting the welfare of children and young people through the provision of adequate financial and human resources, senior management representation and adherence to its policies and procedures (see also the *Working together to safeguard children* guidance, as discussed in chapter 3 at paras 3.157–3.163).

112 Core Document, Children's NSF, p92.
113 Core Document, Children's NSF, p93.
114 Core Document, Children's NSF, p99.

Disabled children's health services and the NSF

5.59   While the core standards of the NSF apply to all children, the needs of disabled children and their families were specifically addressed in Standard 8, the headline standard within which reads as follows:

> Children and young people who are disabled or who have complex health needs receive co-ordinated, high quality child and family centred services which are based on assessed needs, which promote social inclusion and where possible, enable them and their families to live ordinary lives.[115]

5.60   When read with the five core standards of the Children's NSF, Standard 8 provides comprehensive best practice guidance on the provision of health and related services to disabled children.

Identification of disability and the NSF

5.61   Standard 8 of the Children's NSF requires that local authorities, CCGs, NHS Trusts and schools ensure that children with possible impairments have prompt access to a diagnostic assessment facility, that diagnosis is followed and that the assessment includes the parents' and siblings' needs for support.

Hospital services and the NSF

5.62   Disabled children's need to attend hospital appointments can be disruptive to school and family life. Under Standard 8, the NHS should ensure that hospital departments and clinics synchronise their appointment systems as far as possible, so that families make a minimum number of visits and that systems are in place to ensure that children and young people who find it hard to wait, eg those with autistic spectrum disorders, do not have to wait unduly at out-patient clinics or general practice surgeries. Children and young people with complex healthcare needs who are prone to health crises must be seen urgently on request.[116]

5.63   The standard for hospital services for children in the Children's NSF aims to deliver hospital services that meet the needs of children, young people and their parents, and 'provide effective and safe care,

---

115 Disabled Child Standard, Children's NSF, p5.
116 Disabled Child Standard, Children's NSF, p12.

through appropriately trained and skilled staff working in suitable, child-friendly and safe environments'.[117]

5.64   The above requirement for the standard of hospital-based care is considered by the NSF to comprise three distinct elements, namely:

1. Child-centred hospital services[118]

Children and young people should receive care that is integrated and co-ordinated around their particular needs, and the needs of their family. They, and their parents, should be treated with respect, and should be given support and information to enable them to understand and cope with the illness or injury, and the treatment needed. They should be encouraged to be active partners in decisions about their health and care, and, where possible, be able to exercise choice.

2. Quality and safety of care provided[119]

Children and young people should receive appropriate high quality, evidence-based hospital care, developed through clinical governance and delivered by staff who have the right set of skills.

3. Quality of setting and environment[120]

Care will be provided in an appropriate location and in an environment that is safe and well suited to the age and stage of development of the child or young person.

5.65   In meeting these three elements of the standard, hospitals need to recognise and meet the very particular needs of disabled children and involve them and their parents in the planning of services.[121] Disabled children, young people and their parents need to know that staff understand how to support them and have a sound knowledge of the needs of disabled children. Where necessary, this includes how to communicate, support with eating and drinking, the use of specialised aids and equipment, and the delicacy required in dealing with ethical issues, such as consent to intensive therapy.[122] Staff

---

117 Department of Health, *Getting the right start: National Service Framework for Children: Standard for Hospital Services* ('Standard for Hospital Services, Children's NSF'), 2003, p8.

118 Standard for Hospital Services, Children's NSF, p13.

119 Standard for Hospital Services, Children's NSF, p21.

120 Standard for Hospital Services, Children's NSF, p36.

121 Standard for Hospital Services, Children's NSF, p32 at 4.52.

122 See in this respect, Cerebra Legal Entitlements Research Project Digest, Digest of Opinions 2014, 'Terri's Story', Cardiff Law School, 2015, which concerns a disabled young person's strongly expressed wishes concerning the care arrangements for her intimate personal care needs.

need competencies in supporting children with a range of disabilities, including those with learning disabilities or autistic spectrum disorders. There should be procedures for managing challenging behaviour and suitable equipment should be available.[123]

5.66   A multi-agency plan developed and agreed with the disabled child or young person and their parents should be put in place while they are in hospital. For disabled children with complex health needs, this should be expanded into a personal record with a clinical summary of what they require, for example, therapies and equipment, support with eating and drinking, going to the toilet or communicating.[124]

5.67   Sadly it appears that the reality of hospital services for children (including disabled children) remains very different from the NSF's vision. In February 2009, the Healthcare Commission published a report on the care provided to children in NHS hospitals outside of specialist paediatric settings.[125] This reported the need for 'significant improvement' in areas such as child protection, managing children's pain, life support and skills of surgeons and anaesthetists. Specifically, it found almost two-thirds of health trusts did not train enough nurses to administer pain relief to children, and that there was 'very limited progress' in training staff to provide life support to children, with 94 per cent failing to provide basic resuscitation training to surgeons. The CQC made similar findings in its 2012 report into healthcare for disabled children, noting that nearly 60 per cent of primary care providers did not involve disabled children or young people in their assessment processes and that hospital services were disjointed from community services.[126] These are all areas of poor practice that disproportionately affect disabled children.

NHS therapy services

5.68   The importance of disabled children receiving appropriate and timely therapies – such as speech and language therapy or physiotherapy – is emphasised in a number of official documents[127] – not least the

---

123 Standard for Hospital Services, Children's NSF, p32 at 4.54.
124 Standard for Hospital Services, Children's NSF, p33 at 4.55.
125 Healthcare Commission, *Improving services for children in hospital*, 2009.
126 CQC, *Healthcare for disabled children and young people*, March 2012.
127 HM Treasury and Department for Education and Skills, *Aiming high for disabled children: better support for families*, 2007; Department for Children Schools and Families, *The Bercow report: a review of services for children and young people (0–19) with speech, language and communication needs*, 2008;

NSF (see para 5.51). Speech and language therapy should generally be considered as special educational provision and, accordingly, provided by the local education authority where a SEN statement/EHC plan exists.[128] Where there is no statement/plan (or when the child has a need other than an educational need for therapy) then these crucial services must be accorded a high priority by the relevant health body – not least in relation to speech and language therapy since the positive obligation on a state to facilitate a child's right of expression comes within the sphere of fundamental human rights.[129] If delay in providing these supports occurs due to a dispute between an education authority and the NHS, then consideration should be given to making a joint complaint about the failure of these bodies to work together (see para 5.25).

5.69 As noted above (see paras 5.43–5.45 and further in chapter 4 at para 4.139) where an EHC plan exists, it must contain a separate section (G) that provides specific details of the health provision required to address the disabilities which result in the young person's SEN and how this support will help enable him/her to achieve their personal educational outcomes. The Code of Practice[130] notes that this may:

> include specialist support and therapies, such as medical treatments and delivery of medications, occupational therapy and physiotherapy, a range of nursing support, specialist equipment, wheelchairs and continence supplies.

5.70 As also noted above at para 5.45, CFA 2014 s42 creates a specifically enforceable duty in relation to the health care provision specified in the plan – that the CCG must ensure that it is made available to the child or young person.[131]

5.71 Despite the vital importance of such healthcare supports, children and young people's access to rehabilitation and therapy services appears to be inconsistent across regions, with long waits in some areas. In meeting standard 8 of the Children's NSF, local authorities

Department of Health, Department of Education and others, *Improving Children and Young People's Health Outcomes: a system wide response*, 2013.

128 See chapter 4 at para 4.6 and CFA 2014 s21(5).

129 For example, ECHR articles 8 and 10 and UNCRC article 13: this assertion is made by J Morris, *Accessing human rights: Disabled children and the Children Act*, The Who Cares? Trust, London, 1998, p20, and accepted by the Department of Health: see Department of Health, *Assessing children in need and their families: practice guidance*, HMSO, 2000, para 3.125.

130 SEND Code, p167.

131 SEND Code, para 9.141.

and NHS bodies are expected to review local therapy services in order to:

a) Promote self-referral, simplifying the care pathway, and reduce excessive waits that may affect a child's development;
b) Improve administrative systems and processes for referral and discharge, and the effectiveness of outcomes of different therapeutic regimes, such as group sessions; and
c) Ensure that the supply of timely therapy services is sufficient to meet the needs of children and young people who require it, based on assessed needs. This may involve increased capacity to ensure that all children and young people attending early education settings and mainstream or special schools have equal access to therapy.[132]

5.72   Ultimately, local authorities and CCGs need to ensure that:

- parents or carers, children and young people are active partners in decisions about rehabilitation or therapy services, with agreed goals for what it is intended to achieve and how they can help;
- therapeutic interventions are agreed and overseen by specialist paediatric therapists; and
- therapy is delivered in the most appropriate setting, which may include the home or educational settings.[133]

NHS equipment provision

5.73   Section 3 of the NHS Act 2006 requires the NHS to provide – among other things – services and facilities to address people's healthcare needs. The NHS's equipment provision obligations are broad and complementary to those on local authorities concerned with social care support (see chapter 3 at para 3.77). They include, for example, providing specialist beds for children living at home, ceiling rails for hoists, refrigerators for medicines, walking frames, wheelchairs and so on. The provision of such equipment may have to be sanctioned by the local health body although GPs are authorised to provide a wide range of 'appliances', eg medical aids, dressings, pads etc as well as basic equipment to help overcome the effects of disability.[134]

---

132 Disabled Child Standard, Children's NSF, p15.
133 Disabled Child Standard, Children's NSF, p15.
134 NHS (General Medical Services Contracts) Regulations 2004 SI No 291 reg 39.

5.74   Because of concerns over the inadequate nature of equipment services,[135] steps have been taken to require local health bodies and councils to establish joint 'integrated equipment services'.[136] Paragraph 7 of the relevant guidance[137] provides an illustrative list of the type of equipment that might be available from such an integrated service, namely:

> **Community equipment** is equipment for home nursing usually provided by the NHS, such as pressure relief mattresses and commodes, and equipment for daily living such as shower chairs and raised toilet seats, usually provided by local authorities. It also includes, but is not limited to:
>
> - Minor adaptations, such as grab rails, lever taps and improved domestic lighting.
> - Ancillary equipment for people with sensory impairments, such as liquid level indicators, hearing loops, assistive listening devices and flashing doorbells.
> - Communication aids for people with speech impairments.
> - Wheelchairs for short-term loan, but *not* those for permanent wheelchair users, as these are prescribed and funded by different NHS services.[138]
> - Telecare equipment such as fall alarms, gas escape alarms and health state monitoring for people who are vulnerable.

5.75   Notwithstanding the aim of making equipment an integrated support service, disputes inevitably arise as to which authority is responsible for provision. This may be a dispute between a council and a CCG – but disputes can also arise between health bodies themselves. An example would be where a disabled child is attending a school in an area outside his or her home NHS area[139] and the equipment is needed at the school (for example, an additional walking frame). If hardship is caused by such a dispute then a joint complaint or application for judicial review about the failure of these bodies to work together should be considered (see para 5.25 above).

---

135 See, for example, Audit Commission, *Fully equipped: the provision of equipment to older or disabled people by the NHS and social services in England and Wales*, 2000.

136 Department of Health, *Community equipment services guidance*, HSC 2001/0: LAC (2001)13, 27 March 2001.

137 Department of Health, *Community equipment services guidance*, HSC 2001/0: LAC (2001)13, 27 March 2001.

138 See paras 5.77–5.81.

139 In such cases, guidance exists as to how to decide the 'responsible commissioner' – Department of Health, *Who Pays?* 2013.

5.76   A 2007 ombudsman's report[140] concerned such a case, where the patient required a specialist profiling bed and a specialised seating system. The ombudsman considered that one of the health bodies should have funded the necessary equipment as an interim measure, pending the resolution of the dispute – and that a failure to do this amounted to maladministration.

Wheelchair provision

5.77   The provision of publicly funded wheelchairs is an NHS responsibility.[141] The need for a suitable wheelchair will often be capable of being expressed in the language of human rights, for example, in terms of a right under article 8 of the European Convention on Human Rights (ECHR) for a child to be enabled to interact with other people and the environment.[142] Not infrequently, considerable hardship and pain (particularly postural pain) will be caused by the use of an unsuitable wheelchair such that this could be expressed as degrading treatment (contrary to article 3[143]) or contrary to article 8 in relation to the impact on the person's physical and psychological integrity, or dignity.[144]

5.78   Assessments for wheelchairs and their provision are the responsibility of local NHS wheelchair services in England. Assessments are undertaken by specialists, usually an occupational therapist or physiotherapist, although GPs should support children in seeking such equipment and provide advice on the process. As noted above at para 5.77, responsibility for commissioning specialist wheelchairs has transferred from NHS England to CCGs.

---

140 Public Services Ombudsman for Wales, Complaint against Bro Morgannwg NHS Trust, Cardiff & Vale NHS Trust, Vale of Glamorgan Council and Vale of Glamorgan Local Health Board, Case Ref 200501955, 200600591 and 200700641, 28 November 2007 – see pp28 and 30.

141 Under NHS Act 2006, s3: see, for example, Department of Health/Care Services Improvement Partnership, *Out and about: Wheelchairs as part of a whole-systems approach to independence*, 2006, p30.

142 See, for example, *Botta v Italy* (1998) 26 EHRR 241 at [32] and see also paras 2.14–2.19 above.

143 See, for example, *Price v UK* (2002) 34 EHRR 1285.

144 See again *Botta v Italy* (1998) 26 EHRR 241 at [32] and *R (Bernard) v Enfield LBC* [2002] EWHC 2282 (Admin); (2002) 5 CCLR 577.

5.79   Brief guidance on wheelchair provision was issued in 1996[145] albeit that it concentrates on the provision of electrically powered indoor/outdoor wheelchairs (EPIOCs). A voucher scheme also exists that gives the option of purchasing a non-motorised wheelchair from an independent supplier – although in such cases, the user will be responsible for its maintenance and repair. In some cases, powered wheelchairs/scooters can also be purchased through the Motability Scheme by those in receipt of the high rate mobility component of the disability living allowance (DLA) or the enhanced rate of the mobility component of the personal independence payment (PIP).

5.80   The 1996 guidance concerning EPIOCs gave as suggested criteria for their provision that the person is:[146]

- unable to propel a manual chair outdoors;
- able to benefit from the chair through increased mobility leading to improved quality of life; and
- able to handle the chair safely.

5.81   In practice there have been severe concerns about the adequacy of the NHS wheelchair services[147] which have resulted in many families seeking charitable and other support in order to address their child's mobility needs – for example, from charities such as Whizz-Kidz and Cerebra.[148]

145   HSG (96)34, *Powered indoor/outdoor wheelchairs for severely disabled people* and HSG(96)53, *The wheelchair voucher scheme.*

146   NHS Executive, *Powered indoor/outdoor wheelchairs for severely disabled people,* HSG (96)34, May 1996.

147   See, for example, Audit Commission, *Fully equipped 2002: assisting independence,* 2002; Department of Health, *Evaluation of the powered wheelchair and voucher system 2000,* 2002; emPower, *NHS wheelchair and seating services mapping project: final report,* Limbless Association, 2004; and Prime Minister's Strategy Unit, *Improving the life chances of disabled people,* 2005. See also, N Sharma with J Morrison, *Don't push me around! Disabled children's experiences of wheelchair services in the UK,* 2006, a joint report published by Barnardo's and Whizz-Kidz and endorsed by the UK's four Children's Commissioners; the 2010 Inquiry commissioned in Wales – Welsh Assembly Government (2010) Health, Wellbeing and Local Government Committee: Ministerial Evidence session HWLG(3)–04–10-p4: 4 March 2010 and Every Disabled Child Matters, *Disabled children and health,* 2009, p13.

148   See www.whizz-kidz.org.uk and http://w3.cerebra.org.uk/.

Short breaks

5.82   Although short breaks[149] are services most commonly provided by local authorities (and are considered in chapter 3 at paras 3.92–3.97 above), the NHS also has important responsibilities to provide such support. The need for short breaks or respite will now form an important part of the right to a parent carer's assessment under the Children Act 1989 ss17ZD and 17ZE (see chapter 8 at para 8.18 below). The NHS duty was recognised in *R (D) v Haringey LBC*[150] (see para 5.88 below) and is highlighted in a number of important NHS guidance documents.[151] Where, therefore, the child would need access to healthcare supports during a period of short break provision, the NHS should ensure that this service is available. It can do this by providing or funding the short break/respite care or working with the local authority to ensure that the service is available. In the *Haringey* case, the health body was responsible for the service by providing a respite care service in the children's home (or paying a private agency to do this).

5.83   Sometimes, however, the provision of short breaks will be a joint initiative under the 'working together' duties (see para 5.20 above). For example, a respite care centre run by a local authority may not have staff trained to deliver certain healthcare support (such as administering rectal valium) which as a consequence might make the service unavailable to children with certain disabling conditions. Such an impasse could be resolved, if a care assistant at the centre was willing to take on this role and be trained by the NHS in the procedure (and when administering the valium, he or she would be doing this as an agent of the NHS).

5.84   Short breaks have been identified as a key priority for NHS delivery and investment by the Department of Health with a clear expectation that both local authorities and health bodies will deliver additional and better quality short breaks services for disabled children and

---

149 Also known, particularly in the health context, as 'respite care' although the term is not preferred from a disability rights perspective.

150 [2005] All ER (D) 256.

151 See, for example, Department of Health, *The national framework for NHS continuing healthcare and NHS funded nursing care in England*, 2009, para 104; Department of Health *NHS continuing healthcare practice guidance*, March 2010, para 11.1.

their families.[152] In 2013 Department of Health guidance, a best practice case study is set out in which the CCG and the local authority have formally integrated their commissioning for disabled children and have provided additional sessions of respite care.[153]

Continence services

5.85   Achieving continence is a central goal for many disabled children and their families. Yet even when continence assessments are available, parents report real problems in securing the supply of the right sort of continence products for their child, with many experiencing a 'one size fits all' service.[154] NHS guidance in the Children's NSF recommended 'an integrated community based paediatric continence service' in every area. In 2007, the Department of Health issued the Children's Continence Exemplar to support the development of child-centred local delivery.[155]

5.86   Detailed practice guidance concerning the organisation and range of continence services that should be made available has been issued by the Department of Health.[156] This advises that the nature and quantity of continence supplies made available should be determined as a result of an individual assessment of need in every case. Research suggests,[157] however, that despite the requirement for pads to be available on the basis of clinical need, almost 75 per cent of CCGs operate a fixed policy which stipulates a maximum number of continence pads that can be provided over a specified period. The research concerned older people but the experience of disabled

152 Department for Children Schools and Families/Department of Health, *Aiming high for disabled children: short breaks implementation guidance*, 2008 and Department of Health, *Healthy lives, brighter futures – The strategy for children and young people's health*, 2009.

153 Department of Health, Department of Education and others, *Improving Children and Young People's Health Outcomes: A system wide response*, 2013, p32.

154 See in this respect the Cerebra Legal Entitlements Research Project Digest, Digest of Opinions 2013, 'Jinny's Story', Cardiff Law School, 2014, which concerns a NHS body that operated an inflexible policy in relation to a disabled young person's continence needs.

155 Despite these recommendations, the *Every disabled child matters* campaign describes integrated paediatric continence services as 'virtually non-existent': EDCM, 'Disabled children and health', 2009, p30.

156 Department of Health, *Good practice in continence services*, April 2000.

157 Royal College of Physicians, *National audit of continence care for older people*, November 2006, accessible at www.rcplondon.ac.uk/news/news.asp?PR_id=331.

children is similar: such policies are, however, contrary to the guidance, fetter the authorities' discretion and, where individual hardship results, constitute maladministration. If challenged through an application for judicial review, it is highly likely (in the opinion of the authors) that such a policy would be held to be unlawful.

Continuing care

5.87   Although (as noted above, see para 5.22) the local authority will generally be the lead agency in co-ordinating the support services for a disabled child, frequently the package will have funding support from the NHS and the education department (in relation to SEN needs – see chapter 4) as well as from the children's services department of the local authority. In some cases, however, the child's needs are such that the NHS may not only become the lead agency, but it may also assume sole responsibility for funding the child's health and social care needs. In such situations, the child is held to be eligible for 'NHS Continuing Care'.

5.88   *R (T, D and B) v Haringey LBC*[158] is an example of a case involving a disabled child with complex health needs. Her impairment meant that she required a tracheostomy (a tube in the throat) which needed regular suctioning. The child was discharged from hospital and cared for at home, with her mother being trained to manage the tracheostomy with back up from the district nursing service. The issue in the case was which authority – the health body or local authority – was responsible for providing the respite care that the mother required – since when she was attending to the tracheostomy she had to be awake through the night. The court held that in such a situation, the NHS was responsible – meaning that the same principles for NHS continuing healthcare eligibility as applied to adults, applied to children. In the judge's opinion, the 'scale and type of nursing care' was such that it was outside that which could be provided by the local authority.

5.89   The Department of Health has issued guidance specifically concerned with the assessment of children's eligibility for NHS Continuing Care – *The National Framework for Children and Young People's Continuing Care 2010* ('Continuing Care Framework'). The framework is now out of date as it refers to NHS structures which existed prior to the 2012 reforms, for example Primary Care Trusts. However,

---

158 [2005] EWHC 2235 (Admin); (2006) 9 CCLR 58.

the Department of Health consulted on a revised version in Autumn 2015, see para 5.94 below.

5.90   The framework sets out the process for arranging packages of continuing care for children and young people who have health needs that cannot be met by existing universal and specialist services. It requires that every child or young person referred to the NHS with possible continuing care needs should be offered a comprehensive assessment[159] by a nominated children and young people's health assessor.[160] The assessment should (among other things):

- consider the preferences of the child or young person and his or her family;
- be holistic – considering the needs not only of the child or young person but also of his or her family, and where relevant should include a carer's assessment (see chapter 8 at para 8.8);
- consider all relevant reports and risk assessments from the multi-disciplinary team (health, social and education).

5.91   The framework makes the not unreasonable point, that for children even if there is a primary health care need it is unrealistic for all commissioning responsibility to shift to the NHS:

> childhood and youth is a period of rapidly changing physical, intellectual and emotional maturation alongside social and educational development. All children of compulsory school age (5 to 16) should receive suitable education, either by regular attendance at school or through other arrangements. There may also be social care needs. Most care for children and young people is provided by families at home, and maintaining relationships between the child or young person, their family and other carers, and professionals, is a particularly important aspect.[161]

5.92   What is being asserted here is that from a policy perspective, social services and the education agencies should remain involved – even if a child has a primary care need. What the guidance cannot do is over-rule or undermine the law, as detailed in the *Haringey* judgment. The legal position is, therefore, that once a child is eligible for NHS continuing care funding, the children's services department is unable to fund social care services which are related to a child's medical needs – in the same way that the adult legislation (ie the Care Act 2014 s22) prohibits adult services funding services for adults. Services provided by the local authority must not turn the authority 'into a substitute

159 *Continuing Care Framework*, para 50.
160 *Continuing Care Framework*, para 51.
161 *Continuing Care Framework*, para 8.

or additional NHS for children'.[162] Children's services do, however, retain responsibilities for safeguarding and associated social work functions eg:

- helping parents with the emotional problems of caring for disabled children;
- providing carer support services ie services delivered solely to the parents/siblings – bearing in mind that respite care services are generally not of this nature since they are generally delivered to the child (eg a sitting service or overnight care);
- giving information and so on.

5.93   So, for example, if a child's behaviour became very challenging and a safeguarding issue arose then social services would have a role to fulfil. The safeguarding work undertaken by the local authority might flag up that the mother was not coping and that she had a need to develop the skills to address the behaviour and also that the child needed short break care. It would be a health function to provide support to manage challenging behaviour (ie skilled assistants); it would be a health function to train the mother to acquire these skills; and the provision of the short break care too would be a NHS responsibility. This could be provided by skilled assistants coming to the home or the child going to a residential or overnight fostering placement – and, in this case, social services could seek to ensure this happened using its powers under CA 1989 s27.

5.94   At the time of writing in November 2015, the Department of Health expected to publish imminently a new National Framework for Children and Young People's Continuing Care which will replace the 2010 version once it is finalised. The new framework as published in draft for consultation continues to rely on the principles set out in the 2010 framework, but reflects the changes to the organisation of the NHS, the new integrated approach to the commissioning of services introduced by the CFA 2014 and the changes to social care introduced by the Care Act 2014.

Decision support tool

5.95   The framework contains a decision support tool which is based on a tool widely used for adults,[163] and brings together needs from across

---

162 *R (T, D and B) v Haringey LBC* [2005] EWHC 2235 (Admin); (2006) 9 CCLR 58 at [68].

163 For detailed consideration of these tools see L Clements, *Community care and the law*, 6th edn, LAG, 2016.

ten care domains: challenging behaviour, communication, mobility, nutrition – food and drink, continence and elimination, skin and tissue viability, breathing, drug therapies and medicines, psychological and emotional, and seizures. It describes five levels of need, from low to priority, and provides descriptors to assess the level of need for each of the care domains. The framework indicates that three 'high' ratings, one severe rating or one priority rating is likely to indicate that the child or young person has continuing care needs.[164]

5.96   The framework stresses that the decision support tool is not prescriptive and the importance of exercising evidence-based professional judgment in all cases. Following assessment, the framework indicates that a decision as to whether or not the child has a continuing care need should be made by a multidisciplinary or multi-agency forum or panel and, where a decision is made regarding a package of continuing care, processes undertaken to put it in place.

5.97   The framework requires NHS bodies to have a local complaints procedure in place to respond to any disagreements voiced by the child or their family about any aspect of the continuing care process. In addition, once a continuing care package is put in place, regular reviews must be carried out. The framework recommends that a review takes place three months after initial assessment and then annually or more frequently depending on the specific case.

5.98   The new draft national framework (see above at para 5.94) also uses a decision support tool, although it is now integrated into the main text of the framework rather than annexed to it.

The continuing care pathway

5.99   Included in the 2010 framework is a continuing care pathway (Annex B), which shows how the continuing care process should look from the perspective of child or young person and their family.[165] The pathway specifies:

a) three phases – assessment, decision-making and arrangement of provision;
b) seven discrete stages within these phases – identify, assess, recommend, decide, inform, deliver and review;
c) key actions to be undertaken at each stage; and
d) timescales, which should see the child and family informed of the continuing care service provision decision within 28 working

164 *Continuing Care Framework*, Annex A, p53.
165 *Continuing Care Framework*, Annex B, p55.

days of the referral. This is an extremely tight timeframe for the completion of a multidisciplinary assessment process and can be contrasted with the 45 working days allowed for the completion of a child in need assessment under the *Working Together* guidance (see chapter 3 at para 3.33).

5.100   The new framework also contains detailed guidance on the continuing care process and pathway; it provides for an additional phase entitled 'ongoing', which requires a reassessment of the child's continuing care needs initially after three months and annually thereafter. The other timescales remain unchanged.

Continuing care and direct payments/personal budgets

Direct payments

5.101   Where a disabled child is deemed eligible for NHS continuing care funding it means that the care provided is subject to the provisions of the NHS Act 2006 and not the social services statutes (such as CA 1989 and CSDPA 1970, see chapter 3). Like social services authorities, NHS bodies are now able to make direct payments for the provision of certain types of healthcare services under the NHS Acts, including for children.[166] Guidance from NHS England[167] sets out illustrative examples of why a CCG might decide not to provide someone with direct payments – for example, because 'the benefit to that individual of having a direct payment for healthcare does not represent value for money'.

5.102   Before providing direct payments, NHS bodies must prepare a care plan setting out the health services that are to be provided and must advise the patient, or their representative in the case of a child,

---

166 See NHS Act 2006 s12A and National Health Service (Direct Payments) Regulations 2013 SI No 1617 reg 4. Health direct payments for children under must be made to a 'representative' who must act in accordance with reg 4(3); for example they must 'act in the best interests of the patient when securing the provision of services in respect of which the direct payment is made'. See further NHS England, *Guidance on Direct Payments for Healthcare: Understanding the Regulations*, March 2014.

167 NHS England, *Guidance on Direct Payments for Healthcare: Understanding the Regulations*, March 2014, para 33.

of any potential risks arising out of the use of direct payments.[168] The direct payment must be set at a level to secure the agreed provision in any EHC plan (see paras 5.43–5.46) and meet health needs agreed in the personal health budget care plan (see paras 5.105–5.106 below for more on personal health budgets).[169] Guidance from NHS England states that 'direct payments must be set at a level sufficient to cover the full cost of each of the services agreed in the care plan'.[170] For each person receiving a direct payment, the CCG must name a care co-ordinator, and this must be recorded in the care plan.[171] The role of the care co-ordinator includes undertaking or arranging for monitoring and review of the direct payment.

5.103   A health direct payment can only be used to pay an individual living in the same household, a close family member[172] or a friend if the CCG is satisfied that to secure a service from that person is necessary in order to satisfactorily meet the person receiving care's need for that service; or to promote the welfare of a child for whom direct payments are being made.[173]

5.104   Where the CCG or commissioning health body declines a request for a direct payment pursuant to a personal health budget, they must set out their reasons for doing so in writing and provide the individual with the opportunity for a formal review.[174]

Personal health budgets

5.105   Since October 2014, disabled children and young people who are eligible for continuing care have had a right to have a 'personal health

---

168 National Health Service (Direct Payments) Regulations 2013 reg 8. The requirements of the care plan are set out in NHS England, *Guidance on direct payments for healthcare: Understanding the regulations*, March 2014, para 97. See the SEND Code at para 9.124 for how sections G and J of an EHC plan can be modified to fulfil the requirements of a care plan for health direct payments.

169 SEND Code, para 9.120.

170 NHS England, *Guidance on Direct Payments for Healthcare: Understanding the Regulations*, March 2014, para 117. The guidance goes on to emphasise (para 118) that 'hidden costs' such as National Insurance and pension contributions and training costs must be recognised in this calculation.

171 NHS England, *Guidance on Direct Payments for Healthcare: Understanding the Regulations*, March 2014, para 114.

172 The definition of 'close family member' is provided in box 3 at para 154 of NHS England, *Guidance on Direct Payments for Healthcare: Understanding the Regulations*, March 2014

173 NHS England, *Guidance on Direct Payments for Healthcare: Understanding the Regulations*, March 2014, para 153.

174 SEND Code, para 9.114, p182.

budget'.[175] Guidance from NHS England[176] describes personal health budgets as 'an amount of money to support a person's identified health and well-being needs the application of which is planned and agreed between the individual, their representative, or, in the case of children, their families or carers and the local NHS team'. The guidance makes clear that a personal budget can be paid in one of three ways:

1) A notional budget – where the commissioner holds the budget.
2) A third party budget – where an organisation independent of the individual and the NHS manages the budget on the individual's behalf.
3) A direct payment to the individual or their representative (see paras 5.101–5.104 above).

5.106   The guidance states that 'CCGs should ensure all three options are available to enable people to make a choice about the level of control they feel comfortable with'. There may be 'exceptional circumstances' where a personal health budget can be refused; the guidance suggests this could be 'due to the specialised clinical care required or because a personal health budget would not represent value for money as any additional benefits to the individual would not outweigh the extra cost to the NHS'.[177]

Child and adolescent mental health services (CAMHS)

5.107   Many disabled children will experience episodes of mental ill-health. Many will need support from CAMHS: support designed to promote the mental health and psychological well-being of children and young people. The intention of CAMH services is 'to provide high quality,

---

175 See the National Health Service Commissioning Board and Clinical Commissioning Groups (Responsibilities and Standing Rules) (Amendment) (No 3) Regulations 2014 SI No 1611.

176 NHS England, *Guidance on the 'right to have' a personal health budget in adult NHS continuing healthcare and children and young people's continuing care,* September 2014, pp8 and 10. The relevant guidance (see below) states (p11) that: 'In the case of children this refers to the element of their care package that would normally be provided by the NHS once they become CC eligible and not the elements of their package provided by social care or education.'

177 NHS England, *Guidance on the 'right to have' a personal health budget in adult NHS continuing healthcare and children and young people's continuing care,* September 2014, p15.

multi-disciplinary mental health services to all children and young people with mental health problems and disorders to ensure effective assessment, treatment and support, for them and their families'.[178] In February 2011, the government published a mental health strategy for people of all ages, which identified the following objectives:[179]

- More people will have good mental health.
- More people with mental health problems will recover.
- More people with mental health problems will have good physical health.
- More people will have a positive experience of care and support.
- Fewer people will suffer avoidable harm.
- Fewer people will experience stigma and discrimination.

5.108   This strategy was followed, in October 2011, by the government committing £32 million to expanding the availability of talking therapies for children and young people.

5.109   The central importance of mental health provision has been highlighted by the events at the Winterbourne View hospital, where vulnerable people were subjected to terrible abuse. The report into what happened was produced by the Department of Health in December 2012. It addresses important issues relating to mental health care for children and young people, as well as adults:[180]

- Children and young people have a right to be given the support and care that they need in a community-based setting, near to family and friends.
- Each area should have a locally agreed joint plan to ensure high quality care and support services for children with mental health problems, learning disabilities or autism.
- The norm should be that children and young people live in their own homes with the support they need for independent living within a safe environment.

5.110   Unfortunately, CAMHS provision is widely criticised as being disjointed, poor quality and difficult to access. In July 2014, NHS England revealed major problems with CAMHS, including finding that many children and young people were placed in hospitals hundreds

178 Department for Children Schools and Families, *Services supporting the emotional wellbeing and mental health of children and young people*, 2010.
179 *No health without mental health: a cross-government outcomes strategy for people of all ages*, February 2011.
180 Department of Health, *Transforming care: A national response to Winterbourne View Hospital*, 2012.

of miles away from home or were inappropriately placed on adult wards.[181] In October 2014, the House of Commons Health Committee published a report into CAMHS.[182] The report found that there are 'serious and deeply ingrained problems with the commissioning and provision of children's and adolescents' mental health services' that 'run through the whole system from prevention and early intervention through to in-patient services for the most vulnerable young people'.[183]

5.111   In its latest report, the Children and Young People's Mental Health and Wellbeing Taskforce recognised that there are a number of challenges facing CAMHS, including difficulties accessing mental health services generally, and crisis services in particular. The taskforce's key proposals include delivering a joined-up approach between health and social care bodies, simplifying commissioning structures and arrangements and improving access to services.[184]

5.112   The term 'CAMHS' can be used widely to refer to all services which play a part in promoting children's mental well-being, or narrowly to refer to specialist mental health services for children. The narrow meaning of the term is used in the remainder of this section, while recognising the critical importance of wider health and other services in achieving good mental health for disabled children – and their families.

5.113   There is no specific statutory framework for CAMHS. Accordingly, CAMH services are provided under the general obligations created by the NHS Act 2006 and the Mental Health Act (MHA) 1983. Provisions in relation to detention in hospital and compulsory treatment will be found in the MHA 1983, for children as for adults. All issues in relation to mental health treatment should be informed by the 2015 Mental Health Act Code of Practice ('MHA Code') which has statutory force.[185] Particular regard should be had to chapter 19 'Children and young people under the age of 18'.

---

181 NHS England, *Child and Adolescent Mental Health Services (CAMHS) Tier 4 Report*, July 2014.

182 House of Commons Health Committee, *Children's and adolescents' mental health and CAMHS*, third report of session 2014–15.

183 House of Commons Health Committee, *Children's and adolescents' mental health and CAMHS*, third report of session 2014–15, at p3.

184 Children and Young People's Mental Health and Well-being Taskforce, *Future in Mind: Promoting, protecting and improving our children and young people's mental health and wellbeing*, 2015.

185 *R (Munjaz) v Mersey Care NHS Trust* [2006] 2 AC 148.

5.114   Input into CAMHS from children's services within local authorities will be governed by the Children Acts 1989 and 2004, the Chronically Sick and Disabled Persons Act 1970 s2 (see chapter 3 at paras 3.66–3.78) and MHA 1983 s117 (see para 5.130).

5.115   CAMH services are in large part shaped by government policy initiatives and targets. These targets and polices are relevant in that they give an indication of the nature and quality of services that disabled children and their families should expect to receive if they need the help of a specialist mental health service. It is for this reason that the following paragraphs provide a brief overview of the structure of local CAMH services, their guiding principles and the services that they should be able to provide.

5.116   Many disabled children will require input from CAMHS, whether because their primary need is a mental health need or because of secondary mental health problems associated with their disabilities, which may sadly emerge as a result of their needs not being addressed properly. The expectation is that all such children will have 'access to timely, integrated, high quality, multi-disciplinary mental health services to ensure effective assessment, treatment and support'[186] and that CAMHS will provide for four levels of service:

- Tier 1: A primary level of care.
- Tier 2: A service provided by specialist individual professionals relating to workers in primary care.
- Tier 3: A specialised multi-disciplinary service for more severe, complex or persistent disorders.
- Tier 4: Essential tertiary level services such as day units, highly specialised out-patient teams and in-patient units.

5.117   Responsibility for commissioning the first three tiers of CAMHS lies with CCGs. NHS England has responsibility for commissioning Tier 4 of CAMHS.

A comprehensive CAMHS

5.118   A 2003 *Department of Health policy paper*[187] set the expectation that a comprehensive CAMHS would be available in each locality in

---

186 Department of Health/DfES, *National service framework for children young people and maternity services: the mental health and psychological well-being of children and young people: Standard 9*, 2004 ('NSF Standard 9'), p4.

187 Department of Health, *Improvement, expansion and reform: the next 3 years, priorities and planning framework 2003–2006*, 2003.

England by 2006. This has proved to be aspirational, and recent reports suggest that such a service has yet to be achieved.[188]

5.119   In 2004, a specific Children's NSF Standard was published to address the 'Mental Health and Psychological Well-being of Children and Young People'[189] which required that CAMHS should ensure, as part of their underpinning principles:

- access for all children and young people regardless of their age, gender, race, religion, ability, culture, ethnicity or sexuality;[190]
- multi-agency commissioning and delivery of services;[191] and
- participation of children and young people and their families at all levels of service provision.[192]

5.120   The NSF placed great emphasis on early intervention,[193] by (among other things) requiring that health bodies and local authorities ensure CAMH workers are available and accessible within community settings[194] and that all localities have specialist multidisciplinary teams with the resources and skills to provide:

- specialist assessment and treatment services;
- services for the full range of mental disorders in conjunction with other agencies as appropriate;
- a mix of short-term and long-term interventions and care;
- a full range of evidence-based treatments; and
- specialist services that are commissioned on a regional or multi-district basis, including in-patient care.[195]

5.121   Adequate services must be in place for emergencies, including policies that clarify the level of service provided and the criteria for referral. Arrangements need to be in place to ensure that 24-hour cover is provided to meet children's urgent needs and that a specialist mental

---

188 For analysis of what is meant by a 'Comprehensive CAMHS' and whether it has been achieved, see 11 Million, *Out of the shadows?* Children's Commissioner for England, 2008, p42 and the 2008 UK Children's Commissioners' *Report to UN Committee on the rights of the child*, p23. See also House of Commons Health Committee, *Children's and adolescents' mental health and CAMHS*, third report of session 2014–15.

189 NSF Standard 9, p49.

190 NSF Standard 9, p49.

191 NSF Standard 9, p49.

192 NSF Standard 9, p13.

193 NSF Standard 9, eg, pp8–9.

194 NSF Standard 9, p11–12.

195 NSF Standard 9, p50.

health assessment is undertaken within 24 hours or during the next working day where indicated.[196]

5.122   Health bodies and local authorities are also required to develop a long-term strategy to ensure that young people[197] are provided with services which meet their developmental needs. This includes ensuring there are no gaps in service provision and that there is a smooth transition to adult services.

5.123   Adults who receive help from 'secondary mental health services' (for example from community mental health teams (CMHTs), early intervention teams etc) are assessed and supported under a system known as the care programme approach (CPA)[198] and the CPA should also be used on transition from child to adult services (see paras 5.146–5.152 below for more on transition to adult health services).[199]

5.124   It is the responsibility of health bodies and local authorities to ensure that children and young people with learning disabilities receive equal access to mental health services at all tiers of CAMHS. This includes:

- adequately resourced Tiers 2 and 3 learning disability specialist CAMHS with staff with the necessary competencies to address mental health difficulties in children and young people with learning disabilities; and
- access to Tier 4 services providing in-patient, day-patient and outreach units for children and adolescents with learning disabilities and severe and complex neuro-psychiatric problems.[200]

Admission to hospital for treatment of a mental disorder

5.125   The law relating to the admission and treatment of a child or young person with a mental health issue (whether 'informally', with parental consent or under the MHA 1983) is complex and is explained

196 NSF Standard 9, p19.
197 The Mental Health Act Code refers to 'child' or 'children' as under 16s and 'young person' or 'young people' in relation to those aged 16 or 17.
198 Department of Health, *Refocusing the care programme approach policy and positive practice guidance*, 2008, although the CPA is capable of being adapted to meet the needs of children in touch with CAMHS – see Annex B: CPA and Child and Adolescent Mental Health Services. See further the Mental Health Act Code at chapter 34.
199 NSF Standard 9, p22.
200 NSF Standard 9, p24.

in chapter 19 of the MHA Code.[201] A key complicating factor is the difficult relationship that exists between the detention and treatment powers under the 1983 Act, the Mental Capacity Act 2005 (which is of primary relevance for persons aged 16 and over) and the common law as it relates to children's powers to make their own decisions.

5.126   Detailed guidance on assessment and applications for detention in hospital under the MHA 1983 is set out in chapter 14 of the MHA Code[202] which in addition, at chapter 19, provides guidance on particular issues arising in relation to children and young people. An application is usually made by the approved mental health professional (AMHP) and, save in cases of emergency, must be supported by two medical recommendations. Those with parental responsibility (see chapter 2 at paras 2.58–2.62) should be consulted about decisions to admit/treat their child.[203] The person identified as the 'nearest relative'[204] will have additional rights.

Ensuring an age appropriate environment for CAMHS

5.127   MHA 1983 s131A requires that for mental health purposes the hospital environment in which a child or young person is to be accommodated is age appropriate. The requirement applies regardless of whether the admission is informal or formal and its primary purpose is to ensure that children and young people are not admitted inappropriately on to adult psychiatric wards. A detailed briefing published in 2010 by Young Minds[205] explains the nature of the obligation created by section 131A and the very limited circumstance when an admission to an adult psychiatric ward would be permitted – and the obligations that are placed on the hospital in such cases.[206]

201 See further Department of Health, *The legal aspects of the care and treatment of children and young people with mental disorder,* 2009
202 Department of Health, *Code of Practice: Mental Health Act 1983,* TSO, 2015.
203 See MHA Code, para 19.38.
204 See MHA Code at chapter 5 for the definition of 'nearest relative'. See also MHA Code, paras 14.57–14.65.
205 C Parker, *Young Minds briefing on the responsibilities of NHS Trust Boards under section 131A of the Mental Health Act 1983,* Young Minds, 2010.
206 See the MHA Code, paras 19.90–19.104.

Hospital discharge

5.128 The Children's NSF Standard for Hospital Services[207] provides general advice concerning the discharge of children from hospital care – including the need (where appropriate) for effective liaison with the social services – to ensure (for example) that equipment is available and 'that rehabilitation programmes can be continued at home'.[208]

5.129 Good practice guidance is given in the Children's NSF Standard for Mental Health and Psychological Well-being of Children and Young People[209] where the discharge follows a period in an NHS mental health setting (or CAMHS arranged setting). The advice includes:

> The in-patient unit needs to be able to hand over to an appropriately equipped community service. There needs to be a shared understanding of the level of care required on discharge from inpatient services and if the appropriate resources are not available in community services, shared aftercare arrangements should be considered; there may be a continuing role for the in-patient team in the provision of outreach and after-care services.

5.130 Where the discharge of the child or young person follows their formal detention under either section 3 or one of the criminal provisions of the 1983 Act, then they will be entitled to support services, not under the CA 1989 or the Chronically Sick and Disabled Persons Act 1970 (see chapter 3 above) but under MHA 1983 s117 ('section 117 services'). The fact that these services are provided under a distinct statutory provision should not in practice make any material difference to the child, young person or his or her family. Section 117 services do have certain distinct legal characteristics, for example, they are the joint responsibility of both the NHS and the local authority,[210] they must be provided free of charge[211] and can cover a wide spectrum of supports – both health and social care – albeit that they must be required because of a mental health need.[212] A detailed

207 Department of Health, *Getting the right start: national service framework for children: standard for hospital services*, 2003, see para 3.27 onwards.

208 Department of Health, *Getting the right start: national service framework for children: standard for hospital services*, 2003, see paras 3.27 and 3.30.

209 NSF Standard 9, para 9.13 onwards.

210 *R v Mental Health Review Tribunal ex p Hall* (1999) 2 CCLR 361.

211 *R v Manchester CC ex p Stennett and others* [2002] UKHL 34; (2002) 5 CCLR 500.

212 MHA 1983 s117(6) and *R (Mwanza) v Greenwich LBC and Bromley LBC* [2010] EWHC 1462 (Admin); (2010) 13 CCLR 454.

consideration of section 117 services is provided by the MHA 1983 Code of Practice.[213]

Consent to mental health treatment

5.131   In all areas of healthcare, including mental health care and treatment, it will be unlawful to treat a disabled child unless the appropriate consent has been obtained or the treatment is otherwise authorised. A general overview of the law relating to mental capacity and decision-making is provided at chapter 7. Issues of capacity to consent to treatment are dealt with below.

Consent to treatment

Children (under 16s)

5.132   Consent to treatment is a difficult issue for disabled children, as it can be for all children. Consent should be sought for each aspect of the child or young person's treatment as and when it arises, even if the treatment proposed could be given without consent under the MHA 1983.[214] In relation to mental health treatments, reference should be made to the MHA Code at chapter 19 and the Department of Health publication *The legal aspects of the care and treatment of children and young people with mental disorder.*[215]

5.133   Detailed guidance has been issued by the Department of Health concerning treatment decisions relating to children.[216] Children's capacity to consent to treatment is determined by individual assessment. Children who are able to make decisions about their admission to hospital or treatment are referred to as being '*Gillick* competent', a reference to the leading House of Lords case.[217] A '*Gillick* competent' child is a child who has attained sufficient understanding and intelligence to be able to understand fully what is involved in the proposed

---

213 Department of Health, *Code of Practice: Mental Health Act 1983*, 2015, chapter 33.

214 Department of Health, *The legal aspects of the care and treatment of children and young people with mental disorder*, 2009, p56 at 4.3.

215 Department of Health, *The legal aspects of the care and treatment of children and young people with mental disorder*, 2009.

216 Department of Health, *Reference guide to consent for examination or treatment*, 2nd edn, 2009.

217 *Gillick v West Norfolk and Wisbech Area Health Authority* [1986] AC 112.

intervention. Such a child will be regarded as competent to consent to a particular intervention, such as admission to hospital or proposed treatment.[218]

5.134   If a child is not 'Gillick competent', those with parental responsibility may, as a general rule, consent if the decision falls within the 'scope of parental responsibility'. This relatively difficult concept is discussed in detail in chapter 7 at paras 7.17–7.20. The parent's consent should be sought for each aspect of the child or young person's care and treatment as it arises.[219]

5.135   The 'inherent jurisdiction' of the High Court can be invoked to make treatment decisions on behalf of all children, whether competent or otherwise and the court may override treatment consents or refusals if it considers it necessary to do so in the child's 'best interests'.[220] This jurisdiction has no limits other than the requirement to act in the child's best interests, although the House of Lords has held that the Family Division cannot compel a public authority to exercise its public law functions.[221]

Young people (16- and 17-year-olds)

5.136   The law on consent to treatment, including treatment for mental disorder, for young people (aged 16–17 years) is governed by the Mental Capacity Act (MCA) 2005 and Family Law Reform Act (FLRA) 1969 s8. The MCA 2005 creates a rebuttable presumption that all individuals aged 16 or over have capacity to make decisions for themselves, see further chapter 7. FLRA 1969 s8 provides that persons of this age can consent to any surgical, medical or dental treatment.

5.137   MCA 2005 s3 provides that a person is deemed to be incapable of making a specific decision if they cannot understand the information

218 Department of Health, *The legal aspects of the care and treatment of children and young people with mental disorder*, 2009, p18 at 2.10.
219 See the MHA Code, chapter 19.
220 *Re W (A Minor) (Medical Treatment: Court's Jurisdiction)* [1993] Fam 64 and P Bowen, *Blackstone's guide to the Mental Health Act 2007*, OUP, 2007, para 9.33. See further *Re JM (A Child)* [2015] EWHC 2832 (Fam), where the Court approved life-saving invasive surgery to treat cancer in relation to a 10-year-old child whose parents did not consent to the treatment. The court gave guidance that in these cases an application should be made for a specific issue order under CA 1989 s8 as well as under the inherent jurisdiction, see [20]–[28].
221 *A v Liverpool CC* [1982] AC 363. In addition to the High Court's inherent jurisdiction, courts also have jurisdiction under section 8 of the Children Act 1989 to make a 'specific issue order' for the purposes of determining a specific question, including a question relating to medical treatment. See P Bowen, *Blackstone's guide to the Mental Health Act 2007*, OUP, 2007, para 9.35.

about the decision, retain the relevant information in their mind, use or weigh the information as part of the decision-making process or communicate their decision.[222] A person may be incapable of 'understanding' relevant information due to a particularly severe intellectual impairment or because they have a completely distorted sense of reality – for example, a belief that they are obese, when they are in fact emaciated. Likewise, a person's inability to weigh information in their mind as part of the decision-making process, might stem, not from profound cognitive impairment but from an obsessional or compulsive disorder – for example, an uncontrollable phobia.[223]

5.138   The courts have held that, in certain cases, a court (or even a parent) can override a refusal by a competent child or a young person with capacity.[224] While the courts, in the exercise of their inherent jurisdiction, can override certain treatment refusal decisions of even 16- and 17-year-olds,[225] great caution should be exercised in relying on parental consent in relation to a competent child or a young person with capacity. In this context, the MHA Code states at para 19.39 that where a child under 16 has competence or a young person has capacity then it would be inadvisable to rely on parental consent. In such cases, legal advice should be sought and an application made to the relevant court, if necessary on an emergency basis. See, further, the 2009 Department of Health guidance concerning treatment decisions relating to children.[226]

Emergency treatment

5.139   If there is no other lawful basis on which to give the treatment and if the failure to treat is likely to lead to the child or young person's

222 MCA 2005 s3.
223 See, for example, *Re MB (Caesarean Section)* [1997] 2 FLR 426; (1998) 38 BMLR 175.
224 See, for example, *Re R (A Minor) (Wardship: Medical Treatment)* [1991] 4 All ER 177 and *Re W (A Minor) (Medical Treatment)* [1992] 4 All ER 627. In *Re W*, the court also emphasised that the child or young person's refusal is a very important consideration when deciding whether treatment should be given, despite the child or young person's refusal, noting that its importance increases with their age and maturity; see the MHA Code at para 9.23.
225 See for example *Re P (A Child)* [2014] EWHC 1650 (Fam); [2014] Fam Law 1249, where the court granted a declaration overriding the wishes of a 17-year-old girl who had refused to consent to urgent life-saving treatment following a drug overdose.
226 Department of Health, *Reference guide to consent for examination or treatment*, 2nd edn, 2009, pp34–35.

death or to severe injury, it may be possible to treat without consent or formal authorisation.[227] In this context, the 2009 Department of Health guidance concerning treatment decisions relating to children[228] advises:

> A life-threatening emergency may arise when consultation with either a person with parental responsibility or the court is impossible, or the person with parental responsibility refuses consent despite such emergency treatment appearing to be in the best interests of the child. In such cases, the courts have stated that doubt should be resolved in favour of the preservation of life, and it will be acceptable to undertake treatment to preserve life or prevent serious damage to health.

Palliative care

5.140 A group of disabled children whose needs must be given the highest priority are those with life-limiting conditions who require palliative care services. In accordance with Standard 8 of the Children's NSF, high quality palliative care services should be available for all children and young people who need them. As with CAMHS, there is no specific statutory basis for palliative care services, which are provided under the NHS Acts. Palliative care provision for children has been criticised. A 2011 Department of Health report, for example, found that although children and families overwhelmingly wanted a child in the terminal phase of an illness to die at home, 74 per cent of children requiring palliative care died in hospital.[229]

5.141 Since the publication of the Children's NSF in England, local authorities, CCGs and NHS Trusts have been required to ensure that:

- Palliative care services provide high quality, sensitive support that takes account of the physical, emotional and practical needs of the child and their family, including siblings. Services are sensitive to the cultural and spiritual needs of the child and family.

---

227 In the mental health context, see the MHA Code at paras 19.71–19.72. The MHA Code suggests: 'If the failure to treat the child or young person would be likely to lead to their death or to severe permanent injury, treatment may be given without their consent, even if this means overriding their refusal when they have the competence (children) or the capacity (young people and those with parental responsibility), to make this treatment decision.'

228 Department of Health, *Reference guide to consent for examination or treatment*, 2nd edn, 2009, p35, para 18. This guidance is relevant to all under 18s.

229 Department of Health, *NHS at Home: Community children's nursing services*, 2011, p31.

- Services maximise choice, independence and creativity to promote quality of life.
- Services are delivered where the child and family want.
- Services include the prompt availability of equipment to support care, access to appropriate translation services, and workers skilled in using communication aids.
- Services are regularly reviewed with parents or carers, children and young people, and gaps in provision identified and addressed.
- Services are planned in partnership with voluntary sector providers and children and young people's hospices in localities where these exist.
- Provision of services includes, where appropriate:
  a) 24-hour access to expertise in paediatric and family care (often provided by local community children and young people's services to enable continuity of care);
  b) 24-hour expertise in paediatric palliative care (provided by those with specialist palliative care training);
  c) pain and symptom control;
  d) psychological and social support;
  e) spiritual support which takes account of the needs of the whole family;
  f) where required, formal counselling or therapy;
  g) arrangements to avoid unnecessary emergency admission to hospital;
  h) protocols for immediate access to hospital, if needed; and
  i) a process for keeping the general practitioner informed.[230]

5.142   In recognition of the ongoing problems in children's palliative care, the government strategy document *Better care: better lives*[231] provides best practice guidance on children's palliative care services in England. The vision of the guidance is that every child with a life-limiting and life-threatening condition has equitable access to high quality, family-centred care with services built around a philosophy of 'children first'.[232] In order to achieve this, the guidance requires a fully integrated approach among key delivery partners and for all services to be designed around the needs of children and their families.[233]

---

230 Disabled Child Standard, Children's NSF, pp33–34.
231 Department of Health, *Better care: better lives: improving outcomes and experiences for children and young people and their families living with life-limiting and life-threatening conditions*, 2009.
232 *Better care: better lives*, p11.
233 *Better care: better lives*, p12.

5.143   The guidance recognises that all children need to experience life as a child and as such all children with palliative care needs should have equal access to universal and generic services. These universal services should also be able to inform children and their families about what other support is available and work in partnership to ensure support is timely, accessible and effective. A flexible approach should be adopted with recognition that traditional methods of service delivery may need to be reviewed and, in some cases, services may have to be taken to the child.[234] To achieve this, there should be joint assessment and planning, joint funding or aligned budgets and an agreed decision-making formula such as the decision support tool in the National Framework for the Assessment of Children's Continuing Care (see paras 5.95–5.98 above).[235]

5.144   The guidance also aims to ensure that all children have a choice of location of care, 24-hour access to multidisciplinary community teams and, when needed, specialist care advice and services.[236] The independent review of children's palliative care services demonstrated that there is an overreliance on hospital-based care and that there needs to be an increased amount of community-based support through the use of multidisciplinary children's community teams.[237] Access to specialist end of life care is highlighted as a key component of palliative care services. At this stage families need access to the multidisciplinary community team working seven days a week as well as 24-hour specialist support and advice and specialist psychological, emotional and spiritual care and bereavement support.[238]

5.145   Co-ordination of transition between children's and adult services is as critical in palliative care as in every other aspect of disabled children's service provision. A transition support worker or named key worker should ideally be identified for each young person to oversee their transition, ensuring links with a counterpart within the receiving adult service.[239] Concerns have been raised about young adults being able to access services during the transition period,[240] although the Choice in End of Life Care Programme Board has now been

234 *Better care: better lives*, p26.
235 *Continuing Care Framework*, Annex A.
236 *Better care: better lives*, p30.
237 *Better care: better lives*, p31.
238 *Better care: better lives*, p33.
239 *Better care: better lives*, p40.
240 *Report of the Long Term Conditions, Disability and Palliative Care Sub-Group*, Children and Young People's Health Outcomes Forum, 2012; *Making a Difference for Young Adult Patients – Research Briefing*, York University, 2013.

commissioned to provide advice to the government on the quality and experience of end of life care.

Transition from child to adult services

5.146   As set out in detail in chapter 10, the guidance (and in some contexts, the legislation) concerning the respective responsibilities of the NHS, social care and other services differ between children's and adult services. By way of example, the National Framework for NHS Continuing Healthcare and NHS-funded Nursing Care and the supporting guidance only applies to people aged 18 or over. The terms 'continuing care' (in relation to children's services) and 'NHS continuing healthcare' (in relation to adults) also have different meanings, as explained above. It is important that young people and their families are helped to understand this difference and its implications from the start of transition planning.[241] *Transition: moving on well*[242] sets out good practice for health professionals and their partners in transition planning for young people with complex health needs or disabilities and *A transition guide for all services*[243] explains how all relevant services should work together with a young person to identify how they can best support them to help achieve their desired outcomes. All transition planning for young people should take full account of the approaches set out in these documents.[244] The 2014 *From the pond into the sea: Children's transition to adult health services* report sets out the CQC's assessment of transition services. Unfortunately, the report found that there is a significant difference between policy and practice, with many young people falling between the gaps of child and adult service provision.[245]

5.147   The SEND Code sets out general guidance about what children and young people are entitled to when they transition to adult health services:

241   *Continuing Care Framework*, p26 at 79.
242   Department for Children Schools and Families/Department of Health, *Transition: moving on well – a good practice guide for health professionals and their partners on transition planning for young people with complex health needs or a disability*, 2008.
243   Department for Children Schools and Families/Department of Health, *A transition guide for all services: key information for professionals about the transition process for disabled young people*, 2007.
244   *Continuing Care Framework*, p26 at 80.
245   CQC, *From the pond into the sea: children's transition to adult health services*, 2014.

- Health service and other professionals should work with the young person and, where appropriate, their family.
- Health professionals should gain a good understanding of the young person's individual needs, including their learning difficulties or disabilities, to co-ordinate health care around those needs and to ensure continuity and best outcomes for the young person. This means working with the young person to develop a transition plan, which identifies who will take the lead in co-ordinating care and referrals to other services.
- The young person should know who is taking the lead and how to contact them.
- The CCG must co-operate with the local authority in supporting the transition to adult services and must jointly commission services that will help to meet the EHC plan outcomes.
- In supporting the transition from CAMHS to adult mental health services, CCGs and local authorities should refer to *The Mental Health Action Plan, Closing the Gap: Priorities for Essential Change in Mental Health.*[246]

5.148 Children's continuing care teams should identify those young people for whom it is likely that adult NHS continuing healthcare will be necessary and notify the relevant CCG that will hold adult responsibility for them. Such young people should be identified when they reach the age of 14. This should be followed up by a formal referral for screening at age 16 to the adult NHS continuing healthcare team. By the age of 17, an individual's eligibility for adult NHS continuing healthcare should be decided in principle by the relevant CCG in order that, where applicable, effective packages of care can be commissioned in time for the individual's 18th birthday.[247]

5.149 Entitlement for adult NHS continuing healthcare should initially be established through use of the decision-making process set out in the National Framework for NHS Continuing Healthcare and NHS-funded Nursing Care. If a young person receiving children's continuing care has been determined by the relevant CCG not to be eligible for adult NHS continuing healthcare, they should be advised of their non-eligibility and of their rights to request an independent review on the same basis as NHS continuing healthcare eligibility decisions regarding adults.[248] Even where a young person is not entitled to adult NHS continuing healthcare, they may have some health needs that

246 Department of Health, 2014.
247 *Continuing Care Framework*, p27 at 83–85.
248 *Continuing Care Framework*, p27 at 87.

fall within the responsibilities of the NHS. In such circumstances, CCGs should continue to play a full role in transition planning for the young person.[249]

5.150   Guidance from NHS England[250] highlights (at para 88) the abrupt transition at 16 for a child who has previously been receiving health direct payments:

> When a child on whose behalf a representative has consented to direct payments reaches 16, the CCG may continue to make direct payments to the representative or their nominee in accordance with the care plan, providing the child who has reached 16 and the representative and, where applicable the nominee, consent. If the child who has reached 16 does not consent the CCG must stop making direct payments. In either case, the CCG must as soon as reasonably possible review the making of direct payments.

5.151   There is specific guidance relating to the transition from children's to adult health services in different service areas. For example, guidance on the transition from CAMHS to adult mental health services can be found in the MHA Code of Practice.[251]

5.152   Further information on the issues for disabled young people in transition to adult health services can be found in chapter 10.

---

249 *Continuing Care Framework,* p28 at 89.
250 NHS England, *Guidance on Direct Payments for Healthcare: Understanding the Regulations,* March 2014, at para 88.
251 *Mental Health Act 1983: Code of Practice,* paras 19.119–18.120.

CHAPTER 6

Housing

continued

Key points

- Like all children, disabled children and their families need suitable housing. This may mean that specific adaptations are required to meet individual needs, or may mean that accommodation in a particular area or of a particular size or type is needed.
- Housing authorities and other public bodies, including children's services authorities and health bodies, have duties to co-operate to ensure that disabled children's housing needs are met.
- Whilst families with disabled children may benefit from the statutory protection for 'homeless' people, including in situations where they have accommodation but it is so unsuitable for their needs that it is not reasonable for them to continue to live there, recent changes mean that a homelessness application may no longer be an available or appropriate route to suitable social housing.
- Families who need to move to accommodation which meets the needs of their disabled children need to be informed about the policies and practice of the relevant housing providers in the area they want to live in.
- Where inadequate housing is putting a disabled child at risk of harm or impacting on the child's family's ability to meet their needs, this should be addressed in an assessment of the child's need for services under Children Act 1989 s17 (see chapter 3). Any assessment or planning arising from the assessment which ignores housing needs is unlikely to be lawful.
- Families with disabled children who live in accommodation which does not meet their needs may be able to obtain 'priority' to enable them to 'bid' successfully for a suitable home using local authorities' choice based lettings schemes, or persuade a local authority to make a direct allocation of a suitable home. Social workers and other professionals working with the family, including occupational therapists, should liaise with and influence housing authorities when they decide whether to provide alternative accommodation.
- The main route for families with disabled children to secure adaptations to make their home safe and accessible for their child is through a disabled facilities grant (DFG).
- DFGs must be paid to eligible individuals if the mandatory requirements for the grant are met.

continued

- The maximum amount of a DFG is currently £30,000 in England.
- Housing authorities have powers to supplement the DFG to meet the cost of more expensive works or to pay for adaptations which fall outside the criteria for a DFG.
- If a disabled child has an assessed need for an adaptation to his or her home which costs more than the maximum amount for a DFG, the law may require the shortfall to be met by the children's services authority and/or the housing authority.
- It will not be lawful to refuse to make an adaptation to meet an assessed need solely by reason of resource shortfalls (costs or human resources).

Introduction

6.1   Appropriate housing is a foundation of the right to an ordinary life for disabled children. As with many areas covered in this book, disabled children have the same basic housing needs as their non-disabled peers. However, many disabled children also require adaptations to make their homes safe and reasonably accessible for them to live in. For some disabled children, for instance those with autism or those who use bulky equipment, the need may simply be for more space than would be considered necessary for a non-disabled child. 2000 practice guidance to the Children Act (CA) 1989 noted that 'when houses are well adapted for a particular child, the family's life can be transformed'.[1] Yet as has been noted in chapter 1 (para 1.37 above), many families with disabled children currently live in housing which is restrictive and unsuitable for both the child or children and their carers and siblings.

6.2   These families also frequently suffer from overcrowding, which is harder to deal with because of the impact of the needs of their disabled children. Other housing difficulties often have a particularly acute impact on disabled children. For example, in areas of the country where there is a shortage of ground floor accommodation or housing with exclusive access to a garden or play area, disabled children may be more vulnerable to risks such as a risk of falling

---

1 Department of Health, *Assessing children in need and their families: practice guidance*, 2000, para 3.115.

from height, or may find that they are not able to have the access to outdoor space and physical exercise that they require because of difficulties in accessing public play spaces. Some children have health difficulties which are particularly sensitive to common problems in poor quality housing such as cold, damp and mould growth.

6.3   This chapter does not attempt to set out all the duties owed to children and families under the Housing Act 1996 and related legislation. Not only would this be impossible given the limited space, but also a number of other excellent handbooks can provide this information.[2] This chapter instead focuses on the specific housing issues affecting families with disabled children.

6.4   Housing duties are owed by housing authorities, which will be part of the same (unitary) local authority as a social services authority in some areas but in other areas will be a different authority; the housing authority will be the district council whereas the social services authority will be the county council. This chapter focusses in particular on the duty to make adaptations to the home of a disabled child through the use of a disabled facilities grant (DFG) and/or direct provision under the Chronically Sick and Disabled Persons Act (CSDPA) 1970 (see paras 6.41–6.77 below).[3] The chapter also looks specifically at the ways in which families with disabled children may approach their local housing authority for assistance in obtaining suitable accommodation, and briefly at the additional difficulties homeless families with disabled children face at a time of an acute housing shortage. The provision of accommodation under the Children Act (CA) 1989 to homeless children (section 20) is dealt with in chapter 3, see paras 3.136–3.143.[4]

2 See, for example, D Astin, *Housing law handbook*, 3rd edn, LAG, 2015, and A Arden QC, E Orme and T Vanhegan, *Homelessness and allocations*, 9th edn, LAG, 2012.
3 This material draws heavily from L Clements, *Community Care and the law*, 6th edn, LAG, 2016.
4 See I Wise QC, S Broach, J Burton, C Gallagher, A Pickup, B Silverstone and A Suterwalla, *Children in need: local authority support for children and families*, 2nd edn, LAG, 2013, at chapter 6 for the powers and duties to support migrant families, including through the provision of accommodation under CA 1989 s17.

Responsibilities of housing authorities and duties to co-operate

6.5   In meeting their responsibilities to consider housing conditions and provision in their area, housing authorities are obliged under the CSDPA 1970 s3[5] to have specific regard to the needs of disabled people, including disabled children. This duty is exemplified in practice guidance issued in England in 2006[6] which calls for the 'social inclusion of all citizens' and requires housing authorities to counter 'disabling environments' through planning and housing design.

6.6   When deciding who will have priority for public housing in their area, local authorities must give a 'reasonable preference' to individuals (including disabled children) who need to move on medical or welfare grounds. Local authorities are required to publish a set of rules which explain how they decide who gets 'social housing'.[7] The term 'social housing' is used to describe council housing and housing provided by housing associations.[8] These rules are often described as *'allocation schemes'* and the queues or waiting lists for social housing are often referred to as *'housing registers'*. A family's position on the housing register, therefore, becomes a material consideration in relation to any future assessment of their social care needs[9] which would include an assessment under the Children Act 1989 (see paras 3.30–3.46).

6.7   There is an obvious requirement for housing authorities and children's services authorities (as well as the NHS where appropriate) to co-operate to ensure that the housing needs of disabled children are met. The joint working duty is reinforced by statute – prima-

5   As inserted by the Housing (Consequential Provisions) Act 1985 s4 and Sch 2 para 20.

6   Department of Communities and Local Government/Department for Education/Department of Health, *Delivering housing adaptations for disabled people: a good practice guide*, 2006.

7   Housing Act 1996 s166A

8   In some parts of the country all accommodation which was previously provided by the local authority is now owned by housing associations. Elsewhere, social housing is provided by a mix of local authority and housing association landlords but almost all housing association accommodation is now allocated by nominations from local authorities. Nominations are defined as *'allocations'* and so access to housing association accommodation is usually through the local authority's allocation scheme which in most areas provides a single route to social housing.

9   *R (Ireneschild) v Lambeth LBC* [2006] EWHC 2354 (Admin); (2006) 9 CCLR 686. Approved by the Court of Appeal in [2007] EWCA Civ 234 at [64].

rily Children Act (CA) 2004 s10 (see para 2.52 above) and Housing Act (HA) 1996 s213. In relation to this general obligation, 1992 guidance[10] stated:

> Social services authorities and housing should construct an individual's care plan with the objective of preserving or restoring non-institutional living as far as possible, and of securing the most appropriate and cost-effective package of care, housing and other services that meets the person's future needs ...

6.8   Housing authorities are required to have a homelessness strategy which seeks to prevent homelessness, including arrangements for satisfactory provision of support for people at risk of homelessness.[11] The 2006 Homelessness Code of Guidance stresses the importance of social services authorities, including children's services authorities, working together to develop this strategy and prevent homelessness for specific groups, which would include families with disabled children.[12] Examples of collaborative working are listed at para 5.6 of the Code and include joint protocols for referral of clients between agencies.[13]

6.9   The local government ombudsman has held it to be maladministration if a council's housing department receives a homelessness application from someone with clear social care needs (in this case a young woman with schizophrenia) but fails to make an immediate referral to their social services department.[14]

6.10   When a family becomes homeless (including in circumstances where the homelessness duty arises because there is currently no accommodation available which it would be reasonable for the family with a disabled child to continue to occupy: see para 6.18 below), the local housing authority's duty to provide accommodation both pending enquiries[15] and following acceptance of what is

---

10 Department of Health and the Department of the Environment, *Housing and community care*, LAC(92)12/DOE Circular 10/92, para 16. It is unclear as to whether this guidance has been revoked but, in any event, the stated principles of good practice will continue to be valid.

11 Homelessness Act 2002 s3.

12 Department of Communities and Local Government, *Homelessness code of guidance for local authorities*, 2006, para 1.6.

13 See also *R (G) v Southwark LBC* [2009] UKHL 26 at [33]; (2009) 12 CCLR 437.

14 Complaint against Cardiff County Council Public Services Ombudsman for Wales, Case no 2009/00981, 15 March 2011.

15 Housing Act 1996 s188

often referred to as a full housing duty[16] is a duty to provide suitable accommodation.[17]

6.11   Duties to co-operate with housing authorities also extend to health bodies: as we note above (see para 5.20), NHS Act 2006 s82 places an obligation on NHS bodies and local authorities to co-operate with one another in order to 'secure and advance the health and welfare of the people of England and Wales'. Although this longstanding duty has been stressed in many policy documents,[18] the evidence suggests that its operation leaves much to be desired. By way of example, in 2008, the ombudsman criticised as 'appalling' the failure of Kirklees MBC to make suitable adaptations to the home of a quadriplegic young man following his discharge from hospital, with the result that he was confined to two unsuitable rooms without suitable facilities for washing for over 18 months.[19]

Families with disabled children becoming 'homeless'

6.12   Duties owed by local authorities to families with disabled children under Part VII of the Housing Act 1996, which governs support for homeless people, arise when families become 'homeless' for any reason. There may be circumstances where current housing conditions for a disabled child are so unsuitable that even though the family has housing, the family members should be treated as 'homeless'.[20] Families in these circumstances may wish to require a local authority to assess a homelessness application, but should always also ensure that an application for longer-term social housing is also assessed at the same time. A homelessness application will only deal with a family's immediate, urgent housing needs. To obtain settled long-

16 Housing Act 1996 s193
17 Housing Act 1996 s206; see also the Homelessness (Suitability of Accommodation) Orders 2003 (SI No 3326) and 2012 (SI No 2601) and the Code of Guidance (footnote 12 above) in particular at para 17.5
18 See, for example, the hospital discharge guidance in England, Department of Health, *Ready to go?*, 2010, p8; Department of Communities and Local Government, *Homelessness code of guidance for local authorities*, 2006, para 5.14.
19 Complaint no 07/C/05809 against Kirklees MBC, 26 June 2008. The ombudsman recommended a payment of £7,000 to the young man to reflect the unreasonable restriction on his day-to-day life, including his ability to have social contact, caused by its delay and also recommended further payments to the young man's parents.
20 Housing Act 1996 s175(3).

term housing, an application under Part VI of the Housing Act 1996 is required.

6.13 Homeless families which include disabled children face particular difficulties. Many local authorities will not provide temporary accommodation until the day of eviction and will refuse to carry out an assessment about what sort of accommodation is required in advance of the day of eviction. Many families are provided with bed and breakfast or hostel accommodation with shared facilities which may be some distance from the family's previous home and support network. Shared accommodation or accommodation in a different area, far from schools, health and social care services may cause particular difficulties for families with disabled children. Temporary accommodation in a different local authority may also mean that social care and education duties shift from one authority to another. Established routines for travel to and from school may be disrupted. Sharing kitchen or bathroom and toilet facilities may cause particular difficulties.

6.14 Local authorities are likely to assert that there is nothing else available, but families should be aware that the duty to provide suitable accommodation means that the individual circumstances must always be considered and the homelessness duties must be carried out having regard to the particular needs of the disabled child and his or her family.[21] The Code of Guidance specifically provides that authorities must:

> ... consider carefully the suitability of accommodation for applicants whose household has particular medical and/or physical needs. The Secretary of State recommends that physical access to and around the home, space, bathroom and kitchen facilities, access to a garden and modifications to assist sensory loss as well as mobility need are all taken into account. These factors will be especially relevant where a member of the household is disabled.[22]

6.15 If interim accommodation is being provided temporarily whilst enquiries into homelessness are ongoing then the right to suitable accommodation can be enforced by judicial review;[23] if the

---

21 See the approach of the Supreme Court to the needs of children and the suitability of accommodation in *Nzolameso v Westminster City Council* [2015] UKSC 22; (2015) 18 CCLR 201.

22 Department of Communities and Local Government, *Homelessness code of guidance for local authorities*, 2006, para 17.5.

23 Housing Act 1996 s188(1) read with s206.

accommodation is provided following acceptance of a full housing duty[24] then there are statutory review and appeal rights.[25]

6.16   The 2003 Suitability Order[26] provides that bed and breakfast accommodation for families with children (defined by reference to sharing bathroom and kitchen facilities) will only be suitable in an emergency and then only for a maximum of six weeks. The local government ombudsman has repeatedly criticised local authorities for extended use of bed and breakfast accommodation and recommends compensation based on the number of weeks in what is by definition unsuitable accommodation. However, because of the way that bed and breakfast accommodation is defined in the order, many authorities continue to provide shared accommodation but provide it themselves rather than through private providers; this escapes the automatic prohibition on bed and breakfast accommodation for families with children. Additionally, in many areas, hotel rooms have been adapted to provide basic cooking facilities within in bedsitting rooms with en-suite toilet and showers again avoiding the automatic prohibition on bed and breakfast accommodation. It is important to remember that local authority run hostels and rooms with en-suite facilities only escape automatic designation as unsuitable for families. Accommodation must nonetheless be suitable having regard to the particular needs of the family, including the needs of disabled children in the family.

6.17   It will be maladministration if a council's housing department receives a homelessness application from a family with clear social care needs and but fails to make an immediate referral to their social services colleagues.[27]

Families with disabled children who need to move to suitable housing

6.18   Local authorities have specific duties to homeless families (see paras 6.12–6.17 above) and, in some cases, families with disabled children

---

24   Housing Act 1996 s193.

25   Housing Act 1996 ss202 and 204.

26   Homelessness (Suitability of Accommodation) (England) Order 2003 SI No 3326. See further *Department for Communities and Local Government, The Homelessness (Suitability of Accommodation) (England) Order 2003: guidance,* 2006.

27   Complaint against Cardiff County Council Public Services Ombudsman for Wales, Case no 2009/00981, 15 March 2011.

may be living in accommodation that is so unsuitable that there is no real alternative to a homelessness application. Some families will have no option but to request homelessness assistance for other reasons. However, for the majority of families living in accommodation which does not meet the needs of their disabled children, their desired outcome will be an offer of suitable social housing. As set out above, the only route to social housing is via a local authority's allocation scheme or housing register.[28]

6.19   Any family seeking social housing needs to be on the local authority's housing register.[29] Local authorities are free to devise their own criteria for entry to the housing register and determining priorities between competing applicants[30] but in doing so must comply with the requirement to give some groups of applicants a *'reasonable preference'*.[31] The courts have held that qualification criteria which excludes those who are entitled to a reasonable preference are not lawful.[32] Similarly, allocation schemes must comply with other relevant law, for example the prohibition of unlawful discrimination and the duty to make arrangements to safeguard and promote the welfare of children.[33]

6.20   Practice about how an applicant joins the housing register varies. Many authorities do not place homeless applicants on the housing register until the homelessness assessment process is complete, but

28 Housing Act 1996 s159 includes, in the definition of an allocation of housing, a nomination by a local authority to a housing association, and so the other provisions of Part 6 Housing Act 1996 apply to these nominations as well as to the allocation of the authority's own housing.

29 Access to local authority housing registers is restricted in the same way as access to homelessness assistance and welfare benefits by reference to immigration status. Families with disabled children who are not British citizens habitually resident in the UK face myriad barriers to accessing suitable housing which are outside the scope of this chapter. Local authorities can additionally set local criteria determining who can join the housing register.

30 Housing Act 1996 s166A(11).

31 Housing Act 1996 s166A(3)(a).

32 See *R (Jakimaviciute) v Hammersmith and Fulham LBC* [2014] EWCA Civ 1438; [2015] PTSR 822, which concerned the exclusion from the register of homeless people, but the same logic would apply to someone needing to move for welfare or medical reasons or to give or receive support.

33 See for example *R (HA) v Ealing LBC* [2015] EWHC 2375 (Admin), where a policy which excluded applicants who could not meet a five-year residence requirement was found to be unlawful following the approach of the Court of Appeal in *Jakimaviciute*, but also because of unlawful discrimination against women and a failure to comply with CA 2004 s11. At the time of writing (November 2015), this judgment was the subject of an appeal by the local authority.

this approach is not lawful[34] and they should be asked to determine the housing register application at as early a stage as possible. Some authorities require written applications, some require face-to-face interviews whilst others require online applications.

6.21   Many local authorities now operate 'choice based lettings' schemes ('CBLs'). These schemes typically require applicants for housing to 'bid' for accommodation using online bidding schemes. Some schemes also allow for postal or telephone bids. In authorities using CBLs, applicants for housing and those advising them need to be familiar with the schemes and the ways of assessing prospects of bidding successfully. If bidding is required, then suitable accommodation will not be provided to an applicant who does not bid. Applicants for housing are entitled to information to enable them to understand whether or not accommodation appropriate to their needs is likely to become available for allocation to them, and if so, when.[35] This information may be easily available by understanding information published on CBLs' websites, or may be very difficult to obtain. But it is key to understanding what prospects a family has of obtaining the accommodation that they need.

6.22   Once the necessary information has been obtained, families and their advisers can start to understand what further steps may be needed to obtain suitable housing. The key to this may be understanding the local allocation scheme. This is perhaps best seen as a set of criteria which have to be addressed. Some schemes have provision for additional priority to be awarded on medical or welfare grounds. Sometimes, this is reserved to internal or external medical advisers; sometimes, children's services retain nomination rights or the power to place a family in a group or band with overriding priority for housing.

6.23   The starting point for considering how to assist a family with a disabled child in obtaining appropriate housing is likely to be establishing whether there is currently a live application to the housing register in the area in which the family wish to live. Some local authorities treat their existing tenants differently from prospective tenants, but they will still have a policy about how priority is determined for transferring tenants. Tenants of other social landlords (housing associations) should also approach their existing landlord.

---

34 See for example *R (Bilverstone) v Oxford City Council* [2003] EWHC 2434 (Admin). Local authorities should always be specifically asked to make a decision about an applicant's housing register application as well as the homelessness application at as an early a stage as possible

35 Housing Act 1996 s166A(9)(a)(ii).

These tenants may effectively have access to two different pools of housing association properties, that is, those allocated by the local authority and those available for transferring existing tenants.[36]

6.24 Once an application to the local authority for alternative housing has been made, advisers should ensure that it has been determined. What a determination of the application involves will differ from authority to authority. In many areas, applicants will receive a bidding number, details of their band, group or points level, and instructions on how to bid for properties. Other authorities retain schemes which involve only direct offers, and these schemes too may have points-based schemes or operate by sorting applicants into different groups or bands. It is important to understand how the scheme functions, including how and by whom decisions are made and how the scheme works in practice.

6.25 Having understood the workings of the scheme and obtained or attempted to obtain the section 166A(9)(b) information,[37] advisers should consider in detail the authority's allocation scheme, with a view to maximising the family's priority. It is important to look at the family's housing circumstances as a whole and to be realistic about what is likely to be available locally. Not uncommonly, a family will seek rehousing because of the needs of their disabled child but might obtain very high priority for rehousing for an unrelated reason. Other issues impacting on housing needs should not be overlooked because they may result in higher priority for rehousing. For example, local authorities typically give very high priority to those who are occupying a home that is too large, to those in blocks awaiting demolition or refurbishment, to those needing to move because of domestic violence or harassment.

6.26 When considering the detail of an allocation scheme, it is similarly important to understand whether an authority gives cumulative preference based on all of the reasons an applicant needs rehousing. For example a family that needs to move to ground floor accommodation because of a child's mobility problems may also be overcrowded or living in a home that is affected by serious disrepair: can additional priority be awarded under the scheme to reflect these other issues? Does the applicant have to choose which priority group is appropri-

---

36 Those who are existing tenants of housing associations may have additional rights as tenants seeking transfers; to assess these, see the relevant housing provider's own policies. As housing associations are public bodies (see *Donoghue v Poplar HARCA* [2001] EWCA Civ 595; [2002] QB 48), their decisions may be susceptible to judicial review

37 See para 6.21 above.

ate and, if so, how does the applicant make an informed choice? If the scheme awards medical priority which increases depending on how many family members have health issues which are relevant to housing, are there other family members whose less serious medical problems could easily be overlooked? It is almost always worth asking the authority to assess the impact of the housing situation on other family members. In some cases, carers will suffer from anxiety or depressive disorders which are being made worse by the difficulties of providing care in inappropriate housing situations; information to demonstrate this should be provided to the local authority.

6.27   Many local authority schemes provide for priority for rehousing to be awarded on what they describe as welfare grounds distinct from medical grounds. Advisers, therefore, should consider whether families meet the criteria for medical priority, welfare priority, or both. It is always important when making representations about the need to move on medical grounds to provide as much information as possible about how a medical problem is either being made worse by the current housing, or means that a child's needs cannot be properly met in the current accommodation. It will not usually be sufficient simply to describe an illness or disability: linking the health or disability and its impact on the family to the housing conditions will be key to persuading an authority to award medical priority.

6.28   Most authorities have medical assessment forms which need to be completed by applicants seeking to move for medical reasons. Many specifically tell applicants that they need not provide supporting evidence. However, the provision of supporting evidence from professionals will usually be very important in persuading an authority to award additional priority, and in challenging a refusal to do so. The quality of the evidence is likely to be key and so those advocating for the family should be asked to give an opinion not only on the medical or disability issue itself but specifically on why rehousing is needed and what sort of accommodation would be suitable. Reports which describe a medical condition and conclude simply 'please rehouse this family' are likely to be given little weight by authorities.

6.29   Advisers should also make sure they understand insofar as possible what the process is for awarding medical or welfare priority. Many authorities carry out a paper-based exercise, with an internal or external medical adviser looking at the documents provided and providing an opinion. This opinion is not always routinely disclosed to the applicant and should always be requested and carefully considered. Many authorities delegate the decision about welfare priority to a panel and, in some authorities, panels also consider medical priority. It is important, therefore, to try to understand from the authority's allocation scheme not only who makes decisions but what criteria are applicable. Many schemes are silent about important issues like panel composition and guidance provided to the panels. Advisers should ask for relevant information including about decision-makers, panels, criteria and evidence before panels. If a decision is being made by a panel, an applicant may wish to attend to make oral representations. In every case, an understanding of the decision-making process can help applicants and their advisers when preparing and presenting evidence, and will be necessary if a local authority's decision about priority is going to be challenged.

6.30   Once an application has been assessed and the assessment understood, it may be necessary to consider how to challenge the way that the application has been prioritised. There is no statutory right to review a decision about housing register priority.[38] Many schemes, however, will notify applicants of an internal right of review. This may or may not be effective depending on the nature of the decision being challenged. If there is no internal review right, or if that review right is not effective or a review has not been successful, decisions about priority, like other decisions by local authorities, may be susceptible to judicial review or may be dealt with using an authority's complaints procedure followed if necessary by a complaint to the local government ombudsman; see further chapter 11 on remedies.

6.31   Families need to understand not only how to obtain priority for rehousing and what that priority means, but also how an offer of accommodation may be made, what sort of accommodation will be offered and what the consequences of refusing an offer may be. The following questions may be useful:

- Is there a choice-based lettings scheme dependent on the applicant actively bidding?
- If there is a bidding scheme, how does an applicant bid and does the system allow the applicant to see their place in the queue during the bidding process? Can useful information be obtained

---

38 Note that despite a common misconception to the contrary, legal aid is still available from legal aid providers holding housing contracts about housing register applications where there is also an issue about homelessness. This means that any legal aid housing provider should be able to advise on Part 6 of the Housing Act 1996 where either there is also a homelessness application or where it can be argued that the accommodation currently available is not accommodation it would be reasonable for the applicant to continue to occupy, ie there is an argument that the family are homeless as defined by Part 7 of the Housing Act 1996. Advice about a possible judicial review is also available under the legal aid scheme from any supplier holding a contract in public law.

from published results? Is there anyone who can assist with bidding, for example a local authority officer or someone in a local organisation familiar with the scheme?

• How many bids can be made? Are there penalties for not bidding? Are there penalties for refusing properties?

• Do the local authority reserve some lettings for direct allocation? Some families will prefer a direct offer, but others will want to choose where they live. Applicants need to understand when and how they may be made a direct offer and what the penalties for refusing one might be.

• Has the applicant assessed whether their ideas about property type and location are realistic? Conversely, has the applicant considered the consequences of bidding for or accepting a property that may not meet the disabled child's needs or the needs of other family members?

• Is there an agreement about what sort of accommodation is needed? In many areas, there is an acute shortage of ground floor accommodation with a garden. Many authorities have different rules for allocating these properties. These need to be understood. There may be cases where families are awarded what appears to be very high priority for rehousing but because there is no proper assessment of what alternative accommodation is needed, the family have no prospect of getting the sort of accommodation they need (for example because only those assessed as needing a garden can be offered a property with a garden and no such assessment has been carried out).

6.32   In every case, therefore, where a family is not appropriately housed, the first steps should involve ensuring there is a current rehousing application; addressing the priority that application attracts under the local authority's allocation scheme (and the housing association landlord's scheme, if relevant); and gathering evidence and making representations about priority. At the same time, thought should be given to what sort of accommodation is needed (including issues about geographical location, height, access, internal layout, number of bedrooms, toilet and bathroom facilities), how to understand whether an offer is likely, how an offer will be made and whether the applicant is free to refuse it without penalties.

6.33   In some cases, these steps will be effective and suitable accommodation will be provided, particularly if the need for alternative accommodation has been set out clearly by relevant professionals. However, in many other cases, families will find that they have no real prospect of obtaining the sort of accommodation they need quickly enough. In these cases, it will usually be helpful to consider the relationship between the housing authority (or department in a unitary authority) and children's services. An assessment under CA 1989 s17 may be needed if the housing situation is adversely affecting a disabled child and if services are needed to address the housing situation. If an assessment does not deal effectively with the child's home environment then it can be challenged using the complaints procedure or by judicial review.[39]

6.34   Often CA 1989 s17 assessments identify a need for alternative accommodation but simply recommend that a social worker should send a 'letter of support'. This is unlikely to be sufficient to facilitate rehousing, particularly in areas of the country with acute shortages of social housing. If a social worker has recognised the need for alternative accommodation it will be necessary to consider how the housing and children's services authorities work together and whether there are any local protocols or procedures allowing social workers to nominate families for additional priority for rehousing or for direct offers. See further chapter 2 at paras 2.52–2.55 on the duties to co-operate generally.

Benefit reform and disabled children

6.35   There are two recent changes to entitlement to welfare benefits which directly impact on housing for disabled children. When considering the need to move to suitable accommodation, it is necessary to ensure that the suitable accommodation is affordable. For families dependent on assistance from state benefits, the bedroom tax and the benefit cap may impact on their ability to pay the rent.[40]

The bedroom tax

6.36   The social sector size criteria rules (commonly called the bedroom tax) restrict the amount of housing benefit that a family can receive by reference to family size.[41] When these rules were first introduced, there

39 See further chapter 3 at paras 3.30–3.46 re assessments under the CA 1989 and chapter 11 on remedies generally.
40 For detailed coverage of the wide range of welfare benefits issues, see CPAG, *Welfare Benefits and Tax Credits Handbook*, 2015–16.
41 One bedroom is allowed for each couple; each other person over 16, two children of the same sex under 16; two children under 10.

was no exception for disabled children. However, the rules have now been amended so that an additional room is allowed for a *'child who cannot share a bedroom'*. To avoid the reduction[42] in housing benefit which would otherwise result, the child who cannot share a bedroom must be under 16,[43] entitled to the middle or highest rate of DLA care component and the local authority must be satisfied that, because of his/her disability, the child cannot reasonably share a bedroom with another child.[44] However, there are still some circumstances in which the bedroom tax does result in reductions to housing benefit because of a child's disability-related needs.[45]

The benefit cap

6.37   The benefit cap[46] restricts the amount of income available from state benefits including housing benefit to £500 for families with children who are out of work.[47] Where a child is entitled to disability living allowance (DLA) or a personal independence payment (PIP), the benefit cap does not apply, and so many families with disabled children who are out of work will be exempt from the cap. But families should be aware that currently the exemption for families including a disabled child in receipt of PIP or DLA does not apply to adult children and this may mean that when a disabled child eligible for PIP or DLA becomes an adult, the exemption to the benefit cap is lost.[48] For very large families or families living in expensive accommodation, typically in the private rented sector or in temporary accommodation following

---

42   14 per cent where there is 'underoccupation' by one bedroom, 25 per cent where the tenants is underoccupying by two or more bedrooms.

43   Children over 16 are treated as needing their own room.

44   Housing Benefit and Universal Credit (Size Criteria) (Miscellaneous Amendments) Regulations 2013 SI No 2828.

45   See *R (Rutherford) v Secretary of State for Work and Pensions* [2014] EWHC 1631 (Admin), where the bedroom tax applied to reduce housing benefit payable because an additional bedroom was needed for two carers providing respite and staying overnight twice weekly. A challenge to the regulations failed in the High Court but has been heard in the Court of Appeal. As at November 2015 judgment is awaited.

46   Benefit Cap (Housing Benefit) Regulations 2012 SI No 2994.

47   There is currently legislation going through parliament (the Welfare Reform and Work Bill 2015) which, if enacted, will further reduce the maximum amount of welfare benefits available.

48   But see *R (Hurley) v Secretary of State for Work and Pensions* [2015] EWHC 3382 (Admin), where the failure to exempt those caring for disabled adult family members was held to amount to unlawful indirect discrimination against disabled people.

a homelessness application, there may be very high reductions in the amount of housing benefit that they can receive.

Discretionary housing payments and meeting the costs of moving

6.38   Families who cannot pay the rent for the accommodation that they need and are entitled to housing benefit can apply for additional assistance in the form of discretionary housing payments ('DHPs'). DHPs are administered by the local authority. Some authorities will not allow direct applications to the fund, requiring applicants to approach through approved partners. These will usually include local agencies providing services to families with disabled children and the authority's own social workers. Some authorities will allow direct applications. These can usually be found on local authorities' websites.

6.39   Families who succeed in obtaining an offer of suitable accommodation which meets the needs of their disabled children are often required to move very quickly. This can sometimes involve a move from furnished to unfurnished accommodation. Urgent help with the considerable expenses involved in moving may be required. Since the abolition of the social fund, this assistance may be available through localised welfare provision. Applications for assistance with moving including removal expenses and the purchase of essential items such as curtains, carpeting and white goods are usually made directly to the local authority. Information about each local authority's scheme can be easily accessed through the Child Poverty Action Group website.[49] There may well be additional costs arising from the child's disability, and children's services may also be asked to assist with these costs, if necessary through an assessment under CA 1989 s17, see paras 3.30–3.46.

6.40   Housing benefit is usually only payable on one home and this can cause difficulties where rent liability starts almost immediately on accepting a property but for whatever reason a family cannot move straight away. There may for example be delays whilst appropriate adaptations are made. In these circumstances, it may be possible to obtain housing benefit on two properties for a short period of time[50], and/or to ask children's services to assist to meet the shortfall, particularly where the move is as a result of a child's disability-related needs.

49 www.cpag.org.uk/lwas.
50 See Housing Benefit Regulations 2006 SI No 213 reg 7(8).

Disabled facilities grants

6.41   The primary route through which families with disabled children can get public support to meet the costs of adaptations to their homes is through a disabled facilities grant – known as a DFG.[51] Housing authorities are responsible for DFGs, although it is likely that a family will be referred to their housing authority by their social worker or other professional employed by health or children's services.[52] The core funding for DFGs derives from the Better Care Fund.[53] Between 2011 and 2014, demand for DFGs increased by six per cent and during this period, funding for such grants fell by three per cent.[54]

6.42   The purpose of DFGs is to 'modify disabling environments in order to restore or enable independent living, privacy, confidence and dignity for individuals and their families'.[55] Blatant failures to take action to ensure that a property is suitable for the needs of a disabled person may result in a violation of both the private and family life rights within European Convention on Human Rights (ECHR) article 8.[56] They may also be evidence that the award process for DFGs has not been subjected to a proper impact assessment under Equality Act 2010 s149 (see paras 9.97–9.115 below).[57]

6.43   As discussed below, local authorities are under mandatory duty to pay DFGs where a person qualifies and to make the payment within a specified timescale. Despite these legal obligations, research

---

51 For a general briefing on the scheme see W Wilson, *Disabled Facilities Grants (England)*, SN/SP/3011, House of Commons Library, 2013.

52 NHS bodies have extensive statutory powers to transfer funds to social services authorities (including children's services authorities) and these can be used to facilitate housing adaptations.

53 See Department of Health, *Better Care Fund: how it will work in 2015 to 2016. Policy Framework*, 2014, para 3.5 and, generally, Care & Repair, *Disabled Facilities Grant Funding via Better Care Funds – An Opportunity to Improve Outcomes*, 2015.

54 Leonard Cheshire, *The Long Wait For A Home*, 2015.

55 Department of Communities and Local Government/Department for Education/Department of Health, *Delivering housing adaptations for disabled people: a good practice guide*, 2006, para 1.6. The scheme covers mobile homes, houseboats and caravans as well as housing: see L Clements, *Community Care and the Law*, 6th edn, LAG, 2016.

56 *R (Bernard) v Enfield LBC* [2002] EWHC 2282 (Admin); (2002) 5 CCLR 577, and see also Local Government Ombudsman's Report on complaint no 07/A/11108 against Surrey County Council, 11 November 2008, paras 48–49.

57 See Local Government Ombudsman's *Digest of Cases 2008/09* Section F, Housing, p2.

suggests that a third of local authorities routinely breach the legal timescales affecting over 4,000 people every year.[58]

Statutory scheme

6.44 DFGs are made under Part 1 of the Housing Grants, Construction and Regeneration Act (HGCRA) 1996. The duties and powers under the 1996 Act are expanded upon by regulations, principally the Housing Renewal Grants Regulations 1996, which are updated regularly.[59] Separate regulations are made to deal with the maximum amount of the grant[60] (currently set at £30,000 in England[61]) and for other related matters.

6.45 Detailed non-statutory practice guidance on the DFG scheme was issued in England in 2006[62] and is referred to in the remainder of this chapter as 'the 2006 guidance'. 2013 guidance concerning best practice in relation to the award of DFGs has been published by the Home Adaptations Consortium whose membership comprises a broad spectrum of national non-governmental organisations – albeit that the guidance states that it is 'supported by' the Department of Health and the Department for Communities and Local Government.[63] Guidance concerning the process by which local authorities must formulate and consult on their DFG policies is provided in a 2003 circular issued by the (then) Office of the Deputy Prime Minister.[64]

Definition of 'disabled'

6.46 For the purposes of the 1996 Act (s100), a person is disabled if he or she: (a) has sight, hearing or speech which is substantially impaired;

---

58 Leonard Cheshire, *The Long Wait For A Home*, 2015.
59 The most recent updating regulations being the Housing Renewal Grants (Amendment) (England) Regulations 2014 SI No 1829.
60 Disabled Facilities Grants (Maximum Amounts and Additional Purposes) (England) Order 2008 SI No 1189.
61 Disabled Facilities Grants (Maximum Amounts and Additional Purposes) (England) Order 2008 SI No 1189 art 2.
62 Department of Communities and Local Government/Department for Education/Department of Health, *Delivering housing adaptations for disabled people: a good practice guide*, 2006.
63 Home Adaptations Consortium, *Home Adaptations for Disabled People: a detailed guide to related legislation, guidance and good practice* ('2013 Homes Adaptations Consortium Guidance'), Care & Repair, 2013, para 1.15..
64 ODPM circular 05/2003, *Housing Renewal*, 2003, chapter 4 'Preparing A Policy'.

(b) has a mental disorder or impairment of any kind; or (c) is physically substantially disabled by illness, injury, impairment present since birth, or otherwise. Section 100(3) explains that a person under the age of eighteen is to be considered to be disabled if, either they are in the authority's register of disabled children,[65] or if not, the authority is of the opinion that they are a disabled child for the purposes of CA 1989 Part III (see paras 3.13–3.15 above).

Grant-eligible works

6.47 Section 23 of the HGCRA 1996 sets out the purposes for which a grant must be approved, which can be summarised as follows:

a) facilitating access to the home;
b) making the home safe;
c) facilitating access to a room used or usable as the principal family room;
d) facilitating access to, or providing for, a room used or usable for sleeping;
e) facilitating access to, or providing for, a lavatory, or facilitating the use of a lavatory;
f) facilitating access to, or providing for, a bath or shower (or both), or facilitating the use of such;
g) facilitating access to, or providing for, a room in which there is a washbasin, or facilitating the use of such;
h) facilitating the preparation and cooking of food by the disabled occupant;
i) improving any heating system in the home to meet the needs of the disabled occupant or, if there is no existing heating system there or any such system is unsuitable for use by the disabled occupant, providing a heating system suitable to meet his or her needs;
j) facilitating the use of a source of power, light or heat by altering the position of one or more means of access to or control of that source or by providing additional means of control;
k) facilitating access and movement by the disabled occupant around the home in order to enable him or her to care for a person who is normally resident there and is in need of such care; and
l) such other purposes as may be specified by order of the secretary of state.

---

65 In other words, the register maintained under CA 1989 Sch 2 para 2 – see para 3.27 above.

6.48 Since May 2008, local authorities are also required to fund works which facilitate a disabled occupant's access to and from a garden or works which make access to a garden safe for a disabled occupant.[66]

6.49 Entitlement to a DFG arises following an assessment which identifies the need for one or more adaptations to be made (see below)[67] and the duty to make a DFG cannot be avoided by reason of a shortage of resources.[68] The main purposes for which grants must be made to families with disabled children are discussed further in paras 6.50–6.56 below.

Facilitating access

6.50 This heading includes works which are intended to remove or help overcome obstacles to the disabled child moving freely into or around the home and accessing the facilities and amenities within it.[69] These include family rooms, bedrooms and bathrooms.

Making the home safe

6.51 Works under this heading may include adaptations to minimise the risk of danger posed by a disabled child's behavioural problems[70] as well as (for example) the installation of enhanced alarm systems for persons with hearing difficulties.[71] Any grant made under this heading must reduce any identified risk as far as is reasonably practicable, if it is not possible to entirely eliminate the risk.[72]

Room usable for sleeping

6.52 The building of a new room 'usable for sleeping' should only be grant-funded if the adaptation of an existing room is not a suitable option.[73] Grants can be made to expand the size of a shared bedroom used by a disabled child and (for example) a brother or sister.

---

66 Disabled Facilities Grants (Maximum Amounts and Additional Purposes) (England) Order 2008 SI No 1189 art 3.
67 *R (Fay) v Essex CC* [2004] EWHC 879 (Admin) at [28]. The 2013 Homes Adaptations Consortium Guidance notes, however, that the 1996 Act 'makes no reference to assessment of need for an adaptation' (para 7.14).
68 *R v Birmingham CC ex p Taj Mohammed* (1998) 1 CCLR 441.
69 2006 guidance, Annex B, para 16.
70 2006 guidance, Annex B, para 18.
71 2006 guidance, Annex B, para 19.
72 *R (B) v Calderdale MBC* [2004] EWCA Civ 134; [2004] 1 WLR 2017 at [24].
73 2006 guidance, Annex B, para 21.

Bathroom

6.53   The HGCRA 1996 separates out the provision of a lavatory and wash-ing, bathing and showering facilities in order to emphasise that a grant must be available to ensure that a disabled child has access to each of these facilities and is able to use them.[74] Any failure to ensure that a disabled child can access each of these facilities with dignity may be unlawful and/or constitute maladministration.[75] On some occasions, an existing room may be capable of adaptation to provide such facilities – but the ombudsman considers it unreasonable for DFG grants officers to expect disabled persons and their families to give up a family room in order to make way for a ground floor shower/toilet.[76]

Fixtures and fittings

6.54   One potential problem with the DFG scheme is the lack of clarity as to whether fixtures and fittings, including items such as special-ist equipment, come within its terms. The 2006 guidance is silent on this point. However, the previous practice guidance suggested that equipment which requires structural modifications to a build-ing should come within the DFG scheme, with smaller items (for example grab rails, lever taps, small scale ramps etc) remaining the responsibility of children's services departments under the CSDPA 1970 (see para 3.77 above). The 2006 guidance does, however, stress that where major items of equipment have been installed, arrange-ments for servicing and repairs should be made at the time of instal-lation and the costs factored into the grant payable.[77]

6.55   In this context, the 2013 Home Adaptations Consortium Guid-ance advises that in deciding if specialist equipment comes within the terms of the legislation, regard should be had to its primary pur-pose – ie facilitating access; making the dwelling/building safe; pro-viding or improving heating systems and facilitating the preparation and cooking etc. Accordingly:

> The provision of some equipment will clearly contribute to these pur-poses, commonly the use of stair lifts. Other equipment, particularly in the context of assistive technology and monitoring equipment may

---

74 2006 guidance, Annex B, para 22.
75 See, for example, Complaint nos 02/C/8679, 02/C/8681 and 02/C/10389 against Bolsover DC, 30 September 2003.
76 Local Government Ombudsman Complaint no 05/C/13157 (Leeds City Council), 20 November 2007.
77 2006 guidance, para 8.1.

form part of a wider package of care contributed to by health and social care services.[78]

6.56   The 2013 guidance further advises on the potential cost savings to local authorities of bulk buying/recycling the most frequent kinds of equipment such as stair lifts and level access showers.[79]

Individual eligibility for DFGs

Main residence

6.57   DFGs will be available to make adaptations to the disabled person's only or main residence.[80] If the child's parents are separated, this may cause difficulties since the mandatory DFG remains only available for the 'main' residence.[81] Adaptations to the home of the other parent may need to be carried out under CSDPA 1970 s2 if they are assessed as necessary:[82] see para 3.77 above. The 2013 Homes Adaptations Guidance notes that, in addition, authorities 'can use their discretionary powers in considering multiple applications to adapt the homes of disabled children in these situations'.[83] The discretionary powers available to local authorities are considered at paras 6.73–6.75 below.

Tenure

6.58   A DFG is available for the disabled child's main residence regardless of tenure[84] (ie for owner-occupiers, tenants and licensees[85]) and regardless of whether the child is living with his or her parents, foster-carers[86] or others. Where the applicant is a tenant, the consent of the landlord will be required. Authorities should seek to obtain

---

78   2013 Homes Adaptations Consortium Guidance, paras 2.13–2.14.
79   2013 Homes Adaptations Consortium Guidance, para 9.23.
80   HGCRA 1996 ss21(2)(b) and 22(2)(b).
81   Confirmed by the 2006 guidance, Annex B, para 50.
82   For a detailed analysis of this question, see Cardiff Law School, *Cerebra Legal Entitlements Research Project Opinion 'Rosi's Story'*, 2014.
83   Para 7.31: the guidance provides further detail on this issue at Annex C, para 58.
84   In the government's opinion DFGs are 'tenure neutral' see Wendy Wilson *Disabled Facilities Grants (England)* SN/SP/3011, House of Commons Library, 2013, p3.
85   See HGCRA 1996 s19(5) re licensees.
86   The 2013 Homes Adaptations Guidance notes (para 7.32) that in such a case provision may depend upon the type and length of placement.

this consent from private landlords and should offer to 'make good' the adaptations once the family leave the home in appropriate circumstances.[87] The 2006 guidance is clear that the nature of a person's housing tenure is irrelevant in relation to access to a DFG.[88] Any material difference in treatment of applicants who have different tenure (for instance, council tenants and private tenants) would constitute maladministration.[89]

6.59   A problem with the DFG scheme which has been identified by the local government ombudsman is that it only applies to existing tenancies.[90] However, if a family with a disabled child propose to move house and, therefore, acquire a new tenancy, it would be unreasonable and maladministration for an authority not to expedite the works once the family have taken on the new tenancy.[91]

Occupancy requirements

6.60   DFGs are made subject to a requirement that the disabled person lives or intends to live in the accommodation as his or her only or main residence for the grant condition period.[92] This period is currently five years from the date certified by the housing authority as the date on which the works are completed to its satisfaction.[93] The 2006 guidance states that any belief by the assessor that the applicant may not be able to live in the property for five years as a result of their deteriorating condition should not be a reason for withholding or delaying grant approval.[94] However, the guidance somewhat qualifies this otherwise clear statement in a later paragraph which suggests that if the disabled person's 'degeneration' may be 'short-term', this 'should be taken into account when considering the eligible works'.[95] This may be read as little more than a reminder that each applicant's individual circumstances need to be taken into account.

---

87 2006 guidance, para 6.3.
88 2006 guidance, para 3.21.
89 See, for example, the ombudsman reports on complaint 99/B/00012 against North Warwickshire DC, 15 May 2000 and 30 November 2000.
90 HGCRA 1996 s24(2).
91 See, for example, Complaint no 00/C/19154 against Birmingham CC, 19 March 2002.
92 Or for such shorter period as his health and other relevant circumstances permit: HGCRA 1996 ss21(2)(b) and 22(2)(b).
93 HGCRA 1996 s44(3)(a) and (b).
94 2006 guidance, para 6.7; see also para 5.22.
95 2006 guidance, Annex B, para 29.

Decisions on individual eligibility

6.61   The administration of the DFG scheme is the responsibility of the housing authority in whose area the relevant property is located. The housing authority is required to consult the relevant children's services authority (if it is not itself a children's services authority, as it will be in a unitary authority such as a London borough).[96] A housing authority may not approve a DFG application unless it is satisfied that:

- the relevant works are necessary and appropriate to meet the needs of a disabled child; and
- it is reasonable and practicable to carry out the relevant works, having regard to the age and condition of the home.[97]

6.62   The decision as to whether requested works are 'necessary and appropriate' must be taken with reference to the views of the relevant children's services authority on the adaptation needs of disabled people.[98] Although under the CSDPA 1970 all assessed needs must be met once a child is deemed eligible (see para 3.56 above), an authority is entitled to consider a range of ways of meeting the need.[99] The Court of Appeal has stressed that the question of whether the works are of a type which come within the provisions of the scheme must be answered separately and prior to the question of whether the specific works requested are 'necessary and appropriate'.[100]

6.63   A situation may arise where the housing authority would consider it to be more cost-effective to relocate a family with a disabled child, but accepts that, otherwise, the proposed adaptations were 'necessary and appropriate' and 'reasonable and practicable'. It is doubtful whether a refusal to award a DFG to fund adaptations for this reason alone would be lawful although much will depend upon the individual circumstances of the case – especially the practical reality of an alternative property being available. The 2006 guidance[101] suggests that this option should be considered where major adaptations are

---

96   HGCRA 1996 s24(3). It is, however, a matter for the housing authority whether it accepts the children's services authority's advice following consultation: 2006 guidance, Annex B, para 34.
97   HGCRA 1996 s24(3). Guidance is given on the meaning of 'reasonable and practicable' in the 2006 guidance, Annex B, para 37.
98   HGCRA 1996 s24.
99   *R v Kirklees MBC ex p Daykin* (1997–98) 1 CCLR 512.
100   *R (B) v Calderdale MBC* [2004] EWCA Civ 134; [2004] 1 WLR 2017.
101   2006 guidance, para 6.15.

required and it is difficult to provide a cost-effective solution in the existing home – but the 2013 Homes Consortium Guidance notes:

> Experience in recent years has shown that some housing associations and local authority landlords are withholding their approval on the basis that the dwelling is "inappropriate" for adaptation, even when there is no physical reason why the property cannot be adapted. Tenants have been asked to move to alternative property where the DFG applicant is judged by the landlord to be under-occupying the dwelling or where the landlord has decided they do not allow adaptations in certain types of property, i.e. level access showers in accommodation above ground floor level. In such circumstances landlords should be reminded that they *'may not unreasonably withhold their consent'* to the adaptation being undertaken.[102]

Maximum grant

6.64   The maximum mandatory grant awarded as a DFG is £30,000 in England.[103] Local authorities are empowered to make higher awards as discretionary grants: see paras 6.73–6.75 below.

6.65   If an adaptation is required to meet an assessed need and the cost of the works will exceed the maximum cap for a DFG, the remainder should be met either by the housing authority exercising its discretionary powers (see paras 6.73–6.75 below), the children's services authority meeting the additional costs (under CSDPA 1970 s2 – see para 3.72) or by a combination of the two. It will not be lawful for an authority to refuse to make adaptations which have been assessed as necessary solely by reason of cost.

6.66   Difficulties can arise in relation to the provision of advice and assistance with the design, layout and implementation of an adaptation. These costs do of course fall within the meaning of s2(6)(e) of the 1970 Act and it should be noted that section 2(3)(b) of the 1996 Act (and the associated regulations[104]) makes clear that all ancillary costs ought be included in the grant. Additionally, local authorities have power to provide the technical assistance under Local Government and Housing Act 1989 s169.

---

102 2013 Homes Consortium Guidance, para 7.67.
103 Disabled Facilities Grants (Maximum Amounts and Additional Purposes) (England) Order 2008 SI No 1189 art 2.
104 See also Housing Renewal Grants (Services and Charges) Order 1996 SI No 2889 art 2.

Means testing

6.67 Applications for a DFG for a disabled person under the age of 19 are not subject to a means test.[105]

Timescales and grant deferment

6.68 Housing authorities must approve or refuse a DFG application as soon as reasonably practicable and no later than six months after the date of application.[106] The actual payment of the DFG, if approved, may be delayed until a date not more than 12 months following the date of the application.[107] If any hardship is caused by delay even within these timescales, the children's services authority should be pressed to carry out the works under their parallel duties under the CSDPA 1970: see para 3.77.

6.69 Despite these clear statutory provisions, housing authorities routinely adopt a range of extra-statutory procedures to delay the processing of DFG applications. For instance, authorities have been criticised for creating inappropriate administrative hurdles prior to applications being received[108] and for delaying preliminary assessments, citing a shortage of assessors.[109] The 2006 guidance is unhelpfully not as strong in calling for authorities to expedite grant applications as its predecessors.[110]

6.70 The 2006 guidance accepts that some DFG applications will be prioritised ahead of others by housing authorities. Although particular

105 For details of the means test that applies to people over 19 see L Clements, *Community Care and the Law*, 6th edn, LAG, 2016.

106 HGCRA 1996 s34. Any delay beyond six months from the referral by children's services to the execution of the works will generally be considered unjustified and will constitute maladministration: Complaint no 02/C/08679 against Bolsover DC, 30 September 2003.

107 HGCRA 1996 s36.

108 Complaint no 02/C/04897 against Morpeth BC and Northumberland CC, 27 November 2003.

109 Complaint no 90/C/0336, 9 October 1991: delay of nine months for an occupational therapist assessment constituted maladministration. As noted above, the 2013 Homes Adaptations Consortium Guidance notes, at para 7.14, that the 1996 Act 'makes no reference to assessment of need for an adaptation' and it refers to advice from the Department for Communities and Local Government 'that an occupational therapy [(OT)] assessment is not a legislative requirement' and that OT assessments should 'not be used in every case'. See also *R (Fay) v Essex CC* [2004] EWHC 879 (Admin) at [28].

110 See Clements, 2015, for references to the predecessor guidance documents.

priority should be given to those with deteriorating conditions,[111] authorities are also reminded to take a broader approach reflecting the social model of disability, which would consider wider risks to independence.[112] It would of course be unlawful for an authority to operate a blanket policy which discriminated against applications made by families with disabled children in comparison to those made by disabled adults, or to adopt any similar policy which penalised one group of disabled people in relation to any other as a matter of course. The Local Government Ombudsman has found maladministration where a local authority failed to provide clear information to applicants concerning the way its priority system for the processing of DFG applications operated.[113]

6.71   The 2006 guidance provides a table which illustrates a 'possible approach' to target times for each stage of a DFG.[114] The indicative targets for the total process amount to 83 working days for high priority applications, 151 working days for medium priority applications and 259 working days for low priority applications.

6.72   Authorities also have a duty to make interim arrangements to ameliorate any hardship experienced by a disabled child between the assessment of the need for adaptations to their home and the completion of the works. The 2006 guidance states forcefully that it is 'not acceptable' for disabled people to be left for weeks or months without interim help.[115] Furthermore, children's services and housing authorities should consider meeting some or all of the costs occasioned if a family needs to make other arrangements while work is being carried out, and should consider moving the family to temporary accommodation when major works are required.[116] The 2013 Home Adaptations Consortium guidance advises that 'response should be as fast as possible and consideration given to expedited procedures and interim solutions where some measure of delay is inevitable'.[117]

111 2006 guidance, para 4.8.
112 2006 guidance, para 5.21. See L Clements and P Thompson, *Community Care and the Law*, 5th edn, LAG, 2011, paras 15.88–15.93 for further discussion of DFG prioritisation processes.
113 Complaints no 97/B/0524, 0827–8, 1146 and 1760 against Bristol CC 1998.
114 2006 guidance, para 9.3. The table is reproduced in L Clements, *Community Care and the Law*, 6th edn, LAG, 2016.
115 2006 guidance, para 5.40.
116 2006 guidance, paras 5.43–5.44.
117 2013 Homes Consortium Guidance, para 7.33.

Discretionary grants

6.73   Housing authorities in both England and Wales have a wide discretionary power to give assistance in any form for adaptations and
other housing purposes.[118] There is no financial limit on the amount
of assistance that can be given. Specific guidance on the exercise of
this discretion was given by the government in England in 2003.[119]
The 2006 guidance suggests that the types of assistance that can be
provided under this power will include:

- funding for small-scale adaptations not covered by mandatory
  DFGs, or to bypass the lengthy DFG timescales for minor works;
- top-up funding to supplement a mandatory DFG where the necessary works will cost more than the maximum DFG cap; and
- help to buy a new property where the authority considers that this
  will benefit the disabled child at least as much as improving or
  adapting the existing accommodation.[120]

6.74   Discretionary support offered by an authority can be in any form, for
instance as a loan or an outright grant. Any discretionary loan made
to an individual family will not affect their entitlement to a mandatory DFG.[121]

6.75   As with all discretionary powers, housing authorities must exercise their power to fund additional adaptations rationally and reasonably and must ensure like cases are treated alike. It would be unlawful
for an authority to operate a blanket policy of refusing to make any
discretionary payments to fund adaptations; each individual case
must be considered on its merits.

NHS-funded adaptations

6.76   The NHS has power to fund adaptations and brief guidance concerning the use of this power is provided in the 2012 National Framework for NHS Continuing Healthcare (see para 10.67 below).[122] This

---

118 Article 3 of the Regulatory Reform (Housing Assistance) (England and Wales)
Order 2002 SI No 1860.
119 Office of the Deputy Prime Minister, *Housing renewal*, Circular 05/2003, 2003.
120 2006 guidance, para 2.24.
121 2006 guidance, para 6.22.
122 Department of Health, *National Framework for NHS Continuing Healthcare
and NHS-funded Nursing Care November 2012 (Revised)*, DH 2012, – see
PG Guidance (Part 2) and in particular PG 79 and 85–89. Although this
framework applies to adults, the guidance on the principles is relevant to
children.

includes encouragement that partner bodies 'work together locally on integrated adaptations services' and that 'CCGs should consider having clear arrangements with partners setting out how the adaptation needs of those entitled to NHS continuing healthcare should be met, including referral processes and funding responsibilities'.[123] The framework draws attention to the possibility of such adaptations being provided through the use of a DFG although if this is not possible, then the NHS will be responsible for the necessary support. As it notes, where individuals:

> require bespoke equipment (and/or specialist or other non-bespoke equipment that is not available through joint equipment services) to meet specific assessed needs identified in their NHS continuing healthcare care plan. CCGs should make appropriate arrangements to meet these needs.[124]

6.77   Similarly, the National Framework for Children and Young People's Continuing Care (see paras 5.87–5.100 above) requires consideration of whether any adaptations to the child's home are required as part of the completion of the Decision Support Tool to assist with determining eligibility for NHS continuing care.[125]

123 2012 National Framework for NHS Continuing Healthcare, para PG 79.3. This guidance was cited with approval in *R (Whapples) v Birmingham Cross-city Clinical Commissioning Group* [2015] EWCA Civ 435 para 32.

124 2012 National Framework for NHS Continuing Healthcare, para PG 79.2.

125 Department of Health, *National Framework for Children and Young People's Continuing Care,* 2010, p41. At the time of writing (November 2015), the Department of Health is consulting on a revised National Framework, see para 5.94 above.

Decision-making: the legal framework[1]

continued

---

1   With the kind permission of Cerebra, parts of this chapter are taken from C Parker, *Disabled Children's Parent's Guide: decision making, confidentiality and sharing information*, Cerebra, 2013.

Key points

- Decision-making is part of everyday life; it is also crucial to the provision of care and support to disabled children.
- While parents make decisions on behalf of their young children, as those children develop and mature, it will be necessary to determine whether they are able to make decisions for themselves.
- Parents can make decisions on behalf of their children who are unable to make decisions for themselves, provided that such decisions fall within the 'scope of parental responsibility'.
- Children and young people who are unable to make decisions for themselves should still be involved in decisions being made about them.
- The ability of children under 16 years to make decisions for themselves will be depend on whether they are assessed to be '*Gillick* competent'.
- Given that the Mental Capacity Act 2005 (the MCA 2005) applies to people aged 16 and over, it is important that all those working with young people aged 16 and 17 are aware of this Act and its accompanying code of practice.
- Young people aged 16 or 17 will be assumed to be able to make decisions for themselves, unless evidence shows that they lack the capacity to do so.
- Key provisions of the MCA 2005 are summarised, including the assessment of capacity, 'best interests', the role of the Court of Protection and specific issues concerning those aged under 18.
- Under the MCA 2005, decisions can be made on behalf of individuals aged 16 and over who lack the capacity to make such decisions for themselves, provided that this is in the person's best interests and does not give rise to a 'deprivation of liberty'.
- The basis on which children and young people may be considered to be deprived of their liberty is an area of law that is complex and still developing and, accordingly, legal advice should be sought if there are concerns that the decisions being considered may lead to the child or young person being detained.

Introduction

7.1   Decision-making is part of everyday life – ranging from day-to-day decisions such as what to eat for breakfast and what clothes to wear, to more significant decisions such as where to live and whether to agree to medical treatment proposed by healthcare professionals. Adults make such decisions for themselves, unless they lack the 'capacity'[2] to do so, in which case the process for decision-making will be governed by the Mental Capacity Act 2005 (the MCA 2005).[3] The situation is different for under 18s. This is because, in some cases, parents and others with 'parental responsibility'[4] (referred to as 'parents' in this chapter) will be able to make decisions on behalf of their child. Furthermore, although the MCA 2005 applies to those aged 16 and 17, in some areas, there are significant differences in how the MCA 2005's provisions apply to young people, as compared to adults. Given that there are differences in how the law affects the two age groups, this chapter refers to those aged under 16 years as 'children' and those aged 16 and 17 as 'young people'.

7.2   This chapter provides an overview of the legal framework that governs how decisions are made in relation to disabled children and young people's care and support, focusing on two main areas:

- The issues that are specific to children and young people: in particular the circumstances in which parents are able to make decisions on behalf of their child (the concept of the 'scope of parental responsibility') and the assessment of children and young people's ability to make decisions for themselves (the concept of 'Gillick competence' and the relevance of the MCA 2005).
- A summary of the provisions of the MCA 2005 and how they apply to young people (and, more rarely, children).

---

2   MCA 2005 s2 (People who lack capacity). This is discussed below at paras 7.34–7.42

3   Additionally, the High Court can exercise its powers under the inherent jurisdiction to take necessary and proportionate measures to protect adults who, although not lacking capacity under the MCA 2005, are 'vulnerable', for reasons (such as coercion) that prevent that adult from making an autonomous decision: *DL v A Local Authority and Others* [2012] EWCA Civ 253.

4   Children Act (CA) 1989 s3 defines this as: 'the rights, duties, powers, responsibilities and authority which by law a parent has in relation to a child and his property'. Usually, but not always, the parents will have parental responsibility. Unmarried fathers will need to take steps to acquire parental responsibility. Further information is given on parental responsibility in chapter 2 at paras 2.58–2.62.

7.3   Other chapters provide further information on decision-making in the areas of health, education and social care.

An overview of the legal framework for decision-making

7.4   A significant difference between adults, on the one hand, and children and young people on the other, is the decision-making role of parents up until their child reaches adulthood at the age of 18.

7.5   Parents of young children who are not able to make decisions for themselves will make the decisions on behalf of their children. However, as children develop and mature, they will generally become more able to participate in decision-making and to start to make their own decisions, including about their care and support. Developing experience in making decisions for themselves is an important part of growing up and making the transition from childhood to adulthood.

7.6   Accordingly, those working with disabled children and young people, such as health and social care professionals, will start to encourage them to take an active part in planning and reviewing their own care and support. They will need to decide whether the child or young person is able to make decisions for themselves and if not, whether the decision can be made by their parents on their behalf, or in the case of young people who lack capacity under the MCA 2005, whether the decision can be made under that Act. These points are considered below.

Assessing the ability to decide

Children under 16

7.7   Before children reach the age of 16, the law assumes that they are not able to make decisions for themselves and their parents will make decisions for them. This means that parents will routinely be asked to make decisions on behalf of their disabled child; for example, what type of social care support is to be provided, or whether proposed medical treatment should be given to their child. However, as children develop and mature, they will generally become more able to participate in decision-making and start to make their own decisions.[5] For disabled children, this will include decisions about their own care and support.

7.8   In cases where children are considered to have the necessary maturity and understanding to make the decision in question for themselves, they are often referred to as being '*Gillick* competent'. This derives from the House of Lord's decision in *Gillick v West Norfolk and Wisbech Area Health Authority*,[6] which held that a child who has sufficient understanding and intelligence to enable him or her to understand fully what is involved in the proposed intervention will also have the competence to consent to that intervention.

7.9   As discussed in the health chapter of this book (see paras 5.132–5.135), a *Gillick* competent child will be able to consent to a range of interventions, such as treatment and care and admission to hospital. That is not to say that parents are no longer involved in the decision-making process – as a general rule parents should be consulted about decisions concerning their child, but this will be subject to the child's right to confidentiality (see below paras 7.23–7.26).[7]

7.10   Where a child is not *Gillick* competent, his or her parents may be able to make the decision on behalf of the child, but this will depend on whether that decision falls within the 'scope of parental responsibility' (discussed below at paras 7.17–7.18).

7.11   There has been little guidance from the courts on how to assess whether a child is *Gillick* competent. The revised Mental Health Act 1983 Code of Practice issued in 2015 (the MHA Code 2015) provides some assistance in this respect – and this is summarised in Box 1 opposite. Although the primary concern of the MHA Code 2015 relates to mental health care, its guidance in relation to the assessment of *Gillick* competence could be applied in any case in which the child's competence needs to be assessed.

7.12   The MHA Code 2015 adopts similar wording to that of MCA 2005 s3 (inability to make decisions). Whereas individuals can only lack capacity within the meaning of the MCA 2005 if their inability to decide is due to 'an impairment of, or a disturbance in the functioning of the mind or brain', a child might be unable to decide either for this reason, or for some other reason. For example, the child may be unable to understand the relevant information, consider it

---

5   See UN Convention on the Rights of the Child (UNCRC) article 12, which requires the views of children to be given 'due weight in accordance with the age and maturity of the child'.

6   [1986] AC 112.

7   See also Department of Health, Mental Health Act Code of Practice (MHA Code) 2015, paras 19.14–19.16.

and/or reach the decision in question due to a lack of the requisite maturity and intelligence. In either case, the child will lack *Gillick* competence.

> ## Box 1: Assessing '*Gillick* competence'
>
> 19.36 When considering whether a child has the competence to decide about the proposed intervention, practitioners may find it helpful to consider the following questions.
> - Does the child understand the information that is relevant to the decision that needs to be made?
> - Can the child hold the information in their mind long enough so that they can use it to make the decision?
> - Is the child able to weigh up that information and use it to arrive at a decision?
> - Is the child able to communicate their decision (by talking, using sign language or any other means)?
>
> 19.37 A child may lack the competence to make the decision in question either because they have not as yet developed the necessary intelligence and understanding to make that particular decision; or for another reason, such as because their mental disorder adversely affects their ability to make the decision. In either case, the child will be considered to lack Gillick competence.
>
> *Department of Health, Mental Health Act 1983: Code of Practice 2015*

Young people aged 16 or 17

7.13   Given that the MCA 2005 applies to people aged 16 and over, once young people reach the age of 16, health and social care professionals and other practitioners providing care and support to them will work on the basis that they are able to make decisions for themselves, unless this is shown not to be the case.[8] If there are concerns that the young person lacks capacity to make certain decisions, an assessment of their capacity should be undertaken in accordance with the MCA 2005 and the code of practice that accompanies this Act (Mental Capacity Act 2005: Code of Practice (the MCA Code')). More detailed information on the MCA 2005, including how parents should be included in the decision-making process under this Act, is provided below (see paras 7.27–7.62).

8 MCA 2005 s1(2).

7.14   This does not mean that parents will never be asked to make decisions on behalf of their child aged 16 or 17. The MCA Code states that
'a person with parental responsibility for a young person is generally
able to consent to the young person receiving care or medical treatment' where they lack capacity under the MCA 2005.[9]

7.15   Furthermore, in some cases a young person may be unable to
make a decision but will not lack capacity as defined by the MCA
2005 and, therefore, that Act will not apply.[10] This is because in order
to lack capacity the person must be unable to decide 'because of an
impairment of, or a disturbance in the functioning of the mind or
brain'. The young person's inability to decide may be for a different reason, for example they have never been asked to make such
a decision before and they are worrying about the implications of
deciding one way or the other.[11] In such cases, the young person's
parent(s) may be able to make the decision on his/her behalf but
this will depend on whether the decision falls within the 'scope of
parental responsibility' (formerly referred to as the 'zone of parental
control' – this is discussed below (paras 7.17–7.20)).

Involving children and young people in decision-making

7.16   Even if the child lacks the competence, or the young person lacks the
capacity, to make the particular decision, they should be involved in
decisions being made about them. For example, the MHA Code 2015
states that 'children and young people should always be kept as fully
informed as possible' and that they should receive clear and detailed
information concerning their care and treatment, in an age appropriate format and that their views, wishes and feelings should always be
sought and their views taken seriously.[12] The Department of Health's
guide, *Seeking consent: working with children*, states that even if children are not able to give valid consent for themselves they should be
involved 'as much as possible in decisions about their own health':

> Even very young children will have opinions about their healthcare,
> and you should use methods appropriate to their age and understand-
> ing to enable these views to be taken into account. A child who is
> unable to understand any aspects of the healthcare decision may still
> be able to express preferences about who goes with them to the clinic
> or what toys or comforters they would like to have with them while

9   MCA Code, para 12.16.
10 MCA Code, para 12.13.
11 MHA Code 2015, para 19.31.
12 MHA Code 2015, para 19.5.

they are there. Similarly, where treatment choices involve multiple decisions, children may be able to give their own consent to some aspects of their care, even where they are not able to make a decision on the treatment as a whole.[13]

The scope of parental responsibility

7.17   The 'scope of parental responsibility' is a term used by the Department of Health to highlight the fact that while parents will be able to make a range of decisions on behalf of their child, the courts have made clear that there are limits to parents' decision-making powers.[14] The difficulty, however, is that to date there has been little guidance on where those limits are drawn. It will, therefore, be necessary to establish whether the decision in question is one that a parent can authorise.

7.18   Given that the precise circumstances in which parental consent can be relied upon are unclear, the scope of parental responsibility seeks to assist practitioners in assessing whether parental consent can be relied upon to authorise the decision in question, for example admission to hospital and/or medical treatment.[15] Cases in which parental consent is considered to provide sufficient authority for that decision to be made are described as falling within the 'scope of parental responsibility'.[16] Where a decision may fall outside the 'scope of parental responsibility', an application to the High Court under its 'inherent jurisdiction' (or in the case of a young person who lacks capacity under the MCA 2005 to make the relevant decision, the Court of Protection)[17] is likely to be required, for which specialist legal advice will need to be sought. Examples of such cases include where a child or young person is, or may be, deprived of their liberty (see further paras 7.21–7.22 below) or cases involving serious medical treatment, including end of life treatment (see chapter 5 at para 5.138 above).[18]

---

13   Department of Health, *Seeking consent: working with children*, 2001, p9.

14   See for example *Gillick v West Norfolk and Wisbech Area Health Authority* 1986 AC 112; *Hewer v Bryant* [1970] 1 QB 357 at 369; and, *Nielsen v Denmark* (10929/84) 28 November 1988 at [72].

15   P Fennell, *Mental Health Law and Practice*, 2nd edn, Jordans, para 11.42.

16   MHA Code 2015, paras 19.40–19.41.

17   For a discussion on the MCA 2005, see paras 7.27–7.62, in particular 7.49–7.52.

18   However, if the deprivation of liberty concerns the admission to hospital for assessment and/or treatment for mental disorder, the Mental Health Act 1983 might apply.

7.19 The scope of parental responsibility was previously referred to as 'the zone of parental control'. This term was criticised by legal commentators and practitioners alike as being vague and unhelpful.[19] A significant problem with the term 'the zone of parental control' is that it suggests that there is 'a demarcated zone with observable boundaries'[20] which clearly there is not. In response to such criticism, the term has been renamed as the 'scope of parental responsibility' and additional guidance provided as part of the revisions to the MHA Code 2015.[21] Although the guidance in the MHA Code 2015 focuses on mental health care, the principle that there are limits to the type of decisions that parents can make in relation to their child applies to general health care decisions as well.[22] Furthermore, as discussed below, the scope of parental responsibility is relevant to decisions that might give rise to a child's deprivation of liberty.

7.20 The key points from the MHA Code 2015's guidance on the scope of parental responsibility are summarised as follows:

- Parental consent should not be relied upon when the child is competent or the young person has capacity[23] to make the particular decision.[24]
- In relation to children who lack the relevant competence and young people who lack relevant capacity, the question whether parents can consent to a particular decision 'will need to be assessed in the light of the particular circumstances of the case', taking a range of factors into consideration. These fall under two broad questions:

19 See for example, J Watts and R Mackenzie, 'The Zone of Parental Control: a reasonable idea or an unusable concept?' (1996) 18(1) *Tizard Learning Disability Review*, pp38–44; R Sandland, 'Children, Mental Disorder, and the Law' in *Principles of Mental Health Law and Policy* (eds L Gostin, P Bartlett, P Fennell, J McHale and R MacKay), OUP, 2010. This concern was noted in Department of Health, *Stronger Code: Better Care, consultation on the proposed changes to the Code of Practice: Mental Health Act 1983*, July 2014, at para 7.2.

20 B Dolan and S Simlock, 'When is a DOL not a DOL? When parents of a 15 year old agree to it – *Re D (A child: Deprivation of liberty)* [2015] EWHC 922 (Fam)', Serjeants' Inn Chambers, September 2015.

21 MHA Code 2015, chapter 19.

22 Department of Health, *Reference guide to consent for examination or treatment* 2nd edn, 2009, p35.

23 Mental Health Act 1983 s131(4) provides that parental consent cannot override the views of a young person who has capacity to decide about admission to hospital for treatment for mental disorder; see MHA Code 2015, para 19.39, in relation to treatment.

24 MHA Code 2015, para 19.39.

- The first is whether this is a decision that a parent 'should reasonably be expected to make' (covering points such as the type and invasiveness of the proposed intervention, the age maturity and understanding of the child or young person and whether the child or young person is resisting the decision).
- The second question considers whether 'there are any factors that might undermine the validity of parental consent'. This covers points such as whether the parent(s) lacks capacity to make the decision or is unable to focus on what course of action is in the best interests of their child and whether there is a disagreement between the parents (one parent agreeing with the proposed decision but the other objecting to it).[25]

Parental consent: deprivation of liberty and the scope of parental responsibility

7.21   One particular area of confusion about the scope of parental responsibility is how it impacts upon the determination of whether a child has been deprived of his or her liberty for the purposes of article 5 of the European Convention on Human Rights (ECHR)[26], an uncertainty that has been exacerbated by *Trust A v X and Others* (also known as *Re D (A Child: Deprivation of Liberty)*).[27] In that case, Keehan J called into question the Court of Appeal's view that parents cannot authorise the deprivation of liberty of their child[28] and held that the parents of D, a 15-year-old boy with autism, could consent to their son's placement in a locked ward of a psychiatric hospital for 15 months (D was assessed to lack *Gillick* competence to decide about these matters). The judge considered that the parents' decision was within 'the proper exercise of parental responsibility'.[29]

7.22   The decision in *Trust A v X and Others* raises a number of significant concerns, which are set out in Box 3 at the end of this chapter, and for these reasons, the authors would suggest that this decision is not one that should be followed. Indeed Keehan J emphasised that

25 MHA Code 2015, paras 19.40–19.41.
26 See chapter 2 at paras 2.2–2.21 in relation to the concept of deprivation of liberty generally.
27 [2015] EWHC 922 (Fam); [2015] Fam Law 636.
28 *RK v BCC* [2011] EWCA Civ 1305 at [14].
29 *Trust A v X and Others* [2015] EWHC 922 (Fam) at [57]. In *A Local Authority v D and Others* [2015] EWHC 3125 (Admin), Keehan J held that a local authority could not consent to what would otherwise be a deprivation of liberty for a child in its care, see judgment at [29].

his decision was based on the particular facts and he did not propose to give wider guidance on the approach to be taken in relation to children who may be subject to a deprivation of liberty as these decisions are 'fact specific and require a close examination of the "concrete" situation on the ground'.[30]

Confidentiality and sharing information with parents

7.23   As they develop and mature, it is common for children and young people to prefer to discuss personal matters with health, social care and other professionals without their parents being present. Indeed, for some professionals working with young people nearing adulthood, the starting point might be that parents will not be involved unless the young person specifically requests this.

7.24   Like adults, children and young people have the right to confidentiality,[31] so that where children are *Gillick* competent, and young people have the capacity, to make decisions about the use and disclosure of information that they have given in confidence, their views should be respected in the same way as an adult's request for confidentiality. This means that such confidential information may only be disclosed without the child or young person's consent if this can be justified, for example, there is a legal requirement to do so, or there is reasonable cause to suspect that the child or young person is suffering, or at risk of suffering, significant harm.[32]

7.25   The MHA Code 2015 advises that practitioners should encourage children and young people to involve their parents (unless this would not be in the best interests of that child or young person) and that they should 'also be proactive in discussing with the child or young person the consequences of their parent(s) not being involved'.[33] Furthermore:

> Where a child or young person does not wish their parent(s) to be involved, every effort should be made to understand the child or

---

30   *Trust A v X and Others* [2015] EWHC 922 (Fam) at [68].
31   Not least as an aspect of the human right to respect for their private lives under ECHR article 8, see chapter 2 at paras 2.14–2.19.
32   MHA Code 2015, paras 19.14–19.15. See also chapter 10 of the MHA Code 2015. HM Government, *Information Sharing: guidance for practitioners and managers*, 2008 has been superseded by HM Government, *Information sharing advice for practitioners providing safeguarding services to children, young people, parents and carers*, March 2015.
33   MHA Code 2015, para 19.15.

young person's reasons and with a view to establishing whether the child or young person's concerns can be addressed.[34]

7.26 It is suggested that if parents and other carers are concerned that the lack of certain information will prevent them from providing adequate care, they should inform the child or young person's care team and ask that the care plan be reviewed to take account of these concerns.

Mental Capacity Act 2005[35]

7.27 The MCA 2005 provides the legal framework for taking action and making decisions on behalf of individuals aged 16 or over who lack capacity to make such decisions for themselves. It is accompanied by the Mental Capacity Act 2005 Code of Practice (the MCA Code), which provides detailed guidance on the implementation of the MCA 2005.[36]

7.28 The MCA Code notes that while the MCA 2005 seeks to protect people who lack capacity to make decisions for themselves, it also aims 'to maximise their ability to make decisions, or to participate in decision-making, as far as they are able to do so'.[37] The extent to which the MCA 2005 has met these objectives is debatable. Although describing the Act as 'a visionary piece of legislation for its time', a 2014 House of Lords Select Committee concluded that its implementation had not met expectations. It 'has suffered from a lack of awareness and a lack of understanding', which has 'allowed decision-making to be dominated by professionals', without the required input from families and carers about the wishes and feelings of the per-

---

34 MHA Code 2015, para 19.16.
35 A detailed analysis of the MCA 2005 is beyond the scope of this book. More detailed guidance can be found in the following resources: A Ruck Keene, K Edwards, Professor A Eldergill and S Miles, *Court of Protection Handbook – a user's guide*, LAG, revised first edition, 2016; R Jones, *Mental Capacity Act Manual*, Sweet & Maxwell, 6th edn, 2014; Care Quality Commission, *About the Mental Capacity Act*: www.cqc.org.uk/content/about-mental-capacity-act and Mental Capacity Act (MCA) Resource: www.scie.org.uk/publications/mca/.
36 Department for Constitutional Affairs (now Ministry of Justice), *Mental Capacity Act 2005: Code of Practice*, 2007, www.gov.uk/government/publications/mental-capacity-act-code-of-practice.
37 MCA Code, p19.

son who lacks capacity.[38] The committee's comment that '[f]or many who are expected to comply with the Act it appears to be an optional add-on, far from being central to their working lives', is echoed by *Somerset CC v MK (Deprivation of Liberty: Best Interests Decisions: Conduct of a Local Authority).*[39] In that case, the court considered that the various failings by the local authority in relation to the care of a young woman with learning disabilities (including her unlawful deprivation of liberty), illustrated 'a blatant disregard of the process of the MCA and a failure to respect the rights of both P [the young woman] and her family under the ECHR'.[40] The court added:

> ... it is worse than that, because here the workers on the ground did not just disregard the process of the MCA they did not know what the process was and no one higher up the structure seems to have advised them correctly about it.[41]

7.29 Given that the main provisions of the MCA 2005 apply to 16 and 17-year-olds, as well as adults, it is important that everyone working with this age group understands and is able to apply this Act. Accordingly, the following key areas are summarised below:

- MCA 2005 principles;
- Supporting people to make decisions for themselves;
- Capacity under the MCA 2005;
- Determining best interests;
- Decision-making for people who lack capacity;
- Independent Mental Capacity Advocates;
- The Court of Protection and the appointment of deputies;
- Specific issues for children and young people.

Principles

7.30 The MCA 2005 incorporates at the outset five principles which govern all actions and decisions taken under this Act (see Box 2) and underpin the values of the MCA 2005.[42]

---

38 House of Lords, Select Committee on the Mental Capacity Act 2005, Report of Session 2013–14, *Mental Capacity Act 2005: post legislative scrutiny*, HL Paper 139, pp7–8.

39 [2014] EWCOP B25.

40 [2014] EWCOP B25 at [78].

41 [2014] EWCOP B25 at [78].

42 MCA Code, at p19.

Box 2: Principles (MCA 2005 s1)[43]

1) A person must be assumed to have capacity unless it is established that he or she lacks capacity (Presumption of capacity).
2) A person is not to be treated as unable to make a decision unless all practicable steps to help him or her to do so have been taken without success (Provision of support to assist in decision-making).
3) A person is not to be treated as unable to make a decision merely because he or she makes an unwise decision (Right to make unwise decisions).
4) An act done, or decision made, under this Act for or on behalf of a person who lacks capacity must be done, or made, in his or her best interests (Act in person's best interests).
5) Before the act is done, or the decision made, regard must be had to whether the purpose for which it is needed can be as effectively achieved in a way that is less restrictive of the person's rights and freedom of action (Consider less restrictive option).

Supporting people to make decisions for themselves

7.31   The MCA 2005, in particular through Principle 2 (Provision of support to assist decision-making), highlights the importance of supporting and encouraging individuals to make decisions for themselves. Chapter 3 of the MCA Code provides detailed guidance on how this can be done, emphasising the importance of providing information relevant to the decision; communicating with the person in an appropriate way; making the person feel at ease; as well as considering whether others might be able to support the person in making choices or expressing a view. Such support in decision-making should be part of the care planning process.[44]

7.32   The manner in which a person can be helped to make decisions for themselves 'will vary depending on the decision to be made, the time-scale for making the decision and the individual circumstances of the person making it'.[45] This might include choosing where and

43 See MCA 2005 s1 and MCA Code chapter 2.
44 MCA Code, para 3.5.
45 MCA Code, para 3.1.

when is best to talk to the person and ensuring that the information is provided (orally and in writing) in a manner that is appropriate for that individual (taking into account their age and any communication needs). The MCA Code suggests a number of points to consider when seeking to help someone make decisions for themselves. These include asking family members and others who know the person about the best form of communication; whether help is available from people the person trusts (but this would need to be subject to the person's right to confidentiality)[46] and if an advocate might improve communication.[47]

7.33   Those supporting a person in making decisions should ensure that they provide appropriate advice and information but not pressurise the person into making a decision or seek to influence the decision.[48]

Capacity under the MCA 2005

Presumption of capacity

7.34   The starting point for individuals aged 16 and over is that they have the mental capacity to make the decision in question (Principle 1: presumption of capacity). However, if there are concerns that the person lacks capacity to make the particular decision, an assessment of their capacity should be undertaken. The question whether the person lacks capacity will be decided on the balance of probabilities, which 'means being able to show that it is more likely than not that the person lacks capacity to make the decision in question'.[49]

Lacking capacity under the MCA 2005

7.35   Given that the MCA 2005 only allows acts or decisions to be made on behalf of those who lack capacity, it is essential that those seeking to rely on the MCA 2005 understand and are able to apply the MCA 2005's test for capacity in section 2, which is as follows:

> ... a person lacks capacity in relation to a matter if at the material time he is unable to make a decision for himself in relation to the matter because of an impairment of, or a disturbance in the functioning of, the mind or brain.

---

46   See further paras 7.23–7.26 above
47   MCA Code, para 3.10. See also paras 15.4–15.6.
48   MCA Code, para 2.8.
49   MCA Code, para 4.10.

7.36   MCA 2005 s2 makes clear that when considering capacity, the focus is on whether the person is able to make the particular decision at the particular time. There are two elements to lacking capacity under the MCA 2005, both of which must be established: [50]

1) **The 'functional element'**: this requires that the evidence establishes that the person is unable to decide.[51] A person is unable to make a decision if they cannot:

- understand the information about the decision to be made;
- retain the information in their mind;
- use or weigh that information as part of the decision-making process; or
- communicate their decision (by talking, using sign language or any other means).

2) **The 'diagnostic element'**: the person's inability to decide must be 'because of an impairment of, or a disturbance in the functioning of the mind or brain', which can be permanent or temporary. However, if the impairment or disturbance is temporary, the person wishing to make the decision 'should justify why the decision cannot wait until the circumstances change'.[52]

7.37   If the inability to decide is due to something other than 'an impairment of, or a disturbance in the functioning of the mind or brain' the person will not lack capacity for the purposes of the MCA 2005. This is important because the MCA Code suggests that there may be cases in which a young person is unable to decide but does not fall within the MCA 2005 because the reason for the inability to decide is not due to the 'diagnostic element'. The circumstances in which this may arise (which are likely to be rare) are discussed above (see para 7.15).

Assessing capacity

7.38   The MCA Code emphasises that the starting assumption is that the person has capacity, as well as the importance of ensuring that the person's capacity is assessed correctly if this is in doubt.[53] An assessment of a person's capacity must be based on his or her ability to make a particular decision at a particular time.

50 *PC v City of York* [2013] EWCA Civ 478; [2014] Fam 10.
51 Inability to make a decision is defined in MCA 2005 s3. See also the MCA Code, para 4.14.
52 MHA Code 2015, para 13.18.
53 MCA Code, paras 4.34–4.37.

7.39   The MCA Code points out that usually the assessment will be made by the person who is directly concerned with the person at the time the decision needs to be made. Thus, those providing daily care and support (whether they are paid carers or the person's parents, or other relatives) will need to assess the person's capacity to make decisions about that care, for example being helped to get dressed or have a bath.[54] Where health professionals propose treatment or an examination, they must assess the person's capacity.[55] The breadth of the need to assess capacity emphasises the requirement for significant public education about the MCA 2005 which may have been lacking to date, with many family carers unaware of their obligations under the Act.

7.40   Although it is for the person wishing to make the decision to decide whether or not the person has capacity to consent to that decision, in some cases a professional opinion on the person's capacity might be necessary. This might be for a range of reasons such as the serious consequences of the decision in question, or if there are disagreements on whether the person has capacity or not. The MCA Code suggests that this might simply involve contacting the person's GP or it may be appropriate to contact a specialist with experience of working with people with the same condition as the person requiring the assessment, for example, a psychiatrist, psychologist speech and language therapist, occupational therapist or social worker.[56]

7.41   If there are concerns that a disabled young person lacks capacity to make certain decisions, an assessment of his/her capacity should be undertaken, taking into account the following points:

- **Presumption of capacity (Principle 1)**: unless it can be shown that the person lacks capacity, he or she must be assumed to have capacity.
- **Non-discrimination**: the assessment must not be based on assumptions about the person's capacity due to his or her age or appearance; or his or her disability or other condition, or an aspect of his or her behaviour.[57] Thus, the fact that a young person has a disability is not a basis for concluding that s/he lacks capacity to make the decision in question. It must be shown that the disability affects the young person's ability to make the relevant decision at the relevant time.[58]

---

54 MCA Code, para 4.38.
55 MCA Code, para 4.40.
56 MCA Code, paras 4.38–4.43, 4.51 – 4.54.
57 MCA 2005 s2(3).
58 MCA Code, para 4.48.

- **Considering the young person's ability to decide (the 'functional element'):**
  - *Principle 2 (Provision of support to assist in decision-making):* emphasises the importance of encouraging and supporting people to make decisions for themselves. Chapter 3 of the MCA Code provides guidance on helping people to make their own decisions.
  - *Adequacy of the information:* In all cases, the provision of relevant information will be essential.[59] Relevant information will include the nature of the decision, the reason why the decision is needed and the reasonably foreseeable consequences of deciding one way or another, or failing to make the decision.[60] While the provision of a broad explanation, in simple language, may be enough in some cases, in others the nature of the decision (for example if it could have serious consequences) may require more detailed information or access to advice.[61]
  - *Effective communication:* The information needs to be presented in a way that is appropriate to the person's needs and circumstances 'using simple language, visual aids or any other means'.[62] For young people, it will be important that the information is provided in an age appropriate manner as well as being in the most effective form of communication, such as sign language, visual representations and computer support.[63]
  - *Assistance in retaining the relevant information:* it should not be assumed that the fact that a person cannot retain the information for very long means that s/he is unable to make the decision. What will need to be assessed is whether the person is able to hold the information in his/her mind long enough to make an effective decision – and this will depend on the particular circumstances of the case. People can be helped to retain information, by for example, photographs, posters videos and voice recorders.[64]
  - *Assistance in using or weighing information as part of the decision-making process:* individuals must not only be able to understand

---

59 MCA 2005 s3(1).
60 MCA 2005 s3(4) and MCA Code, para 4.19
61 MCA Code, para 4.19.
62 MCA 2005 s3(2) and MCA Code, para 4.17.
63 MCA 2005 s3(2) and MCA Code, paras 4.16–4.19.
64 MCA 2015 S3(3) and MCA Code, para 4.20.

the information but be able to weigh it up and use this to make a decision. People can be supported in doing so, by for example, family members and professional advisers.[65]

— *Assistance in communicating a decision:* before deciding that a person cannot communicate his/her decision, 'it is important to make all practicable and appropriate efforts to help them communicate', which might require the involvement of professionals such as speech and language therapists or specialists in non-verbal communication.[66]

— *Seeking the views of family members and close friends:* people close to the person may be able to provide valuable information, such as the types of decisions the person is able to make (although their views on what they want for the person must not influence the outcome of the assessment).[67]

• **Establishing reasons for inability to decide:** If the young person is unable to decide, it will be necessary to consider whether this is 'because of an impairment of, or a disturbance in the functioning of the mind or brain' ('the diagnostic element'):

— A range of conditions might be covered by 'an impairment of, or a disturbance in the functioning of the mind or brain ... such as psychiatric illness, learning disability, dementia, brain damage or even a toxic confusional state, as long as it has the necessary effect on the functioning of the mind or brain, causing the person to be unable to make the decision'.[68] It also includes physical or medical conditions that cause drowsiness or loss of consciousness, concussion following a head injury and the symptoms of alcohol or drug use.[69]

— As noted above (para 7.15), a young person may be unable to make a decision but for reasons other than 'because of an impairment of, or a disturbance in the functioning of the mind or brain' in which case, the young person will not lack capacity as defined by the MCA 2005 and, therefore, this Act will not apply.[70]

• **Right to make unwise decisions (Principle 3):** the fact that a person makes a decision which others consider to be unwise does not

---

65 *V v R* [2011] EWHC 822 (QB), noted in G Ashton (gen ed), *Court of Protection Practice,* Jordan Publishing, 2015, para 2.82.

66 MCA Code, para 4.24.

67 MCA Code, para 4.52.

68 MCA 2005, Explanatory Notes, para 22.

69 MCA Code, para 4.12.

70 MCA Code, para 12.13.

mean that he or she lacks capacity. This principle applies to young people as well as adults. Nonetheless, it should be noted that:

- While an unwise decision is not in itself a reason for suggesting that a person lacks capacity, factors such as the person repeatedly making 'unwise decisions that put them at significant risk of harm or exploitation'[71] might suggest the need for further investigation (such as an assessment of the person's capacity to make such decisions). Questions to consider include whether the person has developed a medical condition that affects his or her capacity to make particular decisions, is easily influenced by undue pressure or needs information to help them understand the consequences of the decision.[72]

- If a person is making decisions without fully understanding the risks involved or is unable to weigh up the information about the decision, this is relevant to capacity. There is a difference between an 'unwise' decision and a decision that is 'based on a lack of understanding of risks or inability to weigh up the information about a decision'.[73]

Fluctuating capacity

7.42 In some cases, a young person's capacity to make decisions may fluctuate (for example, due to periodic, profound depression). In such cases, social and health care professionals should plan for the times during which the young person is not able to make decisions for him or herself. They can do so by negotiating advance agreements with the young person when s/he has the capacity to consent to such matters, for example medical treatment. Although these are not legally binding, such agreements are helpful in developing trust and understanding between the young person and the care team.[74] They will also help to ensure that the young person's wishes and preferences are taken into account even during periods in which s/he may not be able to express them.[75]

71 MCA Code, para 2.11.
72 MCA Code, para 2.11.
73 *YLA v PM* [2013] EWCOP 4020 at [43](e).
74 For example, see Department of Health, Mental Health Act Code of Practice (the MHA Code) 2015, at para 9.15: 'Encouraging patients to set out their wishes in advance is often a helpful therapeutic tool, encouraging collaboration and trust between patients and professionals.'
75 MCA 2005 s4(6)(a) emphasises the importance of considering relevant written statements. See also MCA Code, paras 5.41–5.45 on the importance of taking into account the person's previously expressed views, in particular, written statements.

Determining best interests

7.43   It is essential to keep in mind that the principle of 'best interests' in decision-making under the MCA 2005 only applies where a person lacks capacity to make a decision or decisions for themselves. People who have capacity are free to make decisions for any reason and are not required to do what is 'best' for them.

7.44   However, anything done for, and any decision made on behalf of, a person without capacity must be done or made in the 'best interests' of that person (Principle 4: Best Interests).[76] This applies to all decisions under the MCA 2005, whether in relation to financial, personal welfare or healthcare decisions and whoever is making the decisions (whether family members, health or social care professionals or individuals appointed to act as the person's deputy).[77]

7.45   The MCA 2005 does not define 'best interests', rather it sets out a range of factors that must be considered when seeking to determine what is in the person's best interests. Decision-makers 'must take into account all relevant factors that it would be reasonable to consider, not just those that are important' and they must not make the decision based on what they would do.[78] The Supreme Court has emphasised the importance of the person's own views, wishes and feelings in determining what is in their best interests.[79]

7.46   Where a young person lacks capacity, the following points will be relevant to determining what is in his or her interests:

- **Non-discrimination**: the determination of best interests must not be based on assumptions about the young person's age or appearance; or his or her disability or other condition, or an aspect of his or her behaviour.[80]
- **Encouraging participation**: wherever possible the young person should be encouraged to be involved in the decision-making process and give their views on matters relevant to the decision and what outcome they would like.[81] Thus, steps will need to be taken

---

76 MCA 2005 s1(5). The MCA Code at para 2.12 notes that there are two exceptions to this – research (which is not covered by this handbook) and advance refusals of treatment (which do not apply to under 18s).

77 MCA Code, para 5.2.

78 MCA Code, para 5.7.

79 *Aintree University Hospitals NHS Foundation Trust v James* [2013] UKSC 67; [2014] AC 591, see Lady Hale at [24]: '... the preferences of the person concerned are an important component in deciding where his best interests lie'.

80 MCA 2005 s4(1).

81 MCA 2005 s4(4) and MCA Code, para 5.22.

to help the young person participate, for example using simple language and/or visual aids to help the young person understand the options and asking the young person about the decision at a time and location where s/he feels the most relaxed and at ease.[82]

- **Considering if the decision can be delayed until the young person has capacity**: although it may not be possible to do so because the decision needs to be made as a matter of urgency, if it is possible to put off the decision until the young person regains capacity, then the decision should be deferred until that time.[83] For many disabled young people there will of course be no prospect that they will gain or regain capacity to make certain decisions.

- **Considering the young person's wishes and feelings: so far as reasonably ascertainable, to consider the following:**
  - The young person's past and present wishes, in particular, any advance statement made when the young person had capacity.
  - The beliefs and values that would be likely to influence the young person if s/he had capacity.
  - The other factors the young person would be likely to consider if s/he had capacity, such as the effect of the decision on other people, providing or gaining emotional support from people close to the young person.[84]

- **Consulting other people close to the young person**: the views of anyone involved in caring for, or interested in the welfare of, the young person, must be taken into account if it is practicable and appropriate to consult them.[85] This should include the young person's deputy if one has been appointed, although a deputy will be entitled to take the relevant decision themselves if it comes within the scope of their powers conferred by the Court of Protection order. Although parents will no longer have parental responsibility once their child becomes 18, they should still be consulted on what is in their adult child's best interests (unless there are good reasons for not doing so, for example there are reasonable grounds to believe that the relationship between the parent and young person is abusive). This is because they will be persons who are 'engaged in caring for' the young person or who are interested

82 MCA Code, para 5.24.
83 MCA 2005 s4(3) and MCA Code, paras 5.25–5.28.
84 MCA 2005 s4(6) and MCA Code, paras 5.37–5.46.
85 MCA 2005 s4(7).

in the young person's welfare.[86] Those consulted should be asked their views on what they think is in the young person's best interests and if they can give any information on the young person's wishes and feelings, beliefs and values.[87]

- **Special consideration for life-sustaining treatment**: when considering whether such treatment is in the young person's best interests, the decision-maker must not be motivated by a desire to bring about his/her death. Where there is any doubt as to what is in the young person's best interests, an application should be made to the Court of Protection.[88]

- **Considering less restrictive principle (Principle 5)**: before an action or decision is taken on behalf of a person who lacks capacity, consideration must be given as to whether there is an alternative approach that would interfere less with the person's basic rights and freedoms,[89] although 'it may be necessary to choose an option that is not the least restrictive alternative if that option is in the person's best interests'.[90]

Decision-making for people who lack capacity

Acts in connection with care or treatment

7.47   MCA 2005 s5 provides that individuals (such as health and social care professionals, parents and other carers) can undertake certain acts 'in connection with the care and treatment' of a person who lacks capacity.[91] Those undertaking such acts must reasonably believe that the person lacks capacity (and have taken reasonable steps to establish whether or not the person does lack capacity) and that it is in the person's best interests to undertake that act. They must also follow the principles set out in section 1 of the MCA 2005 (see Box 2 above).

---

86 MCA 2005 s4(7)(b). See *R (W) Croydon LBC* [2011] EWHC 696 (Admin); (2011) 14 CCLR 247, at [39], for the importance of involving the consultees (in this case, the parents) at the time when the relevant decisions are being made and giving sufficient time 'for adequate time for intelligent consideration and response to be given'.

87 MCA 2005 s4(7) and MCA Code, paras 5.49–5.54.

88 MCA 2005 s4(5) and MCA Code, paras 5.29–5.38.

89 MCA Code, para 2.14. The courts have also taken this approach. See for example *FP v GM and a Health Board* [2011] EWHC 2778 (Fam); [2011] 2 FLR 1375, in which Hedley J at [18], stated that this principle 'in effect, is a principle of minimum intervention consistent with best interests'.

90 MCA Code, para 2.16.

91 See chapter 6 of the MCA Code for further guidance.

7.48   Provided that individuals taking action for a person who lacks capacity have complied with these requirements, they will not incur liability (ie there will not be any civil or criminal penalties) for doing so without the person's consent, so long as the act taken is something that the person could have consented to if s/he had capacity. This means, for example, that a young person who lacks capacity to consent to treatment can be given that treatment by health professionals, or if the young person lacks capacity to feed or dress, those caring for the young person can help the young person to do so, relying on MCA 2005 s5. However, section 5 would not provide a defence to a claim that the person undertaking the act had done so negligently.

Restrictions on acts undertaken

7.49   The acts that can be undertaken under MCA 2005 s5 are subject to the restrictions set out in MCA 2005 s6. Of key importance is that a person who lacks capacity can only be restrained if certain conditions are met. The term 'restraint' covers the use, or threat to use, force to make a person do something that s/he is resisting or restricting a person's liberty of movement, whether or not s/he is resisting.[92] An individual can only use restraint if this is reasonably believed to be necessary to prevent harm to the person who lacks capacity and is a proportionate response to likelihood of the person suffering harm, and the seriousness of that harm.[93] Crucially, acts under MCA 2005 s5 cannot authorise actions that amount to a deprivation of liberty.

7.50   The law relating to the deprivation of liberty of children and young people is particularly complex. Although the Supreme Court's decision in *P v Cheshire West and Chester Council; P and Q v Surrey County Council (Cheshire West)*,[94] has clarified the basis on which the deprivation of liberty of adults who lack capacity under the MCA 2005 to make decisions about their care and treatment is determined, it is not clear how this relates to children and young people. The test formulated in *Cheshire West* (known as 'the acid test') is whether the person is 'under continuous supervision and control and not free to leave'.[95] However, the Law Society's *Deprivation of Liberty: a practical guide* suggests that when assessing whether young people are deprived of their liberty for the purpose of the MCA 2005, a 'nuanced

---

92 MCA 2005 s6(4).
93 See MCA Code, paras 6.40–6.46 for further information.
94 [2014] UKSC 19; [2014] 2 All ER 585.
95 *P v Cheshire West and Chester Council; P and Q v Surrey County Council (Cheshire West)* [2014] UKSC 19; [2014] 2 All ER 585 at [54].

acid test' might be more appropriate. This takes into account 'the liberty-restricting measures that are universally applied to those of the same age and maturity who are free from disability'.[96]

7.51   Another issue is the relevance of parental consent. The MHA Code 2015 notes that it is not clear whether, and if so, in what circumstances, parents can consent to restrictions on their children, which without their consent, would amount to a deprivation of liberty.[97] In the light of *Trust A v X and Others*[98] (discussed above at paras 7.21–7.22), the Law Commission's *Mental Capacity and Deprivation of Liberty – A Consultation Paper* seeks views on the question of the appropriateness of relying on parental consent to the restrictions placed on young people lacking the capacity to consent to their care and treatment.[99]

7.52   Those working with young people will need to consider carefully whether the care regime in community settings such as residential schools or children's homes, gives rise to a deprivation of liberty. If it does, legal authority for this must be sought. Given the current uncertainty in this area of law, legal advice may need to be sought on whether a deprivation has arisen and if so, what action should be taken, which will depend on the circumstances of the case.[100] Where a deprivation of liberty arises in relation to a young person who lacks capacity to make decisions about his or her care, this is likely to require an application to the Court of Protection for an order authorising the young person's care (including the deprivation of liberty) under the MCA 2005.[101] However, if the deprivation of liberty concerns the admission to hospital for assessment and/or treatment for mental disorder, the Mental Health Act 1983 might apply.[102] It is important to note that the deprivation of liberty safeguards under the MCA 2005 do not apply to individuals under the age of 18.[103]

7.53   Furthermore, acts cannot be undertaken under MCA 2005 s5 if they conflict with a decision made by an individual authorised under the MCA 2005 to make decisions for the person who lacks capacity.[104]

---

96 Available at: www.lawsociety.org.uk/support-services/advice/articles/
    deprivation-of-liberty/. See chapter 9.
97 MCA Code 2015, para 19.48.
98 [2015] EWHC 922 (Fam).
99 See paras 15.2–15.12 of the consultation paper.
100 See discussion in Box 3 below and MCA Code, paras 12.23–12.25.
101 *Trust A v X and Others* [2015] EWHC 922 (Fam) at [51].
102 See MHA Code 2015, chapter 19.
103 See MCA 2005 Sch A1.
104 MCA 2005 s6(6) but see s6(7) in relation to life-sustaining treatment.

In the case of a young person, this might be a deputy appointed by the court to make personal welfare and/or financial decisions on behalf of the young person (see below para 7.61).

7.54   Additional restrictions apply to decision-making in relation to those aged 18 and over. For example, adults who have the mental capacity to do so, can appoint another adult to make decisions on their behalf (referred to as a 'Lasting Power of Attorney' (LPA)). These can be either financial decisions or decisions concerning their personal welfare (including healthcare) if in the future they lack the capacity to do so themselves. In cases where the person has made an LPA, actions could not be undertaken if they conflict with the attorney's decision.[105]

Independent Mental Capacity Advocates

7.55   The role of an Independent Mental Capacity Advocate (IMCA) is to represent and support the person who lacks capacity to make the relevant decisions. Support from an IMCA must be made available to people who lack capacity when decisions are being made in relation to 'serious medical treatment' or a long-term change in accommodation and the person has no suitable family or friends who could be consulted on their best interests.

- **'Serious medical treatment'** is 'treatment which involves providing, withholding or withdrawing treatment' which is further described in regulations.[106] The MCA Code notes that it is impossible to set out all types of procedures that may amount to serious medical treatment but suggests that they will include chemotherapy and surgery for cancer, therapeutic sterilisation and major surgery, such as open-heart surgery.[107]
- **Change in accommodation** includes a placement in hospital for longer than 28 days[108] or in a social care setting (eg a care home) for what is likely to be longer than eight weeks.[109]

---

105 MCA 2005 ss9–13; see also chapter 7 of the MCA Code. Other limits apply in relation to adults. For example, medical treatment cannot be given under the MCA 2005 if this conflicts with the adult's valid and applicable advance decision to refuse treatment: see MCA 2005 ss24–26 and also chapter 9 of the MCA Code.

106 MCA 2005 s37(6) and the Mental Capacity Act 2005 (Independent Mental Capacity Advocates) (General) Regulations 2006 SI No 1832, as amended.

107 MCA Code, para 10.45.

108 MCA 2005 s38.

109 MCA 2005 s39.

7.56   Although these provisions for the involvement of IMCAs are available to 16- and 17-year-olds, the Department of Health's reports on the IMCA service shows that the number of referrals to IMCAs for this age group are low (40 in 2011/12 (out of a total of 11,899);[110] 31 in 2012/2013 (out of a total of 12,381)[111] and 34 in 2013/14 (out of a total of 13,301).[112] No explanation is given for these low numbers. It may be because family members or others were available to be consulted. However, it may also be due to the low awareness of the MCA 2005, as highlighted by the House of Lords Select Committee (see para 7.28 above) and, therefore, the issue would appear to merit investigation.

7.57   There is a new right to advocacy under the Care Act 2014 in the assessment and support planning process for adults and young people in transition to adulthood;[113] the statutory guidance to the Care Act makes clear that the same person can be an IMCA and a Care Act advocate, as long as they are suitably qualified for each role.[114]

The Court of Protection and the appointment of deputies[115]

7.58   The Court of Protection (CoP) has a range of powers, which include deciding on whether a person has capacity to make a particular decision and making declarations, decisions or orders in relation to financial or welfare matters affecting those lacking the capacity to make such decisions.[116]

7.59   The CoP can also appoint deputies to make decisions on welfare (including educational or healthcare) decisions as well as property

---

110 The Fifth Year of the Independent Mental Capacity Advocacy (IMCA) Service: 2011/2012, pp18–20.

111 The Sixth Year of the Independent Mental Capacity Advocacy (IMCA) Service: 2012/2013, February 2014, p17.

112 The Seventh Year of the Independent Mental Capacity Advocacy (IMCA) Service: 2013/2014, March 2015, Table 3, p36.

113 Care Act 2014 s67.

114 Department of Health, Care and Support Statutory Guidance, issued under the Care Act 2014, October 2014, para 7.9.

115 See MCA 2005 ss15–21A and chapter 8 of the MCA Code. For a detailed analysis of the role of the Court of Protection, see A Ruck Keene, K Edwards, Professor A Eldergill and S Miles, *Court of Protection Handbook – a user's guide*, LAG, revised first edition, 2016.

116 See MCA 2005 s16 for the power for the court to make decisions on P's behalf and appoint deputies.

and financial matters on behalf of a person who lacks capacity. The deputy is likely to be a family member or someone who knows the person well, but this will not always be the case, for example, the CoP may decide to appoint a professional deputy, such as a solicitor to deal with the person's property or affairs.[117] A representative of the local authority, for example the Director of Adult Services, can also be appointed as a deputy if the CoP considers this to be appropriate but the court will need to be satisfied that the authority has arrangements to avoid possible conflict of interest.[118]

7.60 MCA 2005 s16(4) states that in deciding whether it is in the best interests of the person lacking capacity to appoint a deputy, in addition to the factors set out in section 4 (best interests), the CoP must have regard to the following two principles:

- a decision by the CoP 'is to be preferred to the appointment of a deputy to make a decision'; and
- the powers conferred on a deputy should be 'as limited in scope and duration as is practicably reasonable in the circumstances'.

7.61 The MCA Code anticipates that personal welfare deputies 'will only be required in the most difficult cases'.[119] The CoP has taken a somewhat inconsistent approach to the code's suggestion. In *A Local Authority v TZ (No 2)*,[120] the local authority's application to be appointed as TZ's welfare deputy was rejected on the basis that the court did not consider this to be an appropriate case for the appointment of a welfare deputy. Noting the MCA Code's advice on this point, Baker J added '...for most day to day actions or decisions, the decision-maker should be the carer most directly involved with the person at the time

---

117 MCA Code, para 8.33. See *Re P* [2010] EWHC 1592 (Fam) at [9]: '...the court ought to start from the position that, where family members offer themselves as deputies, then, in the absence of family dispute or other evidence that raises queries as to their willingness or capacity to carry out those functions, the court ought to approach such an application with considerable openness and sympathy'. See also *Re M, N v O & P* 9 April 2013 (COP) (summary available www.39essex.com/cop_cases/re-m-n-v-o-p/) where it was stated that: 'the court prefers to appoint a family member or close friend, if possible, as long as it is in P's best interests to do so' but there would be reasons for not doing so, for example if there had been physical or financial abuse.

118 MCA Code, paras 8.41 and 8.60.

119 MCA Code, para 8.38. See discussion in A Ruck Keene, K Edwards, Professor A Eldergill and S Miles, *Court of Protection Handbook – a user's guide*, LAG, revised first edition, 2016, on the appointment of personal welfare deputies at paras 3.126–3.138.

120 [2014] EWHC 973 (COP).

(paragraph 5.8). That is simply a matter of common-sense'.[121] However, in *SBC v PBA and others*,[122] the court took a different view, stating that the 'unvarnished' words of MCA 2005 s16 set down the test for the appointment of a deputy, and that the MCA Code, with its reference to 'most difficult' health and welfare cases, did not compel the court to be satisfied that the circumstances were difficult or unusual before a deputy could be appointed.

Specific issues for children and young people

7.62   Although the main provisions of the MCA 2005 apply to individuals aged 16 and over, some provisions distinguish between adults and young people aged 16 and 17. Furthermore, in some circumstances, the MCA 2005 can cover those aged under 16. Chapter 12 of the MCA Code provides guidance on how the MCA 2005 applies to under 18s. The key points are summarised below:

- **Planning for possible future incapacity – MCA 2005 ss9–14 and 24–26:** As noted above (para 7.54), young people cannot appoint an attorney under the Lasting Power of Attorney (LPA) provisions, nor can they make an advance refusal of treatment under the MCA 2005 (the age limit for both being 18 and over).[123]
- **Young people with special needs and/or disabilities – MCA 2005 and Children and Families (CFA) Act 2014:** The 2014 Act includes special provisions concerning decision-making where individuals aged 16–25 years lack capacity to make decisions in relation to matters governed by Part 3 of that Act, for example their education, health and care plan or an appeal to the tribunal in relation to such a plan.[124] These provisions are discussed in chapter 11 at paras 11.81–11.87.
- **Children and property and affairs – MCA 2005 s18(3):** The Court of Protection can make decisions in relation to a child's property and affairs if the court thinks it likely that the child will still lack capacity to make financial decisions after reaching the age

---

121 [2014] EWHC 973 (COP) at [82].
122 [2011] EWHC 2580 (Fam). See also A Ruck Keene, 'Getting it right in the balance between autonomy and protection', *Mental Capacity Law and Policy*, 2014.
123 In addition, the Court of Protection's power to make a will does not apply to those aged under 18; see MCA 2005 s18(2).
124 CFA 2014 s80 and the SEND Regs 2014 SI No 1530 regs 63–64.

of 18.[125] For example, this would allow the court to make an order concerning the investment of an award for compensation for the child and/or appoint a deputy to manage the child's property and affairs.[126]

- **Transferring proceedings between a court with jurisdiction under the Children Act 1989 and the Court of Protection – MCA 2005 s21:** Regulations set out a range of considerations to be taken as to which court (ie the Court of Protection or the Family Court) should hear a particular case.[127] The MCA Code notes that a case involving a young person who lacks mental capacity to make a specific decision could be heard in the family courts or in the Court of Protection. It adds:

    If the case might require an ongoing order (because the young person is likely to still lack capacity when they are 18), it may be more appropriate for the Court of Protection to hear the case. For one-off cases not involving property or finances, the Family Division may be more appropriate.[128]

- **Criminal offence (Ill-treatment or neglect – MCA s44):** There appears to be no age limit to this provision which makes it a criminal offence for an individual who is caring for a person who lacks capacity (to make decisions concerning their care[129]) to ill-treat or wilfully neglect that person. The provision could, therefore, apply to a child provided that he or she lacked capacity under MCA 2005 s2, albeit other criminal offences are likely to be applicable whether or not the child lacks capacity, such as offences of child cruelty or neglect.[130]

---

125 MCA 2005 ss2(6) and 18(3).
126 See MCA Code, paras 12.3–12.4.
127 Mental Capacity Act 2005 (Transfer of Proceedings) Order 2007 SI No 1899 art 3(3)(c).
128 MCA Code, paras 12.24; see also para 12.7. *B (A Local Authority) v RM and Others* [2010] EWHC 3802 (Fam) sets out points to be considered by the court when deciding if an application for a care order should be transferred to the Court of Protection to be dealt with under the MCA 2005 instead.
129 *R v Dunn* [2010] EWCA Crim 2935, see also *R v Hopkins* [2011] EWCA Crim 1513 at [43].
130 MCA Code, para 12.5.

Box 3: Case comment

Trust A v X and others [2015] EWHC 922 (Fam)

As noted at paras 7.21–7.22, the decision in *Trust A v X and Others*,[131] which held that the parents of D, a 15-year-old boy with autism, could consent to their son's placement in a locked ward of a psychiatric hospital, raises significant concerns. For the reasons set out below, the authors question whether the parents' consent was within 'the proper exercise of parental responsibility'[132] and would suggest that this decision is not one that should be followed.

One major criticism is that this decision has denied 'the recognition of D's right to liberty'[133] with the result that he was placed in a similar position to that of HL in *HL v United Kingdom*[134] As HL, who had learning disabilities, lacked the capacity to decide about his admission to hospital, the legal basis for his informal admission was the common law doctrine of necessity (the case pre-dates the MCA 2005). The European Court of Human Rights held that HL's admission to hospital breached his right to liberty under ECHR article 5. This was because his admission amounted to a deprivation of liberty and the common law doctrine of necessity lacked sufficient procedural safeguards to protect individuals such as HL from arbitrary detention. There is a similar lack of procedural safeguards for children and young people who are admitted to hospital on the basis of parental consent.[135]

It is not clear to what extent efforts were made to ascertain D's views on his placement; the court noted that the children's guardian's submissions were confined to observing that D was well placed in the hospital and was progressing.[136]

Another concern is that the court failed to consider the limits to the scope of parental responsibility (referred to in the decision as the 'zone of parental responsibility'). Keehan J seemed to assume

---

131 [2015] EWHC 922 (Fam).

132 *Trust A v X and Others* [2015] EWHC 922 (Fam); [2015] Fam Law 636 at [57].

133 A Ruck Keene, 'Baby Bournewood'?', *Mental Capacity Law and Policy*, April 2015. See also B Dolan and S Simlock, 'When is a DOL not a DOL? When parents of a 15 year old agree to it – *Re D (A Child: Deprivation of liberty)* [2015] EWHC 922 (Fam)', Serjeants' Inn Chambers, September 2015.

134 *HL v United Kingdom*, Application no 45508/99, 5 October 2004.

135 See also R Sandland, 'Children, Mental Disorder, and the Law' in *Principles of Mental Health Law and Policy* (eds L Gostin, P Bartlett, P Fennell, J McHale and R MacKay), OUP, 2010, at para 18.107.

136 *Trust A v X and Others* [2015] EWHC 922 (Fam) at [10].

that the fact that D's parents were acting in their (disabled) child's best interests and in line with medical advice, was sufficient to allow them to authorise the significant restrictions placed on D, despite the judge's acknowledgement that such restrictions 'would probably amount to ill treatment' if placed on a non-disabled boy of that age.[137] This is in direct conflict with the principle espoused by Baroness Hale in *P v Cheshire West and Chester Council; P and Q v Surrey County Council (Cheshire West)*,[138] namely: '...what it means to be deprived of liberty must be the same for everyone, whether or not they have physical or mental disabilities'.[139]

Furthermore, although Keehan J seems to adopt the concept of the 'scope of parental responsibility', he does not take into account the guidance on its application. For example, the MHA Code 2015 notes:

> If the decision goes beyond the kind of decisions parents routinely make in relation to the medical care of their child, clear reasons as to why it is acceptable to rely on parental consent to authorise this particular decision will be required.[140]

D's care regime included a range and intensity of restrictions that exceeded, by a long way, the type of restrictions that parents place on their child as part of their parenting responsibilities. For 15 months he was on a locked ward, under constant supervision and control, receiving specialist input from mental health, and other professionals (such as the treating psychiatrist and nursing staff) in an environment that the court acknowledged was not a 'home setting'.

To hold that D's parents could authorise their son to be placed under such intrusive restrictions for such a lengthy duration because of D's 'erratic, challenging and potentially harmful behaviours' appears to the authors to confuse two separate questions. Asking whether restrictions placed on D are justified due to the nature of D's care and support needs is not the same as asking whether D's parents can consent to such restrictions on his behalf. That the parents are doing the best for their child is not the deciding factor when assessing if the care regime imposes restrictions that exceed the limits of parental authority.

---

137 *Trust A v X and Others* [2015] EWHC 922 (Fam) at [57].
138 [2014] UKSC 19; [2014] AC 896.
139 [2014] UKSC 19; [2014] AC 896 at [46].
140 MHA Code, para 19.41.

CHAPTER 8

Carers

continued

Key points

- Carers who are the family or friends of disabled children are entitled to separate carers' assessments – although in practice their needs are generally addressed during the disabled child's assessment.
- The purpose of a parent carer's needs assessment is: (1) to help sustain their caring role (by ensuring that the local authority support provided to disabled child is adequate), and (2) to support parent carers to work or to access education, training or leisure facilities.
- A carer's assessment should provide an opportunity for a 'private discussion' in which carers can candidly express their views.
- When assessing the needs of a carer, professionals should not assume a willingness by the carer to continue caring, or continue to provide the same level of support.
- If the carer's assessment identifies a critical or substantial risk (for example, that the caring role may jeopardise continued involvement in employment or a significant relationship) then there is an obligation on the authority to take steps to prevent this risk occurring.
- The Childcare Act 2006 requires local authorities to take action to secure sufficient childcare services exist to meet the needs of parents of disabled children in their area.
- Local authorities are empowered to provide a wide range of support services and equipment for carers.
- Where a parent carer is a disabled person, the statutory guidance advises that their community care assessment and care plan should provide for adequate supports in order to help them discharge their role as a parent.
- Young carers are entitled to separate carers' assessments and local authorities should offer assessments whenever they identify a young person as a 'carer'.
- The purpose of a young carer's assessment is to ensure that the young carer is not undertaking inappropriate caring roles.
- The young carer's assessment should ensure that the support provided to the disabled person is sufficient so as to avoid the need for a young person to have to provide such care.

Introduction[1]

8.1   Families and friends provide the vast majority of most disabled children's care, and it is well recognised that these caring roles can have adverse impacts in a range of areas (see paras 1.38–1.43 above). Throughout this chapter, we refer to the family and friends of disabled children who provide care to them as 'carers'. This definition excludes paid care workers. The evidence suggests, for instance, that carers lose an average of over £11,000 a year by taking on significant caring responsibilities;[2] that over half of all carers have a caring-related health condition;[3] and that in consequence carers represent one of the UK's most socially excluded groups of people.[4] For parent carers the situation is no less bleak: a 2014 survey of 3,500 families found that due to financial difficulties, a third were going without heating, 31 per cent without food and 84 per cent without leisure and days out.[5]

8.2   Meeting the needs of carers requires effective co-operation between and within a range of public authorities. The main co-operation duties are considered at paras 2.55 and 5.20 above. In relation to the needs of specific carers, there also needs to be co-operation between departments within the same authority – and in particular between children's services and adult services. 2015 guidance[6] refers to a 'Memorandum of Understanding' prepared to aid joint working between children and adult social services and the guidance states that 'an updated version of this document will be made available separately' in due course.[7]

8.3   The 2015 guidance[8] also provides an overview of the strategic approach that local authorities should take to ensure that carers are

---

1   The material in this chapter draws heavily from L Clements, *Carers and their rights*, 6th edn, Carers UK, 2015.

2   Carers UK, 'Out of pocket: the financial impact of caring', 2007.

3   Carers UK, 'Missed opportunities: the impact of new rights for carers', 2003.

4   Office of the Deputy Prime Minister, *Breaking the cycle: taking stock of progress and priorities for the future. A report by the Social Exclusion Unit*, 2004, at para 6.17.

5   Contact a Family, *Counting the costs*, 2014.

6   Department of Health (and others), *The Care Act and Whole-Family Approaches*, 2015, p2.

7   It is understood that this document has been prepared by the Association of Directors of Adult Social Services (ADASS) and the Association of Directors of Children's Services (ADCS) and when published will be available via the Local Government Association's Care Act resources website.

8   Department of Health (and others), *The Care Act and Whole-Family Approaches*, 2015, pp3–6.

identified in all contacts that adult and children's services have with the public and that the full spectrum of carers' rights are addressed in this process. The guidance indicates that this should include the two departments having a formal plan and protocol to ensure their activities are properly co-ordinated.

8.4 Frequently, it is difficult if not impossible to say with precision which particular statutory agency is responsible for providing a particular service, or (put another way) which agency is at fault in any given situation. The experience of practising lawyers is that all too often agencies end up blaming each other and suggesting that it is to the other that complaint should be made.

Parent carers

8.5 The Children Act (CA) 1989 (as amended)[9] defines a 'parent carer' as an adult 'who provides or intends to provide care for a disabled child for whom the person has parental responsibility'.[10] As will be seen below (see para 8.14) this definition does not cover those carers (eg adult relatives) who do not have parental responsibility – and their rights are addressed separately by the legislation.

8.6 'Parent carers' were not mentioned in any legislation prior to the enactment of the Children and Families Act (CFA) 2014. As a consequence, some authorities had been reluctant to undertake separate 'carers' assessments of parents who were caring for a disabled child. This failure was generally unlawful since the Carers (Recognition and Services) Act 1995 s1 placed (and continues to place – see para 8.14 below) a duty on authorities to assess all carers (regardless of their age) who were providing substantial amounts of care on an unpaid basis: a duty referred to on a number of occasions by the courts and ombudsman.[11] Through amendment, the 2014 Act now places significant additional responsibilities on authorities towards 'parent carers'.

9 CA 1989 s17ZA(3) inserted by CFA 2014 s96.
10 CA 1989 s17ZD(2) and see paras 3.13–3.15 above for the definition of a 'disabled child'.
11 *R (LH and MH) v Lambeth LBC* [2006] EWHC 1190 (Admin), 25 May 2006; *HN (A Minor)* [2010] NIQB 86 (a case concerning Children (Northern Ireland) Order 1995 SI No 755 art 18A which in material terms, is indistinguishable from Carers (Recognition and Services) Act 1995 s1(2)); Complaint No 07B 04696 and 07B 10996 against Croydon LBC, 16 September 2009; and, see also Local Government Ombudsman's *Digest of Cases (Education) 2008/09*, Report 06B04654, pp14–15.

Strategic obligations

8.7   CA 1989 s17ZD(14) requires authorities to take reasonable steps to identify the extent to which there are parent carers within their area who have needs for support.

Duty to assess

8.8   CA 1989 ss17ZD and 17ZE[12] oblige local authorities to assess parent carers[13] on the 'appearance of need' – ie if it appears to a local authority that a parent carer may have needs for support (or an assessment is requested by the parent). Such assessments are referred to as 'parent carer's needs assessments'. Having undertaken such an assessment, the authority must then determine whether the parent has needs for support and, if so, what those needs are.

8.9   Parent carers' needs assessments must include 'an assessment of whether it is appropriate for the parent carer to provide, or continue to provide, care for the disabled child, in the light of the parent carer's needs for support, other needs and wishes'[14] and must also have regard to:[15]

- the well-being of the parent carer,[16] and
- the need to safeguard/promote the welfare of the disabled child and any other child for whom the parent carer has parental responsibility.

8.10   The requirement to consider 'well-being' brings with it the duty of the authority to consider a list of factors specified in Care Act 2014 s1. These include such factors as: (a) personal dignity; (b) physical and mental health and emotional well-being; (c) protection from abuse and neglect; (d) control by the individual over day-to-day life (including over care and support, or support, provided to the individual and the way in which it is provided); (e) participation in work, education, training or recreation; (f) social and economic well-being; (g) domestic, family and personal relationships; (h) suitability of living accommodation; (i) the individual's contribution to society.

---

12   Provisions inserted by CFA 2014 s97.
13   Referred to in the Care Act 2014 as 'child's carers': ss60–62; see above.
14   CA 1989 s17ZD(9).
15   CA 1989 s17ZD(10).
16   CA 1989 s17ZD(11): 'well-being' has the same meaning as Care Act 2014 s1 and includes 'control' over day-to-day life and participation in work, education, training or recreation.

8.11 This obligation replicates and broadens the duty under the Carers (Recognition and Services) Act 1995[17] to consider whether the carer: (i) works or wishes to work; or (ii) is undertaking, or wishes to undertake, education, training or any leisure activity. A key ombudsman's report[18] in this context concerned a parent who sought direct payments to enable him to purchase respite care so that he could pursue his University's studies. In the ombudsman's opinion, there was an obligation on the local authority to ensure that the parent was not 'disadvantaged in pursuit of education/training any more than other parents'.

8.12 The legislation provides for a parent carer's assessment to be combined with other assessments – ie the assessment of the disabled child's needs (CA 1989 s17ZE(3)) and (as noted above in relation to young carers) the guidance gives emphasis to assessments adopting 'whole family approach' – see para 8.41. Although a parent carer's assessment can be combined with a disabled child's assessment, they must nevertheless be distinct in the sense that the authority can demonstrate that: (a) it does not have a blanket policy of combining such assessments in every case – ie that it will undertake separate assessments in appropriate cases; (b) the parent carer's specific needs have been identified and addressed (or reasons provided as to why they are not eligible to be addressed); and (c) it has had specific regard to the well-being requirements for the parent carer (see para 8.9 above).

Copies

8.13 Local authorities must provide parent carers and any person they choose with a copy of the assessment.[19] This requirement mirrors the duty under the Care Act (both for adults in need and carers[20]) which, in addition, requires that they be provided with copies of their care and support plans[21] which must be 'in a format that is accessible to the person for whom the plan is intended'.[22] While there is no such explicit obligation in relation to parent carers, the relevant case-law and general principles of public law must require that

---

17 In the Carers (Recognition and Services) Act 1995 s1(2C).
18 Public Service Ombudsman (Wales), Complaint No B2004/0707/S/370 against Swansea City Council, 22 February 2007, see in particular, paras 78, 133 and 137.
19 CA 1989 s17ZD(13).
20 Care and Support (Assessment) Regulations 2014 SI No 2827 reg 3(1) and see also para 6.98 of the *Care and Support Statutory Guidance*, October 2014.
21 Care Act 2014 s25(9) and (10).
22 *Care and Support Statutory Guidance*, October 2014, para 10.87.

authorities provide copies that are intelligible for the relevant family members.[23]

Carers of disabled children who do not have 'parental responsibility

8.14   Due to a drafting oversight, the CFA 2014 failed to secure the rights of adults who provided unpaid care for disabled children but for whom they lacked 'parental responsibility'.[24] As a consequence, a grandparent, adult sibling, relative or a friend providing care would have had no rights to an assessment or support – as well as some unmarried fathers and some stepparents. The omission of such carers was clearly unintended and was resolved by a decision not to repeal the relevant provisions of the Carers (Recognition and Services) Act 1995 s1 that provide for the assessment of (non-parental) carers of disabled children.[25] The effect is that local authorities owe a duty to all unpaid[26] carers of disabled children. The obligation in relation to the assessment process of such carers is as wide ranging as that for those with 'parental responsibility' and (as 2015 guidance[27] makes clear) requires consideration as to:

> whether the carer works or wishes to work, or whether they wish to engage in any education, training or recreation activities. The local authority then has to take the assessment into account when deciding whether to provide any services to the disabled child.

Support services

8.15   Having undertaken a parent carer or other carers assessment, the local authority must then decide whether the parent has needs for

---

23 See for example, *R v Islington LBC ex p Rixon* (1997–98) 1 CCLR 119, QBD, at 128.

24 Parental responsibility (PR) is a legal status governed by CA 1989 s3(1). All mothers and most fathers have legal PR. For an overview of the law concerning PR, see Manjit Gheera, *Parental responsibility*, House of Commons Library Briefing Note, 8 September 2014. Some unmarried fathers of children lack parental responsibility – in the absence of an agreement or court order and this is also the case for some step parents.

25 See Care Act 2014 and Children and Families Act 2014 (Consequential Amendments) Order 2015 SI No 914. This is, however, only a short-term 'patch': the 1995 Act creates a higher assessment threshold for carers than does CA 1989 s17ZD – albeit that in practice, little will turn on this distinction.

26 Carers (Recognition and Services) Act 1995 s1(3)

27 Department of Health (et al), *The Care Act and Whole-Family Approaches*, 2015, p16 – and see also HM Government, *Working together to safeguard children*, 2015, p19, para 27.

support; whether the disabled child has needs for support; and if so whether those needs could be satisfied (wholly or partly) by services under CA 1989 s17. The parent must be given a written copy of the assessment.[28]

8.16   Reference is made to paras 3.62–3.99 above which describe the wide range of services that can be provided under the 1989 Act and also the Chronically Sick and Disabled Persons Act (CSDPA) 1970, s2 which can either support the carer directly (in the case of the 1989 Act) or indirectly (in the case of both the 1989 and 1970 Acts). In this context, the emphasis in CA 1989 Schedule 2[29] is of particular relevance – namely that services must be designed to: (1) minimise the effect of the child's disabilities; (2) give them the opportunity to lead lives which are as normal as possible; and (3) 'to assist individuals who provide care for such children to continue to do so, or to do so more effectively, by giving them breaks from caring'.

8.17   Emphasis is given to the importance of appropriate services in chapter 4 of the *Care and Support Statutory Guidance*. It is noted that:

> ... some parent carers need extra support to juggle caring and paid work after their child leaves full time education. Loss of paid employment can have a significant impact on the carer's wellbeing and self-esteem as well as a significant impact on the family's financial circumstances. Similar issues can affect young carers. Taking a whole family approach to care and support planning that sets out a 'five-day offer' or appropriate supported living options for a young person, and support for a carer to manage an increased caring role (that allows them to stay in paid work if they wish to do so) can help families manage the transition and save money by avoiding unwanted out-of-county placements.

Respite/short break care and disabled children

8.18   The English government's report *Aiming High for Disabled Children: Better Support for Families* (2007)[30] highlighted the importance of short breaks in reducing the 'high levels of stress' present in many families with disabled children, stress that might otherwise 'result in family breakdown.'

---

28 CA 1989 s17ZD(13).
29 CA 1989 Sch 2 Pt 1 para 6 pursuant to section 17(2) of the Act.
30 HM Treasury and the Department for Education and Skills, 2007, para 4.2.

8.19   As a consequence, the Children Act 1989[31] was amended to include a requirement that social services authorities 'assist individuals who provide care for such children to continue to do so, or to do so more effectively, by giving them breaks from caring.' This duty has been the subject of detailed regulations[32] and guidance,[33] which are also covered in chapter 3, see paras 3.92–3.97.

8.20   The regulations require that in making available breaks from caring to assist parents and others who provide care for disabled children, local authorities must:

- ensure that, when making short break provision, they have regard to the needs of different types of carers, not just those who would be unable to continue to provide care without a break;
- provide a range of breaks, as appropriate, during the day, night, at weekends and during the school holidays; and
- provide parents with a short breaks services statement detailing the range of available breaks and any eligibility criteria attached to them.

8.21   The *Short Breaks for Carers of Disabled Children* guidance amplifies the regulations by stressing that local authorities must ensure that:

- short breaks are reliable and regular to best meet families' needs;
- they try to reach groups of parents who may be more difficult to engage;
- parents are engaged in the design of local short breaks services;
- short breaks can build on and be offered by universal service providers;
- they are working in partnership with health services to understand the range of short breaks services in their area and to train the workforce;
- short breaks promote greater levels of confidence and competence for young people moving towards adult life;
- those who use short breaks services have the chance to shape the development of those services; and
- they continue to develop their workforce in relation to short breaks services.[34]

---

31 By Children and Young Persons Act 2008 s25, inserting a new para into CA 1989 Sch 2 – namely para 6(1)(c).
32 Breaks for Carers of Disabled Children Regulations 2011 SI No 707.
33 Department for Education, *Short Breaks for Carers of Disabled Children*, 2011.
34 Department of Education, *Short Breaks for Carers of Disabled Children*, 2011, p5.

Parent carers of disabled children in transition

8.22 The Care Act 2014 places duties on local authorities to assess the needs of disabled children[35] and young carers who are 'in transition' into adulthood (see paras 10.38 and 10.42) and, in addition, it obliges authorities to assess the likely needs of the adult carers of disabled children[36] during the child's transition. In simple terms[37], the Act provides that a local authority must undertake a needs assessment of the carer of a disabled child if it considers that the carer is likely to have needs for support after the child becomes 18 and that the assessment would be of significant benefit to the carer. Such an assessment is referred to as a 'child's carer's assessment'. If a local authority decides not to undertake such an assessment it must give reasons for its refusal. See discussion below in the chapter on transition to adulthood (paras 10.30–10.35) as to how 'significant benefit' and 'likely to have needs' should be construed.

8.23 Such an assessment will generally occur at the same time as the disabled child is having his or her transition assessment. The requirements of the transition assessment are in most respects the same as those for young carers and disabled young people in transition and are analysed at para 10.24 below.

Childcare Act duties

8.24 Childcare Act 2006 s6 requires local authorities to secure, 'so far as is reasonably practicable', sufficient childcare to meet the requirements of parents in their area who require childcare in order to work or to undertake training or education to prepare for work. In relation to disabled children, the obligation extends to childcare facilities up to 1 September after their 18th birthday. In determining whether the provision of childcare is sufficient, councils must have regard to, amongst other things, the needs of parents for childcare eligible for the childcare element of the working tax credit, and for childcare that is suitable for disabled children.

8.25 The High Court has held that a decision by a local authority to reduce its funding of nursery or other child care arrangements will

---

35 Care Act 2014 ss58 and 59.

36 In this context, the parent carer is referred to as a 'child's carer' – see Care Act 2014 ss60–62.

37 The Act, again, contains overly complicated provisions on the issue of consent/capacity to consent and what must be included in the assessment – see footnote above.

be unlawful if it has not had proper regard to its duties under the 2006 Act (to secure childcare sufficient to meet the requirements of parents in the area to enable them to work or undertake education or training).[38]

Young carers

8.26   Carers who are under the age of 18 are generally referred to as 'young carers'. Whilst the 2011 census indicated that there were over 175,000 young carers in the UK, research conducted for the BBC in 2010 suggested that there may in fact be four times as many.[39] A 2004 UK study estimated that a significant number (31 per cent) of children and young people who attended young carers projects and services were offering some form of care to their disabled siblings.[40]

8.27   2015 guidance published by the Department of Health (and others)[41] cited the following statistics:

- One in 12 young carers, cares for more than 15 hours per week and about one in 20 misses school because of their caring responsibilities.
- The average annual income for families with a young carer is £5,000 less than families who do not have a young carer.
- There is no strong evidence that young carers are more likely than their peers to come into contact with support agencies, despite government recognition that this needs to happen.
- Young carers have significantly lower educational attainment at GCSE level, the equivalent to nine grades lower overall than their peers eg the difference between nine Bs and nine Cs.
- Young carers are more likely than the national average to be not in education, employment or training (NEET) between the ages of 16 and 19.

---

38 See *R (West and others) v Rhondda Cyon Taff CBC* [2014] EWHC 2134 (Admin) – the court also considered that the local authority had failed to have regard to the impact these changes would have on its general duties under CA 1989 s17.

39 The Children's Society, *Hidden from View*, 2013.

40 C Dearden, and S Becker, *Young Carers in the UK: The 2004 Report*, Carers UK and The Children's Society, 2004.

41 Department of Health (and others), *The Care Act and Whole-Family Approaches*, 2015, and see also The Children's Society, *Hidden from view*, 2013.

8.28   The Equality and Human Rights Commission's (EHRC) in its 2010 Equality Review,[42] when stressing the importance of addressing the inequality experienced by young carers noted that a disproportionate number were from certain ethnic minority backgrounds (including Bangladeshi, Black African and Black Caribbean and Pakistani).

8.29   The EHRC's emphasis on considering the position of young carers from a human rights perspective is important. As Lord Kerr has observed:[43]

> It is a universal theme of the various international and domestic instruments ... that, in reaching decisions that will affect a child, a primacy of importance must be accorded to his or her best interests. ... . It is a factor ... that must rank higher than any other. It is not merely one consideration that weighs in the balance alongside other competing factors. Where the best interests of the child clearly favour a certain course, that course should be followed unless countervailing reasons of considerable force displace them.

8.30   'Young carers' were not mentioned in any legislation prior to the enactment of the Care Act 2014 and the CFA 2014. As a consequence, some authorities had been reluctant to undertake separate 'carers' assessments of people under 18 who were acting as carers for family or friends. This failure was generally unlawful since there was a duty on such authorities to assess all carers (regardless of their age) who were providing substantial amounts of care on an unpaid basis: a duty referred to on a number of occasions by the courts and ombudsman.[44] The 2014 Acts are now explicit in identifying 'young carers' as rights holders: people for whom local authorities have a duty to assess and where their needs call for support – a duty to provide this under either the Care Act 2014 (if provided to an adult) or the Children Act – see below.

Definition

8.31   The Children Act 1989[45] now defines a young carer as 'a person under 18 who provides or intends to provide care for another person' but it excludes those who provide this care either as part of their

42 Equality and Human Rights Commission, *How fair is Britain?*, 2010, p33.
43 *ZH (Tanzania) v Secretary of State for the Home Department* [2011] UKSC 4.
44 Complaint No 07B 04696 and 07B 10996 against Croydon LBC, 16 September 2009, and see also Cerebra Legal Entitlements Research Project, Digest of Cases 2014 (Kumar's Story at p20 and Peter's Story at p24).
45 CA 1989 s17ZA(3) inserted by CFA 2014 s96.

paid employment of as part of formal 'voluntary work':[46] the same definition is provided by the Care Act 2014.[47] 'Care' in this context includes emotional as well as 'practical support'.[48]

Strategic obligations

8.32   Local authorities are now under a strategic duty to identify the extent to which there are young carers within their area who have needs for support.[49] This strategic planning obligation is reinforced by the *Care and Support Statutory Guidance* which highlights the importance of authorities being proactive in identifying young carers (particularly those not receiving services) who are in transition into adulthood and whose caring role is likely to continue. Authorities are required to consider establishing 'mechanisms in partnership with local educational institutions, health services and other agencies' and gives examples of those who might be targeted, including:

- young people (for example with autism) whose needs have been largely met by their educational institution, but who once they leave, will require their needs to be met in some other way;
- young people and young carers receiving Children and Adolescent Mental Health Services (CAMHS) may also require care and support as adults even if they did not receive children's services from the local authority.[50]

The specific duty to assess young carers

8.33   Local authorities must undertake assessments as to whether a young carer within their area has support needs (and if so, what those needs are) if –

(a) it appears to the authority that the young carer may have needs for support, or

(b) the authority receive a request from the young carer or a parent of the young carer to assess the young carer's needs for support.[51]

8.34   The duty to assess is, therefore, a proactive obligation: one that is triggered by the 'appearance of need' (ie there is no requirement that

---

46 CA 1989 s17ZB(3).
47 Care Act 2014 s63(6).
48 CA 1989 s17ZB(5) and Care Act 2014 s63(9).
49 CA 1989 s17ZA(12).
50 *Care and Support Statutory Guidance*, paras 16.18–16.19.
51 CA 1989 s17ZA(1).

a request is made). The duty arises irrespective of whether the assessment process was initiated under the Care Act or Children Act. Such an assessment is referred to as a 'young carer's needs assessment'.[52]

8.35   When undertaking an assessment, the authority is required to consider whether 'it is appropriate for the young carer to provide, or continue to provide, care for the person in question'.[53] The authority must involve the young carer, his or her parents[54] and any other person any of them wish to be involved[55] and must have regard to:[56]

(a) the extent to which the young carer is participating in or wishes to participate in education, training or recreation, and

(b) the extent to which the young carer works or wishes to work.

8.36   Regulations[57] provide the detail of the local authority 'young carer' assessment obligations. These require that authorities undertake such assessments in a manner 'which is appropriate and proportionate to the needs and circumstances of the young carer' and that in doing so they have particular regard to:

(a) the young carer's age, understanding and family circumstances;

(b) the wishes, feelings and preferences of the young carer;

(c) any differences of opinion between the young carer, the young carer's parents and the person cared for, with respect to the care which the young carer provides (or intends to provide); and

(d) the outcomes the young carer seeks from the assessment.[58]

8.37   As with assessments under the Care Act 2014, authorities are required to provide relevant parties[59] with information 'about the manner and form of the assessment' to enable the effective participation of those involved. The assessor must have sufficient knowledge and skill (having regard amongst other things to the young carer's age, sex and understanding), and be appropriately trained – and where necessary the authority is required to consult third parties with 'expertise

---

52 CA 1989 s17ZA(2).

53 CA 1989 s17ZA(7).

54 CA 1989 s17ZB(2) explains that for this purpose that a 'parent' includes those that do and do not have parental responsibility for the child.

55 CA 1989 s17ZA(9).

56 CA 1989 s17ZA(8).

57 Young Carers' (Needs Assessments) Regulations 2015 SI No 527 made pursuant to the CA 1989 s17ZB(8).

58 Regulation 2(2).

59 Regulation 2(4) specifies that these are: (a) the young carer; (b) the person cared for; (c) the young carer's parents; and (d) any other person whom the young carer or a parent of the young carer requests should participate in the assessment.

and knowledge in relation to the young carer' and consider any other relevant assessments that have been carried out.[60]

8.38   Regulation 4 details what must be determined by the assessment – including:

(a) the amount, nature and type of care which the young carer provides/intends to provide;

(b) the extent to which this care is (or will be) relied upon by the family, including the wider family, to maintain the well-being of the person cared for;

(c) whether the care which the young carer provides (or intends to provide) impacts on the young carer's well-being, education and development;

(d) whether any of the tasks which the young carer is performing (or intends to perform) when providing care are excessive or inappropriate for the young carer to perform having regard to all the circumstances, and in particular the carer's age, sex, wishes and feelings;

(e) whether any of the young carer's needs for support could be prevented by providing services to –
   (i) the person cared for, or
   (ii) another member of the young carer's family;

(f) what the young carer's needs for support would be likely to be if the carer were relieved of part or all of the tasks the young carer performs (or intends to perform) when providing care;

(g) whether any other assessment of the needs for support of the young carer or the person cared for has been carried out;

(h) whether the young carer is a child in need;

(i) any actions to be taken as a result of the assessment; and

(j) the arrangements for a future review.

8.39   In relation to (d) above, the statutory guidance[61] advises that when a 'local authority is determining whether the tasks a child carries out are inappropriate, it should also take into account the child's own view wherever appropriate'.

---

60 Regulation 3.
61 *Care and Support Statutory Guidance*, para 6.73; see also Department of Health (et al), *The Care Act and Whole-Family Approaches*, 2015, p34.

The general assessment obligation under the Children Act 1989

8.40 The enactment of the Children and Families Act 2014 and the publication of the specific regulations[62] concerning the assessment of young carers have created an additional layer of assessment obligations on local authorities: specific duties that remain underpinned by the CA 1989 s17 assessment obligations on such authorities in relation to children in need. These assessment duties are considered at paras 3.33–3.43 above. In this context, however, previous guidance[63] remains relevant, namely that:

> many young people carry out a level of caring responsibilities which prevents them from enjoying normal social opportunities and from achieving full school attendance. Many young carers with significant caring responsibilities should therefore be seen as children in need.[64]

Whole family approach

8.41 Care Act 2014 s12(5) empowers authorities to combine a needs assessment of an adult in need or a carer, with a young carer's assessment as well as any subsequent care and support plan (s25(11)): in both cases, the decision to combine is contingent on the agreement of both parties. In similar terms, CA 1989 s17ZB(7) enables Children Act assessments of young carers to be combined.

8.42 The Young Carers' Assessments Regulations[65] require authorities to consider whether to combine assessments in such cases – and the consultation document accompanying the draft regulations explained that the intention was to promote a 'whole family approach' to assessments:

> ... an assessment that takes into account and evaluates how the needs of the person being cared for impact on the needs of the child who is identified as a possible young carer, or on any other child or on other members of the household. This approach also allows the local authority to combine a young carer's needs assessment with any

62 Young Carers' (Needs Assessments) Regulations 2015 SI No 527 (pursuant to CA 1989 s17ZB(8)).
63 See for example Social Services Inspectorate, Guidance letter CI (95)12, Annex A, para 1.1.
64 See also Department of Health, *The Children Act 1989 Guidance and Regulations, Volume 2*, 1991, para 2.4, which emphasises that 'the definition of "need" in the Act is deliberately wide to reinforce the emphasis on preventive support and services to families'.
65 Young Carers' (Needs Assessments) Regulations 2015 SI No 527 reg 4(5).

other assessment in relation to the young carer, the person cared for or another member of the young carer's family.

8.43   The statutory guidance explains the intention behind the 'whole family approach' and the obligations it places on authorities.[66] This guidance has been augmented by 2015 good practice guidance.[67]

8.44   In summary, the statutory guidance requires that authorities must:

- consider the impact of the needs' of the person cared for on family members (and others);
- identify any children who are involved in providing care;
- 'where appropriate' consider whether the child or young carer should be referred for a young carer's assessment or a needs assessment under the Children Act 1989, or a young carer's assessment under section 63 of the Care Act 2014;
- ensure that adults' and children's care and support services work together – for example by sharing expertise and linking processes;
- (where it appears that a child is involved in providing care) consider:
  - the impact of the person's needs on the young carer's wellbeing, welfare, education and development;
  - whether any of the caring tasks the child is undertaking are inappropriate and if they are, should consider how supporting the adult with needs for care and support can prevent the young carer from undertaking this care. Inappropriate caring responsibilities are defined in the guidance (see para 8.52 below).

8.45   2015 guidance[68] advises that a 'whole-family approach' would ensure that family-related questions are embedded in processes at first contact and subsequently, such as:

- Who else lives in your house?
- Who helps with your support and who else is important in your life?
- Is there anyone that you provide support or care for?

---

66 *Care and Support Statutory Guidance*, paras 6.65–6.73.
67 Department of Health (et al), *The Care Act and Whole-Family Approaches*, 2015, pp8–9.
68 Department of Health (et al), *The Care Act and Whole-Family Approaches*, 2015, pp8–9.

- Is there a child in the family (including stepchildren, children of partners or extended family)?
- Does any parent need support in their parenting role?

8.46 It adds that whatever assessment process is being used/undertaken – in every case a question must be asked as to whether there are any children in the household and if they are undertaking any caring role.[69]

Copies

8.47 Local authorities must provide the young carer, his or her parents, and any person they chose with a copy of the assessment.[70] This requirement mirrors the duty under the Care Act (both for adults in need and carers[71]) which in addition requires that they be provided with copies of their care and support plans[72] which must be 'in a format that is accessible to the person for whom the plan is intended'.[73] While there is no explicit obligation in relation to young carers, the relevant case-law and general principles of public law must require that authorities do provide copies that are intelligible for the relevant family members.[74]

Care planning and the duty to provide support

8.48 Once a local authority has completed a young carers needs' assessment and (almost invariably) an assessment of the needs of the person for whom he or she provides care, the authority must then decide what support it is going to provide. This could take the form of support provided directly to the young carer and/or support for the person being cared for.

8.49 Where a young carer is undertaking inappropriate care, the local authority is under a duty to address this. It has discretion about whether to do this by providing care and support to the person being cared for or by providing support services directly to the young carer

69 Department of Health (et al), *The Care Act and Whole-Family Approaches*, 2015, p15.
70 CA 1989 s17ZA(10).
71 Care and Support (Assessment) Regulations 2014 reg 3(1); see also the *Care and Support Statutory Guidance*, 2014, para 6.98.
72 Care Act 2014 s25(9), (10).
73 *Care and Support Statutory Guidance*, para 10.87.
74 See for example, *R v Islington LBC ex p Rixon* (1997–98) 1 CCLR 119, QBD, at 128.

– but there is a duty to ensure that underlying problem (the inappropriate care) is addressed. As the former Commission for Social Care Inspection noted in this context 'some practitioners appear to think [incorrectly] the discretion is about whether to help carers'.[75]

8.50   If the authority decides that support is required it will be provided under the Children Act 1989 s17 (either to the disabled child or to the carer) although for disabled children support can additionally be provided under the Chronically Sick and Disabled Persons Act 1970 (see paras 3.66–3.78 above). If the young carer is providing support for a disabled adult[76] then any care and support provided to the adult as a consequence (ie to replace the care provided by the young carer) would derive from the Care Act 2014.

8.51   While consideration of the legal duties that arise in cases where a young carer is providing support for a disabled adult is outside the scope of this text[77] it should be noted that the adult in need would be assessed against the scale of eligibility set out in the relevant Eligibility Criteria regulations.[78] Regulation 2(2)(j) of these regulations provides that a significant impact on well-being that arises in consequence of an inability to carry 'any caring responsibilities the adult has for a child' may result in the adult being eligible for care and support services. In such situations (as research has suggested), the local authority should:

> ... 'think parent' and view disabled parents in the same way as non-disabled parents: the vast majority want to parent their children well. They may require additional support to do this, including where mainstream sources of parenting and family support for non-disabled parents are inaccessible to disabled people.[79]

Inappropriate care

8.52   On the definition of 'inappropriate care', consideration of the *Care and Support Statutory Guidance* is of relevance (even though it is directed primarily at young carers who care for adults) since it gives

75 Commission for Social Care Inspection, *Cutting the cake fairly: CSCI review of eligibility criteria for social care*, 2008, para 3.22.
76 A disproportionate number of disabled parents have disabled child, see chapter 1 at para 1.30.
77 For further analysis see L Clements, *Carers and their Rights*, 6th edn, Carers UK, 2015, and L Clements *Community Care and the Law*, 6th edn, LAG, 2016.
78 Care and Support (Eligibility Criteria) Regulations 2015 SI No 313.
79 R Olsen and H Tyers, *Supporting disabled adults as parents*, National Family and Parenting Institute, 2004.

clear examples of what would be considered 'inappropriate'. In this respect, it remedies to some extent the deficiencies in the *Working Together* guidance where such examples ought also to be located The statutory guidance states that:

> Children should not undertake inappropriate or excessive caring roles that may have an impact on their development. A young carer becomes vulnerable when their caring role risks impacting upon their emotional or physical wellbeing and their prospects in education and life. .... A local authority should consider how supporting the adult with needs for care and support can prevent the young carer from under taking excessive or inappropriate care and support responsibilities. Where a young carer is identified, the local authority must undertake a young carer's assessment under Part 3 of the Children Act 1989.[80]

8.53   The *Care and Support Statutory Guidance* advises that when a 'local authority is determining whether the tasks a child carries out are inappropriate, it should also take into account the child's own view wherever appropriate'.[81] The obligation to ensure that young carers do not undertake inappropriate care is picked up again in the guidance which advises that where an authority becomes aware that the child is carrying out such a caring role then the adult should be offered a needs assessment under the Care Act 2014 and the young carer an assessment under either the Care Act 2014 or the Children Act 1989 and whichever route is chosen the local authority must consider:

- the impact of the person's needs on the young carer's wellbeing, welfare, education and development;
- whether any of the caring responsibilities the young carer is undertaking are inappropriate.[82]

8.54   As a result of such an assessment the authority must consider 'how supporting the adult with needs for care and support can prevent the young carer from undertaking excessive or inappropriate care and support responsibilities'.[83] Logically, the same advice would apply if the person being cared for was not a disabled adult, but a disabled child. Examples of the harm that may result to the young carer where there is a lack of support, include impaired access to education (eg regular absence from school or impacts upon their learning)

---

80 *Care and Support Statutory Guidance*, para 2.49.
81 *Care and Support Statutory Guidance*, para 6.73; see also Department of Health, *The Care Act and Whole-Family Approaches*, 2015, p34.
82 *Care and Support Statutory Guidance*, paras 6.68–6.69.
83 *Care and Support Statutory Guidance*, para 6.71.

and impaired ability to build relationships and friendships.[84] The statutory guidance also provides examples of 'inappropriate caring responsibilities' including the young person:

- providing personal care such as bathing and toileting;
- carrying out strenuous physical tasks such as lifting;
- administering medication;
- maintaining the family budget;
- emotional support to the adult.[85]

Providing direct support for a young carer under the Children Act 1989

8.55   There will also be situations where a local authority may decide it is in the best interests of a young carer to provide services directly to him or her. This will generally arise where the caring role is considered unavoidable – or where an older young carer makes an informed decision that they is what they want to do. In such situations, the support would also, generally, be provided under CA 1989 s17 (and the nature of this support is considered at para 3.79 above).

8.56   Whenever it decided that services should be required – these should be 'provided without delay'[86] – and, as the *Working Together* (2015)[87] guidance states:

> A good assessment will monitor and record the impact of any services delivered to the child and family and review the help being delivered. Whilst services may be delivered to a parent or carer, the assessment should be focused on the needs of the child and on the impact any services are having on the child.

8.57   As with care planning duties for adults, support plans should be agreed with other professionals and the child and their family and 'should set out what services are to be delivered, and what actions are to be undertaken, by whom and for what purpose'.[88] They should also 'be reviewed regularly to analyse whether sufficient progress has been made to meet the child's needs and the level of risk faced by the child'.[89]

---

84 *Care and Support Statutory Guidance*, para 6.71.
85 *Care and Support Statutory Guidance*, para 6.72.
86 *Working Together*, 2015, para 30.
87 *Working Together*, 2015, para 30.
88 *Working Together*, 2015, para 53.
89 *Working Together*, 2015, para 55.

Timescale for assessments

8.58 All assessments should be completed without delay and in this respect see the general comments at para 3.34 above.

Young carers in 'transition' to adulthood

8.59 The rights of young carers as they move into adulthood are addressed in chapter 10, see paras 10.42. In essence, carers aged over 18 are entitled to a transition assessment under Care Act 2014 ss63–64 and will be entitled to support in their caring role after this assessment if they meet the Care Act eligibility criteria. Support for young carers must remain in place pending the completion of this assessment and decision-making process (s66).

Parent carers as disabled children 'transition' to adulthood

8.60 Similarly, the rights of parent carers as the child they care for becomes an adult are addressed in chapter 10, see para 10.38. Again, the parent carer is entitled to a transition assessment and will be entitled to support in their caring role after this assessment if the eligibility criteria are met. Again, support must remain in place pending the completion of this assessment and decision-making process (s66).

8.61 Chapter 16 of the *Care and Support Statutory Guidance* provides considerable detail on the way authorities should approach their duties in relation to disabled children; the parents of disabled children and young carers. Importantly, local authorities are not obliged to move responsibility from children's social care to adult care once the young person becomes 18. The statutory guidance expresses the view that in general this move will often begin 'at the end of a school term or another similar milestone, and in many cases should be a staged process over several months or years'.[90]

---

90 *Care and Support Statutory Guidance*, para 16.61.

CHAPTER 9

Equality and non-discrimination

continued

Key points

- Disabled children have had the benefit of protection from discrimination under first the Disability Discrimination Act (DDA) 1995 and then the Equality Act (EqA) 2010, and also under Article 14 of the European Convention on Human Rights (ECHR).
- Despite this, disabled children remain routinely excluded and treated less favourably than others in many areas of public life.
- The EqA 2010 came into force in October 2010 and replaced the DDA 1995 and other previous equality legislation.
- The EqA 2010 outlaws a wide range of discriminatory treatment, alongside harassment and victimisation.
- A failure to make reasonable adjustments so that disabled children are not placed at a substantial disadvantage compared with non-disabled children is also a form of discrimination.
- As well as discrimination against disabled children, family and friends of disabled children will be protected from 'direct discrimination by association'.
- The duties in the EqA 2010 cover every area of public life, including education, service provision and employment.
- The prohibition of discrimination is supported by a Public Sector Equality Duty (PSED) and a general power to take 'positive action' to support the achievement of equality.
- Enforcement action in relation to most of the duties under the EqA 2010 can be taken in the county court. Breaches of the schools duties must be dealt with by the First-tier Tribunal (Special Educational Needs and Disability) in England (except for certain types of admission appeal).

Introduction

9.1   Disabled children in England have had formal legal protection against discrimination since 1995 under the Disability Discrimination Act (DDA). However, disabled children still experience routine exclusion from many parts of public life – whether through being denied access to school trips on alleged health and safety grounds or being told that a playground has no equipment that they are able to use. The vision of ordinary lives for disabled children enshrined in the Children Act 1989 (see chapter 3) requires disabled children to be able to access every opportunity available to non-disabled children. This chapter is about the legislation which seeks to ensure that this happens – now the Equality Act (EqA) 2010. Any reference in this chapter to a section or schedule is, unless the context shows otherwise, a reference to a section in or schedule to the EqA 2010. The chapter also considers the human right to non-discrimination under article 14 of the European Convention on Human Rights (ECHR).

9.2   The EqA 2010 came into force in October 2010. The Equality and Human Rights Commission (EHRC)[1] states that the EqA 2010 '[provides] a modern, single legal framework with clear, streamlined law to more effectively tackle disadvantage and discrimination'.[2] However, in many respects the EqA 2010 codified and built on, rather than replaced, previous legislation, most importantly here the DDA 1995 and its amendments (collectively 'the DDA scheme'). This chapter focuses on the provisions of the EqA 2010 and its related codes of practice and guidance but also draws out the key themes and some of the judgments made both before and since the EqA 2010 came into force.

Legal framework

Discrimination legislation pre-Equality Act 2010

9.3   Protection from discrimination against disabled children in relation to their disabilities was first introduced by the DDA 1995 and then extended by the Special Educational Needs and Disability Act (SENDA) 2001. The DDA scheme followed earlier legislation prohibiting discrimination on the grounds of sex[3] and race.[4] Under the DDA scheme, disabled people (including disabled children) were protected from a number of different forms of discrimination in a wide range of contexts, for example, in the provision of goods and services, education, employment, performance of public authority functions and so on.

---

1 Created by the Equality Act 2006 and replacing (among other bodies) the Disability Rights Commission.
2 See www.equalityhumanrights.com/legal-and-policy/legislation/equality-act–2010.
3 Sex Discrimination Act 1972.
4 Race Relations Act 1976.

European Framework Directive

9.4   The provisions of the EqA 2010 must also be understood in the light of European law on non-discrimination. This was made clearly apparent by the judgment of the Grand Chamber of the European Court of Justice (ECJ) in *Coleman v Attridge Law*.[5] The case examined how a European framework directive[6] which required member states to introduce measures to combat discrimination on various grounds (including disability), should be interpreted. The ECJ held that the directive prohibited discrimination against persons *associated with* a disabled person (in Sharon Coleman's case, the association was as a parent of a disabled child). In particular, the ECJ held[7] that:

> Where it is established that the ... harassment which is suffered by an employee who is not himself disabled is related to the disability of his child, whose care is provided primarily by that employee, such conduct is contrary to the prohibition of harassment laid down by [the framework directive].

9.5   The judgment of the ECJ in *Coleman v Attridge Law* has been reflected in the EqA 2010: see para 9.43.

9.6   The EqA 2010 must also be interpreted in the context of the Human Rights Act (HRA) 1998 and the European Convention on Human Rights (ECHR) since a breach of the provisions of the EqA 2010 may also constitute a violation of ECHR article 14 (the prohibition of certain forms of discrimination), see further para 9.137 below.

Equality Act 2010

9.7   The EqA 2010 extends protection from discrimination to people, with what are termed 'protected characteristics', in almost every area of life. This chapter focuses on the protected characteristic of disability (see paras 9.11–9.18). The Act has two main purposes – to harmonise discrimination law, and to strengthen the law to support progress on equality.[8] The principle of equality underpinning the EqA 2010 'is intended to promote and protect the dignity of all

---

5   (C 223/08) [2008] ECR I–5603.
6   Directive 2000/78/EC ('the framework directive)'.
7   [2008] ECR I–5603 at [63]; ruling at [2].
8   Explanatory Notes to the EqA 2010 at [10].

persons in society'.[9] The policy of the EA is, therefore, to promote equality in every area of public life and as such any exceptions to the duties it imposes are to be interpreted restrictively.[10]

9.8   Despite its intention being to clarify and streamline equalities legislation, the EqA 2010 is 251 pages long and contains 218 sections and 28 schedules. Many of these provisions had different enactment dates and some to date have not yet been enacted. The current government has confirmed that certain parts of the EA will not be brought into force, for example, the socio-economic duty as set out in section 1.[11] Likewise, 'combined discrimination' was referred to in the previous edition of this publication but the government has now confirmed that it does not intend to bring the combined discrimination provisions in the EqA 2010 into force.[12]

9.9   Moreover, the meaning of the EqA 2010's provisions must be interpreted in light of both the court's decisions in relation to its predecessor legislation (in this context the DDA scheme) and the statutory codes of practice. The EHRC has published statutory codes of practice for employment, equal pay and services, public functions and associations ('the Part 3 Code of Practice').[13] The EHRC has also published non-statutory *technical guidance*[14] in the areas of schools,[15] auxiliary aids for disabled pupils, further and higher education and the public sector equality duty (PSED).

9   Part 3 Code of Practice, para 13.2.

10   Part 3 Code of Practice, para 15.5.

11   See Discrimination Law Association Briefing, Vol 53, 'Editorial: Uniting to challenge economic inequality', November 2014.

12   www.equalityhumanrights.com/legal-and-policy/legislation/equality-act–2010/ what-equality-act.

13   The purpose of the codes of practice is 'to provide a detailed explanation of the Act and to apply legal concepts in the Act to everyday situations where services are provided': Part 3 Code of Practice, p9.

14   The EHRC explains that: 'We had originally planned to produce statutory codes of practice on the Public Sector Equality Duty (PSED), which came into force on 5 April 2011, and for statutory codes of practice for Schools and the Further and Higher Education (FEHE) sector. In the light of the Government's position not to lay codes before Parliament, the Commission has decided for now to produce the original text of these codes as technical guidance. Technical guidance is a non-statutory version of a code, however it will still provide a formal, authoritative, and comprehensive legal interpretation of the PSED and education sections of the Act. It will also clarify the requirements of the legislation' – see www.equalityhumanrights.com/legal-and-policy/legislation/ equality-act–2010/equality-act-codes-practice-and-technical-guidance.

15   The English guidance is called *Technical Guidance for Schools in England.*

9.10   This chapter considers the provisions of the EqA 2010 and the codes of practice and guidance of most relevance to disabled children and their families – namely the sections that relate to 'prohibited conduct' (Part 2, Chapter 2), services and public functions (Part 3), education (Part 6), 'advancement of equality', which includes the PSED (Part 11) and to a lesser extent work (Part 5). It also covers the issue of enforcement (Part 9), which is addressed further in chapter 11 on remedies generally. While other areas such as associations (Part 7)[16] and transport (Part 12) may well be of great importance to some disabled children, the aspects of the EqA 2010 listed above are those which should make a difference to the lives of *all* disabled children.

The definition of disability

Equality Act 2010 – a protected characteristic

9.11   Section 4 of the EqA 2010 specifies that disability is a 'protected characteristic' for the purposes of the Act.[17] The definition of 'disability' is provided in section 6(1), which states:

A person (P) has a disability if –
(a) P has a physical or mental impairment,[18] and
(b) the impairment has a substantial and long-term adverse effect on P's ability to carry out normal day-to-day activities.

9.12   This is a deliberately broad definition, and there is no need for a medical diagnosis – what matters is the effect of an impairment, not its cause.[19] The elements of the definition are fleshed out by Schedule 1, which:

• provides for regulations to specify conditions which do or do not fall within the definition of 'impairment' (see para 9.14 below);[20]

---

16 Discrimination by organisations such as the Scouts or the Guides is covered by the provisions of the EqA 2010 in relation to associations: Part 3 Code of Practice, 13.7.

17 The other protected characteristics are age, gender reassignment, marriage and civil partnership, pregnancy and maternity, race, religion or belief, sex and sexual orientation.

18 Which includes a sensory impairment: Part 3 Code of Practice, para 2.7.

19 Part 3 Code of Practice, Appendix 1, p282. Likewise, determination of whether a person is 'disabled' no longer requires specific consideration of the eight capacities, such as mobility or speech, hearing or eyesight, as were set out in the definition of disability under the DDA 1995.

20 Schedule 1 para 1.

- states that an impairment is 'long-term' if it has lasted for 12 months or is likely to last for 12 months;[21]
- states that an impairment is to be judged as to whether it has a substantial impact, irrespective of any medical or other treatment to alleviate the impact of the impairment;[22]
- states that a severe disfigurement is to be treated as an impairment having 'a substantial adverse effect on the ability of the person concerned to carry out normal day-to-day activities'; regulations may prescribe circumstances where a severe disfigurement will not be treated as having such an effect;[23]
- specifies that cancer, HIV infection and multiple sclerosis are all disabilities within the meaning of section 6 (so that a child diagnosed with any of these conditions does not need to fulfil any of the other elements of the section 6 test);[24] and
- states that a person with a progressive condition meets the 'substantial adverse effect' test if the condition is likely to result in such an effect in future, even if it does not at the relevant time.[25]

9.13   The schedule further provides a power[26] for regulations to specify certain symptoms or presentations ('effects of a prescribed description') which may or may not amount to 'substantial adverse effects' within the meaning of section 6.

9.14   The Equality Act (Disability) Regulations 2010[27] (the '2010 Regulations') provide a list of impairments or effects that are excluded from the definition which includes addictions. They also provide that persons who are certified as blind, severely sight impaired, sight impaired or partially sighted by a consultant ophthalmologist are deemed to have a disability.

9.15   Perhaps the most significant exclusion for disabled children under the 2010 Regulations is 'a tendency to physical or sexual abuse of other persons'.[28] In *X v The Governing Body of a School*,[29] the Upper Tribunal dismissed a discrimination appeal against the exclusion of

---

21 Schedule 1 para 2. An impairment will also be 'long term' if it is it is likely to last for the rest of the life of the person affected, where this is less than 12 months.
22 Schedule 1 para 5.
23 Schedule 1 para 3.
24 Schedule 1 para 6.
25 Schedule 1 para 8. Regulations may specify what constitutes a progressive condition: para 8(3).
26 Schedule 1 para 4.
27 SI No 2128 made pursuant to powers set out in EqA 2010 Sch 2 para 1.
28 2010 Regulations, reg 4(1)(c).
29 [2015] UKUT 7 (AAC); [2015] ELR 133.

a six-year-old girl with autism from her school because she had a 'tendency to physical abuse' as evidenced by her violent behaviour. The Upper Tribunal held that it did not matter that this arose out of an impairment (autism) that was itself protected under section 6 of the 2010 Act.

9.16   However, it is clear from the Upper Tribunal's decision that an element of violent conduct on its own may not necessarily mean that a person will be excluded from the definition of 'disability'. The Upper Tribunal stated that '[t]he greater the level of violence, the more readily it will fall within the meaning of "physical abuse".[30] Although the exclusion of a tendency to physical abuse from the definition of 'disability' applies to children as well as adults, the stage of the child's development will be a relevant factor as to whether the exclusion applies in their case.[31]

9.17   It is important to note, however, that even where a child may behave in a way that brings them within this definition, a claim of disability discrimination can still be made in relation to treatment which does not relate to that behaviour but is otherwise related to their disability.[32]

9.18   The 2010 Regulations also provide for the position regarding children under six, when the effect of the impairment may not be long term or have a substantial effect on normal day-to-day activities. An inference can be drawn such that a child who is under six years old is deemed to meet the definition where the impairment would normally have a substantive and long-term adverse effect on a person over six years of age.[33]

No protection for 'non-disabled' people

9.19   The EqA 2010 ensures that the status of being 'non-disabled' is not a protected characteristic. This asymmetrical protection is considered to have stemmed from the need to prohibit the historic discrimination against disabled people. As a result, it will not be discrimination under the EqA 2010 for a service or education provider for example, to treat a disabled person more favourably than they treat a non-disabled person.[34]

---

30 [2015] UKUT 7 (AAC); [2015] ELR 133 at [116].
31 [2015] UKUT 7 (AAC); [2015] ELR 133 at [119].
32 *Edmund Nuttall Law v Butterfield* [2006] ICR 77; [2005] IRLR 751.
33 2010 Regulations, reg 6.
34 EqA 2010 s13(3).

Guidance

9.20   Guidance has been issued about the matters to be taken into account in determining any question for the purposes of considering whether a person is disabled under EqA 2010 s6(1).[35] The guidance highlights the generous approach to the definition of disability by comparison with the definition under the DDA 1995.

'Disability' in international law

9.21   Further guidance on the definition on 'disability' comes from the UN Convention on the Rights of Persons with Disabilities (UNCRPD), approved by the European Union in 2009. As an international agreement, this is binding on and prevails over acts of the European Union.[36] The UNCRPD provides that 'disability is an evolving concept and that disability results from the interaction between persons with impairments and attitudinal and environmental barriers that hinders their full and effective participation in society on an equal basis with others'.[37]

9.22   When deciding whether someone meets the test of a disability for the purposes of either the EqA 2010 or the HRA 1998 (see para 9.137), domestic courts or tribunals may be assisted by a number of European cases concerning the meaning of disability. The European definition is, however, broadly similar to the definition provided for in the EqA 2010, see *HK Danmark v Dansk almennyttigt Boligselskab*,[38] in which the European Court of Justice (ECJ) defined 'disability' as 'a limitation which results in particular from *long-term* physical, mental or psychological impairments which in interaction with various barriers may *hinder* the *full and effective participation* of the person concerned in professional life on an equal basis with other workers'.[39]

---

35   HM Office for Disability Issues, *Equality Act 2010 Guidance – Guidance on matters to be taken into account in determining questions relating to the definition of disability.* Issued under EqA 2010 s6(5) and Sch 1 Pt 2, paras 10–16.

36   Though it does not have direct effect, rather the European directives must be interpreted in a manner consistent with the convention: *Z v A Department*, ECJ, Case C-363/12 [2014] IRLR 563; [2014] EqLR 316, ECJ. See chapter 2 for the role of international conventions such as the UNCRPD in domestic law.

37   Recital (e).

38   Case C-335/11, [2013] IRLR 571, ECJ.

39   Case C-335/11, [2013] IRLR 571, ECJ at [38].

Discrimination – 'prohibited conduct'

9.23   The EqA 2010 effectively outlaws certain forms of behaviour, in so far as they are directed against disabled children, adults and others with 'protected characteristics'. The Act refers to these forms of behaviour as types of 'prohibited conduct', which is described as 'discrimination', and consists of (so far as is particularly relevant to disabled children):

- direct discrimination (section 13);
- discrimination arising from disability (section 15); and
- indirect discrimination (section 19).[40]

9.24   A 'failure to comply with a duty to make reasonable adjustments' also constitutes discrimination: see paras 9.39–9.42. Each of these forms of discrimination is considered below.

Direct discrimination

9.25   Direct discrimination, the most obvious form of discrimination, is prohibited by section 13. In the context of disability, direct discrimination takes place when a decision is taken concerning a disabled person which is based on prejudicial or stereotypical assumptions concerning disability generally, or the specific disability in question. As a general rule,[41] direct discrimination is simply unlawful and incapable of 'justification'.[42]

9.26   The Part 3 Code of Practice suggests that '[l]ess favourable treatment could also involve being deprived of a choice or excluded from an opportunity'.[43] As both of these are routine features of the lives of disabled children, the EqA 2010 has the potential in this respect to require significant changes in the practice of service providers, public authorities and others.

9.27   In most circumstances, direct discrimination requires that the service provider's treatment of the person is less favourable than the

40   Collectively defined as 'disability discrimination': see EqA 2010 s25(2). The EqA 2010 also prohibits instructing, causing or inducing someone to discriminate against, harass or victimise a disabled person and knowingly helping someone discriminate against, harass or victimise another person.
41   For the specific statutory exceptions, see EqA 2010 s191 and Sch 22.
42   Solely in relation to some areas of employment, there is a limited exception for 'genuine occupational requirements' and specifically the provisions relating to disability are disapplied in relation to service or work experience opportunities in the armed forces; Employment Code, para 13.22.
43   Part 3 Code of Practice, para 4.5.

way the service provider treats, has treated or would treat a person who does not have the protected characteristic.[44] This other person is referred to as a 'comparator'; a hypothetical comparator rather than an actual person can be relied on if need be. The EqA 2010 requires that, in comparing people for the purpose of direct discrimination, there must be no material difference between the circumstances relating to each case.[45] However, it is not necessary for the circumstances of the two people to be identical in every way; what matters is that the circumstances which are relevant to the treatment are the same or nearly the same for both them and the comparator. For the purpose of direct discrimination on the grounds of disability the EqA 2010 does state that the circumstances includes a person's abilities.[46]

9.28   While the comparator for direct disability discrimination is the same as for other types of direct discrimination, the relevant circumstances of the comparator and the disabled person, including their abilities, must not be materially different. An appropriate comparator will be a person who does not have the disabled person's impairment but who has the same abilities or skills as the disabled person (regardless of whether those abilities or skills arise from the disability itself).[47]

Discrimination arising from disability

9.29   Discrimination arising from disability, prohibited by section 15, is the government's response to an unexpected 2008 judgment of the House of Lords in the case referred to as *Malcolm*.[48] Prior to this decision, 'less favourable treatment' under the DDA scheme was assessed by comparing the treatment of the disabled person with the treatment of a hypothetical non-disabled person who did not display the same characteristics as the disabled person. A well-known example of this approach involved a child with autism who misbehaved in a dinner queue and was excluded as a result. Under the pre-*Malcolm* approach, this could amount to less favourable treatment if it could be shown that the child's behaviour was a function of his autism and that a non-disabled child would not have misbehaved in the same situation.

---

44   The same analysis would apply to other persons covered by the EqA 2010, for example schools or employers.
45   EqA 2010 s23.
46   EqA 2010 s23(2)(a).
47   EqA 2010 s23(2)(a).
48   *Lewisham LBC v Malcolm* [2008] UKHL 43; [2008] 1 AC 1399.

9.30   Following *Malcolm*, the comparator for 'less favourable treatment' became a non-disabled person with the same characteristics, or who behaved in the same way, as the disabled person. So in the example above, so long as a non-disabled child would have been excluded for misbehaving in the dinner queue, it would not have been less favourable treatment to exclude the disabled child (albeit that in such a case there would have been a requirement to make reasonable adjustments (see paras 9.39–9.42).

9.31   Section 15 attempts to resolve this problem by 're-establishing an appropriate balance between enabling a disabled person to make out a case of experiencing a detriment which arises because of his or her disability, and providing an opportunity for an employer or other person to defend the treatment'.[49] It removes the need for any comparator[50] and specifies instead that a person discriminates against a disabled person if he or she:

- treats him or her unfavourably[51] 'because of something arising "in consequence of" his or her disability';[52] and

- cannot show that the treatment is 'a proportionate means of achieving a legitimate aim'.[53]

9.32   Notably, there is no need to compare a disabled person's treatment with that of another person to prove a claim for discrimination arising from a disability. It is only necessary to demonstrate that the unfavourable treatment is because of something arising in consequence of their disability.

9.33   Unlike direct discrimination, discrimination arising from disability can be justified, if it is a proportionate means of achieving a legitimate aim (the 'justification defence'). Furthermore, no discrimination

49 Explanatory Notes to the EqA 2010 at [70].
50 Part 3 Code of Practice, para 6.7
51 Meaning that the disabled person is put at a disadvantage: Part 3 Code of Practice, para 6.8.
52 Meaning 'anything which is the result, effect or outcome of a disabled person's disability': Part 3 Code of Practice, paras 6.9–6.11.
53 Section 15(1)(a) and (b). Part 3 Code of Practice, para 6.2 refers to this as 'objective justification'. The term 'legitimate aim' is not defined in the EqA 2010, but Part 3 Code of Practice, para 6.19 states that a legitimate aim 'must be legal, must not be discriminatory in itself, and it must represent a real, objective consideration'. A service provider who is simply aiming to reduce costs or improve competitiveness 'cannot expect to satisfy the test': Part 3 Code of Practice, para 6.20. 'Proportionate' is also not defined in the EqA 2010 but for treatment to be proportionate it must be necessary: Part 3 Code of Practice, para 6.20. Again, financial considerations alone cannot render treatment proportionate: Part 3 Code of Practice, para 6.24.

contrary to section 15 occurs if the person did not know, and could not reasonably have been expected to know, that the disabled person 'had the disability'. However, a person relying on this defence must have done all they could reasonably be expected to do to find out if the person has a disability. This is particularly the case where the individual has an on-going relationship with the disabled person.

9.34 Where a person is treated unfavourably because of something arising 'in consequence of' his disability, the onus will generally be on the person responsible for the treatment, to show that what was done was a proportionate means of achieving a legitimate aim. In the 'dinner queue' example above, the 'legitimate aim' might be the protection of the health and safety of teachers and other pupils in the queue – and a proportionate response would be implementation of 'reasonable adjustments' – for example, staff training concerning autistic spectrum disorders and strategies to avoid such difficulties as well as training for the pupil about behaviour in such social situations, such as queuing. In such cases, a failure to make a relevant reasonable adjustment is likely to make it 'very difficult' for an individual to show that any potentially discriminatory treatment was a proportionate means of achieving a legitimate aim.[54]

9.35 The Part 3 Code of Practice gives the following as an example of discrimination arising from disability in a service provision context:

> A mother seeks admission to a privately run nursery for her son who has Hirschprung's disease, which means that he does not have full bowel control. The nursery says that they cannot admit her son because he is not toilet trained and all the children at the nursery are. The refusal to admit the boy is not because of his disability itself; but he is experiencing detrimental treatment as a consequence of his disability.[55]

Indirect discrimination

9.36 Another type of discrimination likely to be relevant to disabled children is indirect discrimination, contrary to section 19. The extension of the prohibition on indirect discrimination to disability is new to the EqA 2010 and follows the *Malcolm* judgment (see paras 9.29–9.30).[56] The indirect discrimination provisions aim to address forms of

---

54 Part 3 Code of Practice, para 7.15; the code also makes the point that unlawful discrimination may still arise even if a reasonable adjustment has been made, if the adjustment is unrelated to the treatment complained of.
55 Part 3 Code of Practice, para 6.4.
56 Explanatory Notes to the EqA 2010 at [81].

discrimination which, while they do not explicitly entail or propose different treatment, in practice disadvantage people with particular protected characteristics.[57] Indirect discrimination occurs if a person applies a 'provision, criterion or practice' which is discriminatory in relation to (in this case) a person's disability.[58] A four-stage test is set out[59] to determine whether a particular 'provision, criterion or practice' is discriminatory in relation to a disabled child; it will be if:

- it applies, or would apply, to people who are not disabled;
- it puts, or would put, disabled people 'at a particular disadvantage'[60] when compared with non-disabled people;
- it puts, or would put, the individual disabled child at that disadvantage; and
- the person applying or operating the provision, criterion or practice cannot show it to be a proportionate means of achieving a legitimate aim.[61]

9.37   The Part 3 Code of Practice suggests[62] that it is 'unlikely' that the protected characteristic in a claim of indirect discrimination will be taken to be disability in general, but rather the individual's specific disability. It may, therefore, be that if an individual with a visual impairment claims to have been indirectly discriminated against, the appropriate comparator would be a person without any visual impairment, rather than a non-disabled person.

9.38   Arguably, because a failure to make reasonable adjustments will also amount to discrimination (see below), it may be that the indirect discrimination provisions of the EqA 2010 add little to the protection afforded to disabled children. However, given the systemic discrimination against disabled people still present in our society there appears to be little harm in taking a 'belt and braces' approach to outlawing all forms of discrimination.

---

57   Part 3 Code of Practice, para 4.4.
58   EqA 2010 s19(1). The terms 'provision, criterion or practice' overlap and should be 'construed widely so as to include, for example, any (formal or informal) policies, rules, practices, arrangements, criteria, prerequisites, qualifications or provisions': Part 3 Code of Practice, para 6.3. The terms also cover proposals and one-off discretionary decisions: Part 3 Code of Practice, para 6.4.
59   EqA 2010 s19(2).
60   EqA 2010 s19(2)(b).
61   See fn 53 above for discussion of the concepts of 'proportionate' and 'legitimate aim'.
62   At para 5.17.

Reasonable adjustments

9.39   The EqA 2010 protects disabled people from discriminatory treatment in specified areas by the imposition of a duty to make reasonable adjustments for them.[63] This duty was central to the DDA scheme and remains a cornerstone of the EqA 2010. The duty is anticipatory[64] continuing and evolving and seeks to level the playing field. The Part 3 Code of Practice explains that in a services context, the policy of the EqA 2010 is to 'provide access to a service as close as it is reasonably possible to get to the standard normally offered to the public at large'.[65]

9.40   There are three elements to the reasonable adjustment duty, not all of which apply in every context as will be explained below:[66]

1) a requirement, where a 'provision, criterion or practice' puts a disabled person at a substantial disadvantage[67] in comparison with persons who are not disabled, to take such steps as is reasonable to avoid the disadvantage;[68]

2) a requirement, where a 'physical feature' puts a disabled person at a substantial disadvantage in comparison with persons who are not disabled, to take such steps as is reasonable to avoid the disadvantage;[69] and

3) a requirement, where a disabled person would, but for the provision of an auxiliary aid, be put at a substantial disadvantage in comparison with persons who are not disabled, to take such steps as is reasonable to 'provide the auxiliary aid'[70] or 'service'.[71]

63 The generic elements of which are set out at EqA 2010 ss20–22.
64 Part 3 Code of Practice, para 7.3.
65 Part 3 Code of Practice, para 7.4.
66 EqA 2010 s20(2).
67 Meaning more than minor or trivial: Part 3 Code of Practice, para 7.11 and EqA 2010 s212(1). Whether disadvantage is substantial is measured by comparison with what the position would be if the disabled person in question did not have a disability. It is more likely to be reasonable for a service provider with substantial financial resources to have to make an adjustment with a significant cost than for a service provider with fewer resources: Part 3 Code of Practice, paras 7.30 and 7.31.
68 EqA 2010 s20(3).
69 EqA 2010 s20(4). This potentially includes removing the feature, altering it or providing a reasonable means of avoiding it: EqA 2010 s20(9). The duty applies to physical features in the broadest sense, including 'any other physical element or quality': EqA 2010 s20(10). A non-exhaustive list of physical features is provided by Part 3 Code of Practice, para 7.60.
70 EqA 2010 s20(6).
71 Services are included within this aspect of the duty by EqA 2010 s20(11). An auxiliary aid or service is 'is anything which provides additional support

9.41 A further specific aspect of the duty is to provide information in accessible formats.[72] Disabled people cannot be charged for the costs of making the reasonable adjustment.[73] The content of the duty in specific areas is governed by schedules to the Act as set out in section 20(13), the most relevant here being services and public functions (Schedule 2) and education (Schedule 13).

9.42 A failure to comply with any of the three aspects of the duty (if applicable) set out above is a breach of the duty[74] and constitutes discrimination.[75]

Discrimination because of association or perception

9.43 The EqA 2010 also protects against direct discrimination because of 'association' or 'perception' about disabilities. Direct discrimination can arise when a person is treated less favourably as a result of their association with a disabled child – for instance a parent denied a business loan simply because he lived with a disabled child. In Sharon Coleman's case (see para 9.4), she argued that her employer made it difficult for her to get time off work to care for her disabled son, whereas it placed no similar restrictions on other employees who took time off for other reasons.[76] What matters is that the less favourable treatment occurred because of the child's disability; ie 'but for' the child's disability, the treatment would not have occurred.

9.44 Although there are limited cases so far addressing claims of discrimination by association, one relevant employment tribunal decision is *Price v Action-Tec Services*.[77] In that case, a telesales executive had just passed her trial period, but was then dismissed after an absence from work related to her husband's leukaemia. The tribunal said the employer made a stereotypical assumption that, because of the disabilities of (herself and) her husband, the claimant would be an unreliable and under-performing employee. Accordingly, there was direct discrimination by way of association.

or assistance to a disabled person', for a list of examples see Part 3 Code of Practice, para 7.47.
72 EqA 2010 s20(6).
73 EqA 2010 s20(7).
74 EqA 2010 s21(1).
75 EqA 2010 s21(2).
76 Part 3 Code of Practice, paras 5.16 and 5.20–21.
77 [2013] EqLR 429.

9.45   Direct discrimination by perception occurs where a person is treated less favourably because their education/service provider or their employer for example mistakenly believes they have a protected characteristic, for example that they are disabled.

9.46   More recently, in *Hainsworth v Ministry of Defence*,[78] the Court of Appeal refused to extend protection to persons associated with a disabled person in the context of the duty to make reasonable adjustments.

9.47   Previously it was viewed that discrimination because of association only applied to direct discrimination. However, the case of *CHEZ Razpredelenie Bulgaria AD v Komisia za zashtita ot diskriminatsias*[79] marks a potentially significant extension of the scope of discrimination because of association to include acts of indirect discrimination (see para 9.36 above). The ECJ decided in that case that a policy (concerning the provision of electricity meters at a certain height) that applied in districts inhabited by people mainly of Roma origin was discriminatory. The case was brought by Ms Nikolova, a woman of non-Roma origin who ran a shop in the district. She brought a race discrimination claim asserting that she suffered the same disadvantage as her Roma neighbours. The ECJ ruled that the Race Discrimination Directive extends to persons who, although not themselves a member of the racial or ethnic group concerned, nevertheless suffer 'less favourable treatment' (ie direct discrimination) or a 'particular disadvantage' (ie indirect discrimination) on the ground of that race or ethnic origin.

9.48   While this case was concerned with the Race Discrimination Directive, a very similar definition of indirect discrimination is used in other EU equality directives. Accordingly, it is very likely that the ECJ's ruling will apply in relation to other protected characteristics, including that of disability.

9.49   The decision in *CHEZ Razpredelenie* is in contrast to the approach of the domestic courts. The Court of Appeal recently held in *Home Office v Essop*[80] that, in order to establish indirect discrimination, claimants have to show: (a) why the practice, criteria or provision relied upon puts the group sharing the protected characteristic (for example disability) at a disadvantage; and (b) that the individual claimant suffered that disadvantage. In light of *CHEZ Razpredelenie*, it is likely decisions following *Essop* will be subject to challenge.

78 [2014] EWCA Civ 763; [2014] EqLR 553.
79 Case C-83/14 EU:C:2015:480; [2015] WLR (D) 314.
80 [2015] IRLR 724.

Harassment and victimisation

9.50   Finally, Part 2 of the EqA 2010 outlaws two specific forms of prohibited conduct, harassment and victimisation. Three different kinds of harassment are prohibited:

1) A person engages in 'unwanted conduct'[81] related to a child's disability and the conduct has the purpose of violating the child's dignity or 'creating an intimidating, hostile, degrading, humiliating or offensive environment'.[82]
2) The conduct is as above but is of a 'sexual nature'.[83]
3) Less favourable treatment of a child because they have submitted to or rejected sexual harassment or harassment relating to sex (or gender reassignment in a further and higher education, services and work context).[84]

9.51   Whether the conduct has the necessary purpose should be judged in all the circumstances, including the perceptions of the disabled child.[85] Clearly in cases involving sexual harassment of a minor, there is other relevant legislation such as that covering criminal behaviour.

9.52   Victimisation occurs if a person is subjected 'to a detriment' because he or she does, or it is believed that he or she has done or may do, a 'protected act'.[86] The 'protected acts' are, in essence, any act done in relation to the EqA 2010, including bringing a claim that there has been disability discrimination.[87] A person can be unlawfully victimised, even though he or she does not have the 'protected characteristic'. Accordingly, a mother of a disabled child could make such a claim if she were told that she would be refused a carer's service (see chapter 8, paras 8.15–8.23) if she complained about the disability discrimination she believed to be taking place in a children's centre. If a school subjects a pupil to a detriment because their parent

---

81   Unwanted conduct can include any kind of behaviour, including spoken or written words or abuse, imagery, graffiti, physical gestures, facial expressions, mimicry, jokes, pranks, acts affecting a person's surroundings or other physical behaviour: Part 3 Code of Practice, para 9.3.
82   EqA 2010 s26(1).
83   EqA 2010 s26(2).
84   EqA 2010 s26(3).
85   EqA 2010 s26(4).
86   EqA 2010 s27(1).
87   EqA 2010 s27(2).

or sibling has carried out a protected act, this will also amount to victimisation of the pupil.[88]

Services and public functions

Provision of services

9.53   Service providers[89] are prohibited from discriminating against disabled children and people with other protected characteristics. However, service providers (and persons performing public functions, see paras 9.59–9.64 below) are not prohibited from discriminating against children on grounds of age.[90] As such, a disabled child could bring a discrimination claim against a service provider in relation to their status as a disabled person but not their status as a child.

The Part 3 Code of Practice states that:

> Part 3 is based on the principle that people with the protected characteristics defined in the Act should not be discriminated against when using any service provided publicly or privately, whether that service is for payment or not.[91]

9.54   The EqA 2010 does not distinguish between service providers of different types or size; the same duties apply to all service providers, although the Part 3 Code of Practice recognises that the way the duties are put into practice may vary between service providers – for example, what might be a reasonable adjustment for a large and well-resourced service provider to make might not be for one that is small and poorly resourced.[92]

---

88 EqA 2010 s86.
89 A 'service provider' is a person concerned with the provision of a service to the public, whether for payment or not: EqA 2010 s29(1). The term encompasses those providing goods and facilities as well as services: EqA 2010 s31(2). It also includes services provided in the exercise of a public function: EqA 2010 s31(3).The EHRC's Technical Guidance for Schools in England makes clear at para 1.4 that early years education providers other than nursery schools maintained by a local authority and nursery education provided by any school (either maintained or independent) have duties under Part 3 of the EqA 2010 as service providers. Local authorities have obligations under the education provisions of the Act where they are the responsible body for the school; in relation to their other education-related functions, most of these will be covered by Part 3 of the Act.
90 See EqA 2010 s28(1)(a): 'This Part does not apply to the protected characteristic of age, so far as relating to persons who have not attained the age of 18.'
91 Part 3 Code of Practice, p7.
92 Part 3 Code of Practice, para 7.30

9.55   In particular, service providers must not:

- discriminate against a disabled child who requires[93] their service by not providing that service[94] (see paras 9.23–9.42 for the meaning of 'discriminate');
- discriminate against a disabled child while providing them with a service by providing it on worse terms or with a poorer quality than that offered to others, terminating the service or 'subjecting [the child] to any other detriment';[95]
- harass a disabled child who requires or is receiving their service[96] (see paras 9.50–9.51 for the meaning of 'harassment'); or
- victimise a disabled child by not providing the service or providing it on worse terms[97] (see para 9.52 for the meaning of 'victimisation').

9.56   Service providers are also subject to the duty to make reasonable adjustments;[98] see paras 9.39–9.42. The Part 3 Code of Practice suggests that service providers are not expected to anticipate the needs of every individual who may wish to use their services, but to consider what reasonable steps may be required to overcome barriers faced by persons with particular kinds of disability – the examples given being visual impairments or mobility impairments.[99] This of course begs the question as to whether it would be 'reasonable' for a service provider not to anticipate the need to make adjustments to ensure access for persons with other types of disability. The Code of Practice does suggest that, once a service provider becomes aware of the requirements of a particular disabled person, it may be reasonable for them to take a particular step to meet their individual needs.[100]

9.57   Service providers also need to take active steps to ensure that discrimination is not occurring in the provision of their services.[101] This is particularly so as a service provider will be liable for unlawful acts committed by their employees unless they have taken reasonable

---

93 'Requiring' a service also means 'seeking to obtain or use the service': EqA 2010 s31(6).
94 EqA 2010 s29(1). 'Not providing the service' also means providing a poorer quality of service or providing it on less favourable terms or in a less favourable manner than it is generally offered to the public: EqA 2010 s31(7).
95 EqA 2010 s29(2).
96 EqA 2010 s29(3).
97 EqA 2010 s29(4) and (5).
98 EqA 2010 s29(7)(a).
99 Part 3 Code of Practice, para 8.22.
100 Part 3 Code of Practice, para 8.24.
101 Part 3 Code of Practice, para 4.10.

steps to prevent such acts.[102] Service providers are advised by the Part 3 Code of Practice to take a number of steps to ensure compliance with their duties, including establishing a policy to ensure equality of access to their services and communicating this policy effectively to their staff.[103]

9.58   The EHRC has issued a range of specific non-statutory guidance concerning, for example, rights to equality in relation to healthcare and social care services (which sets out how the EqA 2010 applies to healthcare services provided both in clinical settings and the home) and in relation to services provided by local councils and government departments.[104]

Performance of public functions

9.59   In addition to duties on service providers, Part 3 of the EqA 2010 places duties on persons performing public functions. Together, these duties mean that every action (or inaction) of a public authority and the exercise of every public function (even if not related to the provision of services) is covered by the EqA 2010 – unless specifically excluded.[105]

9.60   The term 'public function' has the same meaning in the EqA 2010 as the phrase 'function of a public nature' within the HRA 1998.[106] For the purposes of the Act, only those functions of a public authority which are not services and do not fall within Part 4 (premises), Part 5 (work) and Part 6 (education) of the Act are covered by the public

---

102 Part 3 Code of Practice, para 3.10.

103 Part 3 Code of Practice, para 4.11.

104 The latest guidance was published in March 2011 and was last updated in December 2014.

105 EqA 2010 s29(6). The public functions provisions are residual and apply only where other provisions of the EqA 2010 do not: Part 3 Code of Practice, para 12.2. See also Part 3 Code of Practice, para 12.20.

106 EqA 2010 s31(4). This term has been the subject of significant judicial consideration within the Human Rights Act scheme. Although it should be given a broad interpretation, there will be occasions where it will not be obvious if a body is providing a function of a public nature – for instance, a private company carrying out a function under contract from a local authority. See Lester, Pannick and Herberg, *Human rights law and practice*, 3rd edn, LexisNexis, 2009, para 2.6.3. Under s73 of the Care Act 2014, a registered care provider providing care and support to a disabled young person aged over 18 or support to their carer, in the course of providing personal care or residential accommodation, is taken to be exercising a function of a public nature in providing the care or support where the care or support is arranged or paid for by a local authority. However, such organisations would almost certainly be covered as service providers under the EqA 2010 scheme.

function provisions. Often the public authority will be acting under a statutory power or duty when performing such a function. Examples of such activities would be law enforcement or the collection of taxes.[107]

9.61   It is also likely that the public functions duty applies primarily to 'policy' functions such as the setting of budgets and the determination of entitlements to benefits and services, whereas decisions on individual cases are likely to be covered by the service provision or education duties.

9.62   In practice, the duties under the EqA 2010 imposed on persons exercising public functions and those providing a service are 'essentially the same'.[108] The duty in relation to public functions is, however, more clearly expressed: a person carrying out a public function must not 'do anything that constitutes discrimination, harassment or victimisation'.[109] Persons carrying out a public function are also subject to the reasonable adjustments duty.[110]

9.63   There has been limited case-law concerning the duty prohibiting discrimination by public authorities. Under the DDA scheme,[111] the leading authority was *R (Lunt and another) v Liverpool CC*;[112] due to the similarity in the statutory schemes, this case still provides useful guidance. The case involved an application by a vehicle developer for approval of a specific type of taxi in Liverpool. The local authority's refusal was challenged successfully on the ground that the council had failed to take into account a class of wheelchair users with wheelchairs of a certain length and that this failure amounted to unjustified discrimination. The approach taken in *Lunt* was followed by the court in *R (Gill) v Secretary of State for Justice*,[113] where a prisoner had been prevented from accessing offending behaviour programmes in prison because of his learning disability. The court held that the secretary of state had unlawfully breached the duty on public authorities under the DDA scheme and had discriminated against the prisoner by failing to provide programmes which were accessible to him.[114]

---

107 Part 3 Code of Practice, para 11.13
108 Part 3 Code of Practice, para 11.17
109 EqA 2010 s29(6).
110 EqA 2010 s29(7)(b).
111 DDA 1995 s21B.
112 [2009] EWHC 2356 (Admin); [2010] RTR 5.
113 [2010] EWHC 364 (Admin); (2010) 13 CCLR 193.
114 [2010] EWHC 364 (Admin); (2010) 13 CCLR 193 at [80].

9.64   The same approach was adopted by the Court of Appeal in *ZH v Commissioner of Police for the Metropolis*.[115] An autistic boy had become 'stuck' at the side of a swimming pool, and jumped into the water when approached by police. He ended up being restrained by the police, and put in the cage at the back of a police van. The Court of Appeal upheld a decision that the police had failed to make reasonable adjustments (this case was also argued under the DDA scheme). The police should have consulted the boy's carers from the school (at least one carer was present the whole time), to inform themselves properly before taking any action which led to the application of force. Their treatment of him was also in breach of human rights law.

Reasonable adjustments – service providers and public functions

9.65   The operation of the duty to make reasonable adjustments on service providers and persons carrying out a public function is governed by EqA 2010 Schedule 2.[116] The schedule specifies that all three aspects of the reasonable adjustment duty apply:[117] see paras 9.39–9.42. In addition to the duty to help disabled persons avoid the disadvantage they might face in relation to a physical feature, service providers and persons carrying out a public function have an additional duty to 'adopt a reasonable alternative method of providing the service or exercising the function'.[118]

9.66   The meaning of 'substantial disadvantage'[119] in relation to the exercise of a public function is either being placed at a substantial disadvantage in relation to a potential benefit or suffering an 'unreasonably adverse experience' when being subjected to a 'detriment'.[120]

Exceptions

9.67   Schedule 2 contains an important exception to the reasonable adjustment duty on service providers. The duty does not require a service

115 [2013] EWCA Civ 69; (2013) 16 CCLR 109.
116 Schedule 2 para 1 states that the schedule applies where a duty to make reasonable adjustments is imposed by this Part of the Act.
117 Schedule 2 para 2(1).
118 Schedule 2 para 2(3)(b).
119 See para 9.33 and fn 59 above.
120 Schedule 2 para 2(5).

provider to take any step which would 'fundamentally alter' the nature of the service or of the trade or profession of the service provider.[121]

9.68   The use of the phrase 'fundamentally alter' indicates that this is a high threshold which is not intended to be a general 'get out clause' to prevent service providers from making reasonable adjustments in favour of disabled children and others with protected characteristics. A more straightforward exception is also established in relation to persons carrying out a public function, who are not required by the duty to take a step which they have no power at law to take.[122]

9.69   Schedule 3 exempts from the duties on service providers and persons carrying out public functions:

- Parliament;[123]
- the preparation or consideration of legislation in the UK Parliament or the devolved Scottish Parliament and Welsh Assembly;[124]
- judicial functions;[125]
- a decision not to commence or continue criminal proceedings;[126]
- the armed forces;[127]
- the security services;[128]
- specified immigration decisions;[129] and
- transport by air[130] or by land other than in specified vehicles.[131]

9.70   Other than the above specified exceptions, the duties apply to all service providers and all those carrying out a public function. The EqA 2010 thereby obliges a wide range of public and private individuals and organisations to consider their policies, procedures and practices to ensure that they are avoiding discrimination and making necessary reasonable adjustments.

---

121 Schedule 2 para 2(7).
122 Schedule 2 para 8.
123 EqA 2010 Sch 3 para 1.
124 EqA 2010 Sch 3 para 2.
125 EqA 2010 Sch 3 para 3(1)(a).
126 EqA 2010 Sch 3 para 3(1)(c).
127 EqA 2010 Sch 3 para 4.
128 EqA 2010 Sch 3 para 5.
129 EqA 2010 Sch 3 para 16.
130 EqA 2010 Sch 3 para 33.
131 EqA 2010 Sch 3 para 34.

Education

9.71   It is well documented that major inequalities remain for certain groups which prevent some individuals from making the most of their abilities and talents and achieving their full potential. This is certainly the case for disabled pupils (see in this context paras 1.68–1.69 and chapter 4, where the duties in relation to children and young people with special educational needs (SEN) are discussed). In one early DDA case,[132] a disabled child was excluded from his school's nativity play, prevented from making a Christmas card to take home, was not invited to the school disco and was left out of a school trip and a class photograph. The school was ordered to apologise, to revise its policies for disabled pupils and for recruiting staff and the governing body and staff also had to attend disability equality training. While it is hoped that such blatant examples of discrimination will be rare, the equality duties on education providers and, in particular, on schools remain of central importance to the life chances of disabled children.

9.72   Chapter 1 of Part 6 of the EqA 2010 is concerned with education provided by all schools[133] (and local education authorities (LEAs) in the context of accessibility strategies, see paras 9.76 to 9.78).[134] Chapter 2 of Part 6 deals with further and higher education, including further education courses provided by maintained schools, further and higher education courses and recreational and training facilities and recreational and training facilities secured by local authorities.

---

132 Personal correspondence with the authors, 25 July 2010.
133 Meaning schools maintained by the local education authority and independent schools, both special and mainstream: EqA 2010 s85(7). Where schools are providing a non-educational service, for example through renting their premises to a community group, they are covered by the provisions of Part 3 of the EqA 2010 in relation to service providers: Part 3 Code of Practice, para 11.8.
134 See further Philippa Stobbs, *Disabled Children and the Equality Act 2010: What teachers need to know and what schools need to do, including responsibilities to disabled children and young people under the Children and Families Act 2014,* Council for Disabled Children, March 2015.

Schools and LEAs

9.73   The responsible body[135] for a school must not discriminate against a disabled child in relation to admissions,[136] exclusions[137] or the provision of education in the school[138] (see paras 9.23–9.24 for the meaning of 'discrimination') and must not harass[139] or victimise[140] a pupil or prospective pupil (see paras 9.50–9.52 for the meaning of 'harassment' and 'victimisation'). This effectively prohibits[141] discrimination in relation to all aspects of school life and obliges the authorities regularly to review their practices, policies and procedures.

9.74   Although the responsible bodies for schools are also under the duty to make reasonable adjustments[142] (see paras 9.39–9.42) this is limited to the requirement to make adjustments to provisions, criteria or practices and to provide auxiliary aids and services;[143] where the provision, criteria or practice or the need for an auxiliary aid or service involves the provision of information, the duty includes ensuring that information is provided in an accessible format (see para 9.41). The duty to make reasonable adjustments to physical features does not apply to schools because it was argued that the protection

135 Meaning the local authority or governing body of a maintained school, the Academy Trust for academies and the proprietor of an independent school.

136 EqA 2010 s85(1). Although the use of admissions criteria is permitted, schools must ensure that the criteria they use does not discriminate, either directly or indirectly, against anyone with a protected characteristic, and indirect discrimination may occur if admissions criteria exclude a greater proportion of (for example) disabled children: Department of Education, *Non-statutory guidance to the Equality Act 2010 and Schools*, May 2014 (the Education Guidance), paras 1.5, 1.7 and 4.7.

137 EqA 2010 s85(2)(e). Note also the requirement in the School Exclusions Guidance that 'pupils should only be excluded from school as a last resort': see chapter 4, para 4.220.

138 EqA 2010 s85(2)(a).

139 EqA 2010 s85(3).

140 EqA 2010 s85(4) and (5). Disabled children are also protected from victimisation as a result of the conduct of their parents: EqA 2010 s86.

141 The prohibitions do not apply to anything done in relation to the content of the school curriculum: EqA 2010 s89. This ensures that the Act does not inhibit the ability of schools to include a full range of issues, ideas and materials in their syllabus and to expose pupils to thoughts and ideas of all kinds. The way in which the curriculum is taught is, however, covered by the reference to education in EqA 2010 s85(2)(a), so as to ensure issues are taught in a way which does not subject pupils to discrimination: Explanatory Notes to the EqA 2010 at [306].

142 EqA 2010 s85(6).

143 EqA 2010 Sch 13 para 2(2).

this offered is covered by school accessibility plans[144] (see para 9.78). The reasonable adjustment duty applies in relation to disabled pupils generally, not just those already at the school[145], and applies in certain circumstances to pupils who have left the school.[146] A key reasonable adjustment will often be to avoid operating blanket policies – such as a policy that pupils must wear a certain type of trousers when those trousers exacerbated a child's eczema, or a policy that any pupil swearing at a teacher will be excluded when a pupil in the school has difficulties with social communication and expressing his emotions.[147]

9.75   A maintained school governing body or an independent special school proprietor in England can be given directions by the secretary of state[148] if it fails to comply with one of the duties imposed on it by the EqA 2010.[149]

Accessibility strategies and plans

9.76   Two schedules apply in relation to schools. The first, Schedule 10, deals with accessibility for disabled pupils.[150] Under this schedule, local authorities must prepare an accessibility strategy for their maintained schools[151] which sets out a plan for:

- increasing the extent to which disabled pupils can 'participate in the schools' curriculum';[152]
- improving the physical environment of the school for the purpose of increasing access for disabled children;[153] and
- improving the delivery of information for disabled pupils.[154]

---

144 EqA 2010 Sch 10 and EqA 2010 Sch 3 Pt 10.
145 EqA 2010 Sch13 para 2(3)(b).
146 EqA 2010 s108.
147 Both examples of education cases brought under the DDA scheme: personal correspondence with the authors, 25 July 2010.
148 Under Education Act 1996 ss496–497.
149 EqA 2010 s87.
150 Both current and prospective pupils: EqA 2010 Sch 10 para 6(4).
151 EqA 2010 Sch 10 para 1. Maintained schools are those included within the definition in section 20 of the School Standards and Framework Act 1998: Sch 10 para 6(7), being community, foundation and voluntary schools.
152 EqA 2010 Sch 10 para 2(1)(a).
153 EqA 2010 Sch 10 para 1(2)(b).
154 EqA 2010 Sch 10 para 1(2)(c) and (3).

9.77   The accessibility strategy must be in writing,[155] must be kept under review[156] and must be implemented.[157] Adequate resources must be allocated for implementing the strategy[158] and the authority must have regard to any guidance which may be issued by the secretary of state.[159] It is highly likely that the strategy will need to cover staff training, the importance of which in achieving compliance with the EqA 2010 cannot be overestimated.

9.78   At the school level (including independent schools), the responsible body must prepare an accessibility plan.[160] Each school's plan must cover the same matters as an accessibility strategy[161] (see above) and the responsible body is subject to the same procedural requirements as a local authority – producing the plan in writing, keeping it under review and implementing it.[162] Again, adequate resources must be allocated to the implementation of the plan.[163] Importantly, any inspection of the school can review the performance of the responsible body in preparing and implementing its accessibility plan.[164] This gives the duty teeth, as any failure to produce a plan or any seriously inadequate plan is likely to be criticised in inspection reports. However, an individual pupil cannot bring a claim against their school for a failure to make a reasonable adjustment in relation to a physical feature, in other words the 'teeth' given to school pupils are not as sharp as those benefitting students in further and higher education, service users and employees.

Exceptions – selection

9.79   The second schedule relevant to schools is Schedule 11, which sets out the exceptions to duties imposed on schools by the EqA 2010.

155 EqA 2010 Sch 10 para 1(4).
156 EqA 2010 Sch 10 para 1(5).
157 EqA 2010 Sch 10 para 1(6).
158 EqA 2010 Sch 10 para 2(1)(a). The precise duty is to 'have regard to the need to allocate adequate resources for implementing the strategy'.
159 EqA 2010 Sch 10 para 2(1)(b), (2) and (3).
160 EqA 2010 Sch 10 para 3(1).
161 EqA 2010 Sch 10 para 3(2)–(3).
162 EqA 2010 Sch 10 para 3(4)–(6).
163 EqA 2010 Sch 10 para 4(1).
164 EqA 2010 Sch 10 para 3(7)–(8). In England, equality and diversity are now a 'limiting judgement' in Ofsted inspections. This means that if equality measures are not being implemented effectively, this will restrict the overall inspection grade. This is part of the common inspection framework under which Ofsted assess education providers, under the Education and Inspections Act 2006.

Part 3 of this schedule deals with the disability-related exception regarding 'permitted forms of selection'.[165] Selection permitted for maintained schools is that specified in the School Standards and Framework Act 1998.[166] Permitted selection for independent schools is defined as:

> Arrangements which provide for some or all of [a school's] pupils to be selected by reference to general or special ability or aptitude, with a view to admitting only pupils of high ability or aptitude.[167]

9.80   Taken together, these exceptions significantly weaken the duty on schools not to discriminate against disabled pupils in relation to admissions.

9.81   In addition to the EqA 2010 duties, Children and Families Act 2014 s100 imposes further duties on schools in relation to pupils with medical conditions. Statutory guidance has been published to support the implementation of duty.[168] The governing body must ensure that arrangements are in place to support pupils with medical conditions. In doing so, they should ensure that such children can access and enjoy the same opportunities at school as any other child and in particular schools are obliged to comply individual health care plans to assist in achieving this aim. See further chapter 9 at paras 9.93–9.94.

Further and higher education

9.82   Chapter 2 of Part 6 of the EqA 2010 is concerned with the provision of further and higher education. The following paragraphs are concerned with the duties on further and higher education institutions as opposed to those on maintained schools providing further education courses or on local authorities when securing further and higher education courses or recreational and training facilities which are different. These duties are explained more fully in the EHRC's Technical Guidance on Further and Higher Education. Exceptions to the duties on further and higher education institutions are explained in chapter 14 of that guidance.

165 EqA 2010 Sch 11 para 8(1).
166 EqA 2010 ss99 and 104; Sch 11 para 8(2)(a) and (b).
167 EqA 2010 Sch 11 para 8(2)(c).
168 Department of Education, *Supporting Pupils at School with Medical Conditions*, April 2014.

9.83   In relation to admissions, a responsible body[169] of a further or higher education institution must not discriminate[170] against a disabled young person:

- in the arrangements it makes for deciding who is offered admission as a student;
- as to the terms on which it offers to admit the person as a student; or
- by not admitting the person as a student.[171]

9.84   Furthermore, responsible bodies must not discriminate against a disabled person:

- in respect of the way it provides education for the student; or
- in respect of the way it gives the student access to a benefit, facility or service; or
- by excluding the disabled person; or[172]
- by subjecting them to any other detriment.

Harassment[173] and victimisation[174] by responsible bodies are also prohibited.[175]

9.85   Responsible bodies of further education and higher education institutions also have a duty to make reasonable adjustments for current, prospective (and in certain circumstances former) disabled students.[176] All aspects of the duty apply – the obligation to make appropriate changes to their provisions, criteria and/or practices; to provide auxiliary aids and services (including providing information in accessible formats – see para 9.41) and to adapt physical features. See paras 9.39–9.47 for more on the reasonable adjustment duties.[177] Financial assistance to cover the extra costs of studying as a result of a disability (including a long-term health condition, mental health

169 Governing bodies or boards of management: EqA 2010 s91(12).
170 See paras 9.23–9.36 for the meaning of 'discrimination'.
171 EqA 2010 s91(1).
172 EqA 2010 s91(2)(e).
173 EqA 2010 s91(5).
174 EqA 2010 s91(6)–(8).
175 See paras 9.36–9.37 for the meaning of 'harassment' and 'victimisation'.
176 EqA 2010 s91(9). See paras 9.32–9.35 for the duty to make reasonable adjustments under the EqA 2010.
177 EqA 2010 s93.

condition and a specific learning difficulty) is currently available[178] in the form of the disabled students allowances (DSAs), although significant reforms to reduce the role of DSAs have been proposed with greater emphasis to be placed on institutions' reasonable adjustment duties; see further chapter 10 at paras 10.90–10.93.

9.86   However, further and higher education institutions are not required to make reasonable adjustments to 'competence standards' which are defined as academic, medical or other standards that are applied in order to determine whether a person has a particular level of competence or ability[179], such as the ability to play a musical instrument to the standard required for entry onto a performance course. The reasonable adjustments duty does apply to the process by which the competence is assessed.

9.87   If a disabled person is studying on a further or higher education course at one institution but their qualification is conferred by another institution, that other institution also has duties towards them when conferring that qualification.[180]

9.88   If a disabled person is doing a work placement as part of their course, he or she will be protected from discrimination by the work placement provider under the employment provisions of the EqA 2010. Apprenticeship contracts and vocational guidance to training services are also subject to the employment provisions of the EqA 2010.

General qualifications bodies

9.89   The EqA 2010 imposes specific duties on general qualifications bodies[181] which confer academic school and FE qualifications (such as GCSEs) not to discriminate against disabled school children and others with protected characteristics. Part 5 of the EqA 2010 (which

---

178 The government is currently (November 2015) undertaking a review into the working of the DSAs with potential transfer of the financial responsibility to universities and individual students. Unsurprisingly, this review has met with fierce opposition from many in the sector.

179 EqA 2010 Sch 13 para 4(2) and (3).

180 EqA 2010 s91(3)

181 A general qualifications body is an authority or body which can confer a relevant qualification: EqA 2010 s97(2). A 'relevant qualification' is any qualification which may be prescribed by the secretary of state or the Welsh ministers: EqA 2010 s97(3). Responsible bodies of schools are not qualifications bodies (s97(4)(a)) so any in-school examinations will not be covered by this duty, but will be covered by the schools duties.

relates to work) also imposes duties on qualifications bodies[182] which can confer any academic, medical, technical or other standard. As with further and higher education providers, there is no duty on qualifications bodies to make a reasonable adjustment in relation to the application of a competence standard.[183] The application of a competence standard by a qualifications body to a disabled person is not disability discrimination unless it amounts to indirect discrimination.[184]

9.90   The primary duty on general qualifications bodies is not to discriminate against disabled children in their arrangements for deciding 'upon whom to confer a relevant qualification',[185] in setting the terms on which qualifications will be awarded[186] or by not awarding a qualification[187] (see paras 9.23–9.24 for the meaning of 'discrimination'). Furthermore, once a qualification has been awarded, a body must not discriminate against a disabled child by withdrawing the qualification,[188] varying the terms on which it is held[189] or subjecting the child to any other detriment.[190]

9.91   General qualifications bodies are also prohibited from harassing[191] or victimising[192] a disabled child (see paras 9.50 and 9.52 respectively for the meaning of the terms 'harassment' and 'victimisation').

9.92   General qualifications bodies owe the duty to make reasonable adjustments for disabled children.[193] However, the appropriate regulator may (subject to consultation[194]) specify aspects of the body's functions to which the duty does not apply.[195] The Explanatory Notes

182 A qualifications body is an authority or body which can confer a relevant qualification: EqA 2010 s54(2). A 'relevant qualification is an authorisation, qualification, recognition, registration, enrolment, approval or certification which is needed for, or facilitated engagement in a particular trade of profession' (s54(3)). These are separate 'relevant qualifications' to those set out under s97(3).

183 EqA 2010 Sch 8 para 15(2).

184 EqA 2010 s53(7).

185 EqA 2010 s96(1)(a).

186 EqA 2010 s96(1)(b).

187 EqA 2010 s96(1)(c).

188 EqA 2010 s96(2)(a).

189 EqA 2010 s96(2)(b).

190 EqA 2010 s96(2)(c).

191 EqA 2010 s96(3).

192 EqA 2010 s96(4), (5).

193 EqA 2010 s96(6).

194 EqA 2010 s96(9)(a). Equality Act 2010 (General Qualifications Bodies) (Appropriate Regulator and Relevant Qualifications) Regulations 2010 SI No 2245 set up Ofqual as the appropriate regulator for this purpose.

195 EqA 2010 s96(7).

to the EqA 2010[196] suggest that 'it could be specified that the requirement to achieve a particular mark to gain a particular qualification is not subject to reasonable adjustments' or that giving an exemption from a part of an exam would not be a reasonable adjustment.[197] An example given in the Explanatory Notes of a reasonable adjustment by a general qualifications body is as follows:

> A visually impaired candidate is granted a modified paper (enlarged font) by a qualifications body in order that she can read her English GCSE exam.[198]

9.93   In deciding whether to exclude certain functions from the reasonable adjustments duty, the regulator must have regard to the need to:

- minimise the extent to which disabled persons are disadvantaged in attaining the qualification because of their disabilities;[199]
- ensure that the qualification gives a reliable indication of the knowledge, skills and understanding of a person upon whom it is conferred;[200] and
- maintain public confidence in the qualification.[201]

9.94   Arguably, the inclusion of the 'public confidence' factor in the consideration of whether to exempt a general qualifications body's function from the reasonable adjustments duty puts too great an emphasis on the 'standards' agenda and means insufficient weight will be given to the first criterion – the need to minimise the disadvantages faced by disabled people taking public examinations.

9.95   In achieving compliance with the reasonable adjustment duty, general qualifications bodies must have regard to any relevant code of practice.

9.96   Further guidance on the duties on both general qualifications bodies and on qualifications bodies is contained in Appendices 1 and 2 respectively of the EHRC's Technical Guidance on Further and Higher Education.

---

196 Explanatory Notes at [327].
197 For further information see Explanatory Notes at [328] and Appendix 1 of the EHRC's Technical Guidance on Further and Higher Education.
198 Explanatory Notes at [328].
199 EqA 2010 s96(8)(a).
200 EqA 2010 s96(8)(b).
201 EqA 2010 s96(8)(c).

Advancement of equality

Public sector equality duty (the 'PSED')

9.97   Part 11 of the EqA 2010 includes a general PSED[202], replacing the previous public sector duties for the individual equality strands.[203] The PSED gives public bodies legal responsibilities to demonstrate that they are taking action on equality in policy-making, the delivery of services and public sector employment. The PSED is similar in spirit and intention to the pre-existing duties, but is structured differently in some important specific respects.

9.98   In relation to disabled children, the duty on public authorities[204] is to have 'due regard',[205] in the exercise of their functions, to the need to:

- eliminate discrimination, harassment, victimisation and any other conduct that is prohibited under the Act;[206]
- advance equality of opportunity between disabled children and others;[207] and
- foster good relations between disabled children and others.[208]

9.99   The duty applies both to the formulation of policy and to decisions in individual cases, as shown by the Supreme Court's judgment in *Hotak v Southwark LBC*.[209] In *R (Brown) v Secretary of State for Work and Pensions*,[210] the court considered what a relevant body has to do to fulfil its obligation to have due regard to the aims set out in the

---

202 EqA 2010 s149
203 In relation to disability, DDA 1995 s49A, inserted by the DDA 2005.
204 'Public authorities' are defined in EqA 2010 Sch 19 (brought into effect through s150). They include central government departments, health bodies, local government organisations and governing bodies of maintained schools. Further public authorities may be specified by the secretary of state or the Welsh ministers (s151) subject to consultation and consent (s152).
205 The concept of 'due regard' was considered in *R (Baker) v Secretary of State for Communities and Local Government* [2008] EWCA Civ 141; [2009] PTSR 809, where at [31] Dyson LJ said it meant 'the regard that is appropriate in all the particular circumstances'.
206 EqA 2010 s149(1)(a).
207 EqA 2010 s149(1)(b).
208 EqA 2010 s149(1)(c).
209 [2015] UKSC 30; [2015] 2 WLR 1341 per Lord Neuberger at [78]–[79].
210 [2008] EWHC 3158 (Admin); [2009] PTSR 1506.

PSED. The six principles it set out[211] have been accepted by courts in later cases.[212] Those principles are that:

1) Those subject to the PSED must be made aware of their duty to have 'due regard' to the aims of the duty.

2) Due regard is fulfilled before and at the time a particular policy that will or might affect people with protected characteristics is under consideration as well as at the time a decision is taken. Due regard involves a conscious approach and state of mind.

3) A body subject to the duty cannot satisfy the duty by justifying a decision after it has been taken.

4) The duty must be exercised in substance, with rigour and with an open mind in such a way that it influences the final decision. The duty has to be integrated within the discharge of the public functions of the body subject to the duty. It is not a question of 'ticking boxes'. However, the fact that a body subject to the duty has not specifically mentioned EqA 2010 s149[213] in carrying out the particular function where it is to have 'due regard' is not determinative of whether the duty has been performed. But it is good practice for the policy or decision-maker to make reference to section 149 and any code or other non-statutory guidance in all cases where section 149 is in play. 'In that way the decision-maker is more likely to ensure that the relevant factors are taken into account and the scope for argument as to whether the duty has been performed will be reduced.'

5) The duty is a non-delegable one. The duty will always remain the responsibility of the body subject to the duty. In practice, another body may actually carry out the practical steps to fulfil a policy stated by a body subject to the duty.[214]

6) The duty is a continuing one.

---

211 *Brown* at [90]–[96].

212 Including cases about the duty in s149 of the Act. See for example, *R (Greenwich Community Law Centre) v Greenwich LBC* [2012] EWCA Civ 496; [2012] EqLR 572.

213 The equality duty in *Brown* was the disability equality duty in DDA 1995 s49A Later cases have confirmed that the principles in *Brown* also apply to the PSED.

214 In those circumstances, the duty to have 'due regard' to the needs identified will only be fulfilled by the body subject to the duty if: (1) it appoints a third party that is capable of fulfilling the 'due regard' duty and is willing to do so; (2) the body subject to the duty maintains a proper supervision over the third party to ensure it carries out its 'due regard' duty.

9.100 In *R (Bracking) v Secretary of State for Work and Pensions*,[215] the first challenge to the decision to close the Independent Living Fund, the Court of Appeal approved the '*Brown* principles', as well as setting out additional principles that are relevant for a public body in fulfilling its duty to have 'due regard' to the aims set out in the general equality duty. These principles are that:

- The equality duty is an integral and important part of the mechanisms for ensuring the fulfilment of the aims of anti-discrimination legislation.
- The duty is upon the decision-maker personally. What matters is what he or she took into account and what he or she knew.
- A body must assess the risk and extent of any adverse impact and the ways in which such risk may be eliminated before the adoption of a proposed policy.

9.101 In *Bracking*, the Court of Appeal also confirmed the need for a body subject to the duty to have available enough evidence to demonstrate that it has discharged the duty.

9.102 The courts have said that even where the context of decision-making is financial resources in a tight budget, that does not excuse non-compliance with the duty and 'indeed there is much to be said that in straitened times the need for clear, well-informed decision-making when assessing the impacts on less advantaged members of society is as great, if not greater'.[216]

9.103 The 'equality of opportunity' limb of the duty in relation to disabled children requires particular regard to the following needs:

- removing or minimising disadvantages 'suffered' by disabled children that are connected to their disability;[217]
- taking steps to meet the needs of disabled children that are different from non-disabled children;[218] and
- encouraging disabled children to participate in public life.[219]

9.104 The 'foster good relations' limb of the duty requires particular regard to the need to:

---

215 [2013] EWCA Civ 1345; (2013) 16 CCLR 479.
216 *R (Rahman) v Birmingham City Council* [2011] EWHC 944 (Admin); [2011] EqLR 705 at [45].
217 EqA 2010 s149(3)(a).
218 EqA 2010 s149(3)(b). This includes steps to take account of a disabled child's disabilities: s149(4).
219 EqA 2010 s149(3)(c).

- tackle prejudice;[220] and
- promote understanding.[221]

9.105   Any person who is not a public authority but who exercises public functions[222] (eg, a private company providing public services on a contracted-out basis) must also have due regard to these matters in the exercise of their public functions.[223]

9.106   Compliance with the PSED may involve treating disabled children more favourably than others, so long as to do so would not contravene the EqA 2010 in some other way.[224]

9.107   The specific duties were introduced to support the general duty. These vary between England, Wales and Scotland and only apply to authorities which are listed in the relevant parts of Schedule 19 to the EqA 2010 which can be amended by order.

9.108   In England, the specific duties are set out in the Equality Act 2010 (Specific Duties) Regulations 2011.[225] The specific duties require listed public bodies in England to:

- publish information to show their compliance with the Equality Duty, at least annually;
- set and publish equality objectives, at least every four years.

9.109   This information should be published in an accessible format, which should meet the standards set out in the Public Sector Transparency Board's Public Data Principles.

9.110   Detailed guidance about the operation of the PSED can be found in the Technical Guidance published by the EHRC.[226]

9.111   The PSED does not apply to the provision of education in schools in relation to the protected characteristic of age as age is not a protected characteristic in a schools context but does apply to schools in

---

220   EqA 2010 s149(5)(a).
221   EqA 2010 s149(5)(b).
222   A 'public function' is a function of a public nature for the purposes of the Human Rights Act 1998: EqA 2010 s150(5). See fn 91 above for more on the definition of a 'function of a public nature'.
223   EqA 2010 s149(2).
224   EqA 2010 s149(6).
225   SI No 2260.
226   Equality Act 2010 Technical Guidance on the Public Sector Equality Duty England.

relation to disability.[227] Further exemptions from the duty include the courts[228] and parliament.[229]

9.112   A breach of the PSED does not create an individual cause of action.[230] However, such breaches can be (and regularly are) scrutinised by the High Court on an application for judicial review.[231]

9.113   The central importance of the equality duties has been recognised by the courts:

> An important reason why the laws of discrimination have moved from derision to acceptance to respect over the last three decades has been the recognition of the importance not only of respecting rights but also of doing so visibly and clearly by recording the fact.[232]

9.114   In addition to the first successful challenge to the Independent Living Fund decision in *Bracking* (see para 9.100 above), there have been numerous examples where the PSED under the EqA 2010 has been found to have been breached. In *R (Barrett) v Lambeth LBC*,[233] a local authority's decision to withdraw funding from a charity providing services to people with learning disabilities had amounted to a decision to no longer provide such services and was thus a breach of the section 149 equality duty. The services had previously been provided jointly by the local authority and the primary care trust and when an equality impact assessment (EIA) was written, it concluded that there was to be no change in the services provided and that, therefore, there was no perceived adverse impact on people with protected characteristics. The notion that because there would be no change in the services, the duty would not be engaged, misunderstood the duty.

9.115   In *R (RB) v Devon CC*,[234] it was held that both the local authority and the primary care trust had failed to discharge the PSED when deciding to appoint Virgin Care as the preferred bidder for a contract to provide integrated care and health services for children. In

---

227 EqA 2010 Sch 18 para 1(1).

228 EqA 2010 Sch 18 para 3.

229 EqA 2010 Sch 18 para 4.

230 EqA 2010 s156, meaning that an individual may not go to a court or tribunal and seek redress in their individual case for an alleged breach of the duty, other than by way of judicial review (see above).

231 See Part 3 Code of Practice, paras 14.38–14.41 for more on the use of judicial review to remedy breaches of the EqA 2010.

232 *R (Chavda and others) v Harrow LBC* [2007] EWHC 3064 (Admin); (2008) 11 CCLR 187 at [40].

233 [2012] EWHC 4557 (Admin); [2012] BLGR 299.

234 [2012] EWHC 3597 (Admin); [2013] EqLR 113.

R (Winder) v Sandwell MBC,[235] a scheme which imposed a length of residence requirement to access support with council tax payments was held to have been adopted in breach of the PSED. In *Winder,* there was no evidence that the council had conducted any assessment at all of the race or gender impact of the residence requirement before it adopted its scheme.

Positive action

9.116   The EqA 2010 creates a further power to secure the advancement of equality through taking 'positive action'. There is no definition of what constitutes 'positive action' in the EqA 2010. The Explanatory Notes to the EqA 2010 suggest it allows measures to be targeted at particular groups, including training to enable them to gain employment, or health services to address their needs.[236]

9.117   The power to take positive action arises in relation to disabled children if a person reasonably thinks that:

- disabled children suffer a disadvantage in relation to their disabilities;[237]
- disabled children have needs which are different to non-disabled children;[238] or
- participation in an activity by disabled children is disproportionately low.[239]

9.118   The EqA 2010 further specifies that positive action is permitted if it is a proportionate means of achieving one of the following aims:

- enabling or encouraging disabled children to overcome or minimise their disadvantages;[240]
- meeting disabled children's needs;[241] or
- enabling or encouraging disabled children to participate in activities where their participation is disproportionately low.[242]

---

235 [2014] EWHC 2617 (Admin); [2015] PTSR 34 at [92]–[95].
236 Explanatory Notes to the EqA 2010 at [519].
237 EqA 2010 s158(1)(a).
238 EqA 2010 s158(1)(b).
239 EqA 2010 s158(1)(c).
240 EqA 2010 s158(2)(a).
241 EqA 2010 s158(2)(b).
242 EqA 2010 s158(2)(c).

9.119   However, the positive action power does not create a power for a person to do anything which is prohibited under any other Act.[243] Further actions which do not fall within the scope of the duty may be specified by regulations.[244]

9.120   Subject to any qualifications imposed by regulations, the positive action power is extremely broad and should mean that significantly greater thought is given by everyone in public life to the ways in which disabled children can be supported to overcome the disadvantages they face, both as a result of their impairments and as a result of socially constructed barriers to them leading ordinary lives. There is little evidence to date, however, of this power being used.

Enforcement

9.121   The EqA 2010 establishes specific legal routes to enforce breaches of the duties it creates in relation to equality and non-discrimination. The specific routes to enforcement under the EqA 2010 are discussed below; further coverage of enforcement routes generally is found in the Remedies chapter (chapter 11).

9.122   EqA 2010 s113(1) specifies that proceedings relating to a breach of one of the duties in the Act must be brought in accordance with Part 9 'Enforcement'. A key exception to this, however, is that a claim for judicial review is not prevented, albeit that in relation to most of the EqA 2010 the specific enforcement route would provide an alternative remedy which would effectively bar an application for judicial review[245] (see paras11.88–11.103).

9.123   Under Part 9, claims for breach of duties by service providers, further or higher education providers or public authorities must be brought in the county court.[246]

9.124   Claims for breaches of the duties by schools must generally be brought to the First-tier Tribunal (Special Educational Needs and Disability).[247] However, claims relating to the admission of pupils, who do not have an education, health and care plan (EHC plan), to state-funded schools are heard under the appeal arrangements for

---

243 EqA 2010 s158(6).
244 EqA 2010 s158(3).
245 EqA 2010 s113(3)(a). An obvious exception to this is the public sector equality duty, which is only enforceable through an application for judicial review.
246 EqA 2010 s114(1)(a).
247 EqA 2010 s114(3), read with s116(1).

admissions decisions. Details of these will be provided by the school or local authority. See further chapter 11 at para 11.28.

9.125   Claims of breaches of the education duties against a local authority must be brought in the county court under the service provision duties or public function duties: see paras 9.59–9.64 in relation to these duties.

9.126   Discrimination claims against a work placement/apprentice provider must be made to the employment tribunal. Further information can be obtained from the Advisory Conciliation and Arbitration Service (ACAS).

County court – time limits

9.127   Any claim to the county court under the EqA 2010 must be made within six months of the date of the act complained of, or within any other period as the court thinks just and equitable.[248] Where conduct extends over a period, time only starts to run when the period ends.[249] In any complaint in relation to a failure to act, time starts to run when the negative decision was taken.[250] The limitation period is extended to nine months if the matter is referred for conciliation by the EHRC.[251]

County court – remedies

9.128   The county court has available to it all the remedies open to the High Court to grant either on a claim in tort or in an application for judicial

---

248   EqA 2010 s118(1). The wording of the EqA 2010 suggests that this could conceivably be shorter than six months, but Part 3 Code of Practice, para 16.10 states that this means 'such *longer* period as the court thinks is just and equitable' (emphasis added). The date when time stops running is the date the claim form is issued: Part 3 Code of Practice, para 16.12. The court should exercise this discretion having regard to all the circumstances, including the prejudice each party would suffer as a result of the decision: Part 3 Code of Practice, para 16.20.

249   EqA 2010 s118(6)(a). This would also encompass a 'continuing state of affairs', for instance a series of connected acts by different persons employed by the same service provider: Part 3 Code of Practice, para 16.18.

250   EqA 2010 s118(6)(b). In the absence of evidence to the contrary, a failure to act will be 'decided' when a person does something inconsistent with taking the action or on the expiry of the period when a person might reasonably have been expected to do the act: EqA 2010 s118(7).

251   EqA 2010 s118(4): see Equality Act 2006 s27 for the conciliation arrangements.

review.[252] In practice, this means that the court can make a declaration that the EqA 2010 has been breached, grant a mandatory order requiring a party to comply with its duties under the Act or award damages. The ability of the court to award damages for injury to feelings (whether alone or in conjunction with another award) is expressly stated.[253] The court may also award aggravated and/or exemplary damages when the person committing the unlawful act has behaved in a high-handed, malicious, insulting or oppressive manner.[254]

First-tier Tribunal (Special Educational Needs and Disability)

9.129 Claims of disability discrimination by schools must be made to the First-tier Tribunal (Special Educational Needs and Disability) (see para 4.242 and para 11.70 for more on the tribunal). Tribunal claims are governed by the tribunal procedural rules.[255] The limitation period for a discrimination tribunal claim is six months from the date of the act or conduct complained of,[256] although this is extended to nine months where a request for conciliation is made to the EHRC.[257] The tribunal has discretion to consider a claim that is out of time.[258]

9.130   If a breach of duty is identified, the tribunal may make any order that it sees fit to make,[259] other than awarding financial compensation or damages.[260] The tribunal should, in particular, look to 'obviate' or reduce the adverse effect on the disabled child of any discriminatory treatment in deciding how to exercise its discretion to make any order it thinks fit.[261]

---

252 EqA 2010 s119(2). Damages should not, however, be awarded for breaches of s19 (indirect discrimination) unless the court has first considered whether to make any other disposal, unless the court is satisfied that the discrimination was intentional: s119(5) and (6).

253 EqA 2010 s119(4).

254 Part 3 Code of Practice, paras 16.55–16.56.

255 Tribunal Procedure (First-tier Tribunal) (Health, Education and Social Care Chambers) Rules 2008 SI No 2699.

256 EqA 2010 Sch 17 para 4(1). The same provisions apply as in the county court in relation to conduct extending over a period and failures to act: see para 9.93.

257 EqA 2010 Sch 17 para 4(2).

258 EqA 2010 Sch 17 para 4(3).

259 EqA 2010 Sch 17 para 5(2).

260 EqA 2010 Sch 17 para 5(3)(b).

261 EqA 2010 Sch 17 para 5(3)(a).

Employment tribunal

9.131   The time limits for bringing a claim in an employment tribunal is three months from the date of the act complained of.[262] Acts may be seen in certain circumstances as continuing over a period of time (*Hendricks v Commissioner of Police of the Metropolis*[263]) and so the date from which the three-month period will run will be the end of this period. The tribunal has a discretion to extend time, where it would be just and equitable to do so.[264]

9.132   The employment tribunal has the power to order reinstatement to employment if a person has been dismissed unfairly, to award compensation for discrimination and losses caused by that discrimination. Where a personal injury has resulted from discriminatory treatment an employment tribunal can also make an award of damages for the personal injury. For example, if the discriminatory treatment an employee suffered had exacerbated a pre-existing condition then it would be open to a tribunal to make an award of damages to compensate for that.

9.133   Under EqA 2010 s124, a tribunal had the power to make recommendations for an employer to take certain steps within a specified period. These recommendations could be made 'for the purpose of obviating or reducing the adverse effect of any matter to which the proceedings relate'. This was so that recommendations could help prevent similar types of discrimination occurring in future. The Equality Act 2010 Explanatory Notes suggested types of recommendations that could be made:[265]

- introduce an equal opportunities policy;
- ensure its harassment policy is more effectively implemented;
- set up a review panel to deal with equal opportunities and harassment/grievance procedures;
- re-train staff; or
- make public the selection criteria used for transfer or promotion of staff.

---

262 EqA 2010 s123(1)(a).
263 [2002] EWCA Civ 1686; [2003] 1 All ER 654.
264 EqA 2010 s123(1)(b).
265 At para 406.

9.134   As of the 1 October 2015, this power is being repealed and so recommendations can only be made if they will be of benefit to the particular employee bringing the claim.[266]

Burden of proof and general procedural matters

9.135   The EqA 2010 establishes a specific burden of proof for cases alleging breaches of its provisions. If there are facts from which the court or tribunal could decide, in the absence of any other explanation, that a person contravened the provision concerned, the court or tribunal must hold that the contravention occurred.[267] A court or tribunal can look at circumstantial evidence (which may include events before and after the alleged unlawful act) to help establish the basic facts.[268] However, a court or tribunal must not make this finding of a breach of the EqA 2010 if the person can show that they did not contravene the provision.[269] Thus, once a person has established facts from which a court could conclude that there has been an act of unlawful discrimination, harassment or victimisation, the burden of proof shifts to the respondent. To defend a claim successfully, the alleged discriminator will have to prove, on the balance of probabilities, that they did not unlawfully discriminate, harass, victimise or fail to make reasonable adjustments.[270]

9.136   In relation to the need for individuals alleging breaches of the Act to be able to obtain relevant information, the EqA 2010 previously required the relevant minister to prescribe forms through which questions can be put to the alleged discriminator.[271] This requirement has now been removed.[272] Although this procedure is no longer on a statutory footing, parties may still ask questions of each other and answers are admissible as evidence in proceedings.[273] A court or tribunal may still draw adverse inferences from any failure to answer

---

266 See Deregulation Act 2015 s2 and Deregulation Act 2015 (Commencement No 1 and Transitional and Saving Provisions) Order 2015 SI No 994.
267 EqA 2010 s136(2). This includes the First-tier Tribunal and the Special Educational Needs Tribunal for Wales: s136(6)(d) and (e).
268 Part 3 Code of Practice, para 16.25.
269 EqA 2010 s136(3).
270 Part 3 Code of Practice, para 16.26.
271 EqA 2010 s138(2).
272 See Enterprise and Regulatory Reform Act 2013 s66.
273 EqA 2010 s138(3).

a relevant question posed, or from an 'evasive or equivocal' answer. However, this is no longer a statutory requirement.[274]

Article 14 ECHR – the human right to non-discrimination

9.137   In addition to the protection from discrimination under the EqA 2010, disabled children also have the benefit of protection from discrimination in relation to their human rights. This protection comes from ECHR article 14. As with the other ECHR rights, article 14 is incorporated into English law through the Human Rights Act 1998; see chapter 2 at para 2.10.

9.138   ECHR article 14 is not a free-standing prohibition on discrimination, but rather a prohibition on discrimination in the enjoyment of one or more of the substantive Convention rights. The Court of Appeal has highlighted that 'one of the attractions of article 14 is that its relatively non-technical drafting avoids some of the legalism that has affected domestic discrimination law'.[275] In order for a claim under article 14 to succeed the claimant needs to show that:

- the policy or decision gives rise to differential treatment between different groups;
- the relevant group has the necessary 'status';
- the issue is within the 'ambit' of one or more of the substantive Convention rights; and
- the difference in treatment cannot be justified.

Differential treatment

9.139   ECHR article 14 covers what would be thought of under domestic discrimination law as both 'direct' and 'indirect' discrimination (see paras 9.25 and 9.36 for definitions of these concepts).[276] What matters

274 For reference, the previous statutory requirement was contained within EqA 2010 s138(4), subject to the qualifications to this set out in s138(5). This will still apply to acts occurring prior to the repeal of s138 (s66 of the Enterprise and Regulatory Reform Act 2013 repealed the orders made under s138 and came into force on 25 April 2013).

275 *Burnip v Birmingham CC* [2012] EWCA Civ 629; [2013] PTSR 117.

276 See *Burnip* at [11]: 'That article 14 embraces a form of discrimination akin to indirect discrimination in domestic law is well known. Thus, in *DH v Czech Republic* (2007) 47 EHRR 59, para 175, the European Court of Human Rights ... stated: "a general policy or measure that has disproportionately

for the purposes of article 14 is that a claimant can show that a decision or policy has a different effect on them than it would have on a person with a different characteristic or 'status' (see below).

9.140 ECHR article 14 also imposes a positive duty on the state to ensure that Convention rights are secured without discrimination. This includes a failure to discriminate positively in favour of a minority group or a failure to make accommodation to secure substantive equality for persons otherwise disadvantaged by apparently neutral rules. It also gives rise to '[a] positive obligation on the state to make provision to cater for ... significant difference'.[277] The leading case on this positive obligation is *Thlimmenos v Greece*,[278] where the ECtHR said '[t]he right not to be discriminated against in the enjoyment of the rights guaranteed under the Convention is also violated when states without an objective and reasonable justification fail to treat differently persons whose situations are significantly different'.[279] This largely mirrors the reasonable adjustments duties set out under the EqA 2010.

9.141 At the European level, the positive obligation under ECHR article 14 supported arguments concerning reasonable accommodation of children in education. In *Horvath and Kiss v Hungary*, the European Court of Human Rights emphasised the positive obligation of the state to 'undo a history of racial segregation in special schools'[280] and 'in light of the recognised bias in past placement procedures', the court stated 'that the [s]tate has specific positive obligations to avoid the perpetuation of past discrimination or discriminative practices disguised in allegedly neutral tests'.[281] This arguably equally applies to disabled children, an argument that is currently being considered by the ECtHR in the case of *Stoian v Romania*.[282]

9.142 In the domestic courts, the Court of Appeal applied the positive obligation in article 14 in the case of *Burnip*, in which it was held that that article 14 applies to cases where the obligation claimed involves the allocation of state resources – although careful consideration would need to be given to the state's explanation of this and whether

---

prejudicial effects on a particular group may be considered discriminatory notwithstanding that it is not specifically aimed at that group".'.

277 *Burnip v Birmingham CC* [2012] EWCA Civ 629; [2013] PTSR 117 at [15].
278 (2000) 31 EHRR 411.
279 (2000) 31 EHRR 411 at [44].
280 Application no 11146/11, 29 January 2013 at [127].
281 Application no 11146/11, 29 January 2013 at [116].
282 Application no 289/14.

it provided a legal justification for the failure to act (see paras 9.146–9.148 below).[283]

Status

9.143   In order to succeed under article 14, a claimant must show that they have a relevant 'status'. Examples of 'status' are given in the article, including race and sex. Disability generally is an example of 'other status'[284] and so disabled people can claim under article 14 in relation to differential treatment compared with non-disabled people.

9.144   The comparison exercise requires defining who is receiving the differential treatment. This can be 'non disabled people', but it could also be other disabled people who experience disability in a different way. So as with indirect discrimination under the EqA 2010, this would include circumstances where the differential treatment is only apparent when a particular narrower pool of people are considered for comparison, rather than the whole group of people who would qualify as 'disabled'.[285]

Ambit

9.145   As noted above ECHR article 14 is not a free-standing right to be free from discrimination; instead, the differential treatment must be linked to one of the other ECHR rights. This is described as the case being within the 'scope' or 'ambit' of the other right. Lord Wilson clearly enunciated this principle in *Mathieson v Secretary of State for Work and Pensions*,[286] holding that:

> For the purposes of article 14, Mr Mathieson does not need to establish that the suspension of DLA amounted to a violation of Cameron's rights under either of those articles: otherwise article 14 would be redundant. He does not even need to establish that it amounted to an interference with his rights under either of them. He needs to

---

283 *Burnip v Birmingham CC* [2012] EWCA Civ 629; [2013] PTSR 117 at [18].

284 See for example *Botta v Italy* (1998) 26 EHRR 241.

285 An example of this is demonstrated by the decision of the Supreme Court in *Mathieson v Secretary of State for Work and Pensions* [2015] UKSC 47; [2015] 1 WLR 3250. In *Mathieson*, the challenge was to the rule whereby sick disabled children in NHS hospitals lose payment of their disability benefits after 84 days. The question of whether this group had a relevant status, as they were being compared with other individuals who were disabled and in still eligible for disability benefits, this was answered in the affirmative by Lord Wilson at [19]–[23].

286 [2015] UKSC 47; [2015] 1 WLR 3250.

establish only that the suspension is linked to, or (as it is usually described) within the scope or ambit of, one or other of them.[287]

Justification

9.146   The key question in many or most claims under ECHR article 14 will be whether the differential treatment is justified. In every case, once the claimant has established a relevant difference in treatment, the burden is on the state to show justification.[288] In indirect discrimination cases, what has to be justified is not the scheme or measure as a whole but its discriminatory effect.[289]

9.147   In general, a measure will be unjustified and discriminatory if it 'does not pursue a legitimate aim or if there is not a reasonable relationship of proportionality between the means employed and the aim sought to be realised'.[290]

9.148   However, in cases involving social security and potentially other issues involving the allocation of state resources,[291] a higher test for justification is applied. The question in these cases is whether the measure is 'manifestly without reasonable foundation'.[292] Although the court must give the justification advanced careful scrutiny,[293] any reasonable justification will pass this test.

---

287 [2015] UKSC 47; [2015] 1 WLR 3250 at [17].

288 *DH v Czech Republic* (2008) 47 EHRR 3 at [177].

289 *R (SG) v Secretary of State for Work and Pensions* [2015] UKSC 16; [2015] 1 WLR 1449 at [188].

290 *Stec v United Kingdom* (2006) 43 EHRR 1017 at [51].

291 However the standard text of whether the measure was a proportionate means of achieving a legitimate aim was applied in *R (Tigere) v Secretary of State for Business, Innovation and Skills* [2015] UKSC 57; [2015] 1 WLR 3820, a case concerning student loans, see [27]–[33].

292 *Humphreys v Revenue and Customs Commissioners* [2012] UKSC 18; [2012] 1 WLR 1545.

293 Per Lady Hale in *Humphreys* at [22].

CHAPTER 10

Transition to adulthood

Key points

- The process of transition to adulthood involves changes in both the law and service provision for disabled young people.
- This process can be mismanaged and transition to adult services has been described as a 'cliff edge' or 'black hole'.
- The Care Act 2014, the Children and Families Act (CFA) 2014 and the Children Act (CA) 1989 (as amended) contain specific provisions designed to ensure that appropriate transition arrangements are put in place for disabled children.
- Government guidance requires a multi-agency approach to effective transition planning for disabled young people.
- Unless there has been significant social care or health input in the life of a disabled young person, education should generally take the lead in transition planning.
- The education duties are to produce a transition plan following the annual review of a child's education, health and care (EHC) plan or Statement of Special Educational Needs (SEN) at 14 and every review thereafter;
- Disabled young people can continue to receive social care services under the Children Act 1989 and the Chronically Sick and Disabled Persons Act (CSDPA) 1970 s2 even after they have become 18.
- Disabled young people who are accommodated by local authorities as children are entitled to a personal adviser and pathway plan under the leaving care legislation.
- The duties on health bodies generally remain the same when a disabled child becomes an adult. However, the move from paediatric to adult services can be disruptive. Government guidance expects a health transition plan to be developed for every disabled young person with health needs.
- Specific provisions exist to ensure that health and social services authorities manage the transition process for young people eligible (or who may be eligible) for NHS 'continuing healthcare' funding.
- There are a number of accommodation options available for disabled young people outside the family home as they transition into adulthood, including supported living and residential care.
- Disabled young people can access support for higher education through disabled students allowances (DSAs), although the

government intends to reduce the scope of these allowances by reference to the reasonable adjustments duties on higher education institutions.

Introduction

10.1   This chapter deals with the law relating to young disabled people as they move into adulthood.[1] The process is frequently referred to simply as 'transition'. It is often an extremely difficult time for disabled people and their families, as all too frequently the services and supports they may have fought for as children fall away while adult services are not ready to step in: see paras 1.72–1.75 for more on disabled young people's experiences at this life stage. However, as disabled young people move into adulthood, the fundamental duties owed to them by public bodies remain the same – to assess their needs and to use person-centred planning to secure mainstream and specialist services and support that meet these needs.

10.2   At the point of transition to adulthood, legal and organisational arrangements change, new information needs to be accessed and new plans have to be made.[2] System failures in this important stage contribute to negative outcomes and poor quality of life for disabled young people.[3] The report from the parliamentary hearings which informed the 2006 *Aiming High for Disabled Children* review described transition to adulthood as 'the black hole', meaning 'a time when young people have few options, become more isolated and families experience a drop in levels of support'.[4] This language was echoed in a 2007 report from the (then) social care inspectorate, which described the transition process for some disabled young people as a 'nightmare'.[5]

1   As the Children and Families Act (CFA) 2014 creates a single SEN and disability scheme for children and young people aged 0–25 (see chapter 4), this chapter focuses on social care and health duties.

2   J Read, L Clements and D Ruebain, *Disabled children and the law – research and good practice*, Jessica Kingsley Publishers, 2006, p166.

3   J Read, L Clements and D Ruebain, *Disabled children and the law – research and good practice*, Jessica Kingsley Publishers, 2006, pp168–171.

4   *Report of the Parliamentary Hearings on Services for Disabled Children*, 2006, p53.

5   Commission for Social Care Inspection (CSCI), *Growing up matters: better transition planning for young people with complex needs*, 2007.

10.3   As we note below at paras 10.22–10.37, the Care Act 2014 contains major provisions, designed to ensure that the transition process is properly planned in relation to disabled young people's social care needs. It is to be hoped that these reforms will materially improve the experiences of those in the transition process. Equally, it is to be hoped that the extension of education, health and care (EHC) plans from birth to 25 will assist in a more effective transition to adult services for those young people who benefit from them, being young people with significant levels of special educational needs; see further para 10.8 below. The emphasis on the need for effective early preparation for transition to adulthood is made clear by the title of the relevant chapter of the SEND Code (chapter 8): Preparing for adulthood from the earliest years. The benefits of effective transition planning for disabled young people are summarised in the SEND Code.[6] Local authorities now have a duty[7] to offer information and advice which supports children and young people to prepare for adult life.[8] Every 'local offer' (see paras 3.8, 4.72–4.78 and 5.27–5.29) must include provision which will help children and young people prepare for adulthood and independent living.[9]

10.4   This chapter makes many references to court and ombudsman findings concerning serious management failings by health and social care authorities of the transitional process. Such failings cause significant and sometimes long-term hardship to disabled young people and their families. Frequently, the disabled young person is vulnerable and the harm is to their emotional well-being and education/social development,[10] although on occasions it is even more profound, as was the finding of the ombudsmen in a complaint

6   SEND Code, para 8.2. The evidence cited suggests that supporting one person with a learning disability into employment could, in addition to improving their independence and self-esteem, increase that person's income by between 55 and 95 per cent and that equipping a young person with the skills to live in semi-independent rather than fully supported housing could, in addition to quality of life improvements, reduce lifetime support costs to the public purse by around £1 million.

7   Under CFA 2014 s32 and the SEND Code at para 8.3.

8   In addition a wide range of schools are required to ensure pupils from *Year* 8 until year 13 are provided with independent careers guidance; see SEND Code at para 8.27.

9   See CFA 2014 s30 and SEND Regs 2014 SI No 1530 Sch 2 para 10.

10 See for example, a case summarised in Local Government Ombudsman, digest of cases 2007/8, H1, which concerned a young person who had been accommodated by a local authority in a series of inappropriate residential placements for almost two years and in respect of which the ombudsman recommended a compensation payment of over £12,000.

concerning 'Mr W'. In this sad and extreme case, the local government ombudsman[11] found that arrangements by the local authority for this young man's transition into adult accommodation fell significantly below a reasonable standard: indeed Mr W died after a period of deteriorating health.

10.5   The failure of local authorities and health bodies to ensure continuity of care for disabled people moving into adulthood is not a new concern. The problem is primarily organisational, in that at this stage the people responsible for the care planning and commissioning arrangements for the young person generally change: from children's services to adult services; from paediatric services to general adult healthcare, and so on. The creation of separate social services departments in England for children and adults by the Children Act (CA) 2004 has almost certainly exacerbated this profound and long-standing problem.[12] This danger was acknowledged by the statutory guidance concerning the role of directors of adult social services[13] which requires that they, together with their opposite number in children's services, have in place 'adequate arrangements' to ensure 'continuity of care for young disabled people throughout their transition to becoming adults'. It is likely, however, that these long-standing difficulties and failures have been further exacerbated by local authority adult social care budgets being reduced on average by a third during the five years preceding publication of this guide.[14]

10.6   The courts have highlighted the public law requirement that statutory bodies' co-ordinate their actions to protect the wellbeing of individuals – even if responsibility may have transferred from one body to another. In *R (AM) v Havering LBC and Tower Hamlets LBC*,[15] for example, Cobb J held:

> It is trite law that once a public law duty has been engaged ... it is incumbent upon the authority on whom the duty is placed to act reasonably in discharging that duty; where the duty on the authority changes (by virtue for instance of a change of the law, or a change of specific circumstance – ie the family moves from one local authority

---

11   Local Government Ombudsman and Parliamentary and Health Service Ombudsman, *Six lives: the provision of public services to people with learning disabilities* HC 203–201, TSO, 2009, p64.

12   See, for example, L Clements, 'Respite and short break care and disabled children' (2008) 18 *Seen & Heard*, pp23–31.

13   Department of Health, *Guidance on the Statutory Chief Officer Post of Director of Adult Social Services issued under s7(1) Local Authority Social Services Act 1970*, 2006.

14   ADASS Annual Budget Survey June 2015.

15   [2015] EWHC 1004 (Admin).

area to another), the authority remains under a duty to act reasonably and rationally in discharging or relinquishing its duties ... .[16]

10.7   In relation to the particular facts of the *Havering* case, the judge commented:

> Even though there was no ongoing duty ... [to the family] once it had left its area, it was nonetheless ... an inexcusable failure of good social work practice to 'wash its hands' of the family in this way; continuity of social work involvement and practice best meets the obligations under statute and is indeed the most cost-efficient.[17]

10.8   The SEND Regs 2014[18] endeavour to address the problem of transition into adulthood. Chapter 8 of the SEND Code fleshes out this obligation and states that '[t]he principles set out in this chapter apply to all young people with SEN or disabilities, except where it states they are for those with Education, Health and Care (EHC) plans only'.

10.9   The SEND Regs 2014 require that local authorities include in the planning process (from at least year 9 onwards) a focus on preparing for adulthood (a 'preparing for adulthood review').[19] While a period of up to four years to plan for a young person's transition into adulthood might appear a generous timescale, experience suggests that transition planning too often remains poor. Not untypically, councils simply fail to comply with their statutory responsibilities and even when the transition process is instigated, it is frequently characterised by delay, officer turnover, a lack of incisive action, broken undertakings, ignored complaints and a persistent failure to locate suitable placements (which may require a very specific and costly package of care) during which time the authority loses the ability to look at the 'whole child' and his or her spectrum of needs and becomes particularly insensitive to the impact these failures are having on the family carers.[20]

10.10   The basic duty owed to disabled young people in transition, across all service areas, is that the responsible statutory body must assess

---

16 [2015] EWHC 1004 (Admin) at [35]: the judge here cites *R v Secretary of State for the Environment ex p Shelter* 23 August 1996, unreported, and *R v Newham LBC ex p Ojuri (No 5)* [1998] 31 HLR 631 at 637.

17 2015] EWHC 1004 (Admin) at [46].

18 SI No 1530 regs 6, 12, 20 and 21 and see also the SEND Code, chapter 8.

19 See also chapter 8 of the SEND Code, headed 'Preparing for adulthood from the earliest years', at paras 8.9–8.12.

20 There are abundant local government ombudsmen reports which highlight failures of this kind – but for a typical example, see the report on an investigation into complaint 08/001/991 against the Isle of Wight Council, 4 June 2009.

their needs and put in place a plan to ensure that those needs are met. Whatever the type of assessment, it is crucial that the young person and her or his family are made aware of its purpose, how it will be conducted and, most importantly, the nature of the decisions that rest on it. In addition, professionals should adopt a 'person-centred planning' approach:[21] giving disabled young people every opportunity to take decisions about their lives with the necessary support. The SEND Code states that '[l]ocal authorities must place children, young people and families at the centre of their planning, and work with them to develop co-ordinated approaches to securing better outcomes, as should clinical commissioning groups (CCGs)'.[22]

10.11　　Alongside the availability of appropriate provision, a successful transition to adulthood for a disabled young person will almost always depend upon proper planning in which their needs, preferences and wishes and those of their parents are central: not least because this is a legal obligation – see for example CA 1989 ss1(3) and 17(4A) in relation to social care and CFA 2014 s19(1) in relation to education. All too often, it appears that this fundamental prerequisite is overlooked. In a 2008 Report,[23] for example, the local government ombudsman found maladministration through a failure to communicate with and consult a young person who was moved to a residential educational placement, seemingly with almost no reference to his wishes and feelings. The courts have also considered similar failures. *R (CD) v Anglesey CC*[24] concerned a 15-year-old disabled person for whom the local authority's transition care plan was 'substantially contrary' to her wishes and feelings. In a damning judgment, the court castigated the local authority for its failures, observing:

> Of course a 15-year-old who does not suffer substantial disabilities and who is directed to stay at a location to which she or he has strong objection can, as is the frequent experience of the Division, vote with her or his feet. C can do no such thing; but it would, for obvious reasons, be wrong to pay any less respect to her wishes and feelings in consequence.

21　Department of Health, *National service framework for children, young people and maternity services: standard 8*, 2004, p38; Department of Health, *Valuing people: a new strategy for learning disability for the 21st century: towards person centred approaches*, 2002.

22　SEND Code, para 8.1.

23　Local Government Ombudsman, digest of cases 2008/9, Case L3: in a similar vein, see also Local Government Ombudsman, digest of cases 2007/8, Case H4.

24　[2004] EWHC 1635 (Admin); (2004) 7 CCLR 589 at [61].

10.12   Young people in transition and their families should not feel that they have to limit their ambitions. The National Service Framework for Children (England) describes the main focus of transition planning as 'the fulfilment of the hopes, dreams and potential of the disabled young person, in particular to maximise education, training and employment opportunities, to enjoy social relationships and to live independently'.[25] In this context, 2007 Department of Health guidance noted that 'work defines us ... [but] because so few people with learning disabilities do work, there is no expectation from others that they can, and consequently little is done to offer them the opportunity'.[26] Transition planning should, therefore, focus on realistic but ambitious plans for disabled young people in adulthood. This is endorsed by 2009 guidance which stated that planning for employment should be a 'key objective in person centred plans, including person centred transition plans'.[27] In relation to leisure opportunities, local authorities in England have a duty[28] to take reasonable steps to secure leisure activities for young people in their area, including disabled young people up to the age of 25.

10.13   Proper transition planning involves a process that takes time, skill and sensitivity and works to avoid common pitfalls. For example, if the planning starts too late, there is a danger that those involved will simply go through the motions, that young people and their parents will not participate fully and that only limited options will be on offer that do not reflect the range of outcomes which young people might wish to aim for. While people may feel protected by formal procedures, they may also find them inhibiting when it comes to expressing their opinions and aspirations. Some may find it difficult if policy and practice appear to privilege cultural norms that are not their own.[29] Some young people may require forms of communication other than speech and may be prevented from participating if this is

25 Department of Health, *National service framework for children, young people and maternity services: core standards*, 2004, standard 8, p38.

26 Department of Health, *Valuing people now: from progress to transformation*, 2007.

27 HM Government, *Valuing people now: a new three-year strategy for people with learning disabilities*, 2009, 3.29.

28 Education Act 1996 s507B, inserted by Education and Inspections Act 2006 s6(1).

29 L Jones, K Atkin and W Ahmad, 'Supporting Asian deaf young people and their families: the role of professionals and services', (2001) 16 *Disability and Society*, pp51–70.

not fully acknowledged.[30] In what is an essentially personal process, concerns, tensions and differences of view may emerge between family members.

10.14   All these issues need to be addressed for transition planning to succeed in its object of promoting fulfilling lives for disabled young people. Above all, regardless of the formal legal obligations on individual services which are set out below, multi-agency co-operation is essential if satisfactory outcomes are to be achieved for disabled young people.[31] For disabled young people as for their non-disabled peers, autonomy and independence should increase as they reach adulthood, though the meaning and expression of independence and autonomy will differ considerably between individuals.[32]

Social care

10.15   Far too many disabled young people experience a disrupted transition from children to adult social care services. Half the councils responding to a 2007 survey by the Commission for Social Care Inspection reported that young people's care packages changed at, or after, transition to adulthood and that this generally represented a significant reduction in services.[33] The local government ombudsman has repeatedly expressed concern about failures in transition planning and the severe shortfalls in provision at this crucial stage. The ombudsman has in particular emphasised the duty to continue to meet assessed needs and not to 'use available services as a starting point and just fit people into them'.[34]

---

30 P Rabiee, P Sloper and B Beresford, 'Desired outcomes for children and young people with complex health care needs and children who do not use speech for communication', (2005) 135 *Health and Social Care in the Community*, pp478–487. See also (undated) guidance published by the Council for Disabled Children and Participation Works, *How to involve children and young people with communication impairments in decision-making*, available from www.participationworks.org.uk.

31 B Beresford, 'On the road to nowhere? Young disabled people and transition', (2004) 306 *Child: Care, Health and Development*, pp581–587. See also SEND Code, para 9.59.

32 J Read, L Clements and D Ruebain, *Disabled children and the law – research and good practice*, Jessica Kingsley Publishers, 2006, ch 7.

33 CSCI, *Growing up matters: Better transition planning for young people with complex needs*, 2007.

34 Complaint no 03/C/16371 against Stockton-on-Tees BC, 18 January 2005.

10.16   The statutory guidance on the role of director of adult social services requires that 'adequate arrangements' are in place 'to ensure all young people with long-term social care needs have been assessed and, where eligible, receive a service which meets their needs throughout their transition to becoming adults'.[35] To deliver on this expectation, many local areas have set up transition teams – either 'actual', multi-disciplinary teams based together, usually either in children's services or adult social care, or 'virtual' teams which meet regularly and have effective systems for communicating between agencies.

10.17   Because young people with learning disabilities are often particularly disadvantaged in transition to adulthood, 2001 guidance called for person-centred transition planning for these young people to be a priority.[36]

10.18   Despite the abundant guidance in this area, the evidence suggests that all too often local authorities fail properly to manage complex social care transitions. Typically the problem stems from local authorities resource difficulties (both financial and personnel) and inflexible bureaucratic arrangements. Two local government ombudsman investigations illustrate these difficulties. A 2005 report[37] concerned a care plan that had identified a number of suitable placements for a young person as part of his transition from his residential college. The authority's care purchasing panel refused to fund any of the proposed placements and instead determined that he should move to a council-run facility with significantly lower costs. The young person's behaviour deteriorated rapidly at this facility such that he had to be moved again to a secure psychiatric unit where he was sedated for eight months. Once at the unit, which was run by the NHS, the authority withdrew all its funding. In finding maladministration (and recommending compensation of £35,000), the ombudsman held that the placement in the council-run facility 'flew in the face of the assessment'.

---

35 Department of Health, *Guidance on the Statutory Chief Officer Post of Director of Adult Social Services*, 2006, para 27.

36 *Valuing people: a new strategy for learning disability for the 21st century*, Circular HSC 2001/016: LAC(2001)23, para 3.38. Person-centred approaches to transition planning are also required by the DfES/Department of Health, *National service framework for children, young people and maternity services: standard 8: disabled children and young people and those with complex health needs*, 2004, ch 7.

37 Complaint no 04/A/10159 against Southend on Sea BC, 1 September 2005.

10.19   A 2003 ombudsman report[38] concerned a young person due to leave college, for whom his parents had identified a suitable independent residential placement which the social worker agreed met his needs. Although the council was aware that there was considerable demand for this placement and a quick funding decision was needed, it required the funding request to be put to a series of 'panels' (see para 10.18 above) – with the consequence that the placement was delayed by two years. The ombudsman again found maladministration (and recommended similar levels of compensation). In his opinion, once a need such as this had been identified, it had to be met (regardless of resources) and it 'was unacceptable for it not to have made specific budgetary provision that would enable it to respond more quickly once a placement was offered'.

10.20   Given the not infrequent failings of statutory bodies to co-ordinate and plan for a young person's transition into adulthood, it is generally necessary for families to adopt an active and demanding role in the process. In this context, Parker provides the following advice:

> You are going to have to manage a medium term project (a bit like restoring a building). You will need to get various experts to work together; you will need them to agree to work to deadlines and then ensure that they keep to these deadlines. You will need to keep records and to remind the experts of what needs to be done in each phase and by when. If the experts give explanations which you find unconvincing, you may need to challenge these. You will also need to be clear on 'costs'. Generally, councils and NHS bodies must meet the needs of a disabled young person or adult: needs are fundamental and costs are secondary. Vague statements about 'funding panels' or 'cost caps' should be challenged and always clarified in writing.[39]

10.21   The law relating to the provision of social care services to disabled adults is reviewed comprehensively by Clements and Thompson[40] and there is insufficient space in this book to go into the detail of this substantial subject. The following sections, therefore, provide an outline only of the law.

---

38 Complaint no 00/B/18600 against East Sussex CC, 29 January 2003. See also the similar report on complaint no 02/C/17068 against Bolton MBC, 30 November 2004, where the ombudsman found that the service user was not in any way properly prepared for his return to the community on leaving school and that 'there is overwhelming evidence that' the council's reluctance to fund the parents' preferred option was because of the impact this would have 'on the Social Services agency budget'.

39 Camilla Parker, *Transition To Adulthood: A Guide for Parents*, Cerebra, 2014.

40 L Clements, *Community care and the law*, 6th edn, LAG, 2016.

Social care transition responsibilities

10.22   The Care Act 2014 places detailed legal obligations on local authorities to assess and prepare care plans for carers and disabled children whose care and support needs are likely to transfer to the adult social services department. Chapter 16 of the Care and Support Statutory Guidance provides considerable detail on the responsibilities of local authorities to ensure that the transition process is a success. It also articulates the obligations in the language of wellbeing – the importance of young people and their families being in 'control' – and that this encompasses the idea being in control over the move 'from children's services to the adult system without fear of suddenly losing care and support'.[41]

10.23   The Act has a formulaic approach to the duty – essentially that if it appears to an authority that: (1) it is 'likely' that a disabled child and/or the child's carer and/or a young carer will have care and support needs after transition; and (2) it will be of 'significant benefit' to be assessed – then the authority must assess or give reasons if it refuses to assess.

Transitional assessments

10.24   Chapter 16 of the Care and Support Statutory Guidance provides considerable detail on the way authorities should approach their duties in relation to disabled children, the parents of disabled children and young carers. Transition assessments can be combined with those required by other statutory provisions[42] which should always include an assessment of the following:

- current needs for care and support and how these impact on wellbeing;
- whether the child or carer is likely to have needs for care and support after the child in question becomes 18;
- if so, what those needs are likely to be, and which are likely to be eligible needs;
- the outcomes the young person or carer wishes to achieve in day-to-day life and how care and support (and other matters) can contribute to achieving them.[43]

---

41 Care and Support Statutory Guidance, para 1.25.
42 See for example Children Act 1989 s17ZA and s17ZD; Carers (Recognition and Services) Act 1995 s1; and Care and Support Statutory Guidance, para 16.27.
43 Care and Support Statutory Guidance, para 16.24.

10.25 Transition assessments for young carers or adult carers must also consider whether the carer:

- is able to care now and after the child in question turns 18;
- is willing to care now and will continue to after 18;
- works or wishes to do so;
- is or wishes to participate in education, training or recreation.[44]

10.26 The requirement that assessments for carers must consider whether they are *willing* to provide care is of fundamental importance. It needs to be emphasised to carers of disabled adults that there is no legal requirement on them to provide care. Adopting an ongoing caring role for a disabled young person once they turn 18 must be a genuine choice for young person carers and other family members – a choice which should be informed by a proper understanding of the level of support available to them through the assessment and support planning process.

10.27 Authorities should always provide details of the timescale for assessments[45] and should not only identify short, medium and longer-term needs/aspirations – but also be clear about how progress towards achieving these will monitored.[46]

Disabled children in transition

10.28 The Care Act 2014 provisions (sections 58 and 59) relating to disabled children (as well as those concerning carers 'in transition' to adulthood) are overly complicated – as the Act contains considerable detail on the issue of consent/capacity to consent and what must be included in the assessment.[47] Put simply, however, the general formula (above) applies – namely: a local authority must undertake a needs assessment of a disabled child if it considers that the child is likely to have needs for care and support after becoming 18. The assessment must be carried out at the time when it would be of 'significant benefit' to the child to do so. If the young person lacks the necessary mental capacity to agree to the assessment, the local

---

44 Care and Support Statutory Guidance, para 16.25.
45 Care and Support Statutory Guidance, para 16.31.
46 Care and Support Statutory Guidance, para 16.33.
47 Important as these issues are – it is a level of detail one would have expected to find in the regulations rather than the primary statute.

authority must make a best interest determination on this question.[48] Such an assessment is referred to as a 'child's needs assessment'. If a local authority decides not to undertake such an assessment it must give reasons for its refusal together with information about 'about what can be done to prevent or delay the development by the child of needs for care and support in the future'.[49] However, given the low threshold, it should be rare that a request for a transition assessment is refused.

10.29   The mere fact that a disabled child may not require social care support services as an adult is not in itself a conclusive reason for refusing a transitional assessment. As the Care and Support Statutory Guidance advises:

> 16.4 ... The purpose of carrying out transition assessments is to provide young people and their families with information so that they know what to expect in the future and can prepare for adulthood.

> 16.5 Transition assessments can in themselves be of benefit in providing solutions that do not necessarily involve the provision of services, and which may aid planning that helps to prevent, reduce or delay the development of needs for care or support. ...

Likely need

10.30   Paragraph 16.9 of the Care and Support Statutory Guidance advises that a young person or carer is 'likely to have needs' if they have 'any likely appearance of any need for care and support as an adult':

> ... not just those needs that will be deemed eligible under the adult statute. It is highly likely that young people and carers who are in receipt of children's services would be 'likely to have needs' in this context, and local authorities should therefore carry out a transition assessment for those who are receiving children's services as they approach adulthood, so that they have information about what to expect when they become an adult.

---

48 Care Act 2014 s58(3) and see also Care and Support Statutory Guidance, para 16.38, which advises that for those without the requisite capacity a person with parental responsibility will need to be involved in their transition assessment, – or an independent advocate provided if there is no one appropriate to act on their behalf (either with or without parental responsibility). It is difficult to envisage situations in which it would not be in the young person's best interests to undertake an assessment – given that the assessment need not be intrusive and the outcome does not bind the young person to any particular course of action. There may, however, be situations when the timing of the assessment may need to be adjusted: the guidance suggests for example that an assessment might be delayed if a child is sitting their exams: para 16.13.

49 Care Act 2014 s59(5).

Significant benefit

10.31 Paragraph 16.6 advises that it will generally be of 'significant benefit' to assess 'at the point when their needs for care and support as an adult can be predicted reasonably confidently, but will also depend on a range of other factors'. In relation to young people with special educational needs (SEN) who have an EHC plan, the guidance is unequivocal in stating that the transition assessment process should begin from year 9,[50] adding that even 'for those without EHC plans, early conversations with local authorities about preparation for adulthood are beneficial'.[51]

10.32 Paragraph 16.7 gives further guidance as to the point at which the young persons' needs for care and support (as an adult) can be predicted reasonably confidently, stating:

> Transition assessments should take place at the right time for the young person or carer and at a point when the local authority can be reasonably confident about what the young person's or carer's needs for care or support will look like after the young person in question turns 18. There is no set age when young people reach this point; every young person and their family are different, and as such, transition assessments should take place when it is most appropriate for them.

10.33 Paragraph 16.10 states that the considering of 'significant benefit' is 'not related to the level of a young person or carer's needs, but rather to the timing of the transition assessment'. It then provides an illustrative list of factors that should be considered when trying to establish the right time to assess – namely:

- the stage they have reached at school and any upcoming exams;
- whether the young person or carer wishes to enter further/higher education or training;
- whether the young person or carer wishes to get a job when they become a young adult;
- whether the young person is planning to move out of their parental home into their own accommodation;
- whether the young person will have care leaver status when they become 18;
- whether the carer of a young person wishes to remain in or return to employment when the young person leaves full time education;

---

50 SEND Code, para 8.9.
51 Care and Support Statutory Guidance, paras 16.11, 16.12.

- the time it may take to carry out an assessment;
- the time it may take to plan and put in place the adult care and support;
- any relevant family circumstances;
- any planned medical treatment.

10.34   If the authority believes that the timing is such that the assessment should not take place at the particular moment (even though there will be a need for care/support after turning 18), it has responsibility 'to contact the young person or carer to agree the timing of the transition assessment, rather than leaving the young person or carer in uncertainty or having to make repeated requests for an assessment'.[52]

10.35   An informative case study as to the timing of a transition assessment, is provided in the guidance. It concerns a 15-year-old disabled child who attends an education funded residential school and who also receives a funding package from social services – both at the school and on the weekends/holidays with her parents. The parents request a transition assessment on her 16th birthday. After a discussion with the family, the local authority realises that when the young person leaves school at 19 'it will not be appropriate for her to live with her parents and she will require substantial supported living support and a college placement'. The local authority then appreciates that this will necessitate 'a lengthy transition in order to get used to new staff, a new environment and a new educational setting' not least because the 'college has also indicated that that they will need up to a year to plan for her start'. On this basis, the local authority concludes that it would be of 'significant benefit' for the transition assessment to take place.[53]

10.36   A 2008 local government ombudsman report[54] illustrates the problems that can arise where a disabled young person and her family seek a transitional plan that will enable her to live in the family home. In this case, although the young person was in a good quality residential placement and college, she and her parents wanted her to live at the family home – subject to adaptations being undertaken to make it suitable. The local authority failed to progress these adaptations (and the associated disabled facilities grant) with the necessary expedition – such that the ombudsman considered that the young

---

52 Care and Support Statutory Guidance, para 16.15.
53 Care and Support Statutory Guidance, para 16.15.
54 Report on an investigation into complaint no 07 A 11108 against Surrey County Council, 11 November 2008.

person spent at least two-and-a-half years in residential care unnecessarily. The ombudsman also considered that this delay engaged the young person's rights under article 8 of ECHR, and in his opinion:

> The greater a person's disability, the greater is the need to give proper and timely consideration to that person's basic rights and, what concerns me most, the values and principles underlying those rights – such as dignity, equality, fairness and respect.

10.37 Where the young person has an EHC plan then the transitional planning process under the education provisions will 'lead' – and this is considered at para 10.9 above.[55] The same will generally apply for young people with rights under the 'Children Leaving Care' provisions (see para 10.49) where the statutory pathway planning process will generally be the more appropriate process to follow – considered at para 10.54 below. However, it is essential that whichever group of professionals take the lead, there is an accurate and transition assessment completed under the Care Act to ensure there is appropriate social care support in place when the young person turns 18. The SEND Code gives the following guidance in relation to young people with EHC plans and post-18 care needs:

> Where young people aged 18 or over continue to have EHC plans, and are receiving care and support, this will be provided under the Care Act 2014. The statutory adult care and support plan should form the 'care' element of the young person's EHC plan. While the care part of the EHC plan must meet the requirements of the Care Act 2014 and a copy should be kept by adult services, it is the EHC plan that should be the overarching plan that is used with these young people to ensure they receive the support they need to enable them to achieve agreed outcomes.[56]

Parent carers in transition

10.38 Whether disabled young people remain with their families or progress towards living separately, it is important that the rights of family carers are not neglected. Although there is no legal obligation on parents to provide or continue to provide care for their adult children, many continue to offer a great deal of support to their disabled sons and daughters as they become young adults. Local authorities are under a statutory duty, when the young person is being assessed

---

55 See Care and Support Statutory Guidance, para 16.11. See also the SEND Code at paras 8.59–8.64 in relation to transition assessments for young people with EHC plans.

56 SEND Code, para 8.69.

for adult care services, to assess parent carers (see paras 10.24–10.26 above) and to offer other adult carers' an assessment.

10.39 Specific provisions additionally exist for adult carers who are caring for a disabled child in transition. Sections 60 to 62 of the Act places obligations on local authorities to assess the disabled child's adult carers[57] during this transition process. In simple terms,[58] the Act provides that a local authority must undertake a needs assessment of the carer of a disabled child if it considers that the carer is likely to have needs for support after the child becomes 18. The assessment must be carried out at the point it would be of significant benefit to the carer. Such an assessment is referred to as a 'child's carer's assessment'. If a local authority decides not to undertake such an assessment it must give reasons for its refusal together with information about 'about what can be done to prevent or delay the development by the carer of needs for support in the future'.[59] See discussion above at paras 10.30 and 10.31–10.33 as to how 'significant benefit' and 'likely to have needs' should be construed.

10.40 For many parents, the transitional process poses additional challenges with the loss of the regular routine of their child attending school. In this context (illustrating the Care Act's emphasis on carers being able to work or participate in education, training or leisure activities[60]), the guidance to the Care Act 2014 advises as follows:

> ... some carers of disabled children are able to remain in employment with minimal support while the child has been in school. However, once the young person leaves education, it may be the case that the carer's needs for support increase, and additional support and planning is required from the local authority to allow the carer to stay in employment.[61]

10.41 The guidance continues by stressing the importance of full-time programmes for young people aged 16 and over, particularly those who are not in colleges that offer five-day placements. It advises that in such situations, transition assessments should explore the options for other provision (for example volunteering, community

---

57 A child's carer is defined as 'an adult an adult (including one who is a parent of the child) who provides or intends to provide care for the child' (s61(7)) but is not paid to provide the care or a formal volunteer (s61(8)).

58 The Act, again, contains overly complicated provisions on the issue of consent/ capacity to consent and what must be included in the assessment.

59 Care Act 2014 s60(6).

60 The wellbeing principle with its emphasis on 'participation in work, education, training or recreation': Care Act 2014 s1(2)(e).

61 Care and Support Statutory Guidance, para 16.20.

participation or training) which 'not only allows the carer to remain in full time employment, but also fulfils the young person's wishes or equips them to live more independently as an adult'.[62]

Young carers in transition

10.42 The Care Act 2014 ss63 and 64 concern young carers 'in transition'. A young carer is defined as 'a person under 18 who provides or intends to provide care for an adult but is not paid to provide the care or a formal volunteer' (see para 8.31 above). Again the Act (in simple terms)[63] requires that a local authority undertakes a needs assessment of a young carer if it considers that she/he is *likely to have needs* for support after becoming 18 and the assessment must be carried out when it would be of *significant benefit* to him/her. Such an assessment is referred to as a 'young carer's assessment'. If a local authority decides not to undertake such an assessment, it must give reasons for its refusal together with information 'about what can be done to prevent or delay the development by the young carer of needs for support in the future'. See discussion above at paras 10.30 and 10.31–10.33 as to how 'significant benefit' and 'likely to have needs' should be construed. As with assessments of disabled young people, if the young carer lacks the necessary mental capacity to agree to the assessment, the local authority must make a best interest determination on this question.[64]

10.43 Young carers have, in general, significantly lower educational attainments than their non-carer peers.[65] The guidance notes that many of them 'feel that they cannot go to university or enter

---

62 Care and Support Statutory Guidance, para 16.21. See also SEND Code at paras 8.41–8.44.

63 The Act contains overly complicated provisions on the issue of consent/capacity to consent and what must be included in the assessment.

64 Care Act 2014 s53(3). As noted above, it is difficult to envisage situations in which it would not be in the young person's best interests to have an assessment – given that the assessment need not be intrusive and the outcome does not bind the young person to any particular course of action. There may, however, be situations when the timing of the assessment may need to be adjusted: the Care and Support Statutory Guidance suggests for example that an assessment might be delayed if a child is sitting their exams: para 16.13.

65 Young Carers at GCSE achieve the equivalent to nine grades lower overall than their peers, eg, the difference between nine Bs and nine Cs, and are more likely than the national average to be not in education, employment or training (NEET) between the ages of 16 and 19. Department of Health, *The Care Act and Whole-Family Approaches*, 2015, and see also The Children's Society, *Hidden from view*, 2013.

employment because of their caring responsibilities' and advises that the transition process must address this question to support them 'to prepare for adulthood and how to raise and fulfil their aspirations'.[66] This requirement extends to other members of the disabled child's household including the caring impact on:

> ... siblings' school work, or their aspirations to go to university. Young carers' assessments should include an indication of how any care and support plan for the person(s) they care for would change as a result of the young carer's change in circumstances. For example, if a young carer has an opportunity to go to university away from home, the local authority should indicate how it would meet the eligible needs of any family members that were previously being met by the young carer.[67]

Co-operation

10.44   Disabled children with complex needs may have many professionals and different organisations involved in their care. Public bodies have many statutory duties requiring them to cooperate with each other (see para 10.6 above). The guidance to the Care Act makes the traditional exhortation for joint working in relation to transitional planning[68] and notes the frustration that families experience when having to attend 'multiple appointments for assessments, and who have to give out the same information repeatedly'.[69] The guidance contains practical advice on how the various agencies should co-ordinate their assessments and support arrangements including giving emphasis to the value many families attach to having 'one designated person who co-ordinates assessments and transition planning across different agencies, and helps them to navigate through numerous systems and processes that can sometimes be complicated.'[70]

The 18th birthday

10.45   Once a person who has had a transitional assessment becomes 18 (or in the case of a parent carer, their child becomes 18) then the local authority is required to determine whether or not to treat the

---

66   Care and Support Statutory Guidance, para 16.22.
67   Care and Support Statutory Guidance, para 16.23.
68   Care and Support Statutory Guidance, paras 16.41–16.43.
69   Care and Support Statutory Guidance, para 16.44; see also the SEND Code at paras 8.25, 9.33 and 9.47 and its emphasis on the 'tell us once' approach to gathering information; and see also chapter 1 at paras 1.48–1.52.
70   Care and Support Statutory Guidance, paras 16.45–16.49.

assessment as a needs assessment under the 2014 Act.[71] In determining whether this is or is not appropriate, the authority must consider when the assessment was carried out and whether any of the circumstances may have changed since that time.[72] As the guidance to the Care Act advises where it is decided that the young person's or carer's needs are to be met under the Care Act after they have turned 18 the authority must 'undertake the care planning process as for other adults – including creating a care and support plan and producing a personal budget'.[73]

10.46   Section 66 of the Care Act contains a valuable power – enabling the Children Services and the Adult Services departments to determine the best time for transferring their respective responsibilities. As the SEND Code states:

> Under no circumstances should young people find themselves suddenly without support and care as they make the transition to adult services. Very few moves from children's to adult services will or should take place on the day of someone's 18th birthday.[74]

10.47   Section 66 enables an authority to continue providing support under CA 1989 s17 and/or CSDPA 1970 s2 even though the young person has reached the age of 18. If on reaching the 18th birthday the authority decides not to treat it as a needs assessment under the 2014 Act, then it is required to undertake a new assessment and continue with the previous provision to the young person/ carer until it has made an eligibility determination. In this respect the Statutory Guidance to the Care Act stresses[75] the importance of ensuring that families are not faced with a gap in provision of care and support on the relevant 18th birthday and if by that date the necessary care and support not in place then the existing services must be continued until the 'relevant steps have been taken' – which it explains means that the local authority:

- concludes that the person does not have needs for adult care and support; or
- concludes that the person does have such needs and begins to meet some or all of them ...; or

---

71 See Care Act 2014 s59(6) in relation to a disabled child; s61(6) in relation to a parent carer; and s64(7) in relation to a young carer.

72 See Care Act 2014 s59(7) in relation to a disabled child; s61(7) in relation to a parent carer; and s64(8) in relation to a young carer.

73 Care and Support Statutory Guidance, para 16.63.

74 SEND Code, para 8.67.

75 Care and Support Statutory Guidance, para 16.66.

- concludes that the person does have such needs but decides they are not going to meet any of those needs (for instance, because their needs do not meet the eligibility criteria under the Care Act 2014).[76]

10.48   The innovative provisions in section 66 are mirrored by provisions relating to young people with EHC plans[77] and for care leavers in foster placements.[78] As the guidance to the Care Act explains, authorities must have a 'Staying Put' policy[79] 'to ensure transition from care to independence and adulthood that is similar for care leavers to that which most young people experience, and is based on need and not on age alone'.[80]

Duties to disabled young people 'leaving care'[81]

10.49   As detailed in chapter 3 (para 3.144), where a disabled child is accommodated under CA 1989 s20, the child becomes a 'looked after' child. The child is then entitled to the same protection and support as a child who is in the local authority's care under a care order. Disabled young people who are looked after have the same entitlements when leaving care as other looked after young people.[82]

10.50   In recognition of the poor outcomes for children looked after by local authorities, the Children (Leaving Care) Act (CLCA) 2000 introduced significant new duties into the CA 1989, requiring local authorities to continue to support these young people into adulthood. These duties are clarified by regulations and guidance issued

---

76 Care and Support Statutory Guidance, para 16.67.

77 CA 1989 s17ZG.

78 CA 1989 s23CZA which enables local authorities to extend these placements beyond the age of 18.

79 HM Government, *'Staying Put' Arrangements for Care Leavers aged 18 and above to stay on with their former foster carers*, 2013.

80 Care and Support Statutory Guidance, para 16.69.

81 See further chapter 7 of I Wise QC, S Broach, J Burton, C Gallagher, A Pickup, B Silverstone, A Sutterwalla, *Children In Need: Local Authority Support for Children and Families*, 2nd edn, LAG, 2013.

82 Department of Education/Department of Health, *National service framework for children, young people and maternity services: standard 8: disabled children and young people and those with complex health needs*, 2004, para 7.2.

by the Department for Education.[83] This guidance is binding 'policy' guidance issued under Local Authority Social Services Act 1970 s7 (see para 2.41) and states that '[t]he main aim of the Care Leavers Regulations and of this guidance is to make sure that care leavers are provided with comprehensive personal support so that they achieve their potential as they make their transition to adulthood'.[84]

10.51 The general duty on local authorities in relation to children leaving care is to 'advise, assist and befriend [such a child] with a view to promoting his welfare when they have ceased to look after him'.[85] However, the CLCA 2000 also inserts a range of specific duties and powers into the CA 1989 in relation to young people leaving care. These duties and powers generally apply until a young person reaches 21. As an exception to this, help given to meet expenses concerned with education or training may continue to the young person's 24th birthday[86] or, in the case of a former relevant child (see para 10.52), to the end of an agreed programme of education or training as set out in their pathway plan.[87]

10.52 The leaving care duties apply to the following groups of young people:

1) **Eligible children**: children aged 16 and 17 who have been looked after for at least 13 weeks since the age of 14 and who remain looked after.[88]

2) **Relevant children**: children aged 16 and 17 who were looked after for at least 13 weeks since the age of 14, were looked after at some time while 16 or 17 but have stopped being looked after.[89]

3) **Former relevant children**: a young person aged 18–21 who was either an eligible or relevant child.[90] Importantly, if a former relevant child's pathway plan (see paras 10.54 and 10.55) sets out a programme of education or training extending beyond his or her

---

83 Care Leavers (England) Regulations 2010 SI No 2571; Care Planning, Placement and Case Review (England) Regulations 2010 SI No 959 and Department for Education, *The Children Act 1989 guidance and regulations. Volume 3: planning transition to adulthood for care leavers*, 2010 (The CA 1989 Volume 3 Guidance 2015), revised January 2015.

84 The CA 1989 Volume 3 Guidance 2015, para 1.3.

85 CA 1989 Sch 2 para 19A.

86 CA 1989 s24B(3).

87 CA 1989 s23C(7).

88 CA 1989 Sch 2 para 19B(2) and the Care Planning, Placement and Case Review (England) Regulations 2010 SI No 959 reg 40.

89 CA 1989 s23A(2) and the Care Leavers (England) Regulations 2010 SI No 2571 reg 3.

90 CA 1989 s23C(1).

21st birthday, he or she remains a relevant child until that pro-gramme is completed.[91]

10.53 To become an eligible or relevant child, the child must have been accommodated by the local authority and, therefore, 'looked after' for at least 13 weeks since the age of 14. Importantly in relation to disabled children, short-term periods of respite care should be ignored for the purposes of calculating whether 13 weeks have been reached.[92] This means that disabled children who receive residential short breaks lasting less than four weeks at a time but are not otherwise accommodated by the local authority will not become 'care leavers'.

10.54 The CLCA 2000 imposes different duties on local authorities in respect of eligible, relevant and former relevant children. These are:

1) **Eligible children:** in addition to all the provisions of the looked-after system (see paras 3.144–3.147), an eligible child is entitled to a needs assessment leading to a pathway plan[93] and to have a personal adviser[94] (see below).

2) **Relevant children** are also entitled to a pathway plan[95] and person-al adviser.[96] In addition, relevant children must be supported and maintained by the local authority, unless they are satisfied that the child's welfare does not require such support and maintenance.[97] In particular, local authorities must provide assistance (includ-ing cash if required) in order to meet a relevant child's needs in relation to education, training or employment as provided for in his or her pathway plan.[98] If a local authority has lost touch with a relevant child, they must take reasonable steps to re-establish contact.[99]

---

91 CA 1989 s23C(7).
92 Care Leavers (England) Regulations 2010 reg 3(3). This provides that for the purposes of calculating time towards the required 13 weeks 'no account is to be taken of any period in which the child was looked after by a local authority in the course of a pre-planned series of short-term placements, none of which individually exceeded four weeks, where at the end of each such placement the child returned to the care of their parent, or a person who is not a parent but who has parental responsibility for them'.
93 CA 1989 Sch 2 para 19B(4).
94 CA 1989 Sch 2 para 19C.
95 CA 1989 s23B(3).
96 CA 1989 s23B(2).
97 CA 1989 s23B(8).
98 Care Leavers (England) Regulations 2010 reg 9.
99 CA 1989 s23B(11).

3) Former relevant children: local authorities must continue to appoint a personal adviser for a former relevant child and keep his or her pathway plan under review.[100] Furthermore, authorities must provide former relevant children with assistance with employment and education and training.[101] They must also provide other assistance 'to the extent that [the former relevant child's] welfare requires it'.[102] This 'other assistance' can include the provision of accommodation,[103] although only where suitable accommodation is not otherwise available to the young person (for example they are ineligible for accommodation under the Housing Act 1996). Local authorities must take reasonable steps to keep in touch with former relevant children, whether or not the young person remains in their area, and to re-establish contact if they lose touch.[104]

10.55   Eligible, relevant and former relevant children are, therefore, all entitled to both personal advisers and pathway plans. Personal advisers must be appointed by the local authority to support and befriend the young person. The functions of the personal adviser are specified by the regulations[105] and include providing advice and support, co-ordinating the provision of services and participating in pathway planning and reviews. However, the personal adviser must not themselves develop the pathway plan[106] or carry out the review, albeit that particularly in relation to reviews they may play a very active role.[107] Young people should be given a choice of personal adviser.[108] The expectation is that the same personal adviser will remain with the young person once he or she becomes a former relevant child (see above, para 10.54).[109]

10.56   Pathway plans must set out the result of the needs assessment which must be completed within three months of a young person's

100 CA 1989 s23C(3).
101 CA 1989 s23C(4)(a) and (b).
102 CA 1989 s23C(4)(c).
103 As determined by the Court of Appeal in *R (O) v Barking and Dagenham LBC* [2010] EWCA Civ 1101; [2011] 1 WLR 1283.
104 CA 1989 s23C(2).
105 Care Leavers (England) Regulations 2010 reg 8.
106 *R (J) v Caerphilly CBC* [2005] EWHC 586 (Admin); (2005) 8 CCLR 255.
107 *R (A) v Lambeth LBC* [2010] EWHC 1652.
108 The CA 1989 Volume 3 Guidance 2010, paras 3.24 and 3.37. It will be ideal if the range of advisers is sufficiently wide to provide young people with a choice.
109 The CA 1989 Volume 3 Guidance 2010, paras 3.30 and 4.39.

16th birthday.[110] The assessment must address a wide range of issues, including the young person's health and development, need for education, training and employment, financial needs and care and support needs.[111] The young person must be properly involved in the assessment.[112]

10.57   Pathway plans should be produced 'as soon as possible' after the assessment is completed.[113] They should cover all the issues identified in the assessment and the guidance states that young people should be 'central to discussions and plans for their futures and it will be exceptional for decisions about their futures to be made without their full participation'.[114] Pathway plans should contain contingency plans[115] to address potential difficulties and should be reviewed every six months[116] to check that the plan 'continues to respond to all the dimensions of the young person's needs' as well as establishing 'that they have settled into their accommodation and that this is, in practice, suitable in the light of their needs'.[117]

10.58   In *R (J) v Caerphilly CBC*,[118] Munby J (as he then was) considered the assessments and pathway planning produced in relation to a relevant child with complex needs and a history of offending behaviour. The local authority's efforts were all declared to be unlawful, as none of the versions of the plan produced amounted to a 'detailed operational plan' clarifying who would do what and by when to help J.[119] Munby J held that one of the 'telling indicators' of the plan's inadequacy was the failure to identify specialist support for J – a relevant factor in pathway planning for many disabled young people.[120]

---

110 Care Planning, Placement and Case Review (England) Regulations 2010 SI No 959 reg 42(1) – but see also Care Leavers (England) Regulations 2010 SI No 2571 reg 5(2).
111 Care Planning, Placement and Case Review (England) Regulations 2010 reg 42(2) and Care Leavers (England) Regulations 2010 reg 5(4).
112 Care Planning, Placement and Case Review (England) Regulations 2010 reg 42(2) and Care Leavers (England) Regulations 2010 reg 5(4).
113 Care Planning, Placement and Case Review (England) Regulations 2010 reg 43(1) and Care Leavers (England) Regulations 2010 reg 6(1).
114 The CA 1989 Volume 3 Guidance 2015, para 3.32
115 Care Planning, Placement and Case Review (England) Regulations 2010 Sch 8 para 10 and Care Leavers (England) Regulations 2010 Sch 1 para 4.
116 Care Leavers (England) Regulations 2010 reg 7(2).
117 The CA 1989 Volume 3 Guidance 2015, para 3.2.
118 [2005] EWHC 586 (Admin); (2005) 8 CCLR 255.
119 [2005] EWHC 586 (Admin); (2005) 8 CCLR 255 at [45]–[46].
120 [2005] EWHC 586 (Admin); (2005) 8 CCLR 255 at [41].

Munby J further emphasised the need to involve the young person in the planning process, even if they are 'unco-operative'.[121]

10.59   Specific and substantial as are the duties on local authorities in such cases, the evidence suggests that the failures highlighted by the *Caerphilly* judgment (above) are not isolated. While a number of the young people to whom these duties are owed may be unco-operative this was not considered an adequate excuse for failure in the *Caerphilly* judgment. A 2009 local government ombudsman report[122] also concerned a young man who was at times unco-operative and who had been in local authority care since the age of 13, and for whom, therefore, the CLCA 2000 duties were engaged. Sadly, his pathway plans were materially defective and agreed action was not followed through; his personal adviser failed to provide appropriate support and assistance and when he went on sick leave, he was not replaced. During this period, the young man endeavoured to sustain his place on a university course and in his lodgings – although ultimately his lack of support led him to leave the course and to be threatened with eviction for rent arrears. The ombudsman identified multiple maladministration in the way that this case had been handled, and observed:

> In its corporate parenting role the Council should persevere in keeping in touch with the young person. ... In this case I consider that the Council had to take account of the effects of Mr Smith's bouts of depression and to make sure that relevant details of his vulnerability and background were known to those who were working with him ... That made it all the more important for the Council to put effective mechanisms in place to prevent a recurrence of past failures. It did not do so and that was further maladministration by the Council.[123]

10.60   The leaving care scheme offers valuable services and supports to young people who have been accommodated by local authorities. This is a primary reason why it is so important to establish under which statutory provision a disabled child who lives away from her family home is being accommodated. If a child is not in local authority care, it will generally only be if the accommodation is being provided under one of the duties or powers contained in CA 1989 s20 (see para 3.136) that they will benefit from the leaving care provisions.

---

121 2005] EWHC 586 (Admin); (2005) 8 CCLR 255 at [56].

122 Report on an investigation into complaint no 08 013 283 against Lambeth LBC, 18 May 2009.

123 Report on an investigation into complaint no 08 013 283 against Lambeth LBC, 18 May 2009, para 54.

Healthcare responsibilities

10.61   The difficulties that disabled young people experience in relation to the social care transitional process are, sadly, also evident in relation to their healthcare needs. A 2014 Care Quality Commission Report on this issue[124] found that 80 per cent of cases had no transition plan and concluded that the health and social care system was 'not working' and was 'letting down many desperately ill youngsters at a critical time in their lives'; that this was because 'we have put the interests of a system that is no longer fit for purpose above the interests of the people it is supposed to serve.' It considered that the elements of good practice that were not being followed were:

- There should be good planning for transition.
- There should be a good transition plan in place.
- Health passports should be used more widely.
- There should be a lead professional to support young people and their families through transition.
- Health care settings and services should be responsive to the needs of young people and their families when transferring to adult services.
- The needs of parents as carers should be assessed and addressed.
- Responsibility for finding should be agreed early in the process.

10.62   As with social care, there is no legal reason for this system failure, as the duties under the NHS Acts remain fundamentally the same for children and adults (see paras 5.30–5.31). However, a genuine difficulty is created by the fact that many therapeutic interventions, particularly speech and language therapy, are delivered to disabled children through their EHC plans/statements of SEN (see chapter 4) as educational provision and so adult health services will need to take on an additional responsibility for meeting the young person's therapeutic needs.

10.63   Given the potential disruptions in young people's healthcare, the CA 1989 guidance stresses the 'crucial' role of GPs through their knowledge of the whole family and their ability to monitor the individual young person's health and wellbeing.[125] The focus of the guidance is on ensuring that as far as possible disabled young people are not accommodated in hospital on a long-stay basis.

124 Care Quality Commission, *From the Pond to into the Sea*, 2014.
125 Department of Health, *Children Act 1989 Guidance and Regulations*, Vol 6, *Children with disabilities*, 1991, para 16.11.

10.64 Since 2004, the National Service Framework in England (the Children's NSF) has required that health services develop appropriate adolescent/young persons services with a view to enabling smooth transition to comprehensive adult multi-disciplinary care.[126] Standard 4 of the Children's NSF, heading 'Growing up into adulthood', emphasises the importance of age-appropriate services which respond to young people's specific needs as they grow into adulthood.

10.65 A 2008 Department of Health good practice guidance, *Transition: moving on well*,[127] for health services in England on transition to adulthood emphasises the importance of a health transition plan. The guidance is clear that a health transition plan should be 'an integral part of the broader transition plan', linked closely to plans held by education and social care.[128] The health plan should be developed by the young person alongside a multi-disciplinary team (including the GP), supported by the most relevant health professional who can review it regularly with them.[129] Planning should start at the latest when the child is 13.[130] An example of a health transition planning tool is given at Annex B in the guidance. Similarly, *Valuing people*[131] stressed the need for all young people with learning disabilities approaching the end of their secondary schooling to have a health action plan (see chapter 5 at paras 5.47–5.50). These are completed with young people by a range of staff, most commonly a community nurse or a school nurse.

NHS continuing healthcare

10.66 Where a disabled young person has a significant level of health needs, responsibility for meeting those needs may rest with the NHS under the children's continuing care provisions: see paras 5.82–5.100 (and see also paras 5.146–5.152 above where aspects of the transition planning responsibilities of the NHS are also considered).

---

126 DfES/Department of Health, *National service framework for children, young people and maternity services: standard 8: disabled children and young people and those with complex health needs*, 2004, ch 7.

127 Department of Health, *Transition: moving on well. A good practice guide for health professionals and their partners on transition planning for young people with complex health needs or a disability*, 2008.

128 *Transition: moving on well*, pp10–11.

129 *Transition: moving on well*, p11.

130 *Transition: moving on well*, p11.

131 Department of Health, *Valuing people: a new strategy for learning disability for the 21st century*, Circular HSC 2001/016: LAC(2001)23, para 6.15.

10.67   In England, two Department of Health framework documents provide 'strong'[132] guidance concerning the eligibility of adults and young people for NHS Continuing healthcare funding: (1) a 2012 National Framework for NHS Continuing Healthcare and NHS-funded Nursing Care (for adults); and (2) a 2010 National Framework for Children and Young People's Continuing Care. Both these framework documents are under review at the time of writing, albeit that the proposed revisions appear to be minor in scope.

10.68   Paragraph 80 of the 2010 children's framework emphasises the importance of adhering to the key transition guidance for health professionals, *Transition: moving on well* (see above). It requires that all CCGs:

- be actively involved in development and oversight of transition planning processes;
- ensure they are represented in all transition planning meetings regarding individuals who may be eligible for NHS; and
- have systems in place to ensure that appropriate referrals are made when either organisation is supporting a young person who may have a need for services from the other agency on reaching adulthood.[133]

10.69   The guidance then sets out a clear timetable for the transition planning process – requiring that all PCTs (now CCGs) must (paras 83–85):

- at 14, identify young people for whom it is likely that adult NHS continuing healthcare will be necessary and notify the relevant PCT (CCG);
- at 16, make a formal referral for screening to the relevant adult NHS continuing healthcare team;
- by 17, decide eligibility for adult NHS continuing healthcare in principle, so that the PCT (CCG) can:
- by 18, commission an effective package of care.

---

132 The National Health Service Commissioning Board and Clinical Commissioning Groups (Responsibilities and Standing Rules) Regulations 2012 SI No 2996 require that CCGs and the NHS England 'have regard' to the adult National Framework (reg 21(12)) and the courts have treated the guidance as authoritative – see for example *R (Whapples) v Birmingham Cross-city Clinical Commissioning Group* [2015] EWCA Civ 435; (2015) 18 CCLR 300. Given its expert authorship and prescriptive content it is likely, in the views of the authors, that the children's national framework would also be given significant weight in any dispute which came before the courts.

133 Department of Health, *National Framework for Children and Young People's Continuing Care*, 2010, para 81.

10.70 The importance of early assessments for NHS continuing healthcare funding eligibility was highlighted by a 2013 ombudsman report.[134] It concerned a young man in 'transition', and for which it found the health body's eligibility decision to be flawed. The ombudsman found maladministration in relation to the transition planning process. The young man was due to be 18 in November 2011 but the NHS transition process only started in April 2010 when he was 16. Given the complexity of the young man's needs, the ombudsman considered that this was too short a period.

Palliative care

10.71 Young people with life-limiting and life-threatening conditions will have additional support needs at transition to adulthood. As young people with life-limiting conditions are now surviving much longer, this has become an important issue. 2009 guidance[135] summarises the difficulties faced by these young people in transition to adulthood and suggests good practice ways in which these difficulties can be addressed.

Mental health

10.72 The law in relation to meeting the mental health needs of disabled young people is covered extensively in chapter 5, see paras 5.107–5.131. Given the high incidence of mental ill-health among disabled young people, particularly those with learning disabilities, it is essential that child and adolescent mental health services (CAMHS) and adult mental health services engage effectively in transition planning, at an individual and strategic level.[136]

---

134 Public Services Ombudsman for Wales Report on complaint No 201201350 against Aneurin Bevan Health Board, 30 April 2013.

135 National Transition Support Team, *'How to' guide: moving on to adult care services – young people with life-limiting and life-threatening conditions*, NCB, 2009, available at www.transitionsupportprogramme.org.uk/pdf/ACT.pdf. See also ACT, *Transition care pathway: a framework for the development of integrated multi-agency care pathways for young people with life-threatening and life-limiting conditions*, 2007.

136 See National Transition Support Team, *'How to' guide: How to support young people with learning disabilities and mental health issues*, NCB, 2009, available at www.transitionsupportprogramme.org.uk/pdf/HowTo_FPLD.pdf.

Multi-agency disputes

10.73   Problematical as it is for many disabled young people to sustain adequate social care support during their transition into adulthood, these difficulties are frequently compounded if there is (or is thought to be) NHS responsibility for some or all of the package. In such cases, the usual difficulties can be exacerbated as disabled young person and their families find themselves caught in the paralysing crossfire of an inter-authority funding dispute. In this respect, a complaint considered by the Public Services Ombudsman for Wales[137] in 2008 is not untypical: it contains elements of delay, officers leaving their post, disputes over funding and parents being required to make 'snap' decisions about fundamental matters, without having the relevant information.

10.74   The complaint concerned a young person with learning disabilities and extreme challenging behaviour who, when aged 14, was assessed by the local authority as in need (when he left school) of 2:1 support in a community environment. A year later, when aged 15, a transition worker from the council met with the parents and discussed various options – however, nothing came of this and the transition worker left and was not replaced. Three years later (when he became 18), no firm plans had been made and the parents were told that they had to make a quick decision as a potential placement had become available; however, they were unable to act on this, in part because they were unable to visit the placement, due to their son being ill. At this time, the council had formed the view that the young man ought to be funded by the NHS under its continuing healthcare responsibilities – and as a consequence, in the opinion of the ombudsman, there was a 'jockeying for position' between these two bodies over who was to be responsible. The ombudsman held that the failure of the local authority's transitional planning constituted maladministration as did its failure – and that of the NHS bodies – to co-operate (see in this respect paras 5.20–5.26). A consequence of the failure had been that the young man had been cared for over 15 months by his parents in their home with little support. The ombudsman considered that the agencies had thereby profited (because they had avoided funding an expensive package during this time). The ombudsman recommended that an award be paid of £25,000 (£20,000 from the local

137 Report by the Public Services Ombudsman for Wales on an investigation into a complaint against Torfaen Local Health Board Gwent Healthcare NHS Trust and Torfaen County Borough Council, 24 February 2008, Report Reference Numbers 1712/200701931, 1712/200701932 and 1712/200702681.

health board and £5,000 from the council) and that this be placed in trust for the young man, with terms of the trust being agreed with his parents. This case illustrates the imperative for local agencies to meet the needs of disabled young people first, resolving any disputes which may arise as to which agency should take sole or lead funding responsibility only once needs have been met.

Mental capacity

10.75   Issues relating to the capacity of children to consent to decisions which affect them and the changing presumptions as children turn 16 and come within the scope of the Mental Capacity Act 2005 are considered in chapter 7 above.

Housing

Supported housing/supported living

10.76   'Supported living' is a generic term which has come to describe arrangements whereby a disabled person has the benefit of a package of care and support together with accommodation – for which they will ordinarily have a tenancy.[138] The development of such arrangements in the 1990s owed much to the philosophy of the independently living/deinstitutionalisation movement: enabling disabled people to live ordinary lives in the community with the same choices as others.[139] It is likely that 'supported living' will be discussed as an option for many disabled children and young people as they transition into adulthood.

10.77   While a persuasive case has been made about the virtues of 'supported living' much has also been written about the problems such

138   Where a disabled person is not considered to have sufficient mental capacity to enter into a tenancy agreement – procedures exist for the Court of Protection to give authority for the arrangements – see Court of Protection, *Guidance on tenancy agreements*, 2011.

139   For an excellent overview paper see Dr Lucy Series, *A stupid question (about supported living)*, Small Places Blog, 18 February 2015 – which point to the 1990s development of 'supported living' to enable people with learning disabilities to enjoy rights to live in their own homes, with support. The ideal arrangements conform to 'Reach Standards' developed by Paradigm UK which today are little different from the requirements of article 19 of the UN Convention on the Rights of Persons with Disabilities: based on the principle of choice – where to live and with whom, buttressed by high quality supports.

schemes have encountered.[140] As with many of the 'personalisation' initiatives in social care, their enthusiastic adoption by providers and commissioners has frequently been attributable to other policy objectives. Supported living arrangements are often less expensive for local authorities[141] and for many providers they have the twin benefits of being 'lucrative'[142] and less regulated. Not infrequently, a person may have little or no practical choice over their placement in a supported living scheme. Where a disabled person requires a substantial package of care, there are risks with supported living arrangements (unless there is a clear agreement to the contrary with the local authority) which include the risk that the care provider can be changed at short notice and the risk that the person(s) providing the necessary care may have insufficient understanding/expertise to provide adequate the necessary care and support.

10.78   Supported living arrangements separate the delivery of care from the provision of accommodation. Because these are provided by separate entities, the accommodation is not deemed to be a registered care home and so does not have to be registered as such under the relevant legislation.[143] The care provider will, however, generally be required to be registered with the Care Quality Commission. A consequence of not being a registered care home is that those living in such schemes are entitled to claim housing benefit – and crucially housing benefit at higher rates than for non-disabled people.[144] Such

---

140 Mansell highlights the failure, not of the concept, but of 'management and leadership' noting that all too often the problem has been 'wrong buildings, in the wrong places, with the wrong furnishings, staffed by people with the wrong training, managed according to the wrong rules, with the wrong policies, the wrong leadership and the wrong purposes' – see J Mansell, 'The "implementation gap" in supported accommodation for people with intellectual disabilities', foreword to Clement and Bigby, *Group Homes for People with Intellectual Disabilities: Encouraging Inclusion and Participation*, Jessica Kingsley, 2009.

141 Research suggests that significant savings can be made by moving people with learning disabilities into supported living – see Local Government Association, *Learning Disability Services Efficiency Project Interim position report*, 2015.

142 P Kinsella, *Supported living: a new paradigm*, National Development Team, 1993.

143 Health and Social Care Act 2008 (Regulated Activities) Regulations 2014 SI No 2936.

144 Most supported living schemes access higher rates of housing benefit as they are 'exempt accommodation – ie exempt from the general cap on housing benefit by virtue of the maximum 'local reference' rent – Housing Benefit and Council Tax Benefit (Consequential Provisions) Regulations 2006 SI No 217 Sch 3 para 4(10) – ie accommodation provided by a non-metropolitan county

schemes require, however, that the housing body provides care, support or supervision for the tenant.[145]

10.79   Where a local authority has determined that a person has a need that it proposes to meet by way of a supported living arrangement, the individual has the right to 'express a preference' for a particular accommodation[146] and the local authority is required to provide or arrange that accommodation – even if it is in another local authority's area. If the cost of the placement is more than the authority considers necessary, then it can require a 'top-up' payment from a third party to cover the additional cost.[147] Where a local authority funds a supported living package in the area of another authority, the disabled person is 'deemed' to be ordinarily resident in the funding authority's area (ie its continuing responsibility) even though in fact they are resident elsewhere if the accommodation meets the criteria set down in regulations.[148]

10.80   For the purposes of the ordinary residence[149] and choice of accommodation provisions,[150] 'supported living accommodation' means:

(1) (a) accommodation in premises which are specifically designed or adapted for occupation by adults with needs for care and support to enable them to live as independently as possible; and

(b) accommodation which is provided–

(i) in premises which are intended for occupation by adults with needs for care and support (whether or not the premises are specifically designed or adapted for that purpose), and

council in England; a housing association (as defined in Housing Associations Act 1985 s1(1)); a registered charity (as defined in Charities Act 2006 Part 1), or voluntary organisation (as defined in Housing Benefit Regulations 2006 SI No 213 reg 2(1)); see also Commissioner's decisions CH/423/2006, CH/3811/2006 and CH/779/2007 – the 'Turnbull' decision.

145 For example, the provision of an alarm; help ensuring rent is paid; liaising with all relevant agencies, both statutory and voluntary, on the tenant's behalf; assisting people to claim housing benefit and other welfare benefits; helping to keep people safe by monitoring visitors, including contractors and professionals, and by carrying out health and safety and risk assessments of property.

146 Care Act 2014 s30(1).

147 The Care and Support and After-care (Choice of Accommodation) Regulations 2014 SI No 2670.

148 The Care and Support (Ordinary Residence) (Specified Accommodation) Regulations 2014 SI No 2828.

149 The Care and Support (Ordinary Residence) (Specified Accommodation) Regulations 2014 reg 5.

150 The Care and Support and After-care (Choice of Accommodation) Regulations 2014 reg 8.

(ii) in circumstances in which personal care is available if required.

(2) The accommodation referred to in paragraph (1)(a) does not include adapted premises where the adult had occupied those premises as their home before the adaptations were made.

(3) For the purposes of paragraph (1)(b)(ii) personal care may be provided by a person other than the person who provides the accommodation.

Shared lives accommodation/adult placement schemes

10.81   Shared lives (previously known as adult placement) is a care support arrangement that has historically focussed on supporting people with learning disabilities but increasingly is used for the support of a much wider range of individuals 'in need'.

10.82   In general, it applies to adults but schemes can and do cover 16–17-year-olds. As at 2015, there were over 150 shared lives schemes in the UK with over 8,000 shared lives carers.[151] It is the scheme that is registered and regulated in England by the Care Quality Commission.[152] Schemes are most typically local authority led.

10.83   The dramatic growth in shared lives schemes (14 per cent in 2015)[153] is almost certainly due to the significant cost savings they deliver[154] although there is also evidence concerning its potential to materially improve individual wellbeing.[155]

10.84   The purpose of shared lives schemes is to enable the person to live as independently and to have as normal a life in the community as is possible. Placements may be long term or as a transitional arrangement. The individual shares family and community life with the shared lives carer. About half of shared lives arrangements involve

---

151 See generally information at Shared Lives Plus, *What is Shared Lives?*, 2015.

152 Health and Social Care Act 2008 (Regulated Activities) Regulations 2010 SI No 781; Care Quality Commission (Registration) Regulations 2009 SI No 3112 – and see generally The Care Quality Commission, *Supporting Information – Shared Lives schemes*, CQC, 2013.

153 Shared Lives Plus, *What is Shared Lives?*, 2015.

154 See for example Shared Lives Plus, *A Shared Life is a Healthy Life How the Shared Lives model of care can improve health outcomes and support the NHS*, 2015, and The Institute for Research and Innovation in Social Service, *Money matters: Case Study One Shared Lives*, IRISS, 2011.

155 See for example, Shared Lives Plus, *A Shared Life is a Healthy Life How the Shared Lives model of care can improve health outcomes and support the NHS*, 2015.

the disabled person living with their shared lives carer and half visit their shared lives carer for day support or overnight breaks.[156]

10.85   As with supported living placements (see paras 10.76–10.80 above) where a local authority has determined that a person has a need that it proposes to meet by way of a Shared Lives arrangement, the individual has the right to 'express a preference' for a particular accommodation (Care Act 2014 s30(1)) and the local authority is required to provide or arrange that accommodation – even if it is in another local authority area. If the cost of the placement is more than the authority considers necessary, then it can require a 'top-up' payment from a third party to cover the additional cost.[157] Where a local authority funds a Shared Lives package in the area of another local authority, the disabled person is 'deemed' to be ordinarily resident in the funding authority's area (ie its continuing responsibility) even though in fact they are resident elsewhere.[158]

10.86   For the purposes of the ordinary residence[159] and choice of accommodation provisions,[160] 'shared lives scheme accommodation' means:

accommodation which is provided for an adult by a shared lives carer, and for this purpose–

'shared lives carer' means an individual who, under the terms of a shared lives agreement, provides, or intends to provide, personal care for adults together with, where necessary, accommodation in the individual's home;

'shared lives agreement' means an agreement entered into between a person carrying on a shared lives scheme and an individual for the provision, by that individual, of personal care to an adult together with, where necessary, accommodation in the individual's home; and

'shared lives scheme' means a scheme carried on (whether or not for profit) by a local authority or other person for the purposes of–

(a) recruiting and training shared lives carers;

(b) making arrangements for the placing of adults with shared lives carers; and

(c) supporting and monitoring placements.

---

156 Shared Lives Plus, *What is Shared Lives?*, 2015.

157 Care and Support and After-care (Choice of Accommodation) Regulations 2014 SI No 2670.

158 Care and Support (Ordinary Residence) (Specified Accommodation) Regulations 2014 SI No 2828.

159 Care and Support (Ordinary Residence) (Specified Accommodation) Regulations 2014 reg 4.

160 Care and Support and After-care (Choice of Accommodation) Regulations 2014 reg 7.

10.87   CA 1989 s23CZA enables local authorities to extend the foster care placements of care leavers beyond the age of 18 (and in this respect see also CA 1989 Sch 2 para 19B and para 19BA).

Residential care

10.88   For some disabled young people, particularly those with profound and enduring impairments, a placement in a registered care home (with or without nursing) will be the most appropriate care and support arrangement which meets their needs. Such placements have the advantage of being inspected by the Care Quality Commission and are (perhaps) less likely to result in sudden changes: in supported living placements, there is a risk of the local authority changing the care provider with little advance notice. It is important, however, that residential care is a genuine choice and is not forced on the young person by any policies or decisions of the public authority, for example, a policy capping the level of care provided at home at the cost of a residential placement.[161]

10.89   Disabled young people in registered care placements have the right to the full range of support services to meet their needs (ie appropriate daycare/community based supports). As with supported living placements (see paras 10.76–10.80 above) where a local authority has determined that a person has a need that it proposes to meet by way of a residential care arrangement, the individual has the right to 'express a preference' for a particular accommodation[162] and the local authority is required to provide or arrange that accommodation – even if it is in another local authority area. If the cost of the care home is more than the authority considers necessary, then it can require a 'top-up' payment from a third party to cover the additional cost.[163] Where a local authority funds a care home in the area of another local authority, the disabled person is 'deemed' to be ordinarily resident in the funding authority's area (ie its continuing responsibility) even though in fact they are resident elsewhere.[164]

---

161   See the Care and Support Statutory Guidance at para 11.22: 'Local authorities should not have arbitrary ceilings to personal budgets that result in people being forced to accept to move into care homes against their will'.

162   Care Act 2014 s30(1).

163   Care and Support and After-care (Choice of Accommodation) Regulations 2014.

164   Care and Support (Ordinary Residence) (Specified Accommodation) Regulations 2014.

Higher education – disabled student allowances

10.90   As support for disabled young people in further education is now governed primarily by EHC plans which can extend to 25, issues in relation to further education are considered in the Education chapter (see chapter 4).[165]

10.91   For those disabled students able to access higher education,[166] disabled student allowances (DSAs) are grants to help meet the extra course costs students can face as a direct result of a disability, ongoing health condition, mental health condition or specific learning difficulty.[167] DSAs can be used to meet a wide range of additional disability-related costs, including:

- specialist equipment needed for studying – for example, computer software;
- non-medical helpers, such as a note-taker or reader;
- extra travel costs resulting from a student's disability; and
- other costs – for example, tapes or Braille paper.[168]

10.92   The amount of support available through a DSA is dependent on the extent of the person's needs, not their financial circumstances. As at July 2015 the maximum general allowance was £1,741 a year for full-time students and £1,305 a year for part-time students. More significant specific amounts are also available in respect of the provision of specialist equipment and the funding of a non-medical helper[169] to support the student.[170]

10.93   It is important to note that the availability of financial support through DSAs does not absolve higher education providers of their responsibilities under the Equality Act 2010, and in particular their duties to make reasonable adjustments to ensure equality of access for disabled people. These duties are considered at para 9.82 onwards.

---

165 See also chapter 7 of the SEND Code, which deals specifically with the application of the scheme under Part 3 of the Children and Families Act 2014 to further education.

166 See the SEND Code at paras 8.43–8.48 in relation to transition to higher education generally.

167 See www.direct.gov.uk/dsas.

168 See www.direct.gov.uk/dsas.

169 Readers, sign-language interpreters, notetakers and other non-medical assistants.

170 Applications should be made to local authorities using the form DSA1 (disabled students' allowance form), which can be downloaded from the www.direct.gov.uk site.

Indeed the government's policy intention[171] is to reduce availability of DSAs and require higher education institutions to do more by way of reasonable adjustments to ensure that disabled students can access courses on an equal basis to others. Any changes to the DSAs scheme to deliver this policy intention are likely to come into force for the academic year 2016/17. If proposals put out to consultation are taken forward it is likely that only more specialist forms of non-medical help will be routinely available through DSAs in future.

171 See *Disabled students in higher education: funding proposals*, a consultation by the Department for Business, Innovation and Skills which ran from 1 July 2015 to 24 September 2015.

Remedies

continued

Key points

- There are a number of different statutory complaints procedures to deal with disputes relating to education, health and social care.
- The Local Government Ombudsman or Parliamentary and Health Ombudsman is able to investigate complaints about certain matters and has wide ranging powers to make recommendations to remedy injustice including an apology or compensation.
- The First-tier Tribunal (Special Educational Needs and Disability) hears appeals against decisions relating to education, health and care plans (EHC plans) and statements of special educational needs (SEN). This includes refusals to assess or make an EHC plan or statement or to make amendments following annual review. Tribunal claims must be issued within two months of the date of the local authority's decision letter.
- Mediation must be considered before appeals in relation to SEN and provision can be issued with the tribunal. Parents and young people can request mediation in relation to the education, health or social care provision which is in the EHC plan.
- Local authorities are also under a duty to offer dispute resolution arrangements to avoid or resolve disputes.
- If a child or young person has been discriminated against in school, a claim can be brought to the tribunal within six months of the discriminatory act.
- Judicial review is the legal procedure used to challenge decision-making of public bodies in relation to health or social care provision or where special educational provision which is specified in an EHC plan or statement is not being delivered and some other education decisions or failures to act. Judicial reviews must be brought promptly and within three months of the date of the decision.
- Claims in relation to disability discrimination against an early year's provider, further education college or local authority must be made in the county court.
- Legal aid remains available to support disabled children and their parents and young people to access legal advice and assistance in relation to most education, health and social care decisions.

Introduction

11.1   This chapter describes the varying and wide-ranging ways that disabled children and their families can challenge failures and decisions of public bodies. Alongside the traditional remedies such as complaints, the ombudsman and judicial review, this chapter also considers the procedures under the Children and Families Act (CFA) 2014 Part 3, including the introduction of a pilot scheme in the First-tier Tribunal (Special Educational Needs and Disability) (the tribunal) to make recommendations in respect of health and social care disputes, and new rights to independent mediation and disagreement resolution aimed at promoting the early resolution of disagreements at a local level.

11.2   Which route will provide the most effective remedy will depend on a number of factors including:

- whether the matter relates to education, health or social care;
- the type of decision which has been made and whether a specific appeal right has been triggered;
- what the individual wants to achieve through seeking redress;
- the urgency and seriousness of the issue; and
- the funding options available.

11.3   In all cases, it is important to identify from the outset the specific decision or failure which is being challenged and the date that it occurred as there are time limits for most types of remedy.

11.4   It should also be appreciated that there are many non-legal ways of resolving disputes/differences of view, which should always be investigated if at all possible. In exploring these options, as long as legal time limits are not missed, legal rights are not lost (although if a judicial review is being considered, a lawyer should always be consulted first on this question). In many cases (as this chapter explains), mediation must be considered before other legal options become available.

11.5   Disagreement resolution/conciliation/mediation may take different forms, but the essentials are that: (i) they should involve an independent person who has no vested interest in the outcome; (ii) the process must be voluntary; and (iii) unlike with tribunals, courts and arbitration, the independent person's role is to help find a solution acceptable to both parties. They are there to facilitate this and do not have the power to decide the outcome.

Complaints procedures

11.6 Where a disabled child or their family wish to challenge a decision by a public body or educational provider, then formal procedures exist to ensure that these complaints are considered properly.

11.7 A key consideration when deciding whether to pursue a complaint or make a legal challenge is the time it takes for it to be considered and whether it is likely to provide an effective remedy. For example, where the need is urgent the complaints process may be inappropriate (unless the authority has a 'fast track' procedure) whereas an application for interim relief through a judicial review (see below) may be the only effective remedy. In contrast, if an individual wishes to obtain financial redress or an apology for a past delay but where services are now in place then a complaint (if necessary, escalated to the ombudsman) is very likely to be a more effective remedy than a challenge by way of judicial review where the court does not generally have a power to award compensation.[1]

Complaints about children's social care provision

11.8 Local authorities are under a statutory duty to have a procedure for complaints made in relation to the discharge of its functions under the Children Act (CA) 1989, Part 3.[2] This covers such matters as assessments, care planning, reviews, support and services (including for example respite/short breaks support, adaptations, equipment, direct payments) for (among others) disabled children, parent carers and young carers (see chapter 3).

11.9 Complaints may be made by any child or young person 'in need'[3] or by a parent or someone who has parental responsibility. They can also be made by any other person that the local authority considers has sufficient interest in the child or young person's welfare, for example a grandparent. If a child or young person wishes to make a complaint, local authorities are required to provide them with information about advocacy services and offer help to obtain an advocate.

11.10 Generally, complaints must be made within one year of the matter which is the subject of the complaint, although local authorities have a discretion to consider complaints beyond this time limit where it

---

1 Compensation may be awarded if a person's human rights have been breached.
2 Children Act 1989 Representations Procedure (England) Regulations 2006 SI No 1738. Enabling powers: Children Act 1989 ss24D, 26, 26A and 59; Sch 7.
3 See para 3.13 above; a term that includes disabled children and young carers.

is possible to consider it effectively and efficiently or there are good reasons for not bringing the case earlier.

11.11   Where possible, complaints letters should be succinct and should explain in simple terms what the local authority is expected to do as a result of the complaint. The website of the voluntary organisation, Cerebra, provides a precedent children's social services complaint letter as well as a 'toolkit' that outlines problem solving techniques that can be useful in such cases.[4]

11.12   The complaints procedure includes three distinct stages that must be completed within specific timescales, although local authorities remain under a duty to act expeditiously throughout the procedure. Detailed guidance on the procedure for each stage of the complaint can be found in the statutory guidance from the Department of Education and Skills, *Getting the best from complaints: social care complaints and representations from children, young people and others*, 2006 ('the complaints statutory guidance').

11.13   A summary of the procedure and timetables as detailed in the complaints statutory guidance is set out in the table below at para 11.18.

11.14   Local authorities have wide powers to remedy their failings in individual cases, including:

- apologising and/or giving an explanation of what occurred;
- providing conciliation and mediation;[5]
- reassessing the needs of the child/young person/carer;
- taking practical action specific to the particular complainant;
- undertaking a wider review of its practice;
- ensuring that it will monitor the effectiveness of its remedy; and
- providing financial redress – for example, where there has been a quantifiable loss, a loss of a non-monetary benefit, loss of value, lost opportunity, distress; and for time and trouble.[6]

11.15   The complaints statutory guidance[7] also suggests that where the complaint is about a proposed change to a care plan, a placement

---

4 Accessible at https://w3.cerebra.org.uk/help-and-information/legal-entitlements-research-project/precedent-letters/.

5 These are different forms of dispute resolution; where conciliation is more informal, mediation is a formal process which aims to result in a binding agreement between the parties.

6 Local Government Act 2000 s92.

7 Department of Education and Skills, *Getting the best from complaints: social care complaints and representations from children, young people and others*, 2006.

or a service, the decision may need to be deferred (frozen) until the complaint is considered and that:

> ... there should generally be a presumption in favour of freezing, unless there is a good reason against it (for example, if leaving a child or young person where they are would put them at risk).[8]

11.16 There is a separate complaints procedure for complaints made about adult social care. The Citizens Advice Bureau's website provides a precedent adult social services complaint letter as well has a guide to 'complaining about social services'.[9]

Complaints about healthcare provision

11.17 NHS organisations must make arrangements for dealing with complaints about the provision of healthcare services (including services for disabled children). The detail of these procedures are set out in regulations.[10]

11.18 The regulations specify the requirements for complaints handling, which include:

- That each NHS body must make arrangements for the handling and consideration of complaints to ensure that complaints are dealt with efficiently and are properly investigated and that complaints are treated with respect and courtesy, that they receive a timely and appropriate response and action is taken if necessary in light of the outcome.
- The need to identify a 'responsible person': the regulations state that this should be the chief executive officer and a 'complaints manager' (who may be the same person) to deal with complaints.
- That complaints may be made by a person who receives or has received services from a responsible body; or a person who is affected, or likely to be affected, by the action, omission or decision of the responsible body which is the subject of the complaint. Alternatively, a complaint may be made by a person acting on behalf of a child or young person if they lack capacity within the meaning of the Mental Capacity Act (MCA) 2005.

---

8 Complaints Statutory Guidance, para 6.5.2.

9 Accessible at www.citizensadvice.org.uk/healthcare/nhs-and-social-care-complaints/complaining-about-social-care-services/.

10 Local Authority Social Services and National Health Service Complaints (England) Regulations 2009 SI No 309 pursuant to the enabling powers in the Health and Social Care (Community Health and Standards) Act 2003.

Table 1: Complaints procedure for children's social care timetables

Stage	Procedure	Timescale
1. Local resolution	• Complaint is made verbally or in writing on the date it is first received by the local authority. • Staff at the point of service delivery should seek to address as quickly as possible although can agree to move straight to Stage two. • Complaints manager should be informed of outcome and letter should be written to complainant offering right to request reconsideration at Stage two.	10 working days – can be extended by a maximum of a further 10 working days for more complex decisions or if an advocate is required.
2. Investigation	• Complaints manager should arrange for a full and considered investigation of the complaint without delay. • The local authority must appoint an investigating officer (IO) and an independent person (IP). The IO will prepare a written report which should include: – details of findings, conclusions and outcomes are against each point of complaint (i.e. 'upheld' or 'not upheld'; and – recommendations on how to remedy any injustice to the complainant as appropriate. • Good practice states that the IP should also provide a report once he has read the IO's final report. • A senior manager acting as adjudicating officer should then consider the complaints, the IO and IP reports and prepare a response with his decision and actions it will take with timescales – this is the adjudication. • The local authority should then write to the complainant with its response enclosing the IO and IP reports and the adjudication.	The time limit for completing stage two is 25 working days – can be extended to a maximum of 65 working days where there are several agencies or a key witness is unavailable.
	• If the complainant is dissatisfied with the response they have a right to request further consideration at a review panel.	Request must be made within 20 working days.

3. Review panel	• The purpose of the review panel is to consider the adequacy of the Stage two investigation and reach findings and recommendations to try to reach a resolution. • It must consist of three independent people and the complainant has a right to attend. • The review panel should not reinvestigate the complaints or consider substantively new complaints not considered at Stage two. • The guidance suggests that no party should feel they need to be represented by lawyers and states 'and the presence of lawyers can work against the spirit of openness and problem-solving'.[a] • However, the complainant has a right to bring a representative to speak to his/her behalf. • The standard of proof applied by panels should be the civil standard of 'balance of probabilities'. • The review panel must act in accordance with the United Nations Convention on the Rights of the Child and the best interests of the child or young person should be prioritised at all times.[b] • The wishes and feelings of the child and young people should be ascertained, recorded and taken into account	The local authority must convene and hold the review panel within 30 working days of request. Panel papers should be sent to panellists and other attendees, including complainant at least 10 working days before the review panel meets.
After the panel	• Review panel issue a written report of its findings containing a brief summary of the representations and their recommendations for resolution of the issues	Within five working days of panel meeting
	• Local authority must respond to the findings and advise complainant of right to refer complaint to ombudsman.	Within 15 working days

a Complaints Statutory Guidance, para 3.10.3.
b Complaints Statutory Guidance, para 3.11.3.

- The requirement for organisations to co-operate when dealing with a complaint that spans more than one organisation.
- That the complaint should be made within 12 months of either the event being complained about or as soon as the matter came to the attention of the complainant. This time limit can be extended where there are good reasons as long as the complaint can still be investigated effectively and fairly.
- That the complaint must be acknowledged no later than three working days after the day the complaint is received.
- That the complaint must be investigated in an appropriate manner to resolve it speedily and efficiently and, as soon as reasonably practicable after completing the investigation, must send a response to the complainant in writing which includes:
  - an explanation of how the complaint has been considered; and
  - the conclusions reached and whether any remedial action needed.
- That the response must be sent within six months of the date the complaint was agreed unless the NHS body notifies the complainant in writing and explains the reason for the delay.
- The requirement to tell the complainant of their right to put the complaint to the ombudsman if dissatisfied.

11.19   Unlike the statutory procedure for complaints to children's social care services, the regulations regarding NHS complaints (which also apply to complaints in relation to adult social care) do not have specific stages and timescales or any requirement for an independent person.

11.20   If an individual requires support in making the complaint then the NHS is under a duty to provide free and confidential independent advocacy through its NHS Complaints Advocacy Service.[11]

11.21   The Citizens Advice Bureau's website provides a precedent adult social services complaint letter as well has a guide to the 'NHS complaints procedure'.[12]

---

11   National Health Service Act 2006 s248.
12   Accessible at www.citizensadvice.org.uk/healthcare/nhs-and-social-care-complaints/.

Complaints about education

11.22   The foreword from the Local Government Ombudsman Focus Report, *Special Educational Needs: preparing for the future* (March 2014), stated that:

> A common phrase I hear from families when seeking to resolve a complaint about SEN provision is that it feels like a constant battle. It should not have to be this way.

11.23   Often the first challenge for a parent or young person who wishes to complain about inadequacies with education provision is knowing which route to pursue.

11.24   Where a disabled child or their family wish to challenge a decision in respect of special educational needs provision, for example, the contents of an EHC plan, it will usually be more appropriate to pursue disagreement resolution/mediation procedures or an appeal to tribunal (see below) as a formal complaint is unlikely to achieve the outcome required.

11.25   However, where the educational issue cannot appropriately be dealt with through those procedures, complaints in relation to educational issues can be considered by a variety of organisations.

11.26   The starting point will almost always be to use the school or college's internal complaints procedure; the specific requirements for which will vary depending on the type of educational setting but in each case there is a legal process that must be followed.[13]

11.27   If it is not possible to resolve the matter at a local level then there are a number of bodies who are able to investigate complaints as follows:

The responsible local authority

11.28   All local authorities have statutory duties to consider complaints about certain decisions including:

- school admission appeals;[14]
- exclusions;[15]

---

13   The requirements for complaints procedures in academies, free schools and independent schools are set out in Education (Independent School Standards) (England) Regulations 2010 SI No 1997 Part 7; for Early Years providers the requirements are set out in the Early Years Foundation Stage (EYFS) Statutory Framework and for maintained schools under Education Act 2002 s29.

14   School Standards and Framework Act 1998 s94.

15   Education Act 2002 s51A and School Discipline (Pupil Exclusions and Reviews) (England) Regulations 2012 SI No 1033.

- child protection/allegations of abuse;[16]
- school transport.[17]

11.29   All of these decisions also have a further right of complaint to the Local Government Ombudsman if the individual remains dissatisfied following the local authorities' decision (see below at paras 11.36–11.43).

11.30   Local authorities do not have to consider complaints about academies, free schools or independent schools as these educational institutions are independent of the local authority. Complaints about academies and free schools should be addressed to the Education Funding Agency, see below at para 11.32.

Department for Education's (DfE) School Complaints Unit

11.31   The Secretary of State for Education can investigate complaints that either the governing body of a maintained school or a local authority has acted unreasonably or has failed to carry out one of its duties.[18] His officials can also consider complaints about disability discrimination in relation to a pupil at a school.[19] The secretary of state will not intervene in a case where there is another avenue of redress, such as the tribunal.[20] The DfE cannot investigate individual complaints about an independent/private schools but does have powers as a regulator if the school is not meeting required standards in respect of education, welfare etc.[21]

The Education Funding Agency

11.32   The Education Funding Agency investigates complaints about academies and free schools. Part of its role is to make sure academies comply with the terms of their funding agreement which is a contract between the academy and the secretary of state.[22]

---

16   Children Act 1989 s47.
17   Department for Education *'Home to school travel and transport guidance'* statutory guidance for local authorities, July 2014.
18   Education Act 1996 ss496–497.
19   Equality Act 2010 s87.
20   SEND Code, para 11.75.
21   Education Act 2002 s165.
22   See *Education Funding Agency, Procedure for dealing with complaints about academies,* 2013.

Office for Standards in Education, Children's Services and Skills (Ofsted)

11.33   Ofsted can consider complaints about early years' provision and schools where the complaint is about the educational institution as a whole rather than in relation to an individual child and can respond by bringing forward an inspection to look at the issues raised.[23]

Skills Funding Agency

11.34   The Skills Funding Agency, on behalf of the Secretary of State for Education will investigate complaints about further education colleges, apprenticeships and post-19 education and training.[24]

The Information Commissioner

11.35   The Information Commissioner can consider complaints on behalf of parents and young people in relation to access to information in educational establishments including issues such as examination results, taking photos in schools and accessing pupil and official information.[25]

Ombudsmen

11.36   Where an individual has followed the local authority or NHS complaints procedures and the complaint remains unresolved, the complainant can ask for a further investigation by the Local Government Ombudsman (LGO) (where the complaint relates to the local authority or schools) or by the Parliamentary and Health Service Ombudsman (PHSO) (for NHS bodies and government departments). The LGO and PHSO can also carry out joint investigations, for example, where the complaint relates to concerns about the delivery of health provision within an EHC plan. The PHSO can also investigate a number of other organisations: Ofsted, the Education Funding Agency, the Skills Funding Agency, and the Department for Education (including its School Complaints Unit and the Secretary of State

---

23   Education (Investigation of Parents' Complaints) (England) Regulations 2007 SI No 1089 and Education Act 2005, as amended by Education and Inspections Act 2006 s160.

24   For further information see Skills Funding Agency, *Procedure for dealing with complaints about Providers of Education and Training*.

25   See https://ico.org.uk/for-the-public/schools/.

for Education). Both the LGO and the PHSO will generally expect the individual to have completed the organisation's own complaints procedure first.

11.37   A complainant retains the right to approach the ombudsman at any time during the course of the complaint (for example if the complaint is not being investigated fairly or expeditiously). However, the ombudsman would ordinarily expect the local authority or NHS body to consider the complaint initially and may refer the complaint back to the relevant complaints manager if this has not been done. All complaints should usually be made within 12 months of becoming aware of the issue, unless there are good reasons to extend the timeframe. The ombudsman aims to make a decision on whether they will investigate the complaint within 20 working days and in most cases come to a final decision within three months although this will generally be longer in complex cases.

11.38   When deciding what remedy is likely to be most effective, it is important to consider that the ombudsman's remit is only to investigate allegations of 'maladministration'[26] by public bodies which have resulted in some form of injustice. This is different to the test of 'unlawfulness' which is necessary for legal challenges (for example by way of a judicial review). For example, the public body may not have acted 'unlawfully' but its behaviour could have been sufficiently unreasonable that it amounted to maladministration and, in these circumstances, a complaint to the ombudsman would be more appropriate.

11.39   The ombudsman will not consider a complaint where there is an alternative remedy such as tribunal, and importantly, will not (save for limited exceptional circumstances) consider a complaint where legal proceedings have already been commenced.

11.40   The ombudsman does have significant powers that in some cases may provide a better remedy for a disabled child and their family than judicial review. These include recommending that the public body:

- apologises;
- provides a service the disabled child should have had;
- makes a decision that it should have done before;

---

26 The LGO considers that maladministration can include: delay; incorrect action or failure to take any action; failure to follow procedures or the law; failure to provide information; inadequate record-keeping; failure to investigate; failure to reply; misleading or inaccurate statements; inadequate liaison; inadequate consultation; and broken promises; see www.lgo.org.uk/guide-for-advisers/ maladministration-service-failure/.

- reconsiders a decision that it did not take properly in the first place;
- improves its procedures so similar problems do not happen again;
- makes a payment.

11.41 Recent examples of successful complaints to the ombudsman include:

- **School transport:** The complaint alleged that the local authority had wrongly decided to discontinue school transport after the family were forced to move. The family stated that the school transport appeal did not take account of all relevant information. The ombudsman upheld the complaint and found fault causing injustice and recommended the local authority should take the following actions:
  - apologise to the parents
  - put in place home-school transport for the couple's daughter as soon as possible;
  - pay the parents £1,000 to reimburse the costs they incurred as a result of the council's faults; and
  - pay the parents a further £1,000 to acknowledge the avoidable stress the council's faults caused the family.[27]
- **Children's social care:** The complaint alleged that there had been an 11 month delay by a local authority in paying a personal budget to the mother of a disabled child to enable the child to take part in leisure activities. In finding maladministration, the ombudsman recommended that the local authority:
  - pay the mother the original personal budget figure for the 12-month period on a backdated basis; and
  - pay a sum of £2,000 to the mother to recognise the lost opportunity for the child to take part in activities and the mother's time and trouble in pursuing the matter.[28]
- **Health:** the mother of a nine-year-old child with autism made a complaint to the PHSO following delays in arranging a full autistic spectrum disorder assessment following a referral from CAMHS which led to the mother paying for a private assessment. The PHSO found that the waiting time was far longer than the three-month wait specified in relevant guidelines from the National Institute for Health and Care Excellence. Although it

27 Devon County Council (14 009 771).
28 Trafford Council (14 002 965).

found that the Trust was not under an obligation to reimburse the costs of the private treatment, the Trust paid £500 to the mother in recognition of the impact of its poor communication regarding the waiting times and steps it was taking to address them.[29]

11.42   Making a complaint to the ombudsman can, therefore, offer advantages over a legal challenge: not only can the ombudsman make wide recommendations but the process is free and does not expose an individual to the risks of adverse costs if the complaint is not upheld (see para 11.75 below).

11.43   Although a public body does not have to comply with the recommendations in the same way that a court order would be binding, in the vast majority of cases it will, and where a public body fails to comply with the recommendations of an ombudsman that decision could be challenged by way of a judicial review.

Disagreement resolution arrangements

11.44   Since 1 September 2014, local authorities are now under a legal duty to make arrangements with a view to avoiding or resolving disagreements with the parents of disabled children and young people in relation to EHC needs assessments, the preparation and review of review of EHC plans, and re-assessment of educational, health care and social care needs.[30] Local authorities are also under duties to avoid or resolve disagreement between the parents of a child with SEN or young person with SEN and the school or post 16-institution. This process can also be used to resolve disagreements between local authorities and health commissioning bodies that do not involve parents and young people.

11.45   Details of each local authorities' disagreement resolution arrangements should be set out in its local offer (see para 4.72 above). The process must be independent of the local authority and its use is voluntary and must be with the agreement of all parties. Dispute resolution services should be available to be used by all children with SEN (not just those with an EHC plan) and will cover disagreements about any aspect of SEN provision, and any health and social care disagreements that arise during the EHC needs assessment and EHC planning process.

29 Summary 447/ September 2014.
30 CFA 2014 s57.

11.46   The Special Educational Needs and Disability Code of Practice
(SEND Code)[31] states that these services:

> ... can provide a quick and non-adversarial way of resolving disagree-
> ments. Used early in the process of EHC needs assessment and EHC
> plan development they can prevent the need for mediation, once deci-
> sions have been taken in that process, and appeals to the Tribunal.

11.47   Where disagreement resolution is being considered, parents and
young people should ensure that any process is completed in sufficient time to enable them to pursue a legal remedy such as tribunal
or judicial review within the legal time limits if resolution does not
prove possible. The SEND Code states that disagreement resolution
services can be used whilst waiting for tribunal appeals to narrow
issues or reach partial agreement.[32] Disagreement resolution meetings are confidential and without prejudice to the tribunal process.

Mediation

11.48   CFA 2014 Part 3 introduced new rights and requirements in relation to mediation. Mediation is a formal disagreement resolution process where the parties seek to achieve a binding agreement with the
assistance of an independent mediator.

11.49   In particular, where a decision is made against which an appeal to
the tribunal may be brought (see below) or an EHC plan for a child or
young person is made, amended or replaced, then parents and young
people now have a right to mediation.[33] The right to mediation also
extends to mediation in relation to the health and social care parts of
the EHC plan even where there is no tribunal appeal right in relation
to the same.

11.50   However, with this new right, also comes a new requirement
to 'consider mediation' and obtain a mediation certificate from a
mediation adviser before an appeal to the tribunal can be lodged.
The mediation adviser must be contacted within two months after
written notice of the decision is received.[34]

---

31 Department for Education, *Special educational needs and disability code of
practice: 0 to 25 years*, 2014, para 11.7.
32 SEND Code, para 11.8.
33 CFA 2014 s52.
34 SEND Regs 2014 SI No 1530 reg 33. If a parent fails to comply with reg 33 and
the time for obtaining a mediation certificate has elapsed, leave to appeal to the
tribunal may still be sought; see reg 34(3) and Tribunal Procedure (First-tier
Tribunal) (Health, Education and Social Care Chamber) Rules 2008 SI No 2699
r19.

11.51   Importantly, these new rules do not mean that a parent or young person must participate in mediation before they can appeal, only that they must *consider* it after receiving information from a mediation adviser. The SEND Code states that:

> The mediation information which is given to parents and young people:
> • should be factual and unbiased, and
> • should not seek to pressure them into going to mediation. Where there is more than one available, the mediation adviser should not try to persuade the parents or young people to use any particular mediator.[35]

11.52   The mediation adviser must then issue a certificate within three working days of either being informed by the parent or young person that they do not wish to pursue mediation or the conclusion mediation that has been pursued. This will then enable the parents or young person to proceed with the tribunal appeal.

11.53   There is no requirement to consider mediation where the appeal solely relates to a challenge in respect of the school or other institution named in the EHC plan. The mediation advice arrangements also do not apply to disability discrimination claims.

11.54   Mediation must be conducted by an independent person and the public body arranging it must ensure that it is attended by someone who has authority to resolve the issues in dispute.[36] It may be attended by any advocate or other supporter that the child's parent or the young person wishes to attend.[37] This can include legal representation although each party would have to pay for it themselves. The mediator must take reasonable steps to ascertain the wishes of the child or young person. Mediators must have sufficient knowledge of the legislation relating to special educational needs, health and social care to be able to conduct the mediation[38] and must have received accredited training.[39]

11.55   Where a parent or young person wishes to pursue mediation then they must inform the local authority and confirm the issues that they wish to pursue at mediation. If this includes an issue in relation to health care provision in the EHC plan, or the fact there is no health care provision in the EHC plan, the parent or young person must also

---

35 SEND Code, para 11.21.
36 SEND Regs 2014 reg 37.
37 SEND Regs 2014 reg 38.
38 SEND Regs 2014 reg 40.
39 SEND Code, para 11.15.

inform the local authority what health care provision they wish to be specified in the plan and the local authority must notify the relevant commissioning body (generally the clinical commissioning group) within three working days.[40] If the mediation issues are limited to healthcare provision, the commissioning body must arrange the mediation and ensure it is conducted by an independent person and must participate in the mediation.[41]

11.56   If the mediation includes any educational and social care issues, then the local authority must arrange it within 30 days of being informed that the parent or young person wishes to pursue mediation.[42]

11.57   The body responsible for arranging mediation must pay travel costs, loss of earnings, child care and any overnight expenses of the child's parent or young person at a prescribed rate provided prior agreement is obtained where required and upon receipt of supporting evidence of the expenses claimed.[43] The mediation adviser should provide this information to parents and young people.

11.58   The mediation session should be arranged, in discussion with the parents or young people, at a place and a time which is convenient for the parties to the disagreement. The body (or bodies) arranging the mediation must inform the parent or young person of the date and place of the mediation at least five working days before the mediation unless the parent or young person consents to this period of time being reduced.[44]

11.59   The outcome of the mediation must be recorded in writing in a 'mediation agreement' and where the agreement requires the local authority or responsible commissioning group to do something, it must do that thing either within the timescales set out for complying with a tribunal order on the same issue, or, where that doesn't apply, within two weeks of the date of the mediation agreement.[45]

---

40 SEND Regs 2014 reg 35.
41 SEND Regs 2014 reg 35.
42 SEND Regs 2014 reg 36.
43 SEND Regs 2014 reg 41.
44 SEND Regs 2014 reg 37.
45 SEND Regs 2014 reg 42.

Tribunal

11.60   The tribunal has jurisdiction to hear appeals and claims by parents and young people in relation to:

- special educational needs and provision;
- disability discrimination.

11.61   As noted below (paras 11.75–11.80), there is a pilot scheme to allow the tribunal to hear appeals in relation to social care and health provision in the context of EHC plans, although with limited powers of redress in those cases.

Special educational needs

11.62   Subject to the requirement to consider mediation as outlined above, the tribunal hears all appeals against the following decisions:

- a decision of a local authority not to secure an EHC needs assessment for the child or young person;
- a decision of a local authority, following an EHC needs assessment, that it is not necessary for special educational provision to be made for the child or young person in accordance with an EHC plan;
- where an EHC plan is maintained for the child or young person:
  - the child's or young person's special educational needs as specified in the plan (section B);
  - the special educational provision specified in the plan (section F);
  - the school or other institution named in the plan, or the type of school or other institution specified in the plan (section I).
- the fact that no school or other institution is named in the plan;
- a decision of a local authority not to secure a re-assessment of the needs of the child or young person following a request to do so (provided the local authority has not carried out an assessment within the previous six months);
- a decision of a local authority not to secure the amendment or replacement of an EHC plan it maintains for the child or young person following a review or re-assessment; or
- a decision of a local authority to cease to maintain an EHC plan for the child or young person (in these circumstances, the local authority must maintain the plan until the tribunal's decision is made).[46]

46 CFA 2014 s51.

11.63   In addition, the tribunal continues to hear appeals in relation to statements of SEN, including decisions to cease to maintain, and appeals in respect of Parts 2, 3 and 4 following an annual review of the statement pending transfer to an EHC plan. These appeal rights will continue until all children with statements have transferred to EHC plans, the deadline for which is April 2018; see chapter 4 at para 4.44.

11.64   The tribunal does not hear appeals about personal budgets, but will hear appeals about the special educational provision to which a personal budget may apply.[47]

11.65   The procedure for tribunal appeals is set out in the Tribunal Procedure (First-tier Tribunal) (Health, Education and Social Care Chamber) Rules 2008.[48] All appeals must be lodged within two months of the date of the letter of notification from the local authority informing the parent or young person of the decision or within one month of a certificate being issued following mediation or the parent or young person being given mediation information. There are expedited appeals processes, for example, in relation to post-16 transfer appeals, where the tribunal aims to hold a hearing within seven weeks.

11.66   When determining the appeal, the tribunal's powers include dismissing the appeal or ordering the local authority to:

- arrange an EHC needs assessment or re-assessment;
- make and maintain a plan or continue to make a plan;
- name a specified school or other institution in the EHC plan; and
- maintain a plan with specified amendments in respect of the special educational needs and provision.[49]

11.67   Local authorities must comply with decisions of the tribunal within specified time limits.[50]

11.68   The usual order for costs in a tribunal is that each party meets their own costs. There are exceptions to this where a party or its representative has acted unreasonably in bringing, defending or conducting the proceedings.[51]

---

47 See SEND Code, paras 9.108 and 11.45.
48 SI No 2699.
49 SEND Regs 2014 reg 43.
50 SEND Regs 2014 reg 44.
51 Tribunal Procedure (First-tier Tribunal) (Health, Education and Social Care Chamber) Rules 2008 SI No 2699 r10.

11.69   Further help and guidance can be accessed via:

Special Educational Needs and Disability Tribunal
1st Floor, Darlington Magistrates Court
Parkgate
Darlington
DL1 1RU
www.gov.uk/special-educational-needs-disability-tribunal/appeal-to-tribunal
Email: sendistqueries@hmcts.gsi.gov.uk
Telephone: 01325 289 350 Fax: 0870 739 4017

Disability discrimination claims

11.70   The tribunal also has jurisdiction to hear claims on behalf of parents against schools and academies (including independent schools) under the Equality Act 2010 for disability discrimination in relation to:

- the provision of education and associated services and the making of reasonable adjustments, including the provision of auxiliary aids and services;
- fixed-term and permanent exclusions (although parents should be aware of the right to appeal to an independent review panel against permanent exclusions from state-funded schools and academies, see further chapter 4 at para 4.226); and
- admissions to independent and non-maintained special schools (note the tribunal cannot hear a claim for admissions in relation to academies and state-funded schools where there are separate appeal procedures).

11.71   Further coverage of the tribunal's role in determining disability discrimination claims is found in chapter 9 at paras 9.129–9.130.

11.72   The claim for disability discrimination must be received by the tribunal within six months of the alleged discrimination. The tribunal can allow a late claim, but it will only do so if this is considered justified.

11.73   The tribunal has powers to make any remedy to counter-act the alleged discrimination including reinstatement of the child save that it is not able to award financial remedies.

11.74   Where the disability discrimination claim is against an early year's provider, further education college or local authority, the claim must be brought in the county court (see paras 11.104–11.107 below).

Recommendations regarding health and social care needs and provision

11.75   In 2015, regulations made provision for a pilot scheme which enabled the tribunal to consider disputes concerning the health and social care elements of an EHC plan ('the pilot scheme regulations').[52]

11.76   The pilot scheme regulations state that where an appeal is made against a pilot local authority, the tribunal has the power to recommend:

- the health care needs and health provision that should be specified in the EHC plan;
- the social care needs and social care provision that should be specified in the EHC plan.

11.77   This power can be contrasted to the power of the tribunal to *order* the inclusion of special educational needs and provision within the EHC plan and to order that a particular school or institution be named, see para 11.62 above.

11.78   Where recommendations are made in respect of healthcare needs or provision, a copy must be sent by the tribunal to the responsible commissioning body who must respond to the child's parent or young person and the local authority within five weeks to confirm what steps it has decided to take following consideration of the recommendation and give reasons for any decision not to follow the recommendation. Mirror provisions apply to recommendations in respect of social care needs and provision. Although at present, the recommendations are not binding, a failure to give good reasons for departing from the recommendations may give rise to challenge by way of judicial review. There is no right of appeal to the tribunal against these recommendations.

11.79   As at November 2015, the pilot scheme applied to Barking and Dagenham, Bedford, Blackpool, Cheshire West and Chester, Ealing, East Riding, Hackney, Kent, Lambeth, Liverpool, Sandwell, Stockport and Wokingham.

11.80   In non-pilot areas, the main routes for disabled children and their families to challenge health and social care decisions will be through complaints procedures and judicial review. However, dependent on the outcome of the pilot scheme, in the future, the tribunal may provide a more holistic and effective remedy to challenge all the contents of a child or young person's EHC plan.

---

52 Special Educational Needs and Disability (First-tier Tribunal Recommendation Power) (Pilot) Regulations 2015 SI No 358.

Appeal rights for young people

11.81   The CFA 2014 gives significant new rights directly to 'young people', who are brought within the special educational needs system for the first time. A young person is defined as a person over compulsory school age (the end of the academic year in which they turn 16) and under 25.[53] The following decision-making rights are transferred from parents to young people who have capacity to make the relevant decisions (see chapter 7 in relation to mental capacity and decision-making):

- the right to request an assessment for an EHC plan (any time up to their 25th birthday);
- the right to make representations about the content of their EHC plan;
- the right to request that a particular institution is named in their EHC plan;
- the right to request a personal budget;
- the right to appeal to the tribunal.

11.82   Parents, or other family members, can continue to support young people in making decisions, or to act on their behalf, provided that the young person is happy for them to do so, and it is likely that parents will remain closely involved in the great majority of cases. A young person can ask a family member or friend to support them in any way they wish, including, for example, receiving correspondence on their behalf, filling in forms, attending meetings, making telephone calls and helping them to make decisions. However, the final decision rests with the young person, if they have capacity to make the relevant decision.

11.83   The CFA 2014 and the SEND Regs 2014 specify that where a person lacks mental capacity to make a particular decision, that decision will be taken by an 'alternative person' instead of the young person.[54] The alternative person will be either a representative, or where there is no representative, the young person's parent(s). Where the parent(s) themselves lack capacity, then the decision-making power transfers to their representative(s). The decisions which are taken by the 'alternative person' alone are set out in Part 2 of Schedule 3 to the SEND Regs 2014 and are summarised in the Code of Practice. They include decisions in relation to needs assessments, EHC plans and appeals to the tribunal.

53   CFA 2014 s83(2).
54   CFA 2014 s80 and SEND Regs 2014 reg 64.

11.84   The representative can be a deputy appointed by the Court of Protection, or a person who has a lasting or enduring power of attorney.[55] However, in the opinion of the authors, deputies (and attorneys) will only qualify as 'representatives' where they have been appointed to make decisions on education and related health and care matters and, therefore, this would need to be a personal welfare deputy or attorney.[56]

11.85   In the case of a young person who does not have such a representative, the relevant decision will be taken by the young person's parent. The SEND Code suggests that 'this is likely to be the case the majority of the time'. However, the scheme is silent as to what happens in a case where a young person has no parent, or the parent lacks capacity themselves and does not have a representative. In such cases, the authors would suggest that an application needs to be made to the Court of Protection so that an appropriate person is appointed as a personal welfare deputy.[57]

11.86   Where there is a personal welfare deputy for a young person, there does not appear to be a mechanism to allow them to 'step aside' to allow a parent to take the relevant decisions. Regulation 64 creates a hierarchy where 'the alternative person' with decision-making rights and responsibilities is a representative, and it is only where the young person does not have a representative that the parent is able to make the decision. It, therefore, will fall to the deputy to make decisions under Part 3 of the CFA 2014, of course consulting closely with the parents and giving their views significant weight alongside those of the young person themselves. The alternative option is for the parent to apply to become a personal welfare deputy themselves.

11.87   There are some occasions when a local authority must take account of the views of the young person as well as any representative. These are conveniently listed in Annex 1 to the SEND Code.

---

55 CFA 2014 s80(6). In the vast majority of cases, a young person will have a deputy rather than an attorney, as attorneys can only be appointed when a person has capacity to do so.

56 CFA 2014 s80(6)(a) refers to 'a deputy appointed by the Court of Protection … to make decisions on the parent's or young person's behalf in relation to matters within this Part'.

57 SEND Regs 2014 reg 65.

Judicial review

11.88   Judicial review is the legal procedure by which decisions, actions or failures of public bodies can be challenged in the High Court (known as the Administrative Court for such proceedings).[58] It is a remedy of last resort and so cannot be used until other remedies have been exhausted, for example where there is an appeal right to the tribunal in relation to the decision that needs to be challenged or if pursuing the complaints procedure would provide an alternative effective remedy.[59]

Grounds

11.89   A claim for judicial review cannot be brought simply because an individual does not agree with the decision that has been made. The challenge must be brought under one of the recognised public law grounds of claim:

- **Irrationality/unreasonableness:** in this context irrationality and unreasonableness have a legal meaning that describes where the decision is so 'outrageous' or 'absurd' that it 'defies logic' and no reasonable body of persons could have reached it. It is sometimes referred to as '*Wednesbury* unreasonableness' – being named after an early case in which this challenge was defined.[60] Many challenges against individual assessment or service provision decisions are based on grounds of irrationality. A high threshold is to be applied to this test and, therefore, few claims are brought on this ground alone. A public body can also act irrationally if:
  - it takes into account irrelevant considerations or fails to take into account relevant or material considerations; or
  - it has failed to ask the right questions and make sure that it has sufficient information on which a proper decision can be based.[61]
- **Illegality:** this includes where a public body:
  - acts beyond its powers – this is known as acting 'ultra vires';

---

58 For a general guide to judicial review, see J Manning, S Salmon and R Brown, *Judicial Review Proceedings: a practitioner's guide*, LAG, June 2013.

59 *R (Cowl) v Plymouth CC* [2001] EWCA Civ 1935; [2002] 1 WLR 803.

60 *Associated Provincial Picture Houses Ltd v Wednesbury Corporation* [1948] 1 KB 223, CA.

61 *Secretary of State for Education and Science v Tameside MBC* [1977] AC 1014.

- delegates decisions to other bodies or organisations which by law only that public body is permitted to take;
- unlawfully fetters its discretion – for example, by using a blanket policy when applying an eligibility criteria without considering the individual facts of the case or allowing exceptions;
- misdirects itself about the extent of its powers;
- misunderstands its legal obligations and makes an error of law;
- acts in breach of a requirement under a particular statute. In the context of challenges relating to the legal rights of disabled children, this is the most common type of illegality – for example, a local authority may fail to arrange the special educational provision specified in a child's EHC plan and, thereby, breaches the requirements of CFA 2014 s42;
- breaches the Human Rights Act (HRA) 1998. The vast majority of the rights contained in the ECHR are now part of English law as a result of the HRA 1998 and, as a result, it is unlawful for a public body not to act in accordance with those rights. The courts are increasingly willing to consider whether rights contained in other international instruments, for example, the UN Convention on the Rights of the Child and the UN Convention on the Rights of Persons with Disabilities (see for example para 2.24 above), have been breached, particularly in the context of HRA 1998 claims.[62]
- **Procedural fairness/impropriety:** specific grounds of judicial review which fall under this heading includes:
  - a breach of the rules of natural justice;
  - a failure to follow procedural requirements which are set out in law;
  - where there is actual bias or an appearance of bias;
  - where there has been an abuse of power;
  - the right to a fair hearing;
  - there has been a 'procedural' or 'substantive' breach of a legitimate expectation. This may occur where a public body says that it will act in a particular way: such a representation may give rise to a legitimate expectation that the public authority will do as it said it would and the court may enforce this;[63] or

---

62 *R (SG and others) v Secretary of State for Work and Pensions* [2015] UKSC 16; the Supreme Court held that the benefit cap was in breach of the government's obligations to treat the best interests of the child as a primary consideration under the UNCRC.

63 See *R v North and East Devon Health Authority ex p Coughlan* [2001] QB 213.

- failure to consult in a situation where the law requires that there be consultation (for example a substantial reconfiguration of services or the introduction of new charging or eligibility rules).[64]

Procedure and time limits

11.90   A claim for judicial review can be brought by any individual or organisation who has a sufficient interest in the outcome of the legal challenge.[65] For claims brought under the HRA 1998, a narrower test is applied that requires the claimant to be an actual or potential victim of the alleged breaches, although this can include family members.[66]

11.91   To bring a claim for judicial review, it is necessary to have 'litigation capacity', or in plain English to understand the nature and potential consequences of going to court and to have capacity (under the Mental Capacity Act 2005, see further chapter 7) to make the necessary decisions. As many disabled children will not have litigation capacity as a result of their age and/or their impairment(s), any claim brought on their behalf will need to be made by a 'litigation friend'.[67] The test for a person to act as litigation friend is that they can: (a) fairly and competently conduct the proceedings; and (b) have no interest adverse to that of the child.[68] In most cases, one of the parents will act as litigation friend for a disabled child in judicial review proceedings, although this role can also be taken by another family member, a family friend or an advocate.

11.92   Most judicial review cases involving disabled children are reported on an anonymised basis, usually by reference to actual or substitute initials – for example *R (JL) v Islington LBC*[69] and *R (L and P) v Warwickshire CC*.[70] There is no automatic right to anonymity; an application must be made to show that the child's privacy rights under ECHR article 8 outweigh the public interest in free reporting of

---

64 See *R (Moseley) v Haringey LBC* [2014] UKSC 56; [2014] 1 WLR 3947.
65 Senior Courts Act 1981 s31(3).
66 HRA 1998 s7.
67 Civil Procedure Rules (CPR) 21.2.
68 CPR 21.4(3).
69 [2009] EWHC 458 (Admin); (2009) 12 CCLR 322. See, however, *R (Spink) v Wandsworth LBC* [2005] EWCA Civ 302; [2005] 1 WLR 2884 for a case reported under the family's name.
70 [2015] EWHC 203 (Admin); [2015] ELR 271.

court proceedings under ECHR article 10.[71] It is virtually certain in practice that an application for anonymity for a disabled child would be granted. An application for anonymity for a disabled adult who lacks capacity to litigate themselves would also almost certainly be granted.

11.93   It is important to note that any judicial review challenge must be brought 'promptly' and, in any event, within three months after the grounds to make the claim first arose.[72] The time limits may not be extended by agreement between parties. The court has discretion to extend time where it is fair and just to do so but it cannot be assumed that this will happen in any particular case. It is, therefore, essential that individuals seek advice from a specialist legal adviser at the earliest possible stage.

11.94   Before proceedings can be issued, the claimant, or their advisers, must send a letter before claim which complies with the requirements of the Pre-Action Protocol for Judicial Review (the protocol). The requirements to follow the protocol do not affect the time limit for issuing a claim. The protocol requires both claimants and defendants to consider whether some form of alternative dispute resolution procedure would be more suitable and the court may ask for evidence that this has been considered. This could include using the ombudsman or mediation procedures. Defendants should normally be given 14 days to respond, although the timetable can be 'abridged,' or in exceptional emergency cases it may not be necessary to send a letter before claim at all. However, in all cases, the claimant must give some notice to the defendant. Where the court considers that a subsequent claim is made prematurely, it may impose sanctions, including refusing permission for the claim to proceed (see para 11.97 below).

11.95   A judicial review claim can be issued in the Administrative Court Office of the High Court at the Royal Courts of Justice in London, or at one of the regional administrative courts in Birmingham, Leeds or Manchester – or less frequently in other major cities. The procedural requirements for making a claim are outlined in the Civil Procedure Rules (CPR) Part 54 and its accompanying Practice Direction 54A. However, the authors would stress that specialist legal advice should be sought before any claim for judicial review is made. Not only is the procedure technical and relatively complex, there is also the fact

---

71 See *Re Guardian News and Media Ltd and others* [2010] UKSC 1; [2010] 2 AC 697.

72 CPR 54.5(1). If the challenge relates to a planning decision then the time limit is six weeks and in respect of procurement decisions just 30 days.

that, once a claim is issued, the claimant may be ordered to pay the defendant's costs if it fails or is later withdrawn. These costs can run into tens of thousands of pounds if the claim reaches a full hearing but fails at that stage. Claimants with the benefit of legal aid obtained through a specialist solicitor will have the benefit of protection from these costs (see para 11.102 below) in most cases.

11.96   The Administrative Court has a procedure for dealing with urgent cases which allows applications to be made for interim relief – for example to provide a disabled child with accommodation (under CA 1989 s20) pending the final determination of the claim.

11.97   Before a case can proceed to a full hearing, the court must first consider whether to grant permission. At this stage, the court will decide whether there is an 'arguable' case for granting the relief sought by the claimant and if there is any other reason why the claim should not be heard, for example, a failure to exercise an alternative remedy.

11.98   The Administrative Court is required to either refuse permission on an application for judicial review or refuse a remedy if it considers it highly likely that the outcome for the claimant would not have been substantially different if the conduct complained of had not occurred[73] (the so called 'no difference test'). The test does not apply where the court considers that there is an 'exceptional public interest' in the case proceeding (and a court may hold a hearing to determine the issue). Although this is an additional barrier to justice, it should not affect the vast majority of cases involving disabled children in practice.

11.99   Following changes to legal aid rules, where permission for the claim to proceed is refused, a claim may not be made against the legal aid agency for payment of the claimant's own legal costs, although there is a limited discretion to make payment for costs where permission is neither granted nor refused – for example where the defendant concedes the claim after it is issued but before permission is considered by the court.

Remedies

11.100 The Administrative Court has the power to grant wide-ranging remedies, both at interim stage and following a substantive hearing although all remedies are discretionary. Remedies include making:

---

73 Supreme Court Act 1981 s31 as amended by the Criminal Justice and Courts Act 2015 s84.

- A **mandatory order** that a public body must do something. For example, that the public body must carry out an assessment of the disabled child (under CA 1989 s17).
- A **prohibiting order** preventing a public body from doing something. This could include not implementing a decision to close a respite/short break care centre or a reduction in the hours of care provided. Prohibiting orders are often granted at an interim stage pending final determination of the claim.
- A **quashing order** that 'quashes' the decision being challenged, setting it aside so that it is as if the decision was never made.
- A **declaration** that the public body has acted in a way which is unlawful. This can include declarations of incompatibility under the HRA 1998.
- The court can also award **damages** for breaches of the HRA 1998. Apart from this instance, it does not have the power to make financial awards.

11.101 More than one remedy can be granted and they are often used together. For example, the court could make a declaration that a decision made to reduce a disabled child's care arrangements was unlawful, make an order quashing the decision and make a mandatory order to carry out a fresh assessment of the child's needs. In many cases, the relief granted will be limited to a declaration and a quashing order, with the public body expected to then act in the light of the judgment and these orders. Mandatory orders are generally reserved for cases where there is only one lawful action that the public body can take.[74]

Funding

11.102 One of the most significant difficulties with a judicial review challenge is the issue of costs. Not only can the costs of bringing a claim be prohibitively expensive, but in the event that the claim is unsuccessful, even in part, the claimant is exposed to the risk of an adverse costs order being made which means that the claimant will be responsible for the defendant's legal costs as well. Where legal aid is available (see below at paras 11.108–116), it will cover the legal costs of bringing a claim and provide some protection against the liability of an adverse costs order. Although this is not a complete protection, it can be expected that a legally-aided claimant (and any 'litigation friend' if they have one) will not have to pay the other side's costs

74 *R v Ealing LBC ex p Parkinson* (1996) 8 Admin LR 281.

where the correct legal aid certificate is in place unless they act in a wholly unreasonable manner.

11.103   Where legal aid or other forms of funding (such as conditional fee agreements or insurance) are not available, the costs of a judicial review will in most cases represent a barrier for disabled children and their families in accessing the courts to seek a remedy and, in those circumstances, other routes to redress such as the ombudsman will need to be pursued. A specialist solicitor will be able to advise on the potential mechanisms for funding any given claim.

County court claims

11.104   The county court is able to hear a wide range of claims. These include personal injury claims, landlord and tenant disputes and contract disputes.

11.105   The most common types of cases that may be heard in the county court in relation to disabled children and young people are disability discrimination claims under the Equality Act 2010 that cannot be heard by the tribunal (see further chapter 9 at paras 9.123–9.128). This would include:

- claims about access to childcare provision and whether a child-care provider has made reasonable adjustments to enable a child access to a suitable service that meets their needs;
- claims on behalf of students against further or higher education settings, including making reasonable adjustments to its policies, criteria, provision of aids and services and physical features; or
- access to sports, leisure and other recreational facilities.

11.106   A claim must normally be brought within six months of the alleged discrimination. Where there has been a continuing process of discrimination taking place over a period of time, the six months begins at the date of the last discriminatory act. Courts have the discretion to consider a claim brought outside the six-month period if they consider that it is fair to do so.

11.107   Remedies in the county court include damages, injunctions and mandatory orders; see para 11.100 above for more on these remedies.

Availability of legal aid

11.108 Despite the significant cuts to legal aid in many areas, it remains available to provide advice and assistance to children, young people and their parents to challenge decisions of public bodies in relation to most education, health and social care decisions where a 'means' and 'merits' criteria are met.[75]

11.109 There are two main types of legal aid funding for advice relating to services for disabled children:

- **Legal Help:** this level of funding provides general advice and assistance in relation to:
  - preparing for a tribunal appeal including obtaining expert reports; but does not cover the costs of representation at the tribunal hearing itself; and
  - accessing health and social care services, including sending pre-action letters before claim to public bodies in relation to a potential challenge by way of judicial review. It does not cover issuing or conducting court proceedings, instructing an advocate or providing advocacy. This level of funding may cover advice in relation to making complaints.

- **Legal Representation:** this type of funding covers the provision of advice and assistance in relation to proceedings or contemplated proceedings and is provided at two levels:
  - Investigative Representation: this level of funding is used where the prospects of success are unclear and investigatory work is required in order to investigate the merits of a claim, including seeking advice from a barrister and complying with the pre-action protocol for judicial review. It does not cover the issuing of court proceedings. In relation to judicial review claims, the Legal Aid Agency will expect the provider to explain why the work in completing the pre-action protocol could not be completed at Legal Help level; this will usually be where there is evidence that significant investigatory work is required. Before investigative representation funding can be granted, the individual must have notified the proposed defendant of the potential challenge and given a reasonable time for the defendant to respond.[76]
  - Full Representation: this level of funding covers representation in a claim for judicial review and some other proceedings

---

75 See the Legal Aid, Sentencing and Punishment of Offenders Act 2012.
76 Civil Legal Aid (Merits Criteria) Regulations 2013 SI No 104 reg 54(b)(i).

such as health and welfare applications to the Court of Protection in relation to adults who lack capacity under the MCA 2005.

11.110   Legal representation funding is not available for appeals to the tribunal unless the case falls within the Legal Aid Agency 'exceptional funding' criteria – a scheme which has received significant judicial criticism due to the difficulty in accessing funding via this route.[77]

11.111   A financial eligibility or 'means' test will need to be met in every case. For tribunal appeals where the appeal right is with the parent then eligibility will be based on the parents' means. In all other cases, where work is carried out at 'Legal Help' level of funding then the Legal Aid Agency guidance states that when assessing the means of a child, the resources of a parent, guardian or other person who is responsible for maintaining him or who usually contributes substantially to the child's maintenance must be taken into account, as well as any assets of the child. This can be a significant barrier for many families being able to access advice and assistance under the Legal Help scheme.

11.112   There is a discretion not to aggregate assets in this way if it appears inequitable to do so, having regard to all the circumstances including the age and resources of the child and any conflict of interest between the child and the adult(s). The Legal Aid Agency gives as an example that:

> ... in consideration of the age and resources of the child,[78] the provider may determine that it is inequitable to aggregate a child aged 17 years who is estranged from his parents, living separately from them and who is fully financially independent from his parents.
> or
> Where a child is a 'looked-after' child, it would usually be inequitable for his or her foster carer's/social worker's income and capital to be aggregated with that of the child.[79]

11.113   Unless there are exceptional circumstances, legal aid can only be offered by an advice centre or law firm that has a contract with the Legal Aid Agency to provide that type of service in the office where the client wishes to access advice. For example, there are separate

---

77 See for example, *IS v Director of Legal Aid Casework and the Lord Chancellor* [2015] EWHC 1965 (Admin) and *R (Gudanaviciene) v Director of Legal Aid Casework and the Lord Chancellor* [2014] EWCA Civ 1622.

78 For the purposes of legal aid eligibility, a child is a person under the age of 18.

79 Ministry of Justice, *Guide to determining financial eligibility for controlled work and family mediation*, April 2015, para 9.

contracts for community care (which includes judicial reviews in relation to social care and healthcare), education (which includes SEN and discrimination appeals to tribunal) and public law (which includes all judicial review challenges and some human rights act claims). There are also contracts for clinical negligence, actions against the police, housing, family, mental health, crime, welfare benefits, debt and discrimination.

11.114   Since 2013, certain types of advice can only be accessed via a mandatory telephone gateway provided by the Civil Legal Advice (CLA) service on 0345 345 4 345. If a person is eligible, the CLA will provide legal advice, normally by phone, online or by post unless the specialist advice provider assesses them as unsuitable to receive advice in this way. These categories are:

- education;
- debt;
- discrimination.

11.115   There are provisions that allow for certain 'exempt persons' to still be able to access face-to-face advice if they choose.[80] These include a person deprived of their liberty, a person under the age of 18 and a person previously assessed as requiring face-to-face advice within the last 12 months. These provisions will not offer much assistance to families needing to access advice in tribunal appeals as the appeal right will lie with the child's parent until the end of the school year in which the child turns 16 and once the young person turns 18, they will fall back under the mandatory gateway rules.

11.116   In order to find a face-to-face legal adviser in the other categories of work, individuals can go to the 'find a legal adviser' website[81] or telephone the CLA service.

Other sources of advice and support

11.117   Where parents of disabled children or young people find themselves unable to access legal aid for advice and assistance in relation to SEN issues including tribunal appeals, the charitable organisation, Independent Parental Special Education Advice (known as IPSEA), provide invaluable free legal advice and assistance (including tribunal support) via their excellent website. A number of other charities,

---

80   Civil Legal Aid (Procedure) Regulations 2012 SI No 3098 reg 20.
81   http://find-legal-advice.justice.gov.uk/.

including the National Autistic Society and the Downs Syndrome Association, offer condition-specific advice through their helplines. The Contact a Family helpline provides advice on a wide range of issues, including education and benefits. Advice on SEN issues is also available from other charities such as SOS!SEN.[82]

Information, Advice and Support Services

11.118   Under the CFA 2014,[83] local authorities now have specific legal duties to arrange for children and young people for whom they are responsible, and the parents of children for whom they are responsible, to be provided with advice and information about matters relating to the special educational needs and disabilities of the children or young people concerned. These are known as 'Information, Advice and Support (IAS) Services'.

11.119   The local authority must take steps to ensure that these IAS services are known to:

- parents of children in its area;
- children in its area;
- young people in its area;
- head teachers, proprietors and principals of schools and post-16 institutions in its area; and
- other such persons as appropriate.[84]

11.120   Details of how information, advice and support can be accessed and how it is resourced must also be set out in each local authority's local offer.[85]

11.121   These duties are consistent with the key principles set out in the CFA 2014 which all local authorities must have regard to when exercising their functions under the Act and in particular:

> ... the importance of the child and his or her parent, or the young person, being provided with the information and support necessary to enable participation in those decisions.[86]

---

82 www.ipsea.org.uk; advice line on 0800 018 4016 and tribunal helpline on 0845 602 9579.
83 CFA 2014 s32.
84 CFA 2014 s32(3).
85 SEND Regs 2014 Sch 2 para 15.
86 CFA 2014 s19(c).

11.122 The SEND Code states that IAS Services should be free, impartial, confidential and accessible and should have the capacity to handle face-to-face, telephone and electronic enquiries and that children, young people and parents should be involved in the design and commissioning of the service.[87] Local authorities should review and publish information annually about the effectiveness of the information, advice and support provided, including customer satisfaction.[88]

11.123 Although many children will access information, advice and support services via their parents, the local authority must also ensure that it is possible for children to access information, advice and support separately from their parents.[89]

11.124 Young people must be provided with confidential and impartial information, advice and support from staff who are trained to enable them to participate fully in decisions. The SEND Code reflects that young people 'may be finding their voice for the first time' and may need support in exercising choice and control over the support they receive and advocacy should be provided where necessary.[90]

11.125 Local authorities must provide the following types of support through their IAS Services:

- signposting to additional sources of advice, information and support that may be available locally or nationally;
- individual casework and representation for those who need it which should include support in attending meetings, contributing to assessments and reviews;
- help when things go wrong, including arranging or attending early disagreement resolution meetings, supporting in managing mediation, appeals to the First-tier Tribunal, exclusions and complaints on matters related to SEN and disability.[91]

11.126 The SEND Code also states that local authorities should adopt a key working approach which provides children, young people and parents with a single point of contact to help ensure the holistic provision and co-ordination of services and support.[92]

11.127 Further information in relation to IAS services can be accessed via the IASS Network at www.iassnetwork.org.uk.

---

87 SEND Code, para 2.5.
88 SEND Code, para 2.8.
89 SEND Code, para 2.10.
90 SEND Code, para 2.15.
91 SEND Code, para 2.19.
92 SEND Code, paras 2.20–2.22.

Independent Support Programme

11.128   During the implementation of the SEND reforms (see chapter 4 at paras 4.42–4.71); the government has funded a two-year programme of support to children, young people and their parents called the Independent Support Programme. This programme is managed by the Council for Disabled Children and provides a range of time-limited advice and support through the statutory EHC needs assessment and planning process.[93]

---

93 For more information see www.councilfordisabledchildren.org.uk/what-we-do/our-networks/independent-support/what-is-independent-support.

Legislation[1]

CHILDREN ACT 1989

Part III: Local Authority Support for Children and Families

Provision of services for children and their families

Provision of services for children in need, their families and others

17 (1) It shall be the general duty of every local authority (in addition to the other duties imposed on them by this Part)–

(a) to safeguard and promote the welfare of children within their area who are in need; and

(b) so far as is consistent with that duty, to promote the upbringing of such children by their families,

by providing a range and level of services appropriate to those children's needs.

(2) For the purpose principally of facilitating the discharge of their general duty under this section, every local authority shall have the specific duties and powers set out in Part I of Schedule 2.

(3) Any service provided by an authority in the exercise of functions conferred on them by this section may be provided for the family of a particular child in need or for any member of his family, if it is provided with a view to safeguarding or promoting the child's welfare.

(4) The appropriate national authority may by order amend any provision of Part I of Schedule 2 or add any further duty or power to those for the time being mentioned there.

(4A) Before determining what (if any) services to provide for a particular child in need in the exercise of functions conferred on them by this section, a local authority shall, so far as is reasonably practicable and consistent with the child's welfare–

(a) ascertain the child's wishes and feelings regarding the provision of those services; and

(b) give due consideration (having regard to his age and understanding) to such wishes and feelings of the child as they have been able to ascertain.

(5) Every local authority–

(a) shall facilitate the provision by others (including in particular voluntary organisations) of services which it is a function of the authority to provide by virtue of this section, or section 18, 20, 22A to 22C, 23B to 23D, 24A or 24B; and

(b) may make such arrangements as they see fit for any person to act on their behalf in the provision of any such service.

(6) The services provided by a local authority in the exercise of functions conferred on them by this section may include providing accommodation and giving assistance in kind or in cash.

(7) Assistance may be unconditional or subject to conditions as to the repayment of the assistance or of its value (in whole or in part).

(8) Before giving any assistance or imposing any conditions, a local authority shall have regard to the means of the child concerned and of each of his parents.

(9) No person shall be liable to make any repayment of assistance or of its value at any time when he is in receipt of universal credit (expect in such circumstances as may be prescribed) [[*of income support under Part VII of the Social*

Security Contributions and Benefits Act 1992], of any element of child tax credit other than the family element, of working tax credit, of an income-based jobseeker's allowance or of an income-related employment and support allowance.][2]

(10) For the purposes of this Part a child shall be taken to be in need if–

    (a) he is unlikely to achieve or maintain, or to have the opportunity of achieving or maintaining, a reasonable standard of health or development without the provision for him of services by a local authority under this Part;

    (b) his health or development is likely to be significantly impaired, or further impaired, without the provision for him of such services; or

    (c) he is disabled,

    and 'family', in relation to such a child, includes any person who has parental responsibility for the child and any other person with whom he has been living.

(11) For the purposes of this Part, a child is disabled if he is blind, deaf or dumb or suffers from mental disorder of any kind or is substantially and permanently handicapped by illness, injury or congenital deformity or such other disability as may be prescribed; and in this Part–

    'development' means physical, intellectual, emotional, social or behavioural development; and

    'health' means physical or mental health.

[*(12) The Treasury may by regulations prescribe circumstances in which a person is to be treated for the purposes of this Part (or for such of those purposes as are prescribed) as in receipt of any element of child tax credit other than the family element or of working tax credit.]*[3]

Young carers' needs assessments: England

17ZA(1) A local authority in England must assess whether a young carer within their area has needs for support and, if so, what those needs are, if–

    (a) it appears to the authority that the young carer may have needs for support, or

    (b) the authority receive a request from the young carer or a parent of the young carer to assess the young carer's needs for support.

(2) An assessment under subsection (1) is referred to in this Part as a 'young carer's needs assessment'.

(3) In this Part 'young carer' means a person under 18 who provides or intends to provide care for another person (but this is qualified by section 17ZB(3)).

(4) Subsection (1) does not apply in relation to a young carer if the local authority have previously carried out a care-related assessment of the young carer in relation to the same person cared for.

(5) But subsection (1) does apply (and so a young carer's needs assessment must be carried out) if it appears to the authority that the needs or circumstances of the young carer or the person cared for have changed since the last care-related assessment.

(6) 'Care-related assessment' means–

    (a) a young carer's needs assessment;

---

2 Words in square brackets repealed by the Welfare Reform Act 2012 s147, Sch 14 Pt 1 from a date to be appointed.

3 Subs (12) repealed by the Welfare Reform Act 2012 s147, Sch 14 Pt 1 from a date to be appointed.

(b) an assessment under any of the following–
    (i)   section 1 of the Carers (Recognition and Services) Act 1995;
    (ii) section 1 of the Carers and Disabled Children Act 2000;
    (iii) section 4(3) of the Community Care (Delayed Discharges) Act 2003;
    (iv) Part 1 of the Care Act 2014.

(7) A young carer's needs assessment must include an assessment of whether it is appropriate for the young carer to provide, or continue to provide, care for the person in question, in the light of the young carer's needs for support, other needs and wishes.

(8) A local authority, in carrying out a young carer's needs assessment, must have regard to–
(a) the extent to which the young carer is participating in or wishes to participate in education, training or recreation, and
(b) the extent to which the young carer works or wishes to work.

(9) A local authority, in carrying out a young carer's needs assessment, must involve–
(a) the young carer,
(b) the young carer's parents, and
(c) any person who the young carer or a parent of the young carer requests the authority to involve.

(10) A local authority that have carried out a young carer's needs assessment must give a written record of the assessment to–
(a) the young carer,
(b) the young carer's parents, and
(c) any person to whom the young carer or a parent of the young carer requests the authority to give a copy.

(11) Where the person cared for is under 18, the written record must state whether the local authority consider him or her to be a child in need.

(12) A local authority in England must take reasonable steps to identify the extent to which there are young carers within their area who have needs for support.

Young carers' needs assessments: supplementary

17ZB(1) This section applies for the purposes of section 17ZA.

(2) 'Parent', in relation to a young carer, includes–
(a) a parent of the young carer who does not have parental responsibility for the young carer, and
(b) a person who is not a parent of the young carer but who has parental responsibility for the young carer.

(3) A person is not a young carer if the person provides or intends to provide care–
(a) under or by virtue of a contract, or
(b) as voluntary work.

(4) But in a case where the local authority consider that the relationship between the person cared for and the person under 18 providing or intending to provide care is such that it would be appropriate for the person under 18 to be regarded as a young carer, that person is to be regarded as such (and subsection (3) is therefore to be ignored in that case).

(5) The references in section 17ZA and this section to providing care include a reference to providing practical or emotional support.

(6) Where a local authority–
  (a) are required to carry out a young carer's needs assessment, and
  (b) are required or have decided to carry out some other assessment of the young carer or of the person cared for;
  the local authority may, subject to subsection (7), combine the assessments.
(7) A young carer's needs assessment may be combined with an assessment of the person cared for only if the young carer and the person cared for agree.
(8) The Secretary of State may by regulations make further provision about carrying out a young carer's needs assessment; the regulations may, in particular–
  (a) specify matters to which a local authority is to have regard in carrying out a young carer's needs assessment;
  (b) specify matters which a local authority is to determine in carrying out a young carer's needs assessment;
  (c) make provision about the manner in which a young carer's needs assessment is to be carried out;
  (d) make provision about the form a young carer's needs assessment is to take.
(9) The Secretary of State may by regulations amend the list in section 17ZA(6)(b) so as to–
  (a) add an entry,
  (b) remove an entry, or
  (c) vary an entry.

Consideration of young carers' needs assessments

17ZC A local authority that carry out a young carer's needs assessment must consider the assessment and decide–
  (a) whether the young carer has needs for support in relation to the care which he or she provides or intends to provide;
  (b) if so, whether those needs could be satisfied (wholly or partly) by services which the authority may provide under section 17; and
  (c) if they could be so satisfied, whether or not to provide any such services in relation to the young carer.

Parent carers' needs assessments: England

17ZD(1)A local authority in England must, if the conditions in subsections (3) and (4) are met, assess whether a parent carer within their area has needs for support and, if so, what those needs are.
  (2) In this Part 'parent carer' means a person aged 18 or over who provides or intends to provide care for a disabled child for whom the person has parental responsibility.
  (3) The first condition is that–
    (a) it appears to the authority that the parent carer may have needs for support, or
    (b) the authority receive a request from the parent carer to assess the parent carer's needs for support.
  (4) The second condition is that the local authority are satisfied that the disabled child cared for and the disabled child's family are persons for whom they may provide or arrange for the provision of services under section 17.
  (5) An assessment under subsection (1) is referred to in this Part as a 'parent carer's needs assessment'.

(6) Subsection (1) does not apply in relation to a parent carer if the local authority have previously carried out a care-related assessment of the parent carer in relation to the same disabled child cared for.

(7) But subsection (1) does apply (and so a parent carer's needs assessment must be carried out) if it appears to the authority that the needs or circumstances of the parent carer or the disabled child cared for have changed since the last care-related assessment.

(8) 'Care-related assessment' means–
   (a) a parent carer's needs assessment;
   (b) an assessment under any of the following–
      (i)   section 1 of the Carers (Recognition and Services) Act 1995;
      (ii) section 6 of the Carers and Disabled Children Act 2000;
      (iii) section 4(3) of the Community Care (Delayed Discharges) Act 2003;
      (iv) Part 1 of the Care Act 2014.

(9) A parent carer's needs assessment must include an assessment of whether it is appropriate for the parent carer to provide, or continue to provide, care for the disabled child, in the light of the parent carer's needs for support, other needs and wishes.

(10) A local authority in carrying out a parent carer's needs assessment must have regard to–
   (a) the well-being of the parent carer, and
   (b) the need to safeguard and promote the welfare of the disabled child cared for and any other child for whom the parent carer has parental responsibility.

(11) In subsection (10) 'well-being' has the same meaning as in Part 1 of the Care Act 2014.

(12) A local authority, in carrying out a parent carer's needs assessment, must involve–
   (a) the parent carer,
   (b) any child for whom the parent carer has parental responsibility, and
   (c) any person who the parent carer requests the authority to involve.

(13) A local authority that have carried out a parent carer's needs assessment must give a written record of the assessment to–
   (a) the parent carer, and
   (b) any person to whom the parent carer requests the authority to give a copy.

(14) A local authority in England must take reasonable steps to identify the extent to which there are parent carers within their area who have needs for support.

Parent carers' needs assessments: supplementary

17ZE(1) This section applies for the purposes of section 17ZD.

(2) The references in section 17ZD to providing care include a reference to providing practical or emotional support.

(3) Where a local authority–
   (a) are required to carry out a parent carer's needs assessment, and
   (b) are required or have decided to carry out some other assessment of the parent carer or of the disabled child cared for,
   the local authority may combine the assessments.

(4) The Secretary of State may by regulations make further provision about

carrying out a parent carer's needs assessment; the regulations may, in particular–

(a) specify matters to which a local authority is to have regard in carrying out a parent carer's needs assessment;

(b) specify matters which a local authority is to determine in carrying out a parent carer's needs assessment;

(c) make provision about the manner in which a parent carer's needs assessment is to be carried out;

(d) make provision about the form a parent carer's needs assessment is to take.

(5) The Secretary of State may by regulations amend the list in section 17ZD(8)(b) so as to–

(a) add an entry,

(b) remove an entry, or

(c) vary an entry.

Consideration of parent carers' needs assessments

17ZF A local authority that carry out a parent carer's needs assessment must consider the assessment and decide–

(a) whether the parent carer has needs for support in relation to the care which he or she provides or intends to provide;

(b) whether the disabled child cared for has needs for support;

(c) if paragraph (a) or (b) applies, whether those needs could be satisfied (wholly or partly) by services which the authority may provide under section 17; and

(d) if they could be so satisfied, whether or not to provide any such services in relation to the parent carer or the disabled child cared for.

Section 17 services: continued provision where EHC plan maintained

17ZG(1)This section applies where, immediately before a child in need reaches the age of 18–

(a) a local authority in England is providing services for the child in the exercise of functions conferred by section 17, and

(b) an EHC plan is maintained for the child.

(2) The local authority may continue to provide services for the child in the exercise of those functions after the child reaches the age of 18, but may not continue to do so after the EHC plan has ceased to be maintained, except in so far as the authority is required to do so under section 17ZH or 17ZI.

(3) In this section 'EHC plan' means a plan within section 37(2) of the Children and Families Act 2014.

Section 17 services: transition for children to adult care and support

17ZH(1)Subsections (2) to (4) apply where a local authority in England providing services for a child in need in the exercise of functions conferred by section 17–

(a) are required by section 58(1) or 63(1) of the Care Act 2014 to carry out a child's needs assessment or young carer's assessment in relation to the child, or

(b) are required by section 60(1) of that Act to carry out a child's carer's assessment in relation to a carer of the child.

(2) If the local authority carry out the assessment before the child reaches the age

of 18 and decide to treat it as a needs or carer's assessment in accordance with section 59(6), 61(6) or 64(7) of the Care Act 2014 (with Part 1 of that Act applying to the assessment as a result), the authority must continue to comply with section 17 after the child reaches the age of 18 until they reach a conclusion in his case.

(3) If the local authority carry out the assessment before the child reaches the age of 18 but decide not to treat it as a needs or carer's assessment in accordance with section 59(6), 61(6) or 64(7) of the Care Act 2014–

   (a) they must carry out a needs or carer's assessment (as the case may be) after the child reaches the age of 18, and

   (b) they must continue to comply with section 17 after he reaches that age until they reach a conclusion in his case.

(4) If the local authority do not carry out the assessment before the child reaches the age of 18, they must continue to comply with section 17 after he reaches that age until–

   (a) they decide that the duty under section 9 or 10 of the Care Act 2014 (needs or carer's assessment) does not apply, or

   (b) having decided that the duty applies and having discharged it, they reach a conclusion in his case.

(5) Subsection (6) applies where a local authority in England providing services for a child in need in the exercise of functions conferred by section 17–

   (a) receive a request for a child's needs assessment or young carer's assessment to be carried out in relation to the child or for a child's carer's assessment to be carried out in relation to a carer of the child, but

   (b) have yet to be required by section 58(1), 60(1) or 63(1) of the Care Act 2014 to carry out the assessment.

(6) If the local authority do not decide, before the child reaches the age of 18, whether or not to comply with the request, they must continue to comply with section 17 after he reaches that age until–

   (a) they decide that the duty under section 9 or 10 of the Care Act 2014 does not apply, or

   (b) having decided that the duty applies and having discharged it, they reach a conclusion in his case.

(7) A local authority reach a conclusion in a person's case when–

   (a) they conclude that he does not have needs for care and support or for support (as the case may be), or

   (b) having concluded that he has such needs and that they are going to meet some or all of them, they begin to do so, or

   (c) having concluded that he has such needs, they conclude that they are not going to meet any of those needs (whether because those needs do not meet the eligibility criteria or for some other reason).

(8) In this section, 'child's needs assessment', 'child's carer's assessment', 'young carer's assessment', 'needs assessment', 'carer's assessment' and 'eligibility criteria' each have the same meaning as in Part 1 of the Care Act 2014.

Section 17 services: provision after EHC plan no longer maintained

17ZI(1) This section applies where a local authority in England providing services for a person in the exercise, by virtue of section 17ZG, of functions conferred by section 17 are required to carry out a needs assessment in that person's case.

(2) If the EHC plan for the person ceases to be maintained before the local authority reach a conclusion in the person's case, they must continue to comply with section 17 until they do reach a conclusion in his case.

(3) The references to the local authority reaching a conclusion in a person's case are to be read with section 17ZH(7).

(4) In this section, 'needs assessment' has the same meaning as in Part 1 of the Care Act 2014.

Provision of accommodation for children

Provision of accommodation for children: general

20 (1) Every local authority shall provide accommodation for any child in need within their area who appears to them to require accommodation as a result of–
  (a) there being no person who has parental responsibility for him;
  (b) his being lost or having been abandoned; or
  (c) the person who has been caring for him being prevented (whether or not permanently, and for whatever reason) from providing him with suitable accommodation or care.

(2) Where a local authority provide accommodation under subsection (1) for a child who is ordinarily resident in the area of another local authority, that other local authority may take over the provision of accommodation for the child within–
  (a) three months of being notified in writing that the child is being provided with accommodation; or
  (b) such other longer period as may be prescribed.

(3) Every local authority shall provide accommodation for any child in need within their area who has reached the age of sixteen and whose welfare the authority consider is likely to be seriously prejudiced if they do not provide him with accommodation.

(4) A local authority may provide accommodation for any child within their area (even though a person who has parental responsibility for him is able to provide him with accommodation) if they consider that to do so would safeguard or promote the child's welfare.

(5) A local authority may provide accommodation for any person who has reached the age of sixteen but is under twenty-one in any community home which takes children who have reached the age of sixteen if they consider that to do so would safeguard or promote his welfare.

(6) Before providing accommodation under this section, a local authority shall, so far as is reasonably practicable and consistent with the child's welfare–
  (a) ascertain the child's wishes and feelings regarding the provision of accommodation; and
  (b) give due consideration (having regard to his age and understanding) to such wishes and feelings of the child as they have been able to ascertain.

(7) A local authority may not provide accommodation under this section for any child if any person who–
  (a) has parental responsibility for him; and
  (b) is willing and able to–
    (i) provide accommodation for him; or
    (ii) arrange for accommodation to be provided for him,
  objects.

(8) Any person who has parental responsibility for a child may at any time remove the child from accommodation provided by or on behalf of the local authority under this section.

(9) Subsections (7) and (8) do not apply while any person–

(a) who is named in a child arrangements order as a person with whom the child is to live;

(aa) who is a special guardian of the child; or

(b) who has care of the child by virtue of an order made in the exercise of the High Court's inherent jurisdiction with respect to children,

agrees to the child being looked after in accommodation provided by or on behalf of the local authority.

(10) Where there is more than one such person as is mentioned in subsection (9), all of them must agree.

(11) Subsections (7) and (8) do not apply where a child who has reached the age of sixteen agrees to being provided with accommodation under this section.

SCHEDULE 2
Local Authority Support for Children and Families

Sections 17, 23, 29

Part I: Provision of services for families

Identification of children in need and provision of information

1 (1) Every local authority shall take reasonable steps to identify the extent to which there are children in need within their area.

(2) Every local authority shall–

(a) publish information–

(i) about services provided by them under sections 17, 18, 20, 23B to 23D, 24A and 24B; and

(ii) where they consider it appropriate, about the provision by others (including, in particular, voluntary organisations) of services which the authority have power to provide under those sections; and

(b) take such steps as are reasonably practicable to ensure that those who might benefit from the services receive the information relevant to them.

1A [Repealed.]

Maintenance of a register of disabled children

2 (1) Every local authority shall open and maintain a register of disabled children within their area.

(2) The register may be kept by means of a computer.

Assessment of children's needs

3 Where it appears to a local authority that a child within their area is in need, the authority may assess his needs for the purposes of this Act at the same time as any assessment of his needs is made under–

(a) the Chronically Sick and Disabled Persons Act 1970;

(b) Part IV of the Education Act 1996;

(ba) Part 3 of the Children and Families Act 2014;

(c) the Disabled Persons (Services, Consultation and Representation) Act 1986; or

(d) any other enactment.

Prevention of neglect and abuse

4 (1) Every local authority shall take reasonable steps, through the provision of services under Part III of this Act, to prevent children within their area suffering ill-treatment or neglect.

(2) Where a local authority believe that a child who is at any time within their area–

(a) is likely to suffer harm; but

(b) lives or proposes to live in the area of another local authority

they shall inform that other local authority.

(3) When informing that other local authority they shall specify–

(a) the harm that they believe he is likely to suffer; and

(b) (if they can) where the child lives or proposes to live.

Provision of accommodation in order to protect child

5 (1) Where–

(a) it appears to a local authority that a child who is living on particular premises is suffering, or is likely to suffer, ill treatment at the hands of another person who is living on those premises; and

(b) that other person proposes to move from the premises,

the authority may assist that other person to obtain alternative accommodation.

(2) Assistance given under this paragraph may be in cash.

(3) Subsections (7) to (9) of section 17 shall apply in relation to assistance given under this paragraph as they apply in relation to assistance given under that section.

Provision for disabled children

6 (1) Every local authority shall provide services designed–

(a) to minimise the effect on disabled children within their area of their disabilities;

(b) to give such children the opportunity to lead lives which are as normal as possible; and

(c) to assist individuals who provide care for such children to continue to do so, or to do so more effectively, by giving them breaks from caring.

(2) The duty imposed by sub-paragraph (1)(c) shall be performed in accordance with regulations made by the appropriate national authority.

Provision to reduce need for care proceedings etc

7 Every local authority shall take reasonable steps designed–

(a) to reduce the need to bring–

(i) proceedings for care or supervision orders with respect to children within their area;

(ii) criminal proceedings against such children;

(iii) any family or other proceedings with respect to such children which might lead to them being placed in the authority's care; or

(iv) proceedings under the inherent jurisdiction of the High Court with respect to children;

(b) to encourage children within their area not to commit criminal offences; and

(c) to avoid the need for children within their area to be placed in secure accommodation.

Provision for children living with their families

8 Every local authority shall make such provision as they consider appropriate for the following services to be available with respect to children in need within their area while they are living with their families–

(a) advice, guidance and counselling;

(b) occupational, social, cultural, or recreational activities;

(c) home help (which may include laundry facilities);

(d) facilities for, or assistance with, travelling to and from home for the purpose of taking advantage of any other service provided under this Act or of any similar service;

(e) assistance to enable the child concerned and his family to have a holiday.

Provision for accommodated children

8A(1) Every local authority shall make provision for such services as they consider appropriate to be available with respect to accommodated children.

(2) 'Accommodated children' are those children in respect of whose accommodation the local authority have been notified under section 85 or 86.

(3) The services shall be provided with a view to promoting contact between each accommodated child and that child's family.

(4) The services may, in particular, include–

(a) advice, guidance and counselling;

(b) services necessary to enable the child to visit, or to be visited by, members of the family;

(c) assistance to enable the child and members of the family to have a holiday together.

(5) Nothing in this paragraph affects the duty imposed by paragraph 10.

Family centres

9 (1) Every local authority shall provide such family centres as they consider appropriate in relation to children within their area.

(2) 'Family centre' means a centre at which any of the persons mentioned in subparagraph (3) may–

(a) attend for occupational, social, cultural or recreational activities;

(b) attend for advice, guidance or counselling; or

(c) be provided with accommodation while he is receiving advice, guidance or counselling.

(3) The persons are–

(a) a child;

(b) his parents;

(c) any person who is not a parent of his but who has parental responsibility for him;

(d) any other person who is looking after him.

Maintenance of the family home

10 Every local authority shall take such steps as are reasonably practicable, where any child within their area who is in need and whom they are not looking after is living apart from his family–

(a) to enable him to live with his family; or

(b) to promote contact between him and his family,

if, in their opinion, it is necessary to do so in order to safeguard or promote his welfare.

Duty to consider racial groups to which children in need belong

11 Every local authority shall, in making any arrangements–

(a) for the provision of day care within their area; or

(b) designed to encourage persons to act as local authority foster parents,

have regard to the different racial groups to which children within their area who are in need belong.

CHILDREN AND FAMILIES ACT 2014

Part 3: Children and Young People in England with Special Educational Needs or Disabilities

Local authority functions: general principles

Local authority functions: supporting and involving children and young people

19   In exercising a function under this Part in the case of a child or young person, a local authority in England must have regard to the following matters in particular–

(a) the views, wishes and feelings of the child and his or her parent, or the young person;

(b) the importance of the child and his or her parent, or the young person, participating as fully as possible in decisions relating to the exercise of the function concerned;

(c) the importance of the child and his or her parent, or the young person, being provided with the information and support necessary to enable participation in those decisions;

(d) the need to support the child and his or her parent, or the young person, in order to facilitate the development of the child or young person and to help him or her achieve the best possible educational and other outcomes.

Special educational needs etc

When a child or young person has special educational needs

20 (1) A child or young person has special educational needs if he or she has a learning difficulty or disability which calls for special educational provision to be made for him or her.

(2) A child of compulsory school age or a young person has a learning difficulty or disability if he or she–

(a) has a significantly greater difficulty in learning than the majority of others of the same age, or

(b) has a disability which prevents or hinders him or her from making use of facilities of a kind generally provided for others of the same age in mainstream schools or mainstream post-16 institutions.

(3) A child under compulsory school age has a learning difficulty or disability if he or she is likely to be within subsection (2) when of compulsory school age (or would be likely, if no special educational provision were made).

(4) A child or young person does not have a learning difficulty or disability solely because the language (or form of language) in which he or she is or will be taught is different from a language (or form of language) which is or has been spoken at home.

(5) This section applies for the purposes of this Part.

Special educational provision, health care provision and social care provision

21 (1) 'Special educational provision', for a child aged two or more or a young person, means educational or training provision that is additional to, or different from, that made generally for others of the same age in–

(a) mainstream schools in England,

   (b) maintained nursery schools in England,

   (c) mainstream post-16 institutions in England, or

   (d) places in England at which relevant early years education is provided.

(2) 'Special educational provision', for a child aged under two, means educational provision of any kind.

(3) 'Health care provision' means the provision of health care services as part of the comprehensive health service in England continued under section 1(1) of the National Health Service Act 2006.

(4) 'Social care provision' means the provision made by a local authority in the exercise of its social services functions.

(5) Health care provision or social care provision which educates or trains a child or young person is to be treated as special educational provision (instead of health care provision or social care provision).

(6) This section applies for the purposes of this Part.

Identifying children and young people with special educational needs and disabilities

Identifying children and young people with special educational needs and disabilities

22 A local authority in England must exercise its functions with a view to securing that it identifies–

   (a) all the children and young people in its area who have or may have special educational needs, and

   (b) all the children and young people in its area who have a disability.

Duty of health bodies to bring certain children to local authority's attention

23 (1) This section applies where, in the course of exercising functions in relation to a child who is under compulsory school age, a clinical commissioning group, NHS trust or NHS foundation trust form the opinion that the child has (or probably has) special educational needs or a disability.

(2) The group or trust must–

   (a) inform the child's parent of their opinion and of their duty under subsection (3), and

   (b) give the child's parent an opportunity to discuss their opinion with an officer of the group or trust.

(3) The group or trust must then bring their opinion to the attention of the appropriate local authority in England.

(4) If the group or trust think a particular voluntary organisation is likely to be able to give the parent advice or assistance in connection with any special educational needs or disability the child may have, they must inform the parent of that.

Education, health and care provision: integration and joint commissioning

Promoting integration

25 (1) A local authority in England must exercise its functions under this Part with a view to ensuring the integration of educational provision and training provision with health care provision and social care provision, where it thinks that this would–

(a) promote the well-being of children or young people in its area who have special educational needs or a disability, or

(b) improve the quality of special educational provision–

    (i) made in its area for children or young people who have special educational needs, or

    (ii) made outside its area for children or young people for whom it is responsible who have special educational needs.

(2) The reference in subsection (1) to the well-being of children and young people is to their well-being so far as relating to–

(a) physical and mental health and emotional well-being;

(b) protection from abuse and neglect;

(c) control by them over their day-to-day lives;

(d) participation in education, training or recreation;

(e) social and economic well-being;

(f) domestic, family and personal relationships;

(g) the contribution made by them to society.

Joint commissioning arrangements

26 (1) A local authority in England and its partner commissioning bodies must make arrangements ('joint commissioning arrangements') about the education, health and care provision to be secured for–

(a) children and young people for whom the authority is responsible who have special educational needs, and

(b) children and young people in the authority's area who have a disability.

(2) In this Part 'education, health and care provision' means–

(a) special educational provision;

(b) health care provision;

(c) social care provision.

(3) Joint commissioning arrangements must include arrangements for considering and agreeing–

(a) the education, health and care provision reasonably required by–

    (i) the learning difficulties and disabilities which result in the children and young people within subsection (1)(a) having special educational needs, and

    (ii) the disabilities of the children and young people within subsection (1)(b);

(b) what education, health and care provision is to be secured;

(c) by whom education, health and care provision is to be secured;

(d) what advice and information is to be provided about education, health and care provision;

(e) by whom, to whom and how such advice and information is to be provided;

(f) how complaints about education, health and care provision may be made and are to be dealt with;

(g) procedures for ensuring that disputes between the parties to the joint commissioning arrangements are resolved as quickly as possible.

(4) Joint commissioning arrangements about securing education, health and care provision must in particular include arrangements for–

(a) securing EHC needs assessments;

    (b) securing the education, health and care provision specified in EHC plans;

    (c) agreeing personal budgets under section 49.

(5) Joint commissioning arrangements may also include other provision.

(6) The parties to joint commissioning arrangements must–

    (a) have regard to them in the exercise of their functions, and

    (b) keep them under review.

(7) Section 116B of the Local Government and Public Involvement in Health Act 2007 (duty to have regard to assessment of relevant needs and joint health and wellbeing strategy) applies in relation to functions exercisable under this section.

(8) A local authority's 'partner commissioning bodies' are–

    (a) the National Health Service Commissioning Board, to the extent that it is under a duty under section 3B of the National Health Service Act 2006 to arrange for the provision of services or facilities for–

        (i) any children and young people for whom the authority is responsible who have special educational needs, or

        (ii) any children and young people in the authority's area who have a disability, and

    (b) each clinical commissioning group that is under a duty under section 3 of that Act to arrange for the provision of services or facilities for any children and young people within paragraph (a).

(9) Regulations may prescribe circumstances in which a clinical commissioning group that would otherwise be a partner commissioning body of a local authority by virtue of subsection (8)(b) is to be treated as not being a partner commissioning body of the authority.

Review of education and care provision

Duty to keep education and care provision under review

27 (1) A local authority in England must keep under review–

    (a) the educational provision, training provision and social care provision made in its area for children and young people who have special educational needs or a disability, and

    (b) the educational provision, training provision and social care provision made outside its area for–

        (i) children and young people for whom it is responsible who have special educational needs, and

        (ii) children and young people in its area who have a disability.

(2) The authority must consider the extent to which the provision referred to in subsection (1)(a) and (b) is sufficient to meet the educational needs, training needs and social care needs of the children and young people concerned.

(3) In exercising its functions under this section, the authority must consult–

    (a) children and young people in its area with special educational needs, and the parents of children in its area with special educational needs;

    (b) children and young people in its area who have a disability, and the parents of children in its area who have a disability;

    (c) the governing bodies of maintained schools and maintained nursery schools in its area;

    (d) the proprietors of Academies in its area;

(e)　the governing bodies, proprietors or principals of post-16 institutions in its area;

(f)　the governing bodies of non-maintained special schools in its area;

(g)　the advisory boards of children's centres in its area;

(h)　the providers of relevant early years education in its area;

(i)　the governing bodies, proprietors or principals of other schools and post-16 institutions in England and Wales that the authority thinks are or are likely to be attended by–

　　(i)　children or young people for whom it is responsible, or

　　(ii)　children or young people in its area who have a disability;

(j)　a youth offending team that the authority thinks has functions in relation to–

　　(i)　children or young people for whom it is responsible, or

　　(ii)　children or young people in its area who have a disability;

(k)　such other persons as the authority thinks appropriate.

(4)　Section 116B of the Local Government and Public Involvement in Health Act 2007 (duty to have regard to assessment of relevant needs and joint health and wellbeing strategy) applies in relation to functions exercisable under this section.

(5)　'Children's centre' has the meaning given by section 5A(4) of the Childcare Act 2006.

Co-operation and assistance

Co-operating generally: local authority functions

28 (1)　A local authority in England must co-operate with each of its local partners, and each local partner must co-operate with the authority, in the exercise of the authority's functions under this Part.

(2)　Each of the following is a local partner of a local authority in England for this purpose–

(a)　where the authority is a county council for an area for which there is also a district council, the district council;

(b)　the governing body of a maintained school or maintained nursery school that is maintained by the authority or provides education or training for children or young people for whom the authority is responsible;

(c)　the proprietor of an Academy that is in the authority's area or provides education or training for children or young people for whom the authority is responsible;

(d)　the proprietor of a non-maintained special school that is in the authority's area or provides education or training for children or young people for whom the authority is responsible;

(e)　the governing body of an institution within the further education sector that is in the authority's area, or is attended, or likely to be attended, by children or young people for whom the authority is responsible;

(f)　the management committee of a pupil referral unit that is in the authority's area, or is in England and is or is likely to be attended by children or young people for whom the authority is responsible;

(g)　the proprietor of an institution approved by the Secretary of State under section 41 (independent special schools and special post 16 institutions: approval) that is in the authority's area, or is attended, or likely to be attended, by children or young people for whom the authority is responsible;

(h) any other person (other than a school or post-16 institution) that makes special educational provision for a child or young person for whom the authority is responsible;

(i) a youth offending team that the authority thinks has functions in relation to children or young people for whom it is responsible;

(j) a person in charge of relevant youth accommodation–
    (i) in which there are detained persons aged 18 or under for whom the authority was responsible immediately before the beginning of their detention, or
    (ii) that the authority thinks is accommodation in which such persons are likely to be detained;

(k) the National Health Service Commissioning Board;

(l) a clinical commissioning group–
    (i) whose area coincides with, or falls wholly or partly within, the authority's area, or
    (ii) which is under a duty under section 3 of the National Health Service Act 2006 to arrange for the provision of services or facilities for any children and young people for whom the authority is responsible;

(m) an NHS trust or NHS foundation trust which provides services in the authority's area, or which exercises functions in relation to children or young people for whom the authority is responsible;

(n) a Local Health Board which exercises functions in relation to children or young people for whom the authority is responsible.

(3) A local authority in England must make arrangements for ensuring co-operation between–

(a) the officers of the authority who exercise the authority's functions relating to education or training,

(b) the officers of the authority who exercise the authority's social services functions for children or young people with special educational needs, and

(c) the officers of the authority, so far as they are not officers within paragraph (a) or (b), who exercise the authority's functions relating to provision which is within section 30(2)(e) (provision to assist in preparing children and young people for adulthood and independent living).

(4) Regulations may prescribe circumstances in which a clinical commissioning group that would otherwise be a local partner of a local authority by virtue of subsection (2)(l)(ii) is to be treated as not being a local partner of the authority.

Co-operating generally: governing body functions

29 (1) This section applies where an appropriate authority for a school or post-16 institution mentioned in subsection (2) has functions under this Part.

(2) The schools and post-16 institutions referred to in subsection (1) are–

(a) mainstream schools;

(b) maintained nursery schools;

(c) 16 to 19 Academies;

(d) institutions within the further education sector;

(e) pupil referral units;

(f) alternative provision Academies.
(3) The appropriate authority must co-operate with each responsible local authority, and each responsible local authority must co-operate with the appropriate
authority, in the exercise of those functions.
(4) A responsible local authority, in relation to an appropriate authority for a
school or post-16 institution mentioned in subsection (2), is a local authority
in England that is responsible for any child or young person who is a registered pupil or a student at the school or post-16 institution.
(5) The 'appropriate authority' for a school or post-16 institution is–
(a) in the case of a maintained school, maintained nursery school, or institution within the further education sector, the governing body;
(b) in the case of an Academy, the proprietor;
(c) in the case of a pupil referral unit, the management committee.

Information and advice

Local offer

30 (1) A local authority in England must publish information about–
(a) the provision within subsection (2) it expects to be available in its area at
the time of publication for children and young people who have special
educational needs or a disability, and
(b) the provision within subsection (2) it expects to be available outside its
area at that time for–
(i) children and young people for whom it is responsible, and
(ii) children and young people in its area who have a disability.
(2) The provision for children and young people referred to in subsection (1) is–
(a) education, health and care provision;
(b) other educational provision;
(c) other training provision;
(d) arrangements for travel to and from schools and post-16 institutions and
places at which relevant early years education is provided;
(e) provision to assist in preparing children and young people for adulthood
and independent living.
(3) For the purposes of subsection (2)(e), provision to assist in preparation for
adulthood and independent living includes provision relating to–
(a) finding employment;
(b) obtaining accommodation;
(c) participation in society.
(4) Information required to be published by an authority under this section is to
be known as its 'local offer'.
(5) A local authority must keep its local offer under review and may from time to
time revise it.
(6) A local authority must from time to time publish–
(a) comments about its local offer it has received from or on behalf of–
(i) children and young people with special educational needs, and the
parents of children with special educational needs, and
(ii) children and young people who have a disability, and the parents of
children who have a disability, and
(b) the authority's response to those comments (including details of any
action the authority intends to take).

(7) Comments published under subsection (6)(a) must be published in a form that does not enable the person making them to be identified.

(8) Regulations may make provision about–
   (a) the information to be included in an authority's local offer;
   (b) how an authority's local offer is to be published;
   (c) who is to be consulted by an authority in preparing and reviewing its local offer;
   (d) how an authority is to involve–
      (i) children and young people with special educational needs, and the parents of children with special educational needs, and
      (ii) children and young people who have a disability, and the parents of children who have a disability,
   in the preparation and review of its local offer;
   (e) the publication of comments on the local offer, and the local authority's response, under subsection (6) (including circumstances in which comments are not required to be published).

(9) The regulations may in particular require an authority's local offer to include–
   (a) information about how to obtain an EHC needs assessment;
   (b) information about other sources of information, advice and support for–
      (i) children and young people with special educational needs and those who care for them, and
      (ii) children and young people who have a disability and those who care for them;
   (c) information about gaining access to provision additional to, or different from, the provision mentioned in subsection (2);
   (d) information about how to make a complaint about provision mentioned in subsection (2).

Co-operating in specific cases: local authority functions

31 (1) This section applies where a local authority in England requests the co-operation of any of the following persons and bodies in the exercise of a function under this Part–
   (a) another local authority;
   (b) a youth offending team;
   (c) the person in charge of any relevant youth accommodation;
   (d) the National Health Service Commissioning Board;
   (e) a clinical commissioning group;
   (f) a Local Health Board;
   (g) an NHS trust or NHS foundation trust.

(2) The person or body must comply with the request, unless the person or body considers that doing so would–
   (a) be incompatible with the duties of the person or body, or
   (b) otherwise have an adverse effect on the exercise of the functions of the person or body.

(3) A person or body that decides not to comply with a request under subsection (1) must give the authority that made the request written reasons for the decision.

(4) Regulations may provide that, where a person or body is under a duty to

comply with a request to co-operate with a local authority in securing an EHC needs assessment, a detained person's EHC needs assessment or the preparation of an EHC plan, the person or body must comply with the request within a prescribed period, unless a prescribed exception applies.

Advice and information

32 (1) A local authority in England must arrange for children and young people for whom it is responsible, and the parents of children for whom it is responsible, to be provided with advice and information about matters relating to the special educational needs of the children or young people concerned.

(2) A local authority in England must arrange for children and young people in its area with a disability, and the parents of children in its area with a disability, to be provided with advice and information about matters relating to the disabilities of the children or young people concerned.

(3) The authority must take such steps as it thinks appropriate for making the services provided under subsections (1) and (2) known to–
(a) the parents of children in its area;
(b) children in its area;
(c) young people in its area;
(d) the head teachers, proprietors and principals of schools and post-16 institutions in its area.

(4) The authority may also take such steps as it thinks appropriate for making the services provided under subsections (1) and (2) known to such other persons as it thinks appropriate.

Mainstream education

Children and young people with EHC plans

33 (1) This section applies where a local authority is securing the preparation of an EHC plan for a child or young person who is to be educated in a school or post-16 institution.

(2) In a case within section 39(5) or 40(2), the local authority must secure that the plan provides for the child or young person to be educated in a maintained nursery school, mainstream school or mainstream post-16 institution, unless that is incompatible with–
(a) the wishes of the child's parent or the young person, or
(b) the provision of efficient education for others.

(3) A local authority may rely on the exception in subsection (2)(b) in relation to maintained nursery schools, mainstream schools or mainstream post-16 institutions in its area taken as a whole only if it shows that there are no reasonable steps that it could take to prevent the incompatibility.

(4) A local authority may rely on the exception in subsection (2)(b) in relation to a particular maintained nursery school, mainstream school or mainstream post-16 institution only if it shows that there are no reasonable steps that it or the governing body, proprietor or principal could take to prevent the incompatibility.

(5) The governing body, proprietor or principal of a maintained nursery school, mainstream school or mainstream post-16 institution may rely on the exception in subsection (2)(b) only if they show that there are no reasonable steps that they or the local authority could take to prevent the incompatibility.

(6) Subsection (2) does not prevent the child or young person from being educated in an independent school, a non-maintained special school or a special post-16 institution, if the cost is not to be met by a local authority or the Secretary of State.

(7) This section does not affect the operation of section 63 (fees payable by local authority for special educational provision at non-maintained schools and post-16 institutions).

Children and young people with special educational needs but no EHC plan

34 (1) This section applies to a child or young person in England who has special educational needs but for whom no EHC plan is maintained, if he or she is to be educated in a school or post-16 institution.

(2) The child or young person must be educated in a maintained nursery school, mainstream school or mainstream post-16 institution, subject to subsections (3) and (4).

(3) The child or young person may be educated in an independent school, a non-maintained special school or a special post-16 institution, if the cost is not to be met by a local authority or the Secretary of State.

(4) The child or young person may be educated in a special school or special post-16 institution during any period in which any of subsections (5) to (9) applies.

(5) This subsection applies while the child or young person is admitted to a special school or special post-16 institution for the purposes of an EHC needs assessment, if all the following have agreed to his or her admission to the school or post-16 institution–
   (a) the local authority which is responsible for him or her;
   (b) the head teacher of the school or the principal of the Academy or post-16 institution;
   (c) the child's parent or the young person;
   (d) anyone else whose advice is required to be obtained in connection with the assessment by virtue of regulations under section 36(11).

(6) This subsection applies while the child or young person remains admitted to a special school or special post-16 institution, in prescribed circumstances, following an EHC needs assessment at the school or post-16 institution.

(7) This subsection applies while the child or young person is admitted to a special school or special post-16 institution, following a change in his or her circumstances, if all the following have agreed to his or her admission to the school or post-16 institution–
   (a) the local authority which is responsible for him or her;
   (b) the head teacher of the school or the principal of the Academy or post-16 institution;
   (c) the child's parent or the young person.

(8) This subsection applies while the child or young person is admitted to a special school which is established in a hospital and is–
   (a) a community or foundation special school, or
   (b) an Academy school.

(9) This subsection applies while the child is admitted to a special school or special post-16 institution that is an Academy, if the Academy arrangements

made in respect of the school or post-16 institution permit it to admit children and young people with special educational needs for whom no EHC plan is maintained.

(10) This section does not affect the operation of section 63 (fees payable by local authority for special educational provision at non-maintained schools and post-16 institutions).

Children with SEN in maintained nurseries and mainstream schools

35 (1) This section applies where a child with special educational needs is being educated in a maintained nursery school or a mainstream school.

(2) Those concerned with making special educational provision for the child must secure that the child engages in the activities of the school together with children who do not have special educational needs, subject to subsection (3).

(3) Subsection (2) applies only so far as is reasonably practicable and is compatible with–

(a) the child receiving the special educational provision called for by his or her special educational needs,

(b) the provision of efficient education for the children with whom he or she will be educated, and

(c) the efficient use of resources.

Assessment

Assessment of education, health and care needs

36 (1) A request for a local authority in England to secure an EHC needs assessment for a child or young person may be made to the authority by the child's parent, the young person or a person acting on behalf of a school or post-16 institution.

(2) An 'EHC needs assessment' is an assessment of the educational, health care and social care needs of a child or young person.

(3) When a request is made to a local authority under subsection (1), or a local authority otherwise becomes responsible for a child or young person, the authority must determine whether it may be necessary for special educational provision to be made for the child or young person in accordance with an EHC plan.

(4) In making a determination under subsection (3), the local authority must consult the child's parent or the young person.

(5) Where the local authority determines that it is not necessary for special educational provision to be made for the child or young person in accordance with an EHC plan it must notify the child's parent or the young person–

(a) of the reasons for that determination, and

(b) that accordingly it has decided not to secure an EHC needs assessment for the child or young person.

(6) Subsection (7) applies where–

(a) no EHC plan is maintained for the child or young person,

(b) the child or young person has not been assessed under this section or section 71 during the previous six months, and

(c) the local authority determines that it may be necessary for special educational provision to be made for the child or young person in accordance with an EHC plan.

(7) The authority must notify the child's parent or the young person–
    (a) that it is considering securing an EHC needs assessment for the child or young person, and
    (b) that the parent or young person has the right to–
        (i) express views to the authority (orally or in writing), and
        (ii) submit evidence to the authority.

(8) The local authority must secure an EHC needs assessment for the child or young person if, after having regard to any views expressed and evidence submitted under subsection (7), the authority is of the opinion that–
    (a) the child or young person has or may have special educational needs, and
    (b) it may be necessary for special educational provision to be made for the child or young person in accordance with an EHC plan.

(9) After an EHC needs assessment has been carried out, the local authority must notify the child's parent or the young person of–
    (a) the outcome of the assessment,
    (b) whether it proposes to secure that an EHC plan is prepared for the child or young person, and
    (c) the reasons for that decision.

(10) In making a determination or forming an opinion for the purposes of this section in relation to a young person aged over 18, a local authority must consider whether he or she requires additional time, in comparison to the majority of others of the same age who do not have special educational needs, to complete his or her education or training.

(11) Regulations may make provision about EHC needs assessments, in particular–
    (a) about requests under subsection (1);
    (b) imposing time limits in relation to consultation under subsection (4);
    (c) about giving notice;
    (d) about expressing views and submitting evidence under subsection (7);
    (e) about how assessments are to be conducted;
    (f) about advice to be obtained in connection with an assessment;
    (g) about combining an EHC needs assessment with other assessments;
    (h) about the use for the purposes of an EHC needs assessment of information obtained as a result of other assessments;
    (i) about the use of information obtained as a result of an EHC needs assessment, including the use of that information for the purposes of other assessments;
    (j) about the provision of information, advice and support in connection with an EHC needs assessment.

Education, health and care plans

Education, health and care plans

37 (1) Where, in the light of an EHC needs assessment, it is necessary for special educational provision to be made for a child or young person in accordance with an EHC plan–
    (a) the local authority must secure that an EHC plan is prepared for the child or young person, and
    (b) once an EHC plan has been prepared, it must maintain the plan.

(2) For the purposes of this Part, an EHC plan is a plan specifying–

(a) the child's or young person's special educational needs;

(b) the outcomes sought for him or her;

(c) the special educational provision required by him or her;

(d) any health care provision reasonably required by the learning difficulties and disabilities which result in him or her having special educational needs;

(e) in the case of a child or a young person aged under 18, any social care provision which must be made for him or her by the local authority as a result of section 2 of the Chronically Sick and Disabled Persons Act 1970;

(f) any social care provision reasonably required by the learning difficulties and disabilities which result in the child or young person having special educational needs, to the extent that the provision is not already specified in the plan under paragraph (e).

(3) An EHC plan may also specify other health care and social care provision reasonably required by the child or young person.

(4) Regulations may make provision about the preparation, content, maintenance, amendment and disclosure of EHC plans.

(5) Regulations under subsection (4) about amendments of EHC plans must include provision applying section 33 (mainstream education for children and young people with EHC plans) to a case where an EHC plan is to be amended under those regulations.

Preparation of EHC plans: draft plan

38 (1) Where a local authority is required to secure that an EHC plan is prepared for a child or young person, it must consult the child's parent or the young person about the content of the plan during the preparation of a draft of the plan.

(2) The local authority must then–

(a) send the draft plan to the child's parent or the young person, and

(b) give the parent or young person notice of his or her right to–

(i) make representations about the content of the draft plan, and

(ii) request the authority to secure that a particular school or other institution within subsection (3) is named in the plan.

(3) A school or other institution is within this subsection if it is–

(a) a maintained school;

(b) a maintained nursery school;

(c) an Academy;

(d) an institution within the further education sector in England;

(e) a non-maintained special school;

(f) an institution approved by the Secretary of State under section 41 (independent special schools and special post-16 institutions: approval).

(4) A notice under subsection (2)(b) must specify a period before the end of which any representations or requests must be made.

(5) The draft EHC plan sent to the child's parent or the young person must not–

(a) name a school or other institution, or

(b) specify a type of school or other institution.

Finalising EHC plans: request for particular school or other institution

39 (1) This section applies where, before the end of the period specified in a notice under section 38(2)(b), a request is made to a local authority to secure that a particular school or other institution is named in an EHC plan.

(2) The local authority must consult–
- (a) the governing body, proprietor or principal of the school or other institution,
- (b) the governing body, proprietor or principal of any other school or other institution the authority is considering having named in the plan, and
- (c) if a school or other institution is within paragraph (a) or (b) and is maintained by another local authority, that authority.

(3) The local authority must secure that the EHC plan names the school or other institution specified in the request, unless subsection (4) applies.

(4) This subsection applies where–
- (a) the school or other institution requested is unsuitable for the age, ability, aptitude or special educational needs of the child or young person concerned, or
- (b) the attendance of the child or young person at the requested school or other institution would be incompatible with–
  - (i) the provision of efficient education for others, or
  - (ii) the efficient use of resources.

(5) Where subsection (4) applies, the local authority must secure that the plan–
- (a) names a school or other institution which the local authority thinks would be appropriate for the child or young person, or
- (b) specifies the type of school or other institution which the local authority thinks would be appropriate for the child or young person.

(6) Before securing that the plan names a school or other institution under subsection (5)(a), the local authority must (if it has not already done so) consult–
- (a) the governing body, proprietor or principal of any school or other institution the authority is considering having named in the plan, and
- (b) if that school or other institution is maintained by another local authority, that authority.

(7) The local authority must, at the end of the period specified in the notice under section 38(2)(b), secure that any changes it thinks necessary are made to the draft EHC plan.

(8) The local authority must send a copy of the finalised EHC plan to–
- (a) the child's parent or the young person, and
- (b) the governing body, proprietor or principal of any school or other institution named in the plan.

Finalising EHC plans: no request for particular school or other institution

40 (1) This section applies where no request is made to a local authority before the end of the period specified in a notice under section 38(2)(b) to secure that a particular school or other institution is named in an EHC plan.

(2) The local authority must secure that the plan–
- (a) names a school or other institution which the local authority thinks would be appropriate for the child or young person concerned, or
- (b) specifies the type of school or other institution which the local authority thinks would be appropriate for the child or young person.

(3) Before securing that the plan names a school or other institution under subsection (2)(a), the local authority must consult–
- (a) the governing body, proprietor or principal of any school or other institution the authority is considering having named in the plan, and

(b) if that school or other institution is maintained by another local authority, that authority.

(4) The local authority must also secure that any changes it thinks necessary are made to the draft EHC plan.

(5) The local authority must send a copy of the finalised EHC plan to–
(a) the child's parent or the young person, and
(b) the governing body, proprietor or principal of any school or other institution named in the plan.

Independent special schools and special post-16 institutions: approval

41 (1) The Secretary of State may approve an institution within subsection (2) for the purpose of enabling the institution to be the subject of a request for it to be named in an EHC plan.

(2) An institution is within this subsection if it is–
(a) an independent educational institution (within the meaning of Chapter 1 of Part 4 of ESA 2008)–
   (i) which has been entered on the register of independent educational institutions in England (kept under section 95 of that Act), and
   (ii) which is specially organised to make special educational provision for students with special educational needs,
(b) an independent school–
   (i) which has been entered on the register of independent schools in Wales (kept under section 158 of the Education Act 2002), and
   (ii) which is specially organised to make special educational provision for pupils with special educational needs, or
(c) a special post-16 institution which is not an institution within the further education sector or a 16 to 19 Academy.

(3) The Secretary of State may approve an institution under subsection (1) only if its proprietor consents.

(4) The Secretary of State may withdraw approval given under subsection (1).

(5) Regulations may make provision about giving and withdrawing approval under this section, in particular–
(a) about the types of special post-16 institutions which may be approved under subsection (1);
(b) specifying criteria which an institution must meet before it can be approved under subsection (1);
(c) about the matters which may or must be taken into account in deciding to give or withdraw approval;
(d) about the publication of a list of all institutions who are approved under this section.

Duty to secure special educational provision and health care provision in accordance with EHC Plan

42 (1) This section applies where a local authority maintains an EHC plan for a child or young person.

(2) The local authority must secure the specified special educational provision for the child or young person.

(3) If the plan specifies health care provision, the responsible commissioning body must arrange the specified health care provision for the child or young person.

(4) 'The responsible commissioning body', in relation to any specified health care provision, means the body (or each body) that is under a duty to arrange health care provision of that kind in respect of the child or young person.

(5) Subsections (2) and (3) do not apply if the child's parent or the young person has made suitable alternative arrangements.

(6) 'Specified', in relation to an EHC plan, means specified in the plan.

Schools and other institutions named in EHC plan: duty to admit

43 (1) Subsection (2) applies if one of the following is named in an EHC plan–

 (a) a maintained school;

 (b) a maintained nursery school;

 (c) an Academy;

 (d) an institution within the further education sector in England;

 (e) a non-maintained special school;

 (f) an institution approved by the Secretary of State under section 41.

(2) The governing body, proprietor or principal of the school or other institution must admit the child or young person for whom the plan is maintained.

(3) Subsection (2) has effect regardless of any duty imposed on the governing body of a school by section 1(6) of SSFA 1998.

(4) Subsection (2) does not affect any power to exclude a pupil or student from a school or other institution.

Reviews and re-assessments

44 (1) A local authority must review an EHC plan that it maintains–

 (a) in the period of 12 months starting with the date on which the plan was first made, and

 (b) in each subsequent period of 12 months starting with the date on which the plan was last reviewed under this section.

(2) A local authority must secure a re-assessment of the educational, health care and social care needs of a child or young person for whom it maintains an EHC plan if a request is made to it by–

 (a) the child's parent or the young person, or

 (b) the governing body, proprietor or principal of the school, post-16 institution or other institution which the child or young person attends.

(3) A local authority may also secure a re-assessment of those needs at any other time if it thinks it necessary.

(4) Subsections (1) and (2) are subject to any contrary provision in regulations made under subsection (7)(b).

(5) In reviewing an EHC plan maintained for a young person aged over 18, or deciding whether to secure a re-assessment of the needs of such a young person, a local authority must have regard to whether the educational or training outcomes specified in the plan have been achieved.

(6) During a review or re-assessment, a local authority must consult the parent of the child, or the young person, for whom it maintains the EHC plan.

(7) Regulations may make provision about reviews and re-assessments, in particular–

 (a) about other circumstances in which a local authority must or may review an EHC plan or secure a re-assessment (including before the end of a specified phase of a child's or young person's education);

 (b) about circumstances in which it is not necessary for a local authority to review an EHC plan or secure a re-assessment;

(c) about amending or replacing an EHC plan following a review or re-assessment.

(8) Regulations under subsection (7) about re-assessments may in particular apply provisions of or made under this Part that are applicable to EHC needs assessments, with or without modifications.

(9) Regulations under subsection (7)(c) must include provision applying section 33 (mainstream education for children and young people with EHC plans) to a case where an EHC plan is to be amended following a review.

Ceasing to maintain an EHC plan

45 (1) A local authority may cease to maintain an EHC plan for a child or young person only if–

(a) the authority is no longer responsible for the child or young person, or

(b) the authority determines that it is no longer necessary for the plan to be maintained.

in which it is no longer necessary for an EHC plan to be maintained for a child or young person include where the child or young person no longer requires the special educational provision specified in the plan.

(3) When determining whether a young person aged over 18 no longer requires the special educational provision specified in his or her EHC plan, a local authority must have regard to whether the educational or training outcomes specified in the plan have been achieved.

(4) A local authority may not cease to maintain an EHC plan for a child or young person until–

(a) after the end of the period allowed for bringing an appeal under section 51 against its decision to cease to maintain the plan, where no such appeal is brought before the end of that period;

(b) after the appeal has been finally determined, where such an appeal is brought before the end of that period.

(5) Regulations may make provision about ceasing to maintain an EHC plan, in particular about–

(a) other circumstances in which it is no longer necessary for an EHC plan to be maintained;

(b) circumstances in which a local authority may not determine that it is no longer necessary for an EHC plan to be maintained;

(c) the procedure to be followed by a local authority when determining whether to cease to maintain an EHC plan.

Maintaining an EHC plan after young person's 25th birthday

46 (1) A local authority may continue to maintain an EHC plan for a young person until the end of the academic year during which the young person attains the age of 25.

(2) 'Academic year' means the period of twelve months ending on the prescribed date.

Transfer of EHC plans

47 (1) Regulations may make provision for an EHC plan maintained for a child or young person by one local authority to be transferred to another local authority in England, where the other authority becomes responsible for the child or young person.

(2) The regulations may in particular–
- (a) impose a duty on the other authority to maintain the plan;
- (b) treat the plan as if originally prepared by the other authority;
- (c) treat things done by the transferring authority in relation to the plan as done by the other authority.

Release of child or young person for whom EHC plan previously maintained

48 (1) This section applies where–
- (a) a child or young person who has been subject to a detention order (within the meaning of section 562(1A)(a) of EA 1996) is released,
- (b) on the release date, a local authority in England becomes responsible for him or her, and
- (c) an EHC plan was–
  - (i) maintained for him or her immediately before the start of the detention, or
  - (ii) kept for him or her under section 74 during the detention.

(2) The local authority must–
- (a) maintain the plan, and
- (b) review the plan as soon as reasonably practicable after the release date.

(3) Subsection (2)(b) is subject to any contrary provision in regulations under section 44(7)(b).

Personal budgets and direct payments

49 (1) A local authority that maintains an EHC plan, or is securing the preparation of an EHC plan, for a child or young person must prepare a personal budget for him or her if asked to do so by the child's parent or the young person.

(2) The authority prepares a 'personal budget' for the child or young person if it identifies an amount as available to secure particular provision that is specified, or proposed to be specified, in the EHC plan, with a view to the child's parent or the young person being involved in securing the provision.

(3) Regulations may make provision about personal budgets, in particular–
- (a) about requests for personal budgets;
- (b) about the amount of a personal budget;
- (c) about the sources of the funds making up a personal budget;
- (d) for payments ('direct payments') representing all or part of a personal budget to be made to a child's parent or a young person, or a person of a prescribed description in prescribed circumstances, in order to secure provision to which the budget relates;
- (e) about the description of provision to which personal budgets and direct payments may (and may not) relate;
- (f) for a personal budget or direct payment to cover the agreed cost of the provision to which the budget or payment relates;
- (g) about when, how, to whom and on what conditions direct payments may (and may not) be made;
- (h) about when direct payments may be required to be repaid and the recovery of unpaid sums;
- (i) about conditions with which a person or body making direct payments must comply before, after or at the time of making a direct payment;

(j) about arrangements for providing information, advice or support in connection with personal budgets and direct payments.

(4) If the regulations include provision authorising direct payments, they must–

(a) require the consent of a child's parent or a young person, or a person of a prescribed description in prescribed circumstances, to be obtained before direct payments are made;

(b) require the authority to stop making direct payments where the required consent is withdrawn.

(5) Special educational provision acquired by means of a direct payment made by a local authority is to be treated as having been secured by the authority in pursuance of its duty under section 42(2), subject to any prescribed conditions or exceptions.

(6) Subsection (7) applies if–

(a) an EHC plan is maintained for a child or young person, and

(b) health care provision specified in the plan is acquired for him or her by means of a payment made by a commissioning body under section 12A(1) of the National Health Service Act 2006 (direct payments for health care).

(7) The health care provision is to be treated as having been arranged by the commissioning body in pursuance of its duty under section 42(3) of this Act, subject to any prescribed conditions or exceptions.

(8) 'Commissioning body', in relation to any specified health care provision, means a body that is under a duty to arrange health care provision of that kind in respect of the child or young person.

Continuation of services under section 17 of the Children Act 1989

50   After section 17 of the Children Act 1989 (provision of services for children etc) insert–

'Section 17 services: continued provision where EHC plan maintained

17ZG(1) This section applies where, immediately before a child in need reaches the age of 18–

(a) a local authority in England is providing services for the child in the exercise of functions conferred by section 17, and

(b) an EHC plan is maintained for the child.

(2) The local authority may continue to provide services for the child in the exercise of those functions after the child reaches the age of 18, but may not continue to do so after the EHC plan has ceased to be maintained.

(3) In this section 'EHC plan' means a plan within section 37(2) of the Children and Families Act 2014.'

Appeals, mediation and dispute resolution

Appeals

51 (1) A child's parent or a young person may appeal to the First-tier Tribunal against the matters set out in subsection (2), subject to section 55 (mediation).

(2) The matters are–

(a) a decision of a local authority not to secure an EHC needs assessment for the child or young person;

   (b) a decision of a local authority, following an EHC needs assessment, that it is not necessary for special educational provision to be made for the child or young person in accordance with an EHC plan;

   (c) where an EHC plan is maintained for the child or young person–

      (i) the child's or young person's special educational needs as specified in the plan;

      (ii) the special educational provision specified in the plan;

      (iii) the school or other institution named in the plan, or the type of school or other institution specified in the plan;

      (iv) if no school or other institution is named in the plan, that fact;

   (d) a decision of a local authority not to secure a re-assessment of the needs of the child or young person under section 44 following a request to do so;

   (e) a decision of a local authority not to secure the amendment or replacement of an EHC plan it maintains for the child or young person following a review or re-assessment under section 44;

   (f) a decision of a local authority under section 45 to cease to maintain an EHC plan for the child or young person.

(3) A child's parent or a young person may appeal to the First-tier Tribunal under subsection (2)(c)–

   (a) when an EHC plan is first finalised for the child or young person, and

   (b) following an amendment or replacement of the plan.

(4) Regulations may make provision about appeals to the First-tier Tribunal in respect of EHC needs assessments and EHC plans, in particular about–

   (a) other matters relating to EHC plans against which appeals may be brought;

   (b) making and determining appeals;

   (c) the powers of the First-tier Tribunal on determining an appeal;

   (d) unopposed appeals.

(5) Regulations under subsection (4)(c) may include provision conferring power on the First-tier Tribunal, on determining an appeal against a matter, to make recommendations in respect of other matters (including matters against which no appeal may be brought).

(6) A person commits an offence if without reasonable excuse that person fails to comply with any requirement–

   (a) in respect of the discovery or inspection of documents, or

   (b) to attend to give evidence and produce documents,

where that requirement is imposed by Tribunal Procedure Rules in relation to an appeal under this section or regulations under subsection (4)(a).

(7) A person guilty of an offence under subsection (6) is liable on summary conviction to a fine not exceeding level 3 on the standard scale.

Right to mediation

52 (1) This section applies where–

   (a) a decision against which an appeal may be brought under section 51 is made in respect of a child or young person, or

   (b) an EHC plan for a child or young person is made, amended or replaced.

(2) Before the end of the prescribed period after the decision is made, or the plan is made, amended or replaced, the local authority must notify the child's parent or the young person of–

(a) the right to mediation under section 53 or 54, and
(b) the requirement to obtain a certificate under section 55 before making certain appeals.
(3) If the parent or young person wishes to pursue mediation under section 53 or 54, he or she must inform the local authority of–
(a) that fact, and
(b) the issues in respect of which he or she wishes to pursue mediation ('the mediation issues').
(4) If the mediation issues are, or include, the fact that no health care provision, or no health care provision of a particular kind, is specified in the plan, the parent or young person must also inform the local authority of the health care provision which he or she wishes to be specified in the plan.

Mediation: health care issues
53 (1) This section applies where–
(a) the parent or young person informs the local authority under section 52 that he or she wishes to pursue mediation, and
(b) the mediation issues include health care provision specified in the plan or the fact that no health care provision, or no health care provision of a particular kind, is specified in the plan.
(2) The local authority must notify each relevant commissioning body of–
(a) the mediation issues, and
(b) anything of which it has been informed by the parent or young person under section 52(4).
(3) If the mediation issues are limited to the health care provision specified in the plan or the fact that no health care provision, or no health care provision of a particular kind, is specified in the plan, the responsible commissioning body (or, where there is more than one, the responsible commissioning bodies acting jointly) must–
(a) arrange for mediation between it (or them) and the parent or young person,
(b) ensure that the mediation is conducted by an independent person, and
(c) participate in the mediation.
(4) If the mediation issues include anything else–
(a) the local authority must–
(i) arrange for mediation between it, each responsible commissioning body and the parent or young person,
(ii) ensure that the mediation is conducted by an independent person, and
(iii) participate in the mediation, and
(b) each responsible commissioning body must also participate in the mediation.
(5) For the purposes of this section, a person is not independent if he or she is employed by any of the following–
(a) a local authority in England;
(b) a clinical commissioning group;
(c) the National Health Service Commissioning Board.
(6) In this section 'responsible commissioning body'–
(a) if the mediation issues in question are or include the health care provision

specified in an EHC plan, means a body that is under a duty to arrange health care provision of that kind in respect of the child or young person;

   (b) if the mediation issues in question are or include the fact that no health care provision, or no health care provision of a particular kind, is specified in an EHC plan, means a body that would be under a duty to arrange health care provision of the kind in question if it were specified in the plan.

Mediation: educational and social care issues etc

54 (1) This section applies where—

   (a) the parent or young person informs the local authority under section 52 that he or she wishes to pursue mediation, and

   (b) the mediation issues do not include health care provision specified in the plan or the fact that no health care provision, or no health care provision of a particular kind, is specified in the plan.

(2) The local authority must—

   (a) arrange for mediation between it and the parent or young person,

   (b) ensure that the mediation is conducted by an independent person, and

   (c) participate in the mediation.

(3) For the purposes of this section, a person is not independent if he or she is employed by a local authority in England.

Mediation

55 (1) This section applies where a child's parent or young person intends to appeal to the First-tier Tribunal under section 51 or regulations made under that section in respect of—

   (a) a decision of a local authority, or

   (b) the content of an EHC plan maintained by a local authority.

(2) But this section does not apply in respect of an appeal concerning only—

   (a) the school or other institution named in an EHC plan;

   (b) the type of school or other institution specified in an EHC plan;

   (c) the fact that an EHC plan does not name a school or other institution.

(3) The parent or young person may make the appeal only if a mediation adviser has issued a certificate to him or her under subsection (4) or (5).

(4) A mediation adviser must issue a certificate under this subsection to the parent or young person if—

   (a) the adviser has provided him or her with information and advice about pursuing mediation under section 53 or 54, and

   (b) the parent or young person has informed the adviser that he or she does not wish to pursue mediation.

(5) A mediation adviser must issue a certificate under this subsection to the parent or young person if the adviser has provided him or her with information and advice about pursuing mediation under section 53 or 54, and the parent or young person has—

   (a) informed the adviser that he or she wishes to pursue mediation under the appropriate section, and

   (b) participated in such mediation.

Mediation: supplementary

56 (1) Regulations may make provision for the purposes of sections 52 to 55, in particular—

(a) about giving notice;

(b) imposing time limits;

(c) enabling a local authority or commissioning body to take prescribed steps following the conclusion of mediation;

(d) about who may attend mediation;

(e) where a child's parent is a party to mediation, requiring the mediator to take reasonable steps to ascertain the views of the child;

(f) about the provision of advocacy and other support services for the parent or young person;

(g) requiring a local authority or commissioning body to pay reasonable travel expenses and other expenses of a prescribed description, up to any prescribed limit;

(h) about exceptions to the requirement in section 55(3);

(i) about the training, qualifications and experience of mediators and mediation advisers;

(j) conferring powers or imposing requirements on local authorities, commissioning bodies, mediators and mediation advisers.

(2) In section 55 and this section 'mediation adviser' means an independent person who can provide information and advice about pursuing mediation.

(3) For the purposes of subsection (2), a person is not independent if he or she is employed by any of the following–

(a) a local authority in England;

(b) a clinical commissioning group;

(c) the National Health Service Commissioning Board.

(4) In this section 'commissioning body' means a body that is under a duty to arrange health care provision of any kind.

Resolution of disagreements

57 (1) A local authority in England must make arrangements with a view to avoiding or resolving disagreements within subsection (2) or (3).

(2) The disagreements within this subsection are those about the exercise by the local authority or relevant bodies of their functions under this Part, where the disagreement is between–

(a) the local authority or a relevant body, and

(b) the parents of children, and young people, in the authority's area.

(3) The disagreements within this subsection are those about the exercise by the local authority of its functions relating to EHC needs assessments, the preparation and review of EHC plans, and re-assessment of educational, health care and social care needs, where the disagreement is between–

(a) the local authority and a responsible commissioning body, or

(b) a responsible commissioning body and the parents of children, or young people, in the authority's area.

(4) A local authority in England must make arrangements with a view to avoiding or resolving, in each relevant school or post-16 institution, disagreements within subsection (5).

(5) The disagreements within this subsection are those about the special educational provision made for a child or young person with special educational needs who is a registered pupil or a student at the relevant school or post-16 institution concerned, where the disagreement is between–

(a) the child's parent, or the young person, and
(b) the appropriate authority for the school or post-16 institution.
(6) Arrangements within this section must provide for the appointment of independent persons with the function of facilitating the avoidance or resolution of the disagreements to which the arrangements apply.
(7) For the purposes of subsection (6) a person is not independent if he or she is employed by any of the following–
(a) a local authority in England;
(b) a clinical commissioning group;
(c) the National Health Service Commissioning Board.
(8) A local authority in England must take such steps as it thinks appropriate for making the arrangements under this section known to–
(a) the parents of children in its area with special educational needs,
(b) young people in its area with special educational needs, and
(c) the head teachers, governing bodies, proprietors and principals of schools and post-16 institutions in its area.
(9) A local authority in England may take such steps as it thinks appropriate for making the arrangements under this section known to such other persons as it thinks appropriate.
(10) In this section–
'relevant body' means–
(a) the governing body of a maintained school, maintained nursery school or institution within the further education sector;
(b) the proprietor of an Academy;
'relevant school or post-16 institution' means–
(a) a maintained school;
(b) a maintained nursery school;
(c) a post-16 institution;
(d) an Academy;
(e) an independent school;
(f) a non-maintained special school;
(g) a pupil referral unit;
(h) a place at which relevant early years education is provided;
'responsible commissioning body', in relation to any particular health care provision, means a body that is under a duty to arrange health care provision of that kind in respect of the child or young person concerned.
(11) For the purposes of this section, the 'appropriate authority' for a relevant school or post-16 institution is–
(a) in the case of a maintained school, maintained nursery school or non-maintained special school, the governing body;
(b) in the case of a post-16 institution, the governing body, proprietor or principal;
(c) in the case of an Academy or independent school, the proprietor;
(d) in the case of a pupil referral unit, the management committee;
(e) in the case of a place at which relevant early years education is provided, the provider of the relevant early years education.

Appeals and claims by children: pilot schemes

58 (1) The Secretary of State may by order make pilot schemes enabling children in England to–

(a) appeal to the First-tier Tribunal under section 51;

(b) make a claim to the First-tier Tribunal under Schedule 17 to the Equality Act 2010 (disabled pupils: enforcement) that a responsible body in England has contravened Chapter 1 of Part 6 of that Act because of the child's disability.

(2) An order under subsection (1) may, in particular, make provision–

    (a) about the age from which children may appeal or make a claim;

    (b) in respect of appeals under section 51, about mediation and the application of section 55;

    (c) about the bringing of appeals or making of claims by a child and by his or her parent concurrently;

    (d) about determining whether a child is capable of bringing an appeal or making a claim, and the assistance and support a child may require to be able to do so;

    (e) enabling a person to exercise a child's rights under an order under subsection (1) on behalf of the child;

    (f) enabling children to have access to advice and information which is available to a parent or young person in respect of an appeal or claim of a kind mentioned in subsection (1);

    (g) about the provision of advocacy and other support services to children;

    (h) requiring notices to be given to a child (as well as to his or her parent);

    (i) requiring documents to be served on a child (as well as on his or her parent).

(3) An order under subsection (1) may apply a statutory provision, with or without modifications.

(4) In subsection (3), 'statutory provision' means a provision made by or under this or any other Act, whenever passed or made.

(5) This section is repealed at the end of five years beginning with the day on which this Act is passed.

Appeals and claims by children: follow-up provision

59 (1) The Secretary of State may by order provide that children in England may–

    (a) appeal to the First-tier Tribunal under section 51;

    (b) make a claim to the First-tier Tribunal under Schedule 17 to the Equality Act 2010 (disabled pupils: enforcement) that a responsible body in England has contravened Chapter 1 of Part 6 of that Act because of the child's disability.

(2) The Secretary of State may not make an order under subsection (1) until the end of two years beginning with the day on which the first order is made under section 58(1).

(3) An order under subsection (1) may, in particular, make provision–

    (a) about the age from which children may appeal or make a claim;

    (b) in respect of appeals under section 51, about mediation and the application of section 55;

    (c) about the bringing of appeals or making of claims by a child and by his or her parent concurrently;

    (d) about determining whether a child is capable of bringing an appeal or making a claim, and the assistance and support a child may require to be able to do so;

(e) enabling a person to exercise a child's rights under an order under subsection (1) on behalf of the child;

(f) enabling children to have access to advice and information which is available to a parent or young person in respect of an appeal or claim of a kind mentioned in subsection (1);

(g) about the provision of advocacy and other support services to children;

(h) requiring notices to be given to a child (as well as to his or her parent);

(i) requiring documents to be served on a child (as well as on his or her parent).

(4) An order under subsection (1) may–

(a) amend, repeal or revoke a statutory provision, or

(b) apply a statutory provision, with or without modifications.

(5) In subsection (4), 'statutory provision' means a provision made by or under this or any other Act, whenever passed or made.

Equality Act 2010: claims against schools by disabled young people

60 In Part 2 of Schedule 17 to the Equality Act 2010 (disabled pupils: enforcement in tribunals in England and Wales), in paragraph 3 (who may make a claim that a school has contravened Chapter 1 of Part 6 of that Act because of a person's disability) for 'to the Tribunal by the person's parent' substitute

'–

(a) to the English Tribunal by the person's parent or, if the person is over compulsory school age, the person;

(b) to the Welsh Tribunal by the person's parent.'

Special educational provision: functions of local authorities

Special educational provision otherwise than in schools, post-16 institutions etc

61 (1) A local authority in England may arrange for any special educational provision that it has decided is necessary for a child or young person for whom it is responsible to be made otherwise than in a school or post-16 institution or a place at which relevant early years education is provided.

(2) An authority may do so only if satisfied that it would be inappropriate for the provision to be made in a school or post-16 institution or at such a place.

(3) Before doing so, the authority must consult the child's parent or the young person.

Special educational provision outside England and Wales

62 (1) This section applies where a local authority in England makes arrangements for a child or young person for whom it maintains an EHC plan to attend an institution outside England and Wales which specialises in providing for children or young people with special educational needs.

(2) The arrangements may (in particular) include contributing to or paying–

(a) fees charged by the institution;

(b) the child's or young person's travelling expenses;

(c) expenses reasonably incurred in maintaining the child or young person while at the institution or travelling to or from it;

(d) expenses reasonably incurred by someone accompanying the child or young person while travelling to or from the institution or staying there.

Fees for special educational provision at non-maintained schools and post-16 institutions

63 (1) Subsection (2) applies where–

(a) a local authority maintains an EHC plan for a child or young person,

(b) special educational provision in respect of the child or young person is made at a school, post-16 institution or place at which relevant early years education is provided, and

(c) that school, institution or place is named in the EHC plan.

(2) The local authority must pay any fees payable in respect of education or training provided for the child or young person at that school, institution or place in accordance with the EHC plan.

(3) Subsection (4) applies where–

(a) a local authority is responsible for a child or young person for whom no EHC plan is maintained,

(b) special educational provision in respect of the child or young person is made at a school, post-16 institution or place at which relevant early years education is provided, and

(c) the local authority is satisfied that–

(i) the interests of the child or young person require special educational provision to be made, and

(ii) it is appropriate for education or training to be provided to the child or young person at the school, institution or place in question.

(4) The local authority must pay any fees payable in respect of the special educational provision made at the school, institution or place in question which is required to meet the special educational needs of the child or young person.

(5) Where board and lodging are provided for the child or young person at the school, post-16 institution or place mentioned in subsection (2) or (4), the authority must also pay any fees in respect of the board and lodging, if satisfied that special educational provision cannot be provided at the school, post-16 institution or place unless the board and lodging are also provided.

Supply of goods and services

64 (1) A local authority in England may supply goods and services to–

(a) the governing body of a maintained school or maintained nursery school in England;

(b) the proprietor of an Academy;

(c) the governing body of an institution within the further education sector that the authority thinks is or is to be attended by a young person for whom the authority maintains an EHC plan,

but only for the purpose set out in subsection (2).

(2) The purpose is that of assisting the governing body or proprietor in the performance of–

(a) any duty imposed on the body under section 66(2) (duty to use best endeavours to secure special educational provision called for by special educational needs);

(b) in the case of a governing body of a community or foundation special school, any duty imposed on the body.

(3) The goods and services may be supplied on the terms and conditions that the authority thinks fit, including terms as to payment.

(4) A local authority in England may supply goods and services to any authority or other person (other than a governing body or proprietor within subsection (1)), but only for the purpose set out in subsection (5).

(5) The purpose is that of assisting the authority or other person in making special educational provision for a child who is receiving relevant early years education, in a case where the authority has decided that the special educational provision is necessary for the child.

Access to schools, post-16 institutions and other institutions

65 (1) This section applies where a local authority in England maintains an EHC plan for a child or young person.

(2) A person authorised by the authority is entitled to have access at any reasonable time to the premises of a school, post-16 institution or other institution at which education or training is provided in pursuance of the plan, for the purpose of monitoring the education or training.

(3) Subsection (2) does not apply to the premises of a mainstream post-16 institution in Wales.

Special educational provision: functions of governing bodies and others

Using best endeavours to secure special educational provision

66 (1) This section imposes duties on the appropriate authorities for the following schools and other institutions in England–
  (a) mainstream schools;
  (b) maintained nursery schools;
  (c) 16 to 19 Academies;
  (d) alternative provision Academies;
  (e) institutions within the further education sector;
  (f) pupil referral units.

(2) If a registered pupil or a student at a school or other institution has special educational needs, the appropriate authority must, in exercising its functions in relation to the school or other institution, use its best endeavours to secure that the special educational provision called for by the pupil's or student's special educational needs is made.

(3) The 'appropriate authority' for a school or other institution is–
  (a) in the case of a maintained school, maintained nursery school or institution within the further education sector, the governing body;
  (b) in the case of an Academy, the proprietor;
  (c) in the case of a pupil referral unit, the management committee.

SEN co-ordinators

67 (1) This section imposes duties on the appropriate authorities of the following schools in England–
  (a) mainstream schools;
  (b) maintained nursery schools.

(2) The appropriate authority must designate a member of staff at the school (to be known as the 'SEN co-ordinator') as having responsibility for co-ordinating the provision for pupils with special educational needs.

(3) Regulations may–
  (a) require appropriate authorities which are subject to the duty imposed by

subsection (2) to ensure that SEN co-ordinators have prescribed qualifications or prescribed experience (or both);

(b) confer other functions relating to SEN co-ordinators on appropriate authorities which are subject to the duty imposed by subsection (2).

(4) The 'appropriate authority' for a school is—

(a) in the case of a maintained school or maintained nursery school, the governing body;

(b) in the case of an Academy, the proprietor.

Informing parents and young people

68 (1) This section applies if—

(a) special educational provision is made for a child or young person at a maintained school, a maintained nursery school, an Academy school, an alternative provision Academy or a pupil referral unit, and

(b) no EHC plan is maintained for the child or young person.

(2) The appropriate authority for the school must inform the child's parent or the young person that special educational provision is being made for the child or young person.

(3) The 'appropriate authority' for a school is—

(a) in the case of a maintained school or maintained nursery school, the governing body;

(b) in the case of an Academy school or an alternative provision Academy, the proprietor;

(c) in the case of a pupil referral unit, the management committee.

SEN information report

69 (1) This section imposes a duty on—

(a) the governing bodies of maintained schools and maintained nursery schools in England, and

(b) the proprietors of Academy schools.

(2) A governing body or proprietor must prepare a report containing SEN information.

(3) 'SEN information' is—

(a) such information as may be prescribed about the implementation of the governing body's or proprietor's policy for pupils at the school with special educational needs;

(b) information as to—

(i) the arrangements for the admission of disabled persons as pupils at the school;

(ii) the steps taken to prevent disabled pupils from being treated less favourably than other pupils;

(iii) the facilities provided to assist access to the school by disabled pupils;

(iv) the plan prepared by the governing body or proprietor under paragraph 3 of Schedule 10 to the Equality Act 2010 (accessibility plan).

(4) In this section—

'disabled person' means a person who is a disabled person for the purposes of the Equality Act 2010;

'disabled pupil' includes a disabled person who may be admitted to a school as a pupil.

Detained persons

Application of Part to detained persons

70 (1) Subject to this section and sections 71 to 75, nothing in or made under this Part applies to, or in relation to, a child or young person detained in pursuance of–

(a) an order made by a court, or

(b) an order of recall made by the Secretary of State.

(2) Subsection (1) does not apply to–

(a) section 28;

(b) section 31;

(c) section 77;

(d) section 80;

(e) section 83;

(f) any amendment made by this Part of a provision which applies to, or in relation to, a child or young person detained in pursuance of–

(i) an order made by a court, or

(ii) an order of recall made by the Secretary of State.

(3) Regulations may apply any provision of this Part, with or without modifications, to or in relation to a child or young person detained in pursuance of–

(a) an order made by a court, or

(b) an order of recall made by the Secretary of State.

(4) The Secretary of State must consult the Welsh Ministers before making regulations under subsection (3) which will apply any provision of this Part to, or in relation to, a child or young person who is detained in Wales.

(5) For the purposes of this Part–

'appropriate person', in relation to a detained person, means–

(a) where the detained person is a child, the detained person's parent, or

(b) where the detained person is a young person, the detained person;

'detained person' means a child or young person who is–

(a) 18 or under,

(b) subject to a detention order (within the meaning of section 562(1A)(a) of EA 1996), and

(c) detained in relevant youth accommodation,

and in provisions applying on a person's release, includes a person who, immediately before release, was a detained person;

'detained person's EHC needs assessment' means an assessment of what the education, health care and social care needs of a detained person will be on his or her release from detention;

'relevant youth accommodation' has the same meaning as in section 562(1A)(b) of EA 1996, save that it does not include relevant youth accommodation which is not in England.

(6) For the purposes of this Part–

(a) 'beginning of the detention' has the same meaning as in Chapter 5A of Part 10 of EA 1996 (persons detained in youth accommodation), and

(b) 'the home authority' has the same meaning as in that Chapter, subject to regulations under subsection (7) (and regulations under section 562J(4) of EA 1996 made by the Secretary of State may also make provision in relation to the definition of 'the home authority' for the purposes of this Part).

(7) For the purposes of this Part, regulations may provide for paragraph (a) of the definition of 'the home authority' in section 562J(1) of EA 1996 (the home authority of a looked after child) to apply with modifications in relation to such provisions of this Part as may be specified in the regulations.

Assessment of post-detention education, health and care needs of detained persons

71 (1) This section applies in relation to a detained person for whom–
   (a) the home authority is a local authority in England, and
   (b) no EHC plan is being kept by a local authority.
   (2) A request to the home authority to secure a detained person's EHC needs assessment for the detained person may be made by–
   (a) the appropriate person, or
   (b) the person in charge of the relevant youth accommodation where the detained person is detained.
   (3) Where this subsection applies, the home authority must determine whether it may be necessary for special educational provision to be made for the detained person in accordance with an EHC plan on release from detention.
   (4) Subsection (3) applies where–
   (a) a request is made under subsection (2),
   (b) the detained person has been brought to the home authority's attention by any person as someone who has or may have special educational needs, or
   (c) the detained person has otherwise come to the home authority's attention as someone who has or may have special educational needs.
   (5) In making a determination under subsection (3), the home authority must consult–
   (a) the appropriate person, and
   (b) the person in charge of the relevant youth accommodation where the detained person is detained.
   (6) Where the home authority determines that it will not be necessary for special educational provision to be made for the detained person in accordance with an EHC plan on release from detention, it must notify the appropriate person and the person in charge of the relevant youth accommodation where the detained person is detained–
   (a) of the reasons for that determination, and
   (b) that accordingly it has decided not to secure a detained person's EHC needs assessment for the detained person.
   (7) Subsection (8) applies where–
   (a) the detained person has not been assessed under this section or section 36 during the previous six months, and
   (b) the home authority determines that it may be necessary for special educational provision to be made for the detained person in accordance with an EHC plan on release from detention.
   (8) The home authority must notify the appropriate person and the person in charge of the relevant youth accommodation where the detained person is detained–
   (a) that it is considering securing a detained person's EHC needs assessment for the detained person, and

(b) that the appropriate person and the person in charge of the relevant youth accommodation where the detained person is detained each have the right to–
  (i) express views to the authority (orally or in writing), and
  (ii) submit evidence to the authority.

(9) The home authority must secure a detained person's EHC needs assessment if, after having regard to any views expressed and evidence submitted under subsection (8), the authority is of the opinion that–
  (a) the detained person has or may have special educational needs, and
  (b) it may be necessary for special educational provision to be made for the detained person in accordance with an EHC plan on release from detention.

(10) After a detained person's EHC needs assessment has been carried out, the local authority must notify the appropriate person and the person in charge of the relevant youth accommodation where the detained person is detained of–
  (a) the outcome of the assessment,
  (b) whether it proposes to secure that an EHC plan is prepared for the detained person, and
  (c) the reasons for that decision.

(11) Regulations may make provision about detained persons' EHC needs assessments, in particular–
  (a) about requests under subsection (2);
  (b) imposing time limits in relation to consultation under subsection (5);
  (c) about giving notice;
  (d) about expressing views and submitting evidence under subsection (8);
  (e) about how detained persons' EHC needs assessments are to be conducted;
  (f) about advice to be obtained in connection with a detained person's EHC needs assessment;
  (g) about combining a detained person's EHC needs assessment with other assessments;
  (h) about the use for the purposes of a detained person's EHC needs assessment of information obtained as a result of other assessments;
  (i) about the use of information obtained as a result of a detained person's EHC needs assessment, including the use of that information for the purposes of other assessments;
  (j) about the provision of information, advice and support in connection with a detained person's EHC needs assessment.

Securing EHC plans for certain detained persons

72 (1) Where, in the light of a detained person's EHC needs assessment it is necessary for special education provision to be made for the detained person in accordance with an EHC plan on release from detention, the home authority must secure that an EHC plan is prepared for him or her.

(2) Sections 37(2) to (5) and 38 to 40 apply in relation to an EHC plan secured under subsection (1) as they apply to an EHC plan secured under section 37(1), with the following modifications–
  (a) references to 'the child or young person' are to be read as references to the detained person,

(b) references to the local authority are to be read as references to the home authority, and

(c) references to the child's parent or the young person are to be read as references to the appropriate person.

(3) Section 33(2) to (7) apply where a home authority is securing the preparation of an EHC plan under this section as they apply where a local authority is securing a plan under section 37, with the following modifications–

(a) references to 'the child or young person' are to be read as references to the detained person,

(b) references to the local authority are to be read as references to the home authority,

(c) references to the child's parent or the young person are to be read as references to the appropriate person, and

(d) the reference in subsection (2) to section 39(5) and 40(2) is to be read as a reference to those provisions as applied by subsection (2) of this section.

EHC plans for certain detained persons: appeals and mediation

73 (1) An appropriate person in relation to a detained person may appeal to the First-tier Tribunal against the matters set out in subsection (2), subject to section 55 (as applied by this section).

(2) The matters are–

(a) a decision of the home authority not to secure a detained person's EHC needs assessment for the detained person;

(b) a decision of the home authority, following a detained person's EHC needs assessment, that it is not necessary for special educational provision to be made for the detained person in accordance with an EHC plan on release from detention;

(c) where an EHC plan is secured for the detained person–

(i) the school or other institution named in the plan, or the type of school or other institution named in the plan;

(ii) if no school or other institution is named in the plan, that fact.

(3) The appropriate person may appeal to the First-tier Tribunal under subsection (2)(c) only when an EHC plan is first finalised for the detained person in accordance with section 72.

(4) Regulations may make provision about appeals to the First-tier Tribunal in respect of detained persons' EHC needs assessments and EHC plans secured under section 72, in particular about–

(a) making and determining appeals;

(b) the powers of the First-tier Tribunal on determining an appeal;

(c) unopposed appeals.

(5) A person commits an offence if without reasonable excuse that person fails to comply with any requirement–

(a) in respect of the discovery or inspection of documents, or

(b) to attend to give evidence and produce documents,

where that requirement is imposed by Tribunal Procedure Rules in relation to an appeal under this section.

(6) A person guilty of an offence under subsection (5) is liable on summary conviction to a fine not exceeding level 3 on the standard scale.

(7) Section 55(2) to (5) apply where an appropriate person intends to appeal to

the First-tier Tribunal under this section as they apply where a child's parent or young person intends to appeal under section 51, with the following modifications–

(a) references to the child's parent or young person are to be read as references to the appropriate person, and

(b) references to mediation under section 53 or 54 are to be read as references to mediation with the home authority.

(8) Where, by virtue of subsection (7), the appropriate person has informed the mediation adviser that he or she wishes to pursue mediation with the home authority–

(a) the adviser must notify the authority, and

(b) the authority must–

(i) arrange for mediation between it and the appropriate person,

(ii) ensure that the mediation is conducted by an independent person, and

(iii) participate in the mediation.

For this purpose a person is not independent if he or she is employed by a local authority in England.

(9) Regulations under section 56 may make provision for the purposes of subsections (7) and (8) of this section, and accordingly section 56 has effect for those purposes with the following modifications–

(a) the references in subsection (1) to commissioning bodies are to be ignored;

(b) the reference in subsection (1)(e) to a child's parent is to be read as a reference to the parent of a detained person who is a child;

(c) the reference in subsection (1)(f) to the child's parent or young person is to be read as a reference to the appropriate person;

(d) in subsection (3), paragraphs (b) and (c) are to be ignored;

(e) subsection (4) is to be ignored.

Duty to keep EHC plans for detained persons

74 (1) This section applies in relation to a detained person–

(a) for whom a local authority in England was maintaining an EHC plan immediately before the beginning of his or her detention, or

(b) for whom the home authority has secured the preparation of an EHC plan under section 72.

(2) The home authority must keep the EHC plan while the person is detained in relevant youth accommodation.

(3) Regulations may make provision about the keeping of EHC plans under subsection (2), and the disclosure of such plans.

(4) The home authority must arrange appropriate special educational provision for the detained person while he or she is detained in relevant youth accommodation.

(5) If the EHC plan specifies health care provision, the detained person's health services commissioner must arrange appropriate health care provision for the detained person while he or she is detained in relevant youth accommodation.

(6) For the purposes of subsection (4), appropriate special educational provision is–

(a) the special educational provision specified in the EHC plan, or

(b) if it appears to the home authority that it is not practicable for that special educational provision to be provided, educational provision corresponding as closely as possible to that special educational provision, or

(c) if it appears to the home authority that the special educational provision specified in the plan is no longer appropriate for the person, such special educational provision as reasonably appears to the home authority to be appropriate.

(7) For the purposes of subsection (5), appropriate health care provision is–

(a) the health care provision specified in the EHC plan, or

(b) if it appears to the detained person's health services commissioner that it is not practicable for that health care provision to be provided, health care provision corresponding as closely as possible to that health care provision, or

(c) if it appears to the detained person's health services commissioner that the health care provision specified in the plan is no longer appropriate for the person, such health care provision as reasonably appears to the detained person's health services commissioner to be appropriate.

(8) In this section, 'detained person's health services commissioner', in relation to a detained person, means the body that is under a duty under the National Health Service Act 2006 to arrange for the provision of services or facilities in respect of the detained person during his or her detention.

Supply of goods and services: detained persons

75 (1) A local authority in England may supply goods and services to any authority or other person making special educational provision for a detained person, but only for the purpose set out in subsection (2).

(2) The purpose is that of assisting the local authority in the performance of a duty under section 74.

(3) The goods and services may be supplied on the terms and conditions that the authority thinks fit, including terms as to payment.

Information to improve well-being of children and young people with SEN

Provision and publication of special needs information

76 (1) The Secretary of State must exercise the powers listed in subsection (2) with a view to securing, in particular, the provision of special needs information which the Secretary of State thinks would be likely to assist the Secretary of State or others in improving the well-being of–

(a) children in England with special educational needs, and

(b) young people aged under 19 in England with special educational needs.

(2) The powers are those of the Secretary of State under the following provisions of EA 1996 (so far as relating to England)–

(a) section 29 (information from local authorities for purposes of Secretary of State's functions);

(b) section 408 (information in relation to maintained schools);

(c) section 537 (information about schools);

(d) section 537A (information about individual pupils);

(e) section 537B (information about children receiving funded education outside school);

    (f) section 538 (information from governing bodies for purposes of Secretary of State's education functions).

(3) In each calendar year, the Secretary of State must publish, or arrange to be published, special needs information which has been obtained under EA 1996, where the Secretary of State thinks the publication of the information would be likely to assist the Secretary of State or others in improving the well-being of–

    (a) children in England with special educational needs, and

    (b) young people aged under 19 in England with special educational needs.

(4) Information published under subsection (3) must be published in the form and manner that the Secretary of State thinks fit, except that the names of the children and young people to whom the information relates must not be included.

(5) The Secretary of State may make a charge, or arrange for a charge to be made, for documents supplied by virtue of this section.

(6) A charge under subsection (5) must not exceed the cost of supply.

(7) 'Special needs information' means–

    (a) information about children, and young people, in England with special educational needs, and

    (b) information about special educational provision made for those children and young people.

(8) References in this section to the well-being of children and young people with special educational needs are to their well-being so far as relating to–

    (a) physical and mental health and emotional well-being;

    (b) protection from abuse and neglect;

    (c) control by them over their day-to-day lives;

    (d) participation in education, training or recreation;

    (e) social and economic well-being;

    (f) domestic, family and personal relationships;

    (g) the contribution made by them to society.

Code of practice

Code of practice

77 (1) The Secretary of State must issue a code of practice giving guidance about the exercise of their functions under this Part to–

    (a) local authorities in England;

    (b) the governing bodies of schools;

    (c) the governing bodies of institutions within the further education sector;

    (d) the proprietors of Academies;

    (e) the management committees of pupil referral units;

    (f) the proprietors of institutions approved by the Secretary of State under section 41 (independent special schools and special post-16 institutions: approval);

    (g) providers of relevant early years education;

    (h) youth offending teams;

    (i) persons in charge of relevant youth accommodation;

    (j) the National Health Service Commissioning Board;

    (k) clinical commissioning groups;

    (l) NHS trusts;

(m) NHS foundation trusts;
(n) Local Health Boards.
(2) The Secretary of State may revise the code from time to time.
(3) The Secretary of State must publish the current version of the code.
(4) The persons listed in subsection (1) must have regard to the code in exercising their functions under this Part.
(5) Those who exercise functions for the purpose of the exercise by those persons of functions under this Part must also have regard to the code.
(6) The First-tier Tribunal must have regard to any provision of the code that appears to it to be relevant to a question arising on an appeal under this Part.

Making and approval of code

78 (1) Where the Secretary of State proposes to issue or revise a code under section 77, the Secretary of State must prepare a draft of the code (or revised code).
(2) The Secretary of State must consult such persons as the Secretary of State thinks fit about the draft and must consider any representations made by them.
(3) If the Secretary of State decides to proceed with the draft (in its original form or with modifications), the Secretary of State must lay a copy of the draft before each House of Parliament.
(4) The Secretary of State may not take any further steps in relation to–
(a) a proposed code unless the draft is approved by a resolution of each House, or
(b) a proposed revised code if, within the 40-day period, either House resolves not to approve the draft.
(5) Subsection (6) applies if–
(a) both Houses resolve to approve the draft, as mentioned in subsection (4)(a), or
(b) neither House resolves not to approve the draft, as mentioned in subsection (4)(b).
(6) The Secretary of State must issue the code or revised code in the form of the draft, and it comes into force on such date as the Secretary of State may by order appoint.
(7) Subsection (4) does not prevent a new draft of a proposed code (or proposed revised code) from being laid before Parliament.
(8) In this section '40-day period', in relation to the draft of a proposed revised code, means–
(a) if the draft is laid before one House on a later day than the day on which it is laid before the other, the period of 40 days beginning with the later of the two days, and
(b) in any other case, the period of 40 days beginning with the day on which the draft is laid before each House.
(9) For the purposes of subsection (8), no account is to be taken of any period during which Parliament is dissolved or prorogued or during which both Houses are adjourned for more than four days.

Review of resolution of disagreements

79 (1) The Secretary of State and the Lord Chancellor must carry out a review of how effectively disagreements about the exercise of functions under this Part are being resolved.

(2) The Secretary of State and the Lord Chancellor must prepare a report on the outcome of the review.

(3) The Secretary of State and the Lord Chancellor must lay the report before Parliament before the end of the period of three years beginning with the earliest date on which any provision of this Part comes into force.

Supplementary

Parents and young people lacking capacity

80 (1) Regulations may apply any statutory provision with modifications, for the purpose of giving effect to this Part in a case where the parent of a child, or a young person, lacks capacity at the relevant time.

(2) Regulations under subsection (1) may in particular include provision for–

(a) references to a child's parent to be read as references to, or as including references to, a representative of the parent;

(b) references to a young person to be read as references to, or as including references to, a representative of the young person, the young person's parent, or a representative of the young person's parent;

(c) modifications to have effect in spite of section 27(1)(g) of the Mental Capacity Act 2005 (Act does not permit decisions on discharging parental responsibilities in matters not relating to a child's property to be made on a person's behalf).

(3) 'Statutory provision' means a provision made by or under this or any other Act, whenever passed or made.

(4) 'The relevant time' means the time at which, under the statutory provision in question, something is required or permitted to be done by or in relation to the parent or young person.

(5) The reference in subsection (1) to lacking capacity is to lacking capacity within the meaning of the Mental Capacity Act 2005.

(6) 'Representative', in relation to a parent or young person, means–

(a) a deputy appointed by the Court of Protection under section 16(2)(b) of the Mental Capacity Act 2005 to make decisions on the parent's or young person's behalf in relation to matters within this Part;

(b) the donee of a lasting power of attorney (within the meaning of section 9 of that Act) appointed by the parent or young person to make decisions on his or her behalf in relation to matters within this Part;

(c) an attorney in whom an enduring power of attorney (within the meaning of Schedule 4 to that Act) created by the parent or young person is vested, where the power of attorney is registered in accordance with paragraphs 4 and 13 of that Schedule or an application for registration of the power of attorney has been made.

Disapplication of Chapter 1 of Part 4 of EA 1996 in relation to children in England

81   Chapter 1 of Part 4 of EA 1996 (children with special educational needs) ceases to apply in relation to children in the area of a local authority in England.

Consequential amendments

82   Schedule 3 (amendments consequential on this Part) has effect.

Interpretation of Part 3

83 (1) In this Part–

'EA 1996' means the Education Act 1996;

'ESA 2008' means the Education and Skills Act 2008;

'SSFA 1998' means the School Standards and Framework Act 1998.

(2) In this Part–

'appropriate person' has the meaning given by section 70(5);

'beginning of the detention' has the meaning given by section 70(6);

'detained person' has the meaning given by section 70(5);

'detained person's EHC needs assessment' has the meaning given by section 70(5);

'education, health and care provision' has the meaning given by section 26(2);

'EHC needs assessment' has the meaning given by section 36(2);

'EHC plan' means a plan within section 37(2);

'health care provision' has the meaning given by section 21(3);

'the home authority' has the meaning given by section 70(6) (subject to subsection (7) of that section);

'mainstream post-16 institution' means a post-16 institution that is not a special post-16 institution;

'mainstream school' means–

(a) a maintained school that is not a special school, or

(b) an Academy school that is not a special school;

'maintained school' means–

(a) a community, foundation or voluntary school, or

(b) a community or foundation special school not established in a hospital;

'post-16 institution' means an institution which–

(a) provides education or training for those over compulsory school age, but

(b) is not a school or other institution which is within the higher education sector or which provides only higher education;

'proprietor', in relation to an institution that is not a school, means the person or body of persons responsible for the management of the institution;

'relevant early years education' has the meaning given by section 123 of SSFA 1998;

'relevant youth accommodation' has the meaning given by section 70(5);

'social care provision' has the meaning given by section 21(4);

'social services functions' in relation to a local authority has the same meaning as in the Local Authority Social Services Act 1970;

'special educational needs' has the meaning given by section 20(1);

'special educational provision' has the meaning given by section 21(1) and (2);

'special post-16 institution' means a post-16 institution that is specially organised to make special educational provision for students with special educational needs;

'training' has the same meaning as in section 15ZA of EA 1996;

'young person' means a person over compulsory school age but under 25.

(3) A child or young person has a disability for the purposes of this Part if he or she has a disability for the purposes of the Equality Act 2010.

(4) A reference in this Part to 'education'–

    (a) includes a reference to full-time and part-time education, but

    (b) does not include a reference to higher education,

and 'educational' and 'educate' (and other related terms) are to be read accordingly.

(5) A reference in this Part to–

    (a) a community, foundation or voluntary school, or

    (b) a community or foundation special school,

is to such a school within the meaning of SSFA 1998.

(6) A reference in this Part to a child or young person who is 'in the area' of a local authority in England does not include a child or young person who is wholly or mainly resident in the area of a local authority in Wales.

(7) EA 1996 and the preceding provisions of this Part (except so far as they amend other Acts) are to be read as if those provisions were contained in EA 1996.

CHRONICALLY SICK AND DISABLED PERSONS ACT 1970

Provision of welfare services

2 (1) Where a local authority having functions under section 29 of the National Assistance Act 1948 are satisfied in the case of any person to whom that section applies who is ordinarily resident in their area that it is necessary in order to meet the needs of that person for that authority to make arrangements for all or any of the following matters, namely-

(a) the provision of practical assistance for that person in his home;

(b) the provision for that person of, or assistance to that person in obtaining, wireless, television, library or similar recreational facilities;

(c) the provision for that person of lectures, games, outings or other recreational facilities outside his home or assistance to that person in taking advantage of educational facilities available to him;

(d) the provision for that person of facilities for, or assistance in, travelling to and from his home for the purpose of participating in any services provided under arrangements made by the authority under the said section 29 or, with the approval of the authority, in any services provided otherwise than as aforesaid which are similar to services which could be provided under such arrangements;

(e) the provision of assistance for that person in arranging for the carrying out of any works of adaptation in his home or the provision of any additional facilities designed to secure his greater safety, comfort or convenience;

(f) facilitating the taking of holidays by that person, whether at holiday homes or otherwise and whether provided under arrangements made by the authority or otherwise;

(g) the provision of meals for that person whether in his home or elsewhere;

(h) the provision for that person of, or assistance to that person in obtaining, a telephone and any special equipment necessary to enable him to use a telephone,

then, subject to the provisions of section 7(1) of the Local Authority Social Services Act 1970 (which requires local authorities in the exercise of certain functions, including functions under the said section 29, to act under the general guidance of the Secretary of State and to the provisions of section 7A of that Act (which requires local authorities to exercise their social services functions in accordance with directions given by the Secretary of State, it shall be the duty of that authority to make those arrangements in exercise of their functions under the said section 29.

(1A) [Repealed.]

(2) [Repealed.]

(3) Subsections (4) to (6) apply to local authorities in England.

(4) Where a local authority have functions under Part 3 of the Children Act 1989 in relation to a disabled child and the child is ordinarily resident in their area, they must, in exercise of those functions, make any arrangements within subsection (6) that they are satisfied it is necessary for them to make in order to meet the needs of the child.

(5) Subsection (4) is subject to sections 7(1) and 7A of the Local Authority Social Services Act 1970 (exercise of social services functions subject to guidance or directions of the Secretary of State).

(6) The arrangements mentioned in subsection (4) are arrangements for any of the following–
  (a) the provision of practical assistance for the child in the child's home;
  (b) the provision of wireless, television, library or similar recreational facilities for the child, or assistance to the child in obtaining them;
  (c) the provision for the child of lectures, games, outings or other recreational facilities outside the home or assistance to the child in taking advantage of available educational facilities;
  (d) the provision for the child of facilities for, or assistance in, travelling to and from home for the purpose of participating in any services provided under arrangements made by the authority under Part 3 of the Children Act 1989 or, with the approval of the authority, in any services, provided otherwise than under arrangements under that Part, which are similar to services which could be provided under such arrangements;
  (e) the provision of assistance for the child in arranging for the carrying out of any works of adaptation in the child's home or the provision of any additional facilities designed to secure greater safety, comfort or convenience for the child;
  (f) facilitating the taking of holidays by the child, whether at holiday homes or otherwise and whether provided under arrangements made by the authority or otherwise;
  (g) the provision of meals for the child whether at home or elsewhere;
  (h) the provision of a telephone for the child, or of special equipment necessary for the child to use one, or assistance to the child in obtaining any of those things.
(7) Any question arising under this section as to a person's ordinary residence in an area in England or Wales is to be determined by the Secretary of State or by the Welsh Ministers.
(8) The Secretary of State and the Welsh Ministers must make and publish arrangements for determining which cases are to be dealt with by the Secretary of State and which are to be dealt with by the Welsh Ministers.
(9) Those arrangements may include provision for the Secretary of State and the Welsh Ministers to agree, in relation to any question that has arisen, which of them is to deal with the case.

Welfare services: transition for children to adult care and support

2A (1) Subsections (2) to (4) apply where a local authority in England making arrangements for a disabled child under section 2 are required by section 58(1) of the Care Act 2014 to carry out a child's needs assessment in relation to the child.
  (2) If the local authority carry out the assessment before the child reaches the age of 18 and decide to treat it as a needs assessment in accordance with section 59(6) of the Care Act 2014 (with Part 1 of that Act applying to the assessment as a result), the authority must continue to comply with section 2 after the child reaches the age of 18 until they reach a conclusion in his case.
  (3) If the local authority carry out the assessment before the child reaches the age of 18 but decide not to treat it as a needs assessment in accordance with section 59(6) of that Act–
    (a) they must carry out a needs assessment after the child reaches the age of 18, and

(b) they must continue to comply with section 2 after he reaches that age until they reach a conclusion in his case.

(4) If the local authority do not carry out the assessment before the child reaches the age of 18, they must continue to comply with section 2 after he reaches that age until–
  (a) they decide that the duty under section 9 of the Care Act 2014 (needs assessment) does not apply, or
  (b) having decided that the duty applies and having discharged it, they reach a conclusion in his case.

(5) Subsection (6) applies where a local authority in England making arrangements for a disabled child under section 2–
  (a) receive a request for a child's needs assessment to be carried out in relation to the child, but
  (b) have yet to be required by section 58(1) of the Care Act 2014 to carry out the assessment.

(6) If the local authority do not decide, before the child reaches the age of 18, whether or not to comply with the request, they must continue to comply with section 2 after he reaches that age until–
  (a) they decide that the duty under section 9 of the Care Act 2014 does not apply, or
  (b) having decided that the duty applies and having discharged it, they reach a conclusion in his case.

(7) A local authority reach a conclusion in a person's case when–
  (a) they conclude that he does not have needs for care and support,
  (b) having concluded that he has such needs and that they are going to meet some or all of them, they begin to do so, or
  (c) having concluded that he has such needs, they conclude that they are not going to meet any of those needs (whether because those needs do not meet the eligibility criteria or for some other reason).

(8) In this section, 'child's needs assessment', 'needs assessment' and 'eligibility criteria' each have the same meaning as in Part 1 of the Care Act 2014.

EDUCATION ACT 1996

Education in accordance with parental wishes

Pupils to be educated in accordance with parents' wishes

9   In exercising or performing all their respective powers and duties under the Education Acts, the Secretary of State and local authorities shall have regard to the general principle that pupils are to be educated in accordance with the wishes of their parents, so far as that is compatible with the provision of efficient instruction and training and the avoidance of unreasonable public expenditure.

Exceptional provision of education in pupil referral units or elsewhere

19 (1)   Each local authority shall make arrangements for the provision of suitable education at school or otherwise than at school for those children of compulsory school age who, by reason of illness, exclusion from school or otherwise, may not for any period receive suitable education unless such arrangements are made for them.

(1A)   In relation to England, subsection (1) does not apply in the case of a child–

    (a) who will cease to be of compulsory school age within the next six weeks, and

    (b) does not have any relevant examinations to complete.

    In paragraph (b) 'relevant examinations' means any public examinations or other assessments for which the child has been entered.

(2)   Any school established (whether before or after the commencement of this Act) and maintained by a local authority which–

    (a) is specially organised to provide education for *such children* [children falling within subsection (1)], and

    (b) is not a county school or a special school,

    shall be known as a 'pupil referral unit'.

(2A)   Subsection (2) does not apply in relation to schools in England.

(2B)   Any school established in England (whether before or after the commencement of this Act) and maintained by a local authority which–

    (a) is specially organised to provide education for *such children* [children falling within subsection (1)],4 and

    (b) is not a community or foundation school, a community or foundation special school, or a maintained nursery school,

    shall be known as a 'pupil referral unit'.

(3)   A local authority may secure the provision of boarding accommodation at any pupil referral unit.

(3A)   In relation to England, the education to be provided for a child in pursuance of arrangements made by a local authority under subsection (1) shall be–

    (a) full-time education, or

    (b) in the case of a child within subsection (3AA), education on such part-time basis as the authority consider to be in the child's best interests.

(3AA)   A child is within this subsection if the local authority consider that, for reasons which relate to the physical or mental health of the child, it would not

---

4   Words in italics repealed and substituted by words in square brackets by Children, Schools and Families Act 2010 s25 Sch 3 Pt 1.

be in the child's best interests for full-time education to be provided for the child.

(3B) Regulations may provide that the education to be provided for a child in pursuance of arrangements made by a local authority in England under subsection (1) must be provided from a day that, in relation to the pupil concerned, is determined in accordance with the regulations.

(4) A local authority may make arrangements for the provision of suitable education otherwise than at school for those young persons who, by reason of illness, exclusion from school or otherwise, may not for any period receive suitable education unless such arrangements are made for them.

(4A) In determining what arrangements to make under subsection (1) or (4) in the case of any child or young person a local authority shall have regard to any guidance given from time to time by the Secretary of State.

(5) Any child for whom education is provided otherwise than at school in pursuance of this section, and any young person for whom full-time education is so provided in pursuance of this section, shall be treated for the purposes of this Act as a pupil.

(6) In this section–

['*relevant school*' *means*–

(a) *a maintained school,*

(b) *an Academy,*

(c) *a city technology college, or*

(d) *a city college for the technology of the arts;*][5]

'suitable education', in relation to a child or young person, means efficient education suitable to his age, ability and aptitude and to any special educational needs he may have [*(and 'suitable full-time education' is to be read accordingly)*.][6]

(7) Schedule 1 has effect in relation to pupil referral units.

Local authorities

508A(1) A local authority in England must–

(a) prepare for each academic year a document containing their strategy to promote the use of sustainable modes of travel to meet the school travel needs of their area ('a sustainable modes of travel strategy'),

(b) publish the strategy in such manner and by such time as may be prescribed, and

(c) promote the use of sustainable modes of travel to meet the school travel needs of their area.

(2) Before preparing a sustainable modes of travel strategy, an authority must in particular–

(a) assess the school travel needs of their area, and

(b) assess the facilities and services for sustainable modes of travel to, from and within their area.

(3) 'Sustainable modes of travel' are modes of travel which the authority consider may improve either or both of the following–

---

5   Repealed by Children, Schools and Families Act 2010 s25, Sch 4 Pt 1 from a date to be appointed.

6   Repealed by Children, Schools and Families Act 2010 s25, Sch 4 Pt 1 from a date to be appointed.

(a) the physical well-being of those who use them;

(b) the environmental well-being of the whole or a part of their area.

(4) The 'school travel needs' of a local authority's area are–

    (a) the needs of children and persons of sixth form age in the authority's area as regards travel mentioned in subsection (5), and

    (b) the needs of other children and persons of sixth form age as regards travel mentioned in subsection (6).

(5) The needs of children and persons of sixth form age in the authority's area as regards travel referred to in subsection (4)(a) are their needs as regards travel to and from–

    (a) schools at which they receive or are to receive education or training,

    (b) institutions within the further education sector, or 16 to 19 Academies, at which they receive or are to receive education or training, or

    (c) any other places where they receive or are to receive education by virtue of arrangements made in pursuance of section 19(1).

(6) The needs of other children and persons of sixth form age as regards travel referred to in subsection (4)(b) are their needs as regards travel to and from–

    (a) schools at which they receive or are to receive education or training,

    (b) institutions within the further education sector, or 16 to 19 Academies, at which they receive or are to receive education or training, or

    (c) any other places where they receive or are to receive education by virtue of arrangements made in pursuance of section 19(1),

in so far as that travel relates to travel within the authority's area.

(7) The Secretary of State must issue, and may from time to time revise, guidance in relation to the discharge by a local authority of their duties under this section.

(8) Before issuing or revising guidance under subsection (7), the Secretary of State must consult such persons as he considers appropriate.

(9) In discharging their duties under this section an authority must–

    (a) consult such persons as they consider appropriate, and

    (b) have regard to any guidance given from time to time by the Secretary of State under subsection (7).

(10) References in this section to persons of sixth form age are to be construed in accordance with subsection (1) of section 509AC.

(11) In this section, 'academic year' has the same meaning as in section 509AC in the case of local authorities in England.

Local authorities

508B(1) A local authority in England must make, in the case of an eligible child in the authority's area to whom subsection (2) applies, such travel arrangements as they consider necessary in order to secure that suitable home to school travel arrangements, for the purpose of facilitating the child's attendance at the relevant educational establishment in relation to him, are made and provided free of charge in relation to the child.

(2) This subsection applies to an eligible child if–

    (a) no travel arrangements relating to travel in either direction between his home and the relevant educational establishment in relation to him, or in both directions, are provided free of charge in relation to him by any person who is not the authority, or

(b) such travel arrangements are provided free of charge in relation to him by any person who is not the authority but those arrangements, taken together with any other such travel arrangements which are so provided, do not provide suitable home to school travel arrangements for the purpose of facilitating his attendance at the relevant educational establishment in relation to him.

(3) 'Home to school travel arrangements', in relation to an eligible child, are travel arrangements relating to travel in both directions between the child's home and the relevant educational establishment in question in relation to that child.

(4) 'Travel arrangements', in relation to an eligible child, are travel arrangements of any description and include–

(a) arrangements for the provision of transport, and

(b) any of the following arrangements only if they are made with the consent of a parent of the child–

(i) arrangements for the provision of one or more persons to escort the child (whether alone or together with other children) when travelling to or from the relevant educational establishment in relation to the child;

(ii) arrangements for the payment of the whole or any part of a person's reasonable travelling expenses;

(iii) arrangements for the payment of allowances in respect of the use of particular modes of travel.

(5) 'Travel arrangements', in relation to an eligible child, include travel arrangements of any description made by any parent of the child only if those arrangements are made by the parent voluntarily.

(6) 'Travel arrangements', in relation to an eligible child, do not comprise or include travel arrangements which give rise to additional costs and do not include appropriate protection against those costs.

(7) For the purposes of subsection (6)–

(a) travel arrangements give rise to additional costs only if they give rise to any need to incur expenditure in order for the child to take advantage of anything provided for him in pursuance of the arrangements, and

(b) travel arrangements include appropriate protection against those costs only if they include provision for any expenditure that needs to be incurred for the purpose mentioned in paragraph (a) in the case of the child to be met by the person by whom the arrangements are made.

(8) Travel arrangements are provided free of charge if there is no charge for anything provided in pursuance of the arrangements.

(9) Schedule 35B has effect for the purposes of defining 'eligible child' for the purposes of this section.

(10) References to a 'relevant educational establishment', in relation to an eligible child, are references to–

(a) in the case of a child who is an eligible child by virtue of falling within any of paragraphs 2, 4, 6, 9, 11 and 12 of Schedule 35B, the qualifying school (within the meaning of that Schedule) at which the child is a registered pupil referred to in the paragraph in question, and

(b) in the case of a child who is an eligible child by virtue of falling within any of paragraphs 3, 5, 7, 10 and 13 of Schedule 35B, the place other than a school, where the child is receiving education by virtue of arrangements made in pursuance of section 19(1), referred to in the paragraph in question.

(11) Regulations may modify subsections (1) and (2) to provide for their application in cases where there is more than one relevant educational establishment in relation to a child.

Local authorities

508C(1) A local authority in England may make such school travel arrangements as they consider necessary, in relation to any child in the authority's area to whom this section applies, for the purpose of facilitating the child's attendance at any relevant educational establishment in relation to the child.

(2) This section applies to a child who is not an eligible child for the purposes of section 508B.

(3) 'School travel arrangements', in relation to such a child, are travel arrangements relating to travel in either direction between his home and any relevant educational establishment in relation to the child, or in both directions.

(4) 'Travel arrangements', in relation to such a child, are travel arrangements of any description and include–
  (a) arrangements for the provision of transport, and
  (b) any of the following arrangements only if they are made with the consent of a parent of the child–
    (i) arrangements for the provision of one or more persons to escort the child (whether alone or together with other children) when travelling to or from any relevant educational establishment in relation to the child;
    (ii) arrangements for the payment of the whole or any part of a person's reasonable travelling expenses;
    (iii) arrangements for the payment of allowances in respect of the use of particular modes of travel.

(5) A local authority in England may pay, in the case of a child in the authority's area to whom this section applies and in relation to whom no arrangements are made by the authority under subsection (1), the whole or any part, as they think fit, of a person's reasonable travelling expenses in relation to that child's travel in either direction between his home and any relevant educational establishment in relation to the child, or in both directions.

(6) References to a 'relevant educational establishment', in relation to a child to whom this section applies, are references to–
  (a) any school at which he is a registered pupil,
  (b) any institution within the further education sector, or 16 to 19 Academy, at which he is receiving education, or
  (c) any place other than a school where he is receiving education by virtue of arrangements made in pursuance of section 19(1).

Guidance etc in relation to sections 508B and 508C

508D(1) The Secretary of State must issue, and may from time to time revise, guidance in relation to the discharge by a local authority of their functions under sections 508B and 508C.

(2) Before issuing or revising guidance under subsection (1), the Secretary of State must consult such persons as he considers appropriate.

(3) In discharging their functions under sections 508B and 508C an authority must have regard to any guidance given from time to time by the Secretary of State under subsection (1).

(4) Regulations may require a local authority to publish, at such times and in such manner as may be prescribed, such information as may be prescribed with respect to the authority's policy and arrangements relating to the discharge of their functions under section 508B or 508C.

SCHEDULE 35B

MEANING OF 'ELIGIBLE CHILD' FOR PURPOSES OF SECTION 508B

Section 508B

1 For the purposes of section 508B (travel arrangements for eligible children) an 'eligible child' means a child who falls within any of paragraphs 2 to 7 or 9 to 13.

Children with special educational needs, a disability or mobility problems

2 A child falls within this paragraph if–
 (a) he is of compulsory school age and is any of the following–
  a child with special educational needs;
  a disabled child;
  a child with mobility problems,
 (b) he is a registered pupil at a qualifying school which is within walking distance of his home,
 (c) no suitable arrangements have been made by the local authority for enabling him to become a registered pupil at a qualifying school nearer to his home, and
 (d) having regard to whichever of the following are relevant–
  his special educational needs;
  his disability;
  his mobility problems,
 he cannot reasonably be expected to walk to the school mentioned in paragraph (b).

3 A child falls within this paragraph if–
 (a) he is of compulsory school age and is any of the following–
  a child with special educational needs;
  a disabled child;
  a child with mobility problems,
 (b) he is receiving education at a place other than a school by virtue of arrangements made in pursuance of section 19(1), and
 (c) having regard to whichever of the following are relevant–
  his special educational needs;
  his disability;
  his mobility problems,
 he cannot reasonably be expected to walk to that place.

Children who cannot reasonably be expected to walk because of nature of routes

4 A child falls within this paragraph if–

   (a) he is of compulsory school age and is a registered pupil at a qualifying school which is within walking distance of his home,

   (b) no suitable arrangements have been made by the local authority for enabling him to become a registered pupil at a qualifying school nearer to his home, and

   (c) having regard to the nature of the routes which he could reasonably be expected to take, he cannot reasonably be expected to walk to the school mentioned in paragraph (a).

5 A child falls within this paragraph if–

   (a) he is of compulsory school age and is receiving education at a place other than a school by virtue of arrangements made in pursuance of section 19(1), and

   (b) having regard to the nature of the routes which he could reasonably be expected to take, he cannot reasonably be expected to walk to that place.

Children outside walking distance where no suitable alternative arrangements made

6 A child falls within this paragraph if–

   (a) he is of compulsory school age and is a registered pupil at a qualifying school which is not within walking distance of his home,

   (b) no suitable arrangements have been made by the local authority for boarding accommodation for him at or near the school, and

   (c) no suitable arrangements have been made by the local authority for enabling him to become a registered pupil at a qualifying school nearer to his home.

7 A child falls within this paragraph if–

   (a) he is of compulsory school age and is receiving education at a place other than a school by virtue of arrangements made in pursuance of section 19(1),

   (b) that place is not within walking distance of his home,

   (c) no suitable arrangements have been made by the local authority for boarding accommodation for him at or near that place, and

   (d) no suitable arrangements have been made by the local authority for enabling him to become a registered pupil at a qualifying school nearer to his home.

8 (1) Where–

   (a) a child of compulsory school age has been excluded from a relevant school,

   (b) he remains for the time being a registered pupil at the school, and

   (c) the appropriate authority for the school has made arrangements for the provision of full-time education for him otherwise than at the school or at his home during the period of exclusion,

paragraph 6 has effect as if the place at which [the education is provided] were a qualifying school and the child were a registered pupil at that school (and not at the school mentioned in paragraph (b)).

   (2) For the purposes of sub-paragraph (1)–

   (a) 'relevant school' and 'appropriate authority' have the same meaning as in section 444ZA (application of section 444 to alternative educational provision), and [(b) in relation to a maintained school or a pupil referral unit, references in that sub-paragraph to exclusion are references to exclusion under section 51A of the Education Act 2002.

Children entitled to free school meals etc

9 A child falls within this paragraph if–

(a) he has attained the age of 8 but not the age of 11,

(b) he is a registered pupil at a qualifying school which is more than two miles from his home,

(c) no suitable arrangements have been made by the local authority for enabling him to become a registered pupil at a qualifying school nearer to his home, and

(d) the appropriate condition is met in relation to him.

10 A child falls within this paragraph if–

(a) he has attained the age of 8 but not the age of 11,

(b) he is receiving education at a place other than a school by virtue of arrangements made in pursuance of section 19(1),

(c) that place is more than two miles from his home, and

(d) the appropriate condition is met in relation to him.

11 A child falls within this paragraph if–

(a) he has attained the age of 11,

(b) he is a registered pupil at a qualifying school which is more than two miles, but not more than six miles, from his home,

(c) there are not three or more suitable qualifying schools which are nearer to his home, and

(d) the appropriate condition is met in relation to him.

12 A child falls within this paragraph if–

(a) he has attained the age of 11,

(b) he is a registered pupil at a qualifying school which is more than two miles, but not more than fifteen miles, from his home,

(c) his parent has expressed a wish, based on the parent's religion or belief, for him to be provided with education at that school,

(d) having regard to the religion or belief on which the parent's wish is based, there is no suitable qualifying school which is nearer to the child's home, and

(e) the appropriate condition is met in relation to him.

13 A child falls within this paragraph if–

(a) he has attained the age of 11,

(b) he is receiving education at a place other than a school by virtue of arrangements made in pursuance of section 19(1),

(c) that place is more than two miles, but not more than six miles, from his home, and

(d) the appropriate condition is met in relation to him.

14 (1) For the purposes of paragraphs 9 to 13, the appropriate condition is met in relation to a child if condition A or condition B is met.

(2) Condition A is met if the child is within section 512ZB(4) (provision of free school lunches and milk).

(3) Condition B is met if–

(a) a parent of the child, with whom the child is ordinarily resident, is a person to whom working tax credit is awarded, and

(b) the award is at the rate which is the maximum rate for the parent's case or, in the case of an award to him jointly with another, at the rate which is the maximum rate for their case.

Meaning of 'qualifying school' etc

15 (1) The definitions in sub-paragraphs (2) to (5) apply for the purposes of this Schedule.

(2) 'Qualifying school' in relation to a child means–

(a) a community, foundation or voluntary school,

(b) a community or foundation special school,

(c) a school approved under section 342 (non-maintained special schools),

(d) a pupil referral unit,

(e) a maintained nursery school, or

(f) a city technology college, a city college for the technology of the arts or, an Academy school or an alternative provision Academy.

(3) In relation to a child with special educational needs, an independent school, other than a college or Academy falling within sub-paragraph (2)(f), is also a 'qualifying school' if–

(a) it is the only school named in the EHC plan maintained for the child, or

(b) it is one of two or more schools named in that [plan] and of those schools it is the nearer or nearest to the child's home.

(4) 'Disabled child' means a child who has a disability for the purposes of the Equality Act 2010, and 'disability' is to be construed accordingly.

(5) 'Walking distance' has the meaning given by section 444(5).

(6) 'Religion' and 'belief' are to be read in accordance with section 509AD(3).

(7) In the case of a child who is a registered pupil at both a pupil referral unit and at a school other than a unit, references in this Schedule to the school at which he is a registered pupil are to be read as references to the unit.

EQUALITY ACT 2010

Part 2: Equality: Key Concepts

Chapter 1: Protected Characteristics

The protected characteristics

4 The following characteristics are protected characteristics–
age;
disability;
gender reassignment;
marriage and civil partnership;
pregnancy and maternity;
race;
religion or belief;
sex;
sexual orientation.

Disability

6 (1) A person (P) has a disability if–
  (a) P has a physical or mental impairment, and
  (b) the impairment has a substantial and long-term adverse effect on P's ability to carry out normal day-to-day activities.
(2) A reference to a disabled person is a reference to a person who has a disability.
(3) In relation to the protected characteristic of disability–
  (a) a reference to a person who has a particular protected characteristic is a reference to a person who has a particular disability;
  (b) a reference to persons who share a protected characteristic is a reference to persons who have the same disability.
(4) This Act (except Part 12 and section 190) applies in relation to a person who has had a disability as it applies in relation to a person who has the disability; accordingly (except in that Part and that section)–
  (a) a reference (however expressed) to a person who has a disability includes a reference to a person who has had the disability, and
  (b) a reference (however expressed) to a person who does not have a disability includes a reference to a person who has not had the disability.
(5) A Minister of the Crown may issue guidance about matters to be taken into account in deciding any question for the purposes of subsection (1).
(6) Schedule 1 (disability: supplementary provision) has effect.

Chapter 2: Prohibited Conduct

Discrimination

Direct discrimination

13 (1) A person (A) discriminates against another (B) if, because of a protected characteristic, A treats B less favourably than A treats or would treat others.
(2) If the protected characteristic is age, A does not discriminate against B if A can show A's treatment of B to be a proportionate means of achieving a legitimate aim.
(3) If the protected characteristic is disability, and B is not a disabled person, A

does not discriminate against B only because A treats or would treat disabled persons more favourably than A treats B.

(4) If the protected characteristic is marriage and civil partnership, this section applies to a contravention of Part 5 (work) only if the treatment is because it is B who is married or a civil partner.

(5) If the protected characteristic is race, less favourable treatment includes segregating B from others.

(6) If the protected characteristic is sex–
  (a) less favourable treatment of a woman includes less favourable treatment of her because she is breast-feeding;
  (b) in a case where B is a man, no account is to be taken of special treatment afforded to a woman in connection with pregnancy or childbirth.

(7) Subsection (6)(a) does not apply for the purposes of Part 5 (work).

(8) This section is subject to sections 17(6) and 18(7).

Combined discrimination: dual characteristics

14 [not reproduced]

Discrimination arising from disability

15 (1) A person (A) discriminates against a disabled person (B) if–
  (a) A treats B unfavourably because of something arising in consequence of B's disability, and
  (b) A cannot show that the treatment is a proportionate means of achieving a legitimate aim.

(2) Subsection (1) does not apply if A shows that A did not know, and could not reasonably have been expected to know, that B had the disability.

Indirect discrimination

19 (1) A person (A) discriminates against another (B) if A applies to B a provision, criterion or practice which is discriminatory in relation to a relevant protected characteristic of B's.

(2) For the purposes of subsection (1), a provision, criterion or practice is discriminatory in relation to a relevant protected characteristic of B's if–
  (a) A applies, or would apply, it to persons with whom B does not share the characteristic,
  (b) it puts, or would put, persons with whom B shares the characteristic at a particular disadvantage when compared with persons with whom B does not share it,
  (c) it puts, or would put, B at that disadvantage, and
  (d) A cannot show it to be a proportionate means of achieving a legitimate aim.

(3) The relevant protected characteristics are–
  age;
  disability;
  gender reassignment;
  marriage and civil partnership;
  race;
  religion or belief;
  sex;
  sexual orientation.

Adjustments for disabled persons

Duty to make adjustments

20 (1) Where this Act imposes a duty to make reasonable adjustments on a person, this section, sections 21 and 22 and the applicable Schedule apply; and for those purposes, a person on whom the duty is imposed is referred to as A.

(2) The duty comprises the following three requirements.

(3) The first requirement is a requirement, where a provision, criterion or practice of A's puts a disabled person at a substantial disadvantage in relation to a relevant matter in comparison with persons who are not disabled, to take such steps as it is reasonable to have to take to avoid the disadvantage.

(4) The second requirement is a requirement, where a physical feature puts a disabled person at a substantial disadvantage in relation to a relevant matter in comparison with persons who are not disabled, to take such steps as it is reasonable to have to take to avoid the disadvantage.

(5) The third requirement is a requirement, where a disabled person would, but for the provision of an auxiliary aid, be put at a substantial disadvantage in relation to a relevant matter in comparison with persons who are not disabled, to take such steps as it is reasonable to have to take to provide the auxiliary aid.

(6) Where the first or third requirement relates to the provision of information, the steps which it is reasonable for A to have to take include steps for ensuring that in the circumstances concerned the information is provided in an accessible format.

(7) A person (A) who is subject to a duty to make reasonable adjustments is not (subject to express provision to the contrary) entitled to require a disabled person, in relation to whom A is required to comply with the duty, to pay to any extent A's costs of complying with the duty.

(8) A reference in section 21 or 22 or an applicable Schedule to the first, second or third requirement is to be construed in accordance with this section.

(9) In relation to the second requirement, a reference in this section or an applicable Schedule to avoiding a substantial disadvantage includes a reference to—

(a) removing the physical feature in question,

(b) altering it, or

(c) providing a reasonable means of avoiding it.

(10) A reference in this section, section 21 or 22 or an applicable Schedule (apart from paragraphs 2 to 4 of Schedule 4) to a physical feature is a reference to—

(a) a feature arising from the design or construction of a building,

(b) a feature of an approach to, exit from or access to a building,

(c) a fixture or fitting, or furniture, furnishings, materials, equipment or other chattels, in or on premises, or

(d) any other physical element or quality.

(11) A reference in this section, section 21 or 22 or an applicable Schedule to an auxiliary aid includes a reference to an auxiliary service.

(12) A reference in this section or an applicable Schedule to chattels is to be read, in relation to Scotland, as a reference to moveable property.

(13) The applicable Schedule is, in relation to the Part of this Act specified in the first column of the Table, the Schedule specified in the second column.

Part of this Act	Applicable Schedule
Part 3 (services and public functions)	Schedule 2
Part 4 (premises)	Schedule 4
Part 5 (work)	Schedule 8
Part 6 (education)	Schedule 13
Part 7 (associations)	Schedule 15
Each of the Parts mentioned above	Schedule 21

Failure to comply with duty

21 (1) A failure to comply with the first, second or third requirement is a failure to comply with a duty to make reasonable adjustments.

(2) A discriminates against a disabled person if A fails to comply with that duty in relation to that person.

(3) A provision of an applicable Schedule which imposes a duty to comply with the first, second or third requirement applies only for the purpose of establishing whether A has contravened this Act by virtue of subsection (2); a failure to comply is, accordingly, not actionable by virtue of another provision of this Act or otherwise.

Regulations

22 (1) Regulations may prescribe–

(a) matters to be taken into account in deciding whether it is reasonable for A to take a step for the purposes of a prescribed provision of an applicable Schedule;

(b) descriptions of persons to whom the first, second or third requirement does not apply.

(2) Regulations may make provision as to–

(a) circumstances in which it is, or in which it is not, reasonable for a person of a prescribed description to have to take steps of a prescribed description;

(b) what is, or what is not, a provision, criterion or practice;

(c) things which are, or which are not, to be treated as physical features;

(d) things which are, or which are not, to be treated as alterations of physical features;

(e) things which are, or which are not, to be treated as auxiliary aids.

(3) Provision made by virtue of this section may amend an applicable Schedule.

Part 11: Advancement of Equality

Chapter 1: Public Sector Equality Duty

Public sector equality duty

149 (1) A public authority must, in the exercise of its functions, have due regard to the need to–

(a) eliminate discrimination, harassment, victimisation and any other conduct that is prohibited by or under this Act;

(b) advance equality of opportunity between persons who share a relevant protected characteristic and persons who do not share it;

(c) foster good relations between persons who share a relevant protected characteristic and persons who do not share it.

(2) A person who is not a public authority but who exercises public functions must, in the exercise of those functions, have due regard to the matters mentioned in subsection (1).

(3) Having due regard to the need to advance equality of opportunity between persons who share a relevant protected characteristic and persons who do not share it involves having due regard, in particular, to the need to–

    (a) remove or minimise disadvantages suffered by persons who share a relevant protected characteristic that are connected to that characteristic;

    (b) take steps to meet the needs of persons who share a relevant protected characteristic that are different from the needs of persons who do not share it;

    (c) encourage persons who share a relevant protected characteristic to participate in public life or in any other activity in which participation by such persons is disproportionately low.

(4) The steps involved in meeting the needs of disabled persons that are different from the needs of persons who are not disabled include, in particular, steps to take account of disabled persons' disabilities.

(5) Having due regard to the need to foster good relations between persons who share a relevant protected characteristic and persons who do not share it involves having due regard, in particular, to the need to–

    (a) tackle prejudice, and

    (b) promote understanding.

(6) Compliance with the duties in this section may involve treating some persons more favourably than others; but that is not to be taken as permitting conduct that would otherwise be prohibited by or under this Act.

(7) The relevant protected characteristics are–

    age;

    disability;

    gender reassignment;

    pregnancy and maternity;

    race;

    religion or belief;

    sex;

    sexual orientation.

(8) A reference to conduct that is prohibited by or under this Act includes a reference to–

    (a) a breach of an equality clause or rule;

    (b) a breach of a non-discrimination rule.

(9) Schedule 18 (exceptions) has effect.

Chapter 2: Positive Action

Positive action: general

158 (1) This section applies if a person (P) reasonably thinks that–

    (a) persons who share a protected characteristic suffer a disadvantage connected to the characteristic,

    (b) persons who share a protected characteristic have needs that are different from the needs of persons who do not share it, or

    (c) participation in an activity by persons who share a protected characteristic is disproportionately low.

(2) This Act does not prohibit P from taking any action which is a proportionate means of achieving the aim of–
  (a) enabling or encouraging persons who share the protected characteristic to overcome or minimise that disadvantage,
  (b) meeting those needs, or
  (c) enabling or encouraging persons who share the protected characteristic to participate in that activity.
(3) Regulations may specify action, or descriptions of action, to which subsection (2) does not apply.
(4) This section does not apply to–
  (a) action within section 159(3), or
  (b) anything that is permitted by virtue of section 104.
(5) If section 104(7) is repealed by virtue of section 105, this section will not apply to anything that would have been so permitted but for the repeal.
(6) This section does not enable P to do anything that is prohibited by or under an enactment other than this Act.

SCHEDULE 1

Disability: Supplementary Provision

Section 6

Part 1: Determination of Disability

Impairment

1 Regulations may make provision for a condition of a prescribed description to be, or not to be, an impairment.

Long-term effects

2 (1) The effect of an impairment is long-term if–
  (a) it has lasted for at least 12 months,
  (b) it is likely to last for at least 12 months, or
  (c) it is likely to last for the rest of the life of the person affected.
(2) If an impairment ceases to have a substantial adverse effect on a person's ability to carry out normal day-to-day activities, it is to be treated as continuing to have that effect if that effect is likely to recur.
(3) For the purposes of sub-paragraph (2), the likelihood of an effect recurring is to be disregarded in such circumstances as may be prescribed.
(4) Regulations may prescribe circumstances in which, despite sub-paragraph (1), an effect is to be treated as being, or as not being, long-term.

Severe disfigurement

3 (1) An impairment which consists of a severe disfigurement is to be treated as having a substantial adverse effect on the ability of the person concerned to carry out normal day-to-day activities.
(2) Regulations may provide that in prescribed circumstances a severe disfigurement is not to be treated as having that effect.
(3) The regulations may, in particular, make provision in relation to deliberately acquired disfigurement.

Substantial adverse effects

4 Regulations may make provision for an effect of a prescribed description on the ability of a person to carry out normal day-to-day activities to be treated as being, or as not being, a substantial adverse effect.

Effect of medical treatment

5 (1) An impairment is to be treated as having a substantial adverse effect on the ability of the person concerned to carry out normal day-to-day activities if–

(a) measures are being taken to treat or correct it, and

(b) but for that, it would be likely to have that effect.

(2) 'Measures' includes, in particular, medical treatment and the use of a prosthesis or other aid.

(3) Sub-paragraph (1) does not apply–

(a) in relation to the impairment of a person's sight, to the extent that the impairment is, in the person's case, correctable by spectacles or contact lenses or in such other ways as may be prescribed;

(b) in relation to such other impairments as may be prescribed, in such circumstances as are prescribed.

Certain medical conditions

6 (1) Cancer, HIV infection and multiple sclerosis are each a disability.

(2) HIV infection is infection by a virus capable of causing the Acquired Immune Deficiency Syndrome.

Deemed disability

7 (1) Regulations may provide for persons of prescribed descriptions to be treated as having disabilities.

(2) The regulations may prescribe circumstances in which a person who has a disability is to be treated as no longer having the disability.

(3) This paragraph does not affect the other provisions of this Schedule.

Progressive conditions

8 (1) This paragraph applies to a person (P) if–

(a) P has a progressive condition,

(b) as a result of that condition P has an impairment which has (or had) an effect on P's ability to carry out normal day-to-day activities, but

(c) the effect is not (or was not) a substantial adverse effect.

(2) P is to be taken to have an impairment which has a substantial adverse effect if the condition is likely to result in P having such an impairment.

(3) Regulations may make provision for a condition of a prescribed description to be treated as being, or as not being, progressive.

Past disabilities

9 (1) A question as to whether a person had a disability at a particular time ('the relevant time') is to be determined, for the purposes of section 6, as if the provisions of, or made under, this Act were in force when the act complained of was done had been in force at the relevant time.

(2) The relevant time may be a time before the coming into force of the provision of this Act to which the question relates.

Part 2: Guidance

Preliminary

10 This Part of this Schedule applies in relation to guidance referred to in section 6(5).

Examples

11 The guidance may give examples of–
  (a) effects which it would, or would not, be reasonable, in relation to particular activities, to regard as substantial adverse effects;
  (b) substantial adverse effects which it would, or would not, be reasonable to regard as long-term.

Adjudicating bodies

12 (1) In determining whether a person is a disabled person, an adjudicating body must take account of such guidance as it thinks is relevant.
  (2) An adjudicating body is–
    (a) a court;
    (b) a tribunal;
    (c) a person (other than a court or tribunal) who may decide a claim relating to a contravention of Part 6 (education).

Representations

13 Before issuing the guidance, the Minister must–
  (a) publish a draft of it;
  (b) consider any representations made to the Minister about the draft;
  (c) make such modifications as the Minister thinks appropriate in the light of the representations.

Parliamentary procedure

14 (1) If the Minister decides to proceed with proposed guidance, a draft of it must be laid before Parliament.
  (2) If, before the end of the 40-day period, either House resolves not to approve the draft, the Minister must take no further steps in relation to the proposed guidance.
  (3) If no such resolution is made before the end of that period, the Minister must issue the guidance in the form of the draft.
  (4) Sub-paragraph (2) does not prevent a new draft of proposed guidance being laid before Parliament.
  (5) The 40-day period–
    (a) begins on the date on which the draft is laid before both Houses (or, if laid before each House on a different date, on the later date);
    (b) does not include a period during which Parliament is prorogued or dissolved;
    (c) does not include a period during which both Houses are adjourned for more than 4 days.

Commencement

15 The guidance comes into force on the day appointed by order by the Minister.

Revision and revocation

16 (1) The Minister may–

    (a) revise the whole or part of guidance and re-issue it;

    (b) by order revoke guidance.

   (2) A reference to guidance includes a reference to guidance which has been revised and re-issued.

HOUSING GRANTS, CONSTRUCTION AND REGENERATION ACT 1996

Grants: certificate required in case of owner's application

21 (1) A local housing authority shall not entertain an owner's application for a grant unless it is accompanied by an owner's certificate in respect of the dwelling to which the application relates or, in the case of a common parts application, in respect of each flat in the building occupied or proposed to be occupied by a disabled occupant.

(2) An 'owner's certificate', for the purposes of an application for a grant, certifies that the applicant—

(a) has or proposes to acquire a qualifying owner's interest, and

(b) intends that the disabled occupant will live in the dwelling or flat as his only or main residence throughout the grant condition period or for such shorter period as his health and other relevant circumstances permit.

Grants: certificates required in case of tenant's application

22 (1) A local housing authority shall not entertain a tenant's application for a grant unless it is accompanied by a tenant's certificate.

(2) A 'tenant's certificate', for the purposes of an application for a grant, certifies—

(a) that the application is a tenant's application, and

(b) that the applicant intends that he (if he is the disabled occupant) or the disabled occupant will live in the dwelling or flat as his only or main residence throughout the grant condition period or for such shorter period as his health and other relevant circumstances permit.

(3) Except where the authority consider it unreasonable in the circumstances to require such a certificate, they shall not entertain a tenant's application for a grant unless it is also accompanied by an owner's certificate from the person who at the time of the application is the landlord under the tenancy.

Certificates required in case of occupier's application

22A(1) A local housing authority shall not entertain an occupier's application for a grant unless it is accompanied by an occupier's certificate.

(2) An 'occupier's certificate', for the purposes of an application for a grant, certifies—

(a) that the application is an occupier's application, and

(b) that the applicant intends that he (if he is the disabled occupant) or the disabled occupant will live in the qualifying houseboat or caravan (as the case may be) as his only or main residence throughout the grant condition period or for such shorter period as his health and other relevant circumstances permit.

(3) Except where the authority consider it unreasonable in the circumstances to require such a certificate, they shall not entertain an occupier's application for a grant unless it is also accompanied by a consent certificate from each person (other than the applicant) who at the time of the application—

(a) is entitled to possession of the premises at which the qualifying houseboat is moored or, as the case may be, the land on which the caravan is stationed; or

(b) is entitled to dispose of the qualifying houseboat or, as the case may be, the caravan.

(4) A 'consent certificate', for the purposes of subsection (3), certifies that the person by whom the certificate is given consents to the carrying out of the relevant works.

Grants: purposes for which grant must or may be given

23 (1) The purposes for which an application for a grant must be approved, subject to the provisions of this Chapter, are the following–

(a) facilitating access by the disabled occupant to and from–
  (i) the dwelling, qualifying houseboat or caravan, or
  (ii) the building in which the dwelling or, as the case may be, flat is situated;

(b) making–
  (i) the dwelling, qualifying houseboat or caravan, or
  (ii) the building,
  safe for the disabled occupant and other persons residing with him;

(c) facilitating access by the disabled occupant to a room used or usable as the principal family room;

(d) facilitating access by the disabled occupant to, or providing for the disabled occupant, a room used or usable for sleeping;

(e) facilitating access by the disabled occupant to, or providing for the disabled occupant, a room in which there is a lavatory, or facilitating the use by the disabled occupant of such a facility;

(f) facilitating access by the disabled occupant to, or providing for the disabled occupant, a room in which there is a bath or shower (or both), or facilitating the use by the disabled occupant of such a facility;

(g) facilitating access by the disabled occupant to, or providing for the disabled occupant, a room in which there is a washhand basin, or facilitating the use by the disabled occupant of such a facility;

(h) facilitating the preparation and cooking of food by the disabled occupant;

(i) improving any heating system in the dwelling, qualifying houseboat or caravan to meet the needs of the disabled occupant or, if there is no existing heating system there or any such system is unsuitable for use by the disabled occupant, providing a heating system suitable to meet his needs;

(j) facilitating the use by the disabled occupant of a source of power, light or heat by altering the position of one or more means of access to or control of that source or by providing additional means of control;

(k) facilitating access and movement by the disabled occupant around the dwelling, qualifying houseboat or caravan in order to enable him to care for a person who is normally resident there and is in need of such care;

(l) such other purposes as may be specified by order of the Secretary of State.

(2) [Repealed.]

(3) If in the opinion of the local housing authority the relevant works are more or less extensive than is necessary to achieve any of the purposes set out in subsection (1), they may, with the consent of the applicant, treat the application as varied so that the relevant works are limited to or, as the case may be, include such works as seem to the authority to be necessary for that purpose.

Grants: approval of application

24 (1) The local housing authority shall approve an application for a grant for purposes within section 23(1), subject to the following provisions.

(2) Where an authority entertain an owner's application for a grant made by a person who proposes to acquire a qualifying owner's interest, they shall not approve the application until they are satisfied that he has done so.

(3) A local housing authority shall not approve an application for a grant unless they are satisfied–

(a) that the relevant works are necessary and appropriate to meet the needs of the disabled occupant, and

(b) that it is reasonable and practicable to carry out the relevant works having regard to the age and condition of–

(i) the dwelling, qualifying houseboat or caravan, or

(ii) the building.

In considering the matters mentioned in paragraph (a) a local housing authority which is not itself a social services authority shall consult the social services authority.

(4) [Repealed.]

(5) A local housing authority shall not approve a common parts application for a grant unless they are satisfied that the applicant has a power or is under a duty to carry out the relevant works.

Delayed payment of mandatory grant

36 (1) The local housing authority may approve an application for a grant on terms that payment of the grant, or part of it, will not be made before a date specified in the notification of their decision on the application.

(2) That date shall not be more than twelve months, or such other period as may be specified by order of the Secretary of State, after the date of the application.

LOCAL AUTHORITY SOCIAL SERVICES ACT 1970

Local authorities to exercise social services functions under guidance of Secretary of State

7 (1) Local authorities shall, in the exercise of their social services functions, including the exercise of any discretion conferred by any relevant enactment, act under the general guidance of the Secretary of State.

(1A) Section 78 of the Care Act 2014 applies instead of this section in relation to functions given by Part 1 of that Act or by regulations under that Part.

(2), (3) [Repealed.]

International conventions

UN CONVENTION ON THE RIGHTS OF THE CHILD

Article 2

1. States Parties shall respect and ensure the rights set forth in the present Convention to each child within their jurisdiction without discrimination of any kind, irrespective of the child's or his or her parent's or legal guardian's race, colour, sex, language, religion, political or other opinion, national, ethnic or social origin, property, disability, birth or other status.
2. States Parties shall take all appropriate measures to ensure that the child is protected against all forms of discrimination or punishment on the basis of the status, activities, expressed opinions, or beliefs of the child's parents, legal guardians, or family members.

Article 3

1. In all actions concerning children, whether undertaken by public or private social welfare institutions, courts of law, administrative authorities or legislative bodies, the best interests of the child shall be a primary consideration.
2. States Parties undertake to ensure the child such protection and care as is necessary for his or her well-being, taking into account the rights and duties of his or her parents, legal guardians, or other individuals legally responsible for him or her, and, to this end, shall take all appropriate legislative and administrative measures.
3. States Parties shall ensure that the institutions, services and facilities responsible for the care or protection of children shall conform with the standards established by competent authorities, particularly in the areas of safety, health, in the number and suitability of their staff, as well as competent supervision.

Article 4

States Parties shall undertake all appropriate legislative, administrative, and other measures for the implementation of the rights recognized in the present Convention. With regard to economic, social and cultural rights, States Parties shall undertake such measures to the maximum extent of their available resources and, where needed, within the framework of international co-operation.

Article 12

1. States Parties shall assure to the child who is capable of forming his or her own views the right to express those views freely in all matters affecting the child, the views of the child being given due weight in accordance with the age and maturity of the child.
2. For this purpose, the child shall in particular be provided the opportunity to be heard in any judicial and administrative proceedings affecting the child, either directly, or through a representative or an appropriate body, in a manner consistent with the procedural rules of national law.

Article 23

1. States Parties recognize that a mentally or physically disabled child should enjoy a full and decent life, in conditions which ensure dignity, promote self-reliance and facilitate the child's active participation in the community.
2. States Parties recognize the right of the disabled child to special care and shall encourage and ensure the extension, subject to available resources, to the

eligible child and those responsible for his or her care, of assistance for which application is made and which is appropriate to the child's condition and to the circumstances of the parents or others caring for the child.

3. Recognizing the special needs of a disabled child, assistance extended in accordance with paragraph 2 of the present article shall be provided free of charge, whenever possible, taking into account the financial resources of the parents or others caring for the child, and shall be designed to ensure that the disabled child has effective access to and receives education, training, health care services, rehabilitation services, preparation for employment and recreation opportunities in a manner conducive to the child's achieving the fullest possible social integration and individual development, including his or her cultural and spiritual development

4. States Parties shall promote, in the spirit of international cooperation, the exchange of appropriate information in the field of preventive health care and of medical, psychological and functional treatment of disabled children, including dissemination of and access to information concerning methods of rehabilitation, education and vocational services, with the aim of enabling States Parties to improve their capabilities and skills and to widen their experience in these areas. In this regard, particular account shall be taken of the needs of developing countries.

Article 24

1. States Parties recognize the right of the child to the enjoyment of the highest attainable standard of health and to facilities for the treatment of illness and rehabilitation of health. States Parties shall strive to ensure that no child is deprived of his or her right of access to such health care services.

2. States Parties shall pursue full implementation of this right and, in particular, shall take appropriate measures:
   (a) To diminish infant and child mortality;
   (b) To ensure the provision of necessary medical assistance and health care to all children with emphasis on the development of primary health care;
   (c) To combat disease and malnutrition, including within the framework of primary health care, through, inter alia, the application of readily available technology and through the provision of adequate nutritious foods and clean drinking-water, taking into consideration the dangers and risks of environmental pollution;
   (d) To ensure appropriate pre-natal and post-natal health care for mothers;
   (e) To ensure that all segments of society, in particular parents and children, are informed, have access to education and are supported in the use of basic knowledge of child health and nutrition, the advantages of breastfeeding, hygiene and environmental sanitation and the prevention of accidents;
   (f) To develop preventive health care, guidance for parents and family planning education and services.

3. States Parties shall take all effective and appropriate measures with a view to abolishing traditional practices prejudicial to the health of children.

4. States Parties undertake to promote and encourage international co-operation with a view to achieving progressively the full realization of the right recognized in the present article. In this regard, particular account shall be taken of the needs of developing countries.

UN CONVENTION ON THE RIGHTS OF PERSONS WITH DISABILITIES

Article 3 – General principles

The principles of the present Convention shall be:

a. Respect for inherent dignity, individual autonomy including the freedom to make one's own choices, and independence of persons;
b. Non-discrimination;
c. Full and effective participation and inclusion in society;
d. Respect for difference and acceptance of persons with disabilities as part of human diversity and humanity;
e. Equality of opportunity;
f. Accessibility;
g. Equality between men and women;
h. Respect for the evolving capacities of children with disabilities and respect for the right of children with disabilities to preserve their identities.

Article 7 – Children with disabilities

1. States Parties shall take all necessary measures to ensure the full enjoyment by children with disabilities of all human rights and fundamental freedoms on an equal basis with other children.
2. In all actions concerning children with disabilities, the best interests of the child shall be a primary consideration.
3. States Parties shall ensure that children with disabilities have the right to express their views freely on all matters affecting them, their views being given due weight in accordance with their age and maturity, on an equal basis with other children, and to be provided with disability and age-appropriate assistance to realize that right.

Article 9 – Accessibility

1. To enable persons with disabilities to live independently and participate fully in all aspects of life, States Parties shall take appropriate measures to ensure to persons with disabilities access, on an equal basis with others, to the physical environment, to transportation, to information and communications, including information and communications technologies and systems, and to other facilities and services open or provided to the public, both in urban and in rural areas. These measures, which shall include the identification and elimination of obstacles and barriers to accessibility, shall apply to, inter alia:
   a. Buildings, roads, transportation and other indoor and outdoor facilities, including schools, housing, medical facilities and workplaces;
   b. Information, communications and other services, including electronic services and emergency services.
2. States Parties shall also take appropriate measures to:
   a. Develop, promulgate and monitor the implementation of minimum standards and guidelines for the accessibility of facilities and services open or provided to the public;
   b. Ensure that private entities that offer facilities and services which are open or provided to the public take into account all aspects of accessibility for persons with disabilities;

c. Provide training for stakeholders on accessibility issues facing persons with disabilities;

d. Provide in buildings and other facilities open to the public signage in Braille and in easy to read and understand forms;

e. Provide forms of live assistance and intermediaries, including guides, readers and professional sign language interpreters, to facilitate accessibility to buildings and other facilities open to the public;

f. Promote other appropriate forms of assistance and support to persons with disabilities to ensure their access to information;

g. Promote access for persons with disabilities to new information and communications technologies and systems, including the Internet;

h. Promote the design, development, production and distribution of accessible information and communications technologies and systems at an early stage, so that these technologies and systems become accessible at minimum cost.

Article 19 – Living independently and being included in the community

States Parties to this Convention recognize the equal right of all persons with disabilities to live in the community, with choices equal to others, and shall take effective and appropriate measures to facilitate full enjoyment by persons with disabilities of this right and their full inclusion and participation in the community, including by ensuring that:

a. Persons with disabilities have the opportunity to choose their place of residence and where and with whom they live on an equal basis with others and are not obliged to live in a particular living arrangement;

b. Persons with disabilities have access to a range of in-home, residential and other community support services, including personal assistance necessary to support living and inclusion in the community, and to prevent isolation or segregation from the community;

c. Community services and facilities for the general population are available on an equal basis to persons with disabilities and are responsive to their needs.

Article 23 – Respect for home and the family

1. States Parties shall take effective and appropriate measures to eliminate discrimination against persons with disabilities in all matters relating to marriage, family, parenthood and relationships, on an equal basis with others, so as to ensure that:

a. The right of all persons with disabilities who are of marriageable age to marry and to found a family on the basis of free and full consent of the intending spouses is recognized;

b. The rights of persons with disabilities to decide freely and responsibly on the number and spacing of their children and to have access to age-appropriate information, reproductive and family planning education are recognized, and the means necessary to enable them to exercise these rights are provided;

c. Persons with disabilities, including children, retain their fertility on an equal basis with others.

2. States Parties shall ensure the rights and responsibilities of persons with disabilities, with regard to guardianship, wardship, trusteeship, adoption of

children or similar institutions, where these concepts exist in national legislation; in all cases the best interests of the child shall be paramount. States
Parties shall render appropriate assistance to persons with disabilities in the
performance of their child-rearing responsibilities.

3. States Parties shall ensure that children with disabilities have equal rights
   with respect to family life. With a view to realizing these rights, and to prevent concealment, abandonment, neglect and segregation of children with
   disabilities, States Parties shall undertake to provide early and comprehensive information, services and support to children with disabilities and their
   families.

4. States Parties shall ensure that a child shall not be separated from his or her
   parents against their will, except when competent authorities subject to judicial review determine, in accordance with applicable law and procedures, that
   such separation is necessary for the best interests of the child. In no case shall
   a child be separated from parents on the basis of a disability of either the child
   or one or both of the parents.

5. States Parties shall, where the immediate family is unable to care for a child
   with disabilities, undertake every effort to provide alternative care within the
   wider family, and failing that, within the community in a family setting.

Article 24 – Education

1. States Parties recognize the right of persons with disabilities to education.
   With a view to realizing this right without discrimination and on the basis of
   equal opportunity, States Parties shall ensure an inclusive education system
   at all levels and life long learning directed to:
   a. The full development of human potential and sense of dignity and self-
      worth, and the strengthening of respect for human rights, fundamental
      freedoms and human diversity;
   b. The development by persons with disabilities of their personality, talents
      and creativity, as well as their mental and physical abilities, to their fullest
      potential;
   c. Enabling persons with disabilities to participate effectively in a free
      society.

2. In realizing this right, States Parties shall ensure that:
   a. Persons with disabilities are not excluded from the general education sys-
      tem on the basis of disability, and that children with disabilities are not
      excluded from free and compulsory primary education, or from secondary
      education, on the basis of disability;
   b. Persons with disabilities can access an inclusive, quality and free primary
      education and secondary education on an equal basis with others in the
      communities in which they live;
   c. Reasonable accommodation of the individual's requirements is provided;
   d. Persons with disabilities receive the support required, within the general
      education system, to facilitate their effective education;
   e. Effective individualized support measures are provided in environments
      that maximize academic and social development, consistent with the goal
      of full inclusion.

3. States Parties shall enable persons with disabilities to learn life and social
   development skills to facilitate their full and equal participation in education

and as members of the community. To this end, States Parties shall take appropriate measures, including:

   a. Facilitating the learning of Braille, alternative script, augmentative and alternative modes, means and formats of communication and orientation and mobility skills, and facilitating peer support and mentoring;

   b. Facilitating the learning of sign language and the promotion of the linguistic identity of the deaf community;

   c. Ensuring that the education of persons, and in particular children, who are blind, deaf or deafblind, is delivered in the most appropriate languages and modes and means of communication for the individual, and in environments which maximize academic and social development.

4. In order to help ensure the realization of this right, States Parties shall take appropriate measures to employ teachers, including teachers with disabilities, who are qualified in sign language and/or Braille, and to train professionals and staff who work at all levels of education. Such training shall incorporate disability awareness and the use of appropriate augmentative and alternative modes, means and formats of communication, educational techniques and materials to support persons with disabilities.

5. States Parties shall ensure that persons with disabilities are able to access general tertiary education, vocational training, adult education and lifelong learning without discrimination and on an equal basis with others. To this end, States Parties shall ensure that reasonable accommodation is provided to persons with disabilities.

Index

Council for disabled children

The Council for Disabled Children (CDC) is the umbrella body for the disabled children's sector in England, with links to the other UK national organisations, and is hosted by the National Children's Bureau.

Our vision is for a society in which disabled children and young people's rights are respected, their aspirations supported, their needs met and life chances are assured.

We simply want disabled children and children with special educational needs to have full and happy childhoods; fulfil their potential and be active within the community. We want parents of disabled children to be parents first – living ordinary lives.

We do this by influencing government policy, working with local agencies to translate policy into practice and producing guidance on issues affecting the lives of disabled children.

CDC is fully committed to the empowerment of disabled children and young people and their families. For this reason we are delighted to support *Disabled children: a legal handbook*. However, it should be noted that the views of the authors do not necessarily reflect those of CDC.